ALL · IN · ONE

SHRM-CP®/SHRM-SCP®
Certification
EXAM GUIDE

Dory Willer, SHRM-SCP, PCC
William H. Truedell, SHRM-SCP
William D. Kelly, SHRM-SCP, SPHR-CA

New York   Chicago   San Francisco
Athens   London   Madrid   Mexico City
Milan   New Delhi   Singapore   Sydney   Toronto

Library of Congress Cataloging-in-Publication Data

Names: Willer, Dory, author. | Truedell, William H., author. | Kelly, William
   D., 1935- author. | Society for Human Resource Management (U.S.)
Title: SHRM-CP/SHRM-SCP certification all-in-one exam guide / Dory Willer,
   SHRM-SCP, PCC, William H. Truedell, SHRM-SCP, William D. Kelly, SHRM-SCP,
   SPHR-CA.
Description: New York : McGraw-Hill Education, [2019] | Includes index.
Identifiers: LCCN 2018048516| ISBN 9781259583421 (alk. paper) | ISBN
   9781259586224 | ISBN 9781259583414
Subjects: LCSH: Personnel management —Examinations—Study guides. | Personnel
   management—Examinations, questions, etc. | Personnel
   departments—Employees—Certification.
Classification: LCC HF5549.15 .W5455 2019 | DDC 658.30076—dc23
LC record available at https://lccn.loc.gov/2018048516

McGraw-Hill Education books are available at special quantity discounts to use as premiums and sales promotions, or for use in corporate training programs. To contact a representative, please visit the Contact Us pages at www .mhprofessional.com.

SHRM-CP®/SHRM-SCP® Certification All-in-One Exam Guide

6789 LCR 21

ISBN: Book p/n 978-1-259-58622-4 and CD p/n 978-1-259-58341-4
   of set 978-1-259-58342-1

MHID: Book p/n 1-259-58622-7 and CD p/n 1-259-58341-4
   of set 1-259-58342-2

Sponsoring Editor Tim Green	**Copy Editor** Kim Wimpsett	**Composition** Cenveo Publisher Services
Editorial Supervisors Jody McKenzie and Patty Mon	**Proofreader** Lisa McCoy	**Illustration** Cenveo Publisher Services
Project Manager Ishan Chaudhary, Cenveo® Publisher Services	**Indexer** Ted Laux	**Art Director, Cover** Jeff Weeks
Acquisitions Coordinator Claire Yee	**Production Supervisor** James Kussow	

We dedicate this book to all HR professionals who constantly strive to do better.

I dedicate this book to two career-impactful bosses of mine, Peter Raisbeck, CEO, and Jim Benson, COO. They understood the value of what the HR function could be as a business partner for an organization. They mentored me with the foundational knowledge and experience of tying HR operations and strategies into the organization's overall vision, grasping business acumen, and earning a seat at the executive round table.

—Dory

This book is dedicated to the HR professionals who choose to do an increasingly difficult job as our world becomes more complex every day. You are carrying the banner for your employees and employers. Best wishes for a wonderful career.

—Bill T.

I dedicate this book with love to my wife, Cheryl. Through days and nights, thick and thin, and months that have grown into years, you are always there!

—Bill K.

ABOUT THE AUTHORS

Dory Willer, SHRM-SCP, PCC, is a certified executive coach with more than 30 years of experience as a senior HR executive, keynote speaker, and strategic planning facilitator. She has broad and diverse experience working for blue-chip and Fortune 100 companies, leaving her last corporate position as a vice president of HR to open Beacon Quest Coaching based in the San Francisco Bay Area. Willer coaches clients in leadership enhancement, performance improvement, and career renewal, and helps teams unleash their full potential. Additionally, she facilitates strategic planning sessions that stretch paradigms, align activities with behaviors, and hold groups accountable to produce end results. She was among the first graduating classes from Stanford's Executive HR Certification Program (Graduate School of Business, 1994). Willer achieved the designation of SPHR more than 20 years ago, has a B.S. degree in behavioral science from the University of San Francisco, and earned several advanced certifications in professional coaching. If you would like to contact Dory for speaking engagements or individual and team coaching, you may reach her at Dory@BeaconQuest.com.

William H. Truesdell, SHRM-SCP, is president of The Management Advantage, Inc., a personnel management consulting firm. He spent more than 20 years in management with American Telephone and Telegraph in HR and operations. Truesdell is an expert on the subjects of personnel practices, employee handbooks, equal opportunity, and performance management programs. He is a past president of the Northern California Employment Round Table and former HR course instructor at the University of California – Berkeley extension program. Truesdell holds the SPHR certification and a B.S. in business administration from California State University – Fresno.

William D. Kelly, SHRM-SCP, SPHR-CA, is the owner of Kelly HR, an HR consulting services firm specializing in providing generalist HR consulting services and support for small business enterprises. Bill's experience includes more than 40 years of professional-level HR responsibilities that include 22 years within industry at Bechtel and later at Brown and Caldwell as an environmental engineer. His credentials include experience in employee relations, state and federal legal compliance, staffing and recruitment, equal employment opportunity and affirmative action, compensation, benefits, training and development, health and safety, and government contract management. Bill also has 20 years' HR consulting experience that includes providing HR services, support, and advice to a wide range of Northern California clients. He also has 17 years' experience as an instructor for the University of California – Berkeley extension program teaching Management of Human Resources; Recruiting, Selection, and Placement; California Employment Law; and professional HR certification preparation courses. Bill has more than 18 years' experience teaching the Professional PHR/SPHR Certification

Preparation Course as well as 7 years' experience teaching the California HR Certification Preparation Course for the Society for Human Resource Management (SHRM) and the Northern California HR Association (NCHRA). He played a key role in the development of California's HR certification credential; also, he was the project manager for the team of California HR professionals who developed SHRM's first California Learning System in support of the California certification. Bill's professional leadership also included roles on the board of directors and national vice president for the Society for Human Resource Management; the board of directors and president for the HR Certification Institute (HRCI); state director, California State Council of SHRM; the board of directors and president for the Northern California HR Association (NCHRA); and commissioner and chair, Marin County Personnel Commission. Bill received his B.S. in political science from Spring Hill College in Mobile, Alabama, and undertook post-graduate studies in organizational management at the College of William and Mary in Williamsburg, Virginia, and the University of Virginia in Richmond, Virginia. Prior to HR, Bill had a military career achieving the rank of Major in the United States Army with tours of duty in the United States, Germany, Thailand, and Vietnam.

About the Contributing Author

Beverley N. Dance, MBA, SHRM-SCP, SPHR-CA, CCP, is a human resource professional with significant HR management and independent consulting experience. She is the founder and principal of Dance Associates, providing human resource consulting; supporting a variety of clients including commercial businesses, nonprofits, and higher-educational institutions; and coaching leadership and individuals.

Beverly joined the Society for Human Resources Management faculty in 2007 and facilitates SHRM's certification preparation and compensation classes. Beverly also facilitates for the Northern California Human Resources Association where she is a certified facilitator and certified mentor. She is approaching facilitating certification class number 100 and has presented at the HR West conference three times and at an SHRM Annual conference.

Beverly earned a master's degree in business administration from the Haas School of Business at the University of California – Berkeley with a concentration in organizational design and industrial relations. Beverly has earned the Certified Compensation Professional (CCP) and Certified Employee Benefit Specialist (CEBS) certifications.

CONTENTS AT A GLANCE

Part I   The Human Resources Profession

Chapter 1   Human Resource Certification 3

Chapter 2   SHRM's Certification Program 9

Chapter 3   U.S. Laws and Regulations 23

Part II   HR Knowledge and Behavior Competencies

Chapter 4   People 85

Chapter 5   Organization 273

Chapter 6   Workplace 373

Chapter 7   Behavioral Competencies 459

Part III   Appendixes

Appendix A   List of Common HR Acronyms 553

Appendix B   Case Laws by Chapter 575

Appendix C   For Additional Study 585

Appendix D   About the Digital Content 589

Glossary 593

Index 635

CONTENTS

Acknowledgments   xix
Introduction   xxi

Part I   The Human Resources Profession

Chapter 1   Human Resource Certification   3
Professional Human Resources Management Certification   3
Benefits of Certification   4
HR Certification Organizations   4
   The HR Certification Institute   5
   The Society for Human Resource Management   6
Chapter Review   6
   References   7

Chapter 2   SHRM's Certification Program   9
HR Expertise / Knowledge   11
SHRM's BoCK Advisory Panel   11
   SHRM Certification Commission   11
The SHRM Body of Competency and Knowledge   13
SHRM-CP and SHRM-SCP Exam Eligibility   13
HR-Related Degrees   14
   Which Certification Is Right for You?   15
   Application Deadlines and Exam Windows   16
   Exam Delivery, Duration, and Format   16
   Exam Content Outline   16
   Exam Identification and Conduct Guidelines   17
   How Exams Are Scored   20
Chapter Review   21
   References   21

Chapter 3   U.S. Laws and Regulations   23
What You Need to Know Concerning Employee Management   23
1. When You Have One or More Employees   24
   1.1. The Clayton Act (1914)   24
   1.2. The Consumer Credit Protection Act (1968)   24
   1.3. The Copeland "Anti-Kickback" Act (1934)   24

1.4. The Copyright Act (1976) 25
1.5. The Davis-Bacon Act (1931) 25
1.6. The Dodd-Frank Wall Street Reform
  and Consumer Protection Act (2010) 25
1.7. The Economic Growth and Tax Relief
  Reconciliation Act (EGTRRA) (2001) 25
1.8. The Electronic Communications Privacy Act
  (ECPA) (1986) 26
1.9. The Employee Polygraph Protection Act (1988) 26
1.10. The Employee Retirement Income Security Act
  (ERISA) (1974) 26
1.11. The Equal Pay Act (EPA) (Amendment to the FLSA)
  (1963) 27
1.12. The FAA Modernization and Reform Act (2012) 27
1.13. The Fair and Accurate Credit Transactions Act
  (FACT) (2003) 27
1.14. The Fair Credit Reporting Act (FCRA) (1970) 27
1.15. The Fair Labor Standards Act (FLSA) (1938) 28
1.16. The Foreign Corrupt Practices Act (FCPA) (1997) 31
1.17. The Health Information Technology for Economic
  and Clinical Health Act (HITECH) (2009) 31
1.18. The Health Insurance Portability and Accountability Act
  (HIPAA) (1996) 32
1.19. The Immigration and Nationality Act (INA) (1952) ... 32
1.20. The Immigration Reform and Control Act
  (IRCA) (1986) 32
1.21. The IRS Intermediate Sanctions (2002) 33
1.22. The Labor-Management Relations Act
  (LMRA) (1947) 33
1.23. The Labor-Management Reporting
  and Disclosure Act (1959) 33
1.24. The Mine Safety and Health Act (1977) 34
1.25. The National Industrial Recovery Act (1933) 35
1.26. The National Labor Relations Act (NLRA) (1935) 35
1.27. The Needlestick Safety and Prevention Act (2000) 35
1.28. The Norris-LaGuardia Act (1932) 36
1.29. The Occupational Safety and Health Act
  (OSHA) (1970) 36
1.30. The Omnibus Budget Reconciliation Act
  (OBRA) (1993) 39
1.31. The Pension Protection Act (PPA) (2006) 39

1.32. The Personal Responsibility and Work Opportunity
Reconciliation Act (1996) 39
1.33. The Portal-to-Portal Act (1947) 40
1.34. The Railway Labor Act (1926) 40
1.35. The Rehabilitation Act (1973) 40
1.36. The Retirement Equity Act (REA) (1984) 41
1.37. The Revenue Act (1978) 41
1.38. The Sarbanes-Oxley Act (SOX) (2002) 41
1.39. The Securities and Exchange Act (1934) 42
1.40. The Service Contract Act (SCA) (1965) 43
1.41. The Sherman Anti-Trust Act (1890) 43
1.42. The Small Business Job Protection Act (1996)
(SBJPA) 43
1.43. The Social Security Act (1935) 44
1.44. The Tax Reform Act (1986) 45
1.45. The Taxpayer Relief Act (1997) 45
1.46. The Trademark Act (1946) 45
1.47. The Unemployment Compensation Amendments Act
(UCA) (1992) 45
1.48. The Uniformed Services Employment and Reemployment
Rights Act (USERRA) (1994) 45
1.49. The Vietnam Era Veterans Readjustment Assistance Act
(VEVRAA) (1974) [as amended by the Jobs for Veterans Act
(JVA) (2008)] 46
1.50. The Wagner-Peyser Act (1933) [as amended by
the Workforce Investment Act (WIA) (1998)] 47
1.51. The Walsh-Healey Act (Public Contracts Act) (1936) . . . 47
1.52. The Work Opportunity Tax Credit (WOTC) (1996) . . . 47
1.53 Labor-Management Reporting and Disclosure Act
(1959) 49
1.54. Whistleblowing 49
2. When You Have 15 or More Employees 49
2.1. Americans with Disabilities Act (ADA) (1990) 49
2.2. Civil Rights Act (Title VII) (1964) 54
2.3. The Civil Rights Act (1991) 55
2.4. Drug-Free Workplace Act (1988) 55
2.5. The Equal Employment Opportunity Act
(EEOA) (1972) 56
2.6. The Genetic Information Nondiscrimination Act
(GINA) (2008) 56
2.7. Guidelines on Discrimination Because of Sex (1980) . . . 57

2.8. The Lilly Ledbetter Fair Pay Act (2009) 57
2.9. The Pregnancy Discrimination Act (1978) 57
2.10. Uniform Guidelines on Employee Selection
        Procedures (1976) 57
3. When You Have 20 or More Employees 58
    3.1. The Age Discrimination in Employment Act
          (ADEA) (1967) 58
    3.2. The American Recovery and Reinvestment Act (ARRA)
          (2009) 59
    3.3. The Consolidated Omnibus Budget Reconciliation Act
          (COBRA) (1986) 59
    3.4. The Older Workers Benefit Protection Act
          (OWBPA) (1990) 59
4. When You Have 50 to 99, 100, or More Employees 60
    4.1. Executive Order 11246—Affirmative Action (1965) . . . 60
    4.2. The Family and Medical Leave Act (FMLA) (1993) 61
    4.3. The Mental Health Parity Act (MHPA) (1996) 62
    4.4. The Mental Health Parity and Addiction Equity Act
          (MHPAEA) (2008) 62
    4.5. The National Defense Authorization Act (2008) 62
    4.6. The Patient Protection and Affordable Care Act
          (PPACA) (2010) 62
5. When You Have 100 or More Employees 63
    5.1. The Worker Adjustment and Retraining Notification Act
          (WARN) (1988) 63
6. For Federal Government Employees 64
    6.1. The Civil Service Reform Act (1978) 64
    6.2. The Congressional Accountability Act (1995) 65
    6.3. The False Claims Act (1863) 65
    6.4. The Homeland Security Act (2002) 66
    6.5. The Privacy Act (1974) 66
    6.6. The USA PATRIOT Act (2001) 66
Employment Visas for Foreign Nationals 67
    E Nonimmigrant Visas 67
    H Visas 67
    L-1 Intra-Company Transferee 68
    O-1 Alien of Extraordinary Ability in Arts, Science,
        Education, Business, Athletics 69
    P Visa Categories 69
    EB-Employment–Based Visas 69
Chapter Review 70
    Questions 70
    Answers 78
    References 81

Part II HR Knowledge and Behavior Competencies

Chapter 4 People 85

Functional Area 1—HR Strategic Planning 85
 Key Concepts 86
 The Role of Strategy 87
 Strategy Formulation 92
 Developing Strategy 98
 Implementing Strategy Production 107
 Evaluating Strategic Performance 113
 Providing Leadership and Strategy 118
Functional Area 2—Talent Acquisition 130
 Key Concepts 130
 Organizational Staffing Requirements 131
 Strategic Staffing 133
 Planning for Talent Acquisition on a Global Basis 134
 Employment Branding 135
 Job Analysis and Job Documentation 136
 Sourcing and Recruiting 139
 Selection 144
 Orientation and Onboarding 158
Functional Area 3—Employee Engagement & Retention 159
 Key Concepts 159
 Understanding Employee Engagement 161
 Drivers and Role of Organizational Culture in Engagement ... 162
 Challenges to Employee Engagement 163
 HR's Employee Engagement Strategy 164
 Assessing Employee Engagement 164
 Engaging Employees from Hiring to Separation 168
 Performance Management 174
 Retention 180
Functional Area 4—Learning & Development 183
 Key Concepts 183
 Learning and Development in Today's Organizations 184
 Adult Learning 186
 Training and Development 189
 Career Development 194
 Developing Leaders 199
Functional Area 5—Total Rewards 204
 Key Concepts 204
 Total Rewards and Organizational Strategy 205
 Compensation Structure 220
 Compensation Systems 232
 Benefits and Perquisites 244
 Legislation Affecting Compensation and Benefits 257

Chapter Review 261

    Questions 261

    Answers 265

    References 267

Chapter 5   Organization 273

    Functional Area 6—Structure of the HR Function 273

        Key Concepts 274

        The Strategic Role of HR 275

        Understanding the Organization 281

        The HR Organization and Function 288

        Measuring and Demonstrating HR Value 291

        HR's Role in Organizational Strategy 293

    Functional Area 7—Organizational Effectiveness

      & Development 297

        Key Concepts 298

        Overview of Organizational

          Effectiveness and Development (OED) 299

        Organizational Gap Development 305

        Implementing OED Initiatives 306

        Measuring Organizational Effectiveness and Development 310

    Functional Area 8—Workforce Management 311

        Key Concepts 311

        Organizational Workforce Requirements 312

        Workforce Planning 317

        The Staffing Plan 319

        Employee Development 321

        Succession Planning 326

        Knowledge Management 327

    Functional Area 9—Employee and Labor Relations 330

        Key Concepts 330

        The Employment Relationship 332

        Third-Party Influences on Employee Relations 339

        When the Employee Relationship Falters 345

    Functional Area 10—Technology Management 351

        Key Concepts 352

        HR and Technology 352

        HR in the Era of Big Data 354

        HR Information Systems 355

        Policies for Technology Use in the Workplace 357

    Chapter Review 361

        Questions 361

        Answers 367

        References 369

Chapter 6   Workplace 373

Functional Area 11—HR in the Global Context 373
Key Concepts 374
The Global Context 374
Defining the Global Organization 377
Creating a Global Strategy 378
Becoming a Multicultural Organization 386
Managing Global Assignments 391
Navigating the Global Legal Environment 394
Functional Area 12—Diversity and Inclusion 397
Key Concepts 397
Overview: Key Terms 398
Developing a Diversity and Inclusion Strategy 402
HR's Role in the D&I Process 408
Functional Area 13—Risk Management 412
Key Concepts 412
Establishing the Context of Risk 413
Identifying and Analyzing Risk 417
Managing Risks 420
Evaluating Risk Management 424
Functional Area 14—Corporate Social Responsibility 426
Key Concepts 427
The Ever-Changing and Growing CSR 428
Creating a CSR Strategy 429
Philanthropy and Volunteerism 435
Functional Area 15—U.S. Employment Law and Regulations 436
Key Concepts 436
HR and the Legislative and Regulatory Environment 437
Organizational Compliance 438
U.S. Laws and Regulations 438
Employee Records Management 439
SHRM-SCP 450
Chapter Review 451
Questions 451
Answers 455
References 456

Chapter 7   Behavioral Competencies 459

Leadership Cluster 459
Behavioral Competency 1—Leadership and Navigation 460
Key Concepts 460
Definition 460
Proficiency Indicators for All HR Professionals 461
Proficiency Indicators for Senior HR Professionals 464
Summary 467

Behavioral Competency 2—Ethical Practice 467
  Key Concepts 467
  Definition 468
  Proficiency Indicators for All HR Professionals 468
  Proficiency Indicators for Senior HR Professionals 471
  Summary 475
Interpersonal Cluster 475
Behavioral Competency 3—Relationship Management 475
  Key Concepts 476
  Definition 476
  Basic Proficiency Indicators 476
  Proficiency Indicators for Senior HR Professionals 481
  Summary 484
Behavioral Competency 4—Communication 484
  Key Concepts 485
  Definition 485
  Proficiency Indicators for All HR Professionals 485
  Proficiency Indicators for Senior HR Professionals 488
  Summary 491
Behavioral Competency 5—Global and Cultural Effectiveness 491
  Key Concepts 492
  Definition 492
  Proficiency Indicators for All HR Professionals 492
  Proficiency Indicators for Senior HR Professionals 496
  Summary 500
Business Cluster 500
Behavioral Competency 6—Business Acumen 501
  Key Concepts 501
  Definition 501
  Proficiency Indicators for All HR Professionals 501
  Proficiency Indicators for Senior HR Professionals 504
  Summary 510
Behavioral Competency 7—Consultation 511
  Key Concepts 511
  Definition 512
  Proficiency Indicators for All HR Professionals 512
  Proficiency Indicators for Senior HR Professionals 516
  Summary 520
Behavioral Competency 8—Critical Evaluation 520
  Key Concepts 520
  Definition 521
  Proficiency Indicators for All HR Professionals 521
  Proficiency Indicators for Senior HR Professionals 524
  Summary 529

Chapter Review 529
    Questions 530
    Answers 544
    References 548

Part III   Appendixes

Appendix A   List of Common HR Acronyms 553

Appendix B   Case Laws by Chapter 575
Chapter 4: People 575
Chapter 5: Organization 576
Chapter 6: Workplace 581
Chapter 7: Behavioral Competencies 584

Appendix C   For Additional Study 585

Appendix D   About the Digital Content 589
System Requirements 589
Your Total Seminars Training Hub Account 589
    Privacy Notice 589
Single User License Terms and Conditions 589
TotalTester Online 591
    TotalTester Online Practice Exam Software 591
Secured Book PDF 592
Technical Support 592

Glossary 593

Index 635

ACKNOWLEDGMENTS

We'd like to thank our executive editor, Tim Green, and the talented editorial coordinator, Claire Yee, at McGraw-Hill Education for helping this become a written reality. With the many different iterations of its content when SHRM modified its CP and SCP exams, their patience paid off in "getting it right" for you, the reader/exam taker—making sure the material we wrote, and its presentation style, is effective in guiding you to passing your SHRM exam.

Human resources is most likely part of our DNA makeup; we've lived it and breathed it for many decades. To be able to share the knowledge and tactics, we believe that will be helpful for passing the newer CP and SCP exams is our mentorship to budding HR professionals. We've tried to design our book to not only help the SHRM certification exam taker but also create a resource that will have a prominent place on the HR bookshelf as a "go-to" reference book. We hope we've succeeded with that intention.

A special thanks and much appreciation goes to Beverly N. Dance, MBA, SHRM-SCP, SPHR, PHRca, CCP, CEBS, of Dance Associates, who is what we consider to be an expert in teaching HR professionals to pass the new SHRM exams. Beverly is our contributing author for the situational judgment questions in our book's practice exam, which pertain to the eight behavioral competencies that make up 50 percent of the exam's passing grade. Beverly's consultations and guidance, from her experience facilitating SHRM study groups, has helped us develop our approach in describing the behavioral competencies that SHRM has determined HR professionals need in order to be effective in their jobs.

A final recognition goes out to co-author William Kelly, who once again fulfilled the most important role of technical editor for the content of this book. In addition to Bill's treasure trove of advice about all things HR and the various certification exams, as well as his experience as a facilitator/teacher for both the SHRM and HRCI exam study groups, he jumped in and took the SHRM-SCP exam to give you, the reader, a firsthand review of the exam process.

INTRODUCTION

Allow us to be the first to congratulate you on deciding to sit for the SHRM certification and obtain your SHRM Certified Professional (SHRM-CP) or SHRM Senior Certified Professional (SHRM-SCP) certification! Professional certifications are a mark of distinction that sets you apart in the profession and speaks volumes as to your commitment to your craft. In 2017, the Society for Human Resource Management (SHRM) awarded its 100,000th certification, just 2 years after first launching its "next-generation" HR professional certifications. It is our belief that HR professional certifications are important to you in your job as an HR professional because they endorse your knowledge and expertise to employers and clients.

Through this book, we can help you ready yourself for the type of materials you will be expected to have mastered. You bring your own professional experience to the process. Combining the two, you can be better able to answer situational-based and knowledge-based questions about human resource situations that you may find on the exam.

We want you to be successful. Having a professional certification is more critical every day in the world of work. It may be a requirement of your next job assignment or the promotional opportunity you are pining for in your organization. You may find that you want to place certification on the list of required qualifications for the future HR professionals you hire. In either event, we wish you the best professional regards and success in passing your exam and earning the prestigious designation of SHRM-CP or SHRM-SCP.

SHRM Certifications

This book was first written in 2015, which was the first year of the new SHRM exams. Over the next couple of years, SHRM modified some of the material to finally land on its official credentialing. We believe that the dust has settled and that the exam's organization, weightings, and content are now set in stone and you, the reader/exam taker, will find this book of immense help in helping you study and pass your exam.

How to Use This Book

We believe this book covers the entire SHRM Body of Competency and Knowledge (BoCK) identified in the three specific domains that topics are organized into and in the eight behavioral competencies identified by SHRM for application by those in the human resource profession. The manner in which we present the information is based on a learning principle we call *foundational knowledge*. This means we've purposefully organized this book to ensure that the reader first grasps the foundational knowledge items required of the profession. That is why we have placed U.S. laws as one of the first chapter topics; followed by the BoCK knowledge domain chapters of People, Organization, and Workplace; and then the behavioral competency information.

Additionally, within the writing, we have presented the essential "guts" of the information that we feel is minimally necessary for the exam purposes and pointed you to additional resources to discover more information on topics such as theories. It is our belief that as readers progress through the material and progressively move through with a sure-footed understanding of the "what," they will then be able to progress to the "how" of applying the topics to their roles in HR. We know that the information presented in this book for passing the exam is concise—studying for the exam is no cake walk. The presentation of material was specifically designed to help the self-directed learner by covering information they may already be well familiar with, and yet offering new information in a succinct manner for ease of learning.

Chapter 1

In Chapter 1 we explain everything you need to know about the different types of HR certifications and the benefits of professional certification (such as boosting your credibility as an HR professional and providing a platform to show you're ready to take on the next-level challenge for your career).

Chapter 2

In Chapter 2 we explain everything you need to know about the SHRM exams, the development process of the exams, eligibility for each exam, and which exam/certifications is right for you. Know that the CP exam is correlated with HR administration, and the SCP is associated more with strategy. New for 2018, SHRM offers the Academic Eligibility Program, which allows students in a bachelor's or master's degree program in good standing at academically aligned schools to apply for and take the CP exam. This boosts the HR students' value prior to graduating and provides opportunities to be as marketable as possible. Additionally, you'll find information about the process of registering, the actual exam experience, and the style and format of questions on the exams.

Chapter 3

Chapter 3 provides a list of all the current U.S. laws and regulations that you need to know. We placed this information as one of the early chapters, rather than as an appendix, to emphasize the importance of reviewing the laws and regulations prior to diving into the knowledge areas. This should make it easier for you to grasp the reasoning behind the material that is presented in Chapters 4–6. Please remember that laws and regulations change and it's important that you stay apprised of current federal and local laws that impact your organization in which you do business.

Chapters 4–6

Chapters 4–6 go into the detailed topics of HR technical knowledge (i.e., HR expertise) grouped into "domains"—People, Organization, and Workforce. These domains are defined as the principles, practices, and function of effective HR management and are associated with the expertise required for the HR profession. The explanations are designed to be concise and yet effectively communicate the information you'll need for the exam. Their application is facilitated by the behavioral competencies identified in Chapter 7.

SHRM suggests that to be a successful HR practitioner, one must be in command of both the technical HR knowledge (*what* you know) and the behavioral components of an effective HR practice (*how* you apply what you know).

The People domain covers HR strategic planning, talent acquisition, employee engagement and retention, learning and development, and total rewards.

The Organization domain covers structure of the HR function, organizational effectiveness and development, workforce management, employee and labor relations, and technology management.

The Workplace domain covers HR in the global context, diversity and inclusion, risk management, corporate and social responsibility, and the application of U.S. employment law and regulations from Chapter 3.

Chapter 7

Chapter 7 consists of the eight behavioral competencies that have been defined by SHRM as needed for success in any HR role, regardless of organization size or sector. These behavioral competencies provide the foundation for talent management throughout the HR lifecycle. They are grouped into three clusters: Leadership and Navigation, Interpersonal, and Business. Each competency cluster is further divided into subcompetencies that specifically describe its components and is composed of proficiency key behavior indicators—the statements that illustrate effective use in the HR role. Pay close attention to the SHRM BoCK related to the behavioral competencies that we have outlined in this chapter. The situational judgment test questions (SJTs) rely heavily on those descriptions.

Notes   Specially called out *Notes* are part of each chapter, too. These are interesting tidbits of information that are relevant to the topic and point out helpful information.

Practice Questions and Answers   At the end of Chapters 3 through 7 you will find a set of questions and answers to help you test your knowledge and comprehension. Practice, practice, practice—it will pay off on exam day.

Appendixes

We have created three appendixes to supplement the information you need to know.

Appendix A   Appendix A lists acronyms used in the HR profession. The HR profession is notorious for using jargon in HR language, and these acronyms have flowed into the everyday business language of employers, employees, and the public at large. Will there be exam questions related to acronyms? Our guess is that questions may have acronyms in them but not necessarily be a question such as "What does ABC stand for?"

Appendix B   In Appendix B we have listed all the associated legal cases you should know and review. They are organized under each chapter's functional area and include a brief synopsis of what the case addressed. A URL is provided to review the case in more detail, and we recommend you delve into more information about the cases.

Appendix C   Appendix C lists additional resources that are not only helpful for your exam study but are also helpful as you navigate through the lifecycle of your HR career. You should treat this resource list as a "living document," adding new listings as new theories and best practices are developed over the course of your HR career.

Appendix D   Appendix D provides information for the accompanying practice exams we've created. There are 160 questions each with answers that relate to each possible response, both correct and incorrect. These two exams should help you prepare yourself for sitting for the SHRM exam.

You can access the software using the link on the CD-ROM accompanying this book, or you can access the software from an Internet-enabled computer whenever convenient. Access is activated through the registration on https://hub.totalsem.com/mheclaim with the key code printed on the back cover of your book.

Glossary

The glossary of terms has been created for just about every conceivable term in the HR profession that you will encounter. Not only will using this glossary help you review and learn the key terms contained in this material, it will help you move through your HR career lifecycle in human resource management. We recommend you study the glossary, not just review or reference it, because several exam questions may pertain to glossary terms.

Index

In the back of the book is an index that will guide you to the appropriate pages where a term is mentioned or discussed.

The Examinations

The SHRM-CP and SHRM-SCP exams are neither simple multiple-choice nor memory-recall exams. You will be sitting for a 4-hour, 160-question exam with 60 percent of it individual knowledge-based multiple-choice questions and 40 percent of it "situational judgment" scenario-based questions. There will be complex situational questions, short situational questions, formula-based questions, knowledge-based questions, and interpretive questions. Knowing how to get the most out of each question is crucial.

The questions will come in clusters; you'll see 40 knowledge questions and then 40 scenario-based situational judgment questions, in that pattern until all 160 questions have been delivered. When the scenario questions begin, a second page will display like a book. The scenario stays on the left side of the screen, and the questions will be on the right side of the screen, one at a time.

Situational Questions

Situational questions will test your ability to identify the relevant content and are associated with the behavioral competencies. These questions will be lengthy and make up 40 percent of the exam weighting. Pay particular attention to reading and accurately identifying the question so that you can eliminate irrelevant and insignificant information.

Formula-Based Questions

Formula-based questions are more thought-provoking. You must know both the formula and how to perform the calculation to reach a correct answer.

Knowledge-Based Questions

The knowledge-based type of questions will require you to know your facts. These questions test your knowledge of HR theories and laws. Sometimes you are asked to identify an example chart or graph, so pay attention to the figures that are included in the chapters.

Interpretational Questions

An interpretational question will seek your ability to deduce a situation or condition and select the best appropriate answer. All answers may actually be correct, yet selecting the *best* answer could apply.

Specific Technique Questions

With this last type of question format, you will be tested on how to apply a tool or technique. The questions included at the end of the chapters and in the online practice exams will provide you with good examples of these different question types.

Preparing for the Exam

Preparing for any type of certification exam is not about memorizing information. As with the CP/SCP exams, they require that an established HR professional with a minimum number of years' experience be able to demonstrate that they can apply their experience and knowledge in a host of different situations. You have already invested in an education for your career, and investing in serious study time and preparation now will pay off so that you can pass the exam.

For those with more limited or minimal experience, we suggest you begin studying 6 months prior to the exam-taking date. For those with significantly more experience as an HR professional, 3 months should be your yardstick. If you want to "shoot from the hip" and not study the material outlined in this book, your chances of passing one of the professional exams will likely be low—even if you have been in an HR exempt position for eons. We aren't saying that it can't be done, but we know that your chances are much better if you use the information in this book and its accompanying practice exams to prepare for the time when you will sit in that room with 100 other candidates and spend 4 hours selecting the correct answers. Guessing strategies are not foolproof and not a good substitute for solid study habits in preparation for an exam.

Exam Tips

Exam tips are exactly what they sound like—tips to assist you in your preparation for the exam. From Dory's years of experience coaching people to achieve goals and achievements, she has compiled a list of tips from exam takers of all disciplines. First let's start with studying.

- Before studying, go for a brief walk to take in some air and clear your mind in preparation for being focused. Put all the other thoughts and projects of the day on a back burner and allow your mind to be a clean slate, setting the intention that this specific amount of time is for the exclusive attention of SHRM studying.

- Make sure your "do not disturb" sign is on your door if you are at home or in the office and that others clearly know nothing is to disturb you during the hour-long study time. Speaking of an hour, that's plenty of time to devote on a regular schedule to study. Most people find that 4 or 5 hours a week is sufficient for this type of material.

- Clear your study area. It should be void of anything else that might capture and distract you from studying. Keep the focus on the studying at hand, and to add a little incentive, create a bit of visual incentive for yourself—the desired end result, which would be a letter stating you have successfully passed your exam. Spoof a letter from SHRM, print it, put it in a nice picture frame, and place it in front of you every time you begin your study time. What the mind can conceive, you can achieve!

- Select a time of day that is optimum for you to study. Are you best in the wee hours of the early morning with a cup of coffee prior to work, or perhaps it's the noon hour? Maybe your rhythm is one of a person who kicks in just after dinner. Find that sweet hour and make the appointment on your calendar listing it as VIP-SHRM. You are the very important person, and this appointment will cause you to think twice before allowing another activity to slip in on your time slot.

- The old adage "practice makes perfect" is not quite right. "Perfect practice makes perfect" is a better way to state the intention. As you make your study time perfect and practice saying "no thank you" to others and other things that would interrupt your study time, you are practicing the perfect combination that will allow you to stay focused and produce the results you are after.

- As you study the material, you may want to make flash cards to help you shore up areas of knowledge that will help you pass the exam. You can make flash cards using the web site http://www.kitzkikz.com/flashcards/ by taking notes and transferring them to this web site later.

- As you work through this exam guide and discover a term that is new to you, pause long enough to flip to the glossary and look it up. Knowing how a word or phrase is used can be helpful in discovering its application or meaning. Consider adding those terms to your flash cards.

- We strongly recommend you consider using the complement publication to this exam guide, *SHRM-CP®/SHRM-SCP® Certification Practice Exams* by William D. Kelly and Joanne Simon-Walters, to further help you with an assessment of your HR knowledge strengths and weaknesses. Time yourself as you take the mock exams.

- Two days prior to the exam, be sure to get a full night's sleep each night, which is typically 7 to 9 hours for most people. Studies prove that a REM state of sleeping is extremely helpful for brain function.

- Hydrate, hydrate, hydrate the day before and the day of the exam. Try to avoid massive amounts of caffeine (it will keep you awake and rob you of precious H_2O hydration). Water is good for the body but even better for the brain; it brings oxygen that helps your brain functions improve.

Here are a couple of other helpful tips about the SHRM exam in particular:

- Nothing that has occurred in the last 2 years will be covered on your exam. It can take a year or two to process the questions and include them on an exam. So, don't worry about current events or a new law that just passed.

- Trust your gut, your first impression. First impressions of the correct answer are many times the best choice. This should not be confused with "guessing." This refers to topics you know that you know.

- Watch out for basing your answer on what your current organization's policy is. Keep focused on generally accepted HR practices as the correct answer.

- There will be no patterns, so don't even try to look for them. The psychometric exam process used for the SHRM exam prevents questions from falling into patterns.

- Only federal laws apply—don't mix them up with your state laws.

- The most common weakness of HR test takers is over-analyzing the options. Be thorough, but be reasonable in your analysis and selection of the options.

- When stumped, try to eliminate the obvious answers and then just focus on what remains.

- Do read all four answers—it may be that you need to select the *best* answer and yet all answers are correct.

- Use the highlighting tool that the exam has to help you identify key phrases.

- Resist the urge to change your answers—this goes hand in hand with the first tip. If you are absolutely, positively sure that you have an incorrect answer, go ahead. But for the most part, resist the urge to change answers.

- Don't rush. Manage your time. You will have a little over a minute for each question. A clock visible on your monitor screen counts down what amount of time is left.

Lastly, this book has been designed not only to assist SHRM exam takers but also to be a reliable reference book on the shelf in any HR professional's office. There is a lot to remember in the discipline of human resources. It is our desire that you find this book to be a quick resource that guides you in times when something pops up that you may need a refresher on. At a minimum, we hope it provides you with direction to gather more information for your HR circumstances.

Finally, dear reader, thank you for selecting this book. We sincerely hope your SHRM exam goes well and wish you the absolute best on exam day!

PART I

The Human Resources Profession

■ **Chapter 1**   Human Resource Certification
■ **Chapter 2**   SHRM's Certification Program
■ **Chapter 3**   U.S. Laws and Regulations

Human Resource Certification

The skills and abilities that a human resources (HR) professional uses to produce desired results require a mastery of sorts. Mastery of any profession will involve a continuous career-long commitment to learning, and that is a foundational truth within the human resources profession. HR has been, and continues to be, an evolving component of an organization because its basic focus is on the people, otherwise referred to as the human capital of an organization. The constant changes and outside influences on an organization's workforce increase the demands on HR professionals. HR professionals today walk a tight line and must master the art of staying two steps ahead while having one foot firmly planted in the present. Today's HR department needs to be perceived as a strategic player in an organization, positioning itself with developing business approaches while solving problems and being more than a cost center.

Professional Human Resources Management Certification

Certifications demonstrate for professionals what we do and why it matters. Credentialing as an HR professional demonstrates to your colleagues and your organization that you are committed to a higher standard and ethic and dedicated to the HR profession. When you achieve your HR credential, it signals your mastery of core practices and principles in HR management, raising the confidence of an employer and your peers in your abilities. Because the HR profession is constantly changing and evolving, it is important for HR professionals to constantly update their HR competencies and knowledge. Achieving certification and recertification is a good method to do so.

A professional certification should not be confused with a certificate program. Professional certifications are based on work experience and education along with recertification requirements. Certificate programs do not require work experience or an educational component, nor do they require recertification. Competency-based certifications address a critical need in our global marketplace because employers expect more today from their internal experts, and the HR profession must be ready to meet those expectations.

Benefits of Certification

Earning an HR credential adds a level of recognition as an expert in the HR profession. This certification is a distinction that sets you apart in the profession, indicating you have a high level of knowledge and skills. It adds to your career value and to the organization you work in. Your HR certification could mean the difference between you and your competition. In fact, 96 percent of employers say that an HR-certified candidate applying for a job would have an advantage over a noncertified candidate. And HR professionals who hold certifications tend to make more money than their peers who do not.[1] According to PayScale Human Capital, this pattern is true for all industries and metropolitan areas in the United States. HR certification is becoming an important means for employers to recognize HR expertise and for HR professionals to increase their value and worth.

Earning an HR credential can help you:

- Boost your confidence
- Create recognition for you as an HR expert
- Master expert knowledge for the HR profession
- Protect your organization from risk by knowing regulatory compliance
- Stand out from other HR candidates in job searches and promotions
- Broaden your perspective in the HR field
- Keep up with HR innovations, developments, and legislative/law changes
- Demonstrate your commitment to the HR profession

Many organizations, including a number of Fortune 500 organizations, now require or prefer HR certification for their new HR hires or for internal promotions. A May 2014 study from Software Advice, Inc., called "What Employers Are Looking for in HR Positions"[2] reveals that employers will be increasingly demanding certification for their job candidates. The study found the HR certification preferences shown in Table 1-1, broken down by job title.

This survey suggests that certification will be essential for any professional-level HR job candidate. If an individual wants to be considered for a senior-level HR position, then certification is nearly an absolute requirement. Those expectations will be further solidified as time goes on.

HR Certification Organizations

As of 2018, there are two certifying organizations for HR professionals to receive their certifications from, the HR Certification Institute (HRCI) which is accredited, and the Society for Human Resource Management (SHRM). Determining whether to pursue

Job Title Classification	Certification Required	Certification Preferred	Total
HR Business Partner	70%	30%	100%
Associate HR Director	35%	30%	65%
Senior HR Manager	10%+	45%	55%
HR Director	10%	45%	55%
HR Manager	5%	40%	45%
Senior HR Generalist		55%	55%
Senior HR Business Partner		45%	45%
Employee Relations Manager		30%	30%
HR Generalist		15%	15%
Other		30%	30%

Table 1-1   HR Certification Specifications by Job Title

the SHRM Certified Professional (SHRM-CP) or SHRM Senior Certified Profession (SHRM-SCP) or the HRCI credentials is an important decision. Both organizations' certifications test knowledge that the profession requires as their baseline. While they both test knowledge, the SHRM certifications focus as much as 50 percent of their test content on applying that knowledge and the importance of behavioral competency even as they include a more expansive global perspective. The eligibility requirements are more inclusive (as of this writing) for the SHRM exams, and the cost is slightly less than the HRCI exams. They both have their merits, which is why we hold both certifications.

The HR Certification Institute

The HR Certification Institute (www.hrci.org) was established in 1976 as an internationally recognized certifying organization for the human resource profession. Its mission is to develop and deliver the highest-quality certification programs that validate mastery in the field of human resource management and contribute to the continued improvement of individual and organizational performance. More than 145,000 HR professionals in more than 100 countries are certified. Until 2015, HRCI was the only certifying organization for the HR profession and as of this writing is the only accredited certifying organization.

HRCI exists to enhance the professionalism of the HR profession with its various certification processes. The institute is a nonprofit $(501)(c)(3)^3$ separate organization, an IRS designation, from the Society of Human Resource Management, which is a $(510)(c)(6)^4$ organization. HRCI was accredited by the National Commission for Certifying Agencies (NCCA) in 2008.

HRCI's Body of Knowledge (BoK) is a complete set of knowledge and responsibilities statements required to successfully understand and perform generalist HR-related duties associated with each of its eight credentials, Associate Professional in Human Resources (aPHR), Professional in Human Resources (PHR), Professional in Human Resources, California (PHRca), Senior Professional in Human Resources (SPHR), Global Professional in Human Resources (GPHR), Associate Professional in Human Resources, International (aPHRi), Professional in Human Resources, International (PHRi), and Senior Professional in Human Resources, International (SPHRi). The BoK is periodically updated, typically every 5 to 7 years, to ensure it is consistent with and reflects current practices in the HR field. Our book, *PHR/SPHR Professional in Human Resources Certification All-in-One Exam Guide,*[5] provides in-depth preparation for the PHR and SPHR exams.

The Society for Human Resource Management

For more than 65 years, the Society for Human Resource Management (www.shrm.org) has served the human resource profession and HR professionals worldwide. Founded in 1948, SHRM is the world's largest HR membership organization devoted to human resource management. Representing more than 275,000 members in more than 160 countries, SHRM is the leading provider of resources to serve the needs of HR professionals and advance the professional practice of human resource management. SHRM has more than 575 affiliated chapters within the United States and subsidiary offices in China, India, and United Arab Emirates.

HR professionals look to SHRM for resources to help them do their jobs, progress their careers, and partner with government and public and private industry. SHRM focuses on advancing the HR profession as a whole, ensuring that as business needs involving human capital evolve, HR evolves to meet those needs. That was the driving force behind the development of a Body of Competency and Knowledge (BoCK) supporting next-generation credentials in the HR field: the SHRM Certified Professional and the SHRM Senior Certified Professional certifications.

SHRM has a commitment to developing the HR profession globally; SHRM provides resources, global best practices, and a network of more than 9,000 members in more than 160 countries. In addition to delivering certification preparation courses and other educational products and services to members around the world, SHRM partners with volunteers in select countries to lead member forums and encourage local networking among members. SHRM is an active member of the North American Human Resource Management Association (NAHRMA) and the World Federation of People Management Associations (WFPMA) and currently serves as the secretariat for both organizations.

Chapter Review

The number of HR professionals needed in the coming years to manage the human capital in organizations will continue to expand. The U.S. Bureau of Labor Statistics anticipates that the number of HR manager positions will grow 13 percent and will grow 8 percent for HR specialist positions by the year 2022.[6] In addition, employer selection systems will increasingly use certification as an employment screening element. Whether you choose to obtain a certification from SHRM or HRCI, or both, is not going to be as relevant as when you will achieve your credential. The value of certification is being recognized in all levels of the organization and throughout the HR profession. SHRM's new Body of Competency and Knowledge (BoCK) and certification exams raise the stakes for the professional by requiring exam takers to demonstrate an ability to apply the knowledge they know, not simply identify what they know. This certainly moves the mark toward "art" and away from "science" with regard to effectiveness. We're confident that adding the SHRM certification to your résumé will draw special attention to your achievement and to the time and discipline involved in attaining this professional goal.

References

1. PayScale Human Capital research report, "The Market Value of PHR and SPHR Certifications," http://resources.payscale.com (*search on title of report*).

2. Osterhaus, Erin. "What Employers Are Looking for in HR Positions," (*The New Talent Times,* May 27, 2014), http://new-talent-times.softwareadvice .com/what-employers-look-for-hr-jobs-0514/.

3. To be tax-exempt under section 501(c)(3) of the Internal Revenue Code, an organization must be organized and operated exclusively for exempt purposes set forth in section 501(c)(3), and none of its earnings may inure to any private shareholder or individual. In addition, it may not be an action organization, i.e., it may not attempt to influence legislation as a substantial part of its activities and it may not participate in any campaign activity for or against political candidates. Organizations described in section 501(c)(3) are commonly referred to as charitable organizations. Organizations described in section 501(c) (3), other than testing for public safety organizations, are eligible to receive tax-deductible contributions in accordance with Code section 170. IRS Code (https://www.irs.gov/charities-non-profits/charitable-organizations/exemption-requirements-section-501-c-3-organizations).

4. IRC 501(c)(6) provides for exemption of business leagues, chambers of commerce, real estate boards, boards of trade, and professional football leagues (whether or not administering a pension fund for football players), which are not organized for profit and no part of the net earnings of which insures to the benefit of any private shareholder or individual. IRS Code (https://www.irs.gov/pub/irs-tege/eotopick03.pdf).

5. Willer, Dory, and William H. Truesdell. *PHR/SPHR Professional in Human Resources Certification All-in-One Exam Guide* (McGraw-Hill Education, 2015).

6. Bureau of Labor Statistics, U.S. Department of Labor, *Occupational Outlook Handbook, 2014-2015 Edition,* Human Resources Managers, www.bls.gov/ooh/management/human-resources-managers.htm.

SHRM's Certification Program

Today, we live and work in a global economy in which geographic borders are virtually nonexistent, with innovation, agility, and strategy as critical success factors. The HR profession operates at the core of this global economy, ensuring the alignment of organizational strategy with a high-performing workforce. The Society for Human Resource Management (SHRM) certification program[1] has two credentials, SHRM Certified Professional (SHRM-CP) and SHRM Senior Certified Professional (SHRM-SCP), that address these roles in today's world.

In 2011, SHRM decided to invest in the advancement of the HR profession by developing a new competency framework to serve as a foundational resource for all HR professionals. The SHRM Competency Model identifies eight key behavioral competencies: *Leadership & Navigation, Business Acumen, Ethical Practice, Relationship Management, Consultation, Critical Evaluation, Global & Cultural Effectiveness,* and *Communication.* It identifies one technical competency: *HR Expertise (HR Knowledge).* SHRM's studies indicate that these competencies are the foundation of a successful HR career.

The SHRM Competency Model[2] is fundamental to SHRM's two certifications: the SHRM-CP for early to mid-career practitioners and the SHRM-SCP for senior-level practitioners. These certifications address two basic goals:

- For HR professionals, these certifications recognize the importance of both competencies and knowledge as essential elements for successful job performance.
- For employers, they affirm the need to look for competencies and knowledge as key indicators of successful HR job performance.

As a function of its studies, SHRM identified a bank of knowledge topics that are essential and a list of behaviors that are critical to HR professionals' success. SHRM called these the Body of Competency and Knowledge (BoCK). SHRM's credentials are designed to demonstrate to the global business community that the credential holder has

9

strong capabilities in both aspects of HR practice, competency and knowledge, and that both are required for effective job performance.

As part of its research, SHRM conducted more than 100 focus groups involving more than 1,000 HR practitioners to identify nine critical competencies necessary for success as an HR professional. Focus group participants included HR professionals from 33 countries, representing a diversity of both personal and organizational attributes.

SHRM then confirmed the relevance and universality of the SHRM Competency Model through a content validation survey, which drew responses from more than 32,000 HR professionals worldwide. Finally, a series of large-scale multiorganizational criterion validation studies were conducted involving a highly diverse sample of more than 1,500 HR professionals and their supervisors, the purpose of which was to establish that proficiency in these competencies is closely linked to successful job performance. Figure 2-1 illustrates SHRM's Body of Competency and Knowledge[3] building blocks of proficiency for the HR professional.

The SHRM-CP and SHRM-SCP exams were accredited by The Buros Center for Testing in late 2016, a pronouncement that the HR credentials meet the highest standards in testing.

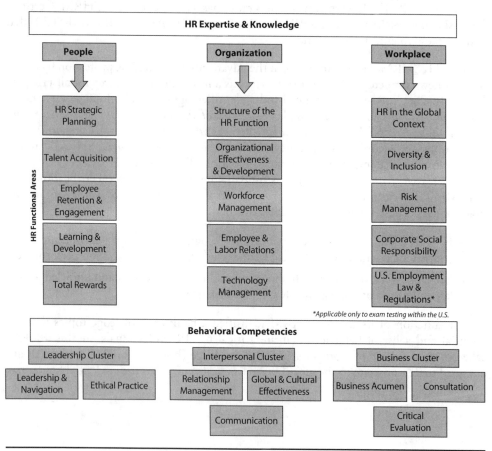

Figure 2-1   SHRM Body of Competency & Knowledge

HR Expertise / Knowledge

A competency model is a set of competencies defining the requirements for effective performance in a specific job, profession, or organization. There are eight behavioral competencies and one technical competency, HR Expertise / Knowledge, in the SHRM Competency Model.

SHRM conducted a knowledge specification exercise to identify the key areas of HR functional knowledge and expertise. SHRM consulted academic and employer surveys regarding the basic functional knowledge needed for participation in the human resources field.

SHRM's BoCK Advisory Panel

Nineteen HR and business leaders from various industries, including retail, research, consulting, health care, and manufacturing, served on SHRM's BoCK Advisory Panel, which was established to validate this framework. The panel reviewed the proposed HR technical knowledge framework for accuracy and comprehensiveness, defined key responsibility statements and knowledge topic areas associated with each knowledge domain and functional area, and developed importance rankings and weights for each knowledge domain. Upon completion, SHRM adopted this framework as the basis for the knowledge component of the SHRM BoCK.

Next, SHRM approached the development of behavioral competencies (see Table 2-1). Competencies can be either technical or behavioral. Technical competencies reflect the knowledge required to perform a specific role. Behavioral competencies describe the knowledge, skills, or abilities (KSAs) that facilitate the application of technical knowledge to job-related behavior. In other words, technical competencies reflect the knowledge HR professionals apply to their jobs, and behavioral competencies reflect how they apply this knowledge. SHRM's moto is "Knowledge + Behavior = Success."

The SHRM BoCK documents the HR behavioral competencies and knowledge domains tested on the SHRM-CP and SHRM-SCP certification exams. The SHRM BoCK is also the basic resource for item writers developing questions and individuals developing exam preparation materials. SHRM operates exam development and study material development as separate, independent functions and has established a strict firewall between these activities to protect the integrity and credibility of the certification exams.

SHRM Certification Commission

The SHRM Certification Commission[4] functions as a technical advisory committee established by SHRM to serve as a governance body for SHRM's certifying activities. The commission is composed of volunteers who have extensive HR and business expertise from industries and organizations throughout the world. The commission's mission is to ensure the highest quality and impartiality of SHRM's certification program. Its responsibilities include reviewing certificant eligibility, approving exam specifications and scoring, ensuring impartiality in certification activities, and ensuring due consideration of appeals and complaints.

Cluster	Competency	Definition
Leadership	Leadership & Navigation	The knowledge, skills, abilities, and other characteristics (KSAOs) needed to navigate the organization and accomplish HR goals, to create a compelling vision and mission for HR that aligns with the strategic direction and culture of the organization, to lead and promote organizational change, to manage the implementation and execution of HR initiatives, and to promote the role of HR as a key business partner.
	Ethical Practice	The KSAOs needed to maintain high levels of personal and professional integrity and to act as an ethical agent who promotes core values, integrity, and accountability throughout the organization.
Interpersonal	Relationship Management	The KSAOs needed to create and maintain a network of professional contacts within and outside of the organization, to build and maintain relationships, to work as an effective member of a team, and to manage conflict while supporting the organization.
	Communication	The KSAOs needed to effectively craft and deliver concise and informative communications, to listen to and address the concerns of others, and to transfer and translate information from one level or unit of the organization to another.
	Global & Cultural Effectiveness	The KSAOs needed to value and consider the perspectives and backgrounds of all parties, to interact with others in a global context, and to promote a diverse and inclusive workplace.
Business	Business Acumen	The KSAOs needed to understand the organization's operations, functions, and external environment, and to apply business tools and analyses that inform HR initiatives and operations consistent with the overall strategic direction of the organization.
	Consultation	The KSAOs needed to work with organizational stakeholders in evaluating business challenges and identifying opportunities for the design, implementation, and evaluation of change initiatives, and to build ongoing support for HR solutions that meet the changing needs of customers and the business.
	Critical Evaluation	The KSAOs needed to collect and analyze qualitative and quantitative data and to interpret and promote findings that evaluate HR initiatives and inform business decisions and recommendations.

Table 2-1   SHRM Behavioral Competency Definitions[5]

Commission members are not financially compensated for their involvement but are reimbursed for their fair and reasonable expenses that are directly related to the commission's business activities.

The SHRM Body of Competency and Knowledge

Increasingly, business leaders understand that effective people management is a strategic imperative. Employers expect that HR professionals will demonstrate, in addition to a basic knowledge of HR concepts and requirements, the behavioral competencies required to effectively apply their knowledge in the modern workplace. Because the HR profession is constantly changing and evolving, it is important for certified professionals to continually update their HR knowledge and competencies. Achieving certification as an SHRM-CP or SHRM-SCP is a first step in this process.

The SHRM Body of Competency and Knowledge[6] (SHRM BoCK) is the basis for the new SHRM credentials. The SHRM BoCK draws heavily from the SHRM Competency Study, as it describes the behavioral competencies and functional areas of knowledge needed for effective job performance. The SHRM BoCK explains not only what HR professionals need to know but also how they must apply this expertise to perform effectively in the workplace.

SHRM-CP and SHRM-SCP Exam Eligibility

Exam applicants are required to meet specific educational and work experience at the time they submit their application.[7] The following general eligibility criteria, shown in Table 2-2, will also apply:

- Applicants must show that they have at least 1,000 hours within a calendar year devoted to HR-related activities. This equates to a year of HR-related experience. (More than 1,000 hours does not equate to more than 1 year of experience.)

Credential	Less than a Bachelor's Degree*		Bachelor's Degree		Graduate Degree	
	HR-related program	Non-HR program	HR-related degree	Non-HR degree	HR-related degree	Non-HR degree
SHRM-CP**	3 years in HR role	4 years in HR role	1 year in HR role	2 years in HR role	Currently in HR role	1 year in HR role
SHRM-SCP	6 years in HR role	7 years in HR role	4 years in HR role	5 years in HR role	3 years in HR role	4 years in HR role

*Less than a bachelor's degree includes working toward a bachelor's degree, associate's degree, some college, qualifying HR certificate program, high school diploma, or GED.

Table 2-2 SHRM-CP and SHRM-SCP Exam Eligibility Criteria

- HR-related experience is any work within the 15 functional areas of HR knowledge that make up the technical competency HR Expertise, as explained in the SHRM BoCK.

- Part-time work qualifies, as long as the 1,000-hour requirement is met within a calendar year.

- HR experience may be in an exempt or nonexempt capacity.

- Applicants are not required to hold an HR title. HR-related work determines eligibility, not the job title.

- Applicants who have mixed roles, such as an office or payroll manager with HR responsibilities, may qualify with their experience, as long as their HR-related duties total at least 1,000 hours in a calendar year (i.e., recruiting, interviewing, onboarding, and benefits enrollment).

- Supervising employees in and of itself is not considered qualifying as HR-related experience.

- SHRM membership is not required to qualify for the exam.

HR-Related Degrees

The following degrees meet the HR-related degree requirements:

- **Graduate (or global equivalent)**   HR-related degrees may include but are not limited to the following: MA in Human Resource Management (HRM), MS in Human Resources (HR), MA or MS in Industrial and Organizational Psychology, MA in Management (MAM) with HR concentration, MBA with concentration in HRM, Organizational Leadership or Leadership Development with HR concentration, Human Capital Development, Organizational Behavior, Labor Relations, and Industrial Relations.

- **Bachelor's (or global equivalent)**   HR-related degrees may include but are not limited to the following: BA or BS in HRM, BA or BS in Management with concentration in HR, BA or BS in Business Administration with concentration in HRM, Bachelor of Business Administration with emphasis in HR, Organizational Behavior, Industrial Relations, Organizational Development, and Management and Leadership.

- **Associate's**   Applicants with less than a bachelor's degree may have HR-related associate's degrees that may include but are not limited to Associate – HR Specialist, Associate – Business: HR Management, and Associate – HR Administration.

- **Certificate program**   Applicants with less than a bachelor's degree may complete an HR Certificate Program from an accredited institution, completing eight courses that cover the fundamentals in HR (i.e., Principles of HRM, Compensation and Benefits, Organizational Development, Recruitment and Selection, Employment Law, Training and Development, Employee Relations, and Performance Management). A qualifying certificate program typically lasts 18 months.

- **Outside the United States**
  - HR-related bachelor's programs may include but are not limited to the following: BBA with emphasis in HRM, Bachelor of Commerce with concentration in Managing People and Organizations, and Bachelor of Business in Pedagogy with concentration in HR.
  - HR-related master's programs may include the following: MA in International HRM, Professional Post-Graduate Diploma in HRM, and Executive Master in HRM.
- **Student eligibility**   Students who are enrolled in their final year of an undergraduate or graduate HR degree program at a college or university that has been approved by SHRM's Academic Initiatives, aligned to SHRM's curriculum guidelines, are eligible to sit for the SHRM-CP exam. Students must have accumulated at least 500 hours of an internship or practical HR experience and must be in good standing with their school.

Which Certification Is Right for You?

Which credential to choose is an important decision that involves several factors. While education and years of experience are the criteria that determine eligibility, it is even more important to consider the nature of your HR experience and the range of your HR responsibilities. The following are general guidelines to consider:

- SHRM-SCP certification is designed for HR professionals at a senior level who operate primarily in a strategic role developing policies and strategies, overseeing the execution of HR operations, analyzing performance metrics, and/or contributing to the alignment of HR strategies to organizational goals.
- SHRM-CP certification is designed for HR practitioners who are engaged primarily in an operational HR role implementing policies, serving as the HR point of contact for staff and stakeholders, and/or performing day-to-day HR functions. If this is your focus, the SHRM-CP is likely your best option, even if you meet the eligibility criteria for the SHRM-SCP.

To ensure that you take the exam that best reflects your experience, first determine your eligibility. Then compare your core responsibilities as reflected in your experience with the key responsibilities that are highlighted in the SHRM BoCK. This should help you, as a test taker, make the choice most appropriate for achieving success.

NOTE   During the winter testing window each year (December to February), SHRM offers both exams in Spanish. Applicants must specifically request the Spanish version when they apply for the exam.

Application Deadlines and Exam Windows

The exam windows are the dates within which the exams are administered.[8] Currently, SHRM has two 75-day exam windows, one in the spring and one in the fall. The testing windows are the dates during which the exams are administered. Candidates can register for the exam between the application's accepted starting date and the regular application deadline. As of this writing, the application fees are $300 USD for SHRM members or $400 USD for non-SHRM members for either the SHRM-CP or SHRM-SCP exam. Candidates who apply after the regular application deadline and before the late application deadline will incur a late application fee. Applications submitted after the late application deadline date will not be accepted.

Go to www.shrm.org/certification/apply for detailed information.

Exam Delivery, Duration, and Format

Prometric is SHRM's test delivery vendor that provides computerized exam administration at more than 8,000 testing centers in 160 countries.[9] The time allowed and the exam format are as follows:

- The exam taker has up to 4 hours to answer a total of 160 multiple-choice questions, of which approximately 60 percent are knowledge-based questions and approximately 40 percent are scenario-based situational judgment items focused on the behavioral competencies.

- Also included are 30 "field test" items that do not count toward an exam taker's final score.

- Two minutes are allotted for applicant confirmation details, eight minutes are allotted for an introduction and tutorial prior to the exam, and another five minutes at the end of the exam are for a survey.

Exam Content Outline[10]

The SHRM-CP and SHRM-SCP exams are based on the SHRM BoCK and its two major aspects of modern HR practice, competencies and knowledge. Accordingly, the exams contain two types of questions:

- **Knowledge items**, which cover the three knowledge domains (People, Organization, and Workplace) associated with the SHRM BoCK's technical competency. There are two categories of stand-alone knowledge-based items on the exams. Items in the first category are referred to as HR-specific *knowledge items* (KIs), covering key concept topics associated with the 15 HR functional areas. Items in the second category, referred to as *foundational knowledge items* (FKIs), cover key concept topics considered foundational to the eight behavioral competencies.

- **Situational judgment items (SJIs)**, which cover the KSAs (knowledge, skills, and abilities) associated with the SHRM BoCK's behavioral competencies.

HR Knowledge Domains	Item Type
People (17 percent)	
Organization (17 percent)	HR-specific knowledge (50 percent)
Workplace (16 percent)	

Behavioral Competency Clusters	Item Type
Leadership (13 percent)	
Business (18.5 percent)	Situational Judgment (40 percent) Foundational Knowledge (10 percent)
Interpersonal (18.5 percent)	

Table 2-3   Exam Score Content Weighting

Answers to these questions determine the final score for the exams. In addition, both exams contain "field test" items, the answers for which will not be scored. Field test items are unscored because they are being presented for the first time for the purpose of statistically determining their validity and reliability. Field test items are randomly distributed throughout the exam. Candidate answers to field test questions will not count toward any part of their final exam scores.

Knowledge items assess candidate understanding of factual information. Examinees are asked questions on particular subject areas. Correct answers receive full credit. Incorrect answers receive no credit.

Situational judgment items assess candidate KSA capabilities and decision-making skills, which are not easily measured using traditional knowledge-based questions. Examinees are presented with realistic work-related scenarios and asked to choose the best of several possible strategies to resolve or address the issues described in each scenario. Because more than one strategy may be effective for addressing actual work-related scenarios, examinees receive full credit for choosing the best possible answer. All other answers, which reflect either less effective or ineffective strategies, receive no credit.

Table 2-3 shows the score weighting for each subject area.

Exam Identification and Conduct Guidelines

The SHRM certification exams are administered in highly secure testing centers.[11] All exam candidates are required to provide proof of identity with an unexpired government-issued photo identification with signature, such as a driver's license, a passport, or a military ID. The name and photo on the primary or secondary ID must exactly match the name on the candidate's authorization to test (ATT) letter.

If the ID used does not have a photo or signature, a second form of identification must be provided that contains the missing information. The name on the second ID must be the same as the name on the first ID.

The following are acceptable forms of secondary identification:

- Valid employer identification card
- Valid credit card with signature
- Valid bank card with photo

If you do not have the appropriate form of ID, contact SHRM at least five business days before your scheduled exam appointment date to determine your options.

Trained proctors, called *test center administrators* (TCAs), supervise the Prometric testing centers. Irregularities observed or suspected by the proctors, or identified by subsequent statistical analysis of your answers on the exam, may result in your removal from participation in the test or invalidation of your score. Irregularities include creating a disturbance, giving or receiving unauthorized information or aid to or from other examinees, and attempting to remove materials from the testing room. SHRM has the right to investigate each incident of misconduct or irregularity.

Testing center rules of conduct include the following:

- You must present an unexpired government-issued ID with a photo and signature to be admitted to the exam.
- Arrive at the testing center at least 30 minutes before your scheduled exam appointment time to check in. Late arrivals are not admitted.
- Note taking and the use of audible beepers, mobile phones, or memory-capable devices are prohibited in the testing room.
- You will be asked to empty and turn out your pockets.
- No breaks are scheduled during the exam. Candidates who have to leave the testing room to take a break will not be given extra time on the exams.
- Candidates cannot leave the testing center during a break.
- Accessing your mobile phone or study materials after your arrival at the testing center or during breaks is prohibited.
- Smoking is prohibited at the testing center and during breaks.
- Religious headwear can be worn into the testing room; however, it may be subject to inspection by a TCA before entry into the testing room is permitted.
- All exams are monitored and may be recorded in both audio and video format.
- Prometric will provide lockers for exam candidates to store their purses, cell phones, jackets, food, drinks, and medical supplies.

My Experience Taking the New SHRM-SCP Examination

To be honest, I was "drafted" into taking the new SHRM-SCP examination as one of the SHRM Study Group instructors. The intention was to use my exam experience as an opportunity to share my experience with people preparing to take the SHRMCP or SHRM-SCP exam for the first time. It was many years ago that I first took my SHRM SPHR exam (then called the "ASPA SPHR exam"), well before there was a Prometric to administer the exam nationwide using the wonderful capabilities of technology.

Following my first exam experience, I promised myself I would never do that again; I would always ensure I had sufficient credits to be able to recertify when the time came for recertification. Now, not only was I being asked to take the exam again, but, even scarier, this was SHRM's new certification program with a heightened presence of international subject matter and focus on behavioral competencies. I had been active in the HR profession for many years, but what if now I failed to pass the new SHRMSCP exam? Well, it was too late to back out. Certainly, as a program instructor, my only choice was to accept this "opportunity" to take the exam.

First, I had to register with SHRM and then with Prometric. I chose a date late in the registration window more out of a lack of excitement (to put it mildly) than anything else. Finally, I registered to take the exam on June 24, scheduled from 1 P.M. to 5 P.M. (to be honest, the four-hour exam window was a bit intimidating by itself). My test location was Alameda, California. Okay, now I am committed I thought; there was no backing out, unless maybe there was an earthquake. Actually, I didn't have much hope that would happen in a timely way. Oh well, time to prepare.

Although I carefully laid out a vigorous study plan (I wasn't going to be embarrassed if I could help it), as I suspected, a thousand unexpected things distracted me. I don't know if that was just my way of avoiding the issue or whether those things were real. Who knows? In any case, I found that the test date was just a week away and I still was only halfway through SHRM's Learning System. By the way, the Learning System is an excellent resource. It is an easy read and covers the subject matter well. But, not surprisingly, I found myself in panic mode a week before my test date. I decided to block big chunks of whatever time there was left to at least read all of the Learning System.

Well, June 24 arrived. Yes, I did read all of the Learning System material but not as well as I should have. There was no backing out now, though. Normally, driving from Walnut Creek, where I live, to Alameda takes no more than an hour in the middle of a workday. I allowed two hours just to be safe. Actually, I drove the distance in less than 45 minutes. The good news was that I had time to kill; the bad news was that I had time to kill but I was too nervous to do any last-minute study. Even experienced HR professionals who have been around the block a few decades can be nervous when being tested on our knowledge and capabilities.

Prometric turned out to be well organized. The staff members were professional but thorough. Test takers really will do well to think of the airport security screening process to mentally prepare for the test center experience. No watches are allowed, not even the lowest-tech models. A metal-detecting wand was used all over, and there was a requirement to lift each pant leg to see whether anything was stashed in socks. We were allowed to take two tissues but instructed to keep them on the surface of the desk. A security camera is focused on every test taker.

(*continued*)

The exam provides 3 hours and 40 minutes for answering 180 questions. Test takers are warned, so they don't feel cheated, especially if they had been timing themselves during their practice runs prior to the real thing. There is a pretest that takes up to 11 minutes, but if you finish early, you are not allowed to use the extra minutes elsewhere. By the way, the pretest is there to help you become familiar with the hardware and software. The remaining time is for survey questions, such as picking the three most important reasons you are testing for your SHRM certification.

A nice feature with the 90 scenario questions is an intuitive highlighter function. It is explained during the pretest. When test takers get to a scenario question, they should hit the "Next" button so they are able to read the first question they will need to answer from the scenario paragraphs. They should feel free to highlight anything that strikes them as being important. The scenario is on the left, and the questions are on the right side of the screen.

For the SHRM-SCP exam, the questions were grouped by styles, that is, knowledge followed by behavioral scenario and then knowledge again followed by scenario. As I recall, it went 30 knowledge questions, followed by 45 scenario questions, followed by 30 more knowledge questions, followed by 45 scenario questions, and finishing with 30 knowledge questions. There were 10 to 15 scenarios in total with several (two to five) multiple-choice questions attached to each of them.

SHRM-SCP test takers would be well served to know their balanced score cards, SWOT analysis, Perlmutter's HQ orientations, details of the WARN Act, and compa-ratios, but I didn't need to do any math.

There is a huge emphasis/bias in the material on large global institutions and big data. This bias may make many HR practitioners with mostly small to medium-size domestic organization experience feel overwhelmed, lost, or frustrated when preparing for this exam. (How do I make sense of this when our HRIS system is an Excel spreadsheet, or what if I don't have a corporate social responsibility manager like the text describes as an answer?)

Well, it turns out that after all was said and done, I passed!

My closing thoughts are that this exam is really not for everyone. Even the experienced HR practitioner whose work experience is mainly with small to medium-size organizations may find the exam experience overwhelming. On the other hand, HR practitioners with large global organization experience will find the experience stimulating. Those who pass the exam certainly can say that they "earned" their certification.

William D. Kelly, author

How Exams Are Scored

The SHRM certification exams are designed to distinguish candidates who have the appropriate levels of competency and knowledge from those who do not.

Your performance on the certification exam is measured against a predetermined standard. The SHRM-CP standard is the level of competency and knowledge that can be reasonably expected of individuals with basic competence in HR management. The SHRM-SCP standard is the level of competency and knowledge that can be reasonably expected of individuals with senior-level competence in HR management.

Your performance is not measured against the performance of other individuals taking the test. Thus, if everyone who takes the test meets the knowledge and competency standards, everyone will pass.

The passing scores for the SHRM-CP and SHRM-SCP exams are set using the Modified Angoff method, a best-practice procedure setting performance standards for certification, licensure, and admissions tests.[12]

Candidates will receive a provisional on-screen pass/did not pass decision at the testing center upon completion of the exam. An electronic version of the provisional report will be e-mailed to the address provided when scheduling the exam. Approximately 3 to 4 weeks after sitting for the exam, candidates will receive an e-mail directing them to retrieve their official results from the SHRM online portal. Those who pass their exam will be able to download a PDF file of their certificate.

Official test results will be sent by postal mail to the primary address in the candidate's online account. To protect confidentiality, results are not provided by e-mail, phone, or fax.

Candidates who pass the exam receive an official score report plus a credential certificate and a lapel pin. The report confirms that they passed the exam, successfully completing the certification process.

Candidates who do not pass the exam receive an official score report with their actual score, plus a diagnostic report outlining their performance. This information is provided to help candidates decide whether to retake the exam and how to prepare.

Chapter Review

Human resource management has evolved over the years into a complex, multidimensional endeavor with expansive global as well as domestic implications. The need to establish competency in today's world requires HR professionals to apply both knowledge and behavioral competencies in order to carry out their responsibilities. The SHRM-Certified Professional (CP) and SHRM-Senior Certified Professional (SCP) certification credentials are designed to test and validate the HR professional's capabilities at all levels in order to meet today's requirements on a global scale.

References

1. The SHRM Body of Competency & Knowledge (BoCK), Introduction, page 1.

2. The SHRM Body of Competency & Knowledge (BoCK), Development of the SHRM BoCK, page 4.

3. BoCK, Competency Definitions, page 4.

4. The SHRM Body of Competency & Knowledge (BoCK), HR Expertise, page 32.

5. SHRM Certification Handbook, The SHRM Certification Commission, page 26.

6. SHRM Certification Handbook, The SHRM Body of Competency & Knowledge, page 4.

7. SHRM Certification Handbook, Exam Eligibility Criteria, page 5.

8. SHRM Certification Handbook, Application Deadlines and Exam Windows, page 107.

9. SHRM Certification Handbook, Preparing for the Exam, page 15.

10. SHRM Certification Handbook, Exam Content Outline, page 16.

11. SHRM Certification Handbook, Taking the Exam, page 18.

12. SHRM Certification Handbook, Test Results, page 21.

U.S. Laws and Regulations

In this chapter we introduce the federal laws and legislation that the human resources professional must know and understand. It is our belief that when you thoroughly read these laws and regulations, it will help you understand the material written in Part II of this book. Knowing these laws can sometimes make the difference for the exam taker on selecting the right, *or almost right*, answer on the SHRM Certified Professional (SHRM-CP) and SHRM Senior Certified Professional (SHRM-SCP) exams. After studying this chapter and completing the practice questions, you should have an understanding of the relevance of these laws in the employment relationship. HR professionals in both small and large companies play an important role in dealing with day-to-day employment issues relating to recruiting, hiring, managing, and training of employees. Ensuring that an employer's policies and actions follow the law and keeping employers out of legal jeopardy are essential functions valued by employers.

What You Need to Know Concerning Employee Management

We have structured this chapter so that it not only covers the necessary knowledge needed for the Society for Human Resource Management (SHRM) exams but can also be used as a reference tool in your day-to-day needs while working in human resources. The laws are summarized and listed in groupings according to the number of employees an organization employs, from 1 to 100+. Included is a reference uniform resource locator (URL) that points to the law's full description. Legal regulation constantly evolves, so when using this guide as a reference book, be sure to check with your attorney about specific state laws that govern your work locations.

- If you have from 1 to 14 employees, there are 54 federal laws and regulations you must abide by.
- If you have from 15 to 19 employees, there are an additional ten federal laws for your attention.

- If you have from 20 to 49 employees, add another four laws to the list.
- If you have from 50 to 99 employees, add another six laws to the list.
- If you have 100 or more employees, there are a total of 67 federal laws you must know and be in compliance with.
- If you are in a federal agency, you must comply with six laws specifically focused on your employee management issues.

In other chapters we will direct you back to this chapter's specific laws for reference. We suggest that you thoroughly explore this chapter's information before moving into subsequent chapters for greater ease with the HR Certification Institute (HRCI) exam's Body of Knowledge. Then gauge your understanding of the laws by using the practice questions at the end of this chapter.

1. When You Have One or More Employees

Employers sometimes forget that the moment they hire their first employee they become subject to a host of legal requirements. Here are 54 laws that will impact an employer with one or more employees on the payroll.

1.1. The Clayton Act (1914)

This legislation modified the Sherman Anti-Trust Act by prohibiting mergers and acquisitions that would lessen competition. It also prohibited a single person from being a director of two or more competing corporations. The act also restricts the use of injunctions against labor and legalized peaceful strikes, picketing, and boycotts.

For more information, see 15 U.S.C. Sec.12, www.law.cornell.edu/uscode/text/15/12, or perform an Internet search for the law by name.

1.2. The Consumer Credit Protection Act (1968)

Congress expressed limits to the amount of wages that can be garnished or withheld in any one week by an employer to satisfy creditors. This law also prohibits employee dismissal because of garnishment for any one indebtedness.

For more information, see www.dol.gov/compliance/laws/comp-ccpa.htm or perform an Internet search for the law by name.

1.3. The Copeland "Anti-Kickback" Act (1934)

This act precludes a federal contractor or subcontractor from inducing an employee to give up any part of his or her wages to the employer for the benefit of having a job. For more information, see www.dol.gov/whd/regs/statutes/copeland.htm or perform an Internet search for the law by name.

1.4. The Copyright Act (1976)

The Copyright Act offers protection of "original works" for authors so others may not print, duplicate, distribute, or sell their work. In 1998, the Copyright Term Extension Act further extended copyright protection to the duration of the author's life plus 70 years for general copyrights and to 95 years for works made for hire and works copyrighted before 1978. If anyone in the organization writes technical instructions, policies and procedures, manuals, or even e-mail responses to customer inquiries, it would be a good idea to speak with your attorney and arrange some copyright agreements to clarify whether the employer or the employee who authored those documents will be designated the copyright owner. Written agreements can be helpful in clearing any possible misunderstandings. For more information, see www.copyright.gov/title17/92appa.pdf or perform an Internet search for the law by name.

1.5. The Davis-Bacon Act (1931)

This law requires contractors and subcontractors on certain federally funded or assisted construction projects over $2,000 in the United States to pay wages and fringe benefits at least equal to those prevailing in the local area where the work is performed. This law applies only to laborers and mechanics. It also allows trainees and apprentices to be paid less than the predetermined rates under certain circumstances. For more information, see www.dol.gov/whd/regs/statutes/dbra.htm or perform an Internet search for the law by name.

1.6. The Dodd-Frank Wall Street Reform and Consumer Protection Act (2010)

This law offers a very wide range of mandates affecting all federal financial regulatory agencies and almost every part of the nation's financial services industry. It includes a nonbinding vote for shareholders on executive compensation, golden parachutes, and return of executive compensation based on inaccurate financial statements. Also included are requirements to report chief executive officer (CEO) pay compared to the average employee compensation and provision of financial rewards for whistleblowers. There are pending proposals for new regulations, so be sure to watch for any final versions of the regulatory requirements. For more information, see www.sec.gov/about/laws/wallstreetreform-cpa.pdf or perform an Internet search for the law by name.

1.7. The Economic Growth and Tax Relief Reconciliation Act (EGTRRA) (2001)

Here are modifications to the Internal Revenue Code that adjust pension vesting schedules, increasing retirement plan limits, permitting pre-tax catch-up contributions by participants over the age of 50 in certain plans (which are not tested for discrimination when made available to the entire workforce), and modification of distribution and rollover rules. For more information, see www.irs.gov/pub/irs-tege/epchd104.pdf or perform an Internet search for the law by name.

1.8. The Electronic Communications Privacy Act (ECPA) (1986)

This is actually a unique law composed of two pieces of legislation, the Wiretap Act and the Stored Communications Act. Combined, they provide rules for access, use, disclosure, interpretation, and privacy protections of electronic communications, and they provide the possibility of both civil and criminal penalties for violations. They prohibit interception of e-mails in transmission and access to e-mails in storage. The implications for HR have to do with recording employee conversations. Warnings such as "This call may be monitored or recorded for quality purposes" are intended to provide the notice required by this legislation. Having cameras in the workplace to record employee or visitor activities is also covered, and notices must be given to anyone subject to observation or recording. Recording without such a notice can be a violation of this act. If employers make observations of employee activities and/or record telephone and other conversations between employees and others and proper notice is given to employees, employees will have no expectation of privacy during the time they are in the workplace.

For more information, see www.justice.gov/jmd/ls/legislative_histories/pl99-508/pl99-508.html or perform an Internet search for the law by name.

1.9. The Employee Polygraph Protection Act (1988)

Before 1988, it was common for employers to use "lie detectors" as tools in investigations of inappropriate employee behavior. That changed when this act prohibited the use of lie detector tests for job applicants and employees of companies engaged in interstate commerce. Exceptions are made for certain conditions, including law enforcement and national security. There is a federal poster requirement. Note: Many state laws also prohibit the use of lie detector tests.

For more information, see www.dol.gov/compliance/laws/comp-eppa.htm or perform an Internet search for the law by name.

1.10. The Employee Retirement Income Security Act (ERISA) (1974)

This law doesn't require employers to establish pension plans but governs how those plans are managed once they are established. It establishes uniform minimum standards to ensure that employee benefit plans are established and maintained in a fair and financially sound manner; protects employees covered by a pension plan from losses in benefits due to job changes, plant closings, bankruptcies, or mismanagement; and protects plan beneficiaries. It covers most employers engaged in interstate commerce. Public-sector employees and many churches are not subject to ERISA. Employers that offer retirement plans must also conform with the Internal Revenue Service (IRS) code in order to receive tax advantages. For more information, see www.dol.gov/compliance/laws/comp-erisa.htm or perform an Internet search for the law by name.

1.11. The Equal Pay Act (EPA) (Amendment to the FLSA) (1963)

Equal pay requirements apply to all employers. The act is an amendment to the FLSA and is enforced by the Equal Employment Opportunity Commission (EEOC). It prohibits employers from discriminating on the basis of sex by paying wages to employees at a rate less than the rate paid to employees of the opposite sex for equal work on jobs requiring equal skill, effort, and responsibility, and which are performed under similar working conditions. It does not address the concept of comparable worth. For more information, see www.eeoc.gov/laws/statutes/epa.cfm or perform an Internet search for the law by name.

1.12. The FAA Modernization and Reform Act (2012)

Congress took these actions in 2012 to amend the Railway Labor Act to change union certification election processes in the railroad and airline industries and impose greater oversight of the regulatory activities of the National Mediation Board (NMB). This law requires the Government Accountability Office (GAO) initially to evaluate the NMB's certification procedures and then audit the NMB's operations every 2 years. For more information, see www.faa.gov/regulations_policies/reauthorization/media/PLAW-112publ95[1].pdf or perform an Internet search for the law by name.

1.13. The Fair and Accurate Credit Transactions Act (FACT) (2003)

The financial privacy of employees and job applicants was enhanced in 2003 with these amendments to the Fair Credit Reporting Act, providing for certain requirements in third-party investigations of employee misconduct charges. Employers are released from obligations to disclose requirements and obtain employee consent if the investigation involves suspected misconduct, a violation of the law or regulations, or a violation of preexisting written employer policies. A written plan to prevent identity theft is required. For more information, see www.gpo.gov/fdsys/pkg/PLAW-108publ159/pdf/PLAW-108publ159.pdf or perform an Internet search for the law by name.

1.14. The Fair Credit Reporting Act (FCRA) (1970)

This was the first major legislation to regulate the collection, dissemination, and use of consumer information, including consumer credit information. It requires employers to notify any individual in writing if a credit report may be used in making an employment decision. Employers must also get a written authorization from the subject individual before asking a credit bureau for a credit report. The Fair Credit Reporting Act also protects the privacy of background investigation information and provides methods for ensuring that information is accurate. Employers who take adverse action against a job applicant or current employee based on information contained in the prospective or current employee's consumer report will have additional disclosures to make to that individual. For more information, see www.ftc.gov/os/statutes/031224fcra.pdf or perform an Internet search for the law by name.

1.15. The Fair Labor Standards Act (FLSA) (1938)

The FLSA is one of a handful of federal laws that establish the foundation for employee treatment. It is a major influence in how people are paid, in employment of young people, and in how records are to be kept on employment issues such as hours of work. The law introduced a maximum 44-hour 7-day workweek, established a national minimum wage, guaranteed "time-and-a-half" for overtime in certain jobs, and prohibited most employment of minors in "oppressive child labor," a term that is defined in the statute. It applies to employees engaged in interstate commerce or employed by an enterprise engaged in commerce or in the production of goods for commerce, unless the employer can claim an exemption from coverage. It is interesting to note that FLSA, rather than the Civil Rights Act of 1964, is the first federal law to require employers to maintain records on employee race and sex identification.

Provisions and Protections

Employers covered under the "enterprise" provisions of this law include public agencies; private employers whose annual gross sales exceed $500,000; those operating a hospital or a school for mentally or physically disabled or gifted children; and a preschool, an elementary or secondary school, or an institution of higher education (profit or non-profit). Individuals can still be covered even if they don't fit into one of the enterprises listed. If the employees' work regularly involves them in commerce between the states, they would be covered. These include employees who work in communications or transportation; regularly use the mail, telephone, or telegraph for interstate communication or keep records of interstate transactions; handle shipping or receiving goods moving in interstate commerce; regularly cross state lines in the course of employment; or work for independent employers who contract to do clerical, custodial, maintenance, or other work for firms engaged in interstate commerce or in the production of goods for interstate commerce. The FLSA establishes a federal minimum wage that has been raised from time to time since the law was originally passed. The FLSA prohibits shipment of goods in interstate commerce that were produced in violation of the minimum wage, overtime pay, child labor, or special minimum wage provisions of the law.

Recordkeeping

FLSA proscribes methods for determining whether a job is exempt or nonexempt from overtime pay requirements of the act. If a job is exempt from those requirements, incumbents can work as many hours of overtime as the job requires without being paid for their overtime. Exempt versus nonexempt status attaches to the job, not the incumbent. So, someone with an advanced degree who is working in a clerical job may be nonexempt because of the job requirements, not their personal qualifications. Employers are permitted to have a policy that calls for paying exempt employees when they work overtime. That is a voluntary provision of a benefit in excess of federal requirements. State laws may have additional requirements. People who work in nonexempt jobs must be paid overtime according to the rate computation methods provided for in the act.

Usually, this is a requirement for overtime after 40 hours of regular time worked during a single workweek. The act also describes how a workweek is to be determined.

Each employer covered by the FLSA must keep records for each covered, nonexempt worker. Those records must include the following:

- Employee's full name and Social Security number.
- Address, including ZIP code.
- Birth date, if younger than 19.
- Sex.
- Occupation.
- Time and day of week when employee's workweek begins.
- Hours worked each day and total hours worked each workweek. (This includes a record of the time work began at the start of the day, when the employee left for a meal break, the time the employee returned to work from the meal break, and the time work ended for the day.)
- Basis on which employee's wages are paid (hourly, weekly, piecework).
- Regular hourly pay rate.
- Total daily or weekly straight-time earnings.
- Total overtime earnings for the workweek.
- All additions or deductions from the employee's wages.
- Total wages paid each pay period.
- Date of payment and the pay period covered by the payment.

There is no limit in the FLSA to the number of hours employees age 16 and older may work in any workweek. There is a provision for employers to retain all payroll records, collective bargaining agreements, sales, and purchase records for at least 3 years. Any time card, piecework record, wage rate tables, and work and time schedules should be retained for at least 2 years. A workplace poster is required to notify employees of the federal minimum wage.

The federal child labor provisions of the FLSA, also known as the child labor laws, were enacted to ensure that when young people work, the work is safe and does not jeopardize their health, well-being, or educational opportunities. These provisions also provide limited exemptions. Workers under 14 years of age are restricted to jobs such as newspaper delivery to local customers; baby sitting on a casual basis; acting in movies, TV, radio, or theater; and working as a home worker gathering evergreens and making evergreen wreathes. Under no circumstances, even if the business is family owned, may a person this young work in any of the 17 most hazardous jobs. See Figure 3-1 for a list of the 17 most hazardous jobs.

- Manufacturing or storing of explosives
- Driving a motor vehicle or working as an outside helper on motor vehicles
- Coal mining
- Forest fire fighting and forest fire prevention, timber tract, forestry service, and occupations in logging and sawmilling
- Using power-driven woodworking machines
- Exposure to radioactive substances and ionizing radiation
- Using power-driven hoisting apparatuses
- Using power-driven metal-forming, punching, and shearing machines
- Mining, other than coal
- Using power-driven meat-processing machines, slaughtering, meat and poultry packing, processing, or rendering
- Using power-driven bakery machines
- Using balers, compactors, and power-driven paper-products machines
- Manufacturing brick, tile, and related products
- Using power-driven circular saws, band saws, guillotine shears, chain saws, reciprocating saws, wood chippers, and abrasive cutting discs
- Working in wrecking, demolition, and ship-breaking operations
- Roofing and work performed on or about a roof
- Trenching or excavating

Source: "U.S. Department of Labor, eLaws Fair Labor Standards Act Advisor"

Figure 3-1   The 17 most dangerous jobs that may not be performed by workers under 18 years of age

For workers aged 14 and 15, all work must be performed outside school hours, and these workers may not work

- More than 3 hours on a school day, including Friday
- More than 18 hours per week when school is in session
- More than 8 hours per day when school is not in session
- More than 40 hours per week when school is not in session
- Before 7 A.M. or after 7 P.M. on any day, except from June 1 through Labor Day, when nighttime work hours are extended to 9 P.M.

Until employees reach the age of 18 it is necessary for them to obtain a work permit from their school district. For workers aged 16 through 17, there are no restrictions on the number of hours that can be worked per week. There continues to be a ban on working any job among the 17 most hazardous industries. All of these conditions must be met, or the employer will be subject to penalties from the U.S. Department of Labor.

Overtime Computation

Overtime is required at a rate of 1.5 times the normal pay rate for all hours worked over 40 in a single workweek. An employer may designate that their workweek begins at a given day and hour and continues until that same day and hour 7 days later. Once selected, that same workweek definition must be maintained consistently until there is a legitimate business reason for making a change. That change must be clearly communicated in advance to all employees who will be affected by the change. No pay may be forfeit because the employer changes its workweek definition. Compensating time off is permitted under the FLSA if it is given at the same rates required for overtime pay.

Enforcement

Provisions of the FLSA are enforced by the U.S. Department of Labor's Wage and Hour Division. With offices around the country, this agency is able to interact with employees on complaints and follow up with employers by making an on-site visit if necessary. If violations are found during an investigation, the agency has the authority to make recommendations for changes that would bring the employer into compliance. Retaliation against any employee for filing a complaint under the FLSA or in any other way availing himself or herself of the legal rights it offers is subject to additional penalties. Willful violations may bring criminal prosecution and fines up to $10,000. Employers who are convicted a second time for willfully violating FLSA can find themselves in prison.

The Wage and Hour Division may, if it finds products produced during violations of the act, prevent an employer from shipping any of those goods. It may also "freeze" shipments of any product manufactured while overtime payment requirements were violated. A 2-year limit applies to recovery of back pay unless there was a willful violation, which triggers a 3-year liability. For more information, see www.dol.gov/whd/regs/statutes/ FairLaborStandAct.pdf or perform an Internet search for the law by name.

1.16. The Foreign Corrupt Practices Act (FCPA) (1997)

The FCPA prohibits American companies from making bribery payments to foreign officials for the purpose of obtaining or keeping business. Training for employees who are involved with international negotiations should include a warning to avoid anything even looking like a bribery payment to a foreign company or its employees. For more information, see www.justice.gov/criminal/fraud/fcpa/ or perform an Internet search for the law by name.

1.17. The Health Information Technology for Economic and Clinical Health Act (HITECH) (2009)

The HITECH Act requires that anyone with custody of personal health records send notification to affected individuals if their personal health records have been disclosed, or the employer believes they have been disclosed, to any unauthorized person. Enacted as part of the American Recovery and Reinvestment Act (ARRA), this law made several changes to the Health Insurance Portability and Accountability Act, including the establishment of a federal standard for security breach notifications that requires covered entities, in the event of a breach of any personal health records (PHI) information, to notify each individual whose PHI has been disclosed without authorization. For more information, see www.hhs.gov/ocr/privacy/hipaa/administrative/enforcementrule/hitechenforcementifr .html or perform an Internet search for the law by name.

1.18. The Health Insurance Portability and Accountability Act (HIPAA) (1996)

This law ensures that individuals who leave or lose their jobs can obtain health coverage even if they or someone in their family has a serious illness or injury or is pregnant. It also provides privacy requirements related to medical records for individuals as young as 12 years old. It also limits exclusions for preexisting conditions and guarantees renewability of health coverage to employers and employees, allowing people to change jobs without the worry of loss of coverage. It also restricts the ability of employers to impose actively-at-work requirements as preconditions for health plan eligibility, as well as a number of other benefits. For more information, see www.hhs .gov/ocr/privacy or perform an Internet search for the law by name.

1.19. The Immigration and Nationality Act (INA) (1952)

The INA is the first law that pulled together all of the issues associated with immigration and is considered the foundation on which all following immigration laws have been built. It addresses employment eligibility and employment verification. It defines the conditions for the temporary and permanent employment of aliens in the United States.

The INA defines an *alien* as any person lacking citizenship or status as a national of the United States. The INA differentiates aliens as follows:

- Resident or nonresident
- Immigrant or nonimmigrant
- Documented and undocumented

The need to curtail illegal immigration led to the enactment of the Immigration Reform and Control Act (IRCA). For more information, see www.dol.gov/compliance/ laws/comp-ina.htm or perform an Internet search for the law by name.

1.20. The Immigration Reform and Control Act (IRCA) (1986)

This is the first law to require new employees to prove both their identity and their right to work in this country. Regulations implementing this law created the Form I-9,[1] which must be completed by each new employee and the employer. Form I-9 has been updated many times since 1986. Please be sure you are using the most current version of the form. There are document retention requirements. The law prohibits discrimination against job applicants on the basis of national origin or citizenship. It establishes penalties for employers who hire illegal aliens. For more information, see www.eeoc.gov/eeoc/history/35th/thelaw/irca.html or perform an Internet search for the law by name.

1.21. The IRS Intermediate Sanctions (2002)

Here we find guidelines for determining reasonable compensation for executives of nonprofit organizations. It was enacted by the IRS and applied to nonprofit organizations that engage in the transactions that inure to the benefit of a disqualified person within the organization. These rules allow the IRS to impose penalties when it determines that top officials have received excessive compensation from their organizations. Intermediate sanctions may be imposed either in addition to or instead of revocation of the exempt state of the organization. For more information, see www .irs.gov/pub/irs-tege/eotopice03.pdf or perform an Internet search for the law by name.

1.22. The Labor-Management Relations Act (LMRA) (1947)

Also called the Taft-Hartley Act, this is the first national legislation that placed controls on unions. It prohibits unfair labor practices by unions and outlaws closed shops, where union membership is required in order to get and keep a job. Employers may not form closed-shop agreements with unions. It requires both parties to bargain in good faith and covers nonmanagement employees in private industry who are not covered by the Railway Labor Act.

For more information, see 29 U.S.C. Sec.141, www.casefilemethod.com/Statuters/ LMRA.pdf or search the Internet for the law by name.

1.23. The Labor-Management Reporting and Disclosure Act (1959)

Also called the Landrum-Griffin Act, this law outlines procedures for redressing internal union problems, protects the rights of union members from corrupt or discriminatory labor unions, and applies to all labor organizations. Specific requirements include the following:

- Unions must conduct secret elections, the results of which can be reviewed by the U.S. Department of Labor.
- A bill of rights guarantees union members certain rights, including free speech.
- Convicted felons and members of the Communist Party cannot hold office in unions.
- Annual financial reporting from unions to the Department of Labor is required.
- All union officials have a fiduciary responsibility in managing union assets and conducting the business of the union.
- Union power to place subordinate organizations in trusteeship is limited.
- Minimum standards for union disciplinary action against its members are provided.

For more information, see www.dol.gov/compliance/laws/comp-lmrda.htm or perform an Internet search for the law by name.

1.24. The Mine Safety and Health Act (1977)

Following a series of deadly mining disasters, the American people demanded that Congress take action to prevent similar events in the future. This law converted the existing Mine Enforcement Safety Administration (MESA) to the Mine Safety and Health Administration (MSHA). For the first time, it brought all coal, metal, and nonmetal mining operations under the same Department of Labor jurisdiction. Regulations and safety procedures for the coal mining industry were not altered, just carried into the new agency for oversight. For more information, see www.dol.gov/compliance/laws/comp-fmsha.htm or perform an Internet search for the law by name.

Provisions and Protections

This law requires the secretaries of labor and health, education, and welfare to create regulations governing the country's mines. All mines are covered if they are involved in commerce, which any active mining operation would be. Regulations that implement this law specify that employees must be provided with certain protective equipment while working in a mine. These devices relate to respiration and fire prevention, among other protections. Protecting against "black lung disease" is a key concern, even today, in the coal mining industry.

Recordkeeping Requirements

Employers engaged in mining operations must inspect their worksites and document the results, reflecting hazards and actions taken to reduce or eliminate the hazards. Employees are to be given access to information related to accident prevention, fatal accident statistics for the year, and instructions on specific hazards they will face while working in the mine. Requirements detail the content of written emergency response plans, emergency mapping, and rescue procedures. Individual employee exposure records must be maintained. Each mine operator is required to conduct surveys of mine exposures and hazards, have a plan to deal with those problems, and keep a record of the results. This information must be made available to MSHA inspectors if they request it.

MSHA Standards

The agency enforces mine safety standards that involve ventilation, chemical exposure, noise, forklifts and other mining equipment, mine shoring, and more. Material safety data sheets (MSDSs) must be available to employees in mining as they are in other industries overseen by the OSHA agency.

MSHA Enforcement

MSHA has a team of federal inspectors that conduct on-site audits of mining operations. MSHA has the authority to cite mine operators for violations of its regulations, and citations can carry a $1,000-per-day penalty in some circumstances.[2]

1.25. The National Industrial Recovery Act (1933)

This was an attempt to help the country get out from the Great Depression. It proposed the creation of "Codes of Fair Competition" for each of several different industries. Essentially, every business would have to identify with and belong to a trade association. The association would then be required to create a Code of Fair Competition for the industry. Antitrust laws would be suspended in favor of the code. Of course, the code would have to be approved by the president of the United States, and the administration would issue federal licenses to every business in the country. If a business refused to participate in the code, its license could be suspended, and that would be the signal for that business to end all operations. There were financial penalties as well. This law didn't fare very well. It was declared unconstitutional by the U.S. Supreme Court in 1935 and was replaced by the National Labor Relations Act later that same year.

For more information, see www.ourdocuments.gov/doc.php?flash=true&doc=66 or perform an Internet search for the law by name.

1.26. The National Labor Relations Act (NLRA) (1935)

This is the "granddaddy" of all labor relations laws in the United States. It initially provided that employees have a right to form unions and negotiate wage and hour issues with employers on behalf of the union membership. Specifically, the NLRA grants to employees the right to organize, join unions, and engage in collective bargaining and other "concerted activities." It also protects against unfair labor practices by employers.

Following on the heels of the National Industrial Recovery Act's failures, this law stepped into the void and addressed both union and employer obligations in labor relations issues. It established the National Labor Relations Board (NLRB), which would help define fair labor practices in the following decades. The NLRB has the power to accept and investigate complaints of unfair labor practices by either management or labor unions. It plays a judicial role within an administrative setting. This law is sometimes called the Wagner Act. The following are some key provisions:

- The right of workers to organize into unions for collective bargaining
- The requirement of employers to bargain in good faith when employees have voted in favor of a union to represent them
- Requirement that unions represent all members equally
- Covers nonmanagement employees in private industry who are not already covered by the Railway Labor Act

For more information, see www.nlrb.gov/national-labor-relations-act or perform an Internet search for the law by name.

1.27. The Needlestick Safety and Prevention Act (2000)

This law modifies the Occupational Safety and Health Act by introducing a new group of requirements in the medical community. Sharps, as they are called, are needles, puncture devices, knives, scalpels, and other tools that can harm either the person using them or someone else. The law and its regulations provide rules related to handling these devices, disposing of them, and encouraging invention of new devices that will reduce or eliminate the risk associated with injury due to sharps. Sharps injuries are to be recorded on the OSHA 300 log with "privacy case" listed and not the employee's name. Blood-borne pathogens and transmission of human blood–borne illnesses such as AIDS/HIV and hepatitis are key targets of this law. Reducing the amount of injury and subsequent illness due to puncture, stab, or cut wounds is a primary objective. There are communication requirements, including employment poster content requirements.

For more information, see www.gpo.gov/fdsys/pkg/PLAW-106publ430/html/PLAW-106publ430.htm or perform an Internet search for the law by name.

1.28. The Norris-LaGuardia Act (1932)

Remember that this was still 3 years before the NLRA came to pass. When unions tried to use strikes and boycotts, employers would trot into court and ask for an injunction to prevent such activity. More often than not, they were successful, and judges provided the injunctions. Congress had been pressured by organized labor to restore their primary tools that could force employers to bargain on issues unions saw as important. The following are key provisions of this law:

- It prohibited "yellow-dog" contracts. Those were agreements in which employees promised employers that they would not join unions. This new law declared such contracts to be unenforceable in any federal court.
- It prohibited federal courts from issuing injunctions of any kind against peaceful strikes, boycotts, or picketing when used by a union in connection with a labor dispute.
- It defined labor dispute to include any disagreement about working conditions.

For more information, see 29 U.S.C., Chapter 6, http://uscode.house.gov/download/pls/29C6.txt, or perform an Internet search for the law by name.

1.29. The Occupational Safety and Health Act (OSHA) (1970)

Signed into law by President Richard M. Nixon on December 29, 1970, the Occupational Safety and Health Act created an administrative agency within the U.S. Department of Labor called the Occupational Safety and Health Administration (OSHA). It also created the National Institute of Occupational Safety and Health (NIOSH), which resides inside the Centers for Disease Control (CDC).

Provisions and Protections

Regulations implementing this legislation have grown over time. They are complex and detailed. It is important that HR professionals understand the basics and how to obtain additional detailed information that applies to their particular employer circumstance. There are many standards that specify what employers must do to comply with their legal obligations. Overall, however, the law holds employers accountable for providing a safe and healthy working environment. The "General Duty Clause" in OSHA's regulations says employers shall furnish each employee with a place of employment free from recognized hazards that are likely to cause death or serious injury. It also holds employees responsible for abiding by all safety rules and regulations in the workplace. Some provisions require notices be posted in the workplace covering some of the OSHA requirements. Posters are available for download from the OSHA website without charge. The law applies to all employers, regardless of the employee population size.

Recordkeeping Requirements

OSHA regulations require that records be kept for many purposes. It is necessary to conduct and document inspections of the workplace, looking for safety and health hazards. It is necessary to document and make available to employees records about hazardous materials and how they must be properly handled. Employers with ten or more people on the payroll must summarize all injury and illness instances and post that summary in a conspicuous place within the workplace. That report must remain posted from February 1 to April 30 each year. Certain employers are exempt from some OSHA recordkeeping requirements. They generally are classified by industry Standard Industrial Classification (SIC) code. A list is available on OSHA's website at www .OSHA.gov. Any time there is a serious or fatal accident, a full incident report must be prepared by the employer and maintained in the safety file. These records must be maintained for a minimum of 5 years from the date of the incident. Known as a log of occupational injury or illness, it must include a record of each incident resulting in medical treatment (other than first aid), loss of consciousness, restriction of work or motion, or transfer or termination of employment. If you are in the medical industry, construction industry, or manufacturing industry, or you use nuclear materials of any kind, there are other requirements you must meet. Key to compliance with OSHA rules is communication with employees. Training is often provided by employers to meet this hazard communication requirement. In summary, then, OSHA recordkeeping involves the following:

- Periodic safety inspections of the workplace
- Injury or illness incident reports
- Annual summary of incidents during the previous calendar year
- Injury and illness prevention program (if required by rules governing your industry)
- Employee training on safety procedures and expectations
- Records of training participation
- Material safety data sheets for each chemical used in the workplace (made available to all employees in a well-marked file or binder that can be accessed at any time during work hours)

Occupational Safety and Health Act Enforcement

OSHA inspections may include the following:

- **On-site visits that are conducted without advance notice**   Inspectors can just walk into a place of employment and request that you permit an inspection. You don't have to agree unless the inspector has a search warrant. In the absence of the warrant, you can delay the inspection until your attorney is present.

- **On-site inspections or phone/fax investigations**   Depending on the urgency of the hazard and agreement of the person filing the complaint, inspectors may telephone or fax inquiries to employers. The employer has 5 working days to respond with a detailed description of inspection findings, corrective action taken, and additional action planned.

- **Highly trained compliance officers**   The OSHA Training Institute provides training for OSHA's compliance officers, state compliance officers, state consultants, other federal agency personnel, and the private sector.

Inspection priorities include the following:

- **Imminent danger**   Situations where death or serious injury are highly likely. Compliance officers will ask employers to correct the conditions immediately or remove employees from danger.

- **Fatalities and catastrophes**   Incidents that involve a death or the hospitalization of three or more employees. Employers must report these incidents to OSHA within 8 hours.

- **Worker complaints**   Allegations of workplace hazards or OSHA violations. Employees may request anonymity when they file complaints with OSHA.

- **Referrals**   Other federal, state, or local agencies; individuals; organizations; or the media can make referrals to OSHA so the agency may consider making an inspection.

- **Follow-ups**   Checks for abatement of violations cited during previous inspections are also conducted by OSHA personnel in certain circumstances.

- **Planned or programmed investigations**   OSHA can conduct inspections aimed at specific high-hazard industries or individual workplaces that have experienced high rates of injuries and illnesses. These are sometimes called *targeted investigations*.

Two Types of Standards

The law provides for two types of safety and health standards. The agency has therefore developed its regulations and standards in those two categories.

Normal Standards   If OSHA determines that a specific standard is needed, any of several advisory committees may be called upon to develop specific recommendations. There are two standing committees, and ad hoc committees may be appointed to examine special areas of concern to OSHA. All advisory committees, standing or ad hoc, must have members representing management, labor, and state agencies, as well as one or more designees of the secretary of Health and Human Services (HHS). The occupational safety and health professions and the general public also may be represented.[3]

Emergency Temporary Standards   "Under certain limited conditions, OSHA is authorized to set emergency temporary standards that take effect immediately. First, OSHA must determine that workers are in grave danger due to exposure to toxic substances or agents determined to be toxic or physically harmful or to new hazards and that an emergency standard is needed to protect them. Then, OSHA publishes the emergency temporary standard in the Federal Register, where it also serves as a proposed permanent standard. It is then subject to the usual procedure for adopting a permanent standard except that a final ruling must be made within six months. The validity of an emergency temporary standard may be challenged in an appropriate U.S. Court of Appeals."[4] For more information, see www.dol.gov/compliance/guide/osha.htm or perform an Internet search for the law by name.

1.30. The Omnibus Budget Reconciliation Act (OBRA) (1993)

Signed into law by President Bill Clinton on August 10, 1993, this legislation reduces compensation limits in qualified retirement programs and triggers increased activity in nonqualified retirement programs. It also calls for termination of some plans. For more information, see www.gpo.gov/fdsys/pkg/BILLS-103hr2264enr/pdf/BILLS-103hr2264enr.pdf or perform an Internet search for the law by name.

1.31. The Pension Protection Act (PPA) (2006)

Focused solely on pensions, this law requires employers that have underfunded pension plans to pay a higher premium to the Pension Benefit Guarantee Corporation (PBGC). It also requires employers that terminate pension plans to provide additional funding to those plans. This legislation impacted nearly all aspects of retirement planning, including changes to rules about individual retirement accounts (IRAs). For more information, see www.dol.gov/ebsa/pensionreform.html or perform an Internet search for the law by name.

1.32. The Personal Responsibility and Work Opportunity Reconciliation Act (1996)

This law requires all states to establish and maintain a new hire reporting system designed to enhance enforcement of child support payments. It requires welfare recipients to begin working after 2 years of receiving benefits. States may exempt parents with children younger than 1 from the work requirements. Parents with children younger than 1 may use this exemption only once; they cannot use it again for subsequent children. These parents also are still subject to the 5-year time limit for cash assistance. HR professionals will need to establish and maintain reporting systems to meet these tracking requirements. For more information, see www.acf .hhs.gov/programs/css/resource/the-personal-responsibility-and-work-opportunity-reconcilliation-act or perform an Internet search for the law by name.

1.33. The Portal-to-Portal Act (1947)

By amending the Fair Labor Standards Act (FLSA), this law defines "hours worked" and establishes rules about payment of wages to employees who travel before and/or after their scheduled work shift. The act provides that minimum wages and overtime are not required for "traveling to and from the actual place of performance of the principal activity or activities which such employee is to perform" or for "activities which are preliminary to or postliminary to said principal activity or activities," unless there is a custom or contract to the contrary. For more information, see 29 U.S.C., Chapter 9, http://uscode .house.gov/download/pls/29C9.txt or perform an Internet search for the law by name.

1.34. The Railway Labor Act (1926)

Originally, this law was created to allow railway employees to organize into labor unions. Over the years, it has been expanded in coverage to include airline employees. Covered employers are encouraged to use the Board of Mediation, which has since morphed into the National Mediation Board, a permanent independent agency. For more information, see www.nmb.gov/documents/rla.html or perform an Internet search for the law by name.

1.35. The Rehabilitation Act (1973)

This replaced the Vocational Rehabilitation Act and created support for states to create vocational rehabilitation programs. The term originally used in this legislation was *handicapped*. The law was later modified to replace that term with *disabled*.

Table 3-1 notes some of the most important sections of the Rehabilitation Act.

Section	Requirement
Section 501	Requires nondiscrimination and affirmative action in hiring disabled workers by federal agencies within the executive branch
Section 503	Requires nondiscrimination and affirmative action by federal contractors and subcontractors with contracts valued at $10,000 or more
Section 504	Requires employers subject to the law to provide reasonable accommodation for disabled individuals who can perform the major job duties with or without accommodation

Table 3-1 Key Employment Provisions of the Rehabilitation Act of 1973

For more information see https://www.disability.gov/rehabilitation-act-1973/ or perform an Internet search for the law by name.

1.36. The Retirement Equity Act (REA) (1984)

Signed into law by President Ronald Reagan on August 23, 1984, the REA provides certain legal protections for spousal beneficiaries of qualified retirement programs. It prohibits changes to retirement plan elections, spousal beneficiary designations, or in-service withdrawals without the consent of a spouse. Changing withdrawal options does not require spousal consent. It permits plan administrators to presume spousal survivors annuity and reduce primary pension amounts accordingly. Specific written waivers are required to avoid spousal annuity. For more information, see www.law.cornell.edu/uscode/text/29/1055 or perform an Internet search for the law by name.

1.37. The Revenue Act (1978)

This law added two important sections to the Internal Revenue Tax Code relevant to employee benefits: Section 125, Cafeteria Benefit Plans, and Section 401(k), originally a pre-tax savings program for private-sector employees known as individual retirement accounts (IRAs), subsequently expanded to a second plan opportunity known as "Roth IRA" that permitted funding with after-tax savings. For more information, see www.irs.gov/pub/irs-utl/irpac-br_530_relief_-_appendix_natrm_paper_09032009.pdf or perform an Internet search for the law by name.

1.38. The Sarbanes-Oxley Act (SOX) (2002)

In response to many corrupt practices in the financial industry and the economic disasters they created, Congress passed the Sarbanes-Oxley Act to address the need for oversight and disclosure of information by publicly traded companies.

Provisions and Protections

This law brought some strict oversight to corporate governance and financial reporting for publicly held companies. It holds corporate officers accountable for proper recordkeeping and reporting of financial information, including internal control systems to assure those systems are working properly. There are also requirements for reporting any unexpected changes in financial condition, including potential new liabilities such as lawsuits. Those lawsuits can involve things such as employee complaints of illegal employment discrimination.

It requires administrators of defined contribution plans to provide notice of covered blackout periods and provides whistleblower protection for employees.

This law protects anyone who reports wrongdoing to a supervisor, appointed company officials who handle these matters, a federal regulatory or law enforcement agency, or a member or committee of Congress. It even extends to claims that prove to be false as long as the employee reasonably believed the conduct is a violation of Security Exchange Commission (SEC) rules or a federal law involving fraud against shareholders.

On March 4, 2014, the U.S. Supreme Court issued its opinion in the case of *Lawson v. FMR LLC.* (No. 12–3).[5] The 6–3 decision held that all contractors and subcontractors of publicly held companies are subject to the Sarbanes-Oxley Act, even if they are not publicly held. The takeaway from this ruling is that nearly everyone is now subject to the whistleblower provisions of the Sarbanes-Oxley Act. As Justice Sotomayor suggested in her dissenting opinion:

> For example, public companies often hire "independent contractors," of whom there are more than 10 million, and contract workers, of whom there are more than 11 million. And, they employ outside lawyers, accountants, and auditors as well. While not every person who works for a public company in these nonemployee capacities may be positioned to threaten or harass employees of the public company, many are.
>
> Under [the majority opinion] a babysitter can bring a ... retaliation suit against his employer if his employer is a checkout clerk for the local PetSmart (a public company) but not if she is a checkout clerk for the local Petco (a private company). Likewise the day laborer who works for a construction business can avail himself of [this ruling] if her company has been hired to remodel the local Dick's Sporting Goods store (a public company), but not if it is remodeling a nearby Sports Authority (a private company).

Recordkeeping Requirements

Internal control systems are required to assure that public disclosure of financial information is done as required. The registered accounting firm responsible for reviewing the company's financial reports must attest to the proper implementation of internal control systems and procedures for financial reporting.

SOX Enforcement

Enforcement of the law is done by private-firm audits overseen by the Public Company Accounting Oversight Board (PCAOB). The PCAOB is a nonprofit corporation created by the act to oversee accounting professionals who provide independent audit reports for publicly traded companies. It essentially audits the auditors.

Companies and corporate officers in violation of the act can find themselves subject to fines and/or up to 20 years imprisonment for altering, destroying, mutilating, concealing, or falsifying records, documents, or tangible objects with the intent to obstruct, impede, or influence a legal investigation. For more information, see http://taft.law.uc.edu/CCL/SOact/soact.pdf or perform an Internet search for the law by name.

1.39. The Securities and Exchange Act (1934)

When companies "go public" by issuing common stock for trade, it is done on the "primary market." This law provides for governance in the "secondary market," which is all trading after the initial public offering. It also created the Securities and Exchange Commission, which has oversight authority for the trading of stocks in this country.

It extends the "disclosure" doctrine of investor protection to securities listed and registered for public trading on any of the U.S. exchanges. For more information, see www .law.cornell.edu/wex/securities_exchange_act_of_1934 or perform an Internet search for the law by name.

1.40. The Service Contract Act (SCA) (1965)

Applying to federal contractors (and subcontractors) offering goods and services to the government, this law calls for payment of prevailing wages and benefit requirements to all employees providing service under the agreement. All contractors and subcontractors, other than construction services, with contract value in excess of $2,500 are covered. Safety and health standards also apply to such contracts.

The compensation requirements of this law are enforced by the Wage and Hour Division in the U.S. Department of Labor (DOL). The SCA safety and health requirements are enforced by the Occupational Safety and Health Administration, also an agency within the DOL. For more information, see 41 U.S.C. 351, www.dol.gov/oasam/regs/ statutes/351.htm or perform an Internet search for the law by name.

1.41. The Sherman Anti-Trust Act (1890)

If you travel back in time to the latter part of the nineteenth century, you will find that big business dominated the landscape. There was Standard Oil, Morgan Bank, U.S. Steel, and a handful of railroads. They were huge by comparison with other similar enterprises at the time. And people were concerned that they were monopolizing the marketplace and holding prices high just because they could. John Sherman, a Republican senator from Ohio, was chairman of the Senate Finance Committee. He suggested that the country needed some protections against monopolies and cartels. Thus, this law was created and subsequently used by federal prosecutors to break up the Standard Oil Company into smaller units. Over the years, case law has developed that concludes that attempting to restrict competition or fix prices can be seen as a violation of this law. Restraint of trade is also prohibited. For more information, see 15 U.S.C. Secs. 1–7, www.law.cornell.edu/ uscode/text/15/1 or perform an Internet search for the law by name.

1.42. The Small Business Job Protection Act (1996) (SBJPA)

This law increased federal minimum wage levels and provided some tax incentives to small business owners to protect jobs and increase take-home pay. It also amended the Portal-to-Portal Act for employees who use employer-owned vehicles. It created the SIMPLE 401(k) retirement plan to make pension plans easier for small businesses. Other tax incentives created by this law include the following:

- Employee education incentive—allowed small business owners to exclude up to $5,250 from an employee's taxable income for educational assistance provided by the employer

- Increased the maximum amount of capital expense allowed for a small business to $7,000 per year

- Replaced the Targeted Jobs Tax Credit with the Work Opportunity Tax Credit
- Provided a tax credit to individuals who adopted a child (up to $5,000 per child) and a tax credit of up to $6,000 for adoption of a child with special needs

For more information, see www.ssa.gov/legislation/legis_bulletin_082096.html or perform an Internet search for the law by name.

1.43. The Social Security Act (1935)

The Social Security program began in 1935 in the heart of the Great Depression. It was initially designed to help senior citizens when that group was suffering a poverty rate of 50 percent. It currently includes social welfare and social insurance programs that can help support disabled workers who are no longer able to earn their wages.

The Social Security program is supported through payroll taxes with contributions from both the employee and the employer. Those payroll tax rates are set by the Federal Insurance Contributions Act (FICA) and have been adjusted many times over the years. There are many programs currently under the control of the Social Security Act and its amendments. These include the following:

- Federal old-age benefits (retirement)
- Survivors benefits (spouse benefits, dependent children, and widow/widower benefits)
- Disability insurance for workers no longer able to work
- Temporary Assistance for Needy Families
- Medicare Health Insurance for Aged and Disabled
- Medicaid Grants to States for Medical Assistance Programs
- Supplemental Security Income (SSI)
- State Children's Health Insurance Program (SCHIP)
- Patient Protection and Affordable Care Act

There is currently a separate payroll deduction for Medicare health insurance, which is also funded by both the employee and employer. The Patient Protection and Affordable Care Act (Obamacare) has been implemented. Congress continues to try to find ways to modify it so the cost of medical health insurance can be reduced to individuals. As with other laws and regulations, events can change rapidly. You must keep up with the news of how health care insurance programs are evolving.

A personal Social Security number is used as a tax identification number for federal income tax, including bank records, and to prove work authorization in this country. Social Security numbers can be used in completing Form I-9, which must be completed for every new employee on the payroll. Also required for the I-9 is proof of identity. For more information, see www.ssa.gov/history/35act.html or perform an Internet search for the law by name.

1.44. The Tax Reform Act (1986)

This law made extensive changes to the Internal Revenue Service tax code, including a reduction in tax brackets and all tax rates for individuals. Payroll withholdings were affected, many passive losses and tax shelters were eliminated, and changes were made to the alternative minimum tax computation. This is the law that required all dependent children to have Social Security numbers. That provision reduced the number of fraudulent dependent children claimed on income tax returns by 7 million in its first year. For HR professionals, answers to employee questions about the number of exemptions to claim on their Form W-4 are greatly influenced by this requirement for dependent Social Security numbers. For more information, see http://archive.org/stream/summaryofhr3838t1486unit/summaryofhr3838t1486unit_djvu.txt or perform an Internet search for the law by name.

1.45. The Taxpayer Relief Act (1997)

Congress wanted to give taxpayers a couple of ways to lower their tax payments during retirement, so the Taxpayer Relief Act was passed to create new savings programs called Roth IRAs and Education IRAs. Many individuals were able to achieve a better tax position through these tools. For more information, see www.gpo.gov/fdsys/pkg/BILLS-105hr2014enr/pdf/BILLS-105hr2014enr.pdf or perform an Internet search for the law by name.

1.46. The Trademark Act (1946)

This is the legislation that created federal protections for trademarks and service marks. Officially it was called the Lanham (Trademark) Act, and it set forth the requirements for registering a trademark or service mark to obtain those legal protections. HR people may well have a role to play in training employees in how to properly handle organizational trademarks and the policies that govern those uses. For more information, see www.uspto.gov/trademarks/law/tmlaw.pdf or perform an Internet search for the law by name.

1.47. The Unemployment Compensation Amendments Act (UCA) (1992)

This law established 20 percent as the amount to be withheld from payment of employee savings accounts when leaving an employer and not placing the funds (rolling over) into another tax-approved IRA or 401(k). For more information, see www.socialsecurity.gov/policy/docs/ssb/v56n1/v56n1p87.pdf or perform an Internet search for the law by name.

1.48. The Uniformed Services Employment and Reemployment Rights Act (USERRA) (1994)

USERRA provides instructions for handling employees who are in the reserves and receive orders to report for active duty. The law protects the employment, reemployment, and retention rights of anyone who voluntarily or involuntarily serves or has served in the uniformed services. It requires that employers continue paying for the employee's benefits to the extent they paid for those benefits before the call to duty. It also requires that employers continue giving credit for length of service as though the military service was equivalent to company service. There are specific detailed parameters for how long an employee may wait to engage the employer in return-to-work conversations after being released from active military duty.

This law and its provisions cover all eight U.S. military services and other uniformed services. They are

- Army
- Navy
- Air Force
- Marines
- Public Health Service Commissioned Corps
- National Oceanic and Atmospheric Administration Commissioned Corps
- Coast Guard
- National Guard groups that have been called into active duty

For more information, see www.dol.gov/compliance/laws/comp-userra.htm or perform an Internet search for the law by name.

1.49. The Vietnam Era Veterans Readjustment Assistance Act (VEVRAA) (1974) [as amended by the Jobs for Veterans Act (JVA) (2008)]

Current covered veterans include the following:

- Disabled veterans
- Veterans who served on active duty in the U.S. military during a war or campaign or expedition for which a campaign badge was awarded
- Veterans who, while serving on active duty in the Armed Forces, participated in a U.S. military operation for which an Armed Forces service medal was awarded pursuant to Executive Order 12985
- Recently separated veterans (veterans within 36 months from discharge or release from active duty)

These requirements apply to all federal contractors with a contract valued at $25,000 or more, regardless of the number of total employees.

This veteran support legislation requires all employers subject to the law to post their job openings with their local state employment service. These are the three exceptions to that requirement:

- Jobs that will last 3 days or less
- Jobs that will be filled by an internal candidate
- Jobs that are senior executive positions

Affirmative action outreach and recruiting of veterans is required for federal contractors meeting the contract value threshold. For more information, see www.dol.gov/compliance/laws/comp-vevraa.htm or perform an Internet search for the law by name.

1.50. The Wagner-Peyser Act (1933) [as amended by the Workforce Investment Act (WIA) (1998)]

The Wagner-Peyser Act created a nationwide system of employment offices known as Employment Service Offices. They were run by the U.S. Department of Labor's Employment and Training Administration (ETA). These offices provided job seekers with assistance in their job search, assistance in searching jobs for unemployment insurance recipients, and recruitment services for employers.

The Workforce Investment Act created the "One Stop" centers within Employment Service Offices. The federal government contracts with states to run the Employment Service Offices and One Stop centers. Funds are allocated to states based on a complicated formula. For more information, see www.doleta.gov/programs/w-pact_amended98.cfm or perform an Internet search for the law by name.

1.51. The Walsh-Healey Act (Public Contracts Act) (1936)

President Franklin Roosevelt signed this into law during the Great Depression. It was designed to assure the government paid a fair wage to manufacturers and suppliers of goods for federal government contracts in excess of $10,000 each. The provisions of the law included the following:

- Overtime pay requirements for work done over 8 hours in a day or 40 hours in a week.
- A minimum wage equal to the prevailing wage.
- Prohibition on employing anyone under 16 years of age or a current convict.
- The Defense Authorization Act (1968) later excluded federal contractors from overtime payments in excess of 8 hours in a day.

For more information, see www.dol.gov/compliance/laws/comp-pca.htm or perform an Internet search for the law by name.

1.52. The Work Opportunity Tax Credit (WOTC) (1996)

This law provides federal income tax credits to employers who hire from certain targeted groups of job seekers who face employment barriers. The amount of tax credit is adjusted from time to time and currently stands at $9,600 per employee.

Targeted groups include the following:

- Qualified recipients of Temporary Assistance to Needy Families (TANF).
- Qualified veterans receiving food stamps (referred to as Supplemental Nutrition Assistance Program [SNAP] today) or qualified veterans with a service connected disability who
  - Have a hiring date that is not more than 1 year after having been discharged or released from active duty, or
  - Have aggregate periods of unemployment during the 1-year period ending on the hiring date that equals or exceeds 6 months
- WOTC also includes family members of a veteran who received food stamps (SNAP) for at least a 3-month period during the 15-month period ending on the hiring date, or a disabled veteran entitled to compensation for a service-related disability hired within a year of discharge or unemployed for a period totaling at least 6 months of the year ending on the hiring date.
- Ex-felons hired no later than 1 year after conviction or release from prison.
- Designated Community Resident—an individual who is between ages 18 and 40 on the hiring date and who resides in an Empowerment Zone, Renewal Community, or Rural Renewal County.
- Vocational rehabilitation referrals, including Ticket Holders with an individual work plan developed and implemented by an Employment Network.
- Qualified summer youth ages 16 through 17 who reside in an Empowerment Zone, Enterprise Community, or Renewal Community.
- Qualified SNAP recipients between the ages of 18 and 40 on the hiring date.
- Qualified recipients of Supplemental Security Income (SSI).
- Long-term family assistance recipients.

These categories change from time to time as well.

In addition to these specific federal laws, there are laws dealing with payroll that HR professionals need to understand. While it is true that accounting people normally handle the payroll function in an employer's organization, occasionally HR professionals get involved and have to work with accounting people to explain deductions and provide input about open enrollment for health care benefit programs, among other things. Those things can include garnishments; wage liens; savings programs; benefit premium contributions; and income tax, FICA, and Medicare withholdings. For more information, see www.gao.gov/new.items/d01329.pdf or perform an Internet search for the law by name.

1.53 Labor-Management Reporting and Disclosure Act (1959)

This law provides for the reporting and disclosure of certain financial transactions and administrative practices of labor organizations and employers to prevent abuses in the administration of trusteeships by labor organizations and to provide standards with respect to the election of officers of labor organizations. It created a bill of rights for members of labor organizations (29 U.S.C. 401-402; 411-415; 431-441; 461-466; 481-484; 501-505).

For more information, see www.dol.gov/olms/regs/statutes/lmrda-act.htm or perform an Internet search for the law by name.

1.54. Whistleblowing

It is important to highlight the issue of whistleblowing. Protections against retaliation are embedded in various laws we cover in this chapter; laws with those provisions and protections include the Civil Rights Acts, OSHA, MSHA, the Sarbanes-Oxley Act, ADA, and more.

Whistleblower laws usually apply to public-sector employees and employees of organizations contracting with the federal government or state governments. They are designed to protect individuals who publicly disclose information about corrupt practices or illegal activities within their employer's organization. Often, such events occur when someone is mishandling money, contracts, or other assets. Construction projects not being built to specifications can result in whistleblowing by governmental employees. Employees of financial services companies (banks, credit unions, stock brokerages, and investment firms) have been in the headlines during recent years. They uncovered and disclosed misbehavior among people in their companies and were protected under whistleblower provisions of various laws. Whistleblowers are protected from disciplinary action, termination, or other penalty. For more information, see www.osc.gov/documents/pubs/post_wb.htm or perform an Internet search for the law by name.

2. When You Have 15 or More Employees

Once employers have added 15 or more employees to their payroll, it becomes necessary to comply with an additional ten major federal laws.

2.1. Americans with Disabilities Act (ADA) (1990)

Prior to this legislation, the only employees who were protected against employment discrimination were the ones working for the federal, state, or local government and federal government contractors. They were captured by the Rehabilitation Act. As a matter of fact, it was the Rehabilitation Act that was used as a model for developing the ADA. Five years after the Rehabilitation Act, the Developmental Disabilities Act of 1978 spoke specifically to people with developmental disabilities. It provided for federally funded state programs to assist people in that category of the population. The ADA had been first proposed in 1988, and it was backed by thousands of individuals around the country who had been fighting for rights of their family members, friends, and co-workers. They thought it was only appropriate for those people to have equal access to community services, jobs, training, and promotions. It was signed into law by President George H. W. Bush on July 26, 1990. It became fully effective for all employers with 15 or more workers on July 26, 1992.

Provisions and Protections

Title I—Employment—applies to employers with 15 or more workers on the payroll. Those employers may not discriminate against a physically or mentally disabled individual in recruitment, hiring, promotions, training, pay, social activities, and other privileges of employment. Qualified individuals with a disability are to be treated as other job applicants and employees are treated. If a job accommodation is required for a qualified individual to perform the assigned job, employers are required to provide that accommodation or recommend an alternative that would be equally effective. The interactive process between employers and employees should result in an accommodation or explanation about why making the accommodation would provide an undue hardship on the employer. Title I is enforced by the Equal Employment Opportunity Commission. Part of the interactive discussion about accommodation requests involves the employer investigating other accommodations that may be equally effective yet lower in cost or other resource requirements. Employers are not obligated to accept the employee's request without alteration.

U.S. Supreme Court Interpretation of the ADA

There were several U.S. Supreme Court cases that interpreted the ADA very narrowly. They limited the number of people who could qualify as disabled under the Court's interpretation of Congress's initial intent. Reacting to those cases, Congress enacted the ADA Amendment Act in September 2008. It became effective on January 1, 2009.

ADA Amendments Act of 2008

Following the U.S. Supreme Court decisions in *Sutton v. United Airlines*[6] and in *Toyota Motor Manufacturing, Kentucky, Inc., v. William*,[7] Congress felt that the Court had been too restrictive in its interpretation of who qualifies as disabled. It was the intent of Congress to be broader in that definition. Consequently, Congress passed the ADA Amendments Act to capture a wider range of people in the disabled classification. A disability is now defined as "an impairment that substantially limits one or more major life activities, having a record of such an impairment, or being regarded as having such an impairment." Although the words remain the same as the original definition, the Amendments Act went further. It said, when determining whether someone is disabled, there may be no consideration of *mitigating circumstances*. In the past, we used to say people who had a disability under control were not disabled. An employee with a prosthetic limb did everything a whole-bodied person could do. An employee with migraines that disappeared with medication wasn't considered disabled. Under the old law, epilepsy and diabetes were not considered disabilities if they were controlled with medication. Now, because the law prohibits a consideration of either medication or prosthesis, they are considered disabilities. You can see that a great many more people are captured within the definition of disabled as a result of these more recent changes. The only specifically excluded condition is the one involving eye glasses and contact lenses. Congress specifically said having a corrected vision problem if eye glasses or contact lenses are worn may not constitute a disability under the law.

An individual can be officially disabled but quite able to do his or her job without an accommodation of any sort. Having more people defined as disabled doesn't necessarily mean there will be more people asking for job accommodations. For more information, see www.eeoc.gov/laws/statutes/adaaa.cfm or perform an Internet search for the law by name.

"Substantially Limits"
Employers are required to consider as disabled anyone with a condition that "substantially limits," but does not "significantly restrict," a major life activity. Even though the limitation might be reduced or eliminated with medication or other alleviation, the treatment may not be considered when determining the limitations. So, people who use shoe inserts to correct a back problem or who take prescription sleeping pills may now be classified as disabled. The same might be said of people who are allergic to peanuts or bee stings. Yet there may be no need for any of them to request a job accommodation.

"Major Life Activities"
Caring for oneself, seeing, hearing, touching, eating, sleeping, walking, standing, sitting, reaching, lifting, bending, speaking, breathing, learning, reading, concentrating, thinking, communicating, interacting with others, and working all are considered "major life activities." Also included are major bodily functions such as normal cell growth, reproduction, immune system, blood circulation, and the like. Some conditions are specifically designated as disabilities by the EEOC. They include diabetes, cancer, HIV/AIDS (human immunodeficiency virus and acquired immunodeficiency syndrome), MS (multiple sclerosis), CP (cerebral palsy), and CF (cystic fibrosis) because they interfere with one or more of our major life activities.

"Essential Job Function"
An essential job function is defined as "a portion of a job assignment that cannot be removed from the job without significantly changing the nature of the job." An essential function is highly specialized, and the incumbent has been hired because he or she has special qualifications, skills, or abilities to perform that function, among others.

"Job Accommodation"
Someone with a disability doesn't necessarily need a job accommodation. Remember that we select people and place them in jobs if they are qualified for the performance of the essential functions, with or without a job accommodation. Someone with diabetes

may have the disease under control with medication and proper diet. No accommodation would be required. However, if it were essential that the employee had food intake at certain times of the day, there could be a legitimate request for accommodating that need. The employer might be asked to consistently permit the employee to have meal breaks at specific times each day.

Job accommodations are situationally dependent. First, there must be a disability and an ability to do the essential functions of the job. Next, there must be a request for accommodation from the employee. If there is no request for accommodation, no action is required by the employer. It is perfectly acceptable for an employer to request supporting documentation from medical experts identifying the disability. There might even be recommendations for specific accommodations, including those requested by the employee.

Once an accommodation is requested, the employer is obliged to enter into an interactive discussion with the employee. For example, an employee might ask for something specific, perhaps a new piece of equipment (a special ergonomic chair) that will eliminate the impact of disability on their job performance. The employer must consider that specific request. Employers are obligated to search for alternatives that could satisfy the accommodation request only when the specific request cannot be reasonably accommodated. This is the point where the Job Accommodation Network (JAN)[8] can become a resource. It can often provide help for even questionable and unusual situations.

The employer must consider if making that accommodation would be an "undue hardship" considering all it would involve. You should note that most job accommodations carry a very low cost. Often they cost nothing. The larger an employer's payroll headcount, the more difficult it is to fully justify using "undue hardship" as a reason for not agreeing to provide an accommodation. Very large corporations or governments have vast resources, and the cost of one job accommodation, even if it does cost some large dollar amount, won't likely cause an undue hardship on that employer.

Recordkeeping Requirements

There is nothing in the Americans with Disabilities Act of 1990, or its amendments, that requires employers to create job descriptions. However, smart employers are doing that in order to identify physical and mental requirements of each job. Job descriptions also make it easy to identify essential job functions that any qualified individual would have to perform, with or without job accommodation. It is easier to administer job accommodation request procedures and to defend against false claims of discrimination when an employer has job descriptions that clearly list all of the job's requirements. It also makes screening job applicants easier because it shows them in writing what the job will entail. Then, recruiters may ask, "Is there anything in this list of essential job functions that you can't do with or without a job accommodation?"

If a job requires an incumbent to drive a delivery truck, driving would be an essential function of that job. A disability that prevented the incumbent from driving the delivery truck would likely block that employee from working—unless an accommodation could be found that would permit the incumbent to drive in spite of the disability.

People are sometimes confused about temporary suspension of duty being a permanent job accommodation. If that temporary suspension means the incumbent no longer is responsible for performing an essential job function, the job could not be performed as it was designed by the employer. It is not necessary for an employer to redesign job content to make a job accommodation. It is possible for such voluntary efforts to be made on behalf of an employee the organization wants to retain. Those situations are not job accommodations, however. They are job reassignments.

EEOC procedures prohibit employers from inviting job applicants to identify their disability status prior to receiving a job offer. Federal regulations related to affirmative action requirements for disabled workers[9] require contractors to invite job applicants to identify their status as disabled and then provide the same invitation to identify themselves as disabled once they have been hired. Federal contractors are also required to conduct a general survey of the entire employee population every 5 years (at a minimum) with an invitation to self-identify as disabled. At any time, employees are permitted to identify themselves as disabled to their employer.

Annual review of job description content is required under the EEOC guidelines. It is important to maintain accurate listings of essential job functions and physical and mental job requirements. Annual review will help assure that you always have current information in your job descriptions.

ADA Enforcement

The EEOC enforces Title I of the ADA. That agency will accept complaints of illegal discrimination based on mental or physical disability. Once an employee has established that he or she is disabled and claims that he or she has been prohibited some employment benefit because of the disability (hiring, promotion, access to training, or inappropriate termination), there is a *prima facie* case (meaning it is true on its surface). Then the EEOC notifies the employer of the complaint and asks for the employer's response. This process can work back and forth from employer response to employee response for several cycles. Ultimately, the agency will determine that the case has cause (was a valid claim of discrimination), the case had no cause (the claim could not be substantiated), or the case was closed for administrative purposes (the employee asked for the case to be closed, or time for an investigation expired). Each of those three outcomes is followed by a "right to sue" letter, allowing the employee to get an attorney and file a lawsuit in federal court seeking remedies under the law.[10]

Once a complaint (called a *charge of illegal discrimination*) is filed with the EEOC, employers are instructed to cease talking about that issue directly with their employee. All conversation about the complaint must be directed through the EEOC. Unfortunately, that complicates the communication process, and it provides a strong incentive for employers to resolve complaints internally before they reach the formal external complaint stage. Working directly with an employee on the subject of accommodation, or any other personnel issue, is preferable to working through an agency such as the EEOC. For more information, see www.ada.gov/ or perform an Internet search for the law by name.

2.2. Civil Rights Act (Title VII) (1964)

Although this was not the first federal civil rights act in the country,[11] it came to us through a great deal of controversy. It was signed into law by President Lyndon Johnson on July 2, 1964. Following the assassination of President John F. Kennedy the previous November, President Johnson took it upon himself to carry the civil rights banner and urge Congress to pass the law.

For more information, see www.eeoc.gov/laws/statutes/titlevii.cfm or perform an Internet search for the law by name.

Employment Protections

Title VII of the act speaks to employment discrimination and cites five protected classes of people. Before the final days when Congress was discussing the issues, there were only four protected classes listed: race, color, religion, and national origin. There was a great deal of opposition in the Senate from Southern states. They decided that they would strategically add another protected category to the list. They thought that if "sex" was added to the list, the bill would surely fail because no one would vote for having women protected in the workplace. Well, it passed…with all five protected categories in place. From that time forward, when making employment decisions, it has been illegal to take into account any employee's membership in any of the protected classifications.

Penalties for Violations

Penalties can be assessed by a federal court. Protocol requires a complaint be filed with the Equal Employment Opportunity Commission, the administrative agency tasked with the duty to investigate claims of illegal employment discrimination. Regardless of the outcome of that administrative review, a "right to sue" letter is given to the complaining employee so the case can move forward to federal court if that is what the employee wants to do next.

Penalties that can be assessed if an employer is found to have illegally discriminated include the following:

- **Actual damages** Costs for medical bills, travel to medical appointments, equipment loss reimbursement, lost wages (back pay), lost promotional increase, lost future earnings (front pay). The limitation is usually 2 years into the past and unlimited number of years into the future.

- **Compensatory damages** Dollars to reimburse the victim for "pain and suffering" caused by this illegal discrimination.

- **Punitive damages** Dollars assessed by the court to "punish" the employer for treatment of the employee that was egregious in its nature. This is usually thought of as "making an example" of one case so as to send a message to other employers that doing such things to an employee or job applicant will be severely punished.

2.3. The Civil Rights Act (1991)

This act modified the 1964 Civil Rights Act in several ways:

- It provided for employees to receive a jury trial if they wanted. Up to this point, judges always heard cases and decided them from the bench.
- It established requirements for any employer defense.
- It placed a limitation on punitive damage awards by using a sliding scale depending on the size of the employer organization (payroll headcount):
  - For employers with 15 to 100 employees, damages are capped at $50,000.
  - For employers with 100 to 200 employees, damages are capped at $100,000.
  - For employers with 201 to 500 employees, damages are capped at $200,000.
  - For employers with more than 500 employees, damages are capped at $300,000.

For more information, see www.eeoc.gov/eeoc/history/35th/1990s/civilrights.html or perform an Internet search for the law by name.

2.4. Drug-Free Workplace Act (1988)

This legislation requires some employers to maintain a drug-free workplace. Employee compliance must be assured by subject employers.

Provisions and Protections

This law applies to federal contractors and all organizations receiving grants from the federal government. If you are covered, you are required to assure that all the employees working on the contract or grant are in compliance with its drug-free requirements. Covered employers are required to have a drug-free policy that applies to its employees. To determine that an employer is in compliance with the requirements, drug testing is usually performed on employees and applicants who have received a job offer. Random drug testing is also used in some organizations to assure employees subject to the law or policy are continuing to comply with the requirements. Those federal requirements do not go away even if laws in your state permit the use of recreational or medical marijuana. The employer is still permitted to have a policy prohibiting the use of drugs by applicants and employees. Any federal contractor under the jurisdiction of the Office of Federal Contract Compliance Programs (OFCCP) in the Department of Labor must comply with this legislation.

Employee notification about the policy must include information about the consequences of failing a drug test. Whenever an employee has been convicted of a criminal drug violation in the workplace, the employer must notify the contracting or granting agency within 10 days.

Recordkeeping Requirements

Covered employers are required to publish a written policy statement that clearly covers all employees or just those employees who are associated with the federal contract or grant. Each covered employee must be given a copy of the policy statement, and it is a good idea, although it is not required, to have employees sign for receipt of that policy statement. The statement must contain a list of prohibited substances. At a minimum it must cite controlled substances.[12]

Some employers choose to include in the policy prohibition of alcohol and prescription drug misuse, although that is not a requirement. Subject employers must also establish a drug-free awareness training program to make employees aware of a) the dangers of drug abuse in the workplace; b) the policy of maintaining a drug-free workplace; c) any available drug counseling, rehabilitation, and employee assistance programs; and d) the penalties that may be imposed on employees for drug abuse violations. Records should be maintained showing each employee who received the training and the date it occurred.

Drug-Free Workplace Act Enforcement

Federal contractors under the jurisdiction of the OFCCP will find that the agency requires proof of compliance when it conducts a general compliance evaluation of affirmative action plans. Any employee who fails a drug test must be referred to a treatment program or given appropriate disciplinary action. Care should be given to treating similar cases in the same way. It is fairly easy to be challenged under Title VII for unequal treatment based on one of the Title VII protected groups.

Each federal agency responsible for contracting or providing grants is also responsible for enforcing the Drug-Free Workplace Act requirements. These responsibilities are spelled out in the Federal Acquisition Regulation (FAR). Failing to maintain a drug-free workplace can result in the following[13]:

- Suspension of payments for contract or grant activities
- Suspension or cancellation of grant or contract
- Up to 5 years' prohibition from any further contracts or grants

For more information, see www.dol.gov/elaws/asp/drugfree/require.htm or perform an Internet search for the law by name.

2.5. The Equal Employment Opportunity Act (EEOA) (1972)

The EEOA amended the Civil Rights Act of 1964 by redefining some terms. It also required a new employment poster for all subject work locations explaining that "EEO is the law."
For more information, see www.eeoc.gov/eeoc/history/35th/thelaw/eeo_1972.html.

2.6. The Genetic Information Nondiscrimination Act (GINA) (2008)

In general terms, GINA prohibits employers from using genetic information to make employment decisions. This legislation was brought about by insurance companies using genetic information to determine who would likely have expensive diseases in the future. That information allowed decisions to exclude them from hiring or enrollment in medical insurance programs. With the implementation of this law, those considerations are no longer legal.

For more information see www.eeoc.gov/laws/statutes/gina.cfm or perform an Internet search for the law by name.

2.7. Guidelines on Discrimination Because of Sex (1980)

The Equal Employment Opportunity Commission (EEOC) published these guidelines to help employers understand what constituted unwanted behavior and harassment. They were issued long before the U.S. Supreme Court considered the leading cases on sexual harassment. This is about the only thing at the time that employers were able to turn to for help in managing the problem of sexual harassment in the workplace.

2.8. The Lilly Ledbetter Fair Pay Act (2009)

This was the first piece of legislation signed by President Barack Obama after he was inaugurated the 44th president of the United States. It was passed in reaction to the U.S. Supreme Court decision in *Ledbetter v. Goodyear Tire & Rubber Co., Inc.,* 550 U.S. 618 (2007).

This law amends the Civil Rights Act of 1964 and states that the clock will begin running anew each time an illegal act of discrimination is experienced by an employee. In Lilly Ledbetter's situation, her pay was less than that for men doing the same job. The old law didn't permit her to succeed in her complaint of discrimination because she failed to file 20 years earlier on the first occasion of her receiving a paycheck for less than her male counterparts. Under the new law, the 180-day statute of limitations for filing an equal-pay lawsuit regarding pay discrimination resets with each new paycheck affected by that discriminatory action. For more information, see www.eeoc.gov/laws/statutes/epa_ledbetter.cfm or perform an Internet search for the law by name.

2.9. The Pregnancy Discrimination Act (1978)

This law modified (amended) the Civil Rights Act of 1964. It defined pregnancy as protected within the definition of "sex" for the purpose of coverage under the Civil Rights Act. It also specifically said that no employer shall illegally discriminate against an employee due to pregnancy. It defines pregnancy as a temporary disability and requires accommodation on the job if it is necessary. It guarantees the employee rights to return to work to the same or similar job with the same pay following her pregnancy disability. For more information, see www.eeoc.gov/laws/types/pregnancy.cfm or perform an Internet search for the law by name.

2.10. Uniform Guidelines on Employee Selection Procedures (1976)

This set of regulations is often overlooked by employers and HR professionals alike. Details can be found in 41 C.F.R. 60-3. For covered employers with 15 or more people on the payroll, this set of requirements is essential in preventing claims of discrimination.

There are two types of illegal employment discrimination: disparate adverse treatment and adverse or disparate impact. The latter almost always results from seemingly neutral policies having a statistically adverse impact on a specific group of people. To avoid illegal discrimination, the guidelines require that all steps in a hiring decision be validated for application to the job being filled. Validity of a selection device can be determined through a validity study or by applying a job analysis to demonstrate the specific relationship between the selection device and the job requirements. Selection devices include things like a written test, an oral test, an interview, a requirement to write something for consideration, and a physical ability test.

Employers can get into trouble when they use selection tools that have not been validated for their specific applications. For example, buying a clerical test battery of written tests and using it to make selection decisions for administrative assistants as well as general office clerks may not be supportable. Only a validity analysis will tell for sure. What specific validation studies have been done for the test battery by the publisher? Any publisher should be able to provide you with a copy of the validation study showing how the test is supposed to be used and the specific skills, knowledge, or abilities that are analyzed when using it. If you can't prove the test measures things required by your job content, don't use the test. According to the Uniform Guidelines, "While publishers of selection procedures have a professional obligation to provide evidence of validity which meets generally accepted professional standards, users are cautioned that they are responsible for compliance with these guidelines."[14] That means the employer, not the test publisher, is liable for the results. For more information, see www.eeoc.gov/policy/docs/factemployment_procedures.html or perform an Internet search for the law by name.

3. When You Have 20 or More Employees

The next threshold for employers occurs when they reach a headcount of 20 employees. At that point another four major federal laws begin their influence on the organization.

3.1. The Age Discrimination in Employment Act (ADEA) (1967)

When this law was first passed, it specified the protected age range of 40 to 70. Anyone younger than 40 or older than 70 was not covered for age discrimination in the workplace. Amendments were made a few years later that removed the upper limit. Today, the law bans employment discrimination based on age if the employee is 40 years old or older. Remedies under this law are the same as under the Civil Rights Act. They include reinstatement, back pay, front pay, and payment for benefits in arrears. Some exceptions to the "unlimited" upper age exist. One example is the rule that airline pilots may not fly commercial airplanes after the age of 65.[15] For more information, see www.eeoc.gov/laws/statutes/adea.cfm or perform an Internet search for the law by name.

3.2. The American Recovery and Reinvestment Act (ARRA) (2009)

The thrust of this legislation was to create government infrastructure projects such as highways, buildings, dams, and such. It was an attempt to find ways to re-employ many of the workers who had become unemployed since the Great Recession began in 2007. There was a provision that provided partial payment of COBRA (The Consolidated Omnibus Budget Reconciliation Act) premiums for people who still had not found permanent job placement. It applied to individuals who experienced involuntary terminations prior to May 31, 2010.

ARRA also modified HIPAA privacy rules. It applies HIPAA's security and privacy requirements to business associates. Business associates are defined under ARRA as individuals or organizations that transmit protected medical data, store that data, process that data, or in any other way have contact with that private medical information. All parties are responsible for proper handling and compliance with the HIPAA rules. For more information, see www.irs.gov/uac/The-American-Recovery-and-Reinvestment-Act-of-2009:-Information-Center or perform an Internet search for the law by name.

3.3. The Consolidated Omnibus Budget Reconciliation Act (COBRA) (1986)

This law requires employers with group health insurance programs to offer terminating employees the opportunity to continue their health plan coverage after they are no longer on the payroll or no longer qualify for benefits coverage due to a change in employment status, i.e., reduction in hours. The cost must be at group rates, and the employer can add a small administrative service charge. It turns out that many employers turn these programs over to vendors who administer the COBRA benefits for former employees. They send out billing statements and provide collection services. Two percent is the maximum administrative overhead fee that can be added. The total cost of COBRA premiums and administrative fees is paid by employees participating in COBRA. The duration of coverage is dependent on some variables, so it may be different from one person to another. For more information, see www.dol.gov/dol/topic/health-plans/cobra.htm or perform an Internet search for the law by name.

3.4. The Older Workers Benefit Protection Act (OWBPA) (1990)

In the 1980s, it was common for employers, particularly large employers, to implement staff reduction programs as a means of addressing expenses. Often those programs were targeted at more senior workers because, generally speaking, their compensation was greater than that of new employees. Reducing one senior worker could save more money than the reduction of a more recently hired worker. Congress took action to prevent such treatment based on age when it passed this law.

The key purposes of the OWBPA are to prohibit an employer from the following:

- Using an employee's age as the basis for discrimination in benefits
- Targeting older workers during staff reductions or downsizing
- Requiring older workers to waive their rights without the opportunity for review with their legal advisor

For more information, see www.eeoc.gov/eeoc/history/35th/thelaw/owbpa.html or perform an Internet search for the law by name.

4. When You Have 50 to 99, 100, or More Employees

Once the employee headcount reaches these higher levels, additional legal obligations become effective for employers. Some of them only apply if the employer is subject to affirmative action requirements as a federal contractor.

4.1. Executive Order 11246—Affirmative Action (1965)

This is the presidential order that created what we now know as employment-based affirmative action. In 1965, President Johnson was past the days when he approved the Civil Rights Act, and he was in the process of examining how it was being implemented around the country by employers. He concluded that the law was pretty much being ignored. He needed something to stimulate implementation of the employment provisions in the Civil Rights Act, Title VII. His staff suggested they require affirmative action programs from federal contractors. A new program was born. President Johnson said that if a company wanted to receive revenue by contracting with the federal government, it would have to implement equal employment opportunity and establish outreach programs for minorities and women. At the time, minorities and women were being excluded from candidate selection pools. If they couldn't get into the selection pools, there was no way for them to be selected.

So, affirmative action programs were created. Outreach and recruiting was the name of the game in these programs. Analysis of the incumbent workforce, the available pool of qualified job candidates, and the training of managers involved in the employment selection process all contributed to a slow movement toward full equality for minorities and women.

The Office of Federal Contract Compliance Programs (OFCCP) is the law enforcement agency that currently has responsibility for enforcing the executive order along with other laws. Federal contractors must meet several conditions in return for the contracting privilege. One is the requirement to abide by a set of rules known as the Federal Acquisition Regulation (FAR). In addition, there is affirmative action for the disabled and veterans. Any business that doesn't want to abide by these requirements can make the business decision to abandon federal revenues and contracts. If you want the contracts, you also have to agree to the affirmative action requirements.[16] For more information, see www.dol.gov/ofccp/regs/statutes/eo11246.htm or perform an Internet search for the law by name.

4.2. The Family and Medical Leave Act (FMLA) (1993)

In general, the Family and Medical Leave Act sets in place new benefits for some employees in the country. If their employer has 50 or more people on the payroll, then they are required to permit FMLA leave of absence for their workers. FMLA provides for leaves lasting up to 12 weeks in a 12-month period, and it is unpaid unless the employer has a policy to pay for the leave time. The 12-month period begins on the first day of leave. A new leave availability will occur 12 months from the date the first leave began. During the leave, it is an obligation of the employer to continue paying any benefit plan premiums that the employer would have paid if the employee had remained on the job. If there is a portion of the premium for health insurance that is normally paid by the employee, that obligation for co-payment continues during the employee's leave time. The 12 weeks leave may be taken in increments of 1 day or less.

To qualify, employees must have more than 1 year of service. The leave is authorized to cover childbirth or adoption; to care for a seriously ill child, spouse, or parent; or in case of the employee's own serious illness. The employee is guaranteed return to work on the same job, at the same pay, under the same conditions as prior to the leave of absence.

There are provisions for "Military Caregiver Leave" lasting up to 26 weeks of unpaid leave of absence for employees with family members needing care due to a military duty–related injury or illness. The 26-week limit renews every 12 months. The law provides for "National Guard and Military Reserve Family Leave." Employees who are family members of the National Guard or Military Reservists who are called to active duty may take FMLA leave to assist with preparing financial and legal arrangements and other family issues associated with rapid deployment or postdeployment activities. An employer may agree to any nonlisted condition as a qualifier for FMLA leave as well.

FMLA provides for "Light Duty Assignments." It clarifies that "light duty" work does not count against an employee's FMLA leave entitlement. It also provides that an employee's right to job restoration is held in abeyance during the light duty period. An employee voluntarily doing light duty work is not on FMLA leave.

There is an employment poster requirement. The notice must be posted at each work location where employees can see it without trouble. A "Medical Certification Process" is part of the new provisions. DOL regulations have specified who may contact the employee's medical advisor for information, written or otherwise, and specifically prohibits the employee's supervisor from making contact with the employee's medical advisor.

Specific prohibitions are made against illegal discrimination for an employee taking advantage of the benefits offered under this law. These provisions are enforced by the EEOC. For more information, see www.dol.gov/whd/fmla/ or perform an Internet search for the law by name.

4.3. The Mental Health Parity Act (MHPA) (1996)

This legislation requires health insurance issuers and group health plans to adopt the same annual and lifetime dollar limits for mental health benefits as for other medical benefits. For more information, see www.dol.gov/ebsa/mentalhealthparity/ or perform an Internet search for the law by name.

4.4. The Mental Health Parity and Addiction Equity Act (MHPAEA) (2008)

This is an amendment of the Mental Health Parity Act of 1996. It requires that plans that offer both medical/surgical benefits and mental health and/or substance abuse treatment benefits provide parity between both types of benefits. All financial requirements (for example, deductibles, copayments, coinsurance, out-of-pocket expenses, and annual limits) and treatment requirements (for example, frequency of treatment, number of visits, and days of coverage) must be the same for treatment of both mental and physical medical problems. For more information, see www.dol.gov/ebsa/newsroom/fsmhpaea.html or perform an Internet search for the law by name.

4.5. The National Defense Authorization Act (2008)

This is the origin of benefit provisions under FMLA for leaves of absence due to military reasons. Qualifying events include notice of deployment, return from deployment, and treatment for an injury sustained while on deployment. The provision is for up to 26 weeks, which can be taken in increments of a day or less if, for example, treatment is required for a service-related injury. For more information, see www.dol.gov/whd/fmla/NDAA_fmla.htm or perform an Internet search for the law by name.

4.6. The Patient Protection and Affordable Care Act (PPACA) (2010)

Signed into law by President Barack Obama on March 23, 2010, this law is commonly referred to as the Affordable Care Act. It has created health insurance trading centers in each state where employees and those who are unemployed can shop for health insurance coverage. These trading centers are the American Health Benefit Exchanges and Small Business Health Options Program (SHOP). Individuals and business owners of organizations with fewer than 100 workers can purchase insurance through these exchanges.

It applies to all employers with 50 or more full-time workers on the payroll. Employers with fewer than 50 full-time workers are exempt from coverage under the law. Effective January 1, 2014, covered employers must either provide minimum health insurance coverage to their full-time employees or face a fine of $2,000 per employee, excluding the first 30 from the assessment. Employers with fewer than 25 employees will receive a tax credit if they provide health insurance to their workers. In 2014, that credit amounted to 50 percent of the employer's contribution to the employee's health care program, if the employer pays at least that amount for insurance costs. A full credit is available for employers with fewer than ten workers earning an average annual wage of less than $25,000. The credit will last for 2 years. For more information, see www.dol.gov/ebsa/healthreform/ or perform an Internet search for the law by name.

5. When You Have 100 or More Employees

The final major threshold for employers is reached when the payroll reaches 100 employees. At that time employers become subject to the WARN Act and are required to submit annual reports to the government summarizing their race and sex demographics. (See Chapter 5 for more information about the Standard Form 100 reports.)

5.1. The Worker Adjustment and Retraining Notification Act (WARN) (1988)

This was the first attempt by Congress to involve local communities early in the private sector's downsizing process. It also prevented employers from just shutting the door and walking away without any worker benefits. It applies to all employers with 100 or more full-time workers at a single facility. The law specifies a qualifying employer to be one that has 100 or more employees who in the aggregate work at least 4,000 hours per week (exclusive of hours of overtime).

Definitions

The term *plant closing* refers to the permanent or temporary shutdown of a single site of employment, or one or more facilities or operating units within a single site of employment, if the shutdown results in an employment loss at the single site of employment during any 30-day period for 50 or more employees, excluding any part-time employees.

The term *mass layoff* refers to a reduction in force that is not the result of a plant closing and results in an employment loss at the single site of employment during any 30-day period for (1) at least 500 employees to be laid off from a workforce of 500 or more; or (2) when at least 33 percent of the workforce (excluding any part-time employees) are going to be removed from the payroll in a layoff where there are a total of 50 to 499 workers before the layoff.

Required Actions

The law requires 60 days' advance notice to employees of plant closing or mass layoffs. Any employment loss of 50 or more people, excluding part-time workers, is considered a trigger event to activate the requirements. Notification of public officials in the surrounding community in addition to notification of employees is a requirement. The local community leaders must be informed and invited to participate in the process of finding new jobs for laid-off workers. There is a provision that says an employer can pay 60 days' separation allowance if it gives no notice to workers who will be terminated.

Exemptions to Notice Requirement

Notice is not required, regardless of the size of layoff, if the layoff, downsizing, or terminations result from the completion of a contract or project that employees understood would constitute their term of employment. It is not uncommon for workers to be hired in a "term" classification that designates them as employees for the life of a project. If they understand that from the beginning of their employment, their termination would not trigger the WARN Act.

WARN is not triggered in the following cases:

- In the event of strikes or lockouts that are not intended to evade the requirements of this law.
- In the event the layoff will be for less than 6 months.
- If state and local governments are downsizing. They are exempt from the notice requirement.
- In the event that fewer than 50 people will be laid off or terminated from a single site.
- If 50 to 499 workers lose their jobs and that number is less than 33 percent of the active workforce at the single site.

For more information, see www.dol.gov/compliance/laws/comp-warn.htm or perform an Internet search for the law by name.

6. For Federal Government Employees

The federal government is subject to some of the same laws as the private-sector employers. Yet there are additional obligations that government employers have. Some of those obligations stem from the United States Constitution. Others come from the following laws.

6.1. The Civil Service Reform Act (1978)

This legislation eliminated the U.S. Civil Service Commission and created three new agencies to take its place:

- **The Office of Personnel Management (OPM)**   This is the executive branch's human resources department. It handles all HR issues for agencies reporting to the president.
- **The Merit Systems Protection Board (MSPB)**   This part of the law prohibits consideration of marital status, political activity, or political affiliation in dealing with federal civilian employees. It also created the Office of Special Counsel, which accepts employee complaints and investigates and resolves them.

- **The Federal Labor Relations Authority (FLRA)** This is the agency that enforces federal civilian employee rights to form unions and bargain with their agencies. It establishes standards of behavior for union officers, and these standards are enforced by the Office of Labor-Management Standards in the U.S. Department of Labor.

For more information, see www.eeoc.gov/eeoc/history/35th/thelaw/civil_service_reform-1978.html or perform an Internet search for the law by name.

6.2. The Congressional Accountability Act (1995)

Until this law was implemented, the legislative branch of the government was exempt from nearly all employment-related requirements that applied to other federal agencies and private employers. This law requires Congress and its affiliated agencies to abide by 11 specific laws that already applied to other employers, in and out of government:

- Americans with Disabilities Act of 1990
- Age Discrimination in Employment Act of 1967
- Employee Polygraph Protection Act of 1988
- Federal Service Labor-Management Relations Statute
- Rehabilitation Act of 1973
- Civil Rights Act of 1964 (Title VII)
- Fair Labor Standards Act of 1938
- Family and Medical Leave Act of 1993
- Occupational Safety and Health Act of 1970
- Veterans Employment Opportunities Act of 1998
- Worker Adjustment and Retraining Notification Act of 1989

For more information, see www.compliance.gov/publications/caa-overview/ or perform an Internet search for the law by name.

6.3. The False Claims Act (1863)

During the Civil War, people were selling defective food and arms to the Union military. This law, sometimes referred to as the Lincoln Law, prohibits such dishonest transactions. It prohibits making and using false records to get those claims paid. It also prohibits selling the government goods that are known to be defective. For HR professionals today, it is wise to train all employees about the need to avoid creating records that are inaccurate or, even worse, fictitious. Doing things that are illegal, just because the boss says you should, will still be illegal. Employees need to understand that concept.

For more information, see www.justice.gov/civil/docs_forms/C-FRAUDS_FCA_Primer.pdf or perform an Internet search for the law by name.

6.4. The Homeland Security Act (2002)

This Cabinet-level organization (Department of Homeland Security) was created by Congress and President George W. Bush to consolidate security efforts related to protecting U.S. geography. Immigration and Customs Enforcement (ICE) is a part of this department. The E-Verify system resides here. Used by federal contractors as part of their affirmative action obligations and other private employers on a voluntary basis, the system is intended to assist in rapid verification of Social Security numbers (SSNs) and confirm that the individual attached to the SSN has a valid right to work in this country. For more information, see https://www.dhs.gov/homeland-security-act-2002 or perform an Internet search for the law by name.

6.5. The Privacy Act (1974)

This law provides that governmental agencies must make known to the public their data collection and storage activities and must provide copies of pertinent records to the individual citizen when requested—with some specific exemptions. Those exemptions include law enforcement, congressional investigations, Census use, "archival purposes," and other administrative purposes. In all, there are 12 statutory exemptions from disclosure requirements. If employees are concerned about employers using their Social Security numbers in records sent to the government, this act ensures privacy. Although such private information is required by the government, the government is prohibited from releasing it to third parties without proper authorization or court order. For more information, see www.justice.gov/opcl/privstat.htm or perform an Internet search for the law by name.

6.6. The USA PATRIOT Act (2001)

The USA PATRIOT Act (Uniting and Strengthening America by Providing Appropriate Tools Required to Intercept and Obstruct Terrorism Act) was passed immediately following the September 11, 2001, terrorist attacks in New York City and at the Pentagon in Virginia. It gives the government authority to intercept wire, oral, and electronic communications relating to terrorism, computer fraud, and abuse offenses. It also provides the authorization for collecting agencies to share the information they collect in the interest of law enforcement. This law can have an impact on private-sector employers in the communications industry. It can also have an impact on any employer when the government asks for support to identify and track "lone wolves" suspected of terrorism without being affiliated with known terrorist organizations. HR professionals may find themselves involved in handling the collection and release of personal, confidential information about one or more employees. When legal documents such as subpoenas and court orders are involved, it is always a good idea to have the organization's attorney review them before taking any other action. For more information, see www.justice.gov/archive/ll/highlights.htm or perform an Internet search for the law by name.

Employment Visas for Foreign Nationals

Under some circumstances, it is possible for people from other countries to come work in the United States. There are several classifications of workers that can be used, depending on the type of work to be done and the level of responsibilities.

E Nonimmigrant Visas

There are two types of E Nonimmigrant Visas, E-1 Treaty Traders and E-2 Treaty Investors. For more information on E Nonimmigrant Visas, see www.uscis.gov/portal/site/uscis.

E-1 Treaty Traders

The individual must be a citizen of the treaty country; there must be substantial trade; the trade must be principally with the treaty country; the individual must have executive, supervisory, or essential skills; and the individual must intend to depart the United States when the trading is completed.

E-2 Treaty Investors

The individual must be a citizen of the treaty country and be invested personally in the enterprise. The business must be a bona fide enterprise and not marginal, and the investment must be substantial. E-2 employees must have executive, supervisory, or essential skills, and E-2 investors must direct and develop the enterprise. The E-2 investor must depart the United States when the investment is concluded.

H Visas

These are visas available to employers and employees for specialized talent or educational requirements.

H1-B Special Occupations and Fashion Models

These visas require a bachelor's or higher degree or its equivalent. The job must be so complex that it can be performed only by a person with the degree. The employer normally requires a degree or its equivalent for this job. Fashion models also fall into this category.

H1-C Registered Nurse Working in a Health Professional Shortage Area

This requires a full and unrestricted nursing license in the country where your nursing education was obtained. Or, you must have received your nursing education and license in the United States. It also requires that you have appropriate authorization from the

U.S. state's Board of Nursing to practice within the United States. H1-C requires that you have passed the examination given by the Commission on Graduates for Foreign Nursing Schools (CGFNS) or have a full and unrestricted license to practice as a registered nurse in the state where you will work.

H-2A Temporary Agricultural Workers

The employer must be able to demonstrate that there are not sufficient U.S. workers who are able, willing, qualified, and available to do the temporary seasonal work. The employer must also show that the employment of H-2A workers will not adversely affect the wages and working conditions of similarly employed U.S. workers.

H-2B Temporary Non-Agricultural Workers

The employer must show that there are not enough U.S. workers who are able, willing, qualified, and available to do the temporary work and that the employment of H-2B workers will not adversely affect the wages and working conditions of similarly employed U.S. workers. The employer must also show that the need for the prospective worker's services is temporary, regardless of whether the underlying job can be described as temporary.

H-3 Nonimmigrant Trainee

To qualify, employees must be trainees receiving training in any field of endeavor, other than graduate medical education, that is not available in their home country. Or, they must be a Special Education Exchange Visitor who will participate in a special education training program focused on the education of children with physical, mental, or emotional disabilities.

L-1 Intra-Company Transferee

This allows a qualifying organization to move an employee from another qualifying country into the United States for a temporary assignment either that is managerial in nature or that requires specialized knowledge.

L1-A Managers and Executives

These are intracompany transferees coming to the United States to work in a managerial or executive capacity. The maximum stay in the United States allowed under this visa is 7 years.

Specialized Knowledge

This is someone with specialized knowledge of the employer's product, service, research, equipment, techniques, management, or other interests and its application in international markets, or an advanced level of knowledge or expertise in the organization's processes and procedures. An L1-B visa holder may stay in the United States for only 5 years.

O-1 Alien of Extraordinary Ability in Arts, Science, Education, Business, Athletics

These people have a level of expertise indicating that they are among the small percentage who have risen to the very top of their field of endeavor. Alternatively, they represent extraordinary achievement in motion picture and television productions, or they have extraordinary ability and distinction in the arts.

P Visa Categories

There are seven variations of athletics-based or art-based visas:

- P1-A Individual Athletes or Athletic Teams
- P1-B Entertainment Groups
- P1-S Essential Support needed for P1-A or P1-B
- P2 Artist or Entertainer Under a Reciprocal Exchange Program
- P2-S Essential Support for P2
- P3 Artist or Entertainer Under a Culturally Unique Program
- P3-S Essential Support for P3

EB-Employment–Based Visas

There are five levels of employment-based visas. They are prioritized so that once the first-level immigrant applicants are processed, the next level of priority will be considered. That will continue until the maximum allotment of visas is reached. In recent years, about 140,000 employment-based visas were permitted each year.

EB-1 Alien of Extraordinary Ability

The employer must demonstrate that the alien has extraordinary ability in the sciences, arts, education, business, or athletics, which has been demonstrated by sustained national or international acclaim and whose achievements have been recognized in the field through extensive documentation. It must also be shown that the work to be done in the United States will continue in the individual's area of extraordinary ability. It shall also be shown how the alien's entry into this country will benefit the United States; 28.6 percent of the total employment-based visas are allocated to this category.

EB-2 Alien of Extraordinary Ability

This is a classification that applies to any job that requires advanced degrees and persons of exceptional ability; 28.6 percent of the employment-based visas are allocated to this category.

EB-3 Skilled Workers

This category requires professionals and even unskilled workers who are sponsored by employers in the United States; 28.6 percent of the employment-based visas are allocated to this category.

EB-4 Certain Special Immigrants

Included here are some broadcasters, ministers of religion, employees or former employees of the U.S. government, Iraqi or Afghan interpreters and translators, and other similar workers; 7.1 percent of the employment-based visas are allocated to this category.

EB-5 Immigrant Investors

These are people who will create new commercial enterprises in the United States that will provide job creation; 7.1 percent of the employment-based visas are allocated to this category.

Chapter Review

While this chapter is not meant to be a comprehensive statement of each law, studying and learning these laws will help you understand the basics as you perform your human resource management responsibilities. As you read through the other chapters in this book, it's important to remember that one or more of these laws will be the underlying basis for SHRM's Body of Knowledge subject matter. Additionally, while using this chapter as a reference guide in your day-to-day application as an HR professional, please consult the statutes and regulations themselves via the URLs we have provided or perform an Internet search for the law by name. A thorough understanding of the various laws and regulations that impact the employment relationship will enhance your ability to protect your organization in matters involving employment and employee relations.

Questions

The following are all questions about U.S. laws and regulations concerning employee management.

1. John, a new employee, has just arrived at the orientation program where everyone completes their payroll forms and signs up for health care benefits. He brings his W-4 form to you and says he isn't subject to payroll withholding because he pays his taxes directly each quarter. What is your response?

    A. "That's okay. We won't process a W-4 form for you. We will give you a Form 1099."

    B. "I'll check with the accounting department to find out whether you can do that."

    C. "Unfortunately, all employees are subject to payroll tax withholding."

    D. "If you can show me a W-10 form you have submitted to the IRS, we can block your paycheck withholding."

2. The Wagner-Peyser Act protects employees who are:

    A. Unemployed

    B. Injured on the job

    C. Unable to work because of pregnancy

    D. Have two or more jobs

3. Mary has had a bad encounter with her supervisor, Henry. That evening after getting home from work, she pulls out her computer and sends a blistering blog post to her Facebook page. She names her company and her supervisor. She calls him unfair, pigheaded, and without principles. What can the company do about her posting?

    A. The company can demand that she remove the offensive post. If she doesn't, the company can file legal action against her.

    B. The company can demand that Facebook remove the offensive post. If it doesn't, the company can file legal action against Facebook.

    C. The company is protected against such employee comments by the Fair and Decent Treatment Act and can take disciplinary action against Mary.

    D. The company is prohibited from any action against Mary because she is engaging in protected concerted activity.

4. Pete is sensitive about security of his personal identity information since his credit card has been stolen twice in the past year. He is trying to clear up his credit rating because of the problems with the stolen cards. Now, he has approached the HR manager at his organization and requested that his Social Security number be removed from all of the company records. He thinks that a mistake could cause him more grief if the Social Security number were to be obtained by thieves. As the HR manager, what should you do?

    A. The company can and should delete the Social Security number from its records to protect Pete.

    B. There is a need for the company to keep the Social Security number for tax reporting.

    C. There is a need for the company to keep the Social Security number for Census reporting.

    D. The company has no need for the Social Security number but should keep it regardless.

5. Pat is talking with her colleagues about illegal discrimination at work. Someone mentions that the company is going to be sending out a request for updated race and sex information. Pat says that isn't legal. The company isn't supposed to track any of that information.

   A. Pat has not understood the FLSA requirements that employers keep race and sex data on employees.

   B. The EEOC has issued guidelines that agree with Pat's belief that it is illegal to maintain that information in company records.

   C. Only federal contractors are required to maintain the race and sex identification for employees.

   D. It is only the public-sector employees who are exempt from providing their race and sex identification to employers.

6. The Tractor and Belt Company (TBC) handles conveyor belt installations for many small firms. Each of the customer projects begins on a day that is most convenient for the customer. Sometimes, that's Monday; sometimes it's Thursday or some other day. The HR manager says that the company will adjust its workweek to begin when the customer's project starts. That way, each installation team has a separate workweek, and those workweeks can shift several times a month. What is your advice about this strategy?

   A. The HR manager is taking advantage of the FLSA's provisions for flexible workweeks that support small business. No change is required.

   B. Once the workweek has been designated to begin on a certain day of the week, it should not be changed by the HR manager.

   C. It depends on state laws and regulations whether the workweek begins on any specific day of the week.

   D. The FLSA says a workweek should always begin on Sunday.

7. Sandy is 15 years old and a sophomore at Central High School. She gets a job at the local hamburger drive-in. Her boss says he needs her to work the following schedule during the Spring Break week: 4 hours at lunch time every day, 9 hours on Saturday, and 6 hours on Sunday. Is that schedule acceptable for Sandy given that she has a work permit from the school?

   A. Because it is a school vacation week, there are no restrictions on the hours that Sandy can work.

   B. Only state laws impact what hours Sandy can work because it happens during a vacation week.

   C. Federal law says Sandy cannot work more than 8 hours a day when it is a vacation week.

   D. Because Sandy won't be working more than 40 hours for the week, there is no problem.

8. Gary is a junior at Southpark High School. He is 17 years old. The school needs some help in its warehouse during the summer, and Gary needs a job so he can save money for college. His boss is the facilities manager. Gary is assigned to work 9 hours every day during the week because one of the other employees is on disability leave. And, because the other employee was the forklift driver, Gary has been given training in how to drive that equipment around the warehouse and loading dock. He likes that duty because he has been driving a car for only a few months. The forklift is cool. Is there any difficulty with the facilities manager's requirements of Gary?

   A. Everything the facilities manager has required Gary to do is permissible under federal laws.

   B. Since there is no restriction to the number of hours Gary can work, everything should be okay.

   C. Whatever the facilities manager wants Gary to do is okay because it's only a summer job.

   D. Even though Gary can work unlimited hours, he cannot be assigned to drive the forklift.

9. Hank puts in the following hours at work: Sunday, 0; Monday, 8; Tuesday, 8; Wednesday, 9; Thursday, 8; Friday, 8; Saturday, 7. His boss says he will give Hank compensating time off for every hour of overtime Hank works. How many compensating hours off should Hank receive for this work time?

   A. 1 day of compensating time off.

   B. 1.5 days of compensating time off.

   C. 7 hours of compensating time off.

   D. Compensating time off is not permitted under the FLSA.

10. The Tractor and Belt Company (TBC) doesn't have an HR manager. HR is handled by the payroll clerk. When a new employee is assigned to the Production Department as an assembler, the payroll clerk raises a question. Should the new person be paid the same as all the other employees, all women, in the department, or is it okay to pay her more because she made more at her former job?

   A. There are no restrictions on the amount a new employee can be paid. It is market driven.

   B. The Fair and Decent Treatment Act requires all people doing the same work to be paid the same amount.

   C. There is no restriction on the amount paid because all the incumbents are women.

   D. Once a valid market survey has been done, it can be used to determine starting pay for new people.

11. Finding a life insurance company to provide benefits to its workforce has been difficult for Joan, the HR manager. She decides to recommend that her company offer a self-insured plan. What controls might Joan have to consider in her planning?

   A. There are no federal restrictions on a company providing its own life insurance plan to employees.

   B. The Employee Retirement Income Security Act regulates welfare benefit plans, including life insurance.

   C. The Life Insurance Benefit Plans Act has control over what Joan is able to do with her idea.

   D. Only state laws will have an influence on Joan's development of a self-insured benefit plan.

12. Simone has just been hired and is asked to complete a Form I-9. She offers her driver's license as proof of her identity. What else is required for her to complete the document?

   A. She may offer any document authorized on the Form I-9 instructions as proof of her authorization to work in this country.

   B. She must have a Social Security number to submit on the form.

   C. Simone has a U.S. passport but is told that she can't use it for her Form I-9.

   D. As long as Simone offers to get a Social Security number in the next 30 days, she can submit her Form I-9.

13. Steve is the HR director for a crane operations company. He just got a phone call from one of his field supervisors with tragic news. One of their units has collapsed and their operator is in the hospital with serious injuries. What should Steve do with that information?

   A. Steve should immediately call the hospital to be sure all the insurance information is on file for their employee.

   B. He should notify the Occupational Safety and Health Administration about the accident and the injuries.

   C. He should notify the Crane Safety Institute of America to be sure they are able to add this accident to its database.

   D. Steve should call the crane operator's spouse to let her know about the tragedy.

14. Every year Donna has to attend training on the use of the company vehicles she drives. She thinks this is a silly waste of time. Donna knows how to drive, and she knows the company vehicles. Why should she attend training every year?

   A. There is no federal requirement for Donna to take yearly training.

   B. OSHA requires training be done only once for vehicle operation.

C. Only state safety provisions govern how frequently training must be done in Donna's situation.

D. Safety programs must be developed that provide for refresher training on all equipment operating procedures.

15. Jerry just arrived at work and found a sink hole in the parking lot. He is early enough that other people have not yet begun arriving for work. Because the hole is about 10 feet across at the moment, what should Jerry be doing about the problem?

A. If Jerry is a management employee, he should take charge of the situation and begin the process of alerting others to the danger posed by the sink hole.

B. If Jerry is a nonmanagement employee, he should give his boss a call and leave a voice mail message, if necessary, about the sink hole.

C. If the sink hole poses an immediate danger of death or serious injury, Jerry should call 911 and report it. He should barricade the perimeter of the sink hole with tape or something else to prevent people from falling in.

D. Jerry should first test the edges of the sink hole to see whether it could grow in size. Then he should barricade the perimeter of the sink hole so no one will fall in.

16. Theresa attended a seminar recently that pointed out the need to post a yearly summary of injury and illness cases. Her boss doesn't want to do that, saying he doesn't want to publicize the problems the organization has had. Theresa should tell him:

A. Posting requirements call for display of the report in a prominent location if there are ten or more people on the payroll.

B. Posting requirements can be met by putting a report on the back of the closet door in the employee lounge.

C. Posting requirements can be met by making the report available in a binder in the HR manager's office.

D. Posting requirements is optional, but good employers are using the report as a "best practice" in safety programs.

17. An employer routinely works with hazardous chemicals, trucking them for delivery to various customer locations. After each load, the truck must be cleaned before being loaded with a different chemical. Cleaning has to be done by someone inside the tanker using special absorbent materials. What else should be considered?

A. Personal protective equipment should be provided by the employer, including breathing apparatus and hazmat suits.

B. Standard coveralls and boot covers should be provided for employees to use if they want.

    C. Workers should never be sent into a tanker truck for any reason.

    D. Breathing equipment is absolutely a requirement if someone will be in the tanker truck for longer than 30 minutes.

18. Shelly has worked for the same dentist for more than 10 years. In all that time, there has been no mention of any special requirements for handling syringes. She arranges the doctor's equipment trays every day and cleans them up after they have been used. She just tosses the used equipment into the autoclave or into the trash if it won't be used again. If you were advising Shelly about the practices used in her dental office, what would you say?

    A. Needles should be broken off before they are thrown into the trash can.

    B. Sharps should be triple wrapped in a stiff paper to protect from sticking someone handling the trash.

    C. Any possible harm can be prevented if used syringes are placed into an approved sharps container.

    D. Putting used syringes into any solid container that is wrapped in red paper is sufficient to meet requirements.

19. The price of gold is climbing, and folks at the Golden Nugget Mine are planning to reopen their operation. They know that safety is an important consideration. But what about federal regulations for gold mines? Are there such things?

    A. There are only OSHA regulations in general. All of those rules still apply.

    B. There are MSHA regulations to be considered, but because they are not in the coal mining business, the Golden Nugget Mine won't have to worry about them.

    C. MSHA rules apply to all mining operations in the United States. The Golden Nugget Mine will have to study those rules and get ready for inspections by the government.

    D. MSHA can tell the mine what to do, but it has no authority to conduct inspections because the Golden Nugget is not a coal mine.

20. Olivia suspects her payroll clerk of embezzlement. She has inspected the records for the past 3 months, and the pattern is clear. But to be sure it is the payroll clerk and not the accounts payable clerk, Olivia wants to confront her and demand she take a lie detector test.

    A. Good going, Olivia. You caught her. Sure enough, demanding that she take a lie detector test is a good way to confirm your suspicions.

    B. While lie detector tests can be used for some employees, accounting employees are exempt. You can't test her.

    C. Lie detector tests are not permitted for any use by any employer. You can't test her.

    D. Lie detector tests can be required only in limited circumstances, and this isn't one of them. You can't test her.

21. For the past 6 years, Sam's company has been a federal contractor working on equipment for the Department of Defense. The company has additional contract opportunities coming up, and Sam isn't sure if there will be an extra burden related to disabled workers because they are subject to both the Americans with Disabilities Act and the Rehabilitation Act.

    A. Sam should rest easy. The ADA and the Rehabilitation Act are identical in their content and requirements.

    B. Sam's company has already met its recruiting obligations and now only has to worry about meeting ADA requirements.

    C. Handling job accommodation requests is a requirement of the ADA but not the Rehabilitation Act. Things should be easier.

    D. Whatever Sam thinks, the ADA and Rehabilitation Act requirements have applied to his company for 6 years already. Adding more contracts won't change his current obligations.

22. Arthur has applied for a job with the AB Transit Company. He is told he must take and pass a urine drug test. If he fails the test and any subsequent random drug test after he is hired, he will be dismissed from the company. Arthur reacts loudly and says, "That's an invasion of my privacy! I won't do it." What happens now?

    A. Arthur can call his lawyer and have the drug test waived since he doesn't want to take it.

    B. Arthur can discontinue his participation in the AB Transit Company's employment process.

    C. Arthur can take the test now and still refuse to participate in random tests later.

    D. Arthur can have his friend take the test for him.

23. Cynthia works for a large multistate manufacturing company and approaches her boss one morning and tells him that her husband has just received orders from the Coast Guard to report for deployment to the Middle East. They have a week to get everything ready for his departure. She wants to know if she can have excused time off during the coming week. If you were her boss, what would you tell her?

    A. She can have the time off, but it will be logged as unpaid and charged as FMLA leave.

    B. She can take the time off, but it will be unexcused because she didn't give more than a week's notice.

    C. If she wants the time off, she will have to use her paid vacation time for the week.

    D. Jennifer has already requested the week off for vacation and only one person can be off at any one time or the unit won't be able to function. Cynthia's request is denied with regrets.

24. Robert works for a congressional representative and suffers a disabling injury in an automobile accident. Robert cannot work more than 3 hours per day according to his doctor. Weeks later, when he returns to work, he asks for a job accommodation and is told that it can't be done. When he presses the point, his supervisor says the reason is:

   A. Congressional staff people aren't covered by the ADA, so they don't have to even discuss his request.

   B. The request he has made would exempt him from several of his job's key responsibilities.

   C. The request he has made would set a precedent that other representatives' offices would have to follow.

   D. Because congressional staff members have to meet the public every day, they can't have people seeing disabled workers in the office. It doesn't look good.

25. Jimmy has heard that he will be getting health care coverage from his company because of the new Affordable Care Act. His company employs only ten people, but Jimmy is excited that he will finally get some insurance. He hasn't been feeling very good lately.

   A. Jimmy might have to wait until he can arrange for insurance through one of the exchanges.

   B. Jimmy should get an enrollment form from his boss because all employees will be covered by the new requirement that employers provide health care coverage to workers.

   C. Jimmy is out of luck. The new law only covers employers with 50 or more people, and there is no way Jimmy will be getting health insurance under the new law.

   D. Jimmy's boss just ran out of forms, but he will get some more from HR and then have Jimmy sign up for his coverage.

Answers

1. **C.** If the new worker is classified as an employee on the payroll, the IRS demands that income tax, Social Security tax, and Medicare tax be withheld. People are not allowed to opt out because they want to file their own tax payments each quarter.

2. **A.** The Wagner-Peyser Act of 1933 provides for federal unemployment insurance and sets guidelines for state unemployment insurance programs.

3. **D.** Mary is protected by the National Labor Relations Act (NLRA) of 1935. The National Labor Relations Board has taken the position that almost all postings on the Internet, whether complaining about supervisors or employers or making charges that employees are treated unfairly, are protected concerted activities under the act.

4. B. Both the FLSA and the IRS regulations require employers to obtain and report Social Security numbers from all employees. A Social Security number is required for completion of the Form I-9 to prove authorization to work in this country. The company may not remove it from its records, regardless of how concerned Pete may be.

5. A. Race and sex data is specifically required by the FLSA. For employers with 15 or more people on the payroll who are engaged in interstate commerce, EEOC regulations also require maintenance of those data records.

6. B. The FLSA requires employers to designate a day as the beginning of the workweek. To change that designation, there should be a significant business reason. Moving the workweek to begin based on projects is not acceptable. FLSA requires consistency because of the need to pay overtime for hours in excess of 40 in a workweek. Constantly moving a workweek could deprive employees of earned overtime.

7. C. The FLSA prohibits people aged 14 and 15 from working more than 8 hours in a day even when school is not in session.

8. D. Driving a "power-driven hoisting apparatus" is one of the 17 most dangerous jobs that may not be performed by workers younger than 18. At Gary's age, the FLSA has no restriction on the hours he may work in a week.

9. B. The FLSA requires all hours of work in excess of 40 in a week be paid overtime at the rate of 1.5 times the normal hourly pay rate. Compensating time off, in lieu of overtime pay, must be given at the rate of 1.5 hours for every overtime hour. So, a day of overtime (8 hours) should be compensated for with 1.5 days of compensating time off.

10. C. The Equal Pay Act requires men and women doing the same work to be paid the same rate. If there are no men in the job, only women, there is no Equal Pay Act issue. If all the incumbents are women, there is no employment discrimination based on sex because there is only one sex represented. So, with those conditions, there is no barrier to paying the new employee more based on her previous job's compensation.

11. B. ERISA specifically regulates welfare benefit plans such as health insurance and life insurance. That is in addition to regulation of pension and retirement plans offered by employers. It makes no difference who underwrites the life insurance—the employer or a vendor. ERISA will still provide requirements.

12. A. The deadline for completing a Form I-9 is 3 days after hire. Any documents listed on the form are acceptable. The employer may not designate certain documents as requirements. A Social Security number is one way to demonstrate authorization to work in this country. A valid U.S. passport is also a way to demonstrate both identity and work authorization.

13. **B**. The company has 8 hours after the accident to file its report of serious injury with OSHA. We don't know how long ago the accident happened, but it was long enough that the operator is now in the hospital. Steve should gather all the information needed for the report and get it called in to the OSHA office.

14. **D**. Injury and Illness Prevention Programs are required by OSHA. Part of the identification and remediation of workplace hazards is employee training. Even if employees have been trained on equipment operation, periodic refresher programs can help overcome bad habits that might have developed. Refresher programs conducted on a yearly basis represent a reasonable interval for Donna's situation.

15. **C**. It doesn't matter if Jerry is a manager or not. All employees should be trained to react to imminent dangers by taking immediate action to prevent anyone from serious injury. And walking up to the edge to see if it is going to collapse is just nuts.

16. **A**. If she must, Theresa should show her boss the requirement in OSHA regulations. A prominent display location excludes places such as the back of a closet door or inside a binder somewhere in the manager's office.

17. **A**. Working inside an enclosed space with dangerous fumes calls for hazmat equipment and adequate breathing equipment. OSHA regulations specify the personal protective equipment (PPE) necessary in this and other working conditions.

18. **C**. The Needlestick Safety and Prevention Act requires all sharps be disposed of in approved sharps containers. It also requires posting of warnings and information about blood-borne pathogens.

19. **C**. The Mine Safety and Health Administration has jurisdiction over all mining operations, not just coal mines. It handles safety complaints and conducts inspections of both above-ground and underground mining operations. All mine operators are required to conduct their internal safety inspections and maintain records of those inspections.

20. **D**. Except for law enforcement, security officers, and people who handle controlled substances, lie detectors are no longer permitted in the workplace. They were commonly used prior to 1988's Employee Polygraph Protection Act.

21. **D**. Sam's company will not incur any additional obligations for disabled workers if they seek additional government contracts. They have been obligated under both laws for 6 years.

22. **B**. Arthur has to decide whether he wishes to continue seeking employment with the AB Transit Company. If so, he must participate in their drug testing program. If he wants to avoid testing, he must drop out of the job application process and seek employment elsewhere.

23. A. Under the FMLA, Cynthia is entitled to unpaid leave of absence as a spouse of a covered medical service worker. It will be logged as unpaid time off, unless she wishes to use some of her accrued paid time off. It will also be logged in her record as FMLA leave.

24. B. Even the congressional offices are subject to the ADA's requirement to consider and discuss requests for job accommodations. Job accommodations must be made to make it easier for an employee to perform one of the job's essential functions. If he can't do that, even with an accommodation, he is not eligible for assignment to that job. If there is no other job available, the employer can't return him to work until his status changes.

25. A. Employers are required to provide health insurance coverage, or pay a penalty in lieu of that insurance, only if they have 50 or more full-time workers. With only ten employees, Jimmy's employer is not obligated to provide health insurance coverage. Jimmy may purchase it for himself through one of the exchanges set up for that purpose.

References

1. "Instructions for Employment Eligibility Verification," U.S. Department of Homeland Security, U.S. Citizenship and Immigration Services, accessed June 20, 2016, www.uscis.gov/files/form/i-9.pdf

2. "Federal Mine Safety & Health Act of 1977, Public Law 91-173, as amended by Public Law 95-164," U.S. Department of Labor, Mine Safety and Health Administration, accessed June 20, 2016, www.msha.gov/regs/act/acttc.htm

3. "OSH Act, OSHA Standards, Inspections, Citations and Penalties," U.S. Department of Labor, Occupational Safety and Health Administration, accessed June 20, 2016, www.osha.gov and search for "Inspections, Citations, and Proposed Penalties."

4. Ibid.

5. *Lawson v. FMR LLC,* U.S. No. 12-3, retrieved from http://www.supremecourt .gov/opinions/13pdf/12-3_4f57.pdf on June 20, 2016

6. *Sutton v. United Air Lines, Inc.,* 527 U.S. 471 (1999)

7. *Toyota Motor Manufacturing, Kentucky, Inc. v. Williams,* 534 U.S. 184 (2002)

8. The Job Accommodation Network, 800-526-7234 or www.askjan.org (accessed on June 20, 2016) is a free resource for employers. It is a service provided by the U.S. Department of Labor's Office of Disability Employment Policy (ODEP). JAN has been providing services for over 25 years.

9. 41 C.F.R.60-741.42(c)

10. "Disability Discrimination," U.S. Equal Employment Opportunity Commission, accessed on June 20, 2016, https://www.eeoc.gov/laws/types/disability.cfm

11. The first was the Civil Rights Act of 1866, which protected the right to enter into contracts regardless of race.

12. A list of controlled substances can be found in Schedules I through V of Section 202 of the Controlled Substances Act (21 U.S.C. 812) and as further defined in Regulation 21 C.F.R. 1308.11-1308.15

13. "eLaws – Drug-Free Workplace Advisor," U.S. Department of Labor, accessed June 20, 2016, http://webapps.dol.gov/elaws/asp/drugfree/screenr.htm

14. 41 C.F.R. 60-3.7

15. Fair Treatment of Experienced Pilots Act (December 13, 2007), Public Law 110-135

16. 41 C.F.R. 60

PART II

HR Knowledge and Behavior Competencies

■ **Chapter 4**   People
■ **Chapter 5**   Organization
■ **Chapter 6**   Workplace
■ **Chapter 7**   Behavioral Competencies

People

The HR expertise domain of People Knowledge counts toward 17 percent for both exams. This domain covers the essential HR knowledge needed for relating to people. The following are the functional areas that fall within the People Knowledge domain:

- Functional Area 1—HR Strategic Planning
- Functional Area 2—Talent Acquisition
- Functional Area 3—Employee Engagement & Retention
- Functional Area 4—Learning & Development
- Functional Area 5—Total Rewards

HR professionals are expected to know how to perform the following Body of Competency and Knowledge (BoCK) statements for the People Knowledge domain:

- **01** Creating and setting the strategic direction of the HR function
- **02** Acquiring or developing the talent necessary for pursuing organizational goals
- **03** Maintaining a satisfied and engaged workforce while minimizing unwanted employee turnover
- **04** Developing a total rewards program that maximizes the effectiveness of the organization's compensation and benefits

Functional Area 1—HR Strategic Planning

Here is SHRM's BoCK definition: "HR Strategic Planning involves the activities necessary for developing, implementing, and managing the strategic direction required to achieve organizational success and to create value for stakeholders."[1]

All career levels of HR are expected to support and contribute to the strategic direction and role of HR. HR professionals must be able to identify and understand the organization's strategic initiatives, plans, and direction for decision-making, as well as contribute to the organization's overall strategy. All of that involves understanding the internal and external environments and utilizing the organization's mission and vision as a focus for determining where HR can support goals and sustain a competitive advantage.

Key Concepts

- Approaches to project management (e.g., traditional, lean, Six Sigma, agile, critical chain) and processes (e.g., initiating, planning and design, launching/executing, monitoring and controlling, closing)
- Concepts of systems thinking (e.g., related parts, input-processes-output) and components of an organizational system (e.g., interdependence, necessity of feedback, differentiation of units)
- Organizational mission, vision and values, and their relation to strategic management and planning
- Project planning, monitoring and reporting methods and tools (e.g., critical path analysis, Gantt charts, variance analysis, outcome monitoring)
- Project leadership, governance, and structures (e.g., team roles, team management, work breakdown structures)
- Role of strategic management and planning in creating and sustaining competitive advantage
- Strategic planning analysis frameworks (e.g., PESTLE analysis, SWOT analysis, industry analysis, scenario planning, growth-share matrix)
- Strategic planning process (e.g., formulation, goal-setting, implementation, evaluation)
- Systems theory and input-process-output models

The following are the proficiency indicators that SHRM has identified as *key concepts*:

For All HR Professionals	For Advanced HR Professionals (SCP Exam)
Uses the perspective of systems thinking to understand how the organization operates	Identifies the ways in which the HR function can support the organization's strategy and goals
Informs business decisions with knowledge of the strategy and goals of HR and the organization	Engages other business leaders in strategic analysis and planning
Develops and implements an individual action plan for executing HR's strategy and goals	Evaluates HR's critical activities in terms of value added, impact and utility, using cost-benefit analysis, revenue, profit-and-loss estimates, and other leading or lagging indicators
Uses benchmarks, industry metrics, and workforce trends to understand the organization's market position and competitive advantage	Provides HR-focused expertise to other business leaders when formulating the organization's strategy and goals
Informs HR leadership of new or overlooked opportunities to align HR's strategy with the organization's	Develops and implements HR strategy, vision, and goals that align with and support the organization's strategy and goals
Provides HR leadership with timely and accurate information required for strategic decision-making	Ensures that HR strategy creates and sustains the organization's competitive advantage

The Role of Strategy

The role of strategy is one that aligns all functions in an organization to "row together" toward defining the organization's goals and direction. The creation of strategic goals requires a vision of growth that is associated with the organization's mission, and, of course, includes the result of value for stakeholders. The development of goals, initiatives, and objectives is a necessary part of strategy to make sure everyone is on the same page, leading in the direction of attaining the defined strategy.

What Is Strategy?

Strategy is the planning of long-range goals and actions to attain those goals. Initiatives, objectives, and tactics are outlined in detail for each specific function in the organization and coordinated over a defined period of time. Strategy will look within the walls of the organization at its strengths, weaknesses, and vulnerabilities, along with looking outward at competition, opportunities, and external issues and influences.

Some theorists believe that strategy emerges in response to environmental threats and opportunities and cannot be planned rationally—because no one person can foresee everything about the future. Theorist Henry Mintzberg[2] is associated with this strategy approach. Others believe that the gathering of data is its core source for setting and choosing direction—much like a control system that would have targets. Michael Porter's perspective of the five forces in planning is aligned with this process.[3] Both concepts and processes have value. Strategic planning is necessary to set the direction and path for an organization, and the management of strategy (*strategic management*) is required in leadership of the organization to ensure that functions in the organization are aligning their activities to help move the organization toward its goals and strategic plans.

Requirements for Strategic Planning and Management   Several strategic-planning processes begin with the extension of the annual operating budget into a typical five-year projection. This can be a valuable exercise, particularly for organizations that have operated on a yearly or even monthly planning cycle. Most organizations soon discover that five-year operational and financial forecasts, in and of themselves, are ineffective as strategic-planning tools because they are predicated on the assumption of no significant change in environmental, economic, and competitive conditions.

There are certain concepts for the creation of strategy and the management of it.

- **Aligning effort**   It's important to ensure that all functions are aligned with the organization's mission and goals. This is where a 10,000-foot helicopter ride is of benefit to have a broader view, ensuring that policies and practices are aligned with the strategy and intention.

- **Controlling drift**   This is important to ensure that an organization is not coasting along doing what it's always done and missing the boat or, at worse, becoming blindsided because of disruption in its marketplace or industry with substitution.

- **Focusing on core competencies**   This means knowing what the organization is good at for its customer base and being sure to focus efforts on those competencies.

- **Systems thinking**   Keep in mind the inter-relations of both internal and external factors, such as stakeholders, industry forces, and the other influences on an organization. This includes looking at both the opportunities and the risks or conflicts and to what degree the risks are acceptable to the organization.

- **Using structure as a strategic level**   Does the structure of the organization support the strategy, or does it hamper it because of current policies and expectations within the organization?

- **Using culture as a strategic level**   Does the culture align itself with the intended strategy? As an example, if the strategy is to have front-line employees make return decisions on the spot with a customer, is the organization's orientation program providing training and demonstrated shadowing for new front-line hires to develop the desired behaviors?

Benefits of Strategy   The benefits of strategy are helping everyone in the organization focus on the future with a written plan that contains goals to further the organization's existence. From top to rank and file, strategy provides a map that gives direction and intention on where the organization plans to use and spend its resources. It helps keep decision-making and activities aligned to ensure that they support the attainment of the planned strategy. It provides a spotlight on what resources are needed, such as talent and development, to progress with the strategy. It also helps determine both positive and negative outcomes for suggested strategies.

Mistakes to Avoid   Organizations can fail to obtain the benefits of strategic planning through their process and/or the management of strategy. They can avoid failing by remembering not to take shortcuts with the process of strategic planning. Analysis such as SWOT (discussed later in this chapter) and an honest look inward, along with valid research externally, are absolutely necessary. Being too comfortable with the status quo and not challenging or assessing the potential risks is another mistake to avoid. Lacking follow-through and alignment of the plan throughout the organization is one of the most common mistakes—creating "the plan" and putting it in a binder on the shelf to just dust it off at next year's planning retreat is a waste of time, effort, and execution. Insufficient involvement or commitment from management will sideline a good strategic plan in its tracks. Lastly, lack of communication throughout the organization on what the strategic plan is, and what it means to each employee and function in the organization, will thwart efforts and should be avoided.

Levels of Strategy   There are three levels of strategy.

- **Organizational level**   This level involves a general vision of the future, typically what the organization plans to grow into, as an umbrella over the entire organization.

- **Business unit level**   This level focuses on the "how" and "where" the organization will focus to create value for its shareholders. The focus is on the business units such as sectors, divisions, regions, and product units.

- **Operational level**   This level focuses on the activities and actions the functions within the organization will take to progress it toward its vision. Finance, manufacturing, R&D, marketing, HR, and so on are operational-level examples.

Role of HR in Strategy   With HR, the operational level is going to be the main focus. HR's policies, programs, and processes will need to correlate, collaborate, and align with the organization's business units. HR's resources will need to be spent on the activities that add value and assist in the business units in fulfilling their work toward the strategic plans. It may be with workforce planning, talent development, or incentive compensation programs.

HR professionals need to develop strategic planning skills—which are discussed in the following sections—such as scanning the environment, formulating strategy, assessing risks, and setting SMART goals and objectives. This role that HR fulfills is the biggest growing role that organizations demand today, which is why the HR job title of *HR business partner* was created.

HR's role includes building bridges with both internal and external stakeholders, where they exist. HR needs to view issues from differing perspectives and seek resolutions to help "bridge" the differing functions in a collaborative effort. There may be a policy within the payroll function of finance that conflicts with a new compensation incentive plan that is being developed with the sales unit to help account management personnel achieve goals that fit the strategic plan. The HR professional will need to view the two conflicting issues and seek resolution for the best of the organization and its strategy.

Role of Value in Strategy

The basic premise with strategic planning and management is to lead activities that yield a great value. Understanding how an organization creates value with its mission is the first step. By value we are not talking cultural values; we are referencing the value it brings to its end customer or stakeholder. What causes the organization to be successful to its customers/stakeholders—that is its value. How well is it achieving its mission, and does its mission still serve its customers/stakeholders?

Value Chain   The value chain is another model by Michael Porter,[4] which describes the process by which a business receives materials and then adds value to the materials through processes that create their finished product or service, which is then sold to customers. Organizations will conduct their value-chain analysis through looking at the steps in their production that are employed to create their product or service and then identifying the way to increase the efficiency of the production chain. The end goal is to create maximum value for the least possible cost, which creates the organization's competitive advantage. Figure 4-1 illustrates Porter's concept of the value chain with primary and secondary activities. It demonstrates the interconnections of various functions in delivering value to the end customer or the organization.

Primary activities, which will vary according to the type of organization's activities, contribute directly to the value that is created for the customer. An example is a food manufacturer that uses distributors and retailers for its product. The value of the primary

Figure 4-1 Porter value chain concept

activities depends on the secondary activities that provide services to the primary functions. HR administration of most HR functions will fall within this area, as will finance and IT.

NOTE Not all businesses will find this value chain concept realistic because their business does not control the entire chain of production and distribution.

A strategist, be it an HR professional or an internal or outside consult, needs to understand the flow in creating value. They need to know which activities in the organization are considered central to its mission, reflecting its *core* activities, and which ones are the most profitable activities or could be profitably outsourced.

Stakeholder Concept R. Edward Freeman offered the stakeholder concept in the mid-1980s[5] as another perspective to the shareholder view of a corporation (which was to create wealth for the shareholders). Freeman's stakeholder concept recognizes the different types of value an organization creates. Yes, there may be monetary value as viewed by investors, but there is also value that a community may perceive via the employment taxes or corporate social responsibility contributions it makes. Figure 4-2 depicts Freeman's stakeholder concept. Understanding the various perceptions from the view of each stakeholder is especially challenging for a global organization. The customer's expectations alone will greatly vary. Employees in other countries will have differing perspectives based on their cultural norms.

HR's Role in Defining and Creating Value The biggest role HR has in defining and creating value for its organization is knowing the workforce. Knowing core competencies of talent, the marketplace for talent that is needed, and the legal environment in which the organization employs its workforce—these are critical value-producing activities for HR.

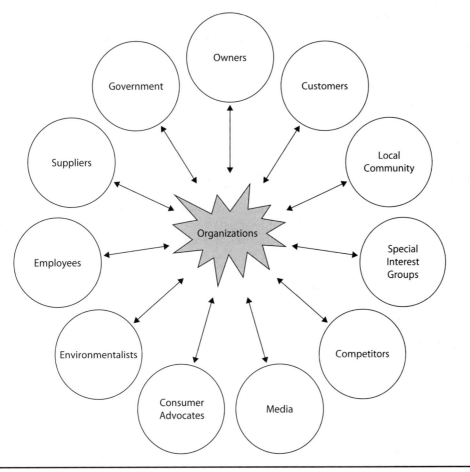

Figure 4-2 Freeman stakeholder concept

The Strategic Planning Process

As we've explained, the strategic creation planning process is about designing the organization for the future. Whether that is a plan that is for 1 year, 5 years, or longer, it will always involve the four basic stages and will be continually dynamic and changing as conditions change for an organization.

- Formulation of the strategy, which is gathering the critical and necessary data.
- Development of the strategy, which is considering the competitive advantage and the markets it competes in.
- Implementation stage, which is creating the specific objectives and initiatives that produce outcomes associated with the goals.
- Evaluation stage, which is the final stage where metrics and achievements are accessed and reported upon to stakeholders.

Strategy Formulation

Strategy formulation is the process by which an organization chooses the most appropriate courses of action to achieve its defined goals.

Information Gathering and Analysis

A major part in strategic planning is the process of gathering data. It should be done prior to and during the creation of the strategic plan and continue on through the implementation and to the monitoring process of the strategic plan. Data can be secondary or primary data and gathered through internal or external means.

Improving Your Business and Organizational "Radar"   Information is the key to business success. When something is "on the radar," it is being tracked. That means someone believes the information is important to the organization's success. So, the question becomes, "What should we be tracking or monitoring?" Get this right and you will be able to keep your eye on all the critical elements surrounding your organization, sort the critical from the mundane, and decide on the future movements of your group with accuracy.

Environmental Scanning

Seeing what is happening in the environment around you is important. Identifying the important information among the plethora of unimportant stuff becomes a challenge.

PESTEL Analysis   One technique for sorting out the important from the unimportant is PESTEL analysis.
    PESTEL stands for:

> P—Political
> E—Economic
> S—Social
> T—Technological
> E—Environmental
> L—Legal

Develop ways that you can gather information in each of these categories, and you will be well out front of your competitors in your ability to make well-informed decisions. According to the Professional Academy, these are the elements and what to look for when gathering information:[6]

- **Political factors**   These are all about how and to what degree a government intervenes in the economy. This can include government policy, political stability or instability in overseas markets, foreign trade policy, tax policy, labor law, environmental law, trade restrictions, and so on.

    It is clear from the earlier list that political factors often have an impact on organizations and how they do business. Organizations need to be able to respond to the current and anticipated future legislation and adjust their marketing policy accordingly.

- **Economic factors** Economic factors have a significant impact on how organizations do business and how profitable they are. Factors include economic growth, interest rates, exchange rates, inflation, disposable income of consumers and businesses, and so on.

  These factors can be further broken down into macro-economics and micro-economics factors. Macro-economic factors deal with the management of demand in any given economy. Governments use interest rate control, taxation policy, and government expenditure as their main mechanisms to influence these demand factors.

  Micro-economic factors are all about the way people spend their incomes. This has a large impact on business-to-consumer organizations in particular.

- **Social factors** Also known as sociocultural factors, these are the areas that involve the shared belief and attitudes of the population. These factors include population growth, age distribution, health consciousness, career attitudes, and so on. These factors are of particular interest as they have a direct effect on how marketers understand customers and what drives them.

- **Technological factors** We all know how fast the technological landscape changes and how this impacts the way we market our products. Technological factors affect marketing of our products and our HR services in three distinct ways.

  - New ways of producing goods and services—using remote access for employee updates directly to the human resource information system (HRIS)

  - New ways of distributing goods and services—providing employee online access to their employee records so they can request changes to correct errors

  - New ways of communicating with target markets—using e-mail, text messages, and a company emergency messaging system to notify employees of critical changes in the work environment

- **Environmental factors** These factors have only really come to the forefront in the last 15 years or so. They have become important because of the increasing scarcity of raw materials, pollution targets, doing business as an ethical and sustainable company, and carbon footprint targets set by governments. If HR were to reduce or eliminate paper records, that could have an impact on the environment (less paper used, fewer trees cut) and cost to the organization (a higher profit, however small a contribution). More and more consumers are demanding that the products they buy are sourced ethically and, if possible, from a sustainable source. HR can make a contribution to that effort and be cited by corporate as an example of how the organization is reducing its impact on the environment.

- **Legal factors** Legal factors include health and safety, equal opportunity, advertising standards, consumer rights and laws, product labeling, and product safety. It is clear that HR professionals need to know what is and what is not legal to avoid embarrassment and bad PR or worse.

After you have completed a PESTEL analysis, you should be able to use this to help you identify the strengths and weaknesses for a SWOT analysis.

SWOT Analysis

SWOT stands for the following:

- **Strengths**   What are the strengths of your HR organization? What do you do really well? What do you want to continue doing into the future? It could be HRIS, sexual harassment prevention, or onboarding.

- **Weaknesses**   These are the areas you know need improvement. Maybe it is the amount and quality of employee training, recruiting for diversity, or benefit program analysis.

- **Opportunities**   A merger or acquisition offers opportunities to examine all HR systems in both organizations and determine which will serve the new employer group best in the future. New reporting requirements imposed by government entities or customer groups give us the chance to determine how they will be met and the information used for improvement in our HR department.

- **Threats**   These are the challenges we face as HR professionals. For example, an outside vendor may propose to deliver benefit program management more cheaply than we can do it in-house. Initially, new government requirements can be perceived as threats. Properly managed, they can sometimes be converted into opportunities.

Industry Analysis

Industry analysis is a tool that facilitates a company's understanding of its position relative to other companies that produce similar products or services. Understanding the forces at work in the overall industry is an important component of effective strategic planning. Industry analysis enables HR professionals to identify the threats and opportunities facing their businesses and to focus their resources on developing unique capabilities that could lead to a competitive advantage.[7] How are HR professionals throughout our industry conducting their business? What are they doing that can be applied within our organization?

Industry Lifecycle   There are four generally recognized phases to the lifecycle of a business or industry.

- **Introduction**   This is the beginning of the organization. It's the entrepreneurial phase where everything is new. Policies and systems are being created as they are needed.

- **Growth**   After the new organization has gotten a foothold in its marketplace, it begins to grow. Growth is influenced by all the factors we have explored in SWOT and PESTEL analyses.

- **Maturity**   This is the time when the organization is comfortable with its size, its influence, and its income.

- **Decline**   The phase when systems have gotten surpassed by technological advances and products and services have become passé. Without updates to its core reasons for existing, the organization will ultimately cease to exist.

Porter's Five Forces   Each employer organization has pressures from both internal and external sources. Those pressures impact the competitiveness the organization will be able to apply to the world in which it operates. Porter first published his suggestion that these five forces are what influence competitiveness. The Harvard Business Review article appeared in 1979.[8] These pressures consist of forces close to a company that affect its ability to serve its customers and make a profit.

The five forces are as follows:

- **Threat of new entrants**   When a company does so well that their success attracts new competitors who want to get in on that success, the competition can drive down profits.

- **Threat of substitutes**   In modern terms, these are the "knock off" products that may even be legal if the original product patents have expired. Other people use different products or services to address the same need that the original product or service solved. Examples are digital watches versus analog watches and cell phones versus land lines.

- **Bargaining power of customers**   When customer orders are large, they can force the lowering of price. Consider the big-box stores and how their orders influence suppliers.

- **Bargaining power of suppliers**   If there are few options for sourcing component parts, raw materials, or other supplies, the supplier can have a strong influence on the cost of end products.

- **Industry rivalry**   Industry competitors greatly influence our ability to succeed in the marketplace. They can often drive our price to end users and force us to clearly differentiate how our products and services are superior to the other industry players.

Strategic Investment Decisions   In evaluating capital expenditure decisions, we should consider three techniques to see how investment decisions are evaluated: accounting rate of return, payback, and discounted cash flow techniques. In HR terms, investments should be evaluated based on the period of time it takes to reclaim the investment (using a new applicant tracking software system), what the payback amount will be (savings in HR payroll expense from new software application), and what impact there will be on cash flow (reduction in HR budget that can put cash back into the organizational P&L statement).

Growth Share Matrix   Sometimes called the *Boston box* or *Boston matrix,* the growth share matrix can be created with plotting on two axes. The x-axis is the relative market share. The y-axis is market growth. Those two axes create four quadrants. When market share increases and market growth does too, the companies are "stars." When market growth is high but market share is low, companies are questionable for investment. When market share is high but growth is low, companies can be good cash cows. Finally, when both market growth and market share are low, companies can be described as *investment dogs.* Figure 4-3 is an example of a growth share matrix.

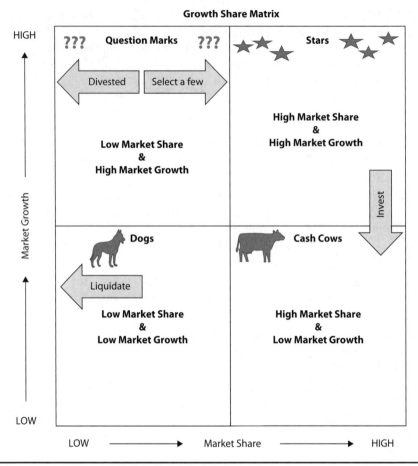

Figure 4-3   Growth share matrix

The GE-McKinsey Nine-Box Matrix   The *nine-box matrix,* shown in Figure 4-4, offers a systematic approach for the decentralized corporation to determine where best to invest its cash. Rather than rely on each business unit's projections of its future prospects, the company can judge a unit by two factors that will determine whether it's going to do well in the future: the attractiveness of the relevant industry and the unit's competitive strength within that industry.[9]

Defining Mission, Vision, and Values

According to SHRM, mission, vision, and values can be defined as follows:

- **Mission**   Mission is a concise explanation of the organization's reason for existence. It describes the organization's purpose and its overall intention. The mission statement supports the vision and serves to communicate purpose and direction to employees, customers, vendors, and other stakeholders.

Figure 4-4
The GE-McKinsey
nine-box matrix
chart

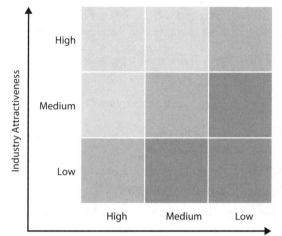

Industry Attractiveness

High

Medium

Low

High   Medium   Low

Competitive Strength of Organization's Business Unit

- **Vision**   Vision looks forward and creates a mental image of the ideal state that the organization wants to achieve. It is inspirational and aspirational and should challenge employees.
- **Values**   Values are the core principles that guide and direct the organization and its culture. In a values-led organization, the values create a moral compass for the organization and its employees.

Mission and Vision Statements   A mission statement answers these questions: What is our organization's purpose? Why does our organization exist? A vision statement answers these questions: What problem are we seeking to solve? Where are we headed? If we achieved all strategic goals, what would we look like 10 years from now?

Organizational Values   Organizational values will answer these questions: What values are unique to our organization? What values should guide the operations of our company? What conduct should our employees uphold?

Articulating the HR Mission, Vision, and Values   HR professionals are accountable for creating the HR mission, vision, and values statements. Beyond that, they are responsible for communicating them to senior executives and to the general employee body in terms that can be well understood. When creating a presentation about the HR role and its place in the overall organization, consider these questions: What will be the impact on me [the executive or employee]? Why should I care about the role of HR in the organization? How will this make my job easier?

Setting Goals

Setting HR goals within the construct of articulated mission, vision, and values statements is the next step. What do we want to accomplish in the coming period of time? The time period could be a month or a year. What contributions can be made by HR to the overall organization's efforts? HR can make a financial impact, for example.

Using the SMART method will ensure that the goals created stand a chance of actually being achieved. Here's an example of an achievable goal:

Implement a new telecommunicating policy that complies with new ERGO standards for the IT department by end of second quarter.

SMART goal setting stands for the following:

- **Specific**   Know exactly what you want to accomplish. Goals must be well defined. They must be clear and unambiguous.

- **Measurable**   Have a yardstick to measure the specific intention.

- **Attainable**   Make the goal achievable.

- **Realistic**   Make the goal realistic to achieve in the time frame and relevant to align with the organization's strategic plan.

- **Timed**   Specify whether this goal has an implementation date.

Composing goals with the SMART outline and using action verbs such as *identify, describe, create, implement,* and *define* will guide the objective of the goal's direction.

A word of caution when goal setting: be careful of the smorgasbord effect, which means getting so excited about creating SMART goals for the HR plan that too many are selected, which can cause a dilution of focus and resources.

Aligning HR Goals and Objectives   Once HR goals are set, it is necessary for a final step in the process. That is to check that HR goals are aligned with organizational goals and objectives. If HR isn't going to be supporting the overall goals of the employer organization, then adjustments should be made. There is no room for "grandstanding" or building personal "kingdoms." HR must be a team player with the other executives in the leadership group. HR's contributions must be clear to the executive team.

Developing Strategy

A strategy is a statement of *how* we are going to get things done. It is less specific than an *action plan.* Once the mission, vision, and values have been established, the logical next step is to ask "How will we accomplish these things?" It is a broad statement about what approach we will take to implement the mission at each point. Then, later, will come the action plan that answers the questions of who, when, and what.

Developing Strategies That Fit

This is according to Community Tool Box: "A good strategy will take into account existing barriers and resources (people, money, power, materials, etc.). It will also stay with the overall vision, mission, and objectives of the initiative. Often, an initiative will use many different strategies—providing information, enhancing support, removing barriers, providing resources, etc.—to achieve its goals.

"Objectives [goals] outline the aims of an initiative—what success would look like in achieving the vision and mission. By contrast, strategies suggest paths to take (and how to move along) on the road to success. That is, strategies help you determine how you will realize your vision and objectives through the nitty-gritty world of action."[10]

It wouldn't make much sense to plan how to do something that isn't part of the mission, vision, or values of the organization. Follow the mission and stay within the boundaries of the vision and values. Strategy will allow you to determine how to implement your mission. If you discover a strategy that isn't speaking to the mission, get rid of it. It will be a distraction at best and a waste of resources at worst.

Business Strategy: How We Will Compete

Each enterprise must assess for itself the missions and strategies that it needs to accomplish its goals. Competing in an open market requires that assessment be updated periodically. After all, world conditions will change with time. Employer organizations need to be flexible to accommodate those shifts.

In HR terms, should the HR functions be performed by in-house staff or by hiring a consultant from the outside? Perhaps contracting with a large vendor would be the more cost-effective approach. Payroll is the obvious example. Oftentimes, vendors can perform the payroll function more cheaply than can internal staff. Other examples are HRIS management or benefit management (employee assistance programs). If you want to compete for rights to deliver any given HR function to your employees, it will be necessary for you to develop a business plan explaining how you will be able to do it better than the external vendors.

Creating Competitive Advantage   Delivering HR services using people on the payroll gives you flexibility because they can often spend a portion of their time working on projects that are not the primary focus of their other work. If you have HR professionals assigned to compensation analysis, they may have some time while waiting for compensation data input that could be used to review policies as part of a two-year review cycle. That efficiency wouldn't be available to you if you hired an outsider to do the compensation analysis.

According to the Priority Metrics Group,[11] there are six ways to differentiate your organization within a competitive marketplace, regardless of where in the world you are located (see Table 4-1).

Types of Differentiation	Methods of Differentiation
Product differentiation	Features, performance, efficacy, conformance, durability, reliability, warranty
Service differentiation	Ordering ease, delivery, installation, customer training, customer consulting, other miscellaneous services
Channel differentiation	Coverage, expertise, performance
Relationship differentiation	Competence, courtesy, credibility, reliability, responsiveness, communication
Reputation/image differentiation	Perception, communication, advertising
Price differentiation	By customer, by quantity, by segment

Table 4-1   Six Ways to Differentiate Your Product or Service

Table 4-2	Scope	Broad	Cost Leadership	Differentiation
Porter's Competitive Strategies		Narrow	Cost Focus	Differentiation Focus
			Cost	Differentiation
			Source of Competitive Advantage	

Porter's Competitive Strategies   What forces drive competition in an industry? What moves will competitors make? How will one's industry evolve? How do strategic planners respond to competitive actions? How can a firm be best positioned to compete in the long run?

In 1985, Porter suggested that there are four primary competitive strategies that organizations can rely on when plotting their future business course.[12] Porter called the generic strategies cost leadership (no frills), differentiation (creating uniquely desirable products and services), and focus (offering a specialized service in a niche market). He then subdivided the focus strategy into two parts: cost focus and differentiation focus (Table 4-2).[13]

Cost Leadership   Within the cost leadership strategy, profits can be increased by reducing costs while maintaining prices at industry average. Market share can be increased by both reducing costs and lowering prices, taking sales away from competitors. The no-frills retailers have opted to cut costs to a minimum and pass their savings on to customers in lower prices. This helps them grab market share and ensure their stores are as full as possible, further driving down cost. Think of Costco, Home Depot, and Lowes. This same thinking can be applied to the HR department if being the lowest-cost HR department in the industry is a mission of the group.

Differentiation   Differentiation involves making your products or services different from and more attractive than those of your competitors. How will you set yourself apart from your competition? Your competition in the HR world are the HR managers in other companies within your industry. Are they running a group that delivers HR services to their employees with a 1:150 HR professional to employee ratio? What if, at the same time, your HR professional to employee ratio was running 2:150? You are spending twice as much for HR professionals as your competitors. If you can differentiate your services based on cost, you should be able to do so based on quality. Being a full-service HR department means you "hold the hand of employees" as they ask for help with benefits enrollment, discrimination complaint processing, and training enrollment. Unless you can be better in either cost or quality, you will lose out to the competition. Important to this approach is that you can actually deliver the differentiated product or service, in high quality and in the time promised. The marketplace will long remember the broken promises made to customers, so beware of making promises you cannot keep.

Focus   When you focus on niche markets, it is possible to use focus as a strategy. Making something that no one else does that serves a specific requirement is one way. Examples are making dog collars using all natural materials or creating a sea-shell shop that imports sea shells from all over the world so customers can have a one-stop shopping experience.

It costs customers less time and money to search the world for what they want when you have it all conveniently located in your offerings.

Companies that use focus strategies concentrate on particular niche markets and, by understanding the dynamics of that market and the unique needs of customers within it, develop uniquely low-cost or well-specified products for the market. Because they serve customers in their market uniquely well, they tend to build strong brand loyalty among their customers. This makes their particular market segment less attractive to competitors.[14]

Impact of Business Strategies on HR Strategy   Business strategy is paramount. HR strategy must support that business strategy. So, begin with questions like these: What is the business mission? What strategies will be used to accomplish that mission? How can HR support those business strategies? HR is one component of the organization, as is finance, accounting, marketing, production, and research. If all of these components are not supporting the business strategy, there is little likelihood that business goals will be accomplished.

Your HR organization and its strategies can have an impact on the overall business strategies if you follow these ten steps to make it happen:[15]

1. *Understand your organization's business.* Spend time every day talking with sales, production, quality, and accounting. Make sure that you know what is going on in that bigger world.

2. *Share responsibility for business goals and plans.* The overall business goals are your goals, too. When you make plans for your department, they should be directed to achieving overall business objectives as well as human resource goals. Developing a performance culture is a goal you'll likely own.

3. *Know the human resource business thoroughly.* Your customers rely on you for correct and insightful information and advice. What more is there to say? You are reliable, credible, trustworthy, and knowledgeable, and you have deep integrity.

4. *Run your department like a business.* Your goals must contribute to the accomplishment of the overall business objectives. Your action plans to achieve the goals need to translate into daily "to-do" lists for your staff. Every significant activity requires a feedback loop or audit so you know that it is being accomplished.

5. *Measure outcomes and goal achievement, not work processes.* Employee and executive surveys are often used to identify how these people see HR performance.

6. *Remember the people in human resources.* Is your office a magnet for people who need help, advice, or a sounding board? Are some of your visitors your senior managers? Even the CEO? If so, you remember that you are there to serve your organization's people so that they can meet your business goals.

7. *Express thoughtful opinions backed by data and study.* You have to understand the numbers. How else can you offer a substantial, intelligent opinion about business direction? Learn everything you can so that you have opinions and so your opinions are backed up with data. You need to understand the effect of decisions that your office makes on the work of the rest of the company. (For example, don't schedule meetings with plant personnel on the last day of their shipping month.)

8. *Harness the benefits of technology.* You'll provide better customer service and free your time for dreaming up new value-added strategies. You cannot overestimate the impact of an effective HRIS. Need reports about attendance? How about salary reports for your whole organization? Interested in turnover and retention figures?

9. *Recommend programs for people who continually improve the business.* When you propose new programs or problem-solve people issues, suggest solutions that support the accomplishment of business goals. You have reasons for suggesting a new variable pay system such as encouraging managers to accomplish business objectives. What's better—the "thank you" card system that appears to help employee motivation and productivity or the attendance system that has reduced absenteeism by 4 percent?

10. *Learn and grow every day through every possible method.* Use your knowledge of how people develop to do what is necessary to continue your growth curve.

- Seek out a more experienced mentor or sounding board. You need someone you can confide in and learn from.

- Attend professional HR conferences, meetings, and events.

- Attend executive leadership and management meetings in addition to your HR professional associations. You seek knowledge that goes beyond the bounds of your discipline and department.

- Attend at least 40 hours of training and education every year. Make sure your staff members attend, too. Cover all aspects of the business and running a business.

- Seek out people who will ask you questions and challenge your beliefs so you can continue to grow. For example, a woman works with a CEO, who asks her questions. She may not always like them, but the questions challenge her to think things through and to follow issues to their logical conclusion. He repeatedly asks, "How will you know if that is working? Happening? Bringing the results you want?" You need to be able to respond.

Corporate Strategy: Where We Will Compete   Whatever the corporate strategy, we need to be able to support it from the HR department. Remember, strategy is how we will meet our goals and objectives. Once we identify how we will get there (what strategies we will use), we can begin developing the action plan that will assign individual responsibilities for each element of the strategy.

Determining which markets to address is a question business strategy must address. If the answer is that expansion into international locations is appropriate, then HR strategic planning will need to address those requirements.

Growth Strategy Options   Growth can happen through market penetration (capturing a greater portion of the existing market with current products/services), market expansion (selling current products in a new market), diversification (selling new products to new markets), and acquisition (purchasing another company to gain broader product or service offerings).[16] Growth requires financial support. HR can contribute by controlling expenses. These are some ways that growth strategy can be a viable option.

- **Market penetration** Increasing market share through options such as lowering prices
- **Market expansion** Developing new markets where current products and services can be sold
- **Product expansion** Increasing the number of products or product features
- **Diversification strategies** Selling new products to new markets
- **Acquisition strategies** Purchasing another organization in an effort to expand product line or markets

Managing Growth Options The key to a long, healthy corporate life is steady growth. According to a 1998 survey, of the companies that enjoyed greater than 10 percent sales growth per year, about 78 percent were still around 6 years after starting. Of the companies with flat or decreasing sales, only 27.5 percent survived for 6 years.[17]

Managing growth requires substantial market intelligence. Researching the needs of the target market, receptivity to product names or applications, and financial requirements of the expansion effort are all concerns that need to be addressed. HR can contribute to those research efforts through identification of employee benefit packages and their costs, specification of employee recruiting techniques and costs, and cultural challenges that will be faced because of the expansion.

Mergers and Acquisitions Mergers and acquisitions (M&As) are transactions in which the ownership of companies, other business organizations, or their operating units are transferred or combined. As an aspect of strategic management, M&As can allow enterprises to grow, shrink, and change the nature of their business or competitive position. From a legal point of view, a merger is a legal consolidation of two entities into one entity, whereas an acquisition occurs when one entity takes ownership of another entity's stock, equity interests, or assets. Mergers and acquisitions are means to new markets, new products or services, or a new management team. All could figure strategically into your future plans.

Sometimes it makes good business sense to purchase another organization or merge with another organization. When markets are different and a combined organization can offer both entities a broader sales base, there is synergy. When product lines can be added through mergers and acquisitions, there is synergy. Then HR interventions are needed that will address cultural blending and employee support systems.

- **HR's role in the mergers and acquisitions strategy** HR is almost always called upon to do due diligence in the investigative phase prior to finalizing a merger or acquisition. What union agreements does the new company have? How will those provisions fit into our organization? What policies does the new company have, and how will they blend with our policies? (Examples are holiday and vacation computations, sick leave policies, and parental leave policies.)

- **Planning the HR integration strategy** An estimated 70 percent to 90 percent of all M&As fail to achieve their anticipated strategic and financial objectives.[18] This rate of failure is often attributed to various HR-related factors, such as incompatible cultures, management styles, poor motivation, loss of key talent, lack of communication, diminished trust, and uncertainty of long-term goals.

Both mergers and acquisitions present significant challenges to HR professionals. The M&A process requires management of both organizations to consider all implications of a proposed merger or acquisition before agreeing to one—which necessarily involves consideration of the "people issues" created by a proposed merger or acquisition. HR professionals are often involved in the process by advising management on human resource matters, including using surveys and other metrics to gather relevant data, identifying potential conflicts or HR challenges between the two companies, integrating HR practices and company cultures after an M&A, and managing talent decisions such as layoffs, to name a few.[19]

Developing integration strategy is like developing any other strategy. It requires asking who the stakeholders are (our company, their company, customers, stockholders, employees) and what benefits can be achieved by successfully completing the merger or acquisition (expanding markets, expanding product line, reducing expenses/costs, gaining customers/market share, and improving customer perception of our business).

Then follow the same basic steps used in other strategic planning sessions.[20]

1. *Identify the vision.* What is the desired future? What is the inspiration? What aspirations will we identify?

2. *Identify the mission.* What is the clear and compelling objective for the integration?

3. *Identify the goals.* What must be achieved? What needs should be met?

4. *Identify the strategies.* What is the plan that will lead us to achieving our mission and goals?

5. *Identify the initiatives.* What tactical and operational plans will be necessary to successfully implement the strategy?

Implementing Once established, the HR strategy for a merger or acquisition needs to be implemented. That requires further analysis of the tactics and operational plans that will be needed for our achieving success. All of the basic support programs needed in running a business must be either blended or transitioned to one of the existing systems.

Here are a few of the keys needed to make a merger/acquisition successful based on the principles of the Accelerating Implementation Methodology (AIM):[21]

- **Define the changes in terms of human behavior** The speed of an integration is determined by how you manage the human elements of the change. Remember to define the changes in terms of what people need to be doing differently. What are we doing? Why are we doing it, and what are the consequences if we don't succeed?

- **Generate sponsorship**   Sponsorship is the single most important factor in ensuring a fast and successful implementation. Every sponsor, from senior management down to the line managers, must express, model, and reinforce their commitment to the change. You will not get a cultural change with minor changes in sponsor behavior!

- **Manage resistance**   Resistance is inevitable even when people see the merger as positive. Resistance is a function of disruption, and an M&A can be very disruptive. Make sure you have a plan on how to manage it, including responding quickly to concerns, rumors, and questions.

- **Tighten up communications**   Every communication sent must include a feedback loop. This way, when a communication goes out, feedback will come back in. Use a variety of communication channels, with an emphasis on the face-to-face method.

- **Manage reinforcements**   The only way to implement actual culture change is to integrate the behavioral elements of the new culture into the daily business activities and then dramatically change the reinforcements—that is, the positive and negative consequences that managers apply on a daily basis with their direct reports.

Monitoring and Evaluating   It is all well and good to know where we want to go and how we want to get there. However, it is equally important to know if we are actually walking the path we outlined for ourselves in the strategic planning. That is what monitoring and evaluating will tell us. Monitoring is the process of continually measuring the progress achievements of a project. It also assesses results that matter. Evaluation is the process of measuring the success of project achievements and the quality of those achievements. Establishing milestones for an M&A project will help you understand if you are on schedule, and quality measures will provide feedback about the success you have had so far with your implementation.

Measuring our incremental success can be great feedback to help us make adjustments where necessary so we can get back on track when necessary. HR can monitor recruiting and staffing functions, benefit design and implementation functions, employee relocation, policy development and implementation, and legal compliance requirements. Each of those functions should be evaluated for progress toward the goal. How many requisitions were filled within 10 days, 30 days, or longer? How quickly were policies developed when they were needed? What compliance requirements were met or not met (EEO discrimination complaint rate, compliance evaluation closures with "no violation" determination from the Department of Labor)? What was the retention rate of new hires? What was the turnover rate at each compensation level within the organization? All these and more are valid measurements that can be used by HR to monitor the progress toward the goal of completing a merger or acquisition.

Divestiture Strategies   The opposite of merger is divestiture. Divestiture is the removal of assets or processes that are no longer needed and that can be converted into cash. As a strategy, "spinning off" pieces of an organization can leave the remainder of the company in a healthier state financially. Splitting up a company can be equally painful and complicated.

For example, in 1982, Judge Green ordered the bifurcation of the Bell System. It was necessary to create a new enterprise that had the legacy telephone company businesses and a new company that would be unregulated and allowed to compete openly in the business communication marketplace. On January 1, 1983, American Bell was born. It was staffed by 100,000 employees who had been transitioned from the 23 legacy operating companies in the Bell System. And the new company had no revenue. It survived the first year or so on loans from the former telephone operating companies. And it was necessary to pay those 100,000 people from the very beginning. The plan called for employee records to be transferred from the 23 operating companies to the new American Bell accounting center in Lakeland, Florida. Well, unfortunately, there were large differences among record storage systems among the 23 companies. So, data fields and formatting requirements were all different. Blending the imported records was not working on a practical level. It was necessary for HR to create a staff that would scrub the employee records to be sure they were both accurate and properly formatted for the new accounting system in Lakeland. Once that was done, things began to run smoothly. In the beginning, approximately 10 to 25 percent of the American Bell staff was not receiving paychecks. Branch sales managers were writing checks on the branch account to their employees as substitute paychecks. It took almost an entire year to unravel all of the payments that were made and reconcile them with payroll.

Identifying how we will accomplish the divestiture seems like a reasonable step to take, and HR professionals can contribute to that planning process by identifying how they will add value to the end result.

Communicating Strategy   "If you don't communicate your strategy in a way that your people understand and find compelling, how can you expect them to help you succeed with it? Research suggests only 5 percent of the people in an organization understand its strategy."[22] According to Harvard Business Review, there are eight ways to effectively communicate your strategy.[23]

- *Keep the message simple but deep in meaning.* Most organizations have a deeper meaning as to why they exist. This tends to influence strategy, decision-making, and behaviors at executive levels but often isn't well articulated for employees. What you call it doesn't matter—your purpose, your why, your core belief, your center. What does matter is that you establish its relevance with employees in a way that makes them care more about the company and about the job they do.

- *Build behavior based on market and customer insights.* For employees to fully understand how your strategy is different and better than the competition, they need to be in touch with market realities. The challenge is in how to effectively convey those realities so that your people can act on them. By building internal campaigns based on market and customer insights, you bring your strategy to life for your employees through this important lens. Package your content so that it can be shared broadly with all departments in your organization but in a hands-on way.

- *Use the discipline of a framework.* Inspire, educate, reinforce.

- *Think broader than the typical CEO-delivered message, and don't disappear.* Employees are more likely to believe what leaders say when they hear similar arguments from their peers, and conversations can be more persuasive and engaging than one-way presentations. Designate a team of employees to serve as ambassadors responsible for delivering important messages at all levels.

- *Put on your "real person" hat.* And take off your "corporate person/executive" hat. The fact is, not many people are deeply inspired by the pieces of communication that their companies put out. Much of it ignores one of the most important truths of communication, especially communication in the early twenty-first century: be real. "Corporate speak" comes off as hollow and lacking in meaning. Authentic messages from you will help employees see the challenges and opportunities as you see them and understand and care about the direction in which you're trying to take the company.

- *Tell a story.* Facts and figures won't be remembered. Stories and experiences will. Use storytelling as much as possible to bring humanity to the company and to help employees understand the relevance of your strategy and real-life examples of progress and shortfalls against it. Ask employees to share stories as well and use these as the foundation for dialogues that foster greater understanding of the behaviors that you want to encourage and enhance versus those that pose risks.

- *Use twenty-first-century media and be unexpected.* Consider the roles of social media, networking, blogs, and games to get the word out in ways that your employees are used to engaging in. Where your message shows up also says a lot. Aim to catch people somewhere that they would least expect it. Is it in the restroom? In the stairwell? On their mobile phone?

- *Make the necessary investment.* Most executives recognize how important their employee audience is. They are the largest expense to the company. They often communicate directly with your customers. They single-handedly control most perceptions that consumers have about the brand. So, if this is a given, why are we so reluctant to fund internal communication campaigns?

Implementing Strategy Production

Implementation is the process that turns strategies and plans into actions in order to accomplish strategic objectives and goals. Implementing your strategic plan is as important, or even more important, than your strategy.[24]

Implementation of Strategy

Implementation requires an action plan. It may be called an *implementation plan.* Regardless of its name, it is a document that assigns responsibility to individuals or specific groups, determines due dates, and sets periodic progress meetings to see whether you are still on track, what unexpected problems have arisen, and what other resources might be needed to fully complete the action plan.

	Strategic Action Plan			
Goal	Strategy (How?)	Assigned To	Complete Target	Actual Complete
New medical insurance provider	Background checks on at least five vendors	HR benefit manager	5/12/2025	?
Upgrade HRIS	Attend vendor training program	HRIS manager	2/15/2025	2/10/2025
Offload employee relocation to a vendor	Analyze at least three vendors for presentation to HR committee	HR director	4/15/2015	?

Table 4-3 Strategic Action Plan

Consider Elon Musk and his SpaceX company. Their mission has been to build and fly a rocket that would launch payloads and then return to a soft landing on a barge in the ocean. Of course, he wanted to reuse the rocket and reduce overall costs in the process. They developed a strategic plan (determining how they would reach their goals) and then assigned responsibilities to specific individuals and groups (to carry out the plan) and had routine meetings to confirm they were still on track with the plan. When the first two rockets landed too hard and blew up as a result, they went back to the drawing board to determine the problem and try again. The third launch got it right, and the company has begun lifting government and private payloads into space ever since.

What Organizations Need for Effective Implementation   First there are objectives. Those are the goals we want to accomplish. Then comes strategy. That is a statement of how we will reach each goal. Then comes the implementation plan (action plan) that answers the questions of who, when, and where. Think of it as a spreadsheet or a table that can be expanded as needed. Table 4-3 is an example.

Allocating Resources

Ultimately, resources come down to budget. But there are many components that can be identified and managed along the way to that bottom-line budget impact. To determine how we will succeed, it is necessary to develop a business case to present to the executive team.

Making a Business Case   A major responsibility falling on the shoulders of HR professionals these days is the development and presentation of a business case for the organizational programs that will solve specific problems. For example, a business case is needed when recommending certain medical insurance programs, particularly if the employer has not provided such benefits in the past.

A business case is a written or oral presentation that identifies a problem, analyzes the various possible solutions, and makes a recommendation for implementing one of them. It will almost always have an analysis of financial impact, personnel impact, and customer impact. It is designed and presented using business terminology. For example, a recommendation for medical insurance would include the current cost plus a forecast of future costs both in total dollars and in dollars per employee. It will have specific information about the way in which the recommendation will solve the problem that has been identified. (For example, the retention of employees is significantly improved if the employer offers medical insurance to workers. Higher retention means less turnover and lower recruiting and training costs.) All of the benefits will have dollar values assigned to them in a business case presentation.

Making a business case means assembling business reasons for taking some action. The case will be ultimately presented to the decision-maker, be it an executive or the board of directors.

Business Case Content	
Executive summary	Short statement that summarizes the problem and recommendation with key reasons for choosing the recommended solution.
Definition of the problem	Identifying the issue that is being addressed in the business case. It could be changes in employee benefits, alterations in payroll, policy changes, or other HR-related issues. The definition should include a statement of how the organization is impacted by the problem.
Objectives	Statements of key results expected in solving the stated problem.
Possible solutions	List of key solutions possible for the stated problem.
Recommended solution	Identification of the solution that is being recommended and why. The list of reasons for making the choice should include statements of impact on the organization, its workforce, its customers/clients, and its other stakeholders. Those impacts should be quantified if possible.
Implementation plan	The steps needed to implement the solution and solve the problem. It could be a short list of steps or something quite complicated. An action plan should always include an action to be taken, who is responsible for that action, and the target date for completion of that action.
Support documents	All documents related to the selection decision. They might include financial analysis, statements of impact on profit and loss or balance sheet, analysis of HR impacts (e.g., turnover, diversity, morale), organizational branding impacts, influences on competitive advantage, corporate responsibility changes, and staffing required for implementation.

Project Management Principles and Practices   Projects come and go in the life of HR professionals. There are projects for the implementation of new benefit programs, assessment of new recruiting sources, and all the projects associated with new paths of business that the organization is embarking on. Being able to juggle all those things at the same time while assuring that each gets the proper amount of attention and actually moves toward a conclusion is the mark of a good project manager.

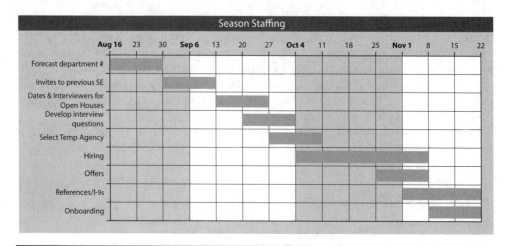

Season Staffing														
	Aug 16	23	30	**Sep 6**	13	20	27	**Oct 4**	11	18	25	**Nov 1**	8	15	22
Forecast department #															
Invites to previous SE															
Dates & Interviewers for Open Houses															
Develop interview questions															
Select Temp Agency															
Hiring															
Offers															
References/I-9s															
Onboarding															

Figure 4-5   Sample Gantt chart

A project consists of a series of activities and tasks that have been identified that need to be performed to accomplish an outcome. Dates are identified, people are assigned to the tasks, and resources such as budget and people are allocated. Overseeing a project is project management.

Project Management Tools   A standard tool used in project management is the Gantt chart, also known as an *activity log* or *milestone chart,* and it is widely available as a template or dedicated software programs. A Gantt chart normally identifies in chronological bar graph order what needs to occur first and simultaneously in a step fashion (see Figure 4-5). The benefit of a Gantt chart is the visual monitoring and communication of who is on first base and doing what task, what needs to occur before progression to second base, and where the results have to be before a run is counted at home plate.

Managing Change

Suffice it to say that managing change is the largest driving force behind employee relations. Change is a process that people and organizations undergo as a response; it is a transformation toward flexibility. HR is involved in managing the people issues resulting from change, either planned change or a reactive change, such as something occurring from an external source like an employment-related law regulating behavior in the workplace.

Helping both employees and management in an organized process through the roller-coaster ride of change, as identified by Elisabeth Kubler-Ross in her book *On Death and Dying,*[25] is an emotional intelligent (EQ) competency skill for HR professionals and leaders. First, shock and denial about the change is awakened within people. Next is the response of anger. Depression eventually sets in about the "loss" of status quo resulting from the change. Then movement toward bargaining and dialogue occurs related to the change. Finally, the roller-coaster ride ends with reaching a level of acceptance about the change. The key knowledge is in understanding the change and the management of the anticipated reactions.

Donald Kirkpatrick's *How to Manage Change Effectively*[26] discusses a model with the seven basic steps in the change management process for HR and organizations to prepare with.

- Determining the need or desire for change
- Preparing the tentative plans for change
- Discussing alternative and probable reactions to the change
- Making a final decision about the change
- Establishing a project plan and associated timetable
- Communicating the change
- Implementing the change and evaluation

Response to Change   Employees are people, and people react to change differently. Fear of the unknown can bring on some strong emotional responses. Here are some of the possibilities of neutral or negative reactions:[27]

- **"Not me!"**   This is when somebody else is better suited for the new job assignment, or it's when there's denial that they are able to make the changes necessary.
- **"What will this do to my job security?"**   Will my job survive the changes?
- **Anger**   Frustration can build to anger when employees believe they are losing control over their work.
- **Gossip**   Uncertainty and frustration can result in employees gossiping about the change. Sometimes this turns to viciousness and vindictiveness, which are problematic.
- **"Who's in charge here?"**   Uncertainty of reporting relationships can be frustrating also. One group in the midst of resizing used to say, "If the boss calls, get her name."
- **Panic**   Emotional upset about the change can cause a severe lack of confidence that can even cause physical illness.
- **"I quit!"**   This is the ultimate response to change by an employee. Unfortunately, the cost to the employee is greater than the cost to the organization.

Here are some examples of positive reactions:

- **"This is a challenge."**   Open minded about the new work arrangement, some employees are confident that they can gain the necessary knowledge to do the work ahead.
- **Enthusiasm**   Eager to accept new assignments, these workers can't wait to dig in.

- **"Maybe I could adjust to this change."** After a period of observation, they agree to give the change a chance.
- **Positive vision** These are people who see the bigger picture and have confidence in the organization's leadership.

Conditions That Make Change Possible Ken Blanchard and Scott Blanchard have listed six steps to ensuring successful change implementation for any organization.[28]

- **Beat communication breakdown** People don't want to be "sold" by executives on the advantages of the changes to come. They want to be able to understand what will be happening and why.
- **Get personal** Help employees answer these questions: What's in it for me to change? Will I win or lose? Will I look good? How will I find the time to implement this change? Will I have to learn new skills? Can I do it?
- **Plan your action** Leaders need to be able to drive forward with answers to these questions: What do I do first, second, third? How do I manage all the details? What happens if it doesn't work as planned? Where do I go for help? How long will this take? Is what we are experiencing typical? How will the organizational structure and systems change?
- **Sell the change** If leaders have done a good job on the previous steps, employees will often sell themselves on the change as a good thing.
- **Collaborate smartly** People begin turning outward to ask who else should be involved with questions such as these: How can we work with others to get them involved in what we are doing? How do we spread the word?
- **Refine for success** Refinement questions are a good sign and show that the people in the organization are focused on continuous improvement. How can we improve on our original idea? How do we make the change even better?

Models for Managing Change If the list of conditions that make change possible aren't enough, you can find more information about managing change in your industry from industry associations and even from your competitors who may already have gone through something similar to your challenge. Specific industry models can be extremely helpful because they are constructed with the language of your industry, not someone else's. HR associations such as SHRM can be helpful with both written reports available and offerings of live expert help to counsel you through your planning and executing change management.

HR's Role in Change Management SHRM suggests that there are four roles HR professionals must play in change management. How that is done will vary according to the type of change being addressed.[29] Here are the four basic roles HR can play under the circumstances:

- **Leader** With management establish vision and clear direction and shape culture to minimize obstacles.

- **Educator**   Coach managers to implement and drive change on their teams, provide necessary training and tools to prepare employees for change, and build a communication road map to resonate with different audiences.

- **Advisor**   Create transparency as a liaison between executives and employees.

- **Demonstrator**   Design methods to reinforce the change, create a mind-set of change by modeling, and encourage other executives to do the same.

Put them together, and the acronym is LEAD.

Evaluating Strategic Performance

SHRM-SCP

Performance management is a systematic process that helps improve organizational effectiveness by providing feedback to employees on their performance results and improvement needs. When individual performance is linked to organizational strategic objectives, employees can see how they help impact accomplishments at the organizational level. It is employee accomplishments and contributions that drive the business results of an organization, so a regular feedback system discussing individual performance is at the core of a good performance management system. It ensures that employees are on course for the completion of tasks and goals that are aligned with the organization's goals and that the resources and support are provided for the employee to perform such functions.

Performance Evaluation and Reporting

Creating and communicating the organization's vision, mission, strategies, specific goals, and values form the foundation that is needed for the performance management system. Then performance standards are agreed upon by both the line management and the employee on what the job requires and what will be measured. At this stage, it is essential that employees clearly understand the standards, including expected behavior standards set forth, for their jobs. Feedback is the next stage and can be both informal and formal. Formal feedback can entail a written performance appraisal.

Defining Performance Objectives

Employees need to know and understand what specific performance is expected of them in performing their jobs and the acceptable behavior. This communication begins with the very first discussion in a job interview and certainly with the job offer and new-hire onboarding orientation. The discussion continues on a consistent basis both with the reinforcement of organizational standards that are outlined in employee handbooks and other written material and with performance appraisal review sessions. The clearer the expectations set for employees, the greater the success in having expectations met.

Effective Performance Measurement   Key to successfully using performance management are the following touchstones:

- Focus on results.

- Develop a culture of accountability.

- Align all organizational activities with overall organizational goals.

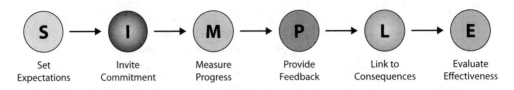

Figure 4-6 Effective performance management touchstones

- Provide a common language for success.
- Make measurements simple to use.

Take a look at Figure 4-6 and you will likely find these concepts easier to grasp.[30]

Using a Balanced Scorecard to Align Objectives with Strategy According to Howard Rohm, CEO of the Balanced Scorecard Institute, "The balanced scorecard is a robust organization-wide strategic planning, management and communications system. These are strategy-based systems that align the work people do with organization vision and strategy, communicate strategic intent throughout the organization and to external stakeholders, and provide a basis for better aligning strategic objectives with resources. In strategy-based scorecard systems, strategic and operational performance measures (outcomes, outputs, process and inputs) are only one of several important components, and the measures are used to better inform decision making at all levels in the organization. In strategy-based systems, accomplishments and results are the main focus, based on good strategy executed well. A planning and management scorecard system uses strategic and operational performance information to measure and evaluate how well the organization is performing with financial and customer results, operational efficiency, and organization capacity building."[31]

Using Benchmarking to Set Performance Objectives According to the Construction Industries Institute (CII), "Benchmarking is the systematic process of measuring one's performance against recognized leaders for the purpose of determining best practices that lead to superior performance when adapted and utilized.[32]

"To be successful, benchmarking should be implemented as a structured, systematic process. It will not be successful if applied in an ad hoc fashion on a random basis. In most cases benchmarking is best-practice-oriented and is part of a continuous improvement program that incorporates a feedback process. Benchmarking requires an understanding of what is important to the organization (sometimes called critical success factors) and then measuring performance for these factors."

Benchmarking can be internal or external. Strategic objectives usually establish comparisons with external sources. An example is found in compensation. Using salary surveys, employers can determine where they rate on compensation scales for any given job content. If the goal is to be in the second quartile, it is easy to determine whether that objective is being met by looking at the external pay for survey participants and the pay offered for the same job content.

SMART Goals/Objectives SMART is the acronym that you can use to guide your goal setting. Its criteria are commonly attributed to Peter Drucker's *Management by Objectives* concept and as discussed in the earlier "Setting Goals" section.

How Many and How Often   Examine your organizational goals and strategies for achieving those goals. You should have as many objectives as you need to identify the work you must do to properly contribute to achieving those organizational goals. Your goals should focus on HR issues, and there should be at least one for each of the major HR functions. Without them, you won't be able to tell how you are really doing in your HR efforts.

Common Organizational Metrics   Here are some common ways that organizations measure their own performance:

- **Marketing metrics**   SEO keyword ranking, web traffic sources
- **Sales metrics**   Sales growth, average sale value, average profit margin
- **Financial metrics**   Debt to equity ratio, working capital
- **Social media metrics**   Social followers versus target
- **Customer feedback metrics**   End-of-transaction survey responses, quarterly survey responses
- **Employee metrics**   Cost per hire, retention rate, health care costs

Financial Statement and Metrics   Financial metrics reveal characteristics of financial data that might not be apparent from a simple review of the numbers.[33]

- **Cash flow metrics**   Businesspeople evaluate streams of cash flow events, such as investment outcomes or business case cash flow estimates.
- **Financial statement metrics**   Businesspeople use these metrics to evaluate a firm's financial position and financial performance, such as liquidity, payback period, and return on investment (ROI).

Nonfinancial Organizational Performance Metrics   Here are any measurements that do not have a financial component. Consider such things as the following:

- Customer satisfaction trends
- Supplier delivery date accuracy
- Recruiting source candidate submission acceptance
- Workplace security and safety performance

Countless other possibilities exist. The challenge is to identify those things that can contribute strategically to your organizational goal achievement. Measure the things that matter. Measuring things that don't matter, or that you have no control over, will only bring a sense of failure and lower morale.

Using Business Intelligence   Business intelligence (BI) refers to the tools, technologies, applications, and practices used to collect, integrate, analyze, and present an organization's raw data to create insightful and actionable business information. BI as a discipline and as a technology-driven process is made up of several related activities, including the following:

- Data mining
- Online analytical processing
- Querying
- Reporting

Today's trend toward using "Big Data" (huge databases with hundreds or even thousands of data elements) makes it essential that employers are able to reach into those databases and extract only those elements that will be useful in monitoring business activities and accomplishments.

Data Analysis Methods   Data can come in large or small files. And the large files can be really large files. The "cloud" is home to many examples of exceptionally large databases. Consider the U.S. Bureau of the Census as one such source. Its 2010 Occupational Database has information about individuals with accompanying information about race, gender, work industry, job category (EEO-1, EEO-3, EEO-4, EEO-5), job title, work location, home location (city, state, ZIP code), and more. If you only want to know about people working in a specific county in the HR professionals job category, you would need some method for extracting that information from the database before you could analyze it. Once you have the data in hand, the following are some ways in which you could analyze the smaller components of interest.

Variance Analysis   Variance analysis is the quantitative investigation of the difference between actual and planned behavior. This analysis is used to maintain control over a business. For example, if you budget for sales to be $10,000 and actual sales are $8,000, variance analysis yields a difference of $2,000. Variance analysis is especially effective when you review the amount of a variance on a trend line so that sudden changes in the variance level from month to month are more readily apparent.[34]

Regression Analysis   This is a technique for isolating which factors really have an impact on the issue you are studying. Does time in service have an impact on current compensation levels? To know, it is necessary to isolate time in service and take away consideration of other variables such as employee age, race, gender, years of experience in the industry, starting compensation amount, and any other variable that might interfere with the analysis of time in service. Regression analysis is generally accepted as the most accurate analysis tool available for assessing such things as employment discrimination like disparate impact.

Trend Analysis   Trend analysis is the process of comparing business data over time to identify any consistent results or trends. You can then develop a strategy to respond to these trends in line with your business goals.

Trend analysis helps you understand how your business has performed and predict where current business operations and practices will take you. Done well, it will give you ideas about how you might change things to move your business in the right direction.[35]

Table 4-4
Requisition by
Month 1

Requisitions by Month	
25	January
15	February
12	March
21	April
18	May
14	June
10	July
8	August
16	September
13	October
24	November
19	December

Let's say you are experiencing what you believe is unfavorable turnover among your production workforce. To begin the process of determining why that may be happening, it can be helpful to determine whether there actually is a turnover trend. Plotting the turnover rates for each month (or year) can allow you to see graphically what is actually happening. If there is an increasing slope in the results, you can begin the process of identifying causes for the trend. If you determine that the results are more or less consistent with an occasional spike in the turnover rate, you may decide that no action is required beyond what you are already doing to control turnover.

Graphic Presentation of Data Analysis   Let's assume we want to see the trend of our job requisitions during the past year. Table 4-4 shows the data.

Figures 4-7 and 4-8 show a couple of ways you might want to display the data in graph format. The months are represented by the numbers 1 through 12. The number of requisitions is shown on the left y-axis.

Figure 4-7
Requisition by
month 2

Figure 4-8
Requisition by
month 3

Communicating Data Analysis   Once you have determined that your data is as accurate as you can get it, then determine what the data says to you. What message is there from the data? Then determine how you will present the data message to your audience. Different audiences sometimes require different presentations. If you are explaining the cost of benefit plans to the general employee body, you may use general cost charts. The same discussion with senior executives or the board of directors may be more detailed. While the subject is the same, the way you convey the message can be different.

Providing Leadership and Strategy

Henry Mintzberg said, "Leaders don't do most of the things that their organizations get done; they do not even make them get done. Rather, they help to establish the structures, conditions, and attitudes through which things get done. And that requires a collaborative mind-set." Leaders' critical focus should be on providing guidance and vision, controlling risks, and providing working environments where employees can contribute their best performance rather than just following directions. Leaders who manage employees should have the key skills of planning, staffing, organizing, controlling yet motivating people, and managing resources and budgets.

The HR professional as a leader will have a dual focus: being a leader for the HR function and being able to assist in identifying and developing the organization's leaders.

Leadership Characteristics

The key characteristics and skills for leadership have been written about for decades by many well-known and publicized authors. The skill set that began as hierarchical in design where coercion and intimidation were main factors has clearly changed in today's organizations. The models and opinions of successful leadership characteristics in the twenty-first century that you'll find associated with the SHRM exam are those of James Kouzes and Barry Posner,[36] Erica Fox,[37] Daniel Goleman,[38] and Marshall Goldsmith.[39]

In their studies and research, Kouzes and Posner found that the following practices made successful leaders:

- **Practice 1: Challenging the process**   Successful leaders will recognize when there is a need for change.

- **Practice 2: Inspiring a shared vision**   Successful leaders will have a vision and get their employees to be inspired by the same vision.

- **Practice 3: Enabling others to act**   Successful leaders will empower their employees to do their best work, bringing out their full potential and encouraging collaboration in the workforce.

- **Practice 4: Modeling the way**   Successful leaders will walk the talk and lead by example.

- **Practice 5: Encouraging the heart**   Successful leaders will help their work groups celebrate the achievements and yet learn from their disappointments and matters of adversity.

Daniel Goleman's research report about emotional intelligence, focused on psychology and neuroscience, offers insight about our "two minds," the rational and the emotional. Goleman delineates the five crucial skills of emotional intelligence for leaders and shows how they determine leaders' success in relationships, work, and physical well-being. The following are the five key emotional intelligence skills associated with successful leadership characteristics:

- **Self-awareness**   A leader knows how they feel and how their emotions or actions can affect people around them.

- **Self-regulation**   This key skill is about staying in control and regulating your actions and communications so to rarely verbally attack others or make rushed or emotional decisions.

- **Motivation**   A self-motived leader will work consistently toward goals and have high standards for the quality of their own work.

- **Empathy**   A leader who has empathy is essential for managing people and teams in today's work environment. They have the ability to put themselves in someone else's shoes. Through empathic skills, they can help develop the people they manage, challenge others who are acting unfairly, give constructive feedback, and also listen deeply for the meaning in conversations.

- **Social skills**   Leaders with emotional intelligence are great communicators. They're just as open to hearing the bad news as the good news. They are great at inspiring their people to a vision, and they are also good at managing change or resolving conflicts diplomatically.

In Erica Fox's research, she sees the successful leader as having a multifaceted personality, what she calls an *inner team*. This inner team draws on the following strengths of characteristics to lead: intuition, reason, emotion, and willpower. As depicted in Figure 4-9, Fox labels these "inner team" members as follows: CEO as the inspirational dreamer, CFO as the analytical thinker, COO as the practical warrior, and the CPO as the emotional lover.

The Leader's Inner Team

Generates vision
Pursues dreams
Has a sense of a
path forward

Focus: Intuition

Applies facts/logic
Considers risks and
consequences
Seeks perspective
from all sides

Focus: Reason

Inspirational
Dreamer

Analytical
Thinker

Practical
Warrior

Emotional
Lover

Speaks the hard
truths
Holds their ground
Takes action

Focus: Willpower

Connects with
emotions
Builds and
maintains trust
Collaborates

Focus: Emotion

Figure 4-9 Fox's inner team leader model

With Marshall Goldsmith's work, he identifies the 21 habits of behavior that derail a leader's effectiveness and holds them back. These behaviors have to change and adapt to the level of leadership a person's career grows into. The 21 bad habits are as follows:

1. **Winning too much**   The need to win at all costs and in all situations.
2. **Adding too much value**   A desire to add two cents to every discussion.
3. **Passing judgment**   The need to evaluate others and impose our standards/values on them.
4. **Making destructive comments**   Sarcasm and cutting remarks.
5. **Starting with "no," "but," or "however"**   The overuse of these negative qualifiers, which conveys "I'm right. You're wrong."
6. **Telling the world how smart we are**   The need to show people we're smarter than they think we are.
7. **Speaking when angry**   Using emotional volatility in communications.
8. **Negativity ("Let me explain why that won't work.")**   The need to share our negative thoughts.
9. **Withholding information**   The refusal to share information for an advantage over others.
10. **Failing to give proper recognition**   The inability to provide praise, rewards, and compliments.

11. **Claiming credit we do not deserve**   The overestimate of our contribution to some success.

12. **Making excuses**   The need to excuse annoying behavior as a permanent fixture so others will excuse us for it.

13. **Clinging to the past**   The need to deflect blame away from ourselves; this is a subset of blaming everyone else.

14. **Playing favorites**   Failing to see that we treat someone unfairly.

15. **Refusing to express regret**   The inability to take responsibility for our actions.

16. **Not listening**   The most passive-aggressive form of disrespect for others.

17. **Failing to express gratitude**   The most basic form of bad manners.

18. **Punishing the messenger**   The misguided need to attack the innocent who are providing information.

19. **Passing the buck**   Blaming everyone but ourselves.

20. **An excessive need to be "me"**   Exalting our faults as virtues simply because they embody who we are.

21. **Refusing to accept any responsibility for needing to change**   "That's just the way I am. Take it or leave it."

Theories About Leadership

In this section on leadership theories, we recognize that your formal education most likely went into great depth about each of the theories. What follows is a refresher on the basics of the leadership theories that will help you with your OD and HR initiatives. There are five basic schools of leadership theories: trait theory, behavioral school, contingency or situational school, leaders and followers, and dispersed leadership.

Trait Theory   The theory of trait leadership was developed from early leadership research, which focused primarily on finding a group of heritable attributes that differentiated leaders from nonleaders. Basically, it asserted that leaders were born and not made, and the focus was on personal characteristics and attributes that included mental and physical abilities. Although this perspective has been criticized immensely over the past century, scholars still continue to study the effects of personality traits on leader effectiveness. Past research has demonstrated that successful leaders differ from other people and possess certain core personality traits that significantly contribute to their success. It has been called the great person leadership theory with its assumption that leaders are different from the average person. The five traits identified are as follows:

- Intelligence
- Dominance
- Self-confidence
- High levels of energy and vitality
- Task or technical relevance knowledge

More current research has failed to identify one set of traits that *always* differentiates a leader.

Behavioral School The behavioral school theory focuses on a leader's ability to manage the performance and contribution of others, those they manage. Douglas McGregor's Theory X and Theory Y and Blake-Mouton apply to the behavioral school theory. Behavioral school identifies two dimensions of leadership behavior—focused on the employee and focused on the job to do. Consideration is the employee-centered behavior; initiating structure is the job-oriented behavior.

McGregor's theory[40] offers two approaches to motivating employees: Theory X, which suggests an authoritative management style because it assumes that employees inherently do not like to work and must be controlled and closely monitored; and Theory Y, which suggests a participative style of management, under the belief that employees dislike controls and inherently want to do their best. It is obvious to see that a Theory Y type of supervisor will provide better leadership and produce greater satisfaction.

Another theory in the behavioral school is the situational leadership model developed originally in 1964 by Robert R. Blake and Jane Mouton[41] and later updated by them. It is a managerial grid model that identifies five different leadership styles based on the concern for people and the concern for production. Figure 4-10 illustrates the Blake-Mouton behavioral leadership theory and the resulting leadership styles.

NOTE The ideal position is a 9 on production and 9 on people.

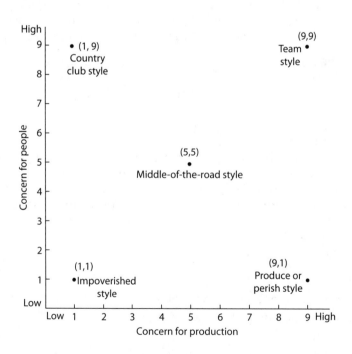

Figure 4-10
Blake-Mouton behavioral leadership theory

The types of leaders/managers are as follows:

- **Impoverished style (1, 1): evade and elude**   In this style, managers have low concern for both people and production. Managers use this style to preserve job and job seniority, protecting themselves by avoiding getting into trouble. The main concern for the manager is not to be held responsible for any mistakes, which results in less innovative decisions.

- **Country club style (1, 9): yield and comply**   This style has a high concern for people and a low concern for production. Managers using this style pay much attention to the security and comfort of the employees, in hopes that this will increase performance. The resulting atmosphere is usually friendly but not necessarily very productive.

- **Produce or perish style (9, 1): control and dominate**   With a high concern for production and a low concern for people, managers using this style find employee needs unimportant; they provide their employees with money and expect performance in return. Managers using this style also pressure their employees through rules and punishments to achieve the company goals. This style is often used in cases of crisis management.

- **Middle-of-the-road style (5, 5): balance and compromise**   Managers using this style try to balance between company goals and workers' needs. By giving some concern to both people and production, managers who use this style hope to achieve suitable performance, but doing so gives away a bit of each concern so that neither production nor people needs are met.

- **Team style (9, 9): contribute and commit**   In this style, high concern is paid both to people and to production. Managers choosing to use this style encourage teamwork and commitment among employees. This method relies heavily on making employees feel like they're constructive parts of the company.

- **The opportunistic style: exploit and manipulate**   Individuals using this style, which was added to the grid theory before 1999, do not have a fixed location on the grid. They adopt whichever behavior offers the greatest personal benefit.

- **The paternalistic style: prescribe and guide**   This style was added to the grid theory before 1999. Managers using this style praise and support but discourage challenges to their thinking.

Contingency or Situational School   The well-known theories for contingency and situational leadership are the ones that accept differing leadership styles and adapt to the situations or people involved.

Widely referred to as the Hersey-Blanchard *situational leadership theory,* the fundamental underpinning of the situational leadership theory is that there is no single "best" style of leadership. Effective leadership is task-relevant, and the most successful leaders are those who adapt their leadership style to the maturity ("the capacity to set high but attainable goals, willingness and ability to take responsibility for the task, and relevant education and/or experience of an individual or a group for the task") of the individual or group they are attempting to lead or influence. Effective leadership varies, not only

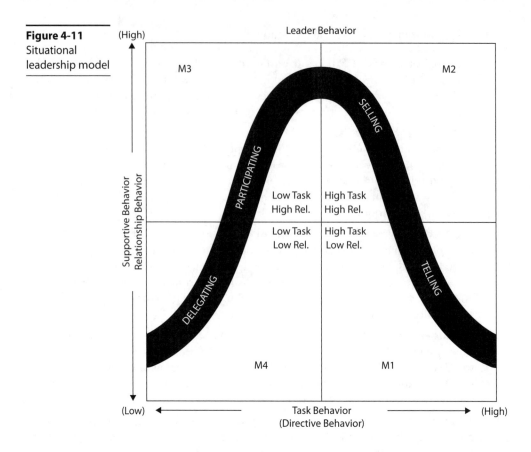

Figure 4-11 Situational leadership model

with the person or group that is being influenced but also depends with the task, job, or function that needs to be accomplished. The Hersey-Blanchard situational leadership theory rests on two fundamental concepts: leadership style and the individual or group's maturity level. Figure 4-11 depicts the situational leadership model.

The Hersey-Blanchard situational leadership theory[42] identifies four levels of maturity, M1 through M4.

High	Moderate		Low
M4	M3	M2	M1
Very capable and confident	Capable but unwilling	Unable but willing	Unable and insecure

- **M1** Employees still lack the specific skills required for the job at hand and are unable and unwilling to do or to take responsibility for this job or task.

- **M2** Employees are unable to take on responsibility for the task being done; however, they are willing to work at the task. They are novice but enthusiastic.

- **M3**   Employees are experienced and able to do the task but lack the confidence or the willingness to take on responsibility.

- **M4**   Employees are experienced at the task and comfortable with their own ability to do it well. They are able and willing to not only do the task but to take responsibility for the task.

Leadership has four tasks based on an employee's maturity.

- **Delegating**   The leader is still involved in decisions; however, the process and responsibility have been passed to the individual or group. The leader stays involved to monitor progress.

- **Participating**   This is where shared decision-making with the work group about how a task is accomplished takes place; the leader is providing less task direction while maintaining high relationship behavior with the group.

- **Selling**   While the leader is still providing the direction, the leader is now using two-way communication and providing the socioemotional support that will allow the individual or group being influenced to buy into the process.

- **Telling**   Characterized by one-way communication in which the leader defines the roles of the individual or group and provides the what, how, why, when, and where to do the task.

The most popular situational contingency theory was developed by Fred Fiedler.[43] The Fiedler contingency theory holds that group effectiveness depends on an appropriate match between a leader's style (essentially a trait measure) and the demands of the situation. Fiedler considers situational control the extent to which a leader can determine what their group is going to do to be the primary contingency factor in determining the effectiveness of leader behavior.

Fiedler's contingency model is a dynamic model where the personal characteristics and motivation of the leader are said to interact with the current situation that the group faces. Thus, the contingency model marks a shift away from the tendency to attribute leadership effectiveness to personality alone.

Fiedler asserts that there are three factors determining the favorableness of the environment for the leader.

- **Leader-member relations**   The degrees of trust, confidence, and respect that employees have in their leader

- **Task structure**   The extent to which the tasks the employees are engaged in are defined (clear or ambiguous, structured or unstructured)

- **Position power**   The degree of power and influence the leader has over their subordinates

Changing one of the three factors is a more effective route rather than trying to change the leadership's trait.

Action-Centered Leadership Action-centered leadership is a model created by John Adair[44] and states that effective leaders accomplish goals and tasks through the efforts of the team they lead. To do so, they must do three things in their leadership of groups.

1. Structure the task and make sure everyone knows what is expected.

2. Develop each team member, review and evaluate their outcomes, coach/motivate, and support.

3. Coordinate the team's workflow, resolve disputes, ensure compliance with rules, and cause collaboration.

Leaders and Followers Jon Katzenback's and Douglas Smith's leadership theory "*Leaders and Followers*" recognizes that the leader is not a hero per se but a team leader and servant to the team. With their leadership theory, leaders ask more questions rather than simply provide answers—a coaching tactic. They share opportunities to lead the team. Working with each other to solve problems is high with this style, along with building a solid foundation of the problems and issues before jumping into work on a resolution. Modern organizations of today generally rely heavily on team leaders and thus this style of leadership.

Dispersed Leadership Sometimes referred to as *emergent leadership*, with the dispersed leadership theory, leaders will emerge from a working group because of their expertise or experience to lead and influence the group working on a situation or task. This typically is not a person who is given authority by way of title, such as manager or supervisor, within the hierarchy. The leader is someone the group has chosen to follow. This style of leadership has grown in the twenty-first century because of more self-managed teams in flat organizational structures.

Transformational and Transactional Leadership Leadership can be either transformational or transactional in nature. A transformational leadership approach is one that stimulates and inspires people to work together toward achieving a common goal. Transformational leaders are charismatic (which instills pride, respect, and trust in the leader's sense of mission and vision); inspirational, with the communication skills necessary to gain engagement; stimulating, where the promotion of intelligence and challenge are at play; and attentive to individual needs, giving personal attention in manners of coaching or mentoring.

Transactional leadership has characteristics associated with contingent reward, where effort is rewarded via accomplishment; management by exception, in which corrective action is taken when standards are not met or protocol is broken; and laissez faire, in which responsibility is abdicated and decision-making is delayed or avoided.

Transactional leadership has been widely used and the norm historically for decades; transformational leadership has been proven to improve productivity and morale in the long run. A blend of both transactional and transformational leadership is typically warranted and the most effective.

Global Leadership Models There are key issues to be aware of in global organizations that apply to global leadership models. Things become more complex because of cultural and language barriers along with geographical and time zone differences. Managing the diverse global workplaces becomes complicated with laws, regulations, and practices differing from country to country. In 2004 and 2007, results from the Global Leadership and Organizational Behavior Effectiveness (GLOBE) Research Program found the data to support the shared cultural dimensions that were derived from Geert Hofstede and other cultural researchers.[46]

Cultural Issues   There are two cultural constructs that have a great influence on communication and training/development activities: power distance and high-context/low-context culture. Dr. Geert Hofstede,[47] well known for his pioneering research of cross-cultural groups in organizations, conducted a study of how workplace values were influenced by culture. He developed a model that identifies five primary dimensions to differentiate cultures. The five dimensions are as follows: *power distance, individualism, uncertainty avoidance, masculinity,* and *long-term orientation.*

Power distance is the extent to which less-powerful members of organizations expect and accept that power is distributed unequally. In high-power distance organizations, the less powerful employee accepts autocratic structures.

Individualism refers to the extent to which people are expected to stand up for themselves. With high individualism, an individual's rights are most important.

Uncertainty avoidance is the extent to which members of a society cope with anxiety by minimizing uncertainty. High uncertainty avoidance cultures like structure and rules.

Masculinity also includes femininity and refers to the value placed on male or female values from a Western culture perspective. Feminine cultures place more value on relationships and harmony, wherein masculine cultures value competitiveness and assertiveness.

Long-term orientation is the degree to which the society embraces long-term devotion to traditional values. High long-term orientation has a respect for loyalty commitments and work ethic is strong.

The American Management Association (AMA) developed a list of global leadership skills, listed in Table 4-5. This list was developed in 2012 via a survey conducted of more than 1,000 global practitioners and emphasizes the essential need for having fluency in local cultures for global organizations.

Key Leadership Skills   More than just business knowledge and expertise, leaders require a number of skills to manage a workforce. Leadership is an ability to influence others toward a strategy, results, and goals. It entails keeping the organization's vision and mission in sight associated with its strategy, providing the direction on how that mission and vision will be accomplished, and providing the tools and means to attain them, while motivating or encouraging people to work toward the vision.

Global Leader Competencies				
Agility	Collaborating with peers	Managing virtual teams	Managing with a matrixed organization	Cross-cultural employee engagement
Managing innovation in multicultural setting	Applying ethical standards in multiple cultures	Mastery of latest advances in virtual technology	Mastery of social network technology	Multicountry supply chain management

Table 4-5   AMA's Global Leader Competencies

Throughout this book, we discuss the multitude of key leadership skills. Those that are associated directly with strategy are focused on motivating a work group, making ethical decisions, having communications skills for aligning with stakeholders, and managing conflicts.

Ethical Behavior One of the key leadership competencies is being the role model for ethical decisions and actions. Being consistent and thoughtful with the challenging ethical decisions is at the core of this key leadership skill. To do so, a leader needs to recognize the ethical situations when they arise. They need to dig in to fully establish the facts about a given situation and their various options. Next they need to evaluate the ethical dimensions of possible actions they can take. These might include religious or cultural beliefs/norms. Then the leader would apply the relevant codes of ethics and behavior toward each option that has been presented in the situation. Consulting with others, perhaps inside the organization such as HR and other senior management levels, or perhaps outside such as legal consultants, should be one of the options. The last parameter is owning the decision once it is made and perhaps learning from the mistakes/errors that are made from the issue/situation—all so that future decisions can be made better.

Communication Communication is absolutely essential for effective leadership—sharing the vision, the strategy, the direction in which the organization is headed, at every level of function. It requires a thorough understanding of what is needed for the listeners to "hear the message" and uses various means to communicate matters appropriately.

Understanding a Listener's Needs and Expectations The leader as a communicator needs to consider the message they want to send, who the "receiver" is intended to be, and in what manner they intend to provide it. A rule of thumb to use in all communications is recalling "MIM," which stands for Message, Intended Receiver, Medium to Be Used. First the communicator should "be in the shoes" of the intended receiver and consider all the varying perspectives that receiver might have. Consider how the receiver might misunderstand the message and what their perception might be.

Planning Communication What is the best manner for the communication to occur for the intended receiver (e.g., verbal, meeting presentation, written)? If the receiver does not have easy access to the Internet or an intranet, that is going to hamper the timeliness of the communication. In planning the communication of strategy, this question is the first one to consider: What information is needed to be communicated, in what order, on what dates, by whom, and specifically to whom? Next, what medium is to be used? Last, what feedback mechanism is in place to ensure the intended communication was received and understood? This feedback will provide an awareness of what may need altering in the message to improve understanding and impact.

Managing Conflict Conflict is natural, and it is bound to happen in all work settings. In most conflicts, neither party is right or wrong; instead, different opinions collide to create disagreement. Is conflict a bad thing? Not necessarily. Conflict can help lead to new discoveries of methods and improvements in matters such as policies and procedures. Interpersonal conflicts are bound to occur when groups of people are working together. There need to be rules of behavior associated with conflict, such as conflict of culture, personal differences, communication styles, and treatment of others. If there is constant conflict, that will surely erode collaboration and relationships in the workplace. Leaders, including HR professionals, should know how to approach conflict proactively and have the skills to resolve it effectively.

Conflict-Resolution Modes   When conflicts need to be resolved, the process of conflict resolution involves techniques to resolve issues and maintain effective working relationships. When a direct supervisor is unable to resolve the conflict, HR is normally brought in as an intervention and mediator. Clear and open communication is the cornerstone of successful conflict resolution, and thus HR professionals must be skilled communicators. This includes creating an open communication environment that encourages the disconnected parties to talk. Listening and probing with nondefensive inquiries will help dissipate the conflict.

Whether it is co-workers who are jockeying for the desk next to the window or the employee who wants the room cooler and the other one who doesn't, immediate conflict resolution is essential. Steps for conflict resolution by a leader involve the following:

- *Acknowledge that an opposing situation exists.* Acquaint yourself with what's happening and be open about the problem.

- *Let the individuals express their feelings.* Emotions fly and feelings of anger and/ or hurt usually accompany conflicts. Before any kind of probing can take place, acknowledge the emotions and feelings.

- *Define the problem.* What is the issue? What is the negative impact on the work or relationships? Are different personality styles part of the problem? Meet with the opposing parties separately at first and gain their perspective about the situation.

- *Determine the underlying need.* There is no goal of deciding which person is right or wrong; the goal is to reach a solution that everyone can live with. Looking first for needs, rather than solutions, is a powerful tool for generating win-win options. To discover needs, you must try to find out why people want the solutions they initially propose. Once you understand the advantages their solutions have for them, you have discovered their needs.

- *Find common areas of agreement.* Agree on the problem; agree on some small change to give a feeling of compromise.

Find solutions to satisfy needs.

- *Generate multiple alternatives.*
- *Determine which actions will be taken.*
- *Make sure involved parties buy into actions.* (Total silence may be a sign of passive resistance.) Be sure you get real agreement from everyone.
- *Determine follow-up to monitor actions and sustained agreements.* Schedule a follow-up check-in to determine how the solutions are working and how those involved feel about how the solutions are working.

What if the conflict goes unresolved? If the conflict is causing a disruption in the workplace and it remains unresolved, you may need to explore other avenues. An outside consultant such as a mediator may be able to offer other insights on solving the conflict problem. In some cases, the conflict becomes a performance issue and may become a topic for coaching sessions, performance appraisals, or disciplinary action.

Negotiation Methods

Some conflict may be to a level that it requires negotiation for a compromise. The methods used in negotiation methods are similar to some used in conflict resolution. Discussed more thoroughly in Chapter 5, negotiation involves knowing the needs and wants of both sides of the conflict. There are several different negotiating styles, yet the most common are the three that are known as *soft, hard,* or *principled.*

Soft negotiations have a focus that is based on the value of the relationship. Hard negotiations have a focus that is associated with win-lose at all costs to the relationship. Principled negotiations have a focus that is aimed at mutual gain for both sides. Principled negotiations are what most organizations expect from their leadership—collaboration and relationship building.

Functional Area 2—Talent Acquisition

This is SHRM's BoCK definition: "Talent Acquisition encompasses the activities involved in building and maintaining a workforce that meets the needs of the organization." [48]

Talent acquisition involves all the HR strategies and processes that are involved in attracting, recruiting, and selecting talent that has the skills, knowledge, and abilities needed in the workforce to meet the organization's needs. HR professionals will analyze and understand the organization's workforce requirements and staffing needs to enable them to assist management with assessing current and future labor needs.

Key Concepts

- Approaches to employee onboarding
- Approaches to sourcing (e.g., external talent pipelines)
- Employment categories (e.g., salaried/hourly, contract, temporary, interns)
- Job analysis and identification of job requirements
- Job offer contingencies (e.g., background investigations, credit checks)
- Job offer negotiations (e.g., salary)
- Methods for creating and maintaining a positive employer value proposition (EVP) and employment brand
- Methods for external and internal employee recruitment (e.g., job ads, career fairs)
- Methods for selection assessment (e.g., ability, job knowledge, noncognitive tests, assessment centers, interviews)
- Talent acquisition metrics (e.g., cost per hire, time to fill)

The following are the proficiency indicators that SHRM has identified as key concepts:

For All HR Professionals	For Advanced HR Professionals (SCP Exam)
Understands the talent needs of the organization or business unit	Analyzes staffing levels and projections to forecast workforce needs
Uses a wide variety of talent sources and recruiting methods to attract qualified applications	Develops strategies for sourcing and acquiring a workforce that meets that organization's needs
Uses technology (e.g., social media, applicant tracking software [ATS]) to support effective and efficient approaches to sourcing and recruiting employees	Establishes an EVP and employment brand that supports recruitment or high-quality job applicants
Promotes and uses the EVP and employment brand for sourcing and recruiting applicants	Designs and oversees effective strategies for sourcing, recruiting, and evaluating qualified job candidates
Uses the most appropriate hiring methods to best evaluate a candidate's technical skills, organizational fit, and alignment with the organization's competencies needs	Designs and oversees employee onboarding and assimilation processes
Conducts appropriate pre-employment screening	Designs and oversees valid and systematic programs for assessing the effectiveness of talent acquisition activities that meet the organization's needs
Implements effective onboarding and orientation programs for new employees	
Designs job descriptions to meet the organization's resource needs	

Organizational Staffing Requirements

Staffing is the lifeblood of an organization as people are required to make any organization run. Getting the right ones into the right jobs is the function known as *staffing*.

Staffing Challenges

At any time, one or more of these challenges can appear to the dismay of HR professionals. Dealing with them effectively is the measure of a skilled HR manager.

Changing Demographics When housing becomes too expensive for job applicants to live close to the job and commute distances are greater than people want to undertake, the workforce demographics can shift, sometimes rapidly. Look at any major metropolitan area these days, and it is easy to identify this problem. Employer responses may be too expensive for practical purposes. Raising the pay scale so new hires have enough money to either rent or buy a home could just be too expensive.

Lack of Skilled Labor According to a Manpower Group survey, more than 40 percent of all employers globally report difficulty filling skilled jobs.[49]

Government and Regulatory Barriers to Hiring   The moment an employer hires its first worker, it becomes subject to more than 50 federal laws that require compliance, everything from safety to payroll and credit reporting. There are untold numbers of state laws that also demand attention, depending on the work locations being used.

Brain Drain   The departure of educated or professional people away from an employer to another employer usually is for better pay or living conditions. Particularly in industries such as high-technology and engineering there is a high cost for key personnel exodus.

Availability of Reliable Data   Workforce planning and strategic staffing initiatives become problematic when there is a lack of current, reliable data. A lack of reliability in either the forecast of job openings or the ability to develop high-quality talent pools from which to draw job candidates will quickly bring the recruiting process to a halt.

Economic Cycles   Economy cycles impact employer headcount levels. Employers are often faced with the challenge of identifying qualified recruits from a scarcity of resources when things get better through growth and demand. Likewise, when the economy turns down, layoffs are often the result.

Business Lifecycles   Recruiting and retention strategies will necessarily change as business moves through four stages, or lifecycles, of existence. In the beginning (startup) and through its growth years, recruiting is typically hectic. Expansion means hiring. In its maturity and decline years, layoffs and downsizing/resizing are frequent impacts. Specific strategies are required for each of these four cycles.

PEST Factors   PEST, i.e., political, economic, social, and technological factors, must be considered when conducting an environmental scan, strategic planning, or being engaged in other forecasting efforts. World events often drive, or at least influence, environmental scans conducted by using the PEST factors.

Employee Lifecycles   Staffing challenges are greatly influenced by employee lifecycles. Here are the relationships:

- **Recruitment and selection**   Finding the best fit between a job and an employee
- **Onboarding and orientation**   Gaining information and tools necessary to succeed in the job and getting acclimated to the organization's culture
- **Training and development**   Promoting engagement and retention by developing an employee's skills and commitment
- **Performance management**   Working with employees helping them achieve their goals and objectives and priming them to become a stronger employee
- **Transition**   Achieving the best match of an employee's capabilities with an organization's needs through transfer, promotion, demotion, resignation, and retirement

Technology Shifts   In years past, recruiting was done with the aid of "position available" advertisements in the local newspaper. Today, social media is the primary source of job candidates. This is a paradigm shift. An example can be found when wristwatches were no longer made with springs but transitioned to models with electronic quartz movements. When robots entered the workplace, helping handle dangerous and repetitive tasks in the automobile industry, employees were tasked with feeding the robot materials and receiving from it the completed subassembly, which was another paradigm shift. When the Bell System used live operators to handle long-distance calls, emergency calls, and questions that are now handled by computer, another paradigm shift took place.

Cherry Picking: Pressure on Salary Levels   Offering more money beyond the approved pay range can effectively entice a desirable job candidate to accept a job offer but can also cause issues for other parts of an organization. If the hiring manager makes a job offer above the pay range maximum, something must happen to bring that individual back into the proper compensation range. Usually, this requires management to "freeze" the new hire's pay level until natural escalation pressures enable the company's pay structure to catch up. The short-term benefit of attracting a desirable job candidate this way is often overcome by general employee discontent and, as a result, discouragement. In addition, state and federal pay requirements, when applicable, must be followed in any case.

Creating a Job vs. Hiring for Work   When an engineering firm encounters an engineer with a certain specialty, experience, and educational credentials to back it up, the company may want to hire that person rather than let them go on to some other firm. In that case, it becomes necessary to create a job opening for the new engineer. As opposed to that scenario, often the practice is to have a job opening identified and then seek candidates for that job with the intent to hire the best qualified out of the batch. Filling a job need is quite different from creating a job for someone special we must hire to save the talent within our employee ranks.

Strategic Staffing

Staffing according to the business strategies requires understanding what those strategies are. Even if strategic plans are not formalized, successful employers need some form of organizational goals to effectively manage their business. HR professionals are uniquely positioned to help managers understand the importance of measurable strategic goals to be successful as HR business partners providing appropriate job candidates to the operations units. When accounting is undertaking a conversion of its financial records processing system or operations is installing a new computer-centric milling system, the HR professional supporting them will need to understand the importance of those changes to accomplishing business goals. HR professionals cannot simply enjoy sitting in the HR world. They must be fluent in the language of their brothers and sisters in other parts of the business. Until they are, they will not be as helpful in staffing jobs in those other organizations as they otherwise could be.

Planning for Talent Acquisition on a Global Basis

 Global staffing depends on recognizing and acquiring talent with precisely the job skills needed in a given work location, even when that work location happens to be halfway around the world.

Global Integration vs. Local Responsiveness Strategy

Strategically, it may be determined that recruiting, processing, and hiring people can be done from a remote location such as at a company's headquarters. Certainly, any talent acquisition program must be able to embrace global requirements. It will come as no surprise that maintaining a local responsiveness to acquisition requirements is also a key to success. It is important that people processing job candidates have the same level of empathy for local needs as local staff. Responsiveness to local management will go a long way toward building a strong working relationship. In the end, it is a customer service relationship that is important.

Orientation and Talent Staffing

Nancy Simonelli at Reliance Staffing and Recruiting says, "Employees who attend a structured orientation program are more likely to remain with the company after 3 years than those who do not. If you are going to spend money and time acquiring top talent and paying them to work, why not prepare them to succeed and stay?"[50] So, a solid strategy for orientation training after a new hire accepts the job offer is to use a structured orientation program. Be sure to cover everything on your checklist, not just payroll and benefit information. Be sure to include things like, "How we do things around here."

Growth Strategies

Identifying growth in workforce needs will allow strategic preparation for recruiting and acquisition of talent that will be needed to permit the growth to be successful. It can take weeks or months to identify specific job candidate needs and then to create a recruiting program that will assimilate those candidates as active participants in the selection process. Starting before you have a specific requisition can be a good strategy for being ready when the time comes.

Maturity of the Global Location

How well can your global locations continue to serve your business needs? Is there a ready workforce with the talent necessary to satisfy your job requirements? In the face of an economic downturn, can you continue to maintain a branding program so that the job candidate market will react positively when openings occur again? Are there competitors in the same locations? Do they seek to attract the same type of talent to their workforce as you want to have in yours? The broader the supply and demand in your areas of talent need, the more likely you will be able to find what you want when you actually start looking.

External Factors

Influences from outside the employer's organization can include such things as local employment laws for wage and hour issues, minimum wage levels, mandated benefit requirements, cultural impacts on production schedules (e.g., holidays), and local commute patterns. All of these and more must be considered as part of your strategic talent acquisition process.

Social Responsibility

Do subcontractors or suppliers participate in pay disparities or racial discrimination because of local cultural practices? It is incumbent upon the employer to determine whether it should even create a work location where those problems exist. And, if so, what will it take to address changes in those cultural standards?

Information Technology

What type of Internet connections are available in the work location chosen for your organization's needs? What types of computer support are available? Will you be using off-the-shelf software programs or something your in-house programmers have created or modified? Is there local support talent that can address these and other related types of infrastructure needs?

Visa Requirements

What type of visa requirements exist in your prospective work location? Can international candidates come and go without difficulty, or are there special work permit requirements they must meet? Are certain countries barred from sending workers to your location? How will you be able to work within those requirements? Talent acquisition can be made more difficult if there are these types of impediments.

Employment Branding

Branding is another word for reputation. What do people in your target workforce think about your company? How can you influence that?

Employment Branding Defined

According to Chris Mossevelde, "Employer branding is the process of promoting a company, or an organization, as the employer of choice to a desired target group, one which a company needs and wants to recruit and retain."[51]

Building a Brand

Mossevelde continues, "The company can only attract current and future employees if it has an identity that is true, credible, relevant, distinctive and aspirational. To achieve this, extensive research needs to be conducted." What does the public think of your organization? What does the group of people you consider a target recruiting source group think of your organization as an employer? Learning what exists will enable you to determine what action steps must be taken to mold your brand into the perceptions you want others to have.

Employee Value Proposition

An employee value proposition (EVP) is the unique set of benefits that an employee receives in return for the skills, capabilities, and experience they bring to a company.

Harnessing Social Media

In mid-2017, CareerBuilder.com posted the results of its latest study regarding the use of social media in the employment process. Here is what that study found: "70 percent of employers use social media to screen candidates before hiring, up significantly from 60 percent last year and 11 percent in 2006."[52] The lesson is clear. Employers must be using social media outlets to find the best talent available. And, social media can influence the employer's brand in the eyes of those it will eventually want to recruit.

Best Practices for Employment Branding

To influence your brand, it is necessary to manage the expectations and perceptions of your job candidate target group. The first step is to identify key words that describe your company as a good place to work. If you say things like exciting, flexible, genuine, and challenging, you may advance to the next step. If you say things like old-fashioned, slow (to change), manipulative, and boring, you may have some work to do before moving to the next step. If you need to work on your employment brand, begin with a task force (group) of employees who can help identify key actions that will be needed to improve your organization's image. Consider focus groups for people in your prime employment recruiting populations to determine what they really think about your organization as an employer.

1. What changes might be necessary if you are to move forward? How can social media become a tool in that change process?

2. Develop and implement your action plan to bring about the changes your organization needs.

3. Evaluate the impact of changes you have created.

4. Repeat as necessary.

Job Analysis and Job Documentation

Establishing job content and determining how the job interacts with other jobs are important. Documenting the results can become what we know as a *job description*. That job description can become the foundation for analyzing its content and plotting its fit into compensation structures.

Job Analysis

Determining the level of responsibility embedded in the job and how it impacts the overall organization is what can be called *job analysis*. In addition to tasks and areas of responsibility assigned to the job, analysis should include the types of physical and mental conditions under which the job operates. That can vary widely from job to job. Consider the physical and mental requirements for an electrical high-tension line technician with those of the computer program coder. One faces the outside weather elements year around. The other sits inside using a computer keyboard to convert thought patterns into code the machine can use. Someone who doesn't like heights or working in rain and snow would probably not be a great candidate for the technician's job. And, someone who has a high need for being outside, working on different job sites each day, would likely not do well in the computer programmer's job.

Job Documentation

Written descriptions of the key elements of a job, its working conditions, and its mental and physical demands will eventually constitute the documentation of the job and its content.

Job Descriptions   Job descriptions follow a general template for content. The same template can be used in constructing a CEO's job description as for an airline pilot. It is the content that falls within the template that varies.

Elements of Job Descriptions   Here is a typical job description template:

Administrative

- Date the job description was prepared
- Title of the job
- FLSA status: Exempt or nonexempt
- Objective: What does the job accomplish and how does it impact other jobs in the organization

Summary of Job Content

Essential job functions: Brief description of the specific tasks, duties, and responsibilities

Mental and educational requirements: Formal education (degrees), certifications, licensing, journey-level craft training, extensive mathematical training (essential job requirements; the job cannot be done without these educational requirements)

Skill requirements: Typing, welding, swimming, running harvesting equipment, docking spacecraft

Physical factors: Hearing, seeing (watching/inspecting), touching, operating, standing, bending, squatting, reaching, lifting, carrying

Environmental factors: Outside weather conditions, inside workplace conditions, confined spaces, heat, cold, wet, dry, odors, dust, hazardous materials

Hours: Number of eight-hour shifts per week, overtime requirements, lunch/break requirements

Unplanned activities: Duties or tasks that could come up, interactions, and support of other jobs

Approvals: Reviews and approvals of management people authorized to design job content

Job Descriptions in the Global Environment Global consistency can be helpful over time. While compensation rates may vary from country to country, the same job content may apply across borders. Having job content consistency may be helpful in the outreach and recruiting efforts your organization makes. Be sure, however, that the wording used accurately communicates the message. Expectations for honesty and forthrightness exist at many locations around the world. Yet, depending on the work location, how the message is expressed may be quite different. In France, value is often placed on open disagreement as discussions move toward consensus. In Mexico, open disagreement is considered rude and disrespectful. In Indonesia, an open disagreement would be considered aggressive and negative because the reputation of the other person can be damaged. International differences do matter.

Job Specifications A job description is a series of statements describing the role, responsibility, duties, and scope of a particular job. A job specification states the minimum qualifications required for performing a that job. What education is required? What physical and mental abilities are a must? What experience is essential? Those answers are posted in the job requisition so potential candidates will be able to assess the match they may have with the job requirements.

Writing and Updating Job Descriptions and Job Specifications It is the duty of the supervisor and/or manager to develop and maintain accurate job descriptions and job specifications. Often this is done with the help of HR professionals. In larger organizations, there is a staff of HR people who are responsible for evaluating, rating, and assigning pay levels to job descriptions and compensation classifications as appropriate. They support line managers and supervisors in documenting their subordinate jobs. An annual review is mandated for all federal contractors who are required to maintain affirmative action plans for the disabled. Those requirements are focused on the need for accurate descriptions of physical and mental job requirements. Essential tasks, duties, and responsibilities are considered in order to determine whether a job accommodation can be made or circumstances call for it.

Accurate job specifications are important when a job opening occurs because the hiring manager often needs to move quickly. Pausing the process to be sure job specifications are accurate will be unnecessary if the specifications are already reviewed and updated.

Employment Categories The term *employment categories* is used by many to mean often conflicting things. The two most often referenced are categories evolving from the Fair Labor Standards Act (FLSA) and those based on company policy. So, SHRM generally considers the following to be employment categories.

These are the FLSA classifications:

- **Nonexempt** Employees are people whose job content is not exempt from the requirements for minimum wage and overtime requirements.

- **Exempt** Employees are people whose job content does not require overtime payment.

These are the company policy classifications:

- *Regular full-time employees* are regularly scheduled to work the company's full-time schedule. Usually, they are eligible for company benefit programs depending on eligibility conditions.

- *Regular part-time workers* are regularly scheduled to work less than the company's full-time schedule. They may be eligible for some company benefit programs.

- *Temporary full-time employees* are interim workers assigned to specific projects or scheduled to work for a specific limited duration. Benefits may or may not be offered.

- *Temporary part-time employees* are hired to temporarily supplement the workforce or to help with a specific project. They are regularly scheduled to work less than the company's full-time schedule for a limited duration. They are usually not eligible for company benefit programs.

- *On-call employees* are scheduled as needed for a nonspecified time period. Normally there is no eligibility for company benefit programs.

- *Interns* may be college or university students, high school students, or post-graduate adults who perform work for a specified period of time, i.e., summer, academic semester, and so on.

Sourcing and Recruiting

Geoff Webb writes on LinkedIn, "A Sourcer finds the passive candidates, the ones not applying through the corporate website or posting on the job boards. A Sourcer is a hunter. A Sourcer creates interest and drives talent to the organization. This means doing research: pouring over org charts, job descriptions, and social media profiles, while sourcing talent by accessing search engines and competitor web pages. This means engaging potential candidates: messaging through social media, sending emails, picking up the phone. And because a hunt often involves a chase, this means repeating, tweaking, and refining these activities—until you have a slate of qualified prospects to hand off to…

"…the Recruiter. The Recruiter manages the relationships, guiding the candidates and the hiring manager through the screening, selection, and hiring process. This means phone calls, meetings, and interviews. This also means administration—a lot of it: posting jobs, reviewing applicant submissions through the corporate website, coordinating schedules, uploading documents, extending offers—going back and forth until all the details come together and the job opening has been filled."[53]

Sourcing and Recruiting in Diverse Markets

McKinsey & Company studied the relationship between diversity and financial returns in business terms. Among their findings were these:[54]

- "In the United States, there is a linear relationship between racial and ethnic diversity and better financial performance: for every 10 percent increase in racial and ethnic diversity on the senior-executive team, earnings before interest and taxes (EBIT) rise 0.8 percent.

- "In the United Kingdom, greater gender diversity on the senior-executive team corresponded to the highest performance uplift in our data set: for every 10 percent increase in gender diversity, EBIT rose by 3.5 percent."

The conclusion is that sourcing and recruiting in diverse markets is a positive thing for the employer and its financial returns.

Recruiting Methods

Finding the right job candidate is a process that has changed little over time. What has changed is where we go to look for that stellar candidate. Two words say it all for external sourcing: social media.

Internal Recruiting   Looking for people who can fill openings often begins by looking internally. Notifying current employees about job openings can be done in any of several ways: sending an e-mail blast to all employees with the announcement, posting the opening announcement on the employee bulletin board, posting the opening announcement on the organization's web site or employee channels, and asking all managers and supervisors to announce the opening to their employee groups. Some organizations believe it is good for morale to give current employees the opportunity to apply for new job openings, especially if it would mean a promotion to the candidate. Whatever the reason, selecting someone from the current employee ranks will cost less than searching for and screening a group of people from outside the organization.

External Recruiting   These are proven external recruiting methods:

- **Job boards**   This includes services such as Monster, ZipRecruiter, Career Bliss, Recruit Net, Jobs2Careers, CareerJet, and Glassdoor.
- **Social media**   This includes LinkedIn, Facebook, Twitter, YouTube, Instagram, and more.
- **Web site**   The employer's Internet site is a perfect place to post job openings and even an application form.
- **Referrals**   Employee referrals are a wonderful source of job candidates. And don't discount referrals from clients, customers, vendors, and the general public.

Other Recruiting Strategies   Employment agencies and temporary help agencies are more traditional, but they still have appeal today. Temporary help workers can "test-drive" the company to see whether it is a good match with their objectives, and the company can "test-drive" the employee to see whether they would be a good match for the employer's culture.

Employment Branding   An employment brand is the market perception of what it's like to work for an organization. It relies heavily on culture and current and former employee testimonials about experience on the payroll.

Robust Sourcing Strategy   Sourcing, as you know, is the art of seeking candidates before they apply for a job. *Hunting* may be a better term. If your sourcing strategy is robust, you have an active presence in the employment market looking for organizations,

Internet sites, and social media accounts that represent the type of individual knowledge, skills, and abilities that you believe you will require now or in the future.

Recruiting Effectiveness

Establishing and maintaining a recruiting program is not cheap. It requires the investment of an internal staff of people dedicated to that activity or the time and effort of consulting support that will offer the same services. The trick is to be sure you are getting your money's worth in the bargain.

Measurers of Recruitment Effectiveness   There are two general areas of interest when measuring recruiting efforts.[55]

- Speed and efficiency
  - Time between opening the requisition and presenting a qualified candidate slate
  - Time for feedback from hiring manager to recruiter
  - Requisition aging
- Quality metrics
  - Number of candidates selected for interview
  - Interview to offer ratio

HR Metrics   In addition to the recruiting measurements, we can measure the quality of new hires (job performance ratings, the percentage of new hires promoted within a year, the percentage of new hires retained after a year) and turnover cost (unemployment insurance expense, workers' compensation expense, cost of training a replacement, cost of recruiting and hiring a new employee).

Cautions Regarding Metrics   We need to be careful that the metrics we choose to use actually report on something that actually matters in our recruiting program. It is easy to get sidetracked into believing something is important when it really isn't. Who really cares about things like the number of typos in a job requisition or the number of people who don't know how to use social media? Be precise in what you measure because if it doesn't tell you something that can help you manage the process, it shouldn't be in your portfolio of metrics.

Peoplepower Reporting   Slicing and dicing the demographics of your workforce can have some value if you are interested in identifying representations of various groups for your diversity program. Here are some things that can be computed and reported.

Headcount   These are the number of people on the payroll, the number of people in candidate pools, the number of people who come from each recruiting source, and so on.

Groups and Subgroups   Numbers can be analyzed for group or unit representations such as department, division, unit, work location, or country. Within these there can be subgroups that might offer additional focus on your recruiting efforts. Focus on what will provide you with the most valuable feedback for the process. You must be able to "do" something with the information you compute. If you don't, there is no point in doing the analysis.

Demographics   Race, gender, disability, veteran status, and national origin are some of the affinity groups that can offer insight into the nature of your workforce composition and the effectiveness of such sourcing options such as employee referrals. You may have reporting requirements as part of your affirmative action program compliance. Be sure there is both value in collecting and analyzing the data and that someone will be doing something with it.

Cost of Hire/Cost per Hire   The American National Standards Institute (ANSI) has some standards for hiring metrics. Along with their partner, the Society for Human Resource Management (SHRM), ANSI has developed and published the following standards.

Cost of Hire   This measurement uses external costs and internal costs to determine overall cost per person hired during any given time period. This formula looks at the number of hires and the costs to obtain them. It enables us to derive expenses for each new hire stated as an average.

$$\text{Cost per Hire} = \frac{(\text{S (External Costs)} + \text{S (Internal Costs)})}{(\text{Total Number of Hires in a Time Period})}$$

External costs are those expenses such as external agency fees, advertising costs, job fair costs, travel costs, and other similar expenses for the time period being analyzed. Internal costs are expenses that can include fully loaded salary and benefits of the recruiting team and fixed costs such as physical infrastructure.

$$\text{Cost per Hire} = \frac{((\text{External Costs} = \$100,000) + (\text{Internal Costs} = \$100,000))}{(\text{Total Number of Hires in Time Period} = 50)}$$

Cost per Hire = \$4,000

Cost per Hire Internal/Comparable   Determining the internal cost per hire uses the same formula but includes only internal costs in the formula numerator. It is possible to compute external cost per hire and compare the two results.

Days to Fill   From the time a requisition is posted until the employment offer has been made can be called the Days to Fill measurement.

Attrition   There are several analyses that could prove helpful when looking at attrition. Consider these:

- Number of employees leaving before the first service anniversary
- Number of employees leaving before the fifth service anniversary
- Number of employees leaving total
- Number of employees leaving voluntarily (within a job or group)
- Number of employees leaving involuntarily (within a job or group)

Recruitment Cost and Yield Ratios   Ratios are the numerical representation of comparisons. They are normally stated as a percentage. The recruiting cost ratio (RCR) is one of those measurements. It is looks at the cost per hire based on compensation rather than headcount.

$$\text{Recruiting Cost Ratio} = \frac{((\text{External Costs} = \$100,000) + (\text{Internal Costs} = \$100,000))}{(\text{Total First Year Compensation of Hires in Time Period})} \times 100$$

The RCR tells you how much you spent recruiting for every dollar of first-year compensation paid to the new hires.

$$\text{Recruiting Cost Ratio} = \frac{((\text{External Costs} = \$100,000) + (\text{Internal Costs} = \$100,000))}{(\text{Total First Year Compensation} = \$2,000,000)} \times 100$$

RCR = 10 percent

Obviously, the lower the percentage, the better (more efficient) the result.

Another measure of recruiting efficiency and effectiveness is the recruitment yield ratio. It can be calculated at each step of the recruiting and hiring process to determine how successful you are at each stage of the process.

- How many people were minimally qualified compared to total responses?
- How many people were sent to the hiring manager compared to minimally qualified?
- How many people were interviewed compared to those sent to the hiring manager?
- How many people were hired compared to those interviewed?

At each state, you can compare a ratio or percentage. The greater the percentage, the better.

$$\text{RYR} = \frac{\text{Number of Hires}}{\text{Number of Interviews}}$$

$$\text{RYR} = 3 / 15 = 20 \text{ percent}$$

Achieving a higher ratio (percentage) means your yield is greater for whatever comparative group you are using. Here is another example:

We have hired 25 new computer programmers. It took an average of four interviews for each new hire. So, our recruitment yield ratio is 25 / 4 = 6.25. If we only required an average of three interviews per new hire, the RYR would be 25 / 3 = 8.33. The higher our RYR, the better. It allows us to recognize that many interviews in the hiring process add to the cost of hiring. Lowering the average number of interviews per hire will raise our ratio.

Workforce Analytics   Looking at the existing incumbent population, we can parse the numbers to tell us things like the representation of PhDs in a given job title or the number of people by gender in trade jobs (carpenter, plumber, electrician, landscaper). Recruiting cost ratio can be computed for job titles, job groups, departmental units, and more.

Leveraging Technology in Sourcing and Recruiting

Even if you are a small employer and don't have access to expensive computer programs, it is still possible to use Excel spreadsheets to provide you with periodic analysis results. Once you have established your spreadsheet to track things like the number of requisitions per month, the time between requisition and job offer, and the cost of hiring at each occupational level, you can create pivot tables that will provide automatic analysis charts once they are set up. Be sure you learn how to create and use pivot tables. They can make your life easier.

Internet Recruiting   Getting candidates from your own organization's web site is a great way to recruit. Other sources can be the state employment service web site, the web site run by your industry, or the web site run by colleges and universities. All of those activities can be tracked and the data analyzed.

Social Media   Social media sites have become a primary recruiting aid in many organizations. It wasn't long ago one expert offered the belief that 70 to 75 percent of jobs are being filled through social media sources. If you are not using social media in your recruiting efforts, you should be considering it.

Selection

Once the recruiting effort has yielded proper candidates qualified for the open position, it is incumbent upon the hiring manager to determine who will get the job offer. That offer should go to the person who is best qualified for the job. That is the best business decision. The best qualified will provide your organization with the greatest return on your investment. Selecting someone other than the best qualified will cost your organization more in the final analysis.

Talent Selection Process

It is helpful sometimes to use a matrix constructed of the job qualifications specified in the job posting, as shown in Table 4-6.

You can easily tell which candidate is the best match for your job requirements when you look at the chart. Candidate 1 is clearly better qualified than the others. Candidate 2 is running a strong second, and should you be unable to hire your first choice, you might feel quite comfortable with Candidate 2 as your alternate. The only possible downside to that individual is independence. Candidate 3 is clearly the poorest of the four candidates. Having fallen asleep during the interview, this candidate received a "minus" score for "Drive/Energy." Candidate 4 is good and solid but not quite as good as the first two. And, then, there is the problem with Candidate 4's ability to travel, which is something the job will require.

Job	Candidate			
	1	**2**	**3**	**4**
Knowledge/Skills/Talents—"Can Do" Items				
Work Experience	+	OK	-	+
Education	OK	OK	OK	OK
Technical Skills	+	+	-	OK
Communication Skills	OK	-	-	OK
Specialized Training	+	+	OK	OK
Analytical Skills	+	OK	+	OK
Behaviors—"Will Do" Items				
Motivation	+	+	-	OK
Interests	+	+	OK	OK
Goals	+	OK	-	OK
Drive/Energy	+	+	-	-
Reliability	+	+	OK	OK
Initiative	+	+	-	OK
Working Conditions—"Compatibility" Issues				
Team Orientation	OK	OK	-	+
Independence	OK	-	+	-
Social Effectiveness	+	OK	-	OK
Interpersonal Style	+	OK	-	OK
Stress Tolerance	OK	OK	OK	OK
Travel	OK	OK	-	-
Overtime	OK	OK	+	OK
Relocation	OK	OK	OK	OK
Weekend Work	OK	OK	OK	OK

Legend:
+ is "better than required."
OK is "meets requirements."
- is "less than required."

Table 4-6　Candidate Selection Factors Chart

Screening

Screening is the process of presorting job candidates to determine who meets minimum eligibility requirements of the job opening.

Screen　The first pass in screening should be to determine whether the candidate meets the job qualifications as specified in the job requisition posting. Anyone who does not meet the job requirements should be removed from the group. No further processing of that group is needed. Sometimes a telephone interview is next in the screening process.

PART II

Then comes an "in-person" interview, with the hiring manager and, possibly, with the HR manager, too. There may be other interviews with people who will be in the same work group or other supervisors. The process should contain decision points that match your organization's requirements.

Lately, video interviews have become popular. That can be helpful to job candidates who are a far distance from the work location.

Tracking Applicants   Data on job applicants is really important. Keeping track of it is even sometimes required. If you are a federal contractor, you will be required to maintain specific applicant-tracking data points. It will be used to analyze disparity in the selection process, comparing females to males and minorities to nonminorities. Disparity analysis can suggest that there is more investigation required, and you will want to do more follow-up to learn more about the specifics of given selections. Ultimately, an enforcement agency, like the Equal Employment Opportunity Commission (EEOC) or the Office of Federal Contract Compliance Programs (OFCCP), would be doing the same type of analysis if a complaint is filed with either or both agencies.

According to EEOC guidelines, it is alright to invite job applicants to self-identify their race/ethnicity and gender. You should use the standard EEOC categories for each.

- **Race/ethnicity**   White, Black/African American, Hispanic, Asian, Native Hawaiian/Pacific Islander, Native American/American Indian, two or more races
- **Gender**   Male, female

Inviting self-identification suggests the information being given is voluntary. If an applicant doesn't want to self-identify, they don't have to. And, employers are not required to have the information for job applicants. Its only use is in disparity analysis. Race/ethnicity information will become mandatory for employer tracking once the applicant accepts a job offer and joins the payroll. The laws enforced by the Equal Opportunity Commission (EEOC) require employers to collect and keep employee race and gender information.

Application Forms   Application forms are not required by any federal law. In addition to being a handy device that can mitigate an employer's risk of discrimination claims, they are a handy way to collect information about job candidates that an employer would like to have. They can also be a test for honesty. It is estimated that as many as 60 percent of job applications have exaggerations or false information in them.

Résumés and Curricula Vitae   Résumés and curricula vitae (CV) are documents prepared by an individual to describe educational and employment history. Résumés are normally used with employers other than educational institutions. CVs are documents with much the same information, but a different format used in educational employment settings. Both résumés and CVs are intended to offer potential employers an overview of the individual's background with a positive "spin." They almost never contain compensation information, information about gaps in the employment timeline, or contact information for reference checking.

Potential Problem Warning Signs   Here are some examples of things that should attract your attention so you can probe more deeply with the applicant:[56]

- Foreign jobs that do not follow a logical pattern of job progression, pay little, or conveniently have the exact requirements you are looking for.

- Jobs at companies that have gone out of business (although there are more legitimate examples these days).

- Too many jobs where the supervisor that the applicant worked for is gone with no forwarding address.

- Jobs at companies whose line of business is the normal line of work of the applicant, but this one position under a long-gone supervisor is the exact type of experience you are looking for. This is especially suspect if this experience is outside the normal work patterns of that company.

- The experience is so long ago that any references would normally have moved on, retired, or died.

- Self-employment where the experience may well have taken more equipment, structure, organization, or industry position than a small self-run company would be able to provide.

- "Volunteer" experience for a company that most probably would not entertain the notion of such an arrangement.

- Volunteer experience for an extended period of time when a means of support would have been required for the applicant.

- A job at a company that has since been merged and cannot find a record of the position having existed.

- Dates of employment that always start and end on exact starts of months or years; January 1, April 1, and so on.

How should you react when you discover one of these flags waving at you from your applicant's résumé? Mark it for follow-up with the applicant, perhaps in an interview. If you know that a claim is untrue, you would be justified in putting that applicant's documentation in a "Suspect" file folder without further consideration.

Interviewing

Interviews are conducted so you can get more information from an applicant and impart information to them about your organization. Sometimes interviews are conducted by HR professionals and other times by hiring managers or groups of people from the hiring department. Interviews can be conducted face to face, on the telephone, or by a video hookup such as Skype. Often, these days, there is more than one interview before a selection decision is made.

Type of Interviews   There are many types of interviews. They are named for the characteristics applied to the process of interviewing. The following are the primary types of interviews used today.

Structured Interview   An interviewer asks every applicant the same questions along with follow-up probes that may be different depending on the initial response. Structured interviews make it possible to gather similar information from all candidates and use it to comparatively measure relative job-based attributes.

Unstructured Interview   While not exactly "freewheeling," these interviews follow threads of information as they are revealed. No two interviews are alike in that regard. The interviewer must discern key information from the overall discussion.

Behavioral Interview   In a behavioral interview, an interviewer focuses on how the applicant previously handled actual situations (real, not hypothetical). The interviewer probes specific situations looking for past behaviors and how the applicant handled those experiences. The questions probe the knowledge, skills, abilities, and other personal characteristics identified as essential to success of the job. The interviewer looks for three things: a description of an actual situation or task, the action taken, and the result or outcome. The principle behind behavioral interviewing is that past performance is the best predictor of future performance.

Competency-Based Interview   In this type of interview, each question probes a specific skill or competency. Candidates are asked about their behavior in certain circumstances. Then, they are asked to explain how that happened in a real-life example.

Group Interview   Group interviews happen when multiple job candidates are interviewed by more than one interviewer at the same time. Group interviews are used in specific situations where several candidates are being considered for the same job in which the duties are limited and clearly defined, such as a merry-go-round operator. A *fishbowl* interview brings multiple candidates together to work with each other in an actual group activity or exercise. It is similar to an in-basket exercise except it involves a group of candidates. A *team interview* typically involves a group of interviewers with a perspective of the actual interactions associated with the job. This might include supervisors, subordinates, peers, customers, and so on. It is like a 360-degree exercise. Finally, in a *panel interview*, questions are distributed among a group of interviewers, typically those most qualified in a particular area. At the end of the panel interview, the panel caucuses with the purpose of coming to a group consensus regarding the result.

Stress Interview   In this type of interview, an interviewer creates an aggressive posture—in other words, deliberately creating some type of stress to see how the candidate reacts to stressful situations. For example, using a room where the candidate has to face an open window with the sun in their eyes can put the candidate under stress. (That could also be problematic if the candidate has serious vision problems that rise to the level of a disability.) This type of interview is used more often in law enforcement, air traffic control, and similar high-stress occupations. The stress interview was more common in the 1970s and 1980s. Today, it is not recommended because of the likelihood that it will be interpreted as personal bias.

Guidelines for Interviews The University of Nebraska at Kearney offers these tips for interviews:[57]

- Directly observe certain aspects of an applicant's behavior, such as ability to communicate, alertness, self-confidence, understanding of necessary technical concepts, and so on.

- Obtain additional information regarding the applicant's education, work experience, relevant community activities, or job-related interests that can supplement or fill gaps on written application materials.

- Identify and assess the extent of the applicant's knowledge, skills, and other characteristics or competencies by inquiring about past performance and achievements.

- Preview the job and what the organization expects of employees and what employees can expect in return—so that the applicants can determine whether they are interested in the position.

- Identify the need for any accommodation that might be required to enable the applicant with a disability to perform the functions of the position.

- Promote a good public image of the institution.

Interview Questions Questions you can and can't ask in an employment interview are described in Table 4-7.[58]

Acceptable	Subject	Not Acceptable
• Street address of residence. • Length of time at current or former residence.	**Address of Residence**	• Inquiries into foreign addresses that would indicate national origin. • Do you own or rent your residence?
• If you are hired, can you show proof that you are older than 18? • If you are younger than 18, can you provide a work permit from your school?	**Age**	• How old are you? • What is your birthday? • When did you graduate from elementary or high school? • Requirement for birth certificate or baptismal record *before* hiring. • Advertisement using words like *young, girl, boy, college student, retired person*, etc.
• If you are hired, can you furnish proof of your right to work in this country?	**Ancestry, Birthplace, or National Origin**	• Where were you born? • Where were your parents born? • How did you learn your languages? • Do you have relatives in any other country?

Table 4-7 Questions You Can and Can't Ask in an Employment Interview *(continued)*

PART II

Acceptable	Subject	Not Acceptable
• Have you ever been *convicted* of a crime that may be related to this job content or responsibilities? • "Ban-the-box" laws, both state and local, have restricted employer rights to inquire about conviction records. Be sure you speak with your attorney to know if this is still appropriate in your jurisdiction.	**Arrests or Convictions**	• Any question related to arrest record. • Some state and local laws and ordinances prohibit employers from inquiring about conviction records. Speak with your attorney about the prohibitions in your jurisdiction.
• Are you a U.S. citizen? (If citizenship is a job requirement because of security clearances, etc.)	**Citizenship**	• Are you a native-born or naturalized citizen? • When did you become a citizen? • Show proof of citizenship or naturalization before hiring.
• Employers may tell applicants that any job offer is made contingent upon their passing a physical examination if such a requirement is made of everyone hired into that specific job. • Requiring applicants to pass a drug screen is usually permitted. • It is acceptable to ask if an applicant is able to perform the essential functions of the job, with or without a job accommodation.	**Disability or Medical Condition**	• Have you ever filed a workers' compensation claim? • Do you have any serious medical condition or disability? • Has anyone in your family ever had cancer, heart disease, or other serious illness? • Have you ever had a job accommodation?
• Please list the college degrees you have earned and the institutions attended. • Please list any continuing education programs, certification, or vocational training you have received related to this job.	**Education**	• Any inquiry into the nationality or racial makeup of the institution. • When did you graduate from elementary or high school?
• There are usually no acceptable questions about financial status.	**Financial Status**	• Have you ever had your wages garnished? • What is your credit rating? • Have you ever filed for bankruptcy? • What is your net worth?

Table 4-7 Questions You Can and Can't Ask in an Employment Interview *(continued)*

Acceptable	Subject	Not Acceptable
• Will you please demonstrate how you would perform job-specific tasks (duties).	**Height and Weight**	• Almost no question about height and/or weight is acceptable.
• Almost no pre-employment inquiry is acceptable.	**Marital Status or Parental Status**	• Are you single, married, divorced, separated, etc.? • What are the names and ages of your spouse and children? • Where does your spouse work? • Are you planning to have more children?
• Please describe any military service experience you believe will help you on this specific job.	**Military Service**	• Have you served in the military of any country other than the United States? • What type of discharge did you receive? • What were the dates of your military service?
• Have you ever used another name that would enable us to check on your employment or education records?	**Name**	• What is your maiden name? • Are you a Mr., Mrs., Miss, Ms., or other designation?
• Please indicate any job-related organizations, clubs, professional societies, or other associations to which you belong. You may omit those that indicate your race, religious creed, color, national origin, ancestry, sex, or age.	**Organization Memberships**	• List all organizations, clubs, societies, and lodges to which you belong. • Do not ask about *paid* work experience without also asking about *unpaid* or *volunteer* work experience.
• Statement that a photograph may be required *after* hiring.	**Physical Description or Photograph**	• Any request for a photograph or physical description prior to a job offer.
• Identifying race following the job offer is often a requirement for governmental reporting. • Inviting applicant self-identification of race and sex is a requirement for affirmative action employers (government contractors). The data must be kept away from the hiring manager.	**Race or color**	• Any inquiry about skin color, hair or eye color, etc. • Any inquiry about race, color, or ethnicity.
• Who referred you to us? • Names of individuals who can provide either personal or professional references for the job applicant.	**References**	• Any request for references that might indicate applicant's race, religion, color, sex, national origin, age, or disability status.

Table 4-7   Questions You Can and Can't Ask in an Employment Interview *(continued)*

Acceptable	Subject	Not Acceptable
• Name and address of person you want to have notified in the event of an emergency. • Name of applicant's relatives who work for the employer. • Names and addresses of guardians of a minor job applicant.	**Relatives or Emergency Contact Information**	• What is the name of the relative you want us to notify in the event of an emergency? • Who is your nearest living relative, and how can we contact them? • Do your relatives speak English?
• Other than absences from work for religious observances, will you be available for work at the following times?	**Religion**	• Who is your pastor (minister, rabbi, or other religious leader)? • What church do you attend? • What religious holidays do you observe?
• Inviting applicant self-identification of race and sex is a requirement for affirmative action employers (government contractors). The data must be kept away from the hiring manager.	**Sex**	• Any inquiry that would indicate preference for one sex over the other. • Advertisement indicating "Men Wanted" or "Women Wanted." • Any preference other than those based upon a bona fide occupational qualification.
• Explanation of work schedule requirements and inquiry about willingness to meet that schedule.	**Work Schedule**	• How will you get to work? • Everyone works through the weekend. Are you willing to do that, too? • Are you willing to work on Christmas, Easter, and Good Friday? • Who will look after your kids while you're at work?

Table 4-7   Questions You Can and Can't Ask in an Employment Interview

Interview Biases   Hiring managers who interview may inadvertently create EEO problems or make ill-fated selection choices without the proper training and guidance from HR. Hiring is typically not a frequent responsibility of a line manager; it may have been several years since they had to hire an employee. A discussion of some common factors that may create problems in interviewing would be helpful from HR. They include the following:[59]

- **Stereotyping**   This involves forming a generalized opinion about how candidates of a particular gender, religion, or race may think, act, feel, or respond. An example would be presuming a woman would prefer to work indoors rather than outdoors.

- **Inconsistency in questioning**   This involves asking different questions of different candidates. An example would be asking only the male candidates to describe a time when they used critical-thinking skills in their last job.

- **First-impression error** This is when the interviewer makes a snap judgment and lets their first impression (be it positive or negative) cloud the entire interview. An example is where added credence is given to a candidate because the person graduated from an Ivy League college.

- **Negative emphasis** This involves rejecting a candidate on the basis of a small amount of negative information. An example is when a male candidate is wearing a large earring plug, and in the interviewer's judgment this is inappropriate, yet the job the candidate is interviewing for is a phone customer service position—there is no customer visual contact.

- **Halo/horn effect** This is when the interviewer allows one strong point that they value to overshadow all other information. Halo is in the candidate's favor, and horn is in the opposite direction.

- **Nonverbal bias** An undue emphasis is placed on nonverbal cues that are unrelated to potential job performance. An example is a distracting mannerism such as biting the nails.

- **Contrast effect** This is when a strong candidate has interviewed after a weak candidate, making the person appear more qualified than they actually are—only because of the contrast.

- **Similar-to-me error** The interviewer selects candidates based on personal characteristics that they share, rather than job-related criteria. An example would be that both the interviewer and the candidate attend the same local NFL sports team home games.

- **Cultural noise** This is when a candidate is masking their response, providing what is considered "politically correct" and not revealing anything or being factual.

Assessing and Evaluating

Assessing candidates and evaluating their assessment tests is helpful in screening to ensure the best qualified for the job position is forwarded on for hiring manager's consideration.

Assessment Methods These are measurement approaches for behavior:

- **Personality tests** These tests are self-reporting, projective techniques (ink blots), and behavioral assessment (role play).

- **Ability tests** These tests tend to have high reliability but risk disparity results for race or gender.

- **Performance tests and work samples** Candidates are asked to perform one or more of the tasks required by the job opening. If the job involves writing, the candidate is given a pencil, paper, and an allotted amount of time to write a sample for consideration. Performance tests can be set up in a workstation model so working conditions can be much the same as on the actual job.

- **Integrity tests**   These are designed to assess the applicant's tendency to be honest, trustworthy, and dependable.
- **Structured interview**   The aim of this approach is to ensure that each interview subject is presented with the same questions in the same order.

Discretionary Assessment Methods   Other methods are used to separate those who will receive a job offer from the other finalists; they might include consideration of the following:

- The person's match to the organization
- Personal motivation level
- Behaviors complementary to organizational personality—doing work in the community outside the individual's assigned job

Contingent Assessment Methods   Job offers can be made contingent upon the applicant succeeding in an assessment exercise. That may be a visit to the job site and interaction with current employees or successful participation in a formal assessment process structured for the job in question.

Cross-Cultural Assessment Tools   This can be a self-assessment tool used extensively in training, consulting, and program evaluation, as well as employment screening, that is designed to address a person's ability to adapt to different cultures. The assessment process should be designed to respond to several needs or practical concerns that are expressed by both culturally diverse and cross-culturally oriented populations.

Criteria for Selecting and Evaluating Selection Methods   There are four important criteria for selecting and evaluating selection methods.

- **Validity**   The extent to which the assessment can predict job behavior (performance)
- **Adverse impact**   The extent to which protected group members (race, gender, age, national origin, disabled, veteran, and other minority groups) score lower on the assessment than those in majority groups
- **Cost**   The cost to develop and administer
- **Applicant reactions**   The extent to which applicants react positively rather than negatively to the assessment process

Establishing Reliability   Reliability is important in the face of an observation or assessment being made by multiple people within the same circumstances.

- **Inter-rater or inter-observer reliability**   Assesses the degree to which different raters/observers give consistent estimates of the same phenomenon
- **Test-retest reliability**   Assesses the consistency of measurements from one time to another

Establishing Validity Since 1978, the government has had specific expectations for employers to offer validation of their employment selection devices. An employment selection device can be a written or oral test, job interview, assessment center participation, or job skill demonstration requirement. Regulations were established by the Equal Employment Opportunity Commission (EEOC) and are published at 41 CFR 60-3. They are known as the *Uniform Guidelines on Employee Selection Procedures*. Validity can be processed in several ways.

- **Construct validity** The extent to which a test actually measures what it claims to measure
- **Content validity** The extent to which a test measures all facets of a job
- **Test-retest or stability** The extent to which a test produces stable and reliable results and the results remain consistent from test to retest

Establishing Equity Determination that the employment test treats people equally, regardless of their personal group membership. Groups include race, gender, age, pregnancy, mental and physical disability, national origin, veteran status, religion, sexual orientation, and additional state-protected groupings.

Establishing Cost-Effectiveness Cost-effectiveness is the relationship between the cost to develop and administer a test and the benefit derived by it.

Background Investigations and Reference Checks Job offers are often conditioned upon successful completion of background checks, reference checks, and sometimes even credit checks. In some instances, a job offer could be conditioned on passing a medical evaluation or drug screen.

Before conducting background checks or credit checks, review the current legal limitations on their use. The EEOC has issued guidelines on consideration of conviction records because the population of convicted felons is so heavily skewed with Blacks and Hispanics. Considering conviction records[60] has a disparate impact on those two racial/ethnic groups. Thus, only if the conviction has a direct relationship to the job content will considering it in the hiring decision be permitted by the EEOC.[61]

International Background Checks Employers will typically use international background checks only if a candidate has lived abroad or if the company has facilities abroad.

Employment, Education, and Reference Checks Résumés and job applications usually contain information about educational background and employment history. While not always successful, verification calls should be made to the organizations on the résumé or job application to confirm the accuracy of the claims.

Select and Offer

Once all screening has been done, a decision must be made. When the best qualified candidate has been selected, a job offer should be made.

Decision Process   There are several steps in the employment decision process.

1. **Summarize information**   Use a summary sheet or matrix to pull together comparative key points about each finalist.

2. **ID and rank candidates**   Using a tool such as the Candidate Selection Factors Chart, it is possible to summarize and rank each candidate against the others.

3. **Collect additional information**   Additional information can include the candidate's willingness to accept the standard benefit package, verification of a professional license, or a pending certification. They all are the loose ends that need to get tied up.

4. **Make an offer**   Offers can be made verbally or in writing. Many employment attorneys counsel their clients to put a job offer in writing.

Contingent Job Offer   A job offer can be made contingent upon any number of conditions.

- Legal right to work in the United States
- Verification of educational degrees
- Verification of professional licensing (medical doctor, lawyer, accountant)
- Confirmation of certification for the job duties (highway flagger, elevator repair technician, HR professional, certified professional accountant)
- Receipt of national security clearance

Employment Offer   An employment offer should include start date, wage, or salary (in weekly or monthly amount[62]), benefits, job title, work location, name of supervisor, restatement that the offer is made under an "employment at will" understanding, and any other pertinent information. In practical terms, phone calls are made to the applicant for confirmation that they are still available and interested in the job. Then, a written offer can be sent to confirm all of the details. A written offer should have a provision for the applicant to sign, accepting the offer and acknowledging the conditions specified. The offer is not considered completed until the signed acceptance is received and any contingency is met.

Employment Contract   You will recall that the alternative to employment at will is an employment contract. A contract can be either oral or written, express or implied. Oral contracts can be created even inadvertently if the employer isn't careful. When a hiring manager tells the newly hired employee something like, "This is a great company. You can spend your whole career here without worry of getting laid off," you run the risk of creating an implied oral contract.

Handing Nonselected Candidates   There may be a few or there may be many job candidates who did not receive a job offer. What do you do with them? Some employers just ignore them. Best HR practices, however, suggests that it is courteous to notify each individual who did not receive a job offer. You do not need to be specific about the reason each person was not selected, but a kind letter can go a long way to boosting your organization's reputation in the marketplace. People will remember for a long time how they felt about their application experience with you and your organization. You can make that a positive memory for them.

Special Considerations: Reasonable Accommodation According to the U.S. Department of Labor's Office of Disability Employment Policy (ODEP)[63] "A reasonable accommodation is any change in the work environment or in the way things are usually done that enables an individual with a disability to participate in the application process, to perform the essential functions (or fundamental duties) of a job, or to enjoy equal benefits and privileges of employment that are available to individuals without disabilities."

Applicants and employees must make their request for accommodation in writing, explaining how the accommodation will help them accomplish the duties of the job or the application process. Then the employer is obligated to review the request, enter into a dialogue about the request, and explore any other accommodations that may be more appealing to the employer (e.g., less expensive) while still permitting the applicant or employee to accomplish the tasks involved in the job or the application process. If the employer feels it cannot make the accommodation requested, it is permitted to decline the request and notify the applicant or employee of the decision.

Job Previewing

A job preview is a way for candidates to see how the job is actually performed. The preview itself can be presented in several different ways.

- **Video preview**   Incumbents can express their thoughts about what they like and dislike about the job.

- **Simulation**   Workstation mock-ups and task processing that can last 8 hours or longer can provide the candidate with a feel for how the job is actually accomplished.

- **Shadowing**   Candidates can spend time on the job with an incumbent to see what happens during the course of a normal workday.

Characteristics of Realistic Job Previews   Job previews must provide an honest picture of the job content. What physical and mental effort is required? What skills are used? What happens when something goes wrong? Honest representation of the job in all respects will give the candidate an opportunity to accept or not accept your invitation to go further in the process. Job previewing can be done after a contingent job offer is made, or it can be done earlier in the employment process. Simulation and shadowing can both be expensive if there are more than a few candidates. Video previews can be much more cost-effective, but they lack the "hands-on" view that a live presence on the job site can provide.

Benefits of a Job Preview   The candidate gets to experience the next best thing to actually performing the job. Seeing incumbents working on the tasks, having a chance to ask questions, and even doing parts of the job can be a great way to gain exposure to how it feels to do that work. It can give candidates the chance to determine whether they will like doing that work. If not, they can resign from further consideration. It also gives the employer a chance to observe each candidate in the working environment and judge their reactions to the work's demands.

Orientation and Onboarding

Orientation and onboarding are two activities that will set the tone for the balance of an employee's line on the job with this employer. If we get off on the right foot with people, the chance for retention success goes up. If we skip this step, we miss the opportunity to define the new employee's image of us as an employer. And, we miss the opportunity to establish the employee's expectations for the rest of their experience with this employer.

It is a common belief that the first 90 days of a worker's experience on a new job will determine how the relationship goes for the balance of their employment. One way to get off on the right foot is to provide a quality orientation program (also referred to as *onboarding*) to every new employee.

A strong orientation program will include such things as follows:

- **Welcome by the CEO/senior executive**   This shows a new hire that senior management cares about employees. Senior executives who believe it isn't worth their time convey a strong message also.

- **Discussion about culture**   An opportunity to discuss "the way we do things around here." What does the employer value? What gets rewarded in the organization? What type of image does the employer want to project to the world? What are expectations of ethics? Assimilating and socializing the new hire into the culture and expectations of behavior that is expected of them while working in the organization is a necessary and important step for orientation and onboarding.

- **Enrollment in benefit programs**   This is an opportunity to complete payroll tax forms, benefit enrollment forms, and self-identification forms for race, sex, disability, and veteran status.

- **Tour of employee common areas**   This can include the cafeteria or break room, the location for labor law compliance posters, and restrooms.

- **Safety equipment and emergency exits**   This is often overlooked when it should be on the orientation agenda. If there are emergency breathing apparatus, eye wash stations, emergency shutdown switches, first-aid stations, or other important safety points of interest, this is the time to show each new worker where they are. Safety training in how to use emergency equipment will come later.

- **Introduction to co-workers and supervisors**   Guide the employees to their new work locations and introduce them to their new co-workers and supervisors, even if they may have met some of them during the interviewing process. Have someone designated to explain where to get office supplies, how to access computer terminals, and whom to ask when questions come up. These things are just common employment courtesy.

Onboarding

Onboarding new employees is the process of integrating them to the organization and its specific culture, as well as getting a new hire the tools and information needed to become a productive contributing member of the organization. Onboarding should be a strategic process that lasts at least 1 year because how employers handle the first few days and months of a new employee's experience is crucial to ensuring a smooth transition into the organization and high retention.

Getting Started with the Onboarding Process   The process of onboarding new employees can be one of the most critical factors in ensuring recently hired talent will be productive and happy workers. Not to be confused with orientation, onboarding is quite different. Orientation involves paperwork and routine tasks to place new hires in the organization's payroll and organization chart. Onboarding is a more comprehensive process involving management and other employees that normally lasts up to a year. An effective onboarding program helps assimilate new hires and addresses the following:

- What impression do you want new hires to walk away with at the end of the first day? First month? First quarter? First year?
- What do new employees need to know about the culture and work environment?
- What role will HR play in the process? What about direct managers? Co-workers?
- What kind of expectations, especially behavioral, do you want to set for new employees?
- Who will be the new employee's sponsor (generally someone out of the direct line of command)?
- How will you gather feedback on the program and measure its success?

Once these questions have been addressed, HR professionals and upper management can devise a plan of action to help new employees quickly assimilate company policies and workflow while getting fully acquainted with the organization's culture.

Functional Area 3—Employee Engagement & Retention

Here is SHRM's BoCK definition: "Employee Engagement and Retention refers to activities aimed at retaining high-performing talent, solidifying and improving the relationship between employees and the organization, creating a thriving and energized workforce, and developing effective strategies to address appropriate performance expectations from employees at all levels."[64]

Key Concepts

- Approaches to developing and maintaining a positive organizational culture (e.g., learning strategies, communication strategies, building values)
- Approaches to recognition (e.g., performance or service awards)

- Creation, administration, analysis, and interpretation of employee attitude surveys
- Creation, planning, and management of employee engagement activities
- Employee lifecycle phases (e.g., recruitment, integration, development, departure)
- Employee retention concepts (e.g., causes of turnover) and best practices (e.g., realistic job previews [RJP])
- Influence of culture on organizational outcomes (e.g., organizational performance, organizational learning, innovation)
- Interventions for improving job attitudes
- Job attitude theories and basic principles (e.g., engagement, satisfaction, commitment)
- Job enrichment/enlargement principles and techniques
- Key components of, and best practices associated with, performance management systems
- Methods for assessing employee attitudes (e.g., focus groups, stay interviews, surveys)
- Principles of effective performance appraisal (e.g., goal setting, giving feedback)
- Retention and turnover metrics (e.g., voluntary turnover rate)
- Types of organizational cultures (e.g., authoritarian, mechanistic, participative, learning, high performance)
- Workplace flexibility programs (e.g., telecommuting, alternative work schedules)

The following are the proficiency indicators that SHRM has identified as key concepts:

For All HR Professionals	For Advanced HR Professionals (SCP Exam)
Designs, administers, analyzes, and interprets surveys of employee attitudes (e.g., engagement, job satisfaction) and culture	In collaboration with other leaders, defines an organizational strategy to create an engaged workforce
Administers and supports HR and organizational programs designed to improve employee attitudes and culture (e.g., social events, telecommuting policies, recognition, job enlargement/enrichment, workplace flexibility)	Implements best practices for employee retention in HR programs, practices, and policies (e.g., RJP, career development programs, employee socialization)
Identifies program opportunities to create more engaging or motivating jobs (e.g., job enrichment/enlargement).	Communicates to other senior leaders the results of surveys of employee attitudes and culture
Monitors changes in turnover and retention metrics and ensures that leadership is aware of such changes	Designs and oversees an action plan to address the findings of employee attitude surveys

For All HR Professionals	For Advanced HR Professionals (SCP Exam)
Coaches supervisors on creating positive working relationships with their employees	Designs and oversees HR and organizational programs designed to improve employee attitudes (e.g., social events, telecommuting policies, recognition, job enlargement/enrichment, workplace flexibility)
Trains stakeholders on the use of organization's performance management systems (e.g., how to enter performance goals, make ratings)	Holistically monitors the organization's metrics on employee attitudes, turnover and retention, and other information about employee engagement and retention
Helps stakeholders understand the elements of satisfactory employee performance and performance management	Designs and oversees best practices–based employee performance management systems that meet the organization's talent management needs
Implements and monitors processes that measure effectiveness of performance management systems	Designs and oversees processes to measure the effectiveness of performance management systems

Maintaining an engaged and satisfied workforce and a culture that employees perceive to be positive is an important function for HR. Employee turnover, along with poor performance, is costly and also disruptive. HR's practices can mitigate these potential problems by monitoring and improving organizational performance and the retention of key talent.

Understanding Employee Engagement

Employee engagement is a broad outcome-driven concept that recognizes certain characteristics that contribute to behaviors that will positively influence employee job performance. HR authorities often define employee engagement in terms of "commitment," that is, the identification with an organization and the commitment to active participation in its future. Engagement is the degree to which employees are psychologically invested in the organization and motivated to contribute to it success. It can also be described as the discretionary effort toward attaining organizational goals.[65]

There are three types of professional HR engagement.

- **Trait engagement** The personality-based elements that make an individual be inclined to be involved, to have a natural curiosity, and to have an interest in addressing and solving problems.

- **Stage engagement** The influence of the workplace environment on an individual's inclination to become involved. Organizational interventions can directly influence this type of engagement.

- **Behavioral engagement** The effect of individual effort that creates the satisfaction from a job well done. Behavioral engagement can occur in cases when both trait and stage engagement are present.

Employee Engagement Levels

While individual surveys differ to some degree, all indicate that the U.S. workforce is typically less engaged than employers expect or hope for. Most results show a relatively low level of employee engagement of about 30 to 40 percent. Other parts of the world show even less engagement.

Benefits of Employee Engagement

A 2013 Gallup study[66] on employee engagement involving 142 countries indicates only 13 percent of employees worldwide are engaged at work; further, 63 percent are not engaged, while 24 percent are actively disengaged. At a regional level, the United States and Canada have the highest proportion of workers who are engaged, 29 percent, followed by Australia and New Zealand. Significant observations indicate that actively disengaged employees outnumber engaged employees by nearly two to one. Gallup describes *engaged employees* as those employees who work with a passion and feel a profound connection to their company. They drive innovation and move their company forward. *Not engaged* employees are essentially "checked out." They're "sleepwalking" through their workday, putting in time but not energy or passion into their work. *Active disengaged* employees are just unhappy at work; they're busy acting out their unhappiness. Every day, these workers undermine what their engaged co-workers accomplish.

In 2012, Gallup conducted a meta-analysis of its research data across 192 organizations, 49 industries, and 34 countries. This study confirmed a well-established connection between employee engagement and a number of performance outcomes. The median differences between top-quartile and bottom-quartile units were as follows:

- 10 percent in customer ratings
- 22 percent in profitability
- 21 percent in productivity
- 25 percent in turnover (high-turnover organizations)
- 65 percent in turnover (low-turnover organizations)
- 48 percent in safety incidents
- 37 percent in absenteeism
- 41 percent in quality defects

Drivers and Role of Organizational Culture in Engagement

Organizational culture is a system of shared assumptions, values, and beliefs that govern how people behave in organizations. These shared values have a significant influence on people in the organization and dictate how they dress, act, and perform their jobs. An organization's ultimate goal is to align its culture and strategy.

Global Engagement Drivers

There are four drivers of engagement from an international perspective.

- The work itself as well as the development opportunities the work provides
- Stability and the confidence that is placed in an organization's leadership
- Rewards and recognition
- The upward and downward flow of communications

These drivers vary from country to country in a global context. Whereas the confidence that career interests can be met, a sense of personal satisfaction, and confidence in the organization's success are primary in the United States, top drivers in Canada include a good work-life balance and being respectfully treated. Other countries value other drivers.

Some international drivers include the need for achievement and competence, but difference occurs between individualist cultures and collectivist cultures. Individualist cultures prefer personal feedback, whereas collectivist cultures prefer group feedback. A need for control is universal, but personal control is preferred in an individualist culture, whereas collective control is preferred in collectivist cultures.

Effective Management and Employee Engagement

Management's behavior is critical to employee engagement and to an employee's well-being. Managers who manage in ways that encourage employee engagement are essential to the engagement of their employees. Recent studies conclude that there is a link between employee engagement and leadership practices that encourage and support employee performance rather than dictate employee performance. The following are three leadership practices that encourage and support employee performance:

- **Transformational leadership**   This is a style of leadership where the leader is charged with identifying the needed change, creating a vision to guide the change through inspiration, and executing the change in tandem with committed members of the group.
- **Authentic leadership**   This is an approach to leadership that emphasizes building the leader's legitimacy through honest relationships with followers who value their input and that is built on an ethical foundation.
- **Supportive leadership**   This is one of the leadership styles found in path-goal theory (a theory based on specifying a leader's style or behavior that best fits the employee and work environment to achieve goals). A supportive leader attempts to reduce employee stress and frustration in the workplace.

Challenges to Employee Engagement

Many external factors present obstacles to effective employee engagement, including global competition, economic conditions, continuous innovation, and new technology. In addition, the blurred line between work and nonwork conditions exacerbates the difficulties faced by employers whose goal is to maximize conditions that support effective employee engagement.

Global competition coupled to less-than-ideal economic conditions places significant pressure on organizational managers to aggressively target production goals. Along with this, continuous innovation and new technology add another layer of pressure on work performance even as they offer new capabilities to the workplace. Further, technology in the form of the Internet and mobile interconnectivity creates a new gray area as to where work time ends and nonwork time begins.

All of this places a new role for HR to create a business case for the need now, more than ever, for managers to invest in the issue of employee engagement.

HR's Employee Engagement Strategy

 As part of its strategic management role, HR is tasked with developing effective strategies incorporating good employee engagement practices designed to best achieve the organization's business goals.

Assessing Employee Engagement

Employee engagement is the level of personal investment an employee has in his or her work. According to the *Harvard Business Review*, "Much has been studied about the impact of employee engagement on company performance, and there is general agreement that increased engagement drives results: Gallup, for example, suggests a 20% or better boost to productivity and profitability for companies with high engagement. Such companies, however, may be few and far between: Gallup also reports that only 30% of American workers, and 13% of global workers, are engaged in their jobs."[67]

Gathering Information About Employee Engagement

If you want to measure employee engagement, consider employee surveys or focus groups. Both can produce a great deal of information about how people feel about their jobs and their contributions to the organization.

Employee Surveys

Perhaps the most frequently used device for gathering information about employee engagement is the employee survey. It can be used to work on issues in the entire employer organization or in only a small part like a department or division. When the accounting department is having problems and a new manager is appointed to manage the department, an employee survey of accounting personnel could be helpful to identify the issues employees want to see improved. Help your employees with the issues they believe are important, and they will react by being nicer to the customers they contact and other employees within the company.

Benefits of Conducting Employee Surveys   Why use an employee survey to measure employee engagement? Well, they are reasonable in cost, can be done fairly quickly, and can provide some great insights into the thinking of your employees. Surveys are versatile and can be done anonymously.

Survey Questions   Questions are constructed so there are no right or wrong answers (unlike the SHRM certification exam). Here are a few examples:

- On a scale of 1 to 10, where 10 is the best, please rate the quality of supervision in your work group.
- What word would you use to describe the company's strategy?
- On a scale of Strongly Agree to Strongly Disagree, how would you rate your views of this statement? The company executive team is open and accessible to all employees.
- Please rank order the following five things on a scale of 1 to 5. Use each number only once.

Developing Surveys   To begin a survey project, you should identify the goals you want to meet by having a survey. If it is to determine levels of employee satisfaction with the new company headquarters building, that would be worthwhile. If it is to see what employees thought of the new office binder supplier, there may be less value to be gained. Once you have the goal in mind, identify the population that you want to invite to participate in the survey. Is it the entire employee body or only the group that is working at a given location? Then determine whether you want to build and implement the survey internally or hire an outside vendor to build and implement the survey for you. Construct the survey questions and test them with your HR staff (and even executives). Once all edits have been made, finalize the survey document and plan for its dissemination to your target audience. Gather and summarize the responses. Prepare a report on results.

Guidelines for Employee Engagement Surveys   Table 4-8 describes the critical drivers to consider when building an employee engagement survey, according to Qualtrics.com.[68]

Online Survey Method   Turn on your computer and start cruising the World Wide Web, and you will be presented with a great many opportunities to participate in customer surveys. There are an equal number of companies that are willing to help you prepare your online survey. Survey fraud is likely the greatest disadvantage of online surveys. You can't be positively sure about who is completing the survey. It could be someone who wants to distort your results, such as a competitor or unscrupulous employee. Yet the costs are low for using online surveys. If you can be sure that only specific people are able to participate, then you may find that this is a survey method you can use in your organization.

Managing Effective Employee Survey Projects   Aside from being careful in the construction of your survey, the most important part of the process is to get senior executive support both for the survey process and for taking actions that are necessary once results have been tabulated. Employee trust can be lost as quickly as you can blink if you ask people for their opinions and then do nothing to fix problems that are unveiled in the process.

Autonomy/empowerment	Are people able to act on their own authority and innovate on the job?
Career progression	Are there opportunities for people to grow and develop in the company?
Collaboration	Are they able to easily work with other teams or colleagues without barriers, and to what extent are people from diverse backgrounds or with diverse opinions able to collaborate?
Communication	Are they able to easily work with other teams or colleagues without barriers?
Company leadership	Do they believe in and trust their senior leaders?
Pay and benefits	Do people feel they're fairly compensated?
Quality of product or ervices	Do people believe in what they (and/or the organization) provide to their customers?
Recognition	Do people feel that they're recognized and appreciated?
Resources	Do they have the right tools (computers, systems, etc.) to do their job, and are there enough people on the team for them to achieve a work-life balance?
Strategy alignment	Do they buy into where the company is going, or do they even know?
Supportive management	Are managers supporting their teams to be successful (this can also include good performance management)?
Training and development	Do people feel they have the training they need to do their job?

Table 4-8 Employee Engagement Survey

Using Focus Groups and Interviews to Gather Engagement Information

When surveying employees, the last question should generally be, "May we contact you to discuss your responses?" Those people who say "yes" become candidates for follow-up interviews or participation in focus groups. Focus groups are designed to gain input from people who meet certain criteria such as more than 2 months of service, working in the engineering department, and within the past 2 years working for one of [named] competitive companies. The focus group can discuss any subject and is highly structured, led by a facilitator who presents questions to get responses from group participants. Sometimes the sessions are recorded for later study. Participants need to be told that to avoid legal complications. There are consulting firms that specialize in focus group facilitation. They assist with designing the questions, the photos or written slogans, advertising, or other company options, and they run the focus group sessions.

One-on-One Interviews   This is a technique for delving more deeply into the opinions expressed by individuals who responded to the employee survey. It can also be used to explore comments and opinions expressed during a focus group session. Someone who has a strong belief that the company benefit program should include paid parental leave could have some valuable input if discussed in a personal interview.

Analyzing Data on Employee Engagement

How do you feel when you are asked for your opinion and then ignored when you give it? That is what happens when employees sense the survey was just an exercise for show, in other words, a PR stunt. When the results are compiled and analyzed and action plans developed based on those results, employees will sense that their opinions actually matter.

Communicating Survey Results   One common failing of employee survey projects is that employees don't get any feedback about what the survey showed. Remember the communication cycle? We must complete the cycle by providing feedback to the employees about the survey results. How that is done can be quite creative. Or, it can be simple. Just be sure to do it. And, let employees know before sending out a press release explaining the results to the world. That sends the message to employees that their input is just being used for a publicity stunt.

Determining Actions from Survey Results   How do you determine what should be done with the survey results? First, summarize the responses so there is a composite view of employee thoughts. Then, analyze those composites to determine what they are saying. Separate them into "urgent," "important," and "later" categories to reflect how quickly the issues should be addressed by the employer. Finally, build an action plan to determine what is to be done, who is assigned the tasks, and when those tasks should be completed. Follow up to check on progress and eventually resurvey the workforce to see how they feel after you have taken the action based on their first input.

Selecting Employee Engagement Initiatives   It is sometimes difficult to know where to start fixing employee engagement problems. Using employee survey results, you can analyze areas of need and then build some plans to address them. Rank ordering the problems is a way to set priorities. And, involving employees in the action plan is a way to further their involvement and engagement. Start with the most important priority and work your way down the list, no matter how long it may take. Keep at it, and tell employees what you are doing from time to time.

Business Case for Engagement

Employee engagement affects nine performance outcomes. Compared with bottom-quartile units, top-quartile units have the following:[69]

- 37 percent lower absenteeism
- 25 percent lower turnover (in high-turnover organizations)
- 65 percent lower turnover (in low-turnover organizations)
- 28 percent less shrinkage
- 48 percent fewer safety incidents
- 41 percent fewer patient safety incidents
- 41 percent fewer quality incidents (defects)
- 10 percent higher customer metrics
- 21 percent higher productivity
- 22 percent higher profitability

It should be rather easy to convert these percentages to dollars in your organizational impact statement. Once that is done, a cost analysis to determine the budget requirements for spending to accomplish those results will help you prove the impact that your employee engagement project will have on the financial bottom line.

Engaging Employees from Hiring to Separation

Employee engagement is not only integral to your organization's workforce satisfaction, it's also imperative to the bottom line. According to the 2015 *Journal of Corporate Finance*, organizations with employee engagement programs saw a 26 percent year-over-year increase in annual company revenue, compared to those that did not have formal programs. Making employees feel like their contribution makes an impact, facilitating opportunities for them to form relationships, and collecting feedback are ways to engage employees.

If you've been tasked with implementing employee engagement initiatives at your organization with a large number of employees, or a company with multiple locations, the task may seem daunting. Start with feedback. Collecting feedback is a great place to start engaging your employees because you can use this feedback to inform the rest of your employee engagement strategy moving forward. For example, new hires are an important group to gather feedback from so you can refine your onboarding process, as are employees who are exiting the organization; they can give you insight into how you can better retain your current employees, if they will be candid with you. There are many different tools you can use to collect feedback. Using Glassdoor to collect feedback gives you a forum by which you can collect and respond to feedback.

Engaging Employees Throughout the Employee Lifecycle

There are critical key points in an employee lifecycle with the organization. Engagement begins with the first contact with the new employee and continues throughout their employment. HR plays an important role in increasing employee overall satisfaction and engagement for the get go.

Engagement Practices During Hiring and Onboarding

HR professionals have a great amount of influence with employee engagement, beginning with the hiring and onboarding phase. The period that begins with the hiring is an important opportunity to begin the engagement process. Gallup's report "State of the American Workplace: Employee Engagement Insights for U.S. Business Leaders" clearly points out that new hires are more engaged in their first 6 months on the job than they are at any other time during their employment. There are five practices that can be employed and used by HR during the hiring and onboarding processes.

- Make the job application process simple and yet informative.
- First impressions count—create an accurate first impression.
- Make the first day on the job organized and meaningful.

- Have a structured onboarding process to provide new hires with 90 days of orientation and fitting in.

- Define and communicate a path to success for the new hires so they are aware of the career advancement paths.

Engagement Practices During an Employee's Career

In the same Gallup report cited earlier, after the first 6 months are done, the honeymoon is over. Gallup stated that engagement fell to 44 percent by the tenth year of employment. There is plenty of opportunity for HR to shift those percentages by developing programs and leadership training that are specifically focused on employee engagement throughout the lifecycle of an employee's career. We address some of the approaches in the functional areas of Learning and Development and Total Rewards in this chapter. They include the topics of job enrichment, compensation, noncompensatory rewards, and career management.

Developing Policies and Procedures to Promote Engagement By helping to create policies, HR professionals are supporting how the organization defines roles and explains what actions and behaviors are acceptable and those that are not. Policies are meant to cover the majority of situations, and yet there will always be an exception to a policy that will occur. Policies lead to the creation of procedures and processes for implementing the policy. HR needs to regularly assess its current policies and how they impact employee engagement. Work-life balance policies are an example of a type of policy that has great impact on employee engagement and that requires review on at least an annual basis.

Work-Life Balance Because of technology growth and social pressures/changes within the family or community, work-life balance (WLB) is growing as an engagement issue for employees and organizations alike. Many organizations offer a number of WLB programs and policies that greatly enhance employee engagement. Telecommuting, child care on-site, gym memberships or gyms on-site, concierge services, and PTO flexibility—the list is growing in innovation.

Developing Policies When developing policies associated with work-life balance, the HR professional can rely on other organizations' best practices. These include having clear guidelines for management to apply and addressing a variety of situations (employee positions/roles) that they will apply to. Policies are created to address a "real need"—be sure that the work-life balance policies do just that in the business unit of the organization. First, identify the "need" for the WLB policy. Next, determine what the policy's content will be in simple language. Avoid rigid rules that must be followed exactly in all circumstances. Move to the next phase of development, which is to obtain stakeholder support. Share the draft with those who will need to apply the policy and look to see where refinement may be needed. Now that the policy is ready to be implemented, go to your communication plan—the when, who, what, where, and how for the policy's launch. As mentioned earlier, keep an eye on the policy to determine when it needs refinement, refreshment, and/or revision.

How Policies Can Affect Employee Engagement Policies can be one of the greatest sources of disenchantment for employee engagement. Notice what is brought up on the list of enhancements during labor relationship and contract negotiations. Pay attention to the exit interviews and preferable the "stay interviews" that provide feedback pointing to ineffective or behind-the-times policies. When it comes to employee engagement, HR can be the keeper of the keys when it comes to policies that affect employee satisfaction.

Using Motivation Theories to Increase Engagement Motivation is essential for engaging employees in their work. Three underlying principles of human behavior are directly linked to motivation.

- All human behavior is caused. This means people have a reason for doing what they do.

- All behavior is focused on achieving an end result or goal. People do things to attain something tangible or intangible. Their behavior is not random, though it could be unconscious.

- Every person has a unique fingerprint and is unique in that no one has the exact experience, heredity, or environmental/relationship influences.

Understanding these principles of human behavior will assist you as an HR professional with motivational pursuits, not just in the learning process but in all matters related to the work and employment relationship, especially engagement.

Motivation is like a shower; it washes off, and you need another in a couple of days. It puts a smiley face on an empty gas tank signal. Inspiration, however, lights up like a fire and grows—it comes from deep within people. Transformational leaders cause people to be inspired, inspiring their employees to take action and providing them with self-esteem versus "shelf-esteem." As an HR professional and one who trains organizational leaders, try to seek the authentic inspirational skills to motivate and engage employees. The event will be lasting and sustained.

There are several other long-standing motivational theories, and we will briefly review them to refresh your memory about what you most likely learned in your secondary educational endeavors.

Maslow's Hierarchy of Needs In Maslow's theory, there are five basic human needs arranged in a pyramid, necessitating that the first level (bottom of the pyramid) must be met first before moving up the pyramid. Figure 4-12 shows Maslow's hierarchy of needs. Lower-level needs on the pyramid will always have some influence on behavior.[70]

You can fulfill these needs in the workplace through the following:

- **Safety and security** Employment security such as an employment contract, pay and benefits, working conditions

- **Belonging and love** Teams, good leadership, participation in groups, employee associations, customer base assignments

- **Esteem** Training, recognition, awards, special assignments

- **Self-actualization** Job growth opportunities, project team participation, becoming a mentor

Figure 4-12   Maslow's hierarchy of needs

 NOTE   It's important to recognize today that not all motivational models of Western culture, like Maslow's hierarchy of needs, are going to apply in many of the global and diverse organizations of today.

Herzberg's Motivation-Hygiene Theory   This theory asserts that employees have two different categories of needs and that they are essentially independent of each other, but they affect behavior in differing ways: hygiene factors, which are considered extrinsic, and motivational factors, which are considered intrinsic. The latter is associated with recognition, achievement, and personal growth–related events in the job, whereas hygiene factors are associated with job security, pay, working conditions, supervision, and co-worker relations that can quickly lead to job dissatisfaction.

Theory X, Y, and Z   McGregor's theories X and Y offer two approaches to motivating employees. Theory X suggests an authoritative management style because it assumes that employees inherently do not like to work and must be controlled and closely monitored. Theory Y suggests a participative style of management, under the belief that employees dislike controls and inherently want to do their best. It is obvious to see that a theory Y type of supervisor will provide better leadership and produce greater satisfaction.

Theory Y is a participative style of management that "assumes that people will exercise self-direction and self-control in the achievement of organizational objectives to the degree that they are committed to those objectives." It is management's main task in such a system to maximize that commitment.

Theory Z management tends to promote stable employment, high productivity, and high employee morale and satisfaction. Theory Z is Dr. William Ouchi's[71] theory called *Japanese management style* popularized during the Japan economic boom of the 1980s. In the 1980s there was a huge demand for Japanese products and imports in America, mostly with the automotive industry. Why were U.S. consumers clambering for cars, televisions, stereos, and electronics from Japan? It was because of two reasons: high-quality products and low prices. The Japanese had discovered something that was giving them the competitive edge. The secret to their success was not what they were producing but how they were managing their people—Japanese employees were engaged, empowered, and highly productive. Ouchi studied Japan's approach to workplace teamwork and participative management. The result was his theory Z: a development beyond McGregor's theory X and theory Y that blended the best of Eastern and Western management practices. For Ouchi, theory Z focused on increasing employee loyalty to the company by providing a job for life with a strong focus on the well-being of the employee, both on and off the job.

Theory Z makes certain assumptions about workers. One assumption is that they seek to build cooperative and intimate working relationships with their co-workers. In other words, employees have a strong desire for affiliation. Another assumption is that workers expect reciprocity and support from the organization. According to theory Z, employees want to maintain a work-life balance, and they value a working environment in which things like family, culture, and traditions are considered to be just as important as the work they do. Under theory Z leadership, not only do workers have a sense of affiliation with their fellow workers, but they also develop a sense of order, discipline, and a moral obligation to work hard. Finally, theory Z assumes that given the right leadership, workers can be trusted to do their jobs and look after their own and their co-workers' well-being.

Skinner's Behavioral Reinforcement Theory One of the most influential American psychologists, B. F. Skinner, developed the theory of behavioral reinforcement that deals with shaping behavior. In Skinner's theory he found that behavior modification has four intervention strategies that are reactions to eventually shape behavior. There is positive reinforcement, negative reinforcement, punishment, and extinction.

- Positive reinforcement involves providing an employee with a desired or appreciated reward to encourage the desired behavior.

- Negative reinforcement involves avoiding an undesirable consequence by giving the employee an appreciated reward when they exhibit a desired behavior.

- Punishment is just as it sounds—something negative occurs when an undesirable behavior occurs by the employee.

- Extinction involves no response. When the behavior is not reinforced through positive, negative reinforcement, or punishment, the employee's behavior will diminish and become nonexistent.

Intrinsic Motivation   Intrinsic motivation is behavior that is driven by internal rewards. The motivation to engage in a behavior arises from within the employee because it is satisfying to them. Author Daniel Pink writes about the research that has been done globally on the topic of motivation. In his book *Drive: The Surprising Truth About What Motivates Us*, Pink states that if-then rewards (pay-for-performance) work well for tasks where there is a simple set of rules and a clear destination, such as accounting and computer programming (the left-brain work).[72] For the tasks that exercise more right-brain, which would be creative, research, and conceptual, a pay-for-performance leads to poorer performance. Science has determined that intrinsic motivation is far more effective for the right-brain types because it is associated with doing tasks, work, and things that matter; because it is interesting; or because the employee likes it.

Using Rewards and Recognition to Increase Engagement   The purpose of having employee recognition and reward programs is to acknowledge the value of employees, their contributions, or some other identification. The intention is to show gratitude, appreciation, loyalty, and trust, as well as to continue engagement and motivation. An effective program highlights valued and desired behaviors. Of course, forms of recognition address the psychological needs of people.

Forms of Rewards and Recognition   There are financial rewards and nonfinancial rewards (explored in the Total Rewards functional area in this book). Rewards need to demonstrate appreciation and are more effective when they are customized to an individual employee, such as tickets to an interest or hobby they may have. HR can be highly effective with designing appropriate recognition rewards through innovation and creativity, looking to other organizations for their best practices, and simply getting to know the employees in their organization. Awards can run the gamut from plaques, jewelry, and certificates to flex time off, conference attendance, tickets to events, and opportunities to fill in for an advanced position on a temporary/interim basis.

Recognition in Multinational Organizations   SHRM conducted research in 2006 that linked performance management and employee engagement in multinational enterprises operating across developed and developing economies. This research had the following key findings:[73]

- Having a broad range of performance appraisal outcomes was positively linked to engagement.
- Key elements of high levels of job/company resources were linked to employee engagement.
- Employee involvement in setting goals is linked positively to engagement.

Consistency and transparency in HR practices were highlighted as being critical.

Role of HR in Employee Recognition In the 2016 SHRM/Globoforce Employee Recognition Survey,[74] the following findings were reported by HR professionals:

- Organizations that had strategic recognition programs reported less frustrated and more engaged employees.
- Programs tied to the organization's values were more effective than programs without ties.
- Empowering employees to give and receive formal recognition had good results.
- When more than 1 percent of payroll was spent on employee recognition, employee engagement was better.

Engagement Practices During Separation

Employee separations happen; it's a fact of the employment cycle. Be it for reasons that are positively focused such as retirement or for reasons that are unpleasant such as terminations for cause or reductions in workforce (RIF). How these separations happen can have a positive or negative effect on employee engagement for those remaining in the workforce. HR can support fair, humane, and yet compliant processes with regard to separation. Exit interviews, as mentioned earlier, can be helpful for feedback on employee engagement. And well-done separations for cause can actually attract better employees capable of engagement and contribution where the departing employee could not. In many organizations, especially in the tech industries, it is not uncommon for former employees to return to the organization with new skills, providing new value at higher-level positions. The level of engagement and treatment at the separation can influence the possibility of key valued employees returning to the organization.

Performance Management

Performance management is a systematic process that helps improve organizational effectiveness by providing feedback to employees on their performance results and improvement needs. Employee accomplishments and contributions drive the business results of an organization, so a regular feedback system discussing individual performance is at the core of a good performance management system. It ensures that employees are on course for the completion of tasks and goals that are aligned with the organization's goals and that the resources and support are provided for the employee to perform such functions.

Employee performance management systems include the following:

- Delegating and planning work
- Setting expectations for performance results
- Continually monitoring performance
- Developing a capacity to perform to new levels for personal and professional growth
- Periodically rating performance in a summary fashion
- Providing recognition and rewarding good performance

Organizational Values and Goals

Creating and communicating the organization's vision, mission, strategies, specific goals, and values form the foundation that is needed for the performance management system. Then performance standards are agreed upon by both the line management and the employee on what the job requires and what will be measured. At this stage, it is essential that employees clearly understand the standards, including expected behavior standards set forth for their jobs. Feedback is the next stage and can be both informal and formal. Formal feedback would entail a written performance appraisal.

When it comes to performance management within a global organization, there are additional considerations. Different cultural values and societal norms will affect the definition of standards and performance criteria as it relates to a global workforce. Different languages will also have to be considered for the interpretation of performance definitions and standards. Recognizing that there are differing behaviors for different cultures can be a challenge for setting the behavioral standards and expectations of individuals.

Performance Standards

Employees need to know and understand what specific performance is expected of them in performing their jobs and the acceptable behavior. This communication begins with the very first discussion in a job interview and certainly with the job offer and new-hire onboarding orientation. The discussion continues on a consistent basis both with the reinforcement of organizational standards that are outlined in employee handbooks and other written material and with performance appraisal review sessions. The clearer the expectations set for employees, the greater the success in having expectations met.

Employee Performance

Job performance means the extent to which an employee generates work output that meets expectations for quality and quantity.

Measurement and Feedback

Everything can be measured, even if it is inherently subjective. Once measured, feedback should be provided to the employees so they can know how they are doing in their job efforts.

Appraisal Methods   Performance appraisals satisfy three purposes.

- Providing feedback and coaching
- Justifying the allocation of rewards and career opportunities
- Helping with employee career planning and development plans

For the organization, performance appraisals can foster commitment and align people to contribute to initiatives with their upcoming performance contributions. The most common performance appraisal method involves just two people: the employee and their direct supervisor. In some companies, others are asked to be involved in the appraisals such as peers, another level of management, and sometimes colleagues in the organization whose job function interacts with the employee. These are known as *360-degree appraisals.*

Methods for rating the performance can be completely narrative, management by objectives (MBO), behaviorally anchored ratings (BARS), category rating, and comparative ratings with others in like functions.

The least complex of the methods is the category rating where the reviewer simply checks a level of rating on a form. These three types of rating formulas are typically used in category ratings:

- **Graphic scale**   The most common type, where the appraiser checks a place on the scale for the categories of tasks and behaviors that are listed. A typical scale is 5 points, where 1 means not meeting expectations or low, and 5 means exceeding expectations or high. These types of performance appraisals normally have a comments section that the appraiser completes that provides justification for the rating.

- **Checklist**   Another common appraisal rating in which the appraiser is provided with a set list of statements/words to describe performance. The appraiser selects the one word or statement that best describes the performance—for example, "Employee consistently meets all deadlines" or "Employee consistently misses deadlines.

- **Forced choice**   A variation of the checklist approach (but in the checklist method, the appraiser is required to check two of four statements). One check is for the statement that is most like the employee's performance, and the other check is for the statement that is least like the employee's performance—a combination of positive and negative statements. This method can be difficult to convey to employees and understand from an employee's perspective.

With comparative methods, employee performance is compared directly with others in the same job. The appraiser will rank the employees in a group from highest to lowest in performance. This causes a forced distribution known as a *bell curve*. Ten percent will fall in the highest and lowest of the rating scale, another 20 percent will fall on either side, and then 40 percent will meet job standards and expectations. An obvious fault with this type of system is suggesting that a percentage of employees will fall below expectations. Figure 4-13 displays a bell curve distribution.

Figure 4-13
Bell curve
distribution

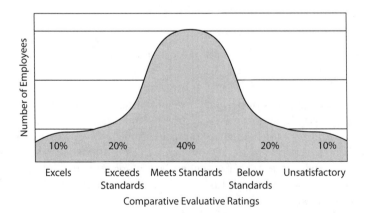

Narrative evaluations are time-consuming for an appraiser to complete, yet they can be the most meaningful to the employee being evaluated. There are three methods that are the most common for the narrative appraisal.

- **Essay format** The appraiser writes an essay describing each category of performance.

- **Critical incident** The appraiser logs the dates and details of both good and not-so-good performance incidents. This method requires the appraiser to keep good, detailed notes on a routine basis during the appraisal period and not rely solely on an employee's most recent performance.

- **Behaviorally anchored rating methods** Referred to as BARS, this appraisal method describes desirable behavior and undesirable behavior. Examples are then compared with a scale of performance level for the rating. BARS works well in circumstances in which several employees perform the same function. A BARS appraisal system requires extensive time to develop and maintain to keep the performance dimensions up-to-date as the job functions change. However, the BARS methods offer a more accurate gauge of performance measurement, provide clearer standards to employees, and have more consistency in rating.

- **Self-assessment** Coupled with the direct supervisory management evaluation, many employees are asked to self-assess their performance. This approach assists with creating a truly two-way dialogue in the evaluation interview and offers an opportunity for the employee to provide their own perception of performance. Additionally, it engages employees in a proactive means of creating goals and objectives, along with triggering a discussion about career development. Figure 4-14 provides an example of a self-assessment—both a category rating and open-ended questions to elicit a narrative commentary.

Errors in Performance Appraisal As with any subjective system, performance appraisals are subjective because they are based on people's perceptions and opinions, so there can be shortcomings. Here are the most common errors made on the part of appraisers:

- **Halo** This occurs when the employee is doing well in one area and is therefore rated high in all areas.

- **Horn** This occurs when an employee is demonstrating a strong weakness and is thus rated low in all other areas.

- **Bias** This happens when the evaluator's bias (consciously or unconsciously) influences and distorts their perspective.

- **Recency** A recency error occurs when more emphasis is placed on a recent occurrence and all earlier performances during the review period are discounted.

- **Primacy** The opposite of recency. The evaluator gives more weight and emphasis to earlier performances, discounting more recent performance.

Self-Assessment Performance Appraisal
For the appraisal period of January 1, 2014 – December 31, 2014

Employee Name: _____ EE # _____

Department: _____
Position Title: _____
Supervisor: _____
Facility: _____

Instructions:
Please complete your self-assessment evaluation and return it to your supervisor by (date)_____.
Your participation in the annual performance appraisal process helps to facilitate a comprehensive evaluation of your performance and accomplishments against set standards, goals, and objectives.

1. Describe your accomplishments and contributions since last review period.
2. Describe the activities you have participated in that have produced favorable outcomes.
3. Since your last appraisal, what new skills have you acquired?
4. Describe skills that you have increased and provide an example of their effective application on the job.
5. List new training and/or development programs you have completed.
6. Describe areas you wish to improve to enhance your job performance and capabilities.
7. State three or more job objectives for this next year and how you plan to achieve them.

Please provide your self-assessment rating in the following categories using the rating scale below.

Rating Scale:

4 - Outstanding   **3** - Very Competent or High Level   **2** - Satisfactory   **1** - Inexperienced or Improvement Needed

Category	Self-Rating
a. Technical Skills (job specific)	_____
b. Job Knowledge (up-to-date on industry, articles, and best practices)	_____
c. Quality of Work Product (comprehensive, accurate, timely)	_____
d. Productivity	_____
e. Professionalism (punctuality, attendance; conduct; responsiveness and follow through)	_____
f. Collaboration & Teamwork	_____
g. Computer Skill Applications	_____
h. Time Management & Organizational Skills	_____
i. Interpersonal Skills	_____
j. Communication Skills - Verbal/Written	_____
k. Innovation or Creativity	_____

Date: _____   Employee Signature: _____

Figure 4-14   Self-assessment performance appraisal

- **Strictness** An evaluator is reluctant to give high ratings, and their standards are higher than other evaluators.

- **Leniency** The evaluator does not provide low scores and instead gives all employees a high rating on their appraisals.

- **Central** An evaluator rates all their employees in the same range and does not take into account differences of actual performance among the group rated.

- **Contrast** The evaluator is providing an employee rating based solely on a comparison to that of another employee and not objective standards.

NOTE These common errors can be avoided with narrative format methods.

Appraisal Meeting Once you have completed the written evaluation of your employee's performance, there are some key factors to consider in planning for the success of your feedback session with the employee. Here is an agenda outline for that meeting:

- Review the purpose of the feedback meeting and the importance of the appraisal process.

- Review results or accomplishments achieved against objectives and explain how these contributed to the work group's efforts.

- Identify reasons for success and causes of problems.

- Agree on action to be taken by you and by the employee, and discuss ideas for development.

- Summarize the discussion and express confidence in the employee's ability to succeed.

Documenting Employee Performance Some performance evaluation systems have elaborate forms that must be filled in by the supervisor. Some require the employee to fill in forms because self-evaluation is part of their system of performance evaluation. Other documentation requirements are rather simple. A simple table with the information shown in Table 4-9 might suffice.

Responsibility	Objective	Result/Accomplishment	Action Plan
Produce monthly employee newsletter	Complete publication by the 15th of each month.	All 12 issues this past year were published on time.	Continue with current performance.
Respond to media inquiries about company	Respond to each inquiry within 1 day.	All but two media inquiries were handled within 24 hours.	Ask for backup if it appears the target will be missed.

Table 4-9 Example of Simple Performance Documentation

Business Results and Employee Growth

Business results and employee success are tightly linked. Employee growth can occur with chances to increase knowledge (learn something new), develop new skills (practice welding), or develop abilities that are new (enhance ability to take off and land an airplane). When a flight school's success depends on the ability of its instructors to help student pilots achieve their licenses, the level of business success cannot be separated from the level of instructor success.

Business Results   Business results can be measured in a host of possible ways. Some of the most common are profit and loss, ranking in the industry among competing companies, number of clients served during the year, and the return on investment for employee training.

Employee Growth and Rewards   In a 2013 Gallop poll,[75] it was discovered that 70 percent of American workers are "not engaged" or "actively disengaged" from their employer's mission. The 30 percent positive result matched the all-time high measured by Gallop since it began the study in 2000. Currently, 52 percent of workers in this country are not engaged in their work. Worse, another 18 percent are actively disengaged in their work. The polling experts estimate that actively disengaged employees cost the United States between $450 billion and $550 billion each year in lost productivity. And, they are more likely to steal from their companies, negatively influence their co-workers, miss workdays, and drive customers away.

The solution harkens back to the basic motivational research results. People want recognition for their work and accomplishments. They want real responsibility, and they want a chance to feel they are achieving good things on their job. All of those are possible if first the basic working conditions, policies, supervisor relationships, and compensation/benefits are acceptable.

Rewarding employees by simply and sincerely thanking them for their contributions can go a long way toward their feeling engaged in their work.

Retention

Once hired, the best business outcome is for the new hire to stick around for a while. Depending on the level of the job in your organization's structure, you can determine how long it will take for you to reach a "break-even" point for the organization to cover the cost of recruiting and hiring.

$$\text{Break-Even Point for New-Hire Retention} = \frac{\text{Monthly Value of New Hire on the Job}}{\text{Cost of Recruiting and Hiring}}$$

$$\text{Break-Even Point for New-Hire Retention} = \frac{\$5{,}000 \text{ per month}}{\$2{,}000^{*}}$$

Break-Even Point for New-Hire Retention = 2.5 months

*Cost of recruiting and hiring includes things such as search fees, HR recruiter expense (salary for time involved), and hiring manager expense (salary for interviews, paper reviews, discussions about candidates)

Business Case for Retention

While many employers say "employees are our greatest asset," in fact, actual business practices have often been inconsistent with this concept. With a relatively high unemployment rate, in many cases employers have adopted a casual attitude toward talent acquisition. In some cases, this has gone so far as to think that a focus on retention is not so important; after all, employees should be happy they are employed. This is a false premise. Companies that don't continuously focus on attracting and retaining the very best talent are companies that will soon find themselves at the "back of the line" when it comes to being a competitive force in the marketplace.

Increasing employee engagement with the goal of keeping key talent on board is not just a matter of making employees feel good. It's about challenging them, asking them to reach their peak productivity, and providing them with meaningful work in which they can take pride. In other words, a poor retention rate means that the business is losing money it could otherwise save.

Satya Radjasa, a reward practice lead with the Hay Group, outlined just how costly it can be when essential employees fly the coop. He noted that there is a series of four different expenses that come up when a valued staff member leaves. The first is the financial cost, which can be particularly high for people tasked with bringing in and keeping revenue streams, such as salespeople and account managers. The second layer of monetary impact, the cost of finding someone to fill the vacated role, can be even more dramatic. "Replacing an employee can cost from 30 to 200 percent of annual salary, depending on their level. So if 15 percent of your 'critical' people are leaving, what would the cost be?"[76]

There is always a need for good talent regardless if there is a high unemployment rate or other adverse employment factors causing a large labor pool. Companies that don't recognize this fact will soon find themselves uncompetitive in the market.

Why Retention Matters   Retention has some level of correlation with morale. If people are constantly coming and going from the payroll, lack of consistency can be a deterrent to productivity. When such things make doing a job more difficult, frustration builds, and people soon become unhappy. Having an organization where people stay for long periods of time means consistency is higher in all respects. Then there is the cost of turnover, which can be controlled or eliminated if the revolving door can be slowed or stopped altogether.

Retention Practices and Strategies

HR professionals don't generally leave retention to chance. There is usually a written plan that describes how the organization will address retention issues.

Drivers of Retention   According to Robert Half, the following are some of the contributors to retention success:[77]

- Onboarding and orientation
- Mentorship programs
- Employee compensation
- Recognition and reward systems
- Work-life balance

- Training and development
- Communication and feedback
- Dealing with change
- Fostering teamwork
- Team celebration

Retention Initiatives   Retention is something that can be addressed like other HR issues. It needs focus and definition. It needs content in business case terms. Then, it needs to be addressed with goals and action planning.

Other Retention Practices   Providing these things can go a long way toward producing better retention results:

- Clear and consistent job expectations
- Supervision
- Training and development
- Promotional opportunities
- Recognition
- Respect
- Perceived equity

Evaluating Retention

Of course, the most obvious means of evaluating a retention program is to monitor the retention rate. That can be done for the organization as a whole or for components like departments, divisions, or service units. Another method for evaluating retention programs is to conduct exit interviews with people who are leaving the payroll. The reasons why they are leaving are really important for survey input. Stay interviews are another source for information. These types of interviews survey key employees and what is causing them to stay with the organization. Analysis of those pieces of intelligence can help identify weaknesses in the employer's organization that can be fixed to bring positive improvement in retention. In the end, it is employees who decide to stay or go. It is up to us as HR professionals to influence their decision to the fullest extent possible.

Retention Measurements   Employee retention is the positive side of employee turnover. You will recall that turnover costs can be computed and over time can give an indication of the impact your retention programs may be having. So, employee turnover is a solid indicator for retention. Absenteeism is another such indicator. Employees who are absent a lot tend to have a lower sense of dedication to their work. Production levels are another indicator of retention program results. Look around, and you will find many more.

Evaluating Employee Engagement

So, you have conducted your employee survey, analyzed the results, and implemented your action plan to improve employee engagement. Ultimately, conducting another employee survey can give you more data about how far you have come in your employee engagement efforts.

Measuring Engagement

Employee engagement is measurable just like other HR variables are measurable. Remember, if you can't measure it, you shouldn't be spending time on it. There is no specific metric called *employee engagement*. We use substitutes based on indicators that employee engagement is rising or falling. Those indicators can be measured. They revolve around what happens in the workplace when employees are happy with their work versus when they are not happy with their work. Absenteeism and turnover are two key variables in that regard. Earlier in this chapter we cited nine outcomes that can represent effectiveness of an employee engagement program.

Engagement Metrics

To measure your results, you need to have a "stake in the ground" from which to stretch your tape. Before you begin the program, take a reading of things such as your absenteeism rate, turnover rate, product/supplies shrinkage, accident rates, customer metrics, quality scores, and productivity rates. Then, once implemented and given time to work, take the same measurements again. That will tell you with empirical clarity how your program is doing.

Functional Area 4—Learning & Development

Here is SHRM's BoCK definition: "Learning and Development activities enhance the knowledge, skills, abilities and other characteristics (KSAOs) and competencies of the workforce in order to meet the organization's business needs."[78]

Key Concepts

- Approaches to coaching and mentoring (e.g., formal, informal mentorship programs)
- Career development
- Developmental assessments (e.g., 360s)
- Knowledge-sharing techniques and facilitation
- Learning and development approaches and techniques (e.g., e-learning, leader development)
- Learning and development program design and implementation (e.g., ADDIE model)

- Learning evaluation (e.g., Kirkpatrick four-level model)
- Learning theories (e.g., adult learning theory)
- Needs analysis types (e.g., person, organizational, training, cost-benefit) and techniques (e.g., surveys, observations, interviews)
- Organizational analysis (e.g., performance analysis).
- Techniques for career development (e.g., career pathing, career mapping)

The following are the proficiency indicators that SHRM has identified as key concepts:

For All HR Professionals	For Advanced HR Professionals (SCP Exam)
Uses best practices to evaluate data on gaps in competencies	Designs and oversees efforts to collect data on critical gaps in competencies
Creates individual development plans (IDPs) in collaboration with supervisors and employees	Provides guidance to identify and develop critical competencies that meet the organization's talent needs
Uses best practices to develop and deliver learning and development activities that close gaps in employees' competencies and skills	Monitors the effectiveness of programs for emerging leaders and leadership development
Uses all available resources (e.g., vendors) to develop and deliver effective learning and development programs	Creates long-term organizational strategies to develop talent
Creates internal social networks to facilitate knowledge sharing among employees	Creates strategies to ensure the retention of organizational knowledge
Administers and supports programs to promote knowledge transfer	

The key function of learning and development plays a vital role for an organization. HR professionals lend their expertise and guidance to enhance the capabilities of employees, aligning their contributions with organizational goals. HR professionals will use their understanding of learning techniques and theories to assess, design, and implement training and learning activities that will develop the workforce for the organization's needs today and in their future.

Learning and Development in Today's Organizations

While the fundamental underpinnings of the learning organization remain aligned to Senge's five disciplines,[79] approaches to organizational learning are changing.

These changes are being driven by a shrinking supply of leaders, in part because of the aging of the "baby boomers," an increasing need to constantly develop and train workers to meet the demands of constantly evolving technology, a growing global marketplace, and issues of reducing turnover as employees seek environments better aligned with their personal values, such as the desire for more flexibility.

A 2014 survey by the Brandon Hall Group[80] states that more than 50 percent of the companies studied had examined their learning strategy less than twice in 5 years, rendering learning, for the most part, stagnant.

This wakeup call has propelled new interest in organizational learning techniques, the most powerful being the use of mobile learning solutions, including mobile learning apps and mobile performance web-based sites. Mobile learning approaches meet the need for global accessibility for employees and excite greater engagement. Current research reveals that only between 4 and 10 percent of companies have adopted these technologies despite the obvious advantages these would bring to attracting and retaining outstanding talent and addressing the increasing demands of the global marketplace.

Further, many companies have only nominally adopted social media tools as a way to enhance continuous learning for their employees. The most powerful of these tools—video and microblogs—are the least used! Less effective tools such as discussion forums are often thought sufficient.

Younger employees expect the latest technologies that allow for flexibility in communication; this group will ultimately be the new breed of leaders needed for sustained business success. Traditional approaches to learning cannot alone inspire employee engagement and retention.

Factors Affecting Learning and Development

Learning doesn't happen in a vacuum. Adult learning takes place in the midst of what is taking place in our personal lives, our work lives, and the stresses associated with both of those environments.

The Learning Organization and Organization Learning   Organizational learning is the process of improving actions through greater knowledge and understanding. Learning organizations are those that support the learning and development of organization members.

Talent Management   Talent management is the forecasting of future people required by organizational needs and then developing plans for meeting those needs.

Knowledge Management   Knowledge management involves actions that capture, develop, share, and effectively use organizational knowledge. According to the University of North Carolina at Chapel Hill, organizational knowledge includes on-the-job discussions, formal apprenticeship, discussion forums, corporate libraries, professional training, and mentoring programs.

Competency Models   Competency models identify the specific competencies needed in each job within the organization. They emphasize basic competencies, or those that are important to everyone in the field, and areas of expertise, which are the specialized knowledge and actions required by specific roles. Sophisticated organizations develop databases that contain standardized competency lists for each job within the organization. When searching for candidates, these competencies are used to advertise for candidates and screen applicants.

Impact of Globalization   Globalization impacts training and development for the simple reason that there is an impact on the organization's competitiveness in the marketplace. When call center staffs are better trained in language skills related to their target audience, the company can achieve a better reputation for support efforts. When sales staff is better trained in cultural expectations for personal interactions, the revenue produced can increase. These are issues that must first be identified and then addressed in the training and development plans of the organization.

Cultural Issues   Learning environments must allow for people to practice and make mistakes. Some high-context cultures place extraordinary importance on expressions and body language during interactions. People in those cultures will be hesitant to practice their learning if they are afraid of making a mistake. Convincing them that mistakes are not only accepted but also expected can take some time. It is wise to explore all cultural issues that will impact a training and development program before implementation begins.

Global Talent Management   There are global implications in talent management because there are cultural differences among global work locations. Cultural differences influence learning and development efforts. They can impact the learning process (expectations for promptness) and the achievement of training objectives (management of confrontation issues). How talent is managed is impacted by the training and development programs available for people within an organization (grow talent internally versus shopping for talent in the open job market).

Adult Learning

Adult learning principles have a single-track focus: trainability. Trainability is concerned with the readiness to learn and its associated motivation. Andragogy is the study of how adults learn, and it is based on five assumptions about learning in adults versus children. As people mature, they shift to the following:

- **Self-concept**   Their concept of self moves toward self-directed and self-sufficiency.
- **Experience**   They accumulate more experience that they tuck away and can access in learning situations.
- **Readiness to learn**   They adjust to a readiness state of learning because of developmental requirements for their stage of life and social roles (e.g., parent, homeowner).
- **Orientation to learning**   They shift from subject-focused to problem-focused learning that has immediate applicability.
- **Motivation to learn**   Motivation for learning comes from an internal source within rather than external.

As training programs are being designed and delivered, these needs of adult learning should be incorporated. Real-world examples and emphasis on how the training is going to be immediately applied is helpful.

Understanding the Adult Learner

All adults have a particular learning style that best suits their ability to learn. Understanding these learning styles will assist you in the creation of a learning environment within your organization, allowing you to accommodate each style with the delivery of training.

Additionally, as a presenter or trainer, knowing your own learning style will enhance your ability to adjust your preference of delivery methods so you won't fall into the comfort of just your style and can shift your delivery to meet the needs of all participants. Also, knowing your own learning style will assist you in your career with problem-solving, conflict management, negotiations, teamwork, and career planning.

There are three learning styles: auditory, visual, and kinesthetic.

- *Auditory learners* tend to benefit most from a lecture style. Present information by talking so they can listen. Auditory learners succeed when directions are read aloud or information is presented and requested verbally because they interpret the underlying meanings of speech through listening to tone of voice, pitch, speed, and other nuances.

- *Visual learners* rely upon a seeing presentation style: "Show me and I'll understand." These learners do best when seeing facial expressions and body language. It helps them understand content of what is being taught because they think in pictures, diagrams, charts, videos, computer training, and written directions. These students will value to-do lists, flip charts, and written notes. They need and want to take detailed notes to absorb the information.

- *Kinesthetic learners* are also called *tactile learners*. They learn via a hands-on approach and prefer to explore the physical aspects of learning. Sitting for long periods of time is difficult for these learners because they need activity in order to learn. Kinesthetic learners are most successful when totally engaged with the learning activity such as in role playing, practicing, and with topics that can use the senses of feeling and imagining.

Active Learning and Retention[81]

The National Training Laboratories in Bethel, Maine, have conducted studies on the subject of learning and retention. Table 4-10 reflects the retention rates measured for each of several different types of learning methods.

It is clear that greater retention comes with greater participation in the learning process, a lesson that should not be lost to any professional trainer.

Table 4-10
Average Learning
Retention Rates

Average Learning Retention Rates*		
Teaching Method	**Method**	**Retention**
Passive teaching	Lecture	5 percent
	Reading	10 percent
	Audiovisual	20 percent
	Demonstration	30 percent
Participatory teaching	Group discussion	50 percent
	Practice	75 percent
	Teaching others	90 percent

*Adapted from National Training Laboratories, Bethel, Maine

Obstacles to Learning

According to K. P. Cross, there are three barriers to adult participation in learning.[82]

- **Situational** Those that arise from one's situation or environment at a given point
- **Institutional** Those practices and procedures that exclude or discourage adults from participating in organized learning activities
- **Dispositional** Those related to the attitudes and self-perceptions about one self as a learner

Learning Styles

Besides having different learning preference styles, adults also learn at different rates. This is referred to as *learning curves* (see Figure 4-15). A learning curve is a graphical representation of the increase of learning (vertical axis) with the experience (horizontal axis). The following are the factors that determine how quickly an adult will learn:

- The person's motivation for learning
- The person's prior knowledge or experience

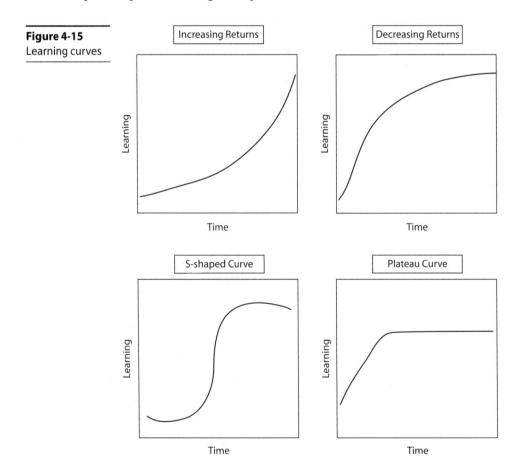

Figure 4-15
Learning curves

- The specific knowledge or task that is to be learned

- The person's aptitude and attitude about the knowledge or skill to learn

- **Increasing returns**   This is the pattern that comes into play when a person is learning something new. The start of the curve is slow while the basics are being learned. The learning increases and takes off as knowledge or skills are acquired. This curve assumes that the individual will continue to learn as time progresses. An example would be when an IT programmer needs to learn a new coding language. Learning will be slow at first until they grasp the new coding protocol, and after mastering the basics, the learning becomes easier and/or quicker as they learn more about the particular language.

- **Decreasing returns**   This pattern is when the amount of learning increases rapidly in the beginning and then the rate of learning slows down. The assumption with this learning curve is that once the learning is achieved, the learning then stops. This occurs with routine tasks learning and is the most common type of learning curve. An example is when a data entry clerk learns how to enter a sales order—the learning is complete.

- **S-shaped**   This learning curve is a blend of the increasing and decreasing returns curves. The assumption with this learning curve is that the person is learning something difficult, such as problem solving or critical thinking. Learning may be slow at the beginning until the person learning becomes familiar with the learning material, and at that point, learning takes off. The cycle continues with a slow to faster progression as new material is presented. An example of this is when a production lead is trained on new equipment, yet this equipment has not been utilized in the production of the product before. There might be a trial and error for adjustments until the new production equipment is working as expected and is adjusted to the new product. Then when another product is introduced, the equipment and process need adjusting again until everything works smoothly.

- **Plateau curve**   Just as the name suggests, learning on this curve is quick in the beginning and then flattens or plateaus. The assumption is that the plateau is not permanent and that with additional coaching, training, and support, the person learning can ramp up again. With this curve, it can be frustrating to the learner if they are not getting the support and additional training needed to master the task. An example of the plateau curve is a salesperson who has met quotas in the past, and when a new line of equipment is introduced into the product line, the salesperson is provided a minimal level of training/knowledge about it but not enough training to answer all the questions of the prospective customers. The anticipation of additional sales with the new product is not being achieved because the salesperson requires more training to pitch the new product and convince the customer to purchase.

Training and Development

All large and many medium-sized employers have one group dedicated to employee training and development. When it doesn't make good economic sense to have a staff dedicated to that function, the programs required for employee training can be purchased "by the seat" from outside consulting organizations, law firms, or industry associations.

Training Design and Development (ADDIE Model)

Originally, this model was developed by Florida State University to explain instructional systems development (ISD) for military applications. It has since been adopted by many in the world of training development. ADDIE, as it is known, stands for Analyze, Design, Develop, Implement, and Evaluate. In practice, evaluation can happen at each of the four primary stages of activity. And, modifications of revisions to the training program can result from each evaluation undertaken.

Analysis

In this phase, data is received and collected to identify where there may be a lack of productivity or gaps in desired performance. Individually, or within groups, this assessment will point the way to what specific knowledge, skills, and abilities are lacking and need to be addressed for training and development objectives.

Cultural Influences on Analysis   Culture is a two-edged sword. There is the culture of the organization that explains values and norms for behavior. Then there is the culture of each individual employee's background. People who come from America are going to see things differently from those who come from Brazil, India, or Russia. Cultural experiences may easily influence how employees behave on the job. And, it is the task of the training organization to create the ability to merge the organization's culture with employee backgrounds to accomplish the organizational objectives.

Design

Training design is the response to gap analysis performed in the first stage of the ADDIE model. The initial information from the assessment phase is decided upon for course content, delivery methods, and tactics for delivery. The result is an outline of what the training design will be and the order of presentation.

Goals and Objectives   Each training effort should begin with a statement of objectives. These objectives should answer the question, "What will participants be able to do when they have completed the training?" Identifying those specific goals will enable the subsequent creation of training content, including experiential exercises.

Cultural Influences on Design   Culture can play an important role in design of training programs when it is known that a large portion of the training participant population will be from a specific cultural background. Customer service representative training may need to explain the reasons why customers in the United States want to have specific appointments made for repair technician visits. In other cultures, specific appointments are not an expectation.

Development

Development of training materials is the phase when pencil meets the paper and actual training materials and coursework are created. Courses and training materials may already be available off the shelf, or a customized or modified creation may occur. For training that is highly specific and customized to the organization, a course may be developed from scratch to fit the specific objectives to reach the desired outcome, such as in a new product launch for a product that has never before existed. An example might be the new Apple Watch.

Learning Activities   Development can produce training that makes use of lectures, small-group exercises, large-group exercises, individual study and feedback, various audiovisual contributions, and other such techniques for getting participants involved with the learning experience.

Training Delivery   There is no one perfect teaching method for every situation. As a matter of fact, the method that should be used will depend upon the training circumstances and the material being covered. There are teacher-centered instructional methods and learner-centered instructional methods. Instructional methods are the manner in which learning materials are presented to students.

Self-Directed Study   Self-directed study, called *auto didacticism,* involves the learner making decisions about what to study and when to study it. Often, people who are self-studying will seek instruction from experts, teachers, parents, friends, or other community members.

Instructor-Led Training   Sometimes called classroom training, this model requires an instructor at the "head of the class" presenting learning material and leading learning exercises.

On-the-Job Training   Learning how to perform specific job functions or how to use equipment and tools required on the job is done on a day-to-day basis in this form of training. Often, on-the-job training involves a supervisor or co-worker showing and then supervising a new worker as tasks are learned and practiced.

Blended Learning   Blended learning involves use of both classroom instruction and computer-based instruction programs. This has become a more popular form of learning since the dawn of the twenty-first century brought an expanded array of computer-based training programs.

Learning Tools   Devices and systems used during the learning process are referred to as *learning tools*. They rely on computer technology.

E-learning   E-learning involves the use of electronic systems in the learning process. Computers and computer-based instructional programs are referred to collectively by the term *e-learning*.

Learning Portals   These are web sites that act as repositories for training materials. They may be reference materials or entire training courses.

Learning Management Systems   As defined by Wikipedia, learning management systems (LMS) are "software applications for the administration, documentation, tracking, reporting and delivery of electronic educational technology education courses or training programs."

Webinars These are Internet-based seminars conducted using an instructor presentation, usually accompanied by visual aids such as slide shows using PowerPoint or another similar program.

Mobile Learning Mobile learning involves the use of tablet computers and smartphones to access training materials or course content along with reference materials important to the learning process. They can be used anywhere there is a phone or Internet connection.

Virtual-World Simulations As applied to the work environment, this type of learning is done by using replications of real-world conditions. Flight simulators are a good example. They offer what appears to be a real airplane cockpit with all the controls and gauges. Computers can be used to simulate actual flying conditions and interject scenarios that should best be practiced in training rather than when the plane is actually flying.

Social Media Internet sites such as Facebook, Instagram, YouTube, LinkedIn, and Twitter, among others, can be learning tools. These services allow the posting of documents, videos, and photos so students can share information and seek feedback about inquiries.

Cultural Influences on Development This is the extent to which culture plays a role in vocational training as it is related to values, expectations, and norms. It has been said that adult development (training) is influenced to a large degree by the cultural background of each individual participant. An example is an expectation for promptness. Training participants are expected to be prompt in their American classroom attendance, yet the same is not always true in other cultures.

Implementation

Once training is designed and constructed, the next phase involves putting it to use.

Pilot Testing This involves a presentation of the training program, with all materials collected to support the program. Someone is designated to observe and take notes about what portions of the program worked well and where there were problems with the materials or presentation. It is difficult for instructors to fill this role, so it is normally filled by the training developer/writer or someone else who is versed in training development and delivery.

Content Revisions Following the pilot test, there is a review of the problems that occurred in the program. Those instances where changes are needed can be identified and changes made so the problems will not occur in future applications of the training.

Translation and Interpretation When training will be offered to multilingual audiences, it is necessary to translate the materials into languages to be used. It is also important to review those translations to be sure the interpretations of the wording used will be acceptable and appropriate. Words and terms used in one culture are not always acceptable in a different culture.

Instructor Selection Instructor selection is identification of the person who will lead the training program. What level of instructor skills are required to present the training successfully? Are facilitation skills more important than skills reading instructions? Candidate recruiting, screening, and selection are all part of this step in the process.

Logistical Considerations   What facilities are required? Will training need to be held in a classroom? Will there be Internet connections required? Will the instructor be needing a computer? What about distribution of course materials? All of these fall into the logistical category for consideration.

Announcing, Implementing, and Supporting   Once the program is prepared and ready for implementation, it must be announced to the target population so people who need the training can be selected for participation. There are issues of participant applications and registration to be handled. And, there are support issues associated with tracking attendance during the program, logging grades, and staffing of any training exercise that is critical to the program.

Evaluation

Evaluation means grading. There may or may not be pass-fail conditions for the training program, but there will almost always be a requirement to track some form of evaluation for participants.

Evaluation Methods—Kirkpatrick's Four Levels[83]   Donald Kirkpatrick was a professor emeritus at the University of Wisconsin. He first published his Four-Level Training Evaluation Model in 1959. The model was updated in 1975 and again in 1994 when he published his "Evaluating Training Programs." The following are the four levels of evaluation he identified:

- **Reaction**   Measuring how participants react to the training
- **Learning**   Measuring how much a participant's knowledge has increased as a result of the training
- **Behavior**   Measuring how participant behavior has changed several weeks following the training
- **Results**   Measuring the outcomes, benefits, or final results of the training (e.g., increased retention, increased production, higher morale, reduced waste, increased sales, higher quality ratings)

Computing the Return on Investment of Training   Return on investment (ROI) is determined by the following:

- Determine the total cost of training (e.g., training development cost, resources cost, salaries of instructors, and participants).
- Determine the total value of the benefits achieved by the training (e.g., increased production, lower waste).
- Determine the net benefit by subtracting the cost from the benefits.
- Determine the percentage of benefits over cost by dividing the cost into the net benefits.
- Multiply the result by 100 to restate the result as a percentage.

Total Dollar Benefits − Cost of Training = Net Benefits
(Net Benefits / Costs) × 100 = ROI of Training

Career Development

Career development is the lifelong individual process that involves planning, managing, learning, and transitions at all ages and stages in work life. In organizations, it is an organized approach used to match employee goals with the business's current and future needs. An individual's work-related preferences and needs continuously evolve throughout life's phases. At the same time, organizations are also continuously adapting to economic, political, and societal changes.

Managing Career Development

There are two processes in career development: career planning and career management. With career planning, the focus is on the individual. Career management has a focus on the organization.

In career planning, assessing an individual's skills, talents, experiences, and potential abilities occurs to give direction to a person's career. HR professionals typically assist with these activities, but many self-assessment instruments are available online for individuals to use.

With career management, this involves implementing and monitoring employee career paths at an organizational level. The individual employee is actively involved; however, the organization is typically providing the development programs and opportunities associated with internal career progression opportunities and succession planning. The intention with career management from the organizational perspective is to assist with aligning existing workforce talent with new business objectives, to create an atmosphere of positive morale, and to retain needed talent.

Roles in Career Development

It is not just the individual employee and HR involved in career development. The direct line of management and the organization's leaders have a role to play, too.

Individuals bear the primary responsibility for their own career. Today, individuals are required to be proactive in planning their career progression and not rely on an organization to direct their career path. Being keenly aware of current assessed traits and skills, along with needs for increased knowledge, skill, and experience associated with the individual's career ambitions, is largely the responsibility of an individual employee. Figure 4-16 shows the stages of an individual's career development.

That said, managers and supervisors perform four roles in assisting employees with their career development.

- **Coach**   Listening, clarifying
- **Appraiser**   Giving feedback, clarifying performance standards
- **Advisor**   Suggesting options, making recommendations
- **Referral agent**   Consulting with employees on action plans and linking them to organizational resources

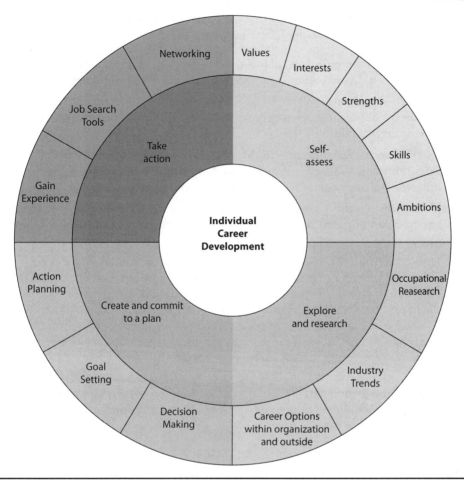

Figure 4-16   Individual career development

Cultural Influences on Career Development

"There are some common career-related issues faced by diverse populations. Their career choices may be constrained by socialization, access to guidance and assessment, tracking into certain fields, societal and self-stereotypes, isolation from networks, and early schooling experiences. Barriers to career development may include lack of developmental feedback or mentors, discrimination in promotion/transfer, tokenism, hostility, plateauing, less access to training, perceived isolation, stress, or self-imposed performance pressure."[84]

Forms of Career Development

Many large organizations create full-fledged career development programs. Some will be self-paced and require individual employees to opt in, and some are created with particular objectives in mind, such as management development programs, where high-potential employees are invited to participate. A typical model for a career development program will include the following stages:

- **Occupational preparation** This stage is where occupations are assessed, an occupation is decided upon, and necessary education and skill levels are pursued.

- **Organizational entry** This is the stage where a person obtains and decides on job offers from organizations they want to work for or internal changes within a current organization.

- **Early career establishment** In this phase, an employee learns a new job, along with organizational norms and rules for fitting into the job, company, or industry. An employee gains work experience and career skills.

- **Midcareer** In this phase, an employee evaluates their career objectives, with an understanding of their current life situation, and may choose to shift career direction.

- **Late-career** In this last phase of career development, employees focus on retirement planning. Their choices in this phase are hugely different than the other career phases. They are more concerned with life considerations such as the hours they want to work and the extra effort they may want to provide, or what work assignments may cause additional mental stress. Climbing a career progression ladder is not normally in their career plans at this phase, yet mentoring employees in early career phases would be.

 NOTE By understanding the focus of each stage, HR professionals are better equipped to prepare and manage the transitions that employees will experience.

Employee Self-Assessment Tools Coupled with the direct supervisory management evaluation, many employees are asked to self-assess their performance. This approach assists with creating a truly two-way dialogue in the evaluation interview and offers an opportunity for the employee to provide their own perception of their performance. Additionally, it engages employees in a proactive means of creating goals and objectives, along with triggering a discussion about career development. Figure 4-14 provides an example of a self-assessment—both a category rating along with open-ended questions to elicit a narrative commentary.

Apprenticeships These are programs that allow untrained individuals to enter a trade or profession through formal on-the-job training, classroom training, and coaching programs. They are usually followed by journey-level status once conditions for ending the apprenticeship have been met. Journey-level traditionally allows an individual to move from location to location or employer to employer within the trade, acknowledged as a skilled technician or professional. Trade unions often offer apprenticeship programs for electricians, plumbers, carpenters, and the like.

Job Rotation, Enlargement, and Enrichment   Job rotation involves an individual spending a short time in each of several job positions. The objective is to gain experience in each type of work but not to become an expert in any of them. Rotating jobs as an engineering technician, for example, might involve some time working on projects in civil engineering, electrical engineering, or mechanical engineering. Job enlargement involves taking on more work of the same type, perhaps additional client or customer assignments, while performing the same type of work for each one. Job enrichment involves taking on added responsibilities, expanding the job assignment's impact. As an example, a traffic enforcement police officer could take on the responsibility for investigating traffic accidents within a given geography.

Projects, Committees, and Team Participation   Assignments to special projects, committees, and designated teams can provide excellent opportunities for growth in a career. These types of experiences can provide developmental opportunities helping an individual get ready for promotions or other assignments with greater responsibility. These are usually temporary assignments. And, they offer exposure to parts of the organization or responsibilities that the individual will need if they will be able to succeed in the next job assignment.

Internal Mobility   There are often opportunities within an employer's organization that can be used for employee career development. They include the following:

- **Promotions**   Promotions are usually defined in government regulations as a job move that involves an increase in job responsibility and an increase in compensation. Employers sometimes take issue with that definition and create their own.

- **Demotions**   When an employee has difficulty performing well at a given level of responsibility, it is sometimes necessary to reduce that responsibility level by moving them to a lower-level job. Demotions are also frequently involved in the disciplinary process as an option that precedes termination of employment.

- **Transfers**   Transfers are normally lateral movements from one job to another at the same level of responsibility and compensation.

- **Relocations and international assignments**   Relocations are geographical movements from one job to another that can help career development by providing experiences that will be necessary when the incumbent is promoted to a new level of responsibility. Relocations are required because the job assignments are not offered at the current work location. International assignments are also career enhancing because they offer exposure to new cultures and new employment challenges.

- **Dual-career ladders**   Dual-ladder career development programs allow mobility for employees without requiring that they be placed into the managerial enclave. Mostly associated with technical, medical, engineering, and scientific occupations, this type of program is a way to advance employees who are not interested in pursuing a management track. These individuals exhibit one or more of the following characteristics:

- Have substantial technical or professional expertise beyond the basic levels
- Have licensure or required credentials
- Are known for innovation
- May or may not be well-suited for management or leadership roles

An objective within a dual-ladder development program is to increase complexity and value to the organization, enabling the organization to increase employee compensation to improve employee retention and satisfaction. Lateral movement may occur within a dual-ladder program such as team membership, internal consultative roles, mentorships, or larger facility rotation. Figure 4-17 shows an example of a dual-ladder career path.

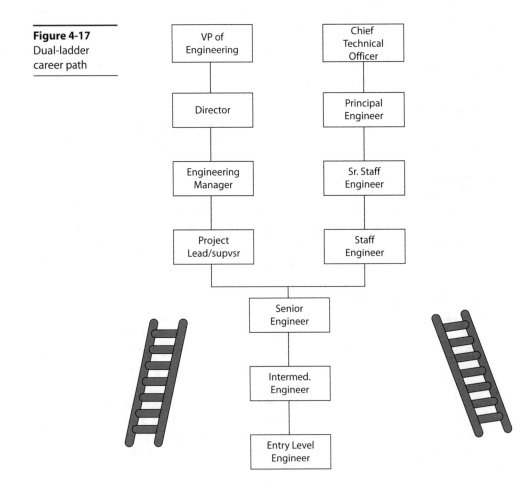

Figure 4-17
Dual-ladder
career path

Individual Coaching/Counseling   When an individual is identified as someone who could advance to the executive level, it is sometimes helpful to provide individual coaching and/or counseling to them. This process can assist people in identifying their developmental needs and providing the skill development and practice necessary for achieving the desired level of performance.

Mentoring   Assignments that involve mentoring other individuals offer involvement with responsibility for the success of other people within the organization. Supporting those who seek to develop their job skills and helping them advance can be a growth experience for the mentor.

Universities, Colleges, Associations, Continuing Education Programs   There are countless programs at universities, colleges, and continuing education curricula that can support employee developmental efforts. It is possible for employers to encourage participation, with the employee underwriting the cost of such programs or the employer sponsoring employees in such programs. There are degree programs that are usually long-term. And, there are certificate programs that generally tend to be shorter-term. Executives will sometimes participate in advanced training for a few weeks or months to gain exposure to cutting-edge theories and methods of management. Networking among executives can be advantageous in itself, offering valuable contacts at other employer organizations that can be accessed later.

Career Development Trends

The single biggest career trend in 2015 is that employees are taking responsibility for their own career development. What used to be left to managers and executive committees is now firmly planted in the lap of each individual employee. Employers are looking for problem-solvers. Volunteering to work with a difficult major customer to satisfy their needs can be a significant career development step. Things don't move in traditional paths anymore. Breaking ground with new jobs, task force membership, and difficult job assignments are all part of career development efforts for individuals who can solve problems for the employer.

Some contemporary trends in career development include the following:

- **Multiple jobs and careers**   Moving from one specialty to another to develop experience
- **Greater individual responsibility**   Moving from one job to another to accept greater responsibility (e.g., managing a small hotel to managing a large hotel)
- **Nontraditional employment**   Work in jobs that have been traditionally done by the opposite sex (e.g., airline pilot, nurse, secretary, truck driver)
- **Temporary contract and contingent work**   Developing experience through brief job assignments in various, untried subject areas or levels of responsibility

Developing Leaders

Leadership skills can be developed within existing employees. People can be taught to be leaders. Here is how that happens.

Leadership Development

Traditional leadership development programs have not been replaced. They have been polished and modified. Key to leadership success is that other people are willing to follow.

Organizational Perspective   From the employer perspective, leaders are essential to ensure the success of the organizational mission(s). Someone decides what the objective is for the current period. It might be a financial objective (returning 7 percent to stockholders through dividend distribution) or an organizational growth objective (opening a new branch in Chicago). With the objective in sight, leaders are needed to create the atmosphere for other people to provide support to the collective effort aimed at reaching the objective. The key to leadership is that others willingly volunteer their efforts each day.

Individual Perspective   From the individual perspective, leadership can be developed by identifying someone senior in the organization who can provide good counsel and advice as a mentor. Seek out and establish that mentor relationship. Solicit feedback and suggestions both before and after decisions are made and plans implemented.

Not all executives are successful, however. For a study on what can sometimes happen, refer to *Why Smart Executives Fail* by Sydney Finkelstein. It includes "Seven Habits of Spectacularly Unsuccessful People."[85]

HR's Role   HR professionals can facilitate leader development by coordinating mentoring programs, establishing and monitoring succession plans, and identifying and fulfilling training needs for employees identified as needing leadership development.

Obstacles to Leadership Development   The single biggest obstacle to leadership development is lack of senior management support for the effort. When senior executives fail to actively support the program, lower-level managers and supervisors will recognize it as having a lower level of importance to the organization. In the end, what the boss wants to have happen will happen. Should leadership development not be on that list of what the boss wants, then leadership development will not happen.

Emotional Intelligence and Leadership Development   According to the American Society for Training and Development (ASTD), leaders "need to be self-aware of their own emotions and clearly understand their strengths and weaknesses. This understanding helps them stay in control of situations and avoid emotionally charged behaviors and decisions."[86]

Assessing Leadership Development Needs

The Center for Creative Leadership has offered some insight into competencies associated with organizational leadership (see Table 4-11).[87]

Assessment Tools   There are a wide range of assessment tools available for determining leadership skills.

Inventories   Inventories are testing devices that measure the quantity of leadership skills an individual displays. Questions pose hypothetical stories and ask the individual to rank responses or identify the most appropriate response in those circumstances. Inventories can be scored and scores compared to successful "norm groups." Multiple media presentations can be used in conducting inventory analysis. Written materials and video and audio

Leading the Organization	Leading Others	Leading Yourself
• Being a quick learner • Change management • Decisiveness • Strategic perspective • Strategic planning	• Building collaborative relationships • Compassion and sensitivity • Confronting problem employees • Employee development • Inspiring commitment • Leading employees • Participative management • Putting people at ease • Respect for differences	• Balancing personal life and work • Career management • Composure • Culturally adaptable • Self-awareness • Taking initiative

Table 4-11   Selected Leadership Competencies

recordings can present various scenarios for consideration. These tools are usually developed by psychologists who have studied the creation of these measurement devices.

Leadership Work Samples, Simulations, and Assessment Centers   The following are examples:

- **Assessment centers**   Actual work examples can be helpful in identifying leadership skills and skill development needs. They offer the individual easy-to-use references to understand what has yet to be done in terms of development.

  Simulations are quite like assessment center exercises. They construct artificial circumstances in which the individual must react to organizational situations. By practicing leadership approaches to these simulated conditions, the individual can gain feedback about successful behaviors and polish those behaviors that have positive outcomes.

  The most sophisticated assessment tool is the skill assessment center. Developed by American Telephone and Telegraph, Inc., in the 1960s, it is based on the Management Progress Study that began in the 1950s and continued for more than 30 years. In an assessment center, candidates are placed in situations where they must solve problems individually and within group settings. During group exercises, observing experts can identify leadership behaviors that are exhibited by each candidate and compare those behaviors with those seen in a control group of successful management people at the same level in the organization. On the other end of the spectrum of assessment tools is the questionnaire that attempts to assess skills through question-and-answer format. There are still other tools that fall within that range including professional assessment by psychologist observation. There are advantages and disadvantages for each.

- **Situational judgment tests (SJTs)**   Situational judgment tests are like inventories in that they offer hypothetical scenarios to individuals and ask for choices of various possible reactions to those scenarios. The SHRM exam includes SJTs for its behavioral competencies.

- **Assessment centers and simulations**   Assessment centers and simulations require a staff of professionals who have studied norm group reactions to the exercises candidates will be asked to participate in. After establishing a reference for the norm group behaviors, the staff of observers can identify behaviors used by the candidate group and compare them to the norm.

Emotional Intelligence Tools   There are three basic types of tools for determining emotional intelligence. Self-assessment is a skill list developed by introspection of the individual. This is usually accomplished by following a prepared list of considerations. Other individual assessment is a list of skills and needs developed by someone else who observes the individual interacting in different real-life circumstances. This can be a boss, supervisor, or mentor. A formal assessment center is usually accomplished in a formal setting with other candidates and requires a professional staff member trained in observation and feedback techniques.

Leadership Development Strategies

Successful leadership development strategies are aligned closely with business strategies. When organizations build a leadership development program that supports, trains, and then selects people who drive their business strategy, the organization thrives. There are no mixed messages. Everyone at all levels hears the same thing. Business strategies are paramount, and good leaders understand that and support them.

Leadership Development Methods   There are many methods for developing leadership skills. Here are some of the more common approaches.

More-Challenging Assignments   Stretching individual high-potential employees with extra responsibilities is a good way to expand skill levels. When the assignments require leadership skills, mentorship programs, coaching, and formal training can be just what is needed to smooth the way to success in the tasks.

Risk Management   Today risks can be salient in financial regulation, markets, and products. There are also risks in employee management, industry evolution, and technological advances. Offering opportunities to lead an organizational effort to address one or more of these risks can result in skill enhancement.

Hardship Testing   The famous American management consultant, Peter Drucker, said there are five types of hardship that can lead to enhanced leadership skills if the manager or executive experiencing them is successful in overcoming the hardship. Career setbacks can teach self-awareness, organizational politics, and identification of what one really wants to do. Personal trauma can teach sensitivity to others, coping with events beyond one's control, perseverance, and recognition of limits. Business mistakes and failures can teach how to handle relationships with humility and how to handle mistakes. Problem employees can teach how to stand firm and improve confrontational skills. Downsizing can teach coping skills, recognition of what's important, and organizational politics.

Real-Life Problem-Solving in a Controlled Environment When problem-solving becomes a process that allows people to grow and get better, the organization has strong leadership. When problem-solving involves chaos, there is likely a large leadership deficiency. Exposing individuals to controlled situations and coaching them through the problem-solving process in the leadership role can give the real-world experience that cannot be totally replicated any other way.

Training Training programs can improve leadership skills, particularly for those people who are just beginning their formal learning experience on the subject. Training exercises, classroom experiences, and personal interactions with other learners are all helpful in the skill development process.

Action Learning Leadership Action learning involves defining the problem, taking action to solve the problem, and then analyzing the results of that action. It is a particularly good method of leadership development when the problem-solving is being done by a team.

Global Considerations in Leadership Development

If getting work done through the efforts of others is the definition of leadership, then that process is complicated considerably when international efforts cause multiple cultures to participate in that process. Working across cultural boundaries and in synchronization with other people who have different ways of getting things done can cause steep inclines in the effort to accomplish goals.

Global Competence and Leadership Development For organizations with a presence in multiple countries, cultural impacts are present every time someone from headquarters issues a new directive. Those instructions just may not be accepted well in remote locations where cultures understand the directive differently from the understanding at headquarters. It is critical that leaders consider all of those cultural influences when attempting to solve problems and steer organizational movement. Without competence in global management and leadership skills needed to gain cooperation, and ultimately success with the problem's solution, it will be difficult or impossible.

Globalization and Leadership Development Programs Traditionally, international companies held key decision-making at headquarters in the home country. It was home-country executives who ascended the executive ladder. Candidates, if there even were some, from other countries and cultures were not provided an opportunity to participate in the selection process. That worked well when foreign markets were just developing.

These days, there is a move to recognize that in developed markets, it is critical to accept cultural influence in the decision-making process. "Developing global leaders with cultural sensitivities and collaborative skills requires greater focus on emotional intelligence, self-awareness, and empowerment than on traditional management skills."[88]

Culturally Related Challenges According to the Center for Creative Leadership,[89] there are six challenges faced by multicultural, international organizations.

- Developing managerial effectiveness
- Inspiring others
- Developing employees
- Leading a team
- Guiding change
- Managing internal stakeholders and politics

There are more similarities in leader challenges from one country to another than there are differences.

Functional Area 5—Total Rewards

Here is SHRM's BoCK definition: "Total Rewards refers to the design and implementation of compensation systems and benefit packages, which employers use to attract and retain employees."[90]

Key Concepts

- Approaches to gathering compensation and benefits-related market and competitive intelligence (e.g., remuneration surveys)
- Basic accounting and financial knowledge for managing payroll (e.g., total compensation statements)
- Compensation philosophies
- Compensation plans for common and special workforce groups (e.g., domestic, global/expatriate, executive, sales)
- Job evaluation for determining compensation and benefits
- Leave plans and approaches (e.g., vacation, holiday, sick, paid/unpaid leave)
- Other benefits (e.g., disability, unemployment insurance, employee assistance programs, family, flex, wellness programs)
- Other compensation (e.g., deferred compensation, direct/indirect compensation, stock options)
- Pay practices and issues (e.g., pay increases, base pay, pay levels, banding, variable pay)
- Remuneration and labor market data collection and interpretation
- Remuneration data analysis (e.g., comparable worth, determining compensation, internal alignment, external competitiveness)
- Retirement planning and benefits (e.g., pension plans)
- Total rewards metrics and benchmarks

The following are proficiency indicators that SHRM has identified as key concepts:

For All HR Professionals	All Advanced HR Professionals (SCP Exam)
Collects, compiles, and interprets compensation and benefits data from various sources (e.g., remuneration surveys, labor market trends)	Designs and oversees organizational compensation and benefits philosophies, strategies, and plans that align with the organization's strategic direction and talent needs
Implements appropriate pay, benefit, incentive, separation, and severance systems and programs	Designs and oversees executive compensation approaches that directly connect individual performance to organizational success
Complies with best practices for all laws and regulations governing compensation and benefits	Ensures the internal equity of compensation systems
Differentiates between government-mandated, government-provided, and voluntary benefit approaches	
Conducts accurate job evaluations to determine appropriate compensation	

Compensation and benefits plans play a key role that help attract and retain talent. HR professionals are responsible for the development and application of an organization's compensation and benefits philosophy, along with benchmarking to determine their competitiveness in the marketplace. A total rewards program will integrate and maximize monetary compensation, benefits, and other forms of compensation that are ideally designed to retain top talent. Total reward encompasses direct and indirect remuneration approaches that employers use to attract, recognize, and retain workers.

Total Rewards and Organizational Strategy

Compensation and benefits are the lifeblood of the employment relationship between the worker and the employer. But this relationship reaches beyond the scope of compensation and benefits alone, including recognition programs and assorted fringe benefits; thus, *total rewards* has become a popular term that best defines this aspect of the employment relationship.

Direct compensation, simply referred to as *compensation,* as a strategic objective, significantly impacts all of the other HR functions, including staffing, performance evaluations, training and development, and employee relations, and these HR functions likewise influence compensation. Compensation affects organizational processes, job satisfaction, productivity, and turnover. Compensation must be viewed not only on the basis of what is legal and motivating but also on the ethical basis of what is fair and just.

Key terms used in this section include the following:

- **Total rewards**   Includes six elements (compensation, benefits, work-life effectiveness, recognition, performance management, and talent development) that collectively define an organization's strategy to attract, motivate, retain, and engage employees.[91]

- **Benefits**   Benefits in kind (also called *fringe benefits* and *perks*) include various types of nonwage compensation paid to employees in addition to their normal wages and salaries. Examples of these benefits include housing (employer-provided or employer-paid), group insurance (health, dental, life, etc.), disability income protection, retirement benefits, daycare, tuition reimbursement, sick leave (paid and nonpaid), vacation (paid and nonpaid), Social Security, profit sharing, funding of education, and other specialized benefits.

- **Compensation**   This includes all of the rewards earned by employees in return for their labor. It includes direct financial compensation consisting of pay received in the form of wages, salaries, bonuses, and commissions provided at regular and consistent intervals.

- **Perquisites**   Colloquially referred to as "perks," these are benefits of a more discretionary nature. Often, perks are given to employees who are doing notably well and/or have seniority. Common perks are company cars, company-paid mobile devices, free refreshments, leisure activities on work time (golf, etc.), allowances for meals, and—when multiple choices exist—first choice of job assignments and vacation scheduling.

- **Incentives**   These are systems of rewarding success and effort in the workplace by allowing employees to earn awards or recognition.

Developing a Total Rewards Strategy

Employers want to attract and retain good, qualified workers who are motivated to a degree of high productivity, but employers must make compensation decisions with competing pressures. Simply paying more or providing better company benefits may make some employees happy but will, in the long term, raise labor costs and make the company less competitive.

A total rewards strategy can be described as a four-step process that consists of assessment, design, implementation, and evaluation. A number of factors affect the planning and design of a total rewards strategy. As an example, if the organization operates in a union environment, the planning and design elements will be affected by collective bargaining requirements. Important HR competencies needed to develop a successful total rewards strategy include excellent interpersonal and communication skills.

Assessment   The assessment stage focuses on a competent evaluation of the organization's current compensation and benefits programs, if any. In particular, attention is paid to the effectiveness of existing programs in fulfilling their purposes in an effective manner. Employee surveys are an important mechanism to develop good information regarding employee attitudes and opinions. Surveys typically address employee pay, benefits and growth, and development issues. During this stage, current policies and practices are also examined. An important result of the assessment phase is producing an assessment report that includes information on the current status of existing compensation and benefits coupled with recommendations for changes based on the assessment findings. Ultimately, the assessment report should address the following:

- Who should be eligible for coverage?
- What behaviors of value should be rewarded?

- What type of rewards will do the best job?
- How will changes, if any, be funded?

Design   The objective of this phase is to identify the best reward strategies for the organization based on the conclusions of the assessment report. To reach this objective, a team of HR leaders and senior management should be taxed with the job of identifying the best combination of pay and benefits needed to accomplish the goals stated in the assessment report. In addition to the direct pay and benefits possibilities, the project team responsible for the design effort should also explore additional benefits such as flexible work scheduled, time off, and similar options as well as personal development opportunities that can be offered such as training and development opportunities.

Implementation   Typically, HR is heavily involved in this phase. A new rewards program needs information planning and material describing the new program's features and benefits. In many cases, additional training will be required. The success of needed changes to an organization's rewards programs is largely dependent on the image that is communicated to the organization's workforce.

Evaluation   An organization's ultimate responsibility is to measure the success of its new rewards programs. Even the best of plans will often require additional attention. Slight modifications may be necessary, but, barring any new unforeseen elements, diligently following these four steps should ensure a successful result.

Objectives of a Total Rewards Strategy

All organizations need to have their compensation and benefits systems support their organization's mission and strategy. Although the degree of sophistication may vary, a good total rewards strategy should hold to some basic principles. That is, in the face of competitive market pressures, all pay decisions should have the following attributes:

- **Be legal**   They must be consistent with numerous federal, state, and local laws.
- **Be adequate**   They must be large enough to attract qualified employees to join the organization and stay.
- **Be motivating**   They should provide sufficient incentives to motivate employees to perform effectively.
- **Be equitable**   Employees should feel that their compensation is internally equitable relative to other employees in the organization and externally equitable relative to employees doing similar work in other organizations.
- **Provide security**   Employees want to feel that their monthly income is secure and predictable. They need to feel that their pay is somewhat insulated from changes in employment, profitability, individual performance, and personal health.
- **Be cost-benefit effective**   The organization must administer its compensation system efficiently and have the financial resources to support it on a continuing basis.

Organizational Mission and Strategy Larger and more mature organizations generally have a written business plan that outlines the organization's mission and strategy. Normally, the compensation and benefits system are an outgrowth of the organization's business plan in these organizations.

A basic principle is that a business must generate sufficient revenue to cover its expenses. When the demand for workers exceeds the supply, there is an upward pressure on pay levels. The degree of competition, the level of market demand, and each industry's overall characteristics influence compensation and benefits programs. Other factors such as the organization's lifecycle stage also play a role. The bottom line is that the objective is to design and implement a total rewards plan that will attract the right people to the right jobs at the right time and the right place at the right cost.

Organizational Culture Regardless of the other factors, a compensation system must fit the organization's culture. By "organizational culture," we mean a system of shared assumptions, values, and beliefs that governs how people behave in organizations. Every organization has a distinct value for each of these characteristics, which, when combined, defines the organization's unique culture. Typically, organizations take one of two basic approaches toward their employees.

Entitlement-Oriented These companies promote a caring, protective feeling and want employees to feel they are part of the family. Sometimes called a *fairness orientation,* or emphasis on people, these companies place a high value on how their decisions affect the people in their organizations. For these companies, it is important to treat their employees with respect and dignity. These organizations feel that employees are entitled to benefits such as health care, employee assistance, or disability insurance as a condition of employment. They place less emphasis on individual contributions and more emphasis on the success of the organization as a whole.

Contribution-Oriented These companies are more performance driven. They put greater emphasis on job performance and the contributions of individual employees. They focus on results but not so much on how the results are achieved. A company that instructs its sales force to do whatever it takes to get sales orders has a culture that places a high value on outcomes. Their compensation systems emphasize performance-based pay, incentives, and shared responsibility for benefits.

Although few organizations have a compensation system based solely on a performance approach, the trend is moving further from an entitlement approach and closer to a performance approach. Most organizations have compensation systems with elements associated with both approaches.

Workforce A rewards program must consider the type of workforce involved. An organization with a large number of entry-level or unskilled workers will likely have a significantly different total rewards program than an organization with mostly high-level, skilled professionals. In either case, an important tool used to measure employee attitudes and opinions is a survey.

Equity Equity is fairness and impartiality toward all concerned, based on the principles of even-handed dealing. Equity implies giving as much advantage, consideration, or latitude to one party as it is given to another. Along with economy, effectiveness, and efficiency, equity is essential for ensuring that the extent and costs of funds, goods, and services are fairly divided among their recipients.

Pay Equity   Pay equity is not equal access to jobs offered by an employer. This is called *employment equity,* which means that women, men, and minorities have equal opportunity when applying for jobs. Nor is pay equity the fact that a person working in company X is being paid $2,000 less than the person of the same gender sitting nearby for exactly the same job. This is called *internal equity* and is unrelated to employment equity. So, what does *pay equity* mean? At first, it meant as equal pay for equal work. However, as organizations tried to achieve pay equity, they quickly realized that it was difficult to compare the same two jobs and their compensation since each one comprised a different set of tasks. The difficulties experienced by organizations with this approach prompted the government to adopt the following definition: "Equal pay for different but equivalent work."

This change ensures that there is no sexist bias in the comparison of compensation so that predominantly female jobs are paid equally to predominantly male jobs of equivalent value. The change also enabled comparisons between jobs of different types but equivalent in terms of tasks. An example of this would be to compare trade and service jobs with clerical jobs of equivalent value.

Internal Equity   Internal equity is a situation that results when people feel that performance fairly determines the pay for each individual with a certain job or that relative difficulty results in appropriate differences in pay rates between jobs. Worker dissatisfaction may arise when internal equity principles aren't met. Internal equity studies analyze the nature of a particular position including skill, effort, responsibility, and working conditions. The internal equity study determines whether there is "pay equity" between like positions. This study ensures compliance with the Federal Equal Pay Act and state laws, thereby avoiding potential lawsuits. Additionally, an internal equity study makes good managerial sense in that employee morale, and consequently productivity, will increase.

External Equity   An effective employee compensation system must balance two factors: worker motivation and labor costs. In designing a company's pay plan, you must consider external equity as well as internal equity. External equity refers to comparisons with other competitive pay structures. An employer's goal should be to pay what is necessary to attract, retain, and motivate a sufficient number of qualified employees. This requires a base pay program that pays competitively. Among others, internal data such as turnover rates and exit interviews can be helpful in determining the competitiveness of pay rates.

As is true for internal equity perceptions, global pay experts indicate that employee external pay fairness perceptions mostly focus on base pay, career development opportunities, and merit increases. Personal recognition perceptions were not as prevalent as base pay, career development, and merit pay. This is probably because it is not easy in the international marketplace for most employees to compare what is done in the employee's own organization compared to other organizations.[92]

Pay Strategies   Employers compete with other employers whose organizations that have similar products and services employ workers with the same experience and skills and employ workers in the same geographical area. Typically, pay strategies are chosen

PART II

Pay Strategy	Description
Lag market	Characteristic of organizations that experience moderate to high turnover in their market. Labor costs are controlled by setting initial pay rates lower than the surrounding market. Examples: Janitorial, security, and fast-food employers
Match market	Wages and benefits comparable to the surrounding market. The objective is to match the competition. Examples: Restaurants, recreation, and entertainment industries
Lead market	Higher wages and better benefits are provided with the objective of attracting the best qualified candidates. The objective is to increase workplace productivity, thus besting the competition. Examples: High-tech companies, selected industry leaders

Table 4-12 Pay Strategies

that will provide the best competitive advantage to the employer. These strategies can be summarized in three ways, as shown in Table 4-12.

Ultimately, an effective pay strategy has to accomplish the following objectives:

- *Attract talented employees.* Rewards should be used to entice talented employees to the company or position. Companies should allocate a certain amount of funds to recruiting and hiring high-caliber employees.

- *Motivate employees to perform optimally.* Most programs focus on the motivational component of rewards. They use rewards to shape employee behavior in the most desired direction. This outcome should be carefully considered when designing a rewards program.

- *Foster personal growth and development.* Rewards should be used to encourage and promote personal growth and professional development. When rewards are used to encourage employees to engage in behavior that will increase their work performance, the company ultimately benefits from a more skilled workforce.

- *Increase employee satisfaction with their work.* Rewards can promote engagement with work, resulting in increased workplace satisfaction. They can motivate an employee to persist in the face of challenges, come up with creative solutions to tackling tasks, and encourage them to derive more pleasure with their work.

- *Keep talented employees from leaving.* When employees love what they do and are rewarded for their performance, they are less likely to leave a company. Keeping talented employees on board should be a priority of any company. Thus, companies should devote resources necessary to ensure that their rewards program meet the needs of their most talented employees.

Global Remuneration Issues and Challenges   HR and compensation professionals in organizations that operate on a global scale often find themselves faced with the task of managing compensation practices across multiple jurisdictions on a regular basis. Many factors increase the complexity of HR operations in a global context. Not only are additional proficiencies required on a daily basis, but there is the need for more collaboration with legal, finance, accounting, tax, and local and country management, which are all key elements in the global environment.

There are two key issues to keep in mind. The concept of "at-will" employment does not generally exist outside of the United States. In the United States, barring a contract to the contrary and in a nonunionized environment, employers are free to hire, fire, and change terms and conditions of employment without notice and without reason (as long as it is not an unlawful reason). Outside the United States, employment is typically a matter of contract, and employers cannot unilaterally change terms and conditions of employment. This limits the ability of an employer to make any changes for its non-U.S. workforce.

Different types of employees have different protections outside the United States. In the United States, the distinctions between type of employee are driven in large part by federal and state minimum wage and overtime laws, i.e., exempt versus nonexempt status. Outside the United States, the distinctions for application of collective bargaining agreements (CBAs) and local labor laws on wage rates, vacation entitlements, and the like are not tied to whether an employee is equivalent to an exempt or nonexempt employee in the United States but rather vary by levels of workers. As an example, in Italy, an executive-level employee, as defined under the applicable CBA, will have different wage entitlements than a blue-collar worker. In France, levels of remuneration are dependent on the coefficient applicable to the position. In Japan, directors can be considered nonemployees, in which case they are generally not protected under the Labor Standards Law.

This presumes that the workforce is composed of employees, as opposed to independent contractors or other contingent workers. Where a company engages nonemployee workers, issues of misclassification of contractors as employees and joint employer liability for contingent workers can arise in almost all jurisdictions, and thus compensation structures for those workers should be carefully managed.[93]

Alignment with Global Staffing   Total rewards must support global talent acquisition and management strategies. Compensation practices must support the hiring and retention of an engaged and productive workforce, domestic and global.

Howard V. Perlmutter first formulated the differences among ethnocentric, polycentric, regiocentric staffing with the geocentric approach to international staffing added later.

The approaches shown in Table 4-13 directly affect the strategies, policies, and practices related to global compensation and benefits.

Global Orientation	Implications for Global Compensation and Benefits Strategy
Ethnocentric Tight control of international operations, little autonomy, compensation, and benefits developed at headquarters and rolled out globally	• This leads to transfer of headquarters total compensation policies, with inadequate consideration of local legal and cultural differences. • Directives to local country management may result in outward consistency but actual rejection of headquarters' practices.
Polycentric Subsidiary treated as its own entity, local compensation and benefits policies, programs, and practices	• Local cultural and legal compensation norms are more likely to be understood and implemented. • Remuneration policies are likely to be consistent and integrated within each subsidiary. • Incentives tend to maximize achievement of local rather than global objectives.
Regiocentric Operations managed regionally, communication and coordination high within the region but less between regions	• There is greater potential for consistency of remuneration approaches within a region. The proximity of countries may lead to the perception that remuneration practices are more similar than they really are. • Regional headquarters may suffer blind spots with respect to country differences, leading to ethnocentrism at the regional level.
Geocentric Organization seen as a single international enterprise with a strategic plan that's global in orientation	• Local compensation strategies are more likely to be consistent with global policies. • A desire for too much global consistency can lead to the imposition of inappropriate policies at the local country level. • The development of consistent and equitable remuneration policies among global managers will facilitate efficient and effective transfers.

Table 4-13 Global Orientation on Global Compensation and Benefits Strategy

Influencing Factors in a Global Environment Many forces influence global remuneration. They include labor market dynamics that exist in the business; regulatory, political, and cultural differences; taxation of compensation and benefits; operational legal and reporting structures in different geographies; and the role that mobility will play in future workforce strategy and deployment. Largely driven by these operational and country specifics, strategies for compensation and benefits delivery are then often capped by market practices.

Table 4-14 describes major issues and challenges, and it notes the general implications for global HR.

Special Considerations in a Total Rewards Strategy

Two factors must be addressed as part of developing a total rewards strategy. They are PEST factors and the employee lifecycle.

Factor	Description	Global HR Implications
Standardization versus localization	Strategies are standardized in keeping with the organization's overall compensation and benefits philosophy. Specific practices are localized to fit the context of the country, regional, or local conditions.	Organization has a long-term plan to support the organizational compensation and benefits philosophy, but local restrictions, tax regimes, and culture are considered.
Culture	Cultural differences require that the value of compensation and benefits programs be in "the eye of the beholder." Local benefits are more highly valued. Differences are often based on deep-seated beliefs, attitudes, and values that are local in nature.	Avoids headquarters biases or replication of headquarters country policies and procedures. Involves local contacts to understand the localized usual and customary compensation and benefits practices.
Competitive labor market	Compensation and benefits required to attract and maintain talent are determined by the competitive demand for that talent. However, the competition for talent may vary across countries and regions, depending on factors such as type of talent, geographic scope of talent market, industries in which the talent may be found, and the mix of remuneration components.	Rates of pay in the relative marketplace are based on the skills needed, the demand for talent, and the best way to compensate different types of workers. Appropriate combinations of pay and benefits are offered that appeal to current or perspective employees. People are employed with similar skills. When industry-specific expertise is in short supply or competition is high, retrain or coach the hires on the job.
Collective bargaining, employee representation, and government mandates	Certain types and categories of employees in most parts of the world are protected from actions that impact their wages and employment conditions. Unions play a strong role in many countries and sometimes include provisions for management as well as employees. Work councils (not to be confused with unions) also offer worker protections.	Comply with requirements of third-party representation. Understand the implications for minimum wages, severance packages, and pensions. Adhere to related government regulations and mandates and industry-wide collective agreements.

Table 4-14   Issues and Challenges in Global Compensation and Benefits (continued)

Factor	Description	Global HR Implications
Economic factors	Many differences exist from one country to the next in terms of the influence of politics and power, the distribution of wealth across a country's citizenry, the unpredictability of events (i.e., rapid changes in rates of inflation and currency levels), as well as the level of unemployment or scarcity of talent.	Unofficial sources of power in a community or region and official governmental personnel may have a large impact on what is considered acceptable. Educational facilities, internal training, child care, or other local services contribute support to the local area. Local inflation/deflation or currency fluctuations are significant factors. Contingency plans may be required to mitigate the risks associated with potential changes in economic factors.
Taxation	Tax regulations differ widely from country to country. Some countries have no income tax, while others have income tax in excess of 50 percent. Some benefits that are taxable in one country are not taxable in geographically adjacent countries, and vice versa. There are complicated and ever-changing tax compliance requirements for nationals from one country working in another.	Experts in local compensation and benefits laws and practices, as well as country taxation, may be required, particularly for long-term assignees. This includes the taxation of cash and noncash compensation, benefits, and perquisites including what is taxed, at what rates, and at what levels. A benefit may be unacceptable depending on how it is taxed.
Laws and statutory regulations	Laws and statutory regulations impact the remuneration of employees in many areas, such as work hours and compulsory time off (paid and unpaid). • Minimum wage • Overtime • Compulsory bonuses • Employment at will • Acquired rights There are significant country-to-country variances as well as some regional and local differences.	Requires an understanding of the differences and similarities in each market. Also, it includes the ability to recognize benefits that are government-provided, mandated by the government, or chosen by the employee. Usually this involves experts in local compensation and benefits laws and regulations as well as country taxation, particularly for expatriates.

Table 4-14   Issues and Challenges in Global Compensation and Benefits

PEST factors address political, economic, social, and technological factors that may influence an organization's total rewards strategy. The following examples describe the conditions that may impact total rewards:

- **Political**   The head of government or legislative body in control most likely has a particular agenda/position on employee pay as well as executive pay. Their approach and legislation impacts an organization's total rewards at least from a legal standpoint (e.g., minimum pay, tax withholding rates).

  HR needs to be proficient in compliance with total rewards–related acts and legislation where the organization does business (e.g., cities, states, countries), as they are charged with (and expected to) provide expertise, particularly in the area of compliance.

- **Economic**   A city, state, or country economy, as well as the global economy, impacts an organization's ability to provide total rewards. Pay may be frozen, and variable compensation may not be paid.

  Poor economies stunt organizational growth and, in turn, the hiring of new talent. The positive outcome of this may be that employee retention increases because of slow job growth/few external opportunities.

  Growing and prosperous economies benefit organizational bottom lines and encourage and promote hiring but accentuate the need for employee retention as more employees will probably be in the job market and look to leave for a better opportunity.

- **Social**   Citizens have views toward organizational pay, particularly that of the C-suite and the CEO. The information on the pay of these individuals is easily accessible if the organization is publicly traded. Even though compensation committees have the ability to control and impact executive total rewards, all too often compensation for the highest levels of an organization is viewed as exorbitant and leads to negative public opinion.

  Organizations come under significant scrutiny when their fired or ousted CEO receives a significant severance package on the way out the door. Many people fail to realize that this may have been contractually negotiated as part of the pre-employment negotiations. At a minimum, this translates to an unfavorable view and perception of the organization or the board of directors.

- **Technological**   An organization's ability to automate, streamline, and improve the efficiency of many transactions that accompany total rewards from regular, periodic base pay to tax withholding to government-mandated reporting and filing are directly impacted by technological advances. Organizations may outsource their technology requirements to third-party vendors that develop and manage applications. However, software may also be licensed so that organizations can perform the function in-house.

  A less common approach is for companies to develop the technology themselves. This usually is because they lack the money, the expertise, and/or the ability to maintain the technology.

Any of these approaches can have a significant impact on employee total rewards, much of which is highly emotional to employees.

Employee lifecycle (ELC) refers to the various stages of the employment process. It starts with the recruitment and ends with termination. The various stages of the employee lifecycle call for different HR management techniques for individual employees. As an example, compensation and benefit practices are increasingly planned and managed in response to the individual employee's lifecycle stage.

Some of the more commonly recognized lifecycle stages include the following:

- **Recruitment** The employee lifecycle begins before the individual employee is even identified. HR considerations begin when the employer begins its planning and engages in its initial search for potential applicants.

- **Onboarding** Most employers agree that complete integration into the workforce is most effective when it begins during the onboarding stage. This is the best time to begin the creation of a productive relationship to make sure the employee is aware of their responsibilities and is comfortable in their new role in the organization.

- **Orientation** During this stage, the employee settles into the job, integrates with the organization's corporate culture, familiarizes himself with co-workers and management, and establishes his role within the organization. Typically, as individuals move through their various lifecycle stages, the value of their contributions increases along with their total rewards.

- **Promotion** An employee who stays with the employer will likely want to advance within the workplace at an average to speedy rate. Managers, supervisors, and HR practitioners must be adept at recognizing changing interests and needs and capable of matching the organization's interests with the individual's needs.

- **Termination** Whether an employee quits, retires, or is terminated by the employer, at some point the employment relationship will end. As planning begins the employee lifecycle, also planning for succession and replacement needs is an ongoing management activity supported by HR counsel and advice that ensures the orderly positioning of the organization toward new opportunities.

Studies show that organizations that are able to effectively adapt to employee lifecycle changes are organizations that succeed.

Communication of the Total Rewards Strategy

A typical total rewards package can include compensation, benefits, work-life balance, performance and recognition, personal development, and career opportunities. Recent strong global competition for talent and shortages of critical-skill workers, particularly in the fast-growing economies of Asia and Latin America, have driven a surge of interest in applying core total rewards principles to designing and delivering workforce programs.

Critically, the total rewards framework is grounded in three core principles of sound design and delivery.

- *Align the total rewards strategy with the organization's business strategy and related workforce goals.* Effective workforce programs are an extension of an organization's business strategy, explicitly supporting key priorities and goals and clearly communicating the level and nature of the contribution the organization expects from its people.

- *Optimize the money spent by allocating it among the programs that matter to employees, and deliver the right return while being sensitive to cost and risk objectives.* Despite the magnitude of spending on reward programs, many organizations don't consistently measure returns or clearly understand the relationship between program costs and the value employees attach to them.

- *Design, communicate, implement, and deliver rewards that drive the specific employee behaviors you need to achieve your business strategy.* Identifying the right mix is not only a function of cost versus value but also of the culture and work environment your company is building and sustaining to meet strategic goals.

The Challenges of Transparency How much to communicate about pay is a continual debate, one for which there is no clear answer. Those in favor of open communication feel that unless employees understand their organization's pay system and how their pay is determined, it will not achieve its primary objective of supporting the achievement of strategic business objectives. But, even proponents of reward program transparency recognize that a level of employee privacy must be preserved. The result of complete openness can foster jealousy and performance problems.

Effective total rewards communications have become even more important now when employees are faced with making a decision between their economic needs (i.e., their pay) and the level of health and retirement benefits they would like to receive.

Today, employers have an array of communication tools to choose from. Technology enables the creation of individualized reports informing employees about reward program eligibility and payouts. Computers make the dissemination of rewards information via e-mails, web sites, webinars, DVDs, and other electronic media fast and cost-effective at work, at home, and, in fact, almost anywhere. Despite this, experts agree that rewards communications are, more times than not, done poorly; for the most part, employees do not understand how they are paid and what factors determine their eligibility for most reward programs.

Effective Communication of Total Rewards Considerations that affect the effective communications of total rewards include the following:

- **Type of Information**
  - **Required communications** Laws and regulations often mandate certain communications such as disclosure and reporting requirements associated with pension benefits plans as well as payroll record and disclosure requirements. It is the organization's responsibility to ensure compliance with these legal requirements.

- **Voluntary communications** Legal compliance is not sufficient to achieve a full objective of employee knowledge and understanding. Organizations must go beyond the legal minimum and fashion communications policies that clearly identify the message outlining policies and procedures as well as management expectations. To be effective, these communications should be of a two-way nature as a direct link between management, HR, and the organization's employees.

- **Communication Plans** The larger the organization, the greater the need for a comprehensive communications plan. A good place to start is with a SWOT analysis (strengths, weaknesses, opportunities, and threats) considering both internal and external factors. Plans vary and should be written. They may include a description of the organization's compensation strategy; its policies, practices, and procedures; and any other pertinent important information.

- **Individualized compensation and benefits statements** Total compensation statements made their appearance in the workplace during the past 20 years. Sometimes they were called *employee benefit statements, hidden paycheck statements,* or *total reward statements,* the purpose is to show true compensation value to employees. This is particularly important in a world where benefit premiums continue to increase while, at the same time, many employers plan to increase salaries minimally. The net result tends to create some negativity in the workplace and grumblings of job searches. The total compensation statement can provide a reassuring picture to your employees and a tangible reminder of the organization's financial commitment to its employees. Total compensation statements contribute to improved employee morale. When employers take the time to present and explain these statements to their employees, they typically improve the employees' overall perceptions of the employer by increasing awareness of the company's total employee benefits (pay and benefits) offering. Total compensation statements also help to attract and retain quality employees by identifying a more rounded picture of both the direct and indirect compensation.

- **Self-service technologies** Employee self-service (ESS) software is an HR technology tool that gives employees the power to manage their own personal data. Employee self-service applications enable employees to view and amend personal data (such as banking details), make requests for leave, easily access corporate policies, access the employee directory, view organizational structuring, access corporate communications, and much more. This gives employees a much higher level of control over the data that pertains to them. Enabling employees to provide input into decision-making is one of the top drivers of employee engagement according to the experts. From the tactical advantages that autonomy can bring to the strategic implications of giving greater responsibility to each employee for their career direction, employee self-service technology is an incredibly powerful tool for engagement when effectively utilized.

- **Consistent key messages** An organization spread across multiple locations requires extra effort to a clearly communicated consistent message. This is even a greater challenge when this is a global organization. Cultures become varied; the same message can be understood in different ways depending on the cultural perspectives. As a result, there is no one way to communicate the organization's compensation and benefits strategy. This results in a number of different approaches that have one objective in common, that is, to create open, effective communications designed to send and receive a clearly understood message.

Evaluation of the Total Rewards Strategy

The last phase of implementing a total rewards program, the evaluation, often is the most overlooked phase of total rewards. In this phase, the actual results of the executed total rewards strategies are compared against the desired results. The objective of this evaluation is to show top management that the company's investment in its total rewards system has paid off. To get the most from the evaluation phase, HR should be encouraged to measure the outcomes of the executed total rewards system and to interpret the findings correctly.

Measures, Metrics, and Analytics Three terms are often play a major role in the evaluation phase.

- **Measures** The process of collecting and tabulating data. This is a standard unit used to express the size, amount, or degree of something.

- **Metrics** Performance parameters based on the relationship between two or more measures. Metrics are a quantifiable measure organizations use to track, monitor, and assess the success or failure of various business processes.

- **Analytics** Convert a metric into a decision-supported insight. This is information resulting from the systematic analysis of data or statistics.

There are three key questions that must be addressed to effectively conduct a total rewards strategy evaluation.

- Is the total rewards strategy in legal compliance?
- Is the total rewards strategy compatible with the organization's mission and strategy?
- Does the total rewards strategy fit the culture?
- Is the total rewards strategy internally equitable and externally competitive?

The following evaluation guidelines are offered to ensure appropriate measures, metrics, and analytics are used in the evaluation phase of a total rewards strategy:

- Align HR measurements to the organizational strategic plan.
- Measure what can help improve employee performance or make better decisions.
- Avoid the problem of gathering data solely for its own sake.

Compensation Structure

People are willing to work in exchange for rewards they receive from the work they do. The objective is to provide a balance between what work is performed and the reward received for doing the work. *Total rewards* includes the financial inducements and rewards (direct pay, cash-based incentives, and benefits) as well as nonfinancial inducements and rewards such as the value of good job content as well as a good working environment. Employers strive to offer an attractive compensation package, including a fair base pay, incentives, and benefits, in addition to a good job match and working environment to attract employees and retain them.

Total rewards includes compensation that is both direct and indirect. Direct compensation (e.g., cash) applies to a variety of pay programs that are, in one way or another, cash-based, whereas indirect compensation (e.g., benefits) applies to programs primarily designed to provide recognition and benefits and, therefore, are indirectly cash-based. Examples of these two types of compensation are listed in Table 4-15.

Some of the direct compensation programs are discretionary (i.e., cash awards, differential pay, and certain bonuses), while others are mandatory and governed by federal, state, and, in some cases, local law and regulation (base pay and incentives). Some of the indirect compensation programs are also discretionary—that is, they are employed at the option of the employer. They include paid vacation, sick leave (four states now offer paid sick leave: Connecticut, California, Massachusetts, and Oregon[94]), paid time off, 401(k) and similar retirement plans, and pensions. Finally, some benefits are mandatory and governed by federal law and regulation. Social Security, workers' compensation, and unemployment insurance are examples. Even discretionary programs are subject to regulation when they are employed.

Compensation System Design

The compensation system design process (Figure 4-18) includes four key activities: job analysis, job documentation, job evaluation, and pay structure.

Table 4-15 Direct and Indirect Compensation	Direct Compensation ("Cash")	Indirect Compensation ("Benefits")
	Base pay (wages and salary)	Social Security
	Commissions	Unemployment insurance
	Bonuses	Disability insurance
	Merit pay	Pensions
	Piece rate	401(k) and other similar programs
	Differential pay	Health care
	Cash award	Vacations
	Profit sharing	Sick leave
	Gainsharing	Paid time off

Figure 4-18 Compensation system design process

Job Analysis

Before we address the process of a job analysis, we should first address what is a job. A job may be best understood as an organization of total work into units or positions. According to Dale Yoder,[95] "A job is a collection of tasks, duties and responsibilities which, as a whole, is treated as assigned duties for individual employees and which is different from other assignments." Thus, a job may be defined as a group of positions involving some duties, responsibilities, knowledge, and skills.

Jobs each have a definite title based on typically accepted business and industry standards. Each job is different from other jobs such as receptionist, accountant, supervisor, and so on. A job such as an accountant may include many positions (i.e., accounting specialist, forensic accountant, and so on). A position is a particular set of duties and responsibilities regularly assigned to an individual.

Job Analysis Defined   Job analysis is the process of collecting information about a job. It refers to the superstructure of the job. According to Herbert G. Heneman III,[96] "A job is a collection of tasks that can be performed by a single employee to contribute to the production of some product or service provided by the organization. Each job has certain ability requirements (as well as certain rewards) associated with it. Job analysis is the process used to identify these requirements."

Job Analysis Considerations   The following considerations must be factors in conducting a job analysis:

- The facts identified must relate to the job and not the job incumbent.
- The duties and responsibilities must be for the job as it actually exists rather than what it is thought to be.
- Job facts must be verified to make sure they are accurate.
- Each duty must be analyzed to ensure it is essential to the job function.
- When there is more than one job incumbent, only one job analysis should be required.

Job Analysis Methods   There are multiple methods that can be used to collect information as part of a job analysis.

- **Observation**   This involves the direct observation of employees performing the tasks of a job, recording observations, and translating them into the necessary knowledge, skills, and abilities. This method provides a realistic view of the daily tasks and activities performed in a job but works best for short-cycle jobs in production rather than long-term jobs.

- **Interview**   This involves a face-to-face interview where the interviewer obtains the necessary information from the employee, peers, supervisors, and team/unit members about the knowledge, skills, and abilities needed to perform the job. The interviewer uses predetermined questions with new ones added as follow-up based on the response of the employee being interviewed. This method is particularly good for professional jobs.

- **Highly structured questionnaire**   This involves questionnaires structured in a way that requires specific responses aimed at determining the frequency certain specific tasks are performed, their relative importance, and the skills required. This method defines a job with a relatively objective approach that also enables analysis that is easily adaptable to using computer models. It's good when a large number of jobs must be analyzed and there are insufficient resources to do it.

- **Open-ended questionnaire**   This involves the use of questionnaires to job incumbents, and sometimes to their supervisors or managers, asking about the knowledge, skills, and abilities necessary to perform the job. After the answers are combined, a composite statement of job requirements is published from which a job description can be refined.

- **Work diary or log**   This is a diary or log is maintained by the employee in this method. Job information, including the frequency and timing of tasks, is recorded in the diary. Logs are usually kept over an extended period of time. They are analyzed, and patterns are identified and translated into duties and responsibilities. While data can be collected over a long period of time with this method, it can result in an enormous amount of information to be culled and summarized.

Job Analysis Outcomes   Possible results from job analysis include the following:

- **Job description**   This is a functional description of what contents the job includes. It is a narration of the job contents, a description of the activities and duties to be performed in a job, the relationship of the job with other jobs, the equipment and tools involved, the nature of supervision, working conditions, and job hazards including physical and mental requirements.

- **Job specifications**   This focuses on the person doing the job, i.e., the job holder. The job specification is a statement of the minimum levels of qualifications, skills, physical and other abilities, experience, judgment, and attributes required to effectively perform the job. It is a statement of the minimum acceptable qualifications that an incumbent must have to perform a given job. It sets forth the knowledge, skills, and abilities required to do the job effectively.

- **Job competencies** Normally focused on "core" or "critical" competencies, these are the measurable or observable knowledge, skills, abilities, and behaviors, sometimes called KSABs, that are critical to successful job performance. Choosing the right competencies allows employers to do the following:
  - Plan how they will organize and develop their workforce.
  - Determine which job classes best fit their business needs.
  - Recruit and select the best employees.
  - Manage and train employees effectively.
  - Develop staff to fill future vacancies.
  - Core competencies may be divided into three categories.
    - **Knowledge competencies** The practical or theoretical understanding of subjects
    - **Skill and ability competencies** The natural or learned capacities to perform acts
    - **Behavioral competencies** Patterns of action or conduct

Job Analysis Uses The following are the many uses of a job analysis:

- **Human resource planning** It can be used to forecast human resource requirements in terms of knowledge and skills.
- **Recruitment** It can be used to find out how and when to hire people for future job openings.
- **Selection** It is not possible to select the right person for the job without a proper understanding of what is to be done on a job.
- **Placement and orientation** After selecting people, we have to place them on jobs best suited to their interests, activities, and aptitude.
- **Training** Required training efforts cannot be initiated if there is any confusion about what the job is and what is supposed to be done.
- **Counseling** Managers can properly counsel employees about their careers when they understand the different jobs in the organization. Likewise, employees can better appreciate their career options when they understand the specific needs of various other jobs.
- **Performance appraisal** The worth of the person doing the job can be assessed by comparing what the person is supposed to be doing (based on job analysis) to what the individual has actually done.
- **Job design and redesign** Once the jobs are properly understood, it becomes easier to locate weak spots and undertake remedial steps.

Job Documentation

Job documentation includes the creation of job descriptions, specifications, and competencies. In the context of a compensation system, job documentation does the following:

- Helps establish evaluation criteria for job performance
- Provides data used to compare pay with that of other organizations
- Helps the assignment of objective classifications or job titles to employees
- Communicates performance expectations to supervisors and employees
- Reduces an organization's liability exposure to discrimination charges allegations
- Assists employers in recognizing and addressing reasonable accommodation and other legal compliance requirements

Job Evaluation

The systematic determination of the relative worth of jobs in an organization is known as *job evaluation*. The importance of job evaluation is that it is a critically important pay equity concept applied through a formalized process designed to prevent internal pay inequities as employers create structure within the organization's cost parameters while responding to its workforce expectations. Conducting a job evaluation is an essential first step in creating an appropriate wage structure that accommodates jobs of different worth, while it preserves the core objective of internal pay equity. Market surveys are a tool that enables organizations to understand and recognize market pressures with an objective of external equity.

Job-Content Based (Internal) Job Evaluation   Job evaluation options can be divided into job-content-based (internal) job evaluation and market-based (external) job evaluation. In job-content-based job evaluation, the relative worth and pay opportunities of different jobs are based on an assessment of their content (e.g., responsibilities and requirements) and their relationship to other jobs within the organization. In a market-based evaluation approach, the relative worth and pay opportunities of different jobs are based on their market value or going rate in the marketplace.

Nonquantitative Job-Content Job Evaluation   Job evaluation methods can be nonquantitative or quantitative. The primary objective of a nonquantitative method is to establish a relative hierarchy of jobs based on each job's relative worth. Nonquantitative methods often are referred to as *whole-job methods* because they rank jobs as a whole based on their perceived worth without placing a numerical value on each job. An example of a nonquantitative method would be to rank a clerical job below a supervisory job on the basis of their relative, nonquantitative worth.

Quantitative job evaluation methods include *point-factor* and *factor comparison* methods. Quantitative methods evaluate factors on a defined measurable scale and provide a score as the result that is a measurable comparison of one job to another (see Table 4-16).

Table 4-16 Job Evaluation Methods		Nonquantitative Methods	Quantitative Methods
	Job-to-job comparison	Job ranking	Factor comparison
	Job-to-predetermined-standard comparison	Job classification	Point-factor

- **Job ranking** The job ranking method is often called a *whole-job* comparison because it is a comparison of the whole job compared to another whole job rather than a comparison based on each job's measurable factors. Job ranking using the whole-job method is quick and easy but not very precise. It is easy to explain which is why it is popular, but it leaves unanswered why one job is worth more than another as well as how much of a "gap" exists between jobs.

  When there are a large number of jobs to evaluate, a *paired-comparison* method of ranking can be used. This method enables each job to be compared with every other job. Jobs are methodically compared to the next job and, depending on the perceived worth, moved up or below the next job. Ultimately, the job with the highest number of upward movements is the highest ranked. Other jobs are ranked accordingly.

- **Job classification** Jobs can be compared to an outside scale. This also can be done on a whole-job basis called a *job classification* method. Job classification is the result of grouping jobs into a predetermined number of grades or classifications. Each classification has a class description. The federal government has a classification system known as the General Schedule. The General Schedule (GS) is the predominant pay scale for federal employees, especially employees in professional, technical, administrative, or clerical positions. The system consists of 15 grades, from the lowest level of GS-1 to the highest level of GS-15. There are also ten steps within each grade. The grade level assigned to a position determines the pay level for that job.

Classes can be further identified by using benchmark jobs that fall into each class. Benchmark jobs have the following characteristics:

- The essential functions and knowledge, skills, and abilities (KSAs) are established and stable.

- They represent the entire range of jobs in each class.

- A significant percentage of workers is employed in these jobs.

- External market rates for these jobs are an acceptable basis for setting wages.

The job classification method is a nonquantitative job evaluation method. In the job classification method, a job may be compared to a similar job or to other jobs in the General Schedule to determine its relative ranking. This is considered a nonquantitative method called a *job-to-predetermined-standard comparison*. Job classification comparisons are a good method when evaluating a large number of jobs and are understandable by employees but may not be effective when jobs overlap as they look only at whole jobs.

Quantitative Methods The difference between nonquantitative job evaluation methods and quantitative job evaluation methods is that quantitative methods use mathematical data, whereas nonquantitative methods use qualitative data. The following methods are two quantitative methods:

- **Point-factor method** The most commonly used job evaluation method is the *point-factor method,* which uses specific compensable factors as its reference points to measure relative job worth. Compensable factors are significant job characteristics that contribute to the value of the work and organization as a whole. Two well-known systems used to identify compensable factors are the following:

- **The Hay plan** Uses a standard criteria comprising three compensable factors: know-how, problem-solving, and accountability.

- **The factor evaluation system (FES)** Determines levels of duties and responsibilities using a point rating system to evaluate selected positions. Uses weighted factors to address the major position characteristics of responsibility, education/experience, job conditions, physical requirements, supervision, training, and so on.

There are five steps involved in the point-factor method of job evaluation:

1. *Identify key jobs.* These are benchmark jobs, not necessarily the most important jobs in the organization but jobs that are equitably paid, stable, and well-defined.

2. *Identify the compensable factors.* These are the factors that will be used to distinguish one job from another. Six to eight factors are generally sufficient. Experience, responsibility, and education are most often used. Other factors that can be considered, depending on their general applicability, include physical demands, mental requirements, skill, working conditions, and supervisory responsibilities.

3. *Weight the factors according to their overall worth.* Usually, the most heavily weighted factors are knowledge, responsibility, experience, education, degree of difficulty, and supervisory responsibilities.

4. *Divide each job factor into degrees that range from high to low.* Assign points to each degree. The number of points assigned to each degree should correspond with the weighting of the factors. As an example, if the factor for skill is weighted 40 percent, the factor of working conditions is weighted 10 percent, and both factors have five degrees, degree two for skill should have four times as many points as degree two for working conditions.

5. *Determine the total points.* This will usually determine the pay grade to which the job will be assigned. The final result will be determined using a table (see Table 4-17) that has a range of points from 50 (the least number, column 1) to 200 (the most, column 5). Based on the point values assigned, the job in this example is 126 on a scale of 50 to 200 points.

Point-Factor Job Evaluation Method						
Compensable Factor	Weighted Percentage	Degrees/Points				
		1	2	3	4	5
Skill	(40 percent)	20	32	48	72	100
Responsibility	(30 percent)	15	24	36	54	75
Effort	(20 percent)	10	16	24	36	50
Working Conditions	(10 percent)	5	8	12	18	25

Example:

Machine Operator	Compensable Factor	Degree	Points
	Skill		48
	Responsibility	3	24
	Effort	2	36
	Working Conditions	4	18
	Total points	4	*126*

Table 4-17   Point-Factor Job Evaluation Method

PART II

- **Factor comparison method**   The *factor comparison method* is more complex than the ranking, classification, or point-factor methods and is rarely used. It involves ranking each job by each compensable factor and then, as an additional step, identifying dollar values for each level of each factor to develop an actual pay rate for the evaluated job.

  The factor comparison method is most often used in union negotiations as part of a labor contract and in limited cases where wages are steady over a period of time and the organization uses a flat rate for each job.

Market-Based (External) Job Evaluation   A market-rate system is not a true job evaluation system; however, in certain cases, market value can be used to price jobs—particularly when the organization is sensitive to competition. These prevailing rates are used to represent the relative worth of the jobs. In this approach, key jobs are measured and valued against the market, and the remaining jobs are inserted into a hierarchy based on their whole-job comparison to the benchmark jobs.

 NOTE   When matching a job with the competition, it is important to compare duties, scope, and reporting relationships but not titles because they are often misleading.

Market-based evaluation can be particularly beneficial when an organization has similar jobs in various locations throughout the United States. The disadvantage of a market-based evaluation is that the data will be reliable only when gathered for a significant number of jobs in the organization. Market-based evaluation results are more vulnerable to legal challenge than job-content approaches. Another disadvantage is that market-based evaluations do not recognize internal job value and, as a result, are more likely to lead to discontent and frustration from within the organization.

Remuneration (Pay) Surveys   Many organizations rely on pay surveys as a systematic way to collect, evaluate, and classify their jobs; adjust pay structures; and provide market information to top management. Pay surveys collect data on prevailing market rates and provide information such as starting wage rates, base pay, pay ranges, overtime pay, shift differentials, and incentive pay plans.

Options to collecting pay survey data include whether the survey should be conducted internally or gathered externally. Organizations that want to maintain maximum control over their pay information often choose to sponsor a custom survey. The advantage of this approach is that the organization has the ability to design the survey, manage its administration, do its own data analysis, and customize its report specifically for its own use. Another advantage is that the organization is able to maximize its control over the transfer of data, thereby reducing the risk of an inappropriate disclosure of highly sensitive confidential information.

While choosing to conduct its own internal survey, an organization should contract with an outside consulting group or independent consultant to design the survey and process the data received in a confidential manner. Using an outside person or group relieves pressure on the organization and ensures compliance with Department of Justice antitrust guidelines.

External surveys have different options. National surveys are widely available through the U.S. Department of Labor and the Bureau of Labor Statistics. Many professional groups such as the Society of Human Resource Management (SHRM) and consulting firms conduct surveys of wage and job data for a wide range of professions and organizations.

Data Analysis

Organizations have an interest in survey data based on their market exposure, completion, product or service, and employees. To be accurate, survey data must be verified and often aged, leveled, and factored for geography.

Survey Data Analysis   Survey data must be verified and may need aging, leveling, and/or factoring for location (geography).

- **Aging**   This is a technique used to make outdated data current, a phenomenon that regularly occurs with printed data as a result of the time lapse between when the data is collected, organized, printed, and published. An example of aging occurs when pay movement or increases average 1.5 percent a year. If you use a pay survey that is 1 year old, to be reasonably accurate, you would increase the survey data by 1.5 percent.

- **Leveling**   Pay surveys provide summary descriptions of each job surveyed. In many cases, this description is close but not an exact match with the organization's job. To accommodate this separation between the two jobs, a leveling technique is used. Leveling consists of adjusting the survey number by an appropriate percentage needed to achieve a match. As an example, an organization's Engineering I job description indicates an approximate 10 percent less scope of responsibility than described in the same job in a pay survey. Reducing the pay survey job data with a 10 percent reduction would be an appropriate technique to provide an accurate match.

Table 4-18	Frequency Distribution and Table		
Frequency Distribution and Table	Survey	Mean Salary	Number of Incumbents
	A	$60,000	2
	B	$65,000	1
	C	$70,000	3
	D	$75,000	4

- **Geography**   While many surveys are developed with a specifically described geographical location identified, in cases where this is not done, it would be appropriate to determine the percent difference in job value for a given location and factor that into the comparison.

Frequencies Distributions and Tables   Frequencies distributions and tables are used to sort salary data gathered from various remuneration (sometimes called *pay* or *salary*) surveys. A frequency distribution is a listing of grouped data, from lowest to highest. A frequency table lists the number of incumbents who receive a specific salary, as shown in Table 4-18.

The following are techniques used to organize data in a logical manner for ease and accuracy of interpretation.

Measures of Central Tendency   Measures of central tendency are another way to analyze salary survey data. Common measures of central tendency are mean (or *average*), median, mode, and quartiles and percentiles.

- **Mean (average)**   The arithmetic average or mean is the average value arrived at by giving equal weight to every participant's actual pay. This method is appropriate when the data to be determined is the average pay for a given job as opposed to actual pay levels applicable to that job. This figure is also known as the *unweighted average*.

- **Weighted average**   This number provides an average result taking into account the number of participants and each participant's pay. This result is known as the *weighted average*.

- **Median**   This number is sometimes referred to in pay surveys as the 50th percentile. This is the middle number in a range. The median is calculated by averaging the two middle numbers in a range when the range data is sorted from lowest to highest.

- **Mode**   This is the most frequently appearing number (or *wage* in a pay survey) in a range.

The following calculations are based on the data shown in Table 4-19:

- The unweighted average is $67,500 ($270,000 ÷ 4 organization salaries = 67,500).
- The weighted average is $69,500 ($695,000 ÷ 10 organization salaries = 69,500).

Organizations	Number of Incumbents	Annual Salary	Total Salary
A	2	$60,000	$120,000
B	1	$65,000	$65,000
C	3	$70,000	$210,000
D	4	$75,000	$300,000
4 organizations	10	$270,000	$695,000

Table 4-19 Weighted and Unweighted Mean Calculation

Pay Structure

After an organization has determined its relative internal job values (i.e., job evaluation) and collected appropriate market survey data through pay surveys, work begins on developing the organization's pay structure, including creating pay grades and establishing pay ranges.

Pay Grades   Pay grades, or job groups, are the way an organization organizes jobs of similar values. The valuation is a result of the job evaluation process. Jobs, even though dissimilar in function, of the same or comparatively the same value are paid within the same pay grade.

No fixed rules apply to creating pay grades; rather, the number of pay grades and their structure are more of a reflection of organizational structure and philosophy. Issues that should be considered include the following:

- The size and structure of the organization
- The "distance" between the lowest and the highest job in the organization
- The organization's pay increase and promotion policy
- The grouping of nonexempt and exempt jobs as well as job families, i.e., clerical, technical, professional, supervisory, and management jobs
- Creating sufficient grades to permit distinguishing difficulty levels but not so many that the difference between adjoining grades is insignificant

Well-structured pay grades enable management to develop a well-coordinated pay system rather than having to create a separate pay range for each job.

Pay Ranges   Pay ranges establish the upper and lower boundaries of each pay grade. Market data for a benchmark job (ideally, a "key" job that will link to market value) in each pay range helps to determine the range midpoint. The range spread reflects the equal dispersion of pay on either side of the midpoint to the lower and upper range boundary.

Quartiles and Percentiles   Quartiles and percentiles show dispersion of data throughout a range. These are commonly recognized reference points an organization uses to measure its position against the market as well as for internal compensation management purposes.

Range Spreads   The range spread is the dispersion of pay from the lowest boundary to the highest boundary of a pay range.

Range Spread Calculation

Range spread is calculated by subtracting the range minimum from the range maximum and dividing that figure by the range minimum. Range spread is expressed as a percentage.

$$\frac{\text{Maximum} - \text{Minimum}}{\text{Minimum}}$$

Example: The range spread for a pay range with a $30,000 minimum and a $45,000 maximum would be as follows:

$$\frac{\$45,000 - \$30,000}{\$30,000} = \frac{\$15,000}{\$30,000} = 50\%$$

Typical range spreads in organizations are as follows:

- Nonexempt jobs: 40 percent
- Exempt jobs: 50 percent
- Executive jobs: 60 percent

Generally, lower-level jobs have a narrow range between minimum and maximum pay ranges. Jobs at a lower level tend to be more skill-based, which provides for more movement opportunity than higher levels where jobs are more knowledge-based and progression is slower.

Ranges should overlap so that progression is steady within a pay grade; as a worker's pay increases with movement to a higher range quartile, the opportunity for managed movement is possible in a measured way.

There also should be a large enough distance between range midpoints so that pay compression between a lower pay grade and a high pay grade does not occur.

Compa-ratios   Compa-ratios are indicators of how wages match, lead, or lag the midpoint, normally an indicator of market value. Compa-ratios are computed by dividing the worker's pay rate by the midpoint of the pay range.

$$\text{The compa-ratio formula is: Compa} - \text{ratio} = \frac{\text{Pay rate}}{\text{Midpoint}}$$

Compa-ratios less than 100 percent (usually expressed as a compa-ratio less than 1.00) mean the worker is paid less than the midpoint of the range. Compa-ratios greater than 100 percent (1.00) mean that wages exceed the midpoint.

Broadbanding   Broadbanding is a recent concept that combines several pay grades or job classifications with narrow range spreads with a single band with a wider spread. Organizations usually adopt broadbanding as a way to simplify their pay levels and reduce management oversight requirements. As a result, broadbanding typically is more popular in large organizations than smaller ones.

While broadbanding has some advantages, it also has some disadvantages. In some cases, broadbanding does not work well with the organization's compensation philosophy. This is particularly true in organizations that focus on promotional opportunities. The reduction of pay grades as a result of broadbanding correspondingly reduces the number of opportunities for promotion.

Compensation Systems

A compensation system is the sum total of all monetary and nonmonetary benefits provided to employees in exchange for their willingness to work.

Base Pay Systems

After an organization has analyzed, evaluated, and priced its jobs, as well as designed its pay structure, the next step is to determine a type of base pay system that will help attract, motivate, and retain employees. In most cases, employees receive some type of base pay, either as an hourly wage (paid to hourly employees) or a salary (a fixed wage that doesn't change regardless of the hours worked). Base pay system choices include single or flat-rate systems, time-based step rate systems, performance-based merit pay systems, productivity-based systems, and person-based systems. Each of these systems is designed to best achieve the objectives of attracting, motivating, and retaining employees each under a different set of circumstances.

Single or Flat-Rate System   A flat-rate pay system compensates all workers at the same rate for each task performed or hour worked, regardless of factors such as performance or seniority. Often, this is used for task-based jobs. It incentivizes workers to complete tasks as quickly as possible but can penalize those unable to meet the established standards and in some cases may encourage workers to sacrifice quality for speed.

Time-Based Step Rate System   The time-based step rate system bases the employee's pay rate on the length of time in the job. Pay increases are published in advance on the basis of time. Increases occur on a predetermined schedule. This system has three variations, as described in the sections that follow.

Automatic Step Rate   In the automatic step rate system, the pay range is divided into several steps, each a predetermined range apart. At the prescribed time interval, each employee with the required seniority receives a one-step pay increase. This system is common in public-sector jobs and in a union environment.

Step Rate with Variability Considerations   The step rate with performance considerations system is similar to the automatic system except that performance can influence the size or timing of the pay increase.

Performance Rating	1st Quartile	2nd Quartile	3rd Quartile	4th Quartile
Exceeds Performance Objectives	6–7 percent	5–6 percent	4–5 percent	3–4 percent
Meets Performance Objectives	4–5 percent	3–4 percent	2–3 percent	1–2 percent
Needs Improvement	2–3 percent	1–2 percent	0–1 percent	0 percent

Table 4-20   Merit Guidelines Example

Combination Step Rate and Performance Structure   In the combination step rate and performance system, employees receive step rate increases up to the established job rate. Above this level, increases are granted only for superior job performance. To work, this system requires a supporting performance appraisal program as well as good communication and understanding by the workers paid under this system.

Performance-Based Merit Pay System   The performance-based merit pay system is based on an employee's individual job performance. A performance-based pay system is often referred to as *merit pay* or *pay for performance*. In this system, employees are typically hired at or near the minimum for their applicable pay range. Pay increases are normally awarded on an annual basis (or annualized if awarded on other than an annual basis) and influenced by the individual's overall job performance. A document identifying the percent pay increase linked to levels of performance and the individual's position in the applicable pay range is communicated to employees as an incentive to increase their performance, thereby earning a higher percentage increase. This document is known as "Merit Guidelines," and Table 4-20 shows an example.

To be effective, the merit pay system must be understood by employees affected by the system. In addition to the merit pay system, a clearly stated performance appraisal program is required to support the merit pay system. Key points that should be addressed in designing and implementing an effective merit pay system include those depicted in Table 4-21.

Merit Pay System	Performance Appraisal Program
Merit pay figures within quartiles can be either a range or a single number depending on the experience of the raters.	Performance ratings should clearly link to documented pre-agreed performance objectives.
Use a range for experienced raters and a single number for inexperienced raters.	Performance ratings are for overall performance.
Use one standard (range) or the other (single number) for the entire program.	Not more than three performance levels should be used (as shown).
The gap between one performance level and the next should be at least 2 percent in order to be a significant incentive.	"Needs Improvement" ratings should be placed into a performance improvement program with a defined period (usually not more than 90 days) to improve overall performance.

Table 4-21   Key Points Applicable to Merit Pay and Performance Appraisals

Productivity-Based System   In the productivity-based system, pay is determined by the employee's output. This system is mostly used on an assembly line in a manufacturing environment. The following sections describe two types of productivity-based systems.

Straight Piece Rate System   With the straight piece rate system, the employee receives a base rate of pay and is awarded additional compensation for the amount of output produced.

Differential Piece Rate System   In the differential piece rate system, the employee receives one rate of pay up to the production standard and a higher rate of pay when the standard is exceeded. Both the straight piece system and the differential piece rate system focus on quantity rather than quality. As a result, other quality control programs may be required to ensure the required quality standard is met.

Person-Based System   In the person-based system, employee capabilities, rather than how the job is performed, determine the employee's pay. For example, two employees do the same work, but one employee with a higher level of skill and experience receives more pay. There are three types of person-based systems, as described here:

- **Knowledge-based system**   In the knowledge-based system, a person's pay is based on the level of knowledge the person has in a particular field. This system is often used in the learned professions such as lawyers and doctors.

- **Skill-based system**   Employees paid in the skill-based system are paid for the number and depth of skills that they have that are applicable to their job. Heavy equipment operators are typically paid in this system.

- **Competency-based system**   In the competency-based system, pay is linked to the level at which an employee can perform in a recognized competency. In HR, a professional with specialty skills in organizational development or labor relations will typically be paid for their competency, for example, organizational development or labor relations in the HR field.

Pay Variations

Pay ranges must be periodically evaluated and adjusted to reflect organizational and market changes. Red circle rates, green circle rates, and cost-of-living adjustments are some of the techniques used to adjust to these changes.

Red Circle Rates   Organizations use red circle rates as a method to increase an employee's pay to a new rate higher than the maximum for the assigned pay range. This situation occurs more often in smaller organizations where promotional opportunities may be limited. When this happens, an employee's next pay raise indicated by the organization's merit guidelines might place the new pay level above the maximum for the applicable pay range.

An example of this is the accounting manager who is paid $95,000 per year, a point less than 5 percent from the top of the range. Based on job performance, the manager would be entitled to a 7 percent increase. The next promotion step is the CFO job.

In this case, the company may decide to process the 7 percent increase as a red circle rate 2 percent above the range maximum for an accounting manager. Typically when this is done, the new pay level is frozen until the maximum of the pay range moves upward to exceed the accounting manager's pay level. This would usually happen when the comparative market numbers increase, thereby allowing a change to the pay range.

Green Circle Rates   Green circle rates occur when a new employee is hired at a pay rate lower than the minimum rate for the applicable grade. It can also happen when a "fast-track" employee is promoted to a new job in a high pay grade under circumstances where the percentage pay increase needed to reach the new grade is excessive and might create an unwanted precedent. In this case, the pay increase may result in a pay level below the minimum level of the new pay grade, thus creating a "green circle rate."

Situations such as this should be avoided whenever possible and should be allowed only as a last resort because they can create serious morale issues and, even worse, may create an arguable case of pay discrimination. In any case, such actions should be carefully considered and justified in writing after all of the possible consequences are considered.

Pay Compression   Pay compression is the situation that occurs when there is only a small difference in pay between employees regardless of their skills or experience. Pay compression is the result of the market rate for a given job outpacing the increases historically given by the organization to high-tenure employees. As a result, employers can only hire newcomers by offering them as much, or sometimes even more, than much more senior professionals.

Pay inequities exist to some degree in all organizations. The most common causes are the result of talent acquisition, overtime, demotions, the demand for technical expertise, reorganizations, reassignments, and seniority. Some organizations conduct wage compression or parity studies to identify pay compression issues and their causes in an effort to achieve levels of internal equity so that people in relatively similar jobs receive equal pay.

Pay Adjustments

This is a term that can be used to signify a pay increase for a number of reasons. In this section, we will examine cost of living adjustments, general pay increases, seniority increases, lump-sum increases, and market-based increases.

Cost-of-Living Increase   Technically, a cost-of-living adjustment (COLA) is an adjustment in pay, usually upward, linked to a predetermined scale, measure, or condition. Employment contracts, pension benefits, and government entitlements, such as Social Security, are linked to a cost-of-living index, typically to the consumer price index (CPI). A COLA adjusts salaries based on changes in a cost-of-living index. Salaries, which are typically adjusted annually, may also be tied to a cost-of-living index that varies by geographic location if the employee moves.

General Pay Increase   In some circumstances, nonunion employers may want to provide a general pay increase to their employees without the potentially precedent-setting basis of a COLA. A general pay increase is a pay increase given to all employees regardless of their job performance and not linked to market pressures. Usually, the only criteria is the desire to provide all employees with a pay increase subject only to the ability to fund the increase. Walmart's recent general pay increase to all of its employees is an example.

Seniority Pay Increase   Whenever a pay increase is given based solely on length of service, it is considered a seniority pay increase. As with a general pay increase, it is simply a basis on which to award a pay increase. Seniority pay increases are common in a unionized setting. In a nonunion setting, pay increases usually combine seniority with performance.

Lump-Sum Increase   A lump-sum increase (LSI) can be either a stand-alone performance bonus or part of an annual pay increase. Because a lump-sum increase is a single lump-sum payment, it has some advantages that other pay increases don't have. Most other pay increases impact a series of wage and benefits actions such as base wage, overtime, shift differentials, sick leave, vacation pay, and holiday pay in that each increases in proportion to the size of the increase. This is because most pay increases are added to base pay and paid over a number of pay periods in a year, in other words, creating a proportional increase in all of these wage and benefits categories.

A lump-sum increase is a single lump-sum payment subject to applicable tax and withholding that is not added to the employee's base rate of pay because of its character as a single lump-sum payment. This provides the full cash payment to the employee in a single lump-sum payment. In a red circle rate situation, the lump-sum increase can be used for the amount that would otherwise exceed the range maximum without increasing the employee's base rate of pay beyond the range maximum.

Market-Based Increase   When employee retention is threatened because employee pay is not competitive with the market, employers can respond by creating a market-based increase to adjust an employee's pay to better match market levels.

Differential Pay

Differential pay is additional compensation paid to an employee as an incentive to accept what would normally be considered adverse working conditions usually based on time, location, or situational conditions. The same differential pay is paid to all employees under the same circumstances or conditions. Differential pay benefits the employer by incentivizing employees to accept work they might not otherwise accept; it benefits the employee as additional compensation for accepting the work.

Time-Based Differential Pay   Also called a *shift differential,* generally time-based differential pay rewards the employee who works hours normally considered undesirable such a night shift or hours that are in addition to the employee's regular work schedule, i.e., overtime. Time-based differential pay may be a specified amount per hour or a percentage of the employee's regular rate of pay. Except for overtime, federal law does not legally require employers to pay a differential rate of pay, although state requirements may differ.

Geographic Differential Pay   Sometimes locations are undesirable because of their remoteness, a lack of amenities, climatic conditions, and other adverse conditions. To attract workers, in some cases employers will add a location-based differential to the employee's pay package. A geographic pay differential is additional compensation paid to an employee to account for variations in cost of labor and/or cost of living between locations. Some companies use the cost of goods and services as a factor to determine geographic pay differentials, but most companies use cost of labor as the primary factor to determine pay differences among locations.

Incentive Pay

Incentive pay is a form of direct compensation where employers pay for performance beyond normal expectations to motivate employees to perform at higher levels. In structured incentives, sometimes called *production incentives,* workers understand ahead of time the precise relationship between performance and the incentive reward. In a casual approach, sometimes called *discretionary incentives,* workers do not know in advance when or how much of a reward will be given.

Types of Incentives   Typically incentives are effective only if they are designed to a specific organization's operational conditions. To accomplish their objective, incentives need to add value to an organization's business objectives. Because of this, incentives generally are grouped into individual, group, and organization-wide applications.

Types of incentives include the following:

- **Individual**   The objective of an individual incentive program is to improve job performance. As such, the individual incentive program must be available to all employees in a particular group. An individual incentive program must be clearly designed and implemented as an incentive separate from an individual's base pay. Individual incentive programs can be either cash-based or non-cash-based.

  - **Cash awards**   Cash award programs reward performance with extra pay based on job performance. The rewards are usually lump-sum rewards such as discretionary bonuses based on the judgment of a supervisor or manager, a performance-based bonus based on predetermined performance criteria, and formula-based bonuses based on a percentage of profits or other pre-established measurement.

  - **Noncash awards**   Noncash awards include prizes, gifts, recognition awards, and other similar noncash items of value to the recipient. Sometimes these awards can be for length of service or contributions in addition to job performance. Although giving cash and noncash awards appears to be pretty straightforward, in fact, it can be more complicated than circumstances suggest. Some awards have tax implications, so advice might be required from accounting or your legal counsel as part of developing a cash or noncash incentive program.

- **Group** Used when teamwork is being rewarded, these programs are designed for groups of employees with the objective of rewarding group job performance considered necessary to accomplish a unit of work or when the desired result requires a team approach to the work. Group incentive programs can reward both short- and long-term work effort. Often, these programs include financial and nonfinancial measures as criteria for success. Group incentive programs include profit-sharing plans, gainsharing plans, and group performance incentives—for example, employee stock ownership plans (ESOPs).

- **Profit-sharing plans** Profit sharing refers to various incentive plans that provide direct or indirect payments to employees that depend on a company's profitability. These payments are in addition to the employees' regular salary and bonuses. In profit-sharing plans, the employer has the discretion to determine when and how much the company will pay into the plan. The contribution and any investment earnings accumulate in the plan on a tax-deferred basis. The IRS taxes these benefits only when employees receive distributions from the plan. A profit-sharing plan can be set up where all or some of the employee's profit-sharing amount can be contributed to a retirement plan. These are often used in conjunction with 401(k) plans.

- **Gainsharing plans** Gainsharing plans are similar to profit-sharing plans except that gainsharing plans measure the gain achieved from one performance period to the next while profit-sharing plans measure the profit to be shared from period to period. In a gainsharing plan, each member of the unit receives the same reward. Gainsharing measures usually apply to productivity terms while profit-sharing plan measures typically apply to profitability. Three types of gainsharing plans are the Scanlon Plan, the Rucker Plan, and the Improshare Plan.

  - **The Scanlon Plan** The Scanlon Plan is the oldest and most widely used type of gainsharing plan. It's based on the historical ratio of labor cost to sales value of production. And, because it rewards labor savings, it is most appropriate for companies that have a "high touch labor" content. The distinctive characteristics of the Scanlon Plan are its philosophy of participative management, administration by a committee of employees and management, and its percentage method of payment. A distinguishing characteristic is that the organization does not have to be profitable for workers to receive an incentive.

  - **The Rucker Plan** The Rucker Plan is based on the premise that the ratio of labor costs to production value is historically stable in manufacturing. The Rucker Plan tracks the value added to a product as a measure of productivity. In the Scanlon Plan, a ratio is calculated that expresses the value of production required for each dollar of the total wage cost.

- **Improshare Plan**   Improshare measures change in the relationship between outputs and the time required to produce them. This plan uses past production records to establish base performance standards. A standard is developed that identifies the expected number of hours to produce something. Any savings between this standard and actual production are shared between the company and the workers. The organization and its employees share 50/50 in all productivity gains. It is minimally affected by changes in sales volume, technology and capital equipment, product mix, or price and wage increases. It's the easiest of the gainsharing plans to understand and install.

- **Executive incentives**   Executives are the people who run the business. Executives form the highest level of management within their organization. In addition to their substantial management responsibilities within their organizations, they develop relationships with people outside their organization with the purpose of improving growth opportunities for their organizations. Their scope of activities and responsibilities impacts their compensation plans in two ways. First, their total compensation package includes their annual cash compensation plus the value of long-term incentives that usually accounts for the larger share of their total package. Second, their incentives are generally linked to the performance of the entire organization's profitability and, in some cases, other nonfinancial measures such as customer satisfaction and/or meeting certain other strategic objectives.

While there is no single compensation package designed for executives, their pay usually consists of a base salary that is "guaranteed," with other forms of variable (incentive) compensation dependent on performance factors.

- **Perquisites**   Special privileges for executives are referred to as *perks*. These privileges include club memberships, company cars, reserved parking, and a host of other noncash benefits. The 1973 Tax Act greatly diminished these perks, but they remain a substantial element in an executive's compensation package.

- **Golden parachutes**   These are provisions included in executive employment contracts that provide special payments or benefits to executives under certain adverse conditions such the loss of their position or if they are otherwise adversely impacted by organizational changes. Most often, these impacts are the result of an organizational merger in which there is a change of control that displaces a senior executive. These "golden parachutes" may provide for accelerated payments or early vesting in nonqualified retirement plan options, among other possibilities.

- **Long-term incentives**   Long-term incentive plans reward employees for attaining results over a long measurement period. For this purpose, *long-term* generally means more than 1 year and typically is between 2 and 5 years. Tax-deferred compensation plans, long-term cash plans, and certain stock-based plans are all considered long-term incentives.

The form of payment from a long-term incentive plan is typically cash or equity. An employer might choose one or the other based on the goals of the plan, the recipients of the awards, and the availability of cash or equity for payment.

- **Organization** Profit-sharing and stock ownership plans
  - **ESOPs** An employee stock ownership plan (ESOP) is a retirement plan in which the company contributes its stock (or money to buy its stock) to the plan for the benefit of the company's employees. The plan maintains an account for each employee participating in the plan. Shares of stock vest over time before an employee is entitled to them. With an ESOP, you never buy or hold the stock directly while still employed with the company. If an employee is terminated, retires, becomes disabled, or dies, the plan will distribute the shares of stock in the employee's account.
  - **Incentive stock options** There are several varieties of stock options, all of which share some basic characteristics. A stock option is a right to purchase a share of stock in the future at a price determined at the grant (or based on a formula defined at the grant). Incentive stock options (ISOs) are a special subset of stock options, satisfying certain criteria promulgated by the Internal Revenue Service and discussed in Internal Revenue Code Section 422.

    One of the primary restrictions is that an ISO can be granted only to an employee; ISOs cannot be granted to outside directors, independent contractors, consultants, or any other nonemployees. Also, the recipient must exercise the ISO within three months of terminating employment.
  - **Employee stock purchase plans (ESPPs)** An ESPP is a company-run program in which participating employees can purchase company shares at a discounted price. Employees contribute to the plan through payroll deductions, which build up between the offering date and the purchase date. At the purchase date, the company uses the accumulated funds to purchase shares in the company on behalf of the participating employees. The amount of the discount depends on the specific plan but can be as much as 15 percent lower than the market price.

    Depending on when you sell the shares, the disposition will be classified as either qualified or not qualified. If the position is sold 2 years after the offering date and at least 1 year after the purchase date, the shares will fall under a qualified disposition. If the shares are sold within 2 years of the offering date or 1 year after the purchase date, the disposition will not be qualified. These positions will have different tax implications.
  - **Phantom stock plan** A phantom stock plan is an employee benefit plan that gives selected employees (senior management) many of the benefits of stock ownership without actually giving them any company stock. This is sometimes referred to as *shadow stock*.

    Rather than getting physical stock, the employee receives "pretend" stock. Even though it's not real, the phantom stock follows the price movement of the company's actual stock, paying out any resulting profits.[4]

- **Restricted stock unit**   A restricted stock unit is compensation offered by an employer to an employee in the form of company stock. The employee does not receive the stock immediately but instead receives it according to a vesting plan and distribution schedule after achieving required performance milestones or upon remaining with the employer for a particular length of time. The restricted stock units (RSUs) are assigned a fair market value when they vest. Upon vesting, they are considered income, and a portion of the shares are withheld to pay income taxes. The employee receives the remaining shares and can sell them at any time.

- **Performance grants**   Public companies can also benefit from linking stock-based compensation to organizational performance. If done properly, such an arrangement can qualify as performance-based compensation, which avoids the deduction limits that can be imposed under Code Section 162(m). Such arrangements can also motivate recipients to achieve goals that are valuable to the organization and its shareholders. The accounting consequences of such arrangements can be tricky, and care should be taken to get the views of the organization's accountants.

All incentive plans must meet the following criteria:

- *They must fit with other programs.* For example, individual sales reward programs must be compatible with larger team recognition and reward programs.

- They must be in the employee's "line of sight." Job performance measures should reflect the results the employee actually controls. For example, a laboratory technician's zero-defect completion of a prescribed number of test results within a specified period of time would be a "line of sight" accomplishment.

- *They must have a "sunset clause."* The incentive plan should be in effect for a specific time period with an identified end date for tracking and measurement purposes.

- *They must incorporate both short- and long-term perspectives.* It should be structured to reward short-term goals (i.e., increased production capacity) and long-term results (i.e., achieving a strategic growth objective). The short-term perspective may be easier to visualize and achieve, but that may not encourage employees to think about long-term results.

Organizational requirements include the following:

- **A stable base pay plan**   A plan must be fair and equitable with long-term stability. Staff must be compensated competitively. An incentive plan will not support a base compensation system that is internally or externally inequitable.

- **An existing strategic plan**   Long-term organizational goals, as expressed in the organization's strategic plan, must be clear, consistent, and measurable. There must be stability as measured through the organization's sales volume, expenses, profitability, and customer satisfaction.

- **Complete commitment** A great deal of effort goes into creating an incentive plan. The plan must be accepted at all levels of management. Continued coaching and training are necessary for long-term stability. Learning must be reinforced by strong support and commitment to achieve desired results using measured output to evaluate performance.

Challenges in Cross-Border Situations In addition to being organization-specific, a successful incentive program has to be culturally sensitive. Cultural attitudes can vary widely from country to country. In addition, incentive programs are impacted by the laws and regulations that govern their application that also vary significantly from one country to another.

Direct Sales Personnel There are several ways to compensate personnel who are responsible for sales, depending on the circumstances surrounding the sales activities. Compensation usually is both *direct,* that is, paid by cash or by cash and incentives (in turn, incentives can be cash-driven—for example, bonuses and commissions), or *indirect,* that is, paid through perks and entitlements (for example, cars and expense accounts, club membership, and allowances).

Factors that influence the design of a salesperson's compensation plan include the following:

- The time involved servicing the account as compared to the time spent in the sale of goods or services
- The ability to objectively measure the sales activity
- The nature of the sales activity is difficult to distinguish from the activity spent providing support services
- The degree and type of motivation associated with the sales activity
- The significance of the sales cost involved in the transaction
- The comparative market place practice

Three types of compensation plans are most commonly used.

- **Straight salary** Of the three types of plans, the straight salary plan is the least used, but it more than likely will be found in situations where most of the time involved is spent servicing the account rather than selling the account. It is also more likely when sales costs would otherwise be higher than acceptable to management and finally when, by comparison, the marketplace is more likely to compensate sales on a straight salary basis.
- **Straight commission** This is the other extreme of the sales compensation spectrum. In this case, a person's entire salary is paid by commission. This most often occurs when the ultimate objective is the increase sales volume with less emphasis or need for service as well as when the marketplace approach is also to compensate by way of a straight commission plan.

In some cases, organizations that use a straight commission form of compensation will provide what is called a *draw* for novice or entry-level sales personnel. Typically, the draw consists of a nonrecoverable or guaranteed commission for a defined period of time, usually not more than 1 year. If, during this period, a salesperson does not earn a commission equal to or exceeding the draw, the salesperson does not owe the organization the difference. The period of time the draw is in place usually conforms with the organization's experience in developing the salesperson's selling capabilities to a point the individual is able to earn at least as much or more than the draw provides.

- **Salary plus commission and/or bonus** In a salary plus commission arrangement, a portion of the total salary is a fixed salary; the remainder is commission. This is the most popular form of sales compensation in that it incorporates parts of both the fixed salary (thus some stability with the individual's income flow) and the commission or the reward for sales success (thus the incentive for greater future success).

Professionals The characteristics unique to professional employees include a focus on their chosen fields of endeavor along with their interest career progression within their chosen field. This requires a company's pay system to provide opportunity and recognize their career progression. Two "tools" enhance management's capability to recognize professional growth.

- **The dual career ladder** Typically describes the progression from entry-level positions to higher levels of pay, skill, responsibility, or authority. The traditional career ladder allows employees to be promoted along either a supervisory or technical track. This program helps retain top talent by offering extended career opportunities with appropriate salary growth to employees in their chosen careers.

- **Maturity curve** Measures salaries based on years of directly related experience since the first educational degree or formal training requirement for job entry was earned. This is most often used to measure market pay for employees engaged in technical work such as engineering, and in particular in research and development, although they are also useful in many other areas. The process assumes that spending more years in the profession equates with more highly valued competencies.

Outside Directors Any member of a company's board of directors who is not an employee or stakeholder in the company is an "outside director." Outside directors are paid an annual retainer fee in the form of cash, benefits, and/or stock options. Corporate governance standards require public companies to have a certain number or percentage of outside directors on their boards as they are more likely to provide an "outside" perspective and offer unbiased opinions.

Metrics

Although there are many metrics applied to the subject of compensation, the following are two of the most common metrics:

- **Compensation ratio**   Also known as *compa-ratio,* this is a measure of the relationship of current pay to the midpoints of the applicable pay ranges. Compa-ratios are computed by dividing a worker's pay rate by the midpoint of the range.

$$\frac{\textit{Employee' rate of pay}}{\textit{Applicable pay range midpoint}}$$

  Example: Compensation ratio data enables managers to comparatively determine whether employees are equitably paid for their job performance.

- **Total company compensation expense**   This identifies all employment-related costs as a percentage of total operating costs.

$$\frac{\textit{Pay + Overtime + Benefits + Bonuses}}{\textit{Total Costs}}$$

  Example: Tracking total compensation as a percentage of total costs helps organizations manage the costs associated with human capital including the use of fixed versus variable compensation.

Benefits and Perquisites

Benefit programs, also called *indirect compensation,* are designed to promote organizational loyalty, reward continued employment, enable employees to live healthy lives, help them care for their families, and help provide for retirement benefits. Examples of benefits include housing (employer-provided or employer-paid), group insurance (health, dental, life, etc.), disability income protection, retirement benefits, daycare, tuition reimbursement, sick leave (paid sick leave in a few states), vacation (paid and non-paid), Social Security, profit sharing, funding of education, and other specialized benefits.

The term *perquisites,* sometimes referred to as *perks,* is often used to refer to benefits that are more discretionary in nature. Perks often are given to employees who are doing notably well, hold senior positions, and/or have seniority. Common perks are take-home vehicles, hotel stays, free refreshments, leisure activities on work time (golf, etc.), and personal stationery.

Benefits Structure

Employee benefits represent a significant financial investment on the part of the employer. To effectively meet its purpose, the employer's total benefits programs must be cost-effective, meet their stated purpose, must be affordable for both the employer and the employee, and must comply with local, state, and federal law. To accomplish these objectives, data must be collected and analyzed to determine whether the employer's benefits programs actually meet its objectives. This process is known as a *benefits needs assessment* (i.e., needs analysis).

Deciding Which Benefits to Offer   Employers must provide monetary compensation as well as certain legally mandated benefits to employees, but most benefits are optional. Providing benefits to your employees also allows you to offer benefits to yourself, and contributions that you make for benefit premiums are often tax-deductible for your business. In addition, if you need to attract employees with a special skill or talent, you're going to have to compete with other employers to get them, which may mean you'll need to offer some benefits to be successful.

So, how do you decide which benefits you should offer? Understanding which benefits you are required to offer is your first consideration because of the impact these requirements can have on your ability to offer optional benefits.

Some of the benefits employers are required to offer include time off to vote, serve on a jury, and perform military service. You must also comply with all of the requirements of workers' compensation, withhold for payroll taxes such as FICA and FUTA, and contribute to state disability programs in states where such programs exist.

Employers don't have to provide paid holidays, vacation, or paid sick leave (except where required by state law), health benefits (except where required by state law), life insurance, or retirement plans.

The pros of offering benefits include the following:

- **Tax advantages**   You may be able to deduct plan contributions.
- **Recruiting advantages**   You can use benefits packages to attract good employees, and you can structure them in such a way to reward and thus retain your best employees.
- **Personal gain**   You may be able to get benefits for yourself for less money, if you also offer them to your employees, than you would procuring them privately for yourself.
- **Alternatives to pay**   Sometimes employees will accept benefits in lieu of higher salaries.

Cost is the biggest "con." Other challenges, particularly for smaller employers, include the following:

- You may have to pay higher rates than larger employers for group health care coverage because there are fewer employees among whom to spread risk.
- There may be difficulty providing life insurance coverage to certain employee groups.
- You may have fewer design choices when offering a retirement plan because of high administrative costs.
- You may be less likely to offer fringe benefits because of administrative complexity.

What benefits should be offered depends on the following:

- What you can afford
- What other businesses are offering
- How the benefit can help your business

Benefits Needs Assessment   A benefits needs analysis consists of several steps that include data collection and analysis culminating in a report called a *gap analysis.*

Gap Analysis   The steps in this analysis are as follows:

- *Review the organization's overall culture and strategy.* The results of this effort will determine the potential coverage and scope of its benefits programs.
- *Collect and analyze the employer's workforce demographics.* This data is key to determining potential benefits needs.
- *Analyze the utilization and costs of existing benefits plans and programs.* The results of this data, coupled with the demographics data, will help determine the nature of coverage desired.
- *Determine the potential benefits coverage and costs.* This analysis will be an important factor for comparing the demographics and benefits utilization data.

The final step is to compare the organizational needs and budget with employee needs and any existing benefits coverage. The end result is a gap analysis, a document that will indicate what a benefits package should and should not include.

Types of Benefits

Employers have found that paid time off as a reward for service provides the employee with relief from the ongoing demands of work as well as benefits the employer with increased morale and commitment. Types of paid leaves are described in the sections that follow.

Paid Time Off   Many employers combine vacation and sick leave into a single program called *paid time off* (PTO). PTO is a concept that allows employees to earn, typically by accrual over time, credits that the employee can then use whenever circumstances require that they be absent from work. PTO does not require justification for an absence; it requires simply an approval in the event of a planned absence or the accrued balance to be used in an unplanned absence. In some states, where PTO is offered, PTO accrual is treated in the same manner as vacation; that is, PTO is subject to the same rules that are applicable to vacation.

Vacation or Holiday Leave in the United States   In the United States, there are paid holidays and vacations.

- **Paid holidays**   While paid holidays are not legally required, employers find that both employers and employees benefit from them. The number of paid holidays vary from 6 to 12 a year, including New Year's Day, Memorial Day, Independence Day, Labor Day, Thanksgiving Day, and Christmas Day. Paid holidays are generally paid on the basis of the employer's schedule for a regular workday.

- **Paid vacation**   The standard vacation is based on an accrual system measured on an employee's length of service. State laws vary on the management of vacation accrual. Some states do not allow a "use-it-or-lose-it" policy, while others are silent on the subject. In some cases, vacation can be carried over from year to year with a provision for a reasonable cap. Many employers have a cash-out policy that allows an employee in states in which there is no rollover who hasn't taken their accrued vacation by the end of the year to receive cash back for their unused accrued vacation. Generally, employees must receive advance approval to use their vacation so as not to disrupt the employer's workflow.

Public or National or Bank Holidays   Most countries provide vacation or holiday time to all employees regardless of job or status. Even in emerging countries, it is common for all employees to be provided a number of days for annual leave plus holidays. Generally, each country has paid public or national or bank holidays, during which firms are required to close. Certain holidays may be observed on a local basis or only by certain industries. Public holidays may be required or they may be only customary. In some Western European countries, most businesses shut down in August when most of their employee take their vacation.

Maternity and Paternity or Parental Leave   At least some portion of maternity leave is paid in most countries. In addition to maternity leave, some countries offer paternity and parental leave. A distinction is sometimes made between the two terms; they can, however, have the same meaning. Generally, parental leave is available to both mothers and fathers.

Leave Related to Illness   There is leave related to illness.

- **Leave in the United States**   Organizations that otherwise have paid vacation policies usually also have paid sick leave policies to provide for time off because of illness or injury. These sick leave programs are primarily intended for the benefit of the employee, although in recent years sick leave programs have often been expanded to cover an employee's time off to care for a family member. Some states mandate that a portion of the employee's sick leave accrual must be allowed for family care.

- **Leave in other countries**   In most countries, it is common to take time off because of illness. Policies vary in terms of the number of days allowed away from work; the amount of ages paid, if any; and in some cases, the applicable waiting period. Sick leave policies may be legally required, may be the result of collective bargaining, or may be determined by the employer.

Other Types of Leave   Some examples of other types of leave available in certain countries include the following:

- Paid leave to trade union officials for participating in trade union duties, union projects, or other activities.
- Paid leave to undergo training.

- In some cases, paid days off when workers get married. This extends to parents who are given paid time off when their children get married.

- In countries predominantly Muslim, paid time off for prayer.

- Time off to carry out specified public duties such as campaigning as an official candidate in an election, voting, or jury duty.

Paid time off is mostly dictated by local laws. As such, it is important to know these laws and practices.

Family-Oriented Benefits The composition of families in the United States has changed significantly in the past few decades. The number of traditional families, in which the man went to work and the woman stayed home to raise children, has declined significantly, while the percentage of two-worker families has more than doubled.

The growth in dual-career couples, single-parent households, and increasing work demands on many workers has accelerated the emphasis employers are placing on family-oriented benefits. Balancing family and work demands is a major challenge facing many workers at all levels of organizations. To provide assistance, employers have established a variety of family-oriented benefits.

Some of the family oriented benefits offered in recent years include: adoption benefits, child care and elder care, flexible work hours, compressed workweeks, and telecommuting.

Flexible Work Hours Flexible work schedules are those that vary from the standard work schedules of an organization. Since flexible schedules must meet the needs of both the employer and the employee, flexible work schedules are based on worker needs within set parameters approved by a supervisor. Table 4-22 lists some of the benefits and challenges of a flexible work schedule.

Flexible Work Schedule		
Benefits to Employee	**Benefits to Employer**	**Challenges**
• Schedule flexibility has been found to be highly associated with job satisfaction. • Employees who perceived having more flexibility on the job reported better sleep, more exercise, and a healthier lifestyle in general than those employees who did not perceive the availability of flexibility.	• Flexible work schedules positively affects work effort, job satisfaction, and improve worker productivity. • Flexible work schedules are positively related to employee engagement.	• Blending employees' schedule requests with business demands. • Using managers' time efficiently (the process of creating numerous schedules can be time-consuming, diverting managers' attention from other responsibilities). • Ensuring fair and equitable practices. • Maintaining customer loyalty (if, for example, the customers interact with different salespeople every time they come in).

Table 4-22 Flexible Schedule: Benefits and Challenges

Compressed Workweek		
Benefits to Employee	**Benefits to Employer**	**Challenges**
• Employees have positive view of the effects of compressed workweek on home and work life. • Employees can schedule doctor appointments, deliveries, repair services, and such on the day that they are not in the office.	• Employers note reduced absenteeism among employees with compressed workweek schedules. • Some studies show improved productivity.	• Fatigue may increase with the initiation of a compressed workweek schedule, which may affect employee stress and, ultimately, productivity and performance. • The results of research have been mixed, with productivity either improving or staying the same after the implementation of a compressed workweek work schedule.

Table 4-23 Compressed Workweek: Benefits and Challenges

Compressed Workweeks The compressed workweek is a special type of flexible schedule that involves working 40 hours per week but in fewer days than found in a typical 9-to-5, 5-day workweek. There are many different configurations to the compressed workweek. For instance, an employee can work 40 hours in 4 days (a 4/40 schedule) or 80 hours in 9 days (a 9/80 schedule). Table 4-23 describes some different configurations of a compressed workweek.

Health and Welfare A group health plan is an employee welfare benefit plan established or maintained by an employer or by an employee organization (such as a union), or both, that provides medical care for participants or their dependents directly or through insurance, reimbursement, or otherwise.

Health plan coverage varies in other countries as indicated here:

- **Australia** In Australia, public coverage is guaranteed to all, but the state encourages wealthier individuals to use a private system by enforcing an additional 1 percent tax on those who fall above a certain income level but use the public system anyway. The Australian government's innovative techniques are evident in their death rate from conditions amenable to medical care, which was a startling 50 percent less than America's in 2003 and 25 percent less than the United Kingdom's.

- **Sweden** Sweden's low health care expenditures ($5,331 USD per capita) in 2011 can in part be attributed to government initiatives that disincentivize sending patients to specialists when their illnesses can be treated by general practitioners. The Swedish government's success with cost efficiency explains why even though public funding accounts for 85 percent of total Swedish health expenditure, this does not place an unreasonable constraint on taxpayers or the government.

- **United Kingdom** The United States and the United Kingdom are worlds apart in terms of health care. In the United Kingdom, the National Health Service (NHS) publicly covers various costs, including preventative services and mental health care. About 88 percent of prescriptions there are exempt from charges. Despite American efforts to increase affordability and equity, the United Kingdom ranked first on indicators of efficiency in a recent Commonwealth Fund study. America could learn a lesson from the United Kingdom's successes at cutting administrative costs and closing loopholes that would otherwise cost the government millions.

- **Germany** With the oldest universal health care system in the world, 90 percent of Germans happily use the public system offered there, and just 10 percent of the population voluntarily uses the private system. Moving past the mythical trade-off between time and cost, Germany is one of the few countries to have quick access to specialty services with very little out-of-pocket costs. Germany spends around half as much as America does on health care per capita, with few differences in quality of services between the two countries.

- **Netherlands** Interestingly, health insurance coverage is statutory in Holland but provided by private insurers competing for business. Insurers can decide by whom and how the care is delivered, which, to capitalists' great relief, allows the insured to choose between alternatives based on quality and costs. This system has proven to be very effective. In 2010, 72 percent of Dutch adults saw their doctor the same or next day when they were sick, compared with only 57 percent of adults in America. And, whereas one third of U.S. adults did not see a doctor when sick, went without recommended care, or failed to fill prescriptions because of costs, only 6 percent of adults in the Netherlands faced these issues.

- **Canada** In the realm of health care, America and its neighbor couldn't be more different. Canada's national health care system consists of a centralized body that sets standards that the 13 Canadian provinces must follow to receive funding. Hospitals are mainly private nonprofit organizations with their own governance structures, lending Canada an interesting balance between privatization and public ownership.[97]

Private Health Insurance In other countries, health care is generally paid for through social insurance funded either by employers, by employees, through general taxation, or by some combination of these sources. By comparison, the United States is ahead of other countries in the use of high-end equipment and procedures. The United States also leads in the use of magnetic resonance imaging (MRI) machines, but the monetary cost of this technology is much higher in the United States than in other countries.

Other comparisons indicate that it is much harder for Americans to get same-day or next-day appointments and to get after-hour appointments. As a result, Americans use high-cost emergency rooms more frequently than in other countries.

Most other countries have a single-payer system but the United States has many different insurance companies with many different plans plus overlapping programs such as Medicare, Medicaid, state plans, and programs for veterans.

Employee Assistance Programs   The employee assistance program (EAP) is an employee benefit programs offered by many employers. EAPs are intended to help employees deal with personal problems that might adversely impact their job performance, health, and well-being. EAPs generally include short-term counseling and referral services for employees and their families. Supervisors may also refer employees (management referral) based upon unacceptable performance or conduct issues.

EAP resources typically provide employees with confidential expert advice and support 24 hours a day, 7 days a week. Nearly all EAPs are outsourced, and most are priced on a "per head" basis. EAPs address a broad and complex body of issues affecting mental and emotional well-being, such as alcohol and other substance abuse, stress, grief, family problems, and psychological disorders. Many EAPs are active in helping organizations prevent and cope with workplace violence, trauma, and other emergency response situations.

Wellness Programs   These are programs intended to improve and promote health and fitness that are usually offered through the workplace, although insurance plans can offer them directly to their enrollees. Wellness programs allow employers to offer premium discounts, cash rewards, gym memberships, and other incentives to participate. Some examples of wellness programs include programs to help employees stop smoking, participate in diabetes management programs, weight loss programs, and preventative health screenings.

Disability   The term *disability* represents a range of conditions differently measured not only from country to country but from program to program within a country. Yet the general characteristics of the disabled are remarkably similar overall. They tend to be the older workers and those with relatively low educational levels and occupational status. When a country has a racial or national minority, members of the minority are more likely to be disabled than members of the majority population. Except in the aftermath of war, women have a higher incidence of disability than do men. The disabled are more likely to be unmarried and live alone than others in the working-age population.

Disability benefits have different meanings in different countries. Generally, disability benefits take the form of payments to employees who are unable to work because of an illness or injury. Benefits may be short-term, long-term, or permanent, sometimes all of these choices.

Short-term benefits usually last up to 6 months; long-term benefits are longer. They usually start where short-term benefits end. Permanent disability may mean the same as a retirement income under health or medical circumstances.

Payments may come from employee contributions, employer contributions, government funding, or a combination of these sources. In some cases, funding may come from multiple agencies depending on factors such as level of income, degree of disability, or even family status.

Life Insurance   In most countries, life insurance is provided by Social Security. Life insurance is mandated in some countries; in many cases, just a small amount is sufficient to cover burial but not sufficient to support a beneficiary. A majority of employers provide life insurance payable upon the death of the employee to a beneficiary as a voluntary company-provided benefit. Additional life insurance can often be purchased through an organization-sponsored group plan.

The situation in third-world countries is very different from the norm in the United States and other richer countries. Poverty, disease, and living conditions directly affect the rate of mortality in many villages in third-world countries. Many people in those countries do not have sufficient food, live in war zones, and have to endure poor working conditions that are physically demanding. Money is used for basic needs such as food and clothing and maybe a roof over their head.

Employees in many Latin American countries receive life insurance that pays for up to 2 years' pay in the case of death. Employees in Peru with 4 or more years of service receive company-provided life insurance. Employees in the United Kingdom receive three to four times their annual salary as a life insurance benefit. Employees in the United States typically receive company-provided life insurance up to the equivalent of 1 year's salary with an option to personally purchase higher amounts of their choosing.

Workers' Compensation   Workers' compensation is a type of insurance paid for by the employer that provides wage replacement income and medical care benefits to employees who suffer work-related injuries or illnesses in return for giving up the employee's right to sue his or her employer for negligence. Benefits are regulated by the states, not the federal government. Individual states prescribe the rules governing coverage, eligibility, types of benefits, and the funding of benefits.

Workers' compensation defines a work-related disability as a physical condition that can result in an accident or illness and is caused, aggravated, precipitated, or accelerated by a work activity or environment. Workers' compensation only covers worker health problems that are identified as work-related disabilities, injuries, or illnesses.

Workers' compensation benefits include the following:

- Paid medical expenses and wage replacement benefits under certain circumstances
- There are four types of workers' wage replacement benefits.
    - **Income benefits**   These benefits replace income that might be lost because of a work-related injury or illness. Income benefits can include temporary income benefits, impairment income benefits, supplemental income benefits, and lifetime income benefits.
    - **Medical benefits**   These benefits pay for necessary medical care to treat a work-related injury or illness.
    - **Death benefits**   These benefits replace a portion of lost family income for eligible family members of employees who are killed on the job.
    - **Burial benefits**   These benefits pay for some of the deceased employee's funeral expenses to the person who paid the expenses.
- Vocational rehabilitation or, in some cases, supplemental job displacement benefits
- Permanent and temporary partial or total disability benefits
- Survivor's benefits in cases of fatal work injuries or illnesses

Workers' compensation law in the United States is derived from European social insurance. It has evolved at the federal and state levels over the past century through a long series of reform (or redesign) initiatives.

Workers' compensation is a European concept, dating back to German Chancellor Otto von Bismarck. By the turn of the twentieth century, all European countries had workers' compensation laws. The German law required employees to pay part of the costs and called for highly centralized administration. Its coverage was broad, was compulsory, and provided for nonprofit mutual employers' insurance funds. Most industrialized nations now have national workers' compensation programs based on the German model.

In European Union (EU) countries, all workers are covered against the risk of wage loss because of temporary sickness through government agencies. Wage-replacement schemes consist of social insurance covering the loss of earnings because of old age, unemployment, temporary sickness, or permanent disability. Coverage typically lasts up to a year, with transition to longer-term disability insurance programs if needed.

Severance Packages   A severance package is pay and benefits an employee receives when leaving employment at a company. In addition to the employee's remaining regular pay, it may include some of the following:

- An additional payment based on length of service.
- Payment for unused vacation time (unless mandated by state law) or sick leave.
- Medical, dental, or life insurance.
- Assistance in searching for new work, such as access to employment services or help in producing a résumé.
- The package may require the severed employee to sign a general release.

Severance pay programs exist in most countries around the world. They typically provide lump-sum cash payments to workers who involuntarily or voluntarily separate from their employers. The size of the payment is usually related to the number of years worked with the last employer and is linked to the last salary in the job. Such payments were provided in many countries by employers before they were required by law. Organization-based severance pay schemes often also exist in parallel to legislated provisions.

Severance packages are required by law in many countries. Employers need to have a thorough understanding of the legal requirements associated with terminating an employee in countries where severance payments are a legal requirement. Some of the issues to address include the following:

- Requirements applicable to warnings for misbehavior or inadequate job performance
- Clearly stated reasons for the termination
- Specifically described severance payments with applicable conditions, if any

Compensation for Termination Support is required for terminated employees in some countries even when they have been terminated for cause. This can become expensive as it often happens at least some degree. If support requirements are ignored, it can be even more expensive because fines and penalties for noncompliance can be costly.

The amount of compensation paid to a terminated employee varies by country, but there may be some similarities within regions. Years of service is often a key factor when determining termination terms and end-of-service calculations. As an example, both Argentina and Bolivia require that a terminated employee receive 1 month's salary for each year worked, up to a defined maximum. Colombia also links the amount paid to the length of service. An employee who worked for a company 10 years is entitled to 45 days' pay, plus an additional 40 days' pay for each full year employed after that up to a defined maximum. Other considerations include the employee's position, any employment agreements, and the employer's current policies and practices. Finally, organizations are responsible for ensuring that severance pay is compliant and fairly compensates terminated employees to avoid discrimination lawsuits and regulatory fines and penalties.

Retirement At some point, employees will reach an age where they no longer desire or are able to work. Retirement plans allow current employees to make financial provisions for the future. Retirement plans differ widely by country. Many retirement programs are mandated by the government and paid for through employee and employer contributions. Supplemental government support is sometimes provided.

The main goal is to provide retirement income to employees with some type of income payable periodically. Characteristics of the two most common types of plans, defined benefit plans and defined contribution plans, are summarized in Table 4-24.

Type of Plan	Description
Defined benefit plan	• The principal goal is to insure against loss of income in the event of retirement, death, or disability. • The employer promises to pay a specific benefit based on pay, age, and service of the member in the event of named contingencies, such as retirement, death, or disability. • The employer is responsible for contributing whatever the promised benefits cost, net of member contributions. • The benefit amount is determined based on a mathematical formula.
Defined contribution plan	• The principal goal is to accumulate savings through deferred compensation and investment earnings. • The employer promises to contribute periodically to each member's individual account. The amount contributed may vary based on pay, age, service, or member contributions. • The employer is responsible for contributing periodically the amount promised to each member's account. • The benefit is the account balance, payable in a lump sum, in installments, or as an annuity for life.

Table 4-24 Types of Retirement Plans

Payments   Most often, payments vary in terms of how they are made. They usually are made in the form of an annuity, paid monthly until death. In other countries, an amount may be paid in a single lump sum. The particular formulas for payment of retirement vary and are often complicated. They may be affected by the nature of the government funding strategies or variations that depend on such factors as age, level in the organization, and family characteristics.

Unemployment Insurance   Unemployment insurance (UI) is a federally mandated program administered by the states that provides unemployment benefits to eligible workers who are unemployed through no fault of their own and who meet other eligibility requirements of applicable state law. UI benefits are designed to provide temporary financial assistance to unemployed workers. Each state administers its own unemployment insurance program within guidelines established by federal law. Eligibility for unemployment insurance, benefit amounts, and the length of time benefits are available are determined by state law. In the majority of states, benefit funding is based solely on a tax imposed on employers. The amount a person receives is based on the person's salary up to a monthly maximum amount.

- **Eligibility**   To qualify for UI, individuals must meet requirements for wages earned or time worked during an established period of time referred to as the *base period*. In most cases, the individual must be unemployed through no fault of their own, must be available and actively seeking work, cannot be terminated for misconduct, and must not be unemployed because of a labor dispute.

    Individuals must file weekly or biweekly claims and respond to questions concerning their continuing unemployment. Any job offers or refusal of work must be reported for the period claimed.

- **Duration**   Most states grant UI benefits for up to 26 weeks, but this is often extended during periods of high unemployment by Congress with the approval of the president.

Social Security   First adopted in Germany in the 1880s, to benefit the workers, Social Security was initially a compulsory sickness insurance for which the worker paid two-thirds of the cost and the employer one-third. In Great Britain, the National Insurance Act was passed in 1911, and a compulsory unemployment insurance program as well as old-age insurance and sickness insurance programs were established. France adopted a program of voluntary unemployment insurance in 1905 and in 1928 made insurance plans for old age and sickness mandatory.

The following are the basic concepts behind Social Security:

- Social insurance in which people receive benefits or services in recognition of their contributions to an insurance program. These services typically include a provision for retirement pensions, disability insurance, survivor benefits, and unemployment insurance.

- Services that are provided by government or by a designated agency responsible for specific Social Security services. While this varies from country to country, it generally covers medical care; financial support during unemployment, sickness, or retirement; health and safety at work; aspects of social work; and even, in some cases, industrial relations.

- Basic security irrespective of participation in specific insurance programs where eligibility would otherwise be an issue. An example is assistance given to newly arriving refugees for basic necessities such as food, clothing, housing, education, money, and medical care.

Perquisites

There are several definitions of *perquisites*; perhaps the most common is "Any monetary or other incidental benefit beyond salary; a gratuity; a privilege or possession held or claimed exclusively by a certain person, group or class."[98]

These are some of the more common perquisites identified by the Society for Human Resource Management (SHRM):

- **Free/discounted products or services**   Employees may be eligible for free products and services or discounts.

- **Mobile devices**   A cell phone, smartphone, personal digital assistant (PDA), or laptop may be provided for business needs.

- **Professional organizations/certifications**   Employee membership in professional associations and fees for professional certifications may be paid.

- **Training programs**   Employer payment for training programs may be available to many levels of employees.

- **Education fees**   Tuition assistance may be provided to employees. An employer may pay all or part of an employee's cost to attend college or university or technical school classes, allowing employees to continue to expand their knowledge and skills while working.

Some of the less common perquisites include the following:

- **Housing**   Accommodations or related allowances are awarded to certain employees; these may be company-owned or company-leased. Allowances may be a fixed monetary amount or a percentage of basic salary. The specifics often depend on employee level. Furnishings may be provided.

- **Company car and/or cash car allowances**   Cars are typically provided on status basis. Some countries offer a car allowance in lieu of a company car. In addition to the cost of the car, organizations often finance car maintenance, taxes, and insurance. Fuel costs are typically reimbursed for business purposes (except for senior executives, where all fuel costs are typically reimbursed).

Benefits Metric	Description	Formula
Benefits costs as a percentage of total payroll costs	Reflects the total cost of benefits compared to the total payroll costs for the organization.	$$\frac{\text{Total benefit costs}}{\text{Total payroll costs}}$$
Value: Pay and benefits combined make up total wage costs for an organization. This metric identifies the proportion of benefits costs to total payroll costs.		
Health care expense per employee	Percentage that measures the health care expense per employee for a given fiscal year. Total health care expenses include employee- and company-paid premiums, stop-loss insurance, and administrative fees.	$$\frac{\text{Total health care expenses}}{\text{No. of employees enrolled in a health care plan}}$$
Value: This measurement can show per-capita cost of employee benefits (e.g., the average per person cost).		
Annual increase/ decrease in benefits costs based on previous years and projected costs	Represents the expected increase/decrease in the organization's health care expense for a given fiscal year.	Compares the current health care expense per employee metric to previous years and project costs.
Value: This measurement alerts an organization to the increasing costs of benefits and helps the organization assess if actions should be taken to control benefit costs (e.g., changing or reducing benefits, sharing the costs with employees, etc.).		

Table 4-25   Benefits Cost Metrics

- **Club memberships**   Entrance fees as well as annual subscriptions for social or sports club memberships are paid by the employer.
- **Meal allowances**   Lunch vouchers, meal tickets, meal subsidies, or subsidized/ free lunches in the company restaurant/canteen may be granted to employees.

Some additional perquisites include financial and legal counseling and, to a lesser extent, medical check-ups, vaccinations, and immunizations; subsidized/low interest loans for the purchase of a house or car; and travel allowances.

Metrics

As with other aspects of HR, knowing how to use metrics as it applies to employee benefits is an important capability for every HR professional. Table 4-25 identifies three metrics applicable to determining the cost of benefits.

Legislation Affecting Compensation and Benefits

A great many things influence the compensation of the employees of any organization. Some of these are external to the organization, such as the labor market and the law. Some are internal to the organization, such as organizational culture and policies. Some are part of the employee, such as skill and performance.

Complexities of Legal Compliance

The legal environment in which U.S. compensation administration is practiced consists of federal and state legislation and the regulations imposed by executive branches of these governments. In the case of some developing legal concepts, case law (court decisions) represents the public position. In these forms, government is stating public intentions or guides to decision-makers. Although private organizations tend to characterize these laws, regulations, and court decisions as constraints, they may also represent opportunities. In essence, the "rules" state that compensation must not be too low or (at times) too high but that within these limits compensation decisions should be left to the parties involved. Also, in the interest of fairness, certain groups have been protected, and all must be paid when wages are due.

As minimum and prevailing-wage laws place a floor under wage rates, Social Security, unemployment insurance, and workers' compensation can be described as placing a floor under benefits. Likewise, the Employee Retirement Income Security Act of 1974 and the 1980 amendments of it applying to multi-employer pensions can be considered assurance-of-benefit-payment laws.

Finally, in the United States, the network of state and federal laws is extensive. Some of the regulations apply only to firms with a specified minimum number of employees; others apply to all employee/employer relationships, regardless of enterprise size. Further, state laws may differ from federal laws. The general rule is to follow the regulation that most benefits or protects the employee when state laws differ from federal laws. (An organization can often do more than the law requires but cannot do less.)

Ultimately, HR practitioners must understand the employment laws, codes, and practices applicable in each of the countries and regions in which the organization operates. This necessitates due diligence on the part of HR practitioners that should include an understanding of the following:

- Standards and regulations set forth by international organizations, such as the International Labor Organization, the Organisation for Economic Cooperation and Development, the United Nations, and the European Union, as well as treaties and agreements, such as the North American Free Trade Agreement or Mercosur (a trade organization of Argentina, Brazil, Paraguay, Uruguay, and Venezuela)
- Country laws and regulations
- Regional and local laws and practices
- Extraterritorial application of national law
- Application of national laws to international-owned subsidiaries operating within a nation's borders

Legal Areas for Compliance

The following legal areas for compliance represent key compensation and benefits topics applicable both in the United States and on a global scale. Keeping in mind the HR professional's responsibility to know, understand, and create compliance with the plethora of applicable laws, the following sections summarize these key topics.

Wage and Hour   To be compliant, employers need to understand the terms and conditions of wage and hour laws and how they apply to various classifications of workers wherever the operations are located. Basic wage and hour terms and conditions and key considerations include the following:

- **Minimum wage and increases**   How are minimum wages set (e.g., hourly or monthly)? If any collective bargaining agreements are in force, do they impose different minimums or minimum wage increases?

- **Overtime pay and holiday pay**   What are the requirements for computing pay for legal overtime and locally worked holiday time (e.g., time-and-a-half, less than time-and-a-half, double-time, or quadruple-time for overtime and holiday work)? If there are no statutory requirements for overtime and holiday pay, do collective bargaining agreements impose any? Who is entitled to overtime (e.g., only hourly employees or managers as well)?

- **Equal pay**   What provisions are there to ensure that individuals doing the same work receive the same compensation?

- **Exemption**   What is the definition of "exempt" work under local law? Does the host country offer any special exemptions?

- **Cap on hours worked**   Is there a flat cap on hours worked (e.g., weekly flat caps or hours of overtime per year)? Are there nominal caps that serve merely as reference points (e.g., a 40-hour "standard" week but with "reasonable additional hours" allowed)?

- **Special issues under local law**   What miscellaneous local wage and hour rules are in place (e.g., paid meal breaks, rules on break time, regulations on night work)?

Tax   Tax systems vary widely around the globe, from no-tax to high-tax regimes. Two commonly withheld taxes are national or federal tax and social tax. In some countries, income tax is dependent upon whether an individual is considered a resident or a nonresident. Bonus payments may be treated differently from other taxable income. Many other variations exist.

Tax issues are quite complex for the employee on an international assignment as well as for the employee's organization. An employee may be subject to both host- and home-country taxes, depending on the countries involved and their tax treaties. Some countries permit residents to "break residency" while on an international assignment, thereby eliminating the need for them to pay into their home-country tax program. Generally, the structure of an employee's remuneration package should take into account various tax arrangements that are available.

Leave   This generally describes an employee benefit that provides paid or unpaid time off work. Country law may require employers to provide specific types of leave, such as time off for legal holidays, a certain amount of vacation each year, maternity and paternity or parental leave, and leave for an illness. Terms and conditions of minimum leave benefits are often stipulated by law. Many countries have generous leave laws. HR must be aware of the organization's legal obligations.

Social Security   Social Security (or social insurance) provides individuals with some level of income when faced with the contingencies of old age, survivorship, incapacity, disability, unemployment, or rearing children. Social Security may also offer access and coverage for curative or preventive health care. According to the International Social Security Association, Social Security can include social insurance programs, social assistance programs, universal programs, mutual benefit schemes, national provident funds, and other arrangements such as market-oriented approaches that, in accordance with national law or practice, form part of a country's Social Security system.

Health Care   Health care laws and regulations are complex. For example, some countries have a statutory universal access/universal coverage health care system. In other countries, employers offer employer-sponsored health insurance. Additionally, health care laws and regulations are often interlocking. Compliance typically cuts across government requirements and labor relations.

To varying degrees, health care affects all organizations, whether they conduct business in one location or multiple jurisdictions worldwide. Simply stated, employers must comply with health care regulations afforded their employees in a given country. Organizations must also comply with the medical privacy protections that are in force.

Disability   The concept of disability benefits varies across the globe. Generally, disability refers to payments made to employees who are physically unable to perform their jobs because of illness or injury. Sometimes it covers only incapacitation because of job-related injuries or illnesses; other times it also covers causes outside the workplace.

Short-term, long-term, and permanent disability are usually differentiated, and the source of funding and the length and amount of the benefit for each disability category may vary.

In addition, employers in some countries may be required to provide unpaid leave as a reasonable accommodation under disability antidiscrimination laws.

Severance   To be compliant, a separation pay policy requires a detailed understanding of the complex laws governing severance and restructuring practices and protections for employees in different markets. Many countries have statutory protections regarding severance provisions. Where country laws dictate the terms of termination and end-of-service calculations, organizations have little room for discretion even if the payments and benefits are significantly more generous than company policy would award in unregulated jurisdictions.

Pensions   Upon retirement, workers in many countries continue to receive monetary compensation from their employer, the government, or a combination of both in the form of a pension. The provision of financial remuneration in retirement is critical for both individuals and societies. There is tremendous diversity in pension systems worldwide, as they are the unique product of each country's particular economic, social, cultural, political, and historical circumstances. Likewise, global pension funding issues are highly complicated.

Fiduciary Responsibility   A fiduciary duty (or fiduciary obligation) implies a legal obligation of one party to act in the best interest of another. The obligated party is typically referred to as a *fiduciary* (e.g., an individual or party entrusted with the care of money or property).

Countries worldwide regard fiduciary duties differently. Some regulations, for example, stipulate a broad view of fiduciary obligation, while other laws adopt more conservative approaches.

Chapter Review

This chapter covered five functional areas of professional HR knowledge and responsibilities. People are the heart of any organization. Until we get to the point where machines are able to run an organization autonomously, we will need to manage people resources. From overall HR strategy and talent acquisition to employee engagement and retention, HR professionals will have an important influence on their employer organizations. Employee learning and development and total rewards are two additional components of people requirements. Complexities abound. Satisfaction is just around the corner. Be ready to influence both the workforce and the employer organization. HR professionals have a unique position and huge responsibilities in this area.

Questions

1. Since 1978 the Uniform Guidelines on Employee Selection Procedures have required that many employers do what?
   - **A.** Validate each step of their employment selection process
   - **B.** Submit their employment selection process to the EEOC
   - **C.** Review their employment selection process to be sure there are sufficient veteran applicants
   - **D.** Publish their employment selection process each year

2. What does PEST mean?
   - **A.** Rodent Tracking and Removal Service
   - **B.** Payroll, employment, systems, and training
   - **C.** Political, economical, social, and technological
   - **D.** Personal, exceptional, systemic and training

3. What are the two primary dimensions of behavioral situational theories of leadership?
   - **A.** Effective leaders let their contributions be known as expertise.
   - **B.** Listening more is helpful to leaders.
   - **C.** Leaders are more logical and analytical rather than intuitive and emotional.
   - **D.** Being more optimistic and less negative about the organization's strategy.

4. What is an employment brand?

   A. The market perception of what it is like to work for an organization

   B. Product name that appears on supermarket packages

   C. Industry-assigned label serial number

   D. A recruiting slogan

5. Reviewing applicant résumés to determine who meets the minimum qualifications for a job opening is:

   A. An example of an employment decision

   B. Subject to disparity testing

   C. Not an employment decision

   D. A way to determine their salary requirements

6. Why is it important to measure turnover, retention rate, and reasons why people leave the payroll?

   A. They are all things the CEO wants to know.

   B. They can contribute to a monthly HR report to the executives.

   C. They are examples of reports HR professionals need clerical support to generate.

   D. They can all help control costs.

7. Why should a job offer always be in writing?

   A. It specifies details of compensation, benefits, and employment-at-will status.

   B. The federal Department of Labor requires it.

   C. State regulations specify that only with written offers can a job be filled.

   D. Actually, they should not be made in writing because that constitutes a contract.

8. Employment interviews and written tests are considered to be what?

   A. Essential to hiring manager acceptance of candidates

   B. Selection devices that must be validated according to federal regulations

   C. HR purview only

   D. Always acceptable if the tests are bought "off the shelf" and not created in-house

9. Training for job selection interviewers is:

   A. Never needed

   B. Essential for all managers and supervisors

   C. Needed for supervisors who are new to employment selection interviewing

   D. A good idea for people who have been hired from competitor's organizations

10. Why are written job descriptions a good strategic tool?

    A. They give incumbents a reference so they don't do something they aren't supposed to do.

    B. It is important to be able to follow responsibility trees in writing.

    C. Federal civil rights enforcement agencies insist on written descriptions.

    D. They provide reference for job seekers as well as incumbents, managers, and supervisors.

11. The key benefit to developing long-term goals is:

    A. Showing the interaction of planning, people, and processes

    B. Separating the effects of culture against the intentions and goals

    C. Increasing the influence on internal factors

    D. Aligning the use of resources with intended strategic goals

12. What are the stages of the strategic planning process?

    A. Formulation, buy-in, communication, evaluation

    B. Formulation, development, implementation, evaluation

    C. Development, communication, buy-in, implementation

    D. Senior management development, communication, implementation, evaluation

13. Herzberg's motivation-hygiene theory is based on which two categories of needs?

    A. Psychological and basic needs

    B. Motivational and security needs

    C. Extrinsic and intrinsic needs

    D. Safety and self-esteem needs

14. Which is considered to be an HR strategic task in an organization?

    A. Developing an ergo training program to reduce repetitive injuries

    B. Ensuring backup and retention of records off-site

    C. Administering new hire orientation

    D. Providing analysis to management to forecast workforce needs

15. The Equal Pay Act prohibits wage discrimination on the basis of what?

    A. Race

    B. Sex

    C. Seniority

    D. Merit

16. You have been asked to develop a 5-year budget for the HR function. In what way would the existence of the organization's strategic plan be of help to you in the development of the multiyear budget?

   A. Because it's a budgeting activity, it will help in providing increase allotments for employees.

   B. The goals identified in the strategic plan will give you an idea of how to allocate monies for each year.

   C. The strategy plan will help you compete for training dollars versus marketing dollars.

   D. It will cause you to identify and prioritize the HR activities and their needed resources that align with the strategic plan's goals.

17. Which of the following laws does not directly relate to a company's compensation or benefits programs?

   A. Equal Pay Act

   B. Fair Labor Standards Act

   C. Port-to-Portal Act

   D. Uniform Guidelines on Employee Selection Procedures

18. Which of the following is not a pay differential?

   A. Hazard pay

   B. Shift pay

   C. Base pay

   D. Overtime

19. A home appliance manufacturer guarantees its installers a base wage plus an extra $25 for each job completed to specifications. The employer is using a:

   A. Merit pay system

   B. Productivity-based pay system

   C. Competency-based system

   D. Flat-rate system

20. An employee elects a $500 annual deferment in his Section 125 Flexible Benefits Plan. His employer pays an FSA claim for $500 in March. In April, the employee terminates his employment after deferring only $290 to his plan. What happens in this situation?

   A. The employee must pay the company $290 for the amount in excess of his actual deferral.

   B. The employer may withhold $290 from the employee's final paycheck.

   C. The employee is entitled to the full reimbursement for $500.

   D. The employee becomes ineligible for the full FSA reimbursement.

21. According to COBRA, a company with 20 or more employees must offer:

    A. Health insurance to its employees

    B. Continued medical insurance coverage to employees terminated for gross misconduct

    C. COBRA benefits to workers if the company terminates its health plan

    D. COBRA benefits to spouses of deceased workers

22. Which of the following is a common action taken in the United States to lower budgets that would most likely violate compensation laws in other countries?

    A. Reduce base salary levels

    B. Offer early retirement packages

    C. Delay or not fill open positions

    D. Downgrade job titles

23. If a leave under FMLA can be reasonably anticipated, how much notice must the employee give the employer?

    A. 7 days

    B. 14 days

    C. 30 days

    D. 90 days

24. An organization establishes an ESOP by:

    A. Deducting a small amount from the individual's pay for the purchase of stock

    B. Using stock as collateral to borrow capital from a financial institution

    C. Providing upper management with a bonus

    D. Having its profits distributed with favorable tax treatment

25. HR manager Sue makes sure that her HR staff has access to leading best practices and theories. What key element of Sue's leadership is she demonstrating according to Kouzes and Posner?

    A. Challenging processes

    B. Inspiring shared vision

    C. Enabling her staff to act

    D. Encouraging spirit

Answers

1. **A**. Each employment selection step must be validated if the employer has 15 or more workers on the payroll.

2. **C**. Political, economical, social, and technological are the components of PEST.

3. **B**. Jon Katzenbach and Douglas Smith's research in "The Wisdom of Teams" identified that a critical behavior for leaders is to listen more.

4. **A**. An employment brand is a positive perception created in the job market for what it is like to work for that organization.

5. **C**. There is no decision when simply determining who meets the minimum qualifications published in the job requisition.

6. **D**. Cost control is the reason for measuring turnover.

7. **A**. Explaining compensation, benefits, and employment-at-will status in writing will minimize any complications later.

8. **B**. Each employment interview and written test is considered a selection device. All must be validated according to the Uniform Guidelines on Employee Selection Procedures.

9. **B**. All interviewers must be properly trained so they will understand what questions they may and may not ask.

10. **D**. Having a written job description provides an anchor for all concerned parties when needing information about job duties and responsibilities.

11. **D**. Strategic planning is the identification of long-term goals, and having long-term goals allows management in an organization to align and appropriate resources to those goals in a consistent yet long-term manner.

12. **B**. The four stages of the strategic planning process are formulation, development, implementation, and evaluation.

13. **C**. Hygiene factors are considered extrinsic and associated with job security, pay, working conditions, and relationships, whereas motivational factors are considered intrinsic, associated with recognition, achievement, and personal growth–related events in the job.

14. **D**. A, B, and C are considered activities and functions of the HR department. Providing analysis for forecasting future workforce needs for, say, a new plant or office opening identified in the strategic plan would be considered an HR strategic task.

15. **B**. The Equal Pay Act requires that men and women be given equal pay for equal work in the same establishment. The jobs need not be identical, but they must be substantially equal. It is job content, not job titles, that determines whether jobs are substantially equal.

16. **D**. Strategic planning assists all function leadership, including the HR function, to allocate and request resources that will be needed to implement initiatives that align with the organization's strategy.

17. **D**. In 1978, the Civil Service Commission, the Department of Labor, the Department of Justice, and the Equal Opportunity Commission jointly adopted the Uniform Guidelines on Employee Selection Procedures to establish uniform standards for employers for the use of selection procedures and to address adverse impact, validation, and recordkeeping requirements. The other choices are laws that directly relate to employers' compensation programs.

18. C. Hazard pay, shift pay, and overtime are all differentials. Base pay is the foundation of an employer's compensation program.

19. B. The employer is using an incentive program based on performance results, which is considered a productivity-based system. A merit-pay system does not address incentive pay. A competency-based system addresses capabilities, whereas a flat-rate system establishes a fixed rate of pay.

20. C. Flexible spending accounts are authorized under Section 125 (Cafeteria) plans. FSAs offer employees a pretax method to defer pay toward their group health plan costs as well as their out-of-pocket medical costs. FSA healthcare claims below the annual elected deferral must be paid by the employer when they are incurred even though the employee's FSA payroll deductions have not created a sufficient balance to cover the expense.

21. D. COBRA provides up to 36 months' continuation of group health benefits in the event of a divorce or death of the employed spouse. None of the other choices is a valid COBRA provision.

22. A. Decreasing an employee's salary is illegal in most countries, particularly in Latin America and Europe. It is legal in the United States.

23. C. The FMLA allows employers to require 30 days advance notice when the leave can be reasonably anticipated. The other choices are incorrect.

24. B. An employee stock ownership plan (ESOP) is an employee-owner method that provides a company's workforce with an ownership interest in the company. In an ESOP, companies provide their employees with stock ownership, often at no up-front cost to the employees. ESOP shares, however, are part of employees' remuneration for work performed. Shares are allocated to employees and may be held in an ESOP trust until the employee retires or leaves the company. The ESOP can borrow money to buy shares, with the company making tax-deductible contributions to the plan to enable it to repay the loan.

25. C. The HR manager is following Practice 3, enabling others to act, which is what Kouzes and Posner discuss in their research about exemplary leaders who encourage collaboration.

References

1. The SHRM Body of Competency and Knowledge, pages 36–37.

2. Mintzberg, Henry. *The Rise and Fall of Strategic Planning*, Free Press, January 1994.

3. Porter, Michael E. *Competitive Strategy: Techniques for Analyzing Industries & Competitors*, Free Press, June 1998.

4. Porter, Michael E. *Competitive Advantage: Creating and Sustaining Superior Performance,* The Free Press, June 1998.

5. Freemen, R. Edward. *Strategic Management: A Stakeholder Approach*, Cambridge University Press, March 1998.

6. https://www.professionalacademy.com/blogs-and-advice/marketing-theories-pestel-analysis

7. https://www.inc.com/encyclopedia/industry-analysis.html

8. Porter, Michael E. *How Competitive Forces Shape Strategy*, Harvard Business Review (March–April 1979).

9. https://www.mckinsey.com/business-functions/strategy-and-corporate-finance/our-insights/enduring-ideas-the-ge-and-mckinsey-nine-box-matrix

10. Community Tool Box, Developing Successful Strategies—Planning to Win, https://ctb.ku.edu/en/table-of-contents/structure/strategic-planning/develop-strategies/main.

11. https://blog.marketresearch.com/6-ways-to-differentiate-your-business-from-the-competition

12. Porter, Michael E. *Competitive Advantage*, Ch. 1, pp 11–15. The Free Press. New York, 1985.

13. Mind Tools, Porter's Competitive Strategies, https://www.mindtools.com/pages/article/newSTR_82.htm.

14. https://www.mindtools.com/pages/article/newSTR_82.htm

15. https://www.thebalancecareers.com/business-strategy-tips-for-hr-manager-1916828

16. http://smallbusiness.chron.com/growth-strategies-business-4510.html

17. Timmons, J. *New Venture Creation* (Burr Ridge, Illinois: Irwin, 1998), 14.

18. Christensen, C.M., R. Alton, C. Rising, and A Waldeck. The Big Idea: The New M&A Playbook. Harvard Business Review, March 2011.

19. https://www.shrm.org/resourcesandtools/tools-and-samples/toolkits/pages/mergersandacquisitions.aspx

20. Wheeler, Gary. The Virtual HR Director LLC, https://www.aligning-hr-to-business-strategy.htm.

21. https://www.imaworldwide.com/resources-aim-methodology

22. Jones, Phil. *Communicating Strategy*, Taylor & Francis, March 2, 2017.

23. https://hbr.org/2011/08/eight-ways-to-energize-your-te

24. https://onstrategyhq.com/resources/strategic-implementation/

25. Kubler-Ross, Elizabeth. *On Death and Dying: What the Dying Have to Teach Doctors, Nurses, Clergy and their Own Families*, Google Books, 1969.

26. Kirkpatrick, Donald L. *How to Manage Change Effectively: Approaches, Methods, and Case Examples*, Jossey-Bass Management Series, 1985.

27. https://peterstark.com/employee-responses-change/

28. https://www.fastcompany.com/3015083/6-steps-for-successfully-bringing-change-to-your-company

29. https://www.shrm.org/resourcesandtools/tools-and-samples/toolkits/pages/managingorganizationalchange.aspx

30. https://www.torbenrick.eu/blog/performance-management/how-to-ensure-successful-performance-measurement/

31. Rohm, Howard. Balanced Scorecards, Balanced Scorecard Institute, 2018.

32. https://www.nap.edu/read/11344/chapter/5#22

33. https://www.business-case-analysis.com/financial-metrics.html

34. https://www.accountingtools.com/articles/what-is-variance-analysis.html

35. https://www.business.qld.gov.au/running-business/growing-business/trend-analysis

36. Kouzes, James M., and Barry Z. Posner. *The Leadership Challenge* Jossey-Bass; sixth edition, April 17, 2017.

37. Fox, Erica Ariel. *Winning from Within: A Breakthrough Method for Leading, Living and Lasting Change*, Harper Business; September 2013.

38. Goleman, Daniel. *Emotional Intelligence*, Bantam Books; 10th edition, September 2005.

39. Goldsmith, Marshall. *What Got You Here, Won't Get You There*, Hachette Books; January 9, 2007.

40. McGregor, Douglas. *The Human Side of Enterprise*, New York: McGraw-Hill Education, 2005.

41. Blake, Robert R., and Jane S. Mouton. *The New Managerial Grid*, Gulf Publishing Company, May 1978.

42. Hersey, Paul, and Ken Blanchard. *Management of Organizational Behavior*, Upper Saddle River, NJ: Prentice Hall, 2012.

43. Fiedler, Fred Edward. *A Theory of Leadership Effectiveness*, New York: McGraw-Hill, 1967.

44. Adair, John. *Action Centered Leadership*, Gower Publishing Company, June 1979.

45. Katzenbach, Jon R., and Douglas K. Smith. *The Wisdom of Teams*, HarperBusiness, July 2006.

46. House, Robert J., Peter W. Dorfman, Mansour Javidan, Paul J. Hanges, and Mary F. Sully de Luque. *Strategic Leadership Across Cultures: GLOBE Study of CEO Leadership Behavior and Effectiveness in 24 Countries*, SAGE Publications, August 2013.

47. Hofstede, Geert. *Culture's Consequences: Comparing Values, Behaviors, Institutions, and Organizations across Nations (2nd ed.)*, Thousand Oaks, CA: SAGE Publications, 2001.

48. The SHRM Body of Competency and Knowledge, page 38.

49. 2016 Survey Results, https://www.manpowergroup.com/talent-shortage-2016, accessed on March 5, 2018.

50. www.reliancestaffing.com/2013/08/employee-orientation-beyond-the-manual, accessed March 6, 2018.

51. https://universumglobal.com/what-is-employer-branding/, accessed on March 6, 2018.

52. http://press.careerbuilder.com/2017-06-15-Number-of-Employers-Using-Social-Media-to-Screen-Candidates-at-All-Time-High-Finds-Latest-CareerBuilder-Study, accessed on March 6, 2018.

53. https://www.linkedin.com/pulse/20141016104025-615702-recruiting-vs-sourcing-a-day-in-the-life/, accessed on March 6, 2018.

54. https://www.mckinsey.com/business-functions/organization/our-insights/why-diversity-matters, accessed on March 6, 2018.

55. https://www.recruiter.com/i/6-key-metrics-to-measure-the-success-of-your-recruiting-process/, accessed on March 7, 2018.

56. Ford, Wayne D. *How to Spot a Phony Résumé*, The Management Advantage, Inc., 1998.

57. Adapted from: *Handbook for Faculty Searches*, the Ohio State University, 1987, https://www.unk.edu/about/compliance/aaeo/hiring_guidelines/guidelines_for_interviews.php, accessed on March 8, 2018.

58. https://www.management-advantage.com/products/QuestionsYouCanandCantAsk.htm, accessed on March 8, 2018.

59. Willer, Dory, William H. Truesdell, William D. Kelly. *aPHR Associate Professional in Human Resources Certification Exam Guide*, McGraw-Hill Education, 2017.

60. Equal Employment Opportunity Commission, "Consideration of Arrest and Conviction Records in Employment Decisions under Title VII of the Civil Rights Act of 1964," www.eeoc.gov/laws/guidance/arrest_conviction.cfm, published on April 25, 2012.

61. U.S. Department of Justice, Bureau of Justice Statistics, "Prisoners in 2012—Advance Counts," www.bjs.gov/content/pub/pdf/p12ac.pdf, published July 2013.

62. Citing yearly compensation on a job offer letter has resulted in employers being obligated for the balance of the yearly amount when they terminated employees earlier than one year. Citing amounts in weekly or monthly terms can reduce that potential liability substantially.

63. https://www.dol.gov/odep/pubs/misc/job.htm

64. The SHRM Body of Competency and Knowledge, pages 39–40.

65. 2014 Modern Survey, Inc.

66. State of the Global Workplace, Employee Engagement Insights for Business Leaders Worldwide 2013, Gallup, Inc.

67. https://hbr.org/2014/11/a-primer-on-measuring-employee-engagement

68. https://www.qualtrics.com/support/wp-content/uploads/2017/10/Qualtrics-EBook-How-to-Design-an-Employee-Engagement-Survey.pdf

69. https://www.torbenrick.eu/blog/employee-engagement/infographic-what-is-the-business-case-for-employee-engagement/

70. Maslow, Abraham. "A Theory of Human Motivation," *Psychological Review*, 50, 370–96, 1943.

71. Ouchi, William. *Theory Z: How American Management Can Meet the Japanese Challenge*, Basic Books, January 1981.

72. Pink, Daniel H. *Drive: The Surprising Truth About What Motivates Us*, Riverhead Books, April 2011.

73. Vance, Robert J. Employee Engagement and Commitment, The SHRM Foundation, 2006, https://www.shrm.org/hr-today/trends-and-forecasting/special-reports-and-expert-views/Documents/Employee-Engagement-Commitment.pdf

74. 2016 SHRM/Globoforce Employee Recognition Survey, https://resources.globoforce.com/globoforce-blog/5-takeaways-from-the-new-shrm-globoforce-recognition-survey

75. State of the American Workplace: Employee Engagement Insights for U.S. Business Leaders, Gallop, Inc., 2013.

76. "How Employee Retention Impacts the Bottom Line," Voice, *The Engage for Success Magazine*, post by David Bator of TemboStatus (www.tembostatus.com/), November 12, 2014.

77. https://www.roberthalf.com/blog/management-tips/effective-employee-retention-strategies, accessed on March 8, 2018.

78. The SHRM Body of Competency and Knowledge, page 41.

79. www.thechangeforum.com/Learning_Disciplines.htm

80. www.trainingmag.com/5-trends-future-learning-and-development

81. www.ntl.org/

82. Cross, K. P. *Adults as Learners,* San Francisco: Jossey-Bass, 1981.

83. www.kirkpatrickpartners.com/

84. www.ericdigests.org/2004-4/career.htm

85. Vii Finkelstein, Stanley. *Why Smart Executives Fail: And What You Can Learn from Their Mistakes*, Portfolio Trade, 2004.

86. https://www.td.org, search for "Leadership Development Through Emotional Intelligence and Meditation Premium Content", September 8, 2014, by Maynard Brusman

87. www.ccl.org/Leadership/pdf/assessments/LGISampleFeedbackReport.pdf

88. www.bloomberg.com/bw/management/a-new-era-for-global-leadership-development-02172012.html

PART II

89. www.ccl.org/Leadership/pdf/research/ChallengesLeadersFace.pdf

90. The SHRM Body of Competency and Knowledge, page 42.

91. *World at Work* website (www.worldatwork.org)

92. Scott, Ph.D., Dow (Loyola University Chicago), Tom McMullen (Hay Group), and Mark Royal, Ph.D. (Hay Group). "Reward Fairness," World at Work, May 2011.

93. Eani, Susan (Baker & McKenzie, WorkSpan). "The Essentials of Managing Global Compensation Practices," World at Work.

94. A Better Balance, the Work and Family Legal Center, Overview of Paid Sick Time Laws in the United States, www.abetterbalance.org, June 24, 2015.

95. Yoder, Dale. *Personnel Management and Industrial Relations*, Prentice-Hall, 1942.

96. Heneman III, Herbert, and Timothy Judge. *Staffing Organizations*, 6th Edition, McGraw-Hill/Irwin, 2008.

97. Jain, Sona. "7 Countries That Show Us How Health Care Should Be Done," June 11, 2013, http://mic.com/articles/46063/7-countries-that-show-us-how-health-care-should-be-done.

98. https://en.wiktionary.org

Organization

The HR expertise domain of Organization Knowledge counts toward 16 percent for both exams. This domain covers the essential HR knowledge needed for relating to the organization. The following are the functional areas that fall within the Organization Knowledge domain:

- Functional area 6—Structure of the HR Function
- Functional area 7—Organizational Effectiveness & Development
- Functional area 8—Workforce Management
- Functional area 9—Employee and Labor Relations
- Functional area 10—Technology Management

HR professionals are expected to know how to perform the following Body of Competency and Knowledge (BoCK) statements for the Organization Knowledge domain:

- **01** Creating an effective HR function fully aligned to the organizational strategy
- **02** Enhancing the effectiveness of the organization at large
- **03** Ensuring that the organization's talent pool has the skills and capabilities to achieve organizational goals
- **04** Promoting positive relationships with employees
- **05** Leveraging technology to improve HR functioning

Functional Area 6—Structure of the HR Function

Here is SHRM's BoCK definition: "Structure of the HR Function encompasses the people, processes, theories, and activities involved in the delivery of HR-related services that create and drive organizational effectiveness."[1]

All career levels of HR are expected to know and support the different types of HR service models and understand how HR services are integrated. The HR organization must be structured to meet the needs of the organization and its stakeholders. Gathering feedback, collecting data, and using the appropriate metrics to determine HR performance and satisfaction all enable HR professionals to evaluate HR's effectiveness and identify areas needing improvement and change.

Key Concepts

- Approaches to HR operational integration (i.e., how HR structures work together)
- Approaches to HR function/service models (e.g., centralized versus decentralized)
- Approaches to HR structural models (e.g., Center of Excellence [COE], shared services)
- Elements of the HR function (e.g., recruiting, talent management, compensation, benefits)
- HR-function metrics (e.g., HR staff per full-time employee, customer satisfaction, key performance indicators, Balanced Scorecard)
- HR staff roles, responsibilities, and functions (e.g., generalists, specialists, HR business partners)
- Outsourcing of HR functions

These are the proficiency indicators that SHRM has identified as key concepts:

For All HR Professionals	Advanced HR Professionals (SCP Exam)
Adapts work style to fit the organization's HR service model (e.g., centralized versus decentralized) to ensure timely and consistent delivery of services to stakeholders	Designs and implements the appropriate HR service model for the organization (e.g., centralized versus decentralized) to ensure efficient and effective delivery of services to stakeholders
Seeks feedback from stakeholders to identify opportunities for HR function improvements	Creates long-term goals that address feedback from stakeholders to identify opportunities for HR function improvements
Acts as HR point-of-service contact for key stakeholders within a division or group	Ensures that all elements of the HR function (e.g., recruiting, talent management, compensation and benefits, learning and development) are aligned and integrated and provides timely and consistent delivery of services to stakeholders
Provides consultation on HR issues to all levels of leadership and management	Identifies opportunities to improve HR operations by outsourcing work or implementing technologies that automate HR functions (e.g., time, payroll)
Coordinates with other HR functions to ensure timely and consistent delivery of services to stakeholders	Designs and oversees programs to collect, analyze, and interpret key performance indicators (e.g., Balanced Scorecard) to evaluate the effectiveness of HR activities in supporting organizational success

For All HR Professionals	Advanced HR Professionals (SCP Exam)
Ensures that outsourced and/or automated HR functions are integrated with other HR activities	
Analyzes and interprets key performance indicators (KPIs) to understand the effectiveness of the HR function	

The Strategic Role of HR

The strategic role of HR professionals is to strengthen the relationship between the employees and the employer.

The Evolving Role of HR Professionals

The role of human resources has evolved over the years, probably more so than any other department function in an organization. In the old days, HR managers simply shuffled paper, keeping payroll records and benefit assignments straight. In the early twentieth century, HR as a specialized function began with a narrow focus of hiring and keeping records of employees, an operational and administrative function. Changes in HR have been stimulated by external changes, and a major change has been the need for HR professionals to participate in strategic planning and then implementation of those plans.

HR's staff typically provided three types of support: advice, service, and control.

- **Advice**   Advising line management on workforce matters including policies and laws, providing solutions and procedural steps, offering assistance and guidance on employee issues, diagnosing problems or gathering facts, and providing resources

- **Service**   Maintaining records, hiring, training, answering, and clarifying information within a broad customer base, including management, employees, legal and regulatory agencies, applicants, retirees, families of employees, and vendors

- **Control**   An authoritative role involved in consistency of policy application, evaluation of employee performance, corrective action, and designing or implementation of employee programs

While the focus continues to have a foundational basis in the day-to-day operational role (acquisition, development, resolving issues, and communications), along with administrative transactional activities (maintaining a human resource information system [HRIS]), the significance of HR's contributions has become more apparent as a business strategist with a forward-thinking, long-term global focus that includes protecting the organization from potential risks. HR professionals have earned a seat at the executive round table, contributing to the organization's direction with strategic solutions for talent management, creating organizational culture, formulating and developing strategies, and balancing the external and internal environments to help the organization achieve its goals. The title of chief human resource officer (CHRO) is common in today's large organizations—a recognition that indicates HR has come a long way up the perceived value-added scale. In today's global competitive business climate, the HR role must contribute in quantifiable business terms, outlining a return on investment (ROI) that ensures the effective and efficient use of its human capital.

Table 5-1 provides a brief historical perspective of the evolution of the human resource function.

HR as a Profession   A job is something you can go to every day, perform the assigned duties, and go home without any further attachment. Human resource management used to fall into this category. Now, however, HR professionals are placed into a role that demands strategic thinking and strategic planning with an eye on overall organizational

Era	HR's Identity	Business Era	Issues for HR
Pre-1900	HR did not exist	Gilded Age—most small businesses and a few large corporations called "trusts"	Responsibilities mostly associated with payroll/hiring done by owners or accounting personnel
1900–19	Referred to as *Labor Relations*	Industrial Revolution	People could be replaced with machinery
1920–39	Referred to as *Employee and Industrial Relations*	World War I and civil service	Formalized processes brought in; workers' rights issues
1940–59	Referred to as *Personnel Administration*	World War II and scientific research	Efficiency productivity experts, benefits administration, women in the workforce
1960–79	Referred to as *Personnel Management*	Civil Rights and government compliance	Legal compliance reporting and policing, policy application consistency
1980–99	Referred to as *Human Resources Management*	Knowledge and service economy; hostile takeovers; M&A; technology	HR theories for employee motivation, training and development, RIFs, immigration hiring
2000–09	Referred to as *People or Talent Management*	9/11 attack on U.S. and homeland security; global competitiveness	Cultural diversity, outsourcing, technology, cultural blending, talent acquisition, offshoring
2010–Present	Evolving: *HR Business Consultants within the Human Asset Department* is trending	Global economy; Mobile Technology Age; Great Recession	Talent retention, organizational restructuring, employee engagement, cost containment

Table 5-1   Evolution of Human Resources

health and success. Early on, "personnel management" was a staff function. Later "human resource management" became a management function. In recent years, HR management has become a strategic function helping the organization achieve its strategic goals.

HR in the Twentieth Century   Following the creation of a "personnel department" in the mid-twentieth century, people in that portion of the organization were expected to shift their focus toward a broader perspective of HR management. It became more than a personnel and payroll support function.

Administrative Services   HR workers were assigned duties including the following:

- Personnel records management
  - Benefits enrollment
  - Attendance tracking
  - Training recordkeeping
  - Employee data management systems such as HRISs
- Employee award tracking
- Office party planning

Operational Services   Direct support of the operational units in the employer organization became necessary. The following were added to the HR responsibilities:

- Labor relations expertise
- Recruiting and staffing
- Training preparation and management such as operations and management skills
- Policy development
- Employee handbook management

HR in the Twenty-First Century   As we transition into the new century, HR professionals find themselves involved more with strategic planning and implementation.

Strategic Administrative Role   The functions handled in the twentieth century still exist, but they have morphed into a strategic support role. Personnel records management is now responsible for assessing employee benefit programs as they contribute to the financial success of the organization. This includes impact analysis on employee recruiting and retention and its effect on the profit and loss performance of the company. Employee award tracking has evolved into a strategic assessment of programs that will improve employee retention and engagement. Office party planning has gone away in many organizations. In its place is the strategic assessment and selection of employee support programs, such as free or low-cost food services, and specific employee motivation programs.

Strategic Operational Role   Labor relations has grown over the years with the transitioning of union contract protections to laws that apply to most employers. Those protections such as wage and hour restrictions now are available to most employees in the country. The benefits offered by labor unions these days are less numerous than they used to be. Most of the old benefits are now legal protections at both the state and federal levels.

Policy development involves a wide swath of topics from employee benefit offerings to disciplinary processes. Those policies are being assessed based on their strategic impact on the organization and its mission. Once policies are developed, employee handbook content can be prepared that communicates those policies to the employee body. Even the designation *employee* is being altered by some organizations. Some of the terms now used include *cast member*, *crew member*, *associate*, and *staff member*.

Changes That Impact the HR Profession

The largest impact on the HR profession has come from state and federal legislative bodies creating new laws that contain employee protections that once were available only to union members within a bargaining unit.

David Ulrich presents his approach in terms of deliverables, or outcomes, for which HR should be responsible in new strategic roles: strategy execution, administrative efficiency, employee contribution, and capacity for change.[2] In the course of delivering in these four areas, he describes four corresponding roles for HR to play within a business: a) as a strategic partner working to align HR and business strategy, b) as an administrative expert working to improve organizational processes and deliver basic HR services, c) as an employee champion, listening and responding to employees' needs, and d) as a change agent managing change processes to increase the effectiveness of the organization. One of unique things about Ulrich's approach is that it includes all of the ways that HR can deliver value to an organization, rather than shifting focus from one area to another.

Workforce/Workplace Changes   According to a recent article in *Work Design Magazine*, "By 2027, global socioeconomic shifts will result in larger changes in worker type, available jobs, and ways of working. The rise of the middle class in emerging markets will have a large impact on the overall workforce. Currently, one-third of the global middle class is located in Asia Pacific. By 2030, this proportion will double, due in large part to expansions of the middle class in countries like China and India. This growth will result in changes in buying habits, ultimately driving economic growth. According to a Morgan Stanley estimate, by 2030 middle-class spending will almost double that of 2010.

"New patterns will emerge in occupations: jobs in service-oriented industries such as healthcare and hospitality sustain growth, but a significant portion of workers gravitate towards more flexible work arrangements and freelance jobs. There will be an influx of jobs enabled by emergent technologies."[3]

Globalization   Globalization is not a fad. It is a movement that will only solidify the ways of doing business as the days go by. The impacts it will have on employer organizations will be profound. Employee groups in remotely operating locations with different laws and customs present challenges to professional HR managers. The role of diversity management will grow even bigger than it is today. Value added will be the operating expectation for every group, including HR. If something can't be measured and shown to add value, the HR organization will be hard-pressed to convince the C suite that it should be done.

Ethics   In the past, HR professionals had to wrestle with different employment laws in the different states where they had employees working. In the future, it will be necessary to wrestle with laws and customs in multiple countries. In some countries there is an expectation that money will be offered to those approving work projects. That is unacceptable to an HR professional's ethics, so dilemmas will arise when the strategic repositioning of workforce groups becomes necessary. It is incumbent upon HR professionals to reconcile those differences so that the work can get done and the local expectations are satisfied without violating U.S. laws.

Organizational Growth or Retraction   When the size of an employment organization increases or decreases, there are considerations for legal compliance and, equally important, for the satisfaction of employee morale requirements. When groups are small, there is a tendency for individuals to bond easily around the mission of the groups. As groups grow, that sense is diluted, and bonding can become more difficult. There can be issues related to who is promoted and who is not or who is given a desirable work assignment and who is passed over. Leadership from HR professionals takes on critical importance. How they communicate and help employees through difficult periods of time will determine how well the organization can meet its strategic objectives.

When organizations reduce their employee headcount, other problems occur that require HR interventions and leadership. Layoffs, downsizing programs, relocations, and constructive discharges can all result in employee dissatisfaction. How HR professionals handle these difficulties will determine how well the force reduction will reach its goals.

Movement of Decision-Making   As new workforce locations are opened in remote countries or even remote locations within the United States, there is a risk that they will experience the "out of sight, out of mind" syndrome. Managing people from a distance involves permitting and even encouraging decision-making by people at those locations. Working out what decisions should be local and what should be held for headquarters becomes an operational requirement that HR can help with.

Extended Organizations   When manufacturing, marketing, or administrative organizations find it necessary to create workforce placement in new, extended locations, HR can help facilitate those movements. Any expansion into an international environment will require some adjustments. It is not so much a need to hire people in the new location as it is a need for cultural adaptation. That is a two-way process. New employees in the remote location must learn about the corporate culture and how to behave within it. The corporation must also learn about the local culture and design ways so that culture can be embraced by the organization.

New Organizational Structures Expansion into international locations is not quite like expanding into additional U.S. locations. There are enough similarities from one U.S. location to another to make the transition easier than when international expansion is undertaken. New locations may mean a different organizational structure is required for the effective management of the remote location. The following are some organizational structures:

- **Functional structure** This type groups all workers within a function under the management of a chief executive for each function. Chief sales and marketing officer, chief administrative support officer, chief human resource officer, and chief financial officer are just examples.

- **Divisional structure** This aligns workers according to product, market, or region. An international expansion can sometimes result in an "Asian division" or a "Customer Product division."

- **Matrix structure** This requires two reporting lines, one to the divisional manager and one to the functional manager.

Changing organizational structures can be as difficult and challenging as merging cultures. Witness the merger of Continental Airlines and United Airlines. In May 2010 the two organizations agreed to a $3 billion merger.[4] In 2018 the combined organization had yet to fully blend its cultures. Union contract provisions for each group of employees were still separate and, in some cases, quite different from one another. Eight years in, and a new airline company has yet to emerge.

Increased Accountability The magazine *Inside HR* suggests, "Today, employees are collaborating in real time on projects across many time zones and geographies. People are working where they want and when they want—more than half of millennials say they want to work in a different country. Companies are moving towards organizational designs centered on project-based teams, matrixed structures and flat hierarchies."[5]

The magazine goes on to add the following:

Possible future #1: expanded HR accountability

This potential future for HR includes increased accountability for workforce productivity, performance, collaboration, innovation and culture. In this future, new core HR competencies would emerge requiring strong technical, analytical and creative skills.

- HR would replace its one-size-fits-all policy focus with a focus on building flexible work environments which support myriad work styles, individual preferences, geographies and time zones.

- HR would replace its focus on ensuring people work the requisite hours with a focus on building technologies that actually facilitate productivity, such as collaborative workspaces and virtual team rooms.

- HR would replace its focus on facilitating an annual performance review with a focus on deploying systems that actually increase performance and engagement, rather than just measuring it.

- HR would replace its focus on developing training curriculum with a focus on enabling real-time, '24/7' learning.

- HR would replace its focus on annual goal-setting with a focus on providing managers with a real-time way to monitor and quantify work.

Possible future #2: decreased HR accountability

The second potential future for HR includes diminished accountability and a narrowing of mission. In this future, there are a couple of different possible paths:

- HR will fail to step into the current accountability vacuum for productivity, performance, collaboration and innovation and would cede enterprise leadership to other areas of the business. In this scenario, the business would drive the changes needed to support emerging work models, and HR would focus primarily on the administrative aspects of HR.

- HR will significantly increase its technical and analytical acumen and provide the business with the tools and data to be more self-sufficient and do for itself many of the things that HR once did for the business (recruiting of talent, measurement of performance, training of staff).

Understanding the Organization

Understanding your organization is fundamental as an HR professional so that you can provide the necessary support required of HR activities to the organization. HR professionals need a thorough understanding of their organization's structure, the internal environment, and the external environment and industry in which it operates. This type of understanding lends itself to helping the HR professional to fulfill the role of a true business partner that can help the operating management with identifying internal needs and the issues they face, along with setting HR goals to address the issues.

Having an understanding of the organization and its design allows you to do the following:

- Be fluent in the nomenclature of the business

- Increase your credibility and the HR function's credibility

- Connect the dots in the strategic planning process

- Educate others in the organization about HR's contributions and value

- Be proactive in affecting outcomes of the organization

The Core Business Functions

Every organization, regardless of size, has basic key business functions: marketing and sales, operations, information technology, and finance and accounting. Larger organizations will have even more, including customer service and relations, research and development, and quality assurance. Each has a connection and collaboration associated with the human resource function. HR professionals need to form partnerships within their organization's key business functions to fully understand the key functional areas in an effort to support and become a strategic business partner. Understanding the core functions and business lines within the organization, including each area's perspectives, challenges, and goals, will be of great use to an HR professional.

Finance and Accounting Similar to the sales and marketing functions, the finance and accounting functions go hand in hand yet are distinctively different. Finance has its focus on funding sources, such as bank loans and stock sales, along with budgeting for income generation and expenses. Accounting, on the other hand, is associated with the movement of the monies going in and out, such as payables and receivables processing, payroll, and taxes.

HR interfaces with finance and accounting by preparing and reviewing budgets.

Budgeting and Financial Analysis Budgeting is the process of estimating the amount of income and expenses that will occur within a given period of time. It is usually done on an annual basis, although budgets can be created for multiple years and for shorter periods of time such as months and quarters. The accuracy of budgeting can be improved when there is some historical data on which to rely. Generally speaking, budgets in the short term can be easier to construct and are usually more accurate than long-range budgets. The reason, simply, is because many unforeseen influences can enter the picture in the long range. Fewer unpredictable influences tend to happen in shorter periods of time. Figure 5-1 illustrates the basis of budgeting.

Whether in a for-profit enterprise, a governmental agency, a nonprofit, or a volunteer service organization, there is a need for money management. Budgeting and financial analysis are critical to any organization large enough to have employees. Understanding how to plan for earnings and expenses, managing the process, and ultimately conducting analyses of what happened after the fact are key to any individual's success in a management role.

There are two key financial reports that any organization should be preparing and studying. One measures the income and expenses over a defined period of time such as a year, a calendar/fiscal quarter, or a month. This is usually called a *profit-and-loss statement*, or P&L. The second is a balance sheet that shows the assets (furniture, buildings, vehicles, cash, and accounts receivable) compared to the liabilities outstanding (accounts payable, taxes payable, credit card balances, and payroll payables). A balance sheet also shows the amount of equity owned by investors in the organization. Equity is the difference between income and liabilities in a for-profit organization. In a nonprofit organization it is called *net assets*.

 NOTE This basic formula helps in understanding balance sheets: assets = liabilities + equity.

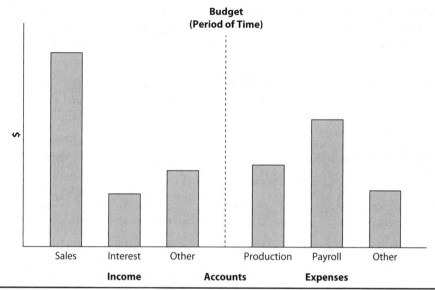

Figure 5-1   Budget chart

There are four basic approaches to budgeting.

- *Zero-based* is a method of budgeting in which all expenses must be justified for each new period. The process of zero-based budgeting starts from a *zero base*, and every function within an organization is analyzed for its needs and costs.

- *Incremental* is a budget prepared using a previous period's budget or actual performance as a basis, with incremental amounts added for the new budget period. It encourages "spending up to the budget" to ensure a reasonable allocation in the next period. It leads to a "spend it or lose it" mentality.

- *Formula* budgeting is based on some predetermined formula.

- *Activity-based* as a method of budgeting is based on an activity framework, using cost driver data in the budget setting and variance feedback processes.

HR professionals at management levels will generally participate in the creation of the HR department's budget to outline anticipated specific expenses, such as office supplies, equipment purchases, and software licenses, but also for other areas in the organization that have compensation and benefits associated with their budgets. Additionally, HR will provide projected budget expenses associated with plans that the organization's strategic plan may pursue that year. An example would be a strategic plan objective that creates a new incentive bonus plan for customer service representatives. HR will project how those additional earnings will impact 401(k) matching contributions.

Marketing and Sales   The marketing function has responsibilities for promoting, pricing, and locating/identifying the customer base. The sales function in an organization is normally the revenue generator. It is responsible for selling the organization's service or product.

Operations   Operations is considered the heartbeat of the organization. Operations will create the goods or services, acquire the resources, and make sure the customer receives those goods or services. This runs off of five concepts: capacity, scheduling, inventory, standards, and control.

Information Technology   Information technology is the brain of today's organizations. The systems, tools, and information required for all other key functions to do what they do are the responsibilities of IT. IT's major focus is to support the integration of data from different systems and processes through an enterprise resource planning (ERP) system. This helps make an organization's data more visible for decisions and in real time.

Research and Development   Research and development (R&D) varies by type of company. It exists not just in the private sector but also in the public sector. The private sector may focus on new product design and the development/expansion of the organization's mission to expand revenue. In the public sector, R&D would be in the form of research institutes and laboratories mostly focusing on theoretical research that promotes science and new technologies of a public interest. Some organizations will have their R&D function in individual business units so that initiatives are focused specifically on that genre. R&D spending and investment vary greatly by organization and industry. According to the 2013 Global Innovation 1000 Study by Booz & Company,[6] R&D spending ranges from 2 percent of revenue in telecommunications to 27 percent in computing and electronics. Globally, R&D spending has increased steadily since 1998.

Organizational Design

The design of an organization determines how it does business. The size and scope of the organization, its functions, its culture, and how it communicates and makes decisions are all part of its design. There are lifecycles for all organizations that take them through phases of growth. Which phase an organization is in will define its structure and its goals. A startup will have a very different design than a more established mature organization, and the focus of HR will vary accordingly.

NOTE   Chapter 4 covered the lifecycle of businesses.

Organizational Structures

Aligning the way the parts of an organization relate to each other is considered the organizational structure. HR professionals need to be familiar with organizational structures so they can act as a guide for management in selecting and determining which structure would be best to gain the highest performance.

Structural Principles   Three key principles guide organizational structure: decision-making authority, layers of hierarchy, and formalization.

There are seven types of organizational structures.

- Departmental
- Chain of command
- Span of control
- Work specialization
- Formalized
- Centralized or decentralized
- Matrix

Departmental   This is where tasks are divided into separate duties grouping people and jobs together. The purpose is so that work can be coordinated. It can be functional in nature, divisional, or matrix.

Chain of Command   This is a structure where an employee typically reports to one manager in an up-down format, with a clear line of decisions and authority. Chain of command is becoming less recognized in organizations today because more and more organizations are pushing decision-making downward matrix lines, which causes the line of authority to look more lateral.

Span of Control   This organizational structure refers to the number of individuals who report to a single supervisor. It's hierarchically in nature through a chain of command. For example, there is an executive at the top, then managers, then supervisors, and then direct reports, much like a pyramid. In organizations where many workers are skilled and require little supervision, they may report to one supervisor; this would be considered a *flat organization*.

Work Specialization   Work specialization was first associated with the assembly line. It is where tasks are divided into specific jobs and workers are considered skilled labor. It may offer a more efficient manner of productivity, yet on the other hand, it can lead to worker boredom. Today's organizations using this organizational structure will typically rotate job functions on a regular basis, training the workers in skills that add variety to their tasks.

Centralized or Decentralized   To centralize or decentralize, that seems to be the question and the cycle of several long-standing organizations. Centralizing pulls decision-making authority to a central level of management, such as headquarters. Decentralizing is pushing the authority level and decisions out to units, such as regional divisions.

Centralizing and decentralizing continuum is also applicable to HR departments. With decentralized structures, corporate headquarters will create policy and develop programs; rollout and application are then carried out by the HR staff in the regional divisions. When the organization is centralized, HR headquarters would make the policy *and* coordinate the rollout activities or administration functions.

Matrix   Matrix structures create a dual chain of command, rather than a singular chain of command. A function, such as HR, would report to the local division executive at a facility, along with a direct reporting function to the head of HR in the headquarters office, which is typically located in another geographical area. As a result, the HR manager at the division location would have two managers, with neither manager having a superior role over the other in this reporting relationship. A huge disadvantage of this type of reporting relationship is the conflicting priorities of the division and the headquarters. The employee with two direct superiors is attempting to follow the direction of one, and the other is competing for their priority. It can be a bit of a tug-of-war.

RACI Matrix   RACI is an acronym standing for responsible (R), accountable (A), consulted (C), and informed (I). The RACI matrix is used by organizations to better define the roles and responsibilities of each member in an organization.

- There should be only one person responsible (R) for a work assignment. Having more than one person responsible for the same task increases the probability that there will be duplication of work or that some portions of the work will not be performed.

- Accountable (A) means an individual is designated to oversee the completion of the assigned tasks.

- Consulted (C) means there are appropriate subject-matter experts when necessary. They will suggest any deviations from the standard procedures that may be necessary.

- Informed (I) are those who have an interest in the task being performed. It could be a manager who oversees the given task or someone who cannot begin the next task until this one is completed.

Structural Alternatives   There are other alternatives to structuring an organization such as functional structure, product structure, geographic structure, and hybrid structure.

Functional Structure   Departments are defined by the services they contribute to the organization in a functional structure. In this type of structure, all of the operations employees report to a single function. In the organizational chart shown in Figure 5-2, each plant has the functions of finance, marketing, and so on, reporting to the plant manager, who in turns reports for those functions collectively to the division president.

Figure 5-2 Functional structure

PART II

Product Structure   With an organization that has a product structure, the functional departments are grouped under major product divisions. As an example, an electronic company may have separate divisions for its printers, cameras, GPS units, and monitors. Each of these divisions will have their own marketing, finance, and sales functions.

Geographic Structure   A geographic structure is similar to a product structure with the exception that the geographic regions, not products, define the organizational chart. Each region has its own complete set of functions such as finance, manufacturing, marketing, and so on. The organizational chart shown in Figure 5-3 depicts a geographic structure.

Hybrid Structures   In a hybrid structure, all the elements of the functional, product, and geographic structures are combined. Because some locations in an organization are not equipped to handle all functional activities such as manufacturing, a hybrid structure is used. A hybrid is generally used when an enterprise is expanding into new geographical areas, such as first going global, and then it will move into a matrix structure.

Other Internal Environment Considerations

Beside understanding the functions within an organization, the HR professional needs to be keen to the important priorities and initiatives that are on the organization's agenda. This might include a shift in customer service performance, a new product or service being developed, or a new focus on vendor relationships. Understanding and knowing the hottest initiatives keeps HR "in the know" to relate its function and services to the initiatives underway.

Figure 5-3 Geographic structure

The External Environment

Equally important to the internal environment is knowing the external environment. PEST is an acronym to follow in learning about the key factors that affect the external environment of an organization.

- **P = Political environment** This political environment includes government regulations or any defined rules for that particular industry or business. It also involves studying tax policy, which includes exemptions (if any), employment laws, environment laws, and so on.

- **E = Economic factors** This includes gauging the economic environment by studying factors in the macro economy such as interest rates, economic growth, exchange rate, and inflation rate. These factors also help in assessing the demand, cost of the product, expansion, and growth.

- **S = Social factors** This forms the macro environment of the organization. It includes the study of demographics, as well as the target customers. These factors help in gauging the potential size of the market. It includes studying population growth, age distribution, career attitude, and so on.

- **T = Technology** Technology changes rapidly. It involves understanding factors that are related to technological advancements and the rate at which technology gets obsolete.

The HR Organization and Function

The function of HR is designed to serve the overall organization and its mission. The structure can take on different arrangements based on the size and needs of the organization. Let's explore the processes, the HR team, the department structure, and ways to demonstrate and measure HR's value.

HR Processes

Grouped in the following categories, these are the HR processes:

- Participating in the implementation and creation of the organization's strategy. Those processes could be
  - Performance management
  - Job design
  - Organizational design
  - Communications
  - Knowledge management
  - HRIS selection, implementation, and integration
  - Strategic planning
  - Hiring

NOTE   You can find additional information on organizational strategy in Chapter 4.

- Creating and following strategy to source, recruit, hire, develop, manage, and retain talent
  - Creating staffing plans
  - Attracting qualified talent
  - Selecting the best talent
  - Offering interviewing assistance to management
  - Onboarding and assimilating new hires into the organization
  - Developing and delivering programs for training, total rewards, employee engagement, communications, and so on
- Collecting data and analyzing it for specific organizational needs
  - Capturing and tracking data to be analyzed
  - Identifying trends in the workforce and the external environment that affect the organization
  - Identifying best practices and processes that would be helpful to the organization and its strategy
- Daily HR operations
  - The processing of data, information, recordkeeping, and requests, typically using an HRIS and applicant tracking system
  - Responding to employee and internal or outside requests

The HR Team

Here again, the HR team will vary depending on the organization's size and needs, yet the following are typical for roles and responsibilities of an HR team:

- **HR leaders**   These can be the most senior of the HR group, and many will be part of the executive team, such as the chief human resource officer (CHRO) reporting directly to the CEO or president. They have a seat at the "round table" where the role lends itself to correlating organizational challenges and strategies to the HR function.
- **Managers**   This role is normally responsible for sections or units with the HR team such as the compensation manager, the talent recruitment manager, and the training manager. They have a direct responsibility in coordinating and managing the activities of their specific function and the people who are within it.

- **Specialists**   This role on the HR team is usually singularly focused with a specific knowledge and ability, such as the benefits specialist, the affirmative action specialist, and the HRIS specialist. They maintain and apply best practices in their specialty.

- **Generalists**   Also called *HR practitioners*, these are the jacks-of-all-trades. They may have a role and responsibility that includes expertise in more than one area. In today's large organizations, generalists are assigned a unit such as a department and become known as the business partner for that unit, guiding the management of that unit with all aspects of HR and serving as a liaison to the HR specialists and management.

HR Structural Alternatives

Organizations will structure HR based on the areas of responsibility they are assigning to the HR function. An important factor is ensuring that the HR structure is aligned with the organization's strategic plan. This may begin to be sounding like a broken record, yet it can't be emphasized enough that creating and sustaining HR's alignment with the organization's strategies is highly important. For example, if one of the organization's strategy's is an initiative and goal to be the employer of choice for its technical engineers in its industry, then it is necessary to ensure that the structure of HR includes the formation of attraction, rewards, retention, and development functions to address those needs for the engineering department.

 NOTE   When aligning HR with the structure, the types of structure also include centralized versus decentralized, as discussed earlier in this chapter.

Shared Services

The shared services model is another structural alternative identified by Ulrich and Brockbank.[7] This model is used in organizations with multiple business units, or *divisions,* as most are referred to as. Each division doesn't need to have its own expertise in every area, such as compensation and benefits. They select what they need from a menu of shared services that are typically transactional that the divisions agree will be shared (e.g., affirmative action compliance, compensation administration).

The most common functions assigned for consolidation are health care, retirement, and compensation. Organizations that have implemented the shared services model have identified four favorable outcomes.

- Reduced administrative time by staff on tasks
- A reduction in administrative costs
- A consolidation of redundant functions
- Better tracking of employee data

NOTE The greatest resistance from implementing a shared services concept generally comes from multinational organizations.

Centers of Excellence   A Center of Excellence is a team, a shared facility, or an entity that provides leadership, best practices, research, support, or training for a focus area. This focus might be a technology (e.g., Oracle), a skill (e.g., negotiation), or a broad area of research (e.g., cancer treatment). A COE, sometimes called a *center of expertise,* is an independent unit that provides services to internal customers within the organization. It is generally funded by fees that other functions using the COE have allotted from their budgeting. COEs may be located anywhere, wherever the internal customers can access the function, for example, an in-house training university.

Third-Party Contractors   Outsourcing and co-sourcing are examples of structural alternatives used by the HR function. Outsourcing is where a third-party vendor provides selected activities, such as administration of benefits. Co-sourcing is when a third party provides dedicated services to HR, which may include having contractors within the HR's organization. An example would be a temporary employment agency on-site hiring and onboarding seasonal labor.

Measuring and Demonstrating HR Value

Organizations have to measure and demonstrate the value they are delivering to their stakeholders—so too does HR to its stakeholders within the organization. Measuring results serves to reinforce HR's role in showing its effectiveness to management. It can also strengthen HR's relationship within the organization by indicating the impact of its services. This affords it the position to seek investment when it comes to budget allocation. Measurement also indicates where things need to be improved. ROI is essential for HR to further the investment requests for its strategic plan serving the organization.

Performance Measures

Key performance indicators are used to measure HR value. A KPI's gauge progresses toward goals and standards of performance that have been agreed to. An example is the number of new hires who have progressed through specific onboarding training such as sexual harassment, ergonomics, and diversity practices.

Balanced Scorecards   A *Balanced Scorecard* is a performance metric used to identify and improve various internal functions and their resulting outcomes. It is used to measure and provide feedback. HR measurement using a Balanced Scorecard method would be focused on specific functions or initiatives—as an example, recruiting—reducing length of time to fill a position. The performance metrics would include financial, processes, customers, and learning and growth.

To be effective, a Balanced Scorecard must include the following:

- Accountability and measurable results
- Measures, metrics, and targets that are understandable and supported by data
- Measures that have actionable items associated with them that can be measured
- Meaningful measures that focus on results
- Carefully planned, focused on end results, and executed

 NOTE   You can find more information on Balanced Scorecards in Chapter 4.

HR Audits   An HR audit is a systematic and comprehensive evaluation of HR's policies, procedures, and practices that protect the organization, create best practices, and identify areas needing improvement. Audits also identify gaps in performance and outcomes and are usually identified in priority order to be corrected. There are different types of audits, such as those caused by legal embattlements with a lawsuit or regulatory compliance and those that are done to achieve a level of world-class acknowledgment such as being recognized for a best practice.

Types of HR Audits	
Type	**Purpose**
Compliance	Determines the compliance with a law or regulation
Best practice	Compares its function with other organizations
Strategic	Reviews strengths and weaknesses of functions to align with the organization's strategic plan and initiatives
Function-specific	Has a specific focus on a function or process (e.g., records retention)

Metrics   There are many different metrics to select from, and the formulas can vary. It's important to use a consistent formula when benchmarking HR practices. Here are the typical metrics used for measuring the HR value:

- Absence rate
- Applicant yield
- Cost per hire
- Human capital ROI
- Human capital value added
- Key talent retention

- Promotion pattern
- Success ratio
- Training ROI
- Transfer/relocation
- Turnover costs
- Turnover rate
- Vacancy costs

NOTE   You can find more information on metrics in Chapter 4.

HR's Role in Organizational Strategy

The role of HR as a function within the strategic plan of the organization has transformed from the traditional administrative and operations roles into becoming more strategic in nature, helping the organization plan how it will achieve its goals and objectives with regard to talent management.

NOTE   You can find more information about strategy in Chapter 4.

HR and the Strategic Process

HR brings significant expertise, knowledge, and perspective to the organization's strategic planning process when it has a place at the table during a planning retreat. What is discussed, decided, and shared in these types of planning meetings helps the senior management team have a full 360-view of the workforce and talent implications of plans and allows HR to ensure its goals and plans are aligned with the overall plans of where the organization is going.

HR's Role

HR plays an important role in the strategic process. It contributes perspective and ensures that all HR implications are considered, such as laws and regulations, community, union contracts, and so on. It plays a role in influencing and voicing an opinion for leadership and stakeholders at large. And it uses its strengths and technology to be applied and aligned with the direction set.

The administrative activities of HR are directly aligned with all aspects of the organization's strategy. Tasks that HR performs may be high in strategic value, such as orientation of new hires, or low in value, such as activities that third-party vendors can provide (e.g., benefits administration). The core functions are what need consideration as to how they stack up to the value that HR lends to the organization's strategy and goals.

Leveraging HR's Strengths   The value of HR in an organization, specifically with the strategic planning process, is that HR knows the entire organization. This includes the functionality of the organization. This is because of the involvement it has in managing the talent, training, recruiting, risk management, policy administration, and so on. HR can be the ringmaster in helping coordinate and integrate the stakeholders listed here:

- **Employees**   HR needs to know the nuances of each geographical area in the organization and what laws or cultural issues are impacting each area.

- **Suppliers**   HR's knowledge of the suppliers and challenges they may pose such as ethical behavior is of great value within the strategic process.

- **Communities**   With HR's role in CSR and interacting with the communities of the organization that it operates in, this allows HR to identify potential conflicts or agreements with its communities associated with new strategic plans on the table.

- **Government**   Yes, there is "big brother" to contend with, and outside of the industry regulatory matters, the matters concerning workforce would be an arena that HR would have an antennae up in.

- **Labor groups**   For those organizations with labor unions, HR has its finger on the pulse of the affected labor unions when a strategy is considered that may affect a workforce union group.

Contributing the HR Perspective   HR professionals can contribute an important perspective during the strategic planning process. Although the main focus is to execute the organization's strategy, they have a ton of expertise and perspective they can add in the planning stages. For example, HR can add value when the organization is formulating a strategy to expand into a new geographical area by pointing out their perspective and knowledge about the issues with local laws for employment in that area.

Negotiating and Influencing   Negotiation is when two or more parties work together to reach an agreement in a matter or with an issue. The HR professional needs to know and work the process, which has six phases to it.

- **Preparation**   Identify the needs and wants that would be concessions.
- **Relationship building**   Personal character is involved here, and within the strategic planning process, this means having the trust of the others at the planning table.
- **Information exchange**   A thorough understanding of both sides of the issue is necessary.
- **Persuasion**   This means seeking what are the mutually beneficial options rather than going for the win-lose positioning. When HR professionals have a broader understanding of the other's interests, they can seek solutions that satisfy both sides of the issue.

- **Concessions**   There can be small concessions that count. They find the "wants" that are not essential and decide whether giving them helps the negotiation process.

- **Agreement**   When both sides have agreed, confirm it in writing. With formal negotiations such as union contracts, legal investigations, etc., these agreements must be in the form of a written document. Within the parameters of strategic planning, think of confirmation memos.

Influencing is an ability that goes hand in hand with credibility. Much more than just having knowledge and expertise, the HR professional needs to have credibility, which is part of building the personal relationship with trust mentioned earlier. HR professionals need to use their influence to provide the added value for the formulation of strategy to add what they know and their opinion of how the strategy can happen or what it's challenges might be.

Due Diligence   Due diligence refers to digging in and looking at all factors surrounding a matter. In strategic planning, it may involve reaching the local employment laws in the example of an organization wanting to expand into a new geographical area. Due diligence would also involve learning the landscape of the potential applicant pool for the new area and a 360-degree look at being an employer in that area. In Chapter 4 we discussed due diligence with mergers and acquisitions, which is the same process that would apply during the due diligence phase in strategic planning.

Aligning the HR Function and the Strategic Plan of the Organization

HR's administrative and operational activities are directly aligned with the organizational strategy and objectives. As we explained in Chapter 4 with SWOT analysis, it is important for HR professionals to understand the business and industry they support and to know all of the business function's own strategic plans.

HR Strategic Alignment   HR serves the entire organization and the needs of each business unit. Thus, having HR participate at each unit's planning session would be helpful, just as it is when HR sits as a participant to the senior team's strategic planning meeting. The same level of expertise, influence, and perspective is necessary at all levels of planning. When part of the organization's strategy involves entering a new market, HR's recruitment plans and sources will require a specific direction to be able to fulfill the workforce needs of the new markets. The goals of HR in, say, talent acquisition, may be focused on the nature of the talent required for the new market and how to manage the advertising that might go along with it. Forecasting the human resource needs is an important and essential role of HR in strategy.

Ensures That HR Fulfills Its Basic Mission   HR's basic mission is to help the organization achieve its vision with a highly engaged and talented workforce. That is the same with all other business units. Yet in regard to HR's mission, it will cross into all business functions because there are employees in each of those functions. Bringing HR into the fold as a true business partner for each of those units in order to help them accomplish their goals and plans that support the organization is the bottom line of the mission of

HR. HR must understand how all business units perform their work and their own priorities, values, and business plans in order to design their processes to fit in.

Learn About Your Organization's History   Learning and talking "story" is an important function of HR, not just in attracting potential talent and onboarding them but in keeping the foundational values, desired culture, and history alive for the organization. HR professionals are generally the first impression in the talent arena and can be in the community too. Knowing the "story" of where the organization has been, how it began, and where it intends to go is necessary for keeping it alive and communicating it to all "who enter the double doors." Add to that the "story" of the industry and how the organization fits in, as well as the communities it exists in. Building this knowledge will help HR professionals make useful recommendations during the planning process.

Use Facts and Objective Data as Support   As a participant in the planning process, you'll need to have tangible evidence to back up your opinions and recommendations. An HR professional needs to be fluent in measuring strategic outcomes that they anticipate in order to be influential, have credibility, and build solid business cases for their recommendations.

Contribute to Measuring Strategic Success   Common measures used, besides the many discussed in Chapter 4, include the ones associated with human capital measurements. They are as follows:

- Productivity
- Employee attitudes
- Employee capability and capacity
- Human capital investment
- Leadership and management
- Total rewards
- Compliance and safety
- Employee relations
- Job recruitment
- Job creation
- Workforce retention
- Workforce profile

Developing the HR Strategy

HR needs to develop a strategy that is aligned with the capabilities needed to implement the organization's overall strategy. Becker, Huselid, and Beatty wrote in *The Differentiated Workforce*[8] that HR must shift its focus from employees to one of strategy, and it needs to commit to diverting a greater share of its resources from developing the entire workforce to developing strategic talent. It needs to "assess the big picture" and get out of the weeds.

The HR Strategic Process   Chapter 4 goes into detail on what creating strategy entails. For the HR strategic process, the steps are similar yet more specific.

1. Assess the big picture. Get an understanding of the organizational context and the previous strategic plans. Identify what goals will involve HR processes and support.

2. Do SWOT analysis, which will review the matters affecting the people side of the business. PEST analysis will also be used in this stage. These analyses are explained in greater detail in Chapter 4.

3. HR's own mission and vision statements need to be either created at this phase or reviewed. They need to reflect and fit into the organization's overall strategies.

4. Conduct detailed HR analysis, which would include a thorough review of the current systems and processes in place. The goal in this phase is to identify gaps that may exist with current systems/processes and the future system needs. Focus is generally in the total rewards, talent acquisition, performance management, and training/development functions. Here again a SWOT analysis and PEST analysis could be utilized. Addressing these gaps to align with the organizational direction is the crux of the HR strategy.

5. Determine what are the critical people issues. During this phase, the future talent needs and existing workforce will be compared, and again, the gaps are considered and addressed with a strategic plan of action. An example is when a plant is going to bring in new automated equipment. How does that affect the current workforce? Will there be a need for retraining to operate the new equipment? Will there be a need to reallocate workers to a different job or downsize?

6. Develop HR's own goals, metrics, consequences, and solutions. At this phase, the specific actions HR will take and how they will be measured occur. Audits and balanced scorecards tools may be utilized (explained in Chapter 4).

7. Developing an implementation and evaluation plan is the last step. Here HR will provide clear direction on the resources, risks, timing, and support that each of their goals and initiatives will require. A project Gantt chart may be used as additional support for budget requests.

Functional Area 7—Organizational Effectiveness & Development

Here is SHRM's BoCK definition: Organizational Effectiveness & Development concerns the overall structure and functionality of the organization, and involves measurement of long- and short-term effectiveness and growth of people and processes, and implementation of necessary organizational change initiatives.[9]

Organizational effectiveness and development (OED) is a complex effort whose objectives are to change the beliefs, attitudes, values, culture, and structure of organizations so that they can be in a better position to adapt to new technologies, markets, and challenges. These changes occur through planned interventions designed to accomplish better results. In simple terms, OD is a systematic approach that enables the company to implement improvements in a consistent way.

Key Concepts

- Application of behavioral assessments (e.g., personality assessments)
- Intergroup dynamics (e.g., intergroup conflict)
- Intragroup dynamics (e.g., group formation, identity, cohesion, structure, influence on behavior)
- Organizational design structures and approaches (e.g., customer, functional, geographic, matrix, program)
- Organizational performance theories, structures, and approaches

The following are the proficiency indicators that SHRM has identified as key concepts:

For All HR Professionals	Advanced HR Professionals (SCP Exam)
Ensures that key documents and systems (e.g., job postings and descriptions, performance management systems) accurately reflect workforce activities	Aligns HR's strategy and activities with the organization's mission, vision, values, and strategy
Supports change initiatives to increase the effectiveness of HR systems and processes	Regularly monitors results against performance standards and goals in support of the organization's strategy
Identifies areas in the organization's structures, processes, and procedures that need change	Establishes measurable goals and objectives to create a culture of accountability
Provides recommendations for eliminating barriers to organizational effectiveness and development	Consults on, plans, and designs organizational structures that align with the effective delivery of activities in support of the organization's strategy
Collects and analyzes data on the value of HR initiatives to the organization	Assesses organizational needs to identify critical competencies for operational effectiveness
	Designs and oversees change initiatives to increase the effectiveness of HR systems and processes
	Ensures that HR initiatives demonstrate measurable value to the organization

Overview of Organizational Effectiveness and Development (OED)

A major HR responsibility and function is to regularly monitor and analyze an organization's metrics to identify and analyze major operating, workforce, and cultural health information to plan and implement organizational effectiveness and development efforts in a way that adds value to the organization. To do this, the HR professional must do the following:

- Recognize and support the alignment of key strategic and tactical business plans and program objectives. Each unit's tactical plans should be designed to support one or more strategic business objectives for the organization. Each unit's operational tactics need to be coordinated with other plans and objectives. In much the same manner, all HR and OED objectives must be aligned with the organization's overall strategy, with each other's activities, and with country-specific requirements.

- Focus on the organization's skills and capabilities; for example, all of the organization's business units, including HR, need to identify, focus, and improve the organization's talent acquisition capabilities.

OED Process

The OED process is based on an action research model that begins with an identified problem or need for change and proceeds with assessing, planning an intervention, implementing the intervention, gathering data to evaluate the intervention, and determining whether satisfactory progress has been made or whether there is need for further intervention. The process is cyclical and ends when the desired developmental result is obtained.

The OED process begins when an organization recognizes that a problem exists that impacts the mission or culture of the organization and change is desired. It can also begin when leadership has a vision of a better way and wants to improve the organization. An organization does not always have to be in trouble to implement organization development activities.

Once the decision is made to change the situation, the next step is to assess the situation to fully understand it. This assessment can be conducted in many ways including documentation review, organizational sensing, focus groups, interviewing, or surveying. The assessment could be conducted by outside experts or by members of the organization.

After the situation is assessed, defined, and understood, the next step is to plan an intervention. The type of change desired determines the type of intervention needed. Interventions can include training and development, team interventions, structural interventions, or individual interventions. Examples are team building for management or employees and establishing change teams. Once the intervention is planned, it is implemented.

During and after the implementation of the intervention, relevant data is gathered. The data to be gathered is determined by the change goals. For example, if the intervention is training and development for individual employees, the data would measure changes in knowledge and competencies.

PART II

This data is used to determine the effectiveness of the intervention. It is reported to the organization's decision-makers. The decision-makers determine whether the intervention met its goals. If the intervention met its goals, the process can end, which is reflected by raising the development bar. If it did not, the decision is made whether to continue the cycle and to plan and carry out another intervention or to end it.

OED Strategies

One approach depicts three basic strategies to achieving successful organizational change. The three strategies are not mutually exclusive, and all three could be used concurrently to bring about systemic change. One or the other, however, may be more conducive to the type of change needed in a particular organization. For this purpose, they are shown as being three different strategies.[10]

The Behavioral Strategy: Talent Development Talent development takes an employee training and development approach. It is based on the premise that employee learning would bring about the organizational change needed. Learning consists of gaining knowledge, skills, and new attitudes that lead to new behaviors. These new behaviors then lead to improved quality and performance.

The Technical Strategy: Performance Improvement Performance improvement takes a continuous improvement approach. Its premise is that processes in the areas of customer focus, product and service delivery, support, and supplier and partnering can be improved. This strategy also maintains that technology be continuously updated and aligned with the processes of production and service to make work more efficient and effective. Continuous process improvement with aligned technology leads to improved quality and performance.

Performance Problems[11]		
Problem	**Description**	**Possible Solutions**
Behavioral	Often manifested as communication problems, this involves a lack of collaborative effort between people or groups, inadequate team performance levels, or performance quality issues. They are frequently the result of inadequate leadership or of unclear performance expectations, such as insufficient communication of performance standards or inconsistent use of metrics or accountability standards.	• Clarified expectations and work processes. • Education. • Consistent workplace practices. • Strong leadership. • Conflict-resolution practices.
Cognitive	These are deficiencies in knowledge or skills.	• On-the-job training, work expansion. • Coaching/mentoring. • Training.

Performance Problems[11]		
Problem	**Description**	**Possible Solutions**
Technological	These are problems with the equipment, materials, and information used to perform the work, including their accessibility, availability, and accuracy.	Address problems associated with inadequate, inaccessible, faulty, or inaccurate equipment, materials, or information that employees rely on to perform their jobs.
Process-related	Problems with how the work is done can stem from inefficient systems, outdated practices, a lack of process measurement data, impractical procedures, or cumbersome reporting structures.	• Review systems to obtain feedback and conduct regular audits. • Determine process measures and data collection techniques. • Identify problems before they become significant obstacles. • Design and implement process improvement strategies.
Cultural	Problems within the workplace atmosphere or environment tend to be the most challenging to remedy. Matters concerning employee satisfaction, leader-employee relationships, leadership styles, corporate responsiveness to change, and policy flexibility are all examples of cultural changes.	• Typically, cultural shifts require multifaceted OED interventions. • Solutions derived from internal sources may be the most desirable, as credibility and familiarity levels are high. • Conversely, using an external tool or facilitator may provide a more holistic and objective perspective, thereby balancing the emotional components associated with internal relationships and performance history.

The Structural Strategy: Organizational Design   The organizational design premise is that organization structure and design should be aligned (or realigned) consistent with the vision, direction, mission, or goals of the organization. Structural strategy will incorporate changes in the organization chart. Employees, units, divisions, and departments can be realigned to optimize resources. For example, hierarchies can be flattened, and decision-making can be placed closer to the point of action. Significant work can be done in chartered, self-directed teams. Such realigned relationships lead to improved quality and performance.

OED Benefits   OED is the practice of planned, systemic change in the beliefs, attitudes, and values of employees for individual and company growth. The purpose of OED is to enable an organization to better respond and adapt to industry/market changes and technological advances. The following are five benefits of OED that range from continuous improvement to increased profits:[12]

- **Continuous improvement**   Companies that engage in organizational effectiveness and development commit to continually improving their business and offerings. The OED process creates a continuous cycle of improvement whereby strategies are planned, implemented, evaluated, improved, and monitored. Organizational effectiveness development is a proactive approach that embraces change (internal and external) and leverages it for renewal.

- **Increased communication**   One of the key advantages to OED is increased communication, feedback, and interaction within the organization. The goal of improving communication is to align all employees to shared company goals and values. Candid communication also leads to increased understanding of the need for change within the organization. Communication is open across all levels of the organization, and relevant feedback is recurrently shared for improvement.

- **Employee development**   Organizational effectiveness/development focuses on increased communication to influence employees to bring about desired changes. The need for employee development stems from constant industry and market changes. This requires an organization to regularly enhance employee skills to meet evolving market requirements, which is achieved through a program of learning, training, skills/competency enhancement, and work process improvements.

- **Product and service enhancement**   A major benefit of OED is innovation, which leads to product and service enhancement. Innovation is achieved through employee development, which focuses on rewarding successes and boosting motivation and morale. In this scenario, employee engagement is high, leading to increased creativity and innovation. Organizational effectiveness and development also increases product innovation by using competitive analysis, market research, and consumer expectations and preferences.

- **Increased profits**   Organizational effectiveness/development affects the bottom line in a variety of ways. Through raised innovation and productivity, efficiency and profits are increased. Costs are also reduced by minimizing employee turnover and absenteeism. As OED aligns objectives and focuses on development, product/service quality and employee satisfaction are increased. The culture shift to one of continuous improvement gives the company a distinct advantage in the competitive marketplace.

In its publication "Traits of Truly Agile Businesses," Accenture reported the results of a survey it conducted in 2013 that investigated business agility in strategy, organization, marketing, operations, and finance. Because of this research, five critical enablers of company agility emerged. Agile companies had leaders who did the following:

- **Actively build seasoned, diverse leaders and management teams**   Leaders ensure that managers up and down the organization are fully accountable and have the right competencies to handle a diverse set of circumstances.

- **Speed up decision-making**   They establish a culture of making critical decisions quickly, always ensuring that those decisions are tuned to market conditions.

- **Prioritize strategic decisions**   They distinguish between the decisions that affect everyday operations and the bigger decisions that concern the company's strategic direction.

- **Prepare their ecosystems to act quickly**   They arm their business ecosystems—suppliers, customers, and a range of third-party partners—with their sources, information, and tools to take decisive, well-orchestrated action and to quickly measure the results and correct their course when needed.

- **Invest in and make more use of data and analytics to run the business**   Leaders understand the competitive value of deeper insights and know how to mine many sources of data—not just their own—to obtain those insights.[13]

Opportunities for OED   In recent years many companies became good at delivering their core products and services with limited resources by adopting a "do more with less" operating style. Many companies reaped some short-term benefits because of certain cost savings. However, some of these short-term benefits have the potential to inflict long-term problems on the organization's overall capabilities, organizational structure, business processes, and levels of workforce engagement. The unintended result of attempting to get along with less over the long term can, in many cases, become very problematic. These same problems can become opportunities for alert HR professionals. Examples include the following:

- **Diminished capacity, capability, and agility**   Not being properly staffed can directly influence a company's cost structure, cash flow, and ability to deliver goods or services. Ultimately, diminished capacity and lagging response times will affect an organization's ability to remain competitive.

- **Misaligned organizational structure**   Many of these reorganizations produced structural gaps in roles, work processes, accountabilities, and critical information flows. Structural gaps can occur when companies eliminate jobs without eliminating the work, forcing employees to take on additional responsibilities. This can create problems because lower-level employees who step in may be ill-equipped to perform the required duties, and higher-level executives, who must take on more-tactical responsibilities, may feel that their leadership skills are being minimized.

- **Broken business processes**   Many organizations will admit that, even prior to the economic downturn, many core business processes were not documented, were not supported by technology, and relied too heavily on the "tribal knowledge" of long-term employees. Many businesses have not analyzed the impact from their cuts and the corresponding critical gaps that have developed. By failing to address these issues in a timely manner, companies risk losing core efficiencies, thus damaging the customer experience—a primary driver of revenue sustainability.

- **Declining workforce engagement** While doing more with less can improve productivity, it can also damage employee morale. More workers (managers and individual contributors alike) are juggling additional responsibilities, working longer hours, missing family time, and performing jobs that are one or two levels above or below their pay grade.

To ensure long-term viability, organizations need to realign their critical elements to fit the new economic realities without diminishing their core capabilities and competitive differentiation.

HR's Role in OED HR should be involved in major organizational changes from the beginning. HR's early involvement can facilitate the improvement of employee understanding of change and communication between management and nonmanagement employees. Positive outcomes of communication efforts can include the following:

- Identification and mitigation of potential risks
- Increased employee buy-in and satisfaction
- Increased trust between management and non-managerial employees
- Identification of needed change-related training initiatives to improve employee skills and proficiency throughout the change process
- Increased leadership cohesiveness

In its 2014 publication "Future Insights," SHRM outlined the top OED trends according to an HR subject-matter expert panel. The panel identified several trends. HR professionals must do the following:

- Increase their focus on the development and engagement of highly professional talent and high-potential employees who possess deep expertise, drive innovation, and uniquely contribute to the organization's value proposition.
- Take responsibility to educate line management and help them acquire skills to become more proactive in managing and coaching talent.
- Become skilled in organizational design and change management required to effectively implement enhanced organizational structures.
- Develop superior communication and situational leadership skills, motivation, energy, and learning agility. Leaders must have the ability to recognize and respect cultural differences and to reconcile the issues cultural diversity creates.
- Integrate the workforce planning process with career planning and employee engagement to provide information and support for employees to help them identify and choose from available career paths and job opportunities.
- Interact with technology specialists to produce accurate models to use in planning and managing the workforce, including decision support tools and predictive analytics.
- Use creative development tools such as mobile technologies for just-in-time learning via "pulled" rather than "pushed" instruction.[14]

Organizational Gap Development

Organizational effectiveness and development involves more than just specialized interventions; its practice should be integrated into the organization's daily operations. When a "gap" begins to develop between what is going on in your organization compared to a standard or benchmark in your industry or other comparator, you may be seeing a problem in the making.

Assessments and Targets

The means to identify an organizational gap is to first isolate the area of interest. That may be customer service, employee skills, leadership skills, employee training, and countless others. Pick one. If your concern is employee skills, first identify the specific skill (running scientific machinery, answering employee benefit questions, or management communication skills). Next, identify the benchmark or industry standard for the skill (number of hours managers spend working directly with employees each month, number of research grants obtained each quarter, successful merger or acquisition for employee policies).

Change Readiness   Developing and implementing change programs should follow the articulation of specific needs. If efficiencies can be improved through implementing new technologies (for example, use of robots on the automobile assembly line to perform routine repetitive actions), plans can be made to implement that change.

Normally, implementation plans should involve these steps:

1. Documenting goals and specific actions required to achieve them

2. Meeting with employees to discuss the changes and vision that requires those changes

3. Soliciting employee support and participating in the change process

4. Measuring the results

Organizational changes should always be consistent with the employer's strategic plan. Changes should represent the means to achieve missions or goals. There should always be a link between the change and the organizational strategy.

Cultural Assessment   Perhaps the greatest need for cultural assessment comes in the wake of mergers and acquisitions (M&A). When organizations try to combine their operations, there will inevitably be conflicts in policy, management style, and "the way we do things around here." One consulting firm, the Turknett Leadership Group, uses a written survey to gather input from employees on both sides of the corporate mix. Then, it conducts in-depth one-on-one interviews with a sampling of employees from each group.[15] In those interviews, they ask questions such as the following:

- "Give me ten words you would use to describe the organization."
- "Who really gets ahead in this organization?"
- "What and who is really rewarded around here?"

- "What are some of the war stories or legendary events in the organization's history?"
- "What does the CEO or leader pay the most attention to? Where does the CEO's energy get expended, and what do they reward?"

With the answers to those and other similar questions, it will soon become apparent where work should be focused for cultural improvement.

Implementing OED Initiatives

According to SHRM, "Unfortunately, many OED interventions are incorrectly implemented in response to symptoms of the dysfunction rather than by following a thorough diagnostic analysis, or organizational assessment, to reveal core problems. To avoid this, employers must use caution and make certain a comprehensive data collection process is followed."[16] When correctly assessed, plans for intervention can be built and then implemented.

OED Initiatives

Organizational development involves more than just specialized interventions; its practice should be integrated into the organization's daily operations. One of the simplest tools OED practitioners use is the ADDIE model.[17] ADDIE is an instructional systems design framework that many instructional designers and training developers use to develop courses. It can be used when dealing with other problems and issues, too. It involves the following:

- Analysis
- Design
- Development
- Implementation
- Evaluation

OED initiatives often involve transformational change including efficiency and effectiveness initiatives, organizational restructurings, organizational capabilities development, rebuilding trust initiative, and culture change. Nearly any aspect of the organization is fair game.

Workforce Support of OED Initiatives

To a large extent, whether employees support your OED initiatives will depend upon the quality of leadership that shepherds the effort. But it is a sure thing that unless employees do support your OED initiatives, there is little hope for success in that effort. Getting employee buy-in is critical.

OED Tools

Here are some tools and techniques that can help you in your OED initiatives.

Team Building   Achieving the state where individual team members actually trust one another to do their work and support others in the group is the objective of any team building program. Some groups work better together as teams than others. How the supervisor or manager treats each employee will influence how likely there will be a cohesiveness to the group. People want to work where they like the people they work with. They don't like to work with people who steal the credit for accomplishments of others, tattle to the supervisor about each small infraction of rules, or actively work to discredit others. Team building can overcome some of those behaviors, but not all. Progressive discipline is sometimes needed to eliminate really bad behavior before the group is willing to be a team. The question in the minds of employees who see the bad behavior all the time is, "Will the boss actually do something about it?"

Group Decision-Making   Group decision-making is a type of participatory process in which multiple individuals acting collectively analyze problems or situations, consider and evaluate alternative courses of action, and select from among the alternatives a solution or solutions.[18] In organizations many decisions of consequence are made after some form of group decision-making process is undertaken. However, groups are not the only form of collective work arrangement. Group decision-making should be distinguished from the concepts of teams, teamwork, and self-managed teams. Although the words *teams* and *groups* are often used interchangeably, scholars increasingly differentiate between the two. The basis for the distinction seems to be that teams act more collectively and achieve greater synergy of effort.

- The group has a definite leader, but the team has shared leadership roles.
- Members of a group have individual accountability; the team has both individual and collective accountability.
- The group measures effectiveness indirectly, but the team measures performance directly through their collective work product.
- The group discusses, decides, and delegates, but the team discusses, decides, and does real work.

There are several types of group decision-making methods.

- **Brainstorming**   This is freewheeling idea generation.
- **Dialectical inquiry**   Opposing groups debate the pros and cons of selected solutions or decisions.
- **Nominal group technique**   This is a structured decision-making process in which group members are required to compose a comprehensive list of their ideas or proposed alternatives in writing.
- **Delphi technique**   Group members are in different remote locations, and the group develops successive rounds of ideas, evaluation, refinement, and choices.

Diversity Programs Changing workforce demographics and new organizational forms are increasing the diversity of work teams in general and decision-making teams in particular. Given these environmental changes, work teams that are diverse in terms of sex, race, ethnicity, national origin, area of expertise, organizational affiliation, and many other personal characteristics are increasingly common.[19]

Striving to increase workplace diversity is not an empty slogan; it is a good business decision. A 2015 McKinsey report on 366 public companies found that those in the top quartile for ethnic and racial diversity in management were 35 percent more likely to have financial returns above their industry mean, and those in the top quartile for gender diversity were 15 percent more likely to have returns above the industry mean.[20]

In a global analysis of 2,400 companies conducted by Credit Suisse,[21] organizations with at least one female board member yielded higher return on equity and higher net income growth than those that did not have any women on the board.

In recent years, a body of research has revealed another, more nuanced benefit of workplace diversity: nonhomogenous teams are simply smarter. Working with people who are different from you may challenge your brain to overcome its stale ways of thinking and sharpen its performance.

Quality Initiatives Focusing on quality issues can happen in any workgroup within an organization. Of course, quality is important on the production line, but it is also important in the accounting department and in HR. What would be the consequence of HR publishing incorrect information about company benefit programs just before open enrollment? There are a few different ways to address quality.

Systems Theory Systems theory is less of a management methodology as it is a way of analyzing and thinking about organizations. It puts forth the premise that organizations, like living organisms, are made up of numerous component subsystems that must work together in harmony for the larger system to succeed. Systems theory states that organizational success relies on synergy, interrelations, and interdependence between different subsystems. As arguably the most valuable component of a company, employees make up various vital subsystems within an organization. Departments, work groups, business units, facilities, and individual employees can all be considered component systems of the organizations.[22]

Systems theory is an alternative approach to understanding, managing, and planning organizations. Employee relations is a human resource discipline concerned with strengthening ties between employers and employees. Systems theory can provide a fresh perspective for approaching employee-relations initiatives, allowing managers to understand their employees' importance and position as a vital system in the organization, rather than viewing employees as an expense through the lens of accounting.

Quality Standards The International Organization for Standardization (ISO) has now published four standards for human resource management. These are considered the benchmark against which all employers should measure themselves in these specific areas of HR.

The standards are as follows:[23]

- **ISO 30400, Human resource management – Terminology** This standard provides a common understanding of the fundamental terms used in human resource management standards.

- **ISO 30405, Human resource management – Guidelines on recruitment** This standard provides guidance on effective recruitment processes and procedures. It is designed for use by anyone involved in recruiting.

- **ISO 30408, Human resource management – Guidelines on human governance** This standard provides the guidelines to create an effective human governance system that can both respond effectively to organizational and operational needs but also foster greater collaboration across all stakeholders, anticipate and manage risks in human resources, and develop a company culture that is aligned with its values.

- **ISO 30409, Human resource management – Workforce planning** This standard helps organizations respond more effectively to their current and projected requirements for staffing.

You can expect that there will be more standards developed related to human resource management as time goes on.

Quality Control Tools The following are the seven tools of quality:

- **Cause-and-effect diagram** Also known as the *fishbone* or Ishikawa diagram.

- **Check sheet** Chart of event/occurrence by date or time with stroke tally of times the event happened.

- **Control chart** Plot of quality conformance at times throughout the day.

- **Histogram** Column chart showing frequency/intervals on the y-axis and the event being measured along the x-axis.

- **Pareto chart** Column chart showing types of quality problems on the x-axis and frequency of occurrence on the y-axis.

- **Scatter diagram** Graph showing plot of individual quality results using any two variables. Plot points can be used to determine the slope of a trend.

- **Stratification** Flow chart or run chart.

Theory of Constraints The Theory of Constraints (TOC) says in essence that "a chain is no stronger than its weakest link." That means quality depends on the weakest point in the process, whether it is a machine or a person. Quality failures can most often be traced back to that single point that constrains the quality results. It may also come to pass that there is more than one constraint interfering with the quality results.

Six Sigma   Six Sigma methodologies can be rolled out in a matter of months or over the course of years. From large international companies to midsize firms, many high-profile companies have implemented Six Sigma strategies as a way of saving corporate dollars, increasing quality, and leveraging the competitive edge.[24]

One of the guiding principles behind Six Sigma is that variation in a process creates waste and errors. Eliminating variation, then, will make that process more efficient, cost-effective, and error-free. This may sound like a relatively straightforward concept, but its application in a complex and highly integrated business environment can be far from simple. The term *Sigma* refers to a scale of measurement of quality in processes such as manufacturing. When using this particular scale, Six Sigma equates to just under 3.4 defects per million opportunities (DPMO).

HR's Role in Implementation

HR can be called on to support OED changes in other portions of the enterprise, or it can take on an OED change program within its own department. HR can help by training managers and employees how the process will work, what the changes will be, and what expectations they should have for the results. They can provide tracking systems if necessary to document the program implementation.

Communicating OED Changes   Communication is basically relating the objectives of the organizational redesign to the organization's strategies and tactical plans. Employees need to understand how they will fit into the new organization, the new process, or the new work assignment. They will need to know that there is training, team building, or individual coaching on the horizon. Communication is more than an e-mail blast to everyone in the organization. It is conversation with groups and individuals. The more employees are included in the OED development process, the more communication they will be receiving along the way.

Measuring Organizational Effectiveness and Development

First comes the goal or objective. Then comes the measurement. There are two types of measurements you can use to determine whether you have reached your goal.

- **Lagging indicators**   These confirm performance or lack of performance. They measure the results of past actions.
- **Leading indicators**   These predict performance. They measure actions that will affect future organizational effectiveness.

Demonstrating Value

It is rather easy to demonstrate value. Simply gather the results you have measured and show how your performance has met or exceeded the goals you set. Goals are established to create value for the organization. If you reach them, or better yet, exceed them, there is clearly value for the organization.

Cultural Assessment   There are tools that companies can use to identify both their current and desired culture. One of the most well-known of these tools is the Organizational Culture Assessment Instrument (OCAI)[25] developed by Kim Cameron and Robert Quinn at the University of Michigan. Cameron and Quinn analyzed 39 organizational effectiveness indicators and identified two key dimensions, as listed here:[26]

- Internal focus and integration versus external focus and differentiation
- Stability and control versus flexibility and discretion

Four organizational culture types emerged from these studies.[27]

- **Clan culture**   Similar to a large family. People have a lot in common. The organization is held together by loyalty and tradition. There is great involvement.
- **Adhocracy culture**   A creative working environment where employees take risks. Experiments and innovation are the bonding agents within the organization.
- **Market culture**   Results-oriented culture emphasizing finishing work and getting things done. The emphasis on winning keeps the organization together.
- **Hierarchy culture**   A formal, structured environment. Procedures decide what people do. Formal rules and policy keep the organization together.

Functional Area 8—Workforce Management

Here is SHRM's BoCK definition: Workforce Management refers to HR practices and initiatives that allow the organization to meet its talent needs (e.g., workforce planning, succession planning) and close critical gaps in competencies.[28]

With workforce management, this is where HR will continually be evaluating the ability of the organization's workforce to meet the competency and talent needs of the organization. Development, productivity, staffing, and effectiveness initiatives will be the core functions of HR's responsibility within workforce management. Workforce planning and employment is where you will find all the information about staffing, recruiting, interviewing, and employee performance management. Master these, and you will have a strong foundation for HR performance in your employment group.

Key Concepts

- Analysis of labor supply and demand
- Approaches to restructuring (e.g., mergers and acquisitions, downsizing)
- Best practices and techniques for knowledge management, retention, and transfer
- Leadership development and planning (e.g., high-potential development programs)
- Success planning programs and techniques

- Techniques for organizational need-gap analysis (e.g., examination of HR records, interviews, focus groups)
- Workforce planning approaches, techniques, and analyses (e.g., attrition, gap and solution, implementation and evaluation, reduction in force, supply and demand, workforce profile)

The following are the proficiency indicators that SHRM has identified as key concepts:

For All HR Professionals	Advanced HR Professionals (SCP Exam)
• Identifies gaps in workforce competencies and misalignment of staffing levels	• Evaluates how the organization's strategy and goals align with future and current staffing levels and workforce competencies
• Implements approaches (e.g., buy or build) to ensure the appropriate organization goals and objectives	• Develops strategies to maintain a robust workforce that has the talent to carry out the organization's current and future strategy and goals
• Plans short-term strategies to develop workforce competencies that support the organization's goals and objectives	• Coordinates with business leaders to create strategies (e.g., succession planning, leadership development, training) that address the organization's leadership needs
• Administers and supports approaches (e.g., succession plans, high-potential development programs) to ensure that the organization's leadership needs are met	
• Supports strategies for restructuring the organization's workforce (e.g., mergers and acquisitions, downsizing)	• Develops strategies for restructuring the organization's workforce (e.g., mergers and acquisitions, downsizing)

Organizational Workforce Requirements

Organizational staffing needs expand and contract with the level of organizational productivity requirements. It's not always a straight-line relationship that would indicate continuous steady growth. Living organizations inhale and exhale, and workloads grow and contract, often at irregular intervals. Workforce requirements expand and contract with those production requirements.

Workforce Requirements

Forecasting results can be converted into employee headcount and budget impact, and the consequences can demand other staffing needs. Adding production workers can cause an increase in payroll support work levels, for example.

Identifying job openings before they exist is the activity known as *forecasting*. It is best performed with the aid of operations managers who will be supervising the new positions. Given what is anticipated for growth (or force reduction), a manager is able to convert workloads into staff requirements. Determining the portion of jobs that will be part-time versus those that will be full-time is another contribution of the forecasting process.

Forecasting staffing needs is usually done in terms of the number of full-time equivalent people. That unit value is also favored for budgeting activities. Here is the formula:

Full-time equivalent (FTE) people required = total functional workload / workload handled by one person

Organizational Structure

Aligning the way the parts of an organization relate to one another is considered the organizational structure. HR professionals need to be familiar with organizational structures so they can act as a guide for management in selecting and determining which structure would be best to gain the best performance.

There are six types of organizational structures. (See descriptions in the "Understanding the Organization" section earlier in this chapter.)

- Departmental
- Chain of command
- Span of control
- Work specialization
- Formalized
- Centralized or decentralized
- Matrix

Restructuring

The act of restructuring the structures of an organization for the purpose of making it more profitable, or better organized, is known as *corporate restructuring*. Additional changes can necessitate restructuring such as a change of ownership or a bankruptcy filing. Restructuring can include selling off portions, or *divesting,* to reduce debt or operations. The 1980s experienced a heyday of restructuring because of the rampant undervaluation of publicly traded organizations that attracted hostile takeover attempts. If the targeted organization was lucky enough to find a major investor to ward off the hostile takeover attempt (known as a *white knight*), the aftermath usually involved a tremendous amount of debt and then restructuring and divesting to pay off the white knight and debt.

During the recent great recession, corporate restructuring occurred as a result of economic decline to reduce financial losses from the lack of revenue. The basic nature of restructuring is a zero-sum game. It can quickly reduce financial losses and simultaneously reduce the tensions between major stakeholders (shareholders) and the overriding condition prompting the distressed situation.

Drivers of Restructuring   Two major reasons for restructuring are divestiture and mergers and acquisitions.

Forms of Restructuring   There are perhaps seven different forms of restructuring. Each is based on specific needs generated just prior to the restructuring efforts.

PART II

Downsizing   When production demand drops, for whatever reason, the number of employees required to meet the production requirements will also fall. Adjusting to that diminished level of production is called *downsizing, layoff, rightsizing, smart-sizing,* or *bad luck*. It doesn't matter what percentage of the workforce will be impacted through layoffs. For each individual who receives a pink slip notice, the number is 100 percent. How that process is handled is a topic to be discussed elsewhere.

When the Bell System underwent a seismic rupture in 1982 because Judge Green ordered it to divest the unregulated portions of the Bell Telephone companies, there were more workers than needed in the new unregulated company. Before the judge's order, the Bell System was composed of 23 operating companies, AT&T, Western Electric, and Bell Labs. Together they were the largest employer in the country with 1,100,000 employees. After the spin-off, the new company was called American Bell and began its life on January 1, 1983, with 100,000 employees and zero revenue. It operated on loans from the other companies. Its reason for being was to sell private branch exchange telephone service to business customers. So, there were marketing people and technical people, too many of each in fact. Thus, it became necessary to develop the first mass industrial layoff in history. The company started with a layoff of 24,000 people in 1983 and followed it with additional large groups of downsizing in subsequent years. That represented a 24 percent reduction in workforce in the first wave of cuts. By any standard, that was substantial downsizing.

Divestiture   This is what the Bell System underwent in 1983. It had to divest itself of the unregulated portion of its business to allow other companies to compete for that customer money. It can also be done when the parent company wants to become more competitive in new business ventures.

In 1911, the U.S. Supreme Court ruled that Standard Oil was an illegal monopoly. Standard Oil at the time was producing, transporting, refining, and marketing oil, gasoline, and other oil-related products such as grease and kerosene. It was ordered to divest itself of the various components into smaller companies so it would be possible for others to enter the marketplace.

Restructuring   As you have seen, restructuring can be done voluntarily or involuntarily. The Bell System and Standard Oil breakups were court-ordered. When done voluntarily, the effort is sometimes called *unbundling*. Some options for unbundling include sell-offs, spin-offs, carve-outs, and buyouts.

Redistribution of Decision-Making Authority   Organizational structure can determine decision-making authority. Centralizing the organization can pull decision-making into the core headquarters establishment. Decentralizing the organization can push decision-making out into the remote locations. This can be true whether the remote locations happen to have independent corporate identity.

Extended Organization   In 2000 Sara Lee began merging various brands to "create smaller, customer-focused teams. In meats alone, for instance, Sara Lee had 10 different brands, including Ball Park, Hillshire Farms, Bryan, and Jimmy Dean."[29] As a result, supermarkets had to deal with ten different sales reps and process ten different invoices each month. "The new customer-focused teams reduced duplication and were more convenient for buyers—a win-win situation. National retailers responded by increasing their orders for Sara Lee products."[30]

Mergers and Acquisitions (M&A) and Divestiture   Mergers, acquisitions, and divestiture are daily occurrences in organizations for restructuring an organization. In some industries, it's become an annual expected event to restructure, and in others, such as technology, M&A has become the norm. HR professionals need to know the importance of their role with workforce planning when it comes to these activities.

Divestiture   Organizations divest to refocus, rethink, and restructure their core business capabilities with an ultimate goal to be leaner and more cost effective. Going from big to smaller, or refocusing on the core product/service that the organization offers by selling off a separate line of business arms, can present a variety of challenges for HR. To minimize the disruption of operations and employees during divestiture, HR may need to redefine some of the organizational structure that is currently in place. Reviewing re-employment policies, severance packages, and employee classifications and job descriptions for either increased or decreased responsibilities are just a few considerations.

Mergers and Acquisitions   Mergers and acquisitions (M&A) are intended to enhance an organization by accessing market share or increasing assets. It is best to involve HR right from the get-go to plan for the effects that mergers and acquisitions have on an organization, such as culture blending, job function redundancy, and comparison of benefits/compensation/job titles, along with effects on HR information systems, policies/procedures/ethics, and, if there is a union, collective bargaining.

The M&A process has four basic phases, which are covered in the following sections.

Preparation   You must first ascertain whether the HR staff has the necessary knowledge, strategic planning, and project management skills for managing the transition of an M&A.

Due Diligence Production   The due diligence stage is next, which includes scrutinizing not just the financials but many of the other risks associated with HR. The organization's workforce-related risks are just the tip of the iceberg. Factoring in people matters are more difficult to quantify and yet absolutely crucial.

Research and investigation are needed on the proposed M&A organization to determine the technology differences and needs, structural and talent risks, and cultural issues that will arise. The sheer recognition that two cultures must be brought together and blended to create a collaborative, high-performance new organization is daunting. Compliance, corporate governance, and legal claims/lawsuit information—those in process and those that appear on the horizon as a potential threat—would additionally be reviewed and understood at this phase. It is important to understand that oversimplifying these risks can lead to misguided integration planning, unexpected costs, and loss of critical talent.

Integration Planning   Here's where a good strategic planning process resulting in goals and objectives is necessary, along with project management implementation. A change management plan associated with a culture blending process, communication strategies, and consolidation activities occurs during this phase.

Implementation, Measurement, and Monitoring Results   The process is not complete when the organizations are finished with the M&A. HR plays a vital role in monitoring the pulse and mood, assisting with workforces that have blended successfully, and helping to troubleshoot new issues that may have occurred during integration. Employees, after all, will be the implementers of the changes to enable an organization to realize the goals of the merger. Creating metrics and milestones that measure the intended results the organization set out to achieve, with respect to the people related value of the deal, is the last phase for HR.

Transition Tactics   During a major transition, management often expects leadership transitions to happen without major changes in the acquired business. When clarity and trust are most needed, it's possible that leadership may appear more focused on itself (individuals impacted personally by the transition) than on taking care of its anxious people. Employees can't help noticing the disconnection between leadership's actions and words, with potentially damaging effects of costly turnover of valued employees and serious morale and productivity problems. Poor people management and communication drain financial value from many changeovers.

Having a clear vision and consistent frequent communication about organizational transition is vital. Creating a strategic blueprint should revolve around communication, not just to the workforce but also to other stakeholders such as the customers and communities served by the organization (plural in the case of M&A). The best transition tactics revolve around trust and communication. Leadership groups must move forward together, fully aligned, and "owning" the strategic blueprint of the newly created vision in sharing its messages. If the messages and themes that are expressed to all parties are not consistent, then confusion, fear, and a lack of faith in the transition process will likely occur. Those signals could send tremors of uncertainty throughout the organization. The workforce can surely be counted on to fill a vacuum of information with worse-case scenario rumors, in terms of who will be retained, who will be let go, and how the everyday rules of the game will change.

Downsizing   Downsizing is the act of reducing the size of a workforce. It can be done for many different reasons, but the end result is fewer people work at the employer than in the past. In the past few decades, corporate downsizing has become a widely used tool. The impact on individual employees has been immense. To help mitigate that impact, employers have sometimes offered incentive programs with cash buyouts based on the length of service and/or retirement qualification enhancements. Offers have sometimes included months- or years-long support in a job search (providing an office, telephone, computer, e-mail, secretarial support), formal outplacement service through a third-party vendor, and occupational training programs to provide new skills necessary for a career in a new field.

Organizational Interventions

Aside from redesigning the organizational structure, the science of organizational development (OD) can be used to help solve problems with organizations through various interventions.

- Team building
- Creating common values
- Creating a vision
- Creating a specific role for each organizational segment
- Facilitating problem-solving sessions focused on organizational structure

Workforce Planning

The exercise known as *workforce planning* is based on the notion that you want a balance between the work to be done and the workers available to do it. Over time, that balance will change, shifting toward one side of the equation or the other.

Workforce Planning Process

There are many approaches you can take to workforce planning. All of them, ultimately, boil down to one thing, analyzing the gap between what you estimate will be the staffing requirement and the staff you have available to meet that requirement. Once the gap is determined, then plans can be laid to identify action steps that will be necessary to narrow that gap.

Supply Analysis   This is a strategic evaluation of supply chain options such as sourcing alternatives, plant locations, and warehouse locations. Will the workforce you need be available in the location where you want it?

Trend and Ratio Analysis Projections   Ratio analysis compares current results or historic results but always at a point in time. Trend analysis compares historical results with current results and identifies what may happen in the future based on the trend of data in the past.

Turnover Analysis   There are many possible reasons for employees leaving the payroll, including resignation, dismissal, death, long-term disability, and transfer to another subordinate company within the same parent company. Identifying the reasons that employees are leaving provides the data needed to analyze trends and identify potential problems within the organization. If supervisors are causing high resignation rates, it may be appropriate to train the supervisors or take some other action to reduce the rate at which their subordinates are leaving.

Flow Analysis   This can involve analysis of data, analysis of production line movement, or analysis of order processing, among other possibilities. How processes operate and how flows of products, data, or other items go through those processes are the objective of this type of monitoring.

Demand Analysis

It is interesting to look forward to determine what customers, clients, or patrons will want in the future.

Judgmental Forecasts These are projections based on subjective inputs. This method is often used when there is a short time to draw a conclusion or data is outdated or unavailable.

Statistical Forecasts These approaches to analysis use mathematical formulas to identify patterns and trends. Once identified, the trends are analyzed again for mathematical reasonableness.

Gap Analysis

Measuring the distance (or difference) between where you are and where you want to be is known as *gap analysis*. If you have to train all employees in certain safety procedures, you can use gap analysis to determine what portion of the population has yet to receive the training, or any portion of the training.

Prioritizing the Gaps Identifying the gaps is the first step. Then, it is a good idea to determine the relevant importance of each portion of the results that need attention. Safety training may be more important (and greater priority) than training on the new benefit forms. Product feature training may be higher priority than updates on vacation scheduling procedures. Setting priorities for all components of the gap is important.

Defining Tactical Objectives "Tactical plans are sometimes called short-term action plans because they break down bigger-picture goals and strategies into narrower, actionable tasks. The key to a well-developed tactical plan is having specifically stated actions assigned to particular employees with specific deadlines."[31] So, identifying specific objectives to be worked on and determining who will do what by what date is the tactical planning component. The following action plan is an example of tactical objectives:

Example of Tactical Objectives		
Objective: Workforce Reduction of 500 People		
☒ Action Step	Responsible Party	Completion Date
Prepare offer of voluntary separation with incentives	CHRO and CFO	Estimated: 1/15/XX
File WARN notice as required	CHRO	Estimated: 11/15/XX
Complete separation notices	CHRO	Estimated: 4/15/XX

Solution Analysis

In problem-solving, once the problem has been identified, identifying potential solutions comes next. Every solution suggested should be written on a list, regardless of whether you think it might actually work. After identifying all the possible solutions you can, begin writing a list of criteria that are absolutely required of any solution you choose. These are the must-haves. Criteria tell us that no solution will work if it doesn't meet all of these requirements. Next, compare each suggested solution with the list of criteria and scratch off the list any solution that does not fully meet all of the criteria requirements. What is left will be a list of solutions that can each satisfy the criteria. You may then make a selection from the surviving list of solutions.

When multiple solutions meet all the criteria, using regression analysis can help you decide which one is best for you. For example, it might be possible to solve the problem of turnover by creating a management skills training program. It also might be possible to solve the turnover problem by providing different employee benefits that are more appealing to the workers. It could also be that offering continuing education to employees would have an impact on turnover. Each of those solutions could work. You can determine how well each works by using regression analysis to calculate the contribution each could make to the problem of turnover control. This analysis considers that there is some value to be contributed by each different solution. If you can't choose all of them, where will you get the greatest impact for your investment of time and money?

The Staffing Plan

Once a list of organizational objectives is determined, it is possible to begin the process of determining the quantity of employees that will be needed in each function to accomplish those objectives.

Statement of Purpose

The purpose of your staffing plan should be simply stated. Universally, staffing involves the activities associated with filling job openings. Candidates can come from both internal and external sources. So, the purpose can be stated like this: "Our staffing plan is designed to meet our employment needs with the right skills in the right jobs at the right time."

Stakeholders

Everyone who has something at risk if the job openings are not filled with qualified individuals at the proper time is considered a stakeholder. This includes the HR manager, the staffing manager, recruiters, operations managers and supervisors, production managers and supervisors, job candidates, interns, job advertising vendors, Internet sources, and more.

Everyone who has a "stake" in the success of your staffing efforts will fall into this grouping. Not all stakeholders will have the same level of interest or amount of risk involved, however. The supervisor trying to fill the job opening will have the most to gain or lose in the successful completion of the staffing efforts. The HR department's reputation will rise or fall depending on how well it develops the staffing plan and then implements its actions.

Activities and Tasks

What is involved in a staffing plan and its implementation? More or less it depends on the size of your organization. The larger the organization, the more complex the staffing plan will be. Larger organizations have more complex policies and procedures. Small organizations are more flexible and less encumbered by detailed policies.

Some of the activities you will find in staffing plans are as follows:

- Identify the organizational goals needing employee support
- Identify the quantity of full-time equivalent (FTE) employees each goal will need
- Specify the knowledge, skills, and abilities (KSAs) each position will require
- Identify candidate sources, considering diversity efforts and KSA requirements
- Solicit job applications or resumes from qualified candidates
- Screen candidates for qualifications
- Select candidates who will likely "fit best" into the job requirements
- Forward candidate records to selecting manager for consideration
- Schedule interviews with selecting manager and/or others in the department
- Administer any other screening device/step such as written tests or skill demonstrations
- Make employment selection decision
- Follow up months later to assess the success of the employment selection
- Make any procedural adjustments for the future based on that assessment

Team Members

Staffing processes involve multiple individuals in organizations of any size. In large organizations, there will be individuals who specialize in given segments of the process. In smaller organizations, there will be greater emphasis on generalists who handle multiple functions.

For example, the HR department may have only one person, the HR manager, who is responsible for all phases of the staffing process. However, in the larger counterpart, there may be an entire staff of recruiters working for the HR department. There can even be psychologists involved in employment screening for some large, sophisticated organizations.

Resources

Staffing resources include all of the people, assets, and funding needed to successfully place qualified people into the job openings. If there is a competitive marketplace where you must try to get your qualified candidates, your competitors may be trying to do the same thing. You will need to distinguish your organization from the competition so you can be successful in attracting the people you want on your staff.

There are internal resources from which you can make your staffing selections. Succession plans will help you identify who is "Ready Now" for promotion, who is capable of a lateral transfer, and who still needs some additional training or experience before being considered "Ready Now" for the job in question. While succession plans normally apply to the executive ranks, employee skills inventories can help you determine who is capable of filling job openings through a database of employee KSAs.

In organizations with labor union representation, it is not uncommon to have union-represented jobs filled based on employee seniority. Internal training centers can produce qualified job candidates with each graduating class.

Don't forget employee referrals. "I know a guy…" can sometimes provide some very appropriate talent for the staffing needs.

External resources include state employment services, veterans groups, state rehabilitation services for disabled job candidates, educational institutions, job fairs, Internet sources such as Monster.com, LinkedIn, Craigslist, school alumni sites, and a host of other service vendors. And, you shouldn't forget your own organization's web site. That can be an excellent avenue for job applicants to enter your selection process.

Communication Plan

A staffing plan won't be very effective unless people important to its success know what should be happening. Letting employees and people outside the organization know that you are hiring and the type of skill sets you want will boost the placement rate and reduce selection time.

Continuous Improvement

As with any other portion of the enterprise, staffing should be the focus of continuous improvement efforts. Small goals that are frequently reached can result in large progress over the course of longer time periods. *Kaizen* to the Japanese, making frequent assessments of performance and then setting new improvement goals, will result in substantial performance improvement. Japan's automobile industry overtook the American market because Honda and Toyota presented better-quality products in the 1980s and 1990s.

Employee Development

Employee development programs are an important aspect of talent management, providing employees with opportunities to learn new knowledge and skills, preparing them for future responsibilities and job changes, and increasing their capacity to perform in their current jobs. Job rotation, job enlargement, and job enrichment represent some approaches to employee development. Another could be an apprenticeship program that relates to skills training.

 NOTE The U.S. apprenticeship system is regulated by the Bureau of Apprenticeship and Training (BAT).

Higher education tuition reimbursement programs are also offered by many organizations as part of their employee development program. The pursuit of education is normally restricted to an employee's current occupation or an occupation that exists within the organization.

Other employee development programs that are increasingly on the rise within organizations are those associated with wellness training, stress management, and work-life balance.

Development of Employees

Next to strong retention efforts, employee development is a staffing effort that can lower overall costs and improve morale in the workforce. Giving people the opportunity to expand their skill set when they want to leads to their taking on more responsibility with higher levels of satisfaction. Blocking the wish for learning new skills can only lead to disappointment and discontent.

Talent Management

Talent management involves all the HR strategies and processes that are involved in attracting, developing, engaging, and retaining the KSAs of the workforce to meet the organization's needs. Talent management goals are simple: manage the human resources initiatives that directly result in employee productivity and that address current and future business needs.

Talent Pools   It's not just best practice. "Creating and maintaining current skills inventories allow employers to develop succession plans based on current employee skills sets and identify key employees for future openings critical to the company's leadership and business success. Skills inventories should be reviewed on an ongoing basis and employers should take steps to ensure employees keep their own skills inventory current and updated. By doing so, employers can help ensure the success of their strategic plans and achievement of their company's short- and long-term goals."[32]

Talent Management Strategies   It is less expensive to tap into the organization's internal talent pool than it is to conduct an external search for the skills needed in a particular job. So, skill inventories are something that can pay off handsomely. Succession planning, if maintained well, can reduce the panic felt when key people are suddenly out of the picture (death, resignation, long term-illness, or injury). Knowing in advance who has the skills and abilities to do the job, plus the interest and willingness, will accelerate placement efforts.

Addressing the Changing Needs of Employees   Nothing in the world is static for very long, and employee needs are no different. Life goes on, and work is just part of our lives. So, when new babies arrive, someone gets seriously ill, or tragedy strikes and an employee has a death in the family, the employer will be faced with some attendance issues and perhaps some ongoing adjustment requests.

Flexible Staffing Growing in popularity, telecommuting is an alternative to traditional staffing where everyone reported to a given work location every day. And, there are other flexible staffing options.

- **Job sharing** Job sharing is an employment technique that you hear about more and more these days. It offers two or more workers the opportunity to collectively constitute one full-time equivalent employee. One person works the job in the morning, and another works the same job in the afternoon. Considerations involve briefing the "job sharing partner" on the current issues to be dealt with during the next portion of work time. There are some financial considerations, too. Each employee will require the employer's full contribution toward Social Security and Medicare. That may cost the employee more than if one person were to occupy the position.

NOTE Job sharing can increase morale and provide staffing in situations that otherwise might be difficult.

- **Shortened workweeks** One option is four 10-hour days per week. Another option involves eight 9-hour days plus one 8-hour day every two weeks, which allows a three-day weekend every other week.

- **Phased retirement** As opposed to instant full-time retirement, phased retirement is another alternative to full-time employment, which allows an individual to take partial retirement while continuing to work a reduced schedule. It can take the form of job sharing, part-time, seasonal, temporary, or project work.

NOTE A major advantage of phased retirement is that is allows employees to get used to working less and having more time to themselves. It prevents the sudden shock of not having a work routine that comes with traditional retirement.

Alternative Staffing When looking for alternatives to the FTE 40-hour workweek stereotype, there are some options.

- **Project employees** Using project hires and contract labor is an alternative to full-time employment. Project hires are people who are recruited and placed on the payroll with the understanding that their employment will be terminated once the project is completed. It is common in organizations that seek out projects from client organizations. A staff is hired for the project and then let go when the project comes to an end.

Contract labor refers to people who are hired for a specific period of time. An organization may believe that the workload will last until this time next year. So, it contracts with people to handle that workload for the year. At the end of the contract, those folks will come off the payroll, whether or not the project has concluded. They could be "extended" (payroll status maintained) for a designated period of time if the workload has not diminished.

- **Temporary employees**   One change to full-time employment is the use of temporary employees. It is not necessary to hire people by putting them on the payroll. Employers can expand their workforce quickly and easily by contracting with temporary talent agencies to satisfy their need for additional people. Temporary workers can be used on production lines, in accounting departments, or in any other portion of an organization experiencing a workload that cannot be handled by the permanent staff. Agencies pay their employees, take care of payroll withholding and tax reporting, add a profit margin, and then pass the final rate to the employer contracting for that help.

- **Payrolling**   When a job needs to be done and the organization does not want to hire someone onto its own payroll to do that job, an alternative is to contract with a vendor who will hire someone to do the job at the client organization. Contractor payrolling is used when you need to adjust to seasonal fluctuations, fill a vacancy while searching for a permanent replacement, bridge the gap in personnel when there is unexpected growth, or use interns for a set period of time. It has many applications, and the greatest benefit is in protecting against charges that the person hired is not an independent contractor but an employee, a problem that cost the company Microsoft just under $100 million in payroll taxes, penalties, fines, and legal fees. This is usually a process used for less than an entire workforce. When single employees or small groups of employees are needed, payrolling services can solve the need.

- **Employee leasing through a professional employer organization (PEO)** Similar to payrolling, employee leasing is a process of moving employees to another company's payroll as a service for a client organization. Typically, PEOs will take over the entire workforce in a client company. PEOs provide payroll services, tax tracking and depositing, retirement program management, health care benefit program management, and even employee counseling and support services. In essence, employee leasing is the outsourcing of the human resource department and the payroll function together. Employees usually become employees of both organizations, the client where they perform their work, and the vendor (PEO) that handles the payroll and HR functions for the client. It means both employers are liable for legal compliance.

- **Outsourcing and managed service providers (MSPs)**   Another alternative is outsourcing. Outsourcing is shifting a workload out of the organization through a contract with another employer organization, either here in this country or somewhere else in the world. Managed service providers offer to manage functions as part of a strategic decision to move operations or support functions out of an employment organization to a vendor that can perform them less expensively. Such a decision is designed to allow the client company to focus on key activities within its core business while a vendor handles support activities for the client.

- **Temp-to-lease programs**   When a need exists for employees on a seasonal basis or for jobs that will last longer than a few days or weeks, it is possible for employers to lease their workers from a vendor organization. The vendor provides the underlying employment relationship with the worker. When temporary needs stretch into longer-term needs, it still may not be wise to increase payroll in the client organization. That's when contracting for temporary agency workers can be converted into long-term employee leases. These workers often have no benefits provided to them. The client organization pays an employment agency a fee in addition to the pay received by the worker assigned to the client. All payroll operations are maintained by the temporary service agency.

- **Rehires and transfers**   When workloads rise unexpectedly, it is sometimes difficult to bring in new hires quickly enough to respond to that increased demand. Rehiring laid-off workers and bringing in transfers from other portions of the organization can sometimes be good solutions. Rehired workers are already trained and can be productive immediately. Transfers from other portions of the organization have the advantage of already knowing the culture and, if coming from similar or identical types of work, can also be productive rather quickly.

- **Relocation**   Moving workers from one location to another outside the normal commute radius requires finding them new living quarters. This can be done on a temporary or permanent basis. If relocation is used to respond to union strikes or increased workload, it will likely be a temporary condition. Employers sometimes rent blocks of rooms in long-term hotel facilities so workers can have cooking and laundry facilities along with living quarters.

Permanent relocation can involve workers selling and buying homes and packing household belongings and shipping them long distances, sometimes across the country or internationally. There are many variables in such action on the part of the employer. Enticing employees to accept relocation can be a high hurdle to overcome. Forcing the change for a spouse's employment, moving children from one school to another, and accepting a higher cost of living at the new location can require employers to provide financial incentives. Those incentives can include such things as the following:

- **Home purchase/lease escape fees**   A strategy is offering a guaranteed purchase of the employee's old home following an appraisal of value. The employee can accept or reject the company's offer if it might be possible to achieve a higher selling price some other way. When there is a fee involved for canceling property leases, employers can pay that fee for employees.

- **Real estate processing fees**   Escrow fees for selling and buying real property can amount to many dollars. Paying these expenses for a relocating employee can lift that burden and remove another objection to relocating.

PART II

- **Mortgage subsidy** In an inflationary economy, mortgage rates rise. It can sometimes be necessary for employers to pay a portion or all of the increased mortgage rate to get an employee to accept relocation.

- **Packing/shipping/unpacking** Paying the bill for a moving company to pack, ship, and unpack at the destination is another way to relieve employees of financial burden.

- **Funds for taxes on increased taxable income** When there are income tax consequences for employees as a result of a relocation, employers sometimes compute a "tax obligation roll-up" and pay that to the employee in a lump sum as withholdings.

Work-Life Balance According to the web site www.worklifebalance.com, the proper definition of the term is meaningful daily achievement and enjoyment in four life quadrants, namely, work, family, friends, and self. That doesn't mean an equal amount of time spent in each life area. It means whatever is necessary for personal satisfaction. And, employers can help facilitate that achievement if they are sophisticated about employee management and contemporary issues.

Measuring Talent Management Effectiveness Talent management can be defined as putting the right people in the right positions at the right time…and keeping them there. So, measuring that must go more than skin deep into the organization's policies and procedures.

An ADP white paper on the topic suggests that talent management should "connect investments in human capital with the immutable facts of financial performance." Here are some basic measurements it suggests organizations consider. All relate to the return on investment (ROI) employers can expect from their human capital.[33]

- Overall talent retention rate
- Cost to hire talent
- Revenue per full-time employee
- Time it takes to hire talent
- Time to full productivity per full-time employee
- Diversity statistics
- Impact of voluntary and involuntary employee loss rates on revenue
- Average tenure of new hires
- Number of senior positions and the depth of bench strength
- Number of promotions made from within the organization

Succession Planning

 Succession planning systematically identifies, assesses, and develops talent as a key component for business success. It is an ongoing process that enables an organization to plan or recover when critical talent is lost. An effective succession plan includes a focus on identifying, developing, and preparing the placement of high-potential employees for future opportunities. It is foolish to assume that key players would provide adequate notice of resignation. Succession planning is not just for the planned events such as retirements; it serves for replacement planning such as when a key player is relocating because of family or perhaps perished in an accident. Succession should be developed to anticipate managerial staffing needs or key employee positions that would interrupt the business process if an incumbent were to vacate.

NOTE Be careful not to exclude employees from a succession plan solely based on their age.

A succession plan contains an identification of high-risk positions along with those positions with known or potentially known vacancy dates (as with retirements). Competencies for those positions are identified, and a gap analysis is conducted with the current workforce potential candidates. Individuals within are identified as high-potential employees, which might include their interest/aspiration in the position. After all, not every individual may be interested in moving into a more responsible position. Tentative plans are created for shortages, which may include seeking outside candidates.

HR is typically responsible for maintaining a candidate database of skills and career development plans, along with the monitoring of development activities. Additionally, HR is responsible for sourcing or creating training needs for candidates. Figure 5-4 provides a typical progression of steps in succession planning.

Knowledge Management

Knowledge management (KM) is a term that relates to the retention and distribution of organizational knowledge. It is the efficient process of capturing, developing, sharing, and handling of information or resources within a business. KM efforts will generally focus on competitive advantage, innovation, the sharing of lessons from the past, integration, and the renewal cycle of continuous improvement in an organization. Its focus is on the management of internal knowledge held by incumbents as a strategic asset and the mentorship in sharing this knowledge.

Managing Organizational Knowledge

In managing organizational knowledge, organizations identify their collective knowledge to compete, including the creation, storage/retrieval, transfer, and application of knowledge that is pertinent to conducting business. Referred to as *knowledge assets*, they are one of an organization's most valuable assets. Knowledge assets include both explicit knowledge (e.g., documented concepts, procedures, and processes) and tacit knowledge (e.g., know-how) that are highly specific to an organization.

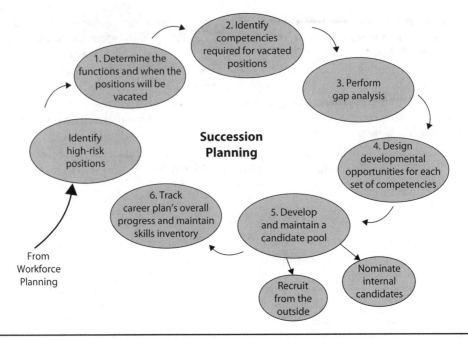

Figure 5-4   Succession planning

Knowledge Management Systems

Today, many organizations and industries as a whole are taking advantage of advanced technologies such as database tools and web-based applications to effectively manage knowledge that their workforce has. Over the last two decades, organizations have leveraged these technologies in their KM initiatives. The ultimate goal of these technologies is to introduce a standardized process to promote a more efficient and effective flow of information and knowledge throughout the organization.

Knowledge Management Process   A knowledge management process is creating, sharing, using, and managing the information and knowledge within an organization. It is a multidisciplinary approach to achieving organizational objectives by making the best use of knowledge.

Uses of Knowledge Management Systems   There are various uses for knowledge management systems, yet generally they all focus on transferring knowledge seamlessly. "Document, document, document" has been the cry in IT for many years because IT has felt the pain of what it's like to have a programmer "keep the coding in their head." when an employee has abruptly and unexpectedly left their employment. An example of a KM system is a central database that stores customer data that is used for sales and marketing analytics. The resulting information that the sales/marketing folks place in the database is *knowledge,* which is then transferred and shared across the organization. A retrieval tool such as a query system could be used to have a new sales or marketing person learn who is the rep for a particular client and what the status is of that particular relationship in the sales cycle.

Strategies for Effective Knowledge Management Systems   Using information systems to manage the knowledge is often a difficult, time-consuming, and tedious task. The following internal and external strategies could help to ensure effective implementation and management of KM systems:

Internal Strategies

- *Identify business challenges.* This is related to knowledge management and then capturing essential pieces of knowledge. Focus on knowledge that is important to capture and feasible to maintain.

- *Obtain executive support.* Executives in the organization need to be on board with supporting knowledge management initiatives from both a strategic perspective and a financial perspective. The probability of success increases when the knowledge management effort is a top priority.

- *Be patient.* Creating a knowledge management system is time-consuming. Managing knowledge is a difficult task with no hard-and-fast rules.

- *Get buy-in and input from the users.* Many KM initiatives have failed because the system designers neglect user feedback. Involve users at early stages in the design process and incorporate user input on system design requirements. Remember, the objective is to implement a system that users willfully use, not one that is technically sound but remains underutilized because of a lack of buy-in from potential users.

- *Celebrate small wins.* Use a "control tower" approach, where a specific function is mandated to develop a knowledge management action plans, such as accounts payable. This can result in a favorable approach to ensure small wins throughout the organization by showing how a function created their KM.

- *Manage employee behavior.* One of the signals of effective KM initiatives is evidence of employee participation. Project leaders should champion changes in KM practices and ensure that the technology provides added value. Moreover, employees should be actively involved in the knowledge management efforts because it is their knowledge that will be leveraged and retained for future.

External Strategies

- *Attend KM-oriented training sessions and conferences.* KM is a new frontier for many organizations. Attending training sessions and discussing knowledge management problems and best practices with others will serve as an introduction to the challenges.

- *Establish a peer network.* Establish forums where colleagues are able to demonstrate the latest best practices.

- *Benchmark your knowledge management practices.* Benchmark your organization's knowledge management process against competitors to identify areas of strength and weakness.

- *Hire a knowledge management expert.* Knowledge management experts provide credibility to the organization's KM efforts especially to stakeholders. Traditional management consultants may be insufficient because they lack the appropriate expertise needed to address KM issues.

Social Sharing of Knowledge   Knowledge sharing via enterprise social media (ESN) is increasingly being introduced into large organizations. ESN focuses on the use of online social networks among the employees who share the same roles and responsibilities, generally in large organizations, such as matrix positions (e.g., HR business partners in each manufacturing plant who report to both the plant manager and the headquarters' HR director). Internally, an enterprise social software may be part of the organization's intranet. ESNs are also used externally and not just within a particular organization, such as software programmers seeking knowledge shared on blogs and networks to figure out how to code a particular challenge.

Functional Area 9—Employee and Labor Relations

Here is SHRM's BoCK definition: Employee and Labor Relations refers to any dealings between the organization and its employees regarding the terms and conditions of employment.[34]

Human Resources Management as a functional area within employer organizations didn't always exist in its current configuration. It began as a kinship department associated with accounting and was primarily responsible for taking care of payroll issues and for record keeping. From that it evolved into a labor relations department responsible for union interactions. In recent years HR has had responsibility for employee management legal compliance and today is involved in strategic issues of employee resource management.

Key Concepts

- Approaches to retaliation prevention
- Approaches to union-organization relations (e.g., collective bargaining, contract negotiation, contract administration process)
- Causes of and methods for preventing and addressing strikes, boycotts, and work stoppages
- Disciplinary procedures and approaches
- Employment rights, standards, and concepts (e.g., labor rights, living wage and fair concepts, standard workday), according to the International Labor Organization (ILO)
- Techniques for disciplinary investigations
- Techniques for grievance and complaint resolution

- Types and development of compliance and ethics programs (e.g., design, implementation, performance measures)
- Types and structures of organized labor (e.g., unions, works councils, trade union federations, other employee collectives)
- Types of alternative dispute resolution (ADR) (e.g., mediation, arbitration) and their advantages and disadvantages
- Unfair labor practices, according to the ILO
- Unionization approaches, methods, and management (e.g., acceptance, avoidance strategies)

The following are the proficiency indicators that SHRM has identified as key concepts:

For All HR Professionals	Advanced HR Professionals (SCP Exam)
• Supports interactions with union and other employee representatives	• Manages interactions and negotiations with union and other employee representatives (e.g., governmental, legal)
• Supports the organization's interests in union-management activities	• Serves as the primary representative of the organization's interests in union management activities (e.g., negotiations, dispute resolution)
• Assists and supports the organization in the collective bargaining process	
• Participates in or facilitates ADR processes (e.g., arbitration, mediation)	• Manages the collective bargaining process
• Makes recommendations for addressing other types of employee representation (e.g., governmental legal)	• Consults on and develops an effective organized labor strategy (e.g., avoidance, acceptance, adaptation) to achieve the organization's desire impact on itself and its workforce
• Develops and implements workplace policies, handbooks, and codes of conduct	• Educates employees, managers, and leaders at all levels about the organization's labor strategy (e.g., avoidance, acceptance, adaptation) and its impact on the achievement of goals and objectives
• Provides guidance to employees on the terms and implications of their employment agreement and the organization's policies and procedures (e.g., employee handbook)	• Educates employees at all levels about changes in the organization's policies
• Consults managers on how to supervise difficult employees, handle disruptive behaviors, and respond with the appropriate level of corrective action	• Coaches and counsels managers on how to operate within the parameters of organizational policy, labor agreements, and employment agreements
• Conducts investigations into employee misconduct and suggests disciplinary action when necessary	• Oversees employee investigations and discipline
• Manages employee grievance and discipline processes	
• Resolves workplace labor disputes internally	

The Employment Relationship

According to the government, people are either employees or not employees. That begs the question, "What is an employee?" A quick look in our glossary will reveal an employee is "A person in the service of another under any contract of hire, express or implied, oral or written, where the employer has the power or right to control and direct the employee in the material details of how the work is to be performed."

Toward "Employee Relations"

Organizational culture is often defined, at least in part, by the type of employee relations programs that exist. We are talking about structured programs that are designed to help employees feel part of the organization in positive ways. Creating a positive culture is not a simple matter and is an essential influential factor for recruiting and retaining talent. HR devotes much effort and time to champion a positive culture with effective employee relations programs. The human resource department also serves as an employee advocate. Culture is defined by the way an organization treats its employees, customers, and others. It is also influenced by the way power is distributed within the organization and the amount of power employees sense they have. What follows is an overview of different types of employee relationship programs.

Employer and Employee Rights

Under the laws of the United States both employers and employees have rights related to their relationship.

Employer Rights Under the Law   Employers used to be able to treat employees in any way they wanted. That is what brought about the rise of labor unions. Unions protested ill treatment of workers and fought for employee benefits and wages. Over the decades, much of what the unions accomplished for their membership have been transported into laws that protect all employees, not just unionized workers. Equal Employment Opportunity (EEO) is a prime example. Employers may make their decisions about employees based on any factor that is job related. Things such as race, religion, sex, or national origin may no longer be considered in that decision-making process.

As things stand today, employers can do virtually anything they want as long as it doesn't violate law or public policy. That includes the covenant of good faith and fair dealing. Employers are expected to give workers more consideration the longer they have served the employer. And all workers are due fair treatment. That is a constant expectation.

Intellectual Property   While there are some exceptions, the general rule is that employers own the rights to work-related copyrights, patents, and trademarks developed by employees even if the work was done on the employee's own time. In the absence of written agreements to the contrary, employers are ordinarily the owners of such work products by their employees.

Employee Rights Under the Law   There are dozens of labor laws on the books today. They have been created to provide protections to employees in the workplace. You can scan the list of federal laws in Chapter 3. Case laws (Appendix B) also bring influence to the subject. All U.S. employers are influenced in one way or another by these requirements.

Employees are usually given the "benefit of the doubt" when it comes to disciplinary treatment or complaint against an employer. Remember, they are always afforded consideration under the covenant of good faith and fair dealing. Employers must treat people fairly, even though they may be categorized as "employment at will" employees.

Employment at will is a form of employment relationship that has been amended over the years. Now, there are many restrictions to an employer's termination of a worker without cause. And, fair treatment influences strongly employee attitudes and, in turn, production levels.

International Human Rights and Labor Standards   While the United States and other first-world countries lead the pack for employee rights, other countries also recognize the need to protect workers against inhumane treatment and bad employer conduct.

- **International Labor Organization**   In 1919, the International Labor Organization (ILO) was created. It was later adopted by the United Nations as a component of that international body; 185 of 193 UN member states also belong to the ILO.[35] There are four key principles of the ILO.

  - Freedom of association and the effective recognition of the right to collective bargaining
  - Elimination of all forms of forced or compulsory labor
  - Effective abolition of child labor
  - Elimination of discrimination in respect of employment and occupation

- **Organisation for Economic Co-operation and Development (OECD)**
  The OECD was formed in 1961 to stimulate economic progress and world trade. Current members are Australia, Austria, Belgium, Canada, Chile, the Czech Republic, Denmark, Finland, France, Germany, Greece, Hungary, Iceland, Ireland, Israel, Italy, Japan, South Korea, Luxembourg, Mexico, the Netherlands, New Zealand, Norway, Poland, Portugal, Slovakia, Slovenia, Spain, Sweden, Switzerland, Turkey, the United Kingdom, and the United States. Member countries produce two-thirds of the world's goods and services.[36]

  By maintaining contact with many governmental and international agencies, such as the International Monetary Fund, the OECD has become a clearinghouse for a vast amount of economic data. It publishes hundreds of titles annually on a variety of subjects that include agriculture, scientific research, capital markets, tax structures, energy resources, lumber, air pollution, educational development, and development assistance.

- **World Trade Organization (WTO)**   The WTO has been headquartered in Geneva, Switzerland, since its creation in January 1995. Its 161 member countries focus on global rules of trade between nations. Its main function is to ensure that trade flows as smoothly, predictably, and freely as possible.[37]

Treaties and Trade Agreements   Treaties are formal contracts between nations that, in the United States, must be approved by the U.S. Senate before they become binding on the government. Trade agreements are administrative arrangements generally made by the executive branch of the government that do not require approval of the U.S. Senate. Under international law, both types of agreement are considered binding, even though we only see treaties as enforceable under our laws.

Relevant Employment Laws   Federal laws applying to employee relations include the following:

Davis-Bacon Act of 1931	Electronic Communications Privacy Act of 1986
Employee Polygraph Protection Act of 1988	Equal Pay Act of 1963
Fair and Accurate Credit Transactions Act of 2003	Fair Credit Reporting Act of 1970
Fair Labor Standards Act of 1938	Immigration and Nationality Act of 1952
Immigration Reform and Control Act of 1986	Labor-Management Relations Act of 1947 (Taft-Hartley Act)
Labor-Management Reporting and Disclosure Act of 1959 (Landrum-Griffin Act)	National Labor Relations Act of 1935
Norris-LaGuardia Act of 1932	Portal-to-Portal Act of 1947
Railway Labor Act of 1926	Service Contract Act of 1965
Federal Insurance Contributions Act of 1935 (Social Security Act)	Uniformed Services Employment and Reemployment Rights Act of 1994
Vietnam Era Veterans Readjustment Assistance Act of 1974	Wagner-Peyser Act of 1933 (amended by Workforce Investment Act of 1998)
Walsh-Healey Act of 1936 (Public Contracts Act)	Civil Rights Act of 1964 (Title VII)
Civil Rights Act of 1991	Drug-Free Workplace Act of 1988
Genetic Information Nondiscrimination Act of 2008	Lilly Ledbetter Fair Pay Act of 2009
Pregnancy Discrimination Act of 1978	Uniform Guidelines on Employee Selection Procedures of 1976
Age Discrimination in Employment Act of 1967	Worker Adjustment and Retraining Notification Act of 1988

- **Data privacy**   Privacy of employee-related data is a prime concern these days, especially with weekly revelations about computer hackers breaking into one database after another. And, the grand prize of all was reached when hackers accessed millions of records in the Office of Personnel Management database. Both current and former employee records were involved. The hack was attributed to Chinese government groups. It is among a growing list of invasions into personal information collections maintained by employers and governments around the country.

Some of the key requirements are shown here:

National Requirement for Employee Data Protection	
Jurisdiction	**Law or Agreement**
United States of America	Health Insurance Portability and Accountability Act (HIPAA).
	Genetic Information Nondiscrimination Act (GINA).
	Fair and Accurate Credit Transactions Act (FACTA).
	Data breech notification requirements (49 states and territories have enacted notification requirements in some form when personal data is compromised or illegally accessed).
European Economic Area	European Union's data protection Directive 95/46/EC (the "EU Directive") recognizes personal data privacy as a fundamental right and establishes a comprehensive scheme to protect such information.
Non-European Economic Area countries	Countries with comprehensive laws covering data protection and nondisclosure include Argentina, Australia, Canada, China, India, Japan, and Mexico.

- **Separation of employment**   Separation of employment includes every form of voluntary and involuntary employment termination category. Voluntary separations include resignation, retirement, and job abandonment. Involuntary separations include death, discharge, layoff/downsizing, or incapacitation.

Employment Contracts   Employment relationships can exist under a contract or without a contract. Contracts can exist either as oral agreements or as written documents. Either form of agreement will obligate each party to certain performance behaviors. Employers will be obligated for certain compensation, and employees will be obligated for certain work. Contracts spell out how the contract can be ended, meaning how the employment can come to an end. Usually, there is a requirement for a "just cause" before an employer can dismiss a contractual employee.

Written employment contracts will typically contain several sections, such as the following:

- **Job description**   Lists duties and responsibilities.
- **Statement of authority**   Details expenditure limits, hiring authority, and what conditions require approval of the board of directors or other authority.
- **Agreement length**   Identifies the beginning and ending dates of the contract.

- **Performance requirements**   Documents performance requirements for compensation increases or bonuses. These can include revenue targets, sales targets, or other measurable performance standard.

- **Compensation and benefits**   Details the base rate of pay, pay calculation (hourly, salaried, commissioned), how increases will be achieved, how bonuses will be achieved, how compensation will be paid (cash, stock, bonds, future payments), pension program (company and employee contribution scheme), healthcare benefits programs (medical, dental, vision, individual or family), perks (company car, airplane, driver, concierge, entertainment tickets for concerts and sporting events), and any other compensation condition upon which the relationship will be based.

- **Other important issues**   Can include agreements about who owns copyright and patent rights to things produced by the employee during the contract period, nondisclosure agreements for employer intellectual property protection, and noncompete provisions.

- **Termination provisions**   Can include personal behavior and ethics requirements and other reasons or "causes" for separating the employee from the organization. In many contracts these reasons are specified in great detail. If there is to be a "buyout" for time remaining on the agreement, that should be specified here. "Golden parachutes" are often large sums representing the buyout for early separation such as in a merger.

Oral Employment Contracts   Oral employment contracts can be expressly made, or made by mistake, and still be valid and enforceable, much to the dismay of employers who fall into those traps.

Oral contracts can be created in some unusual circumstances. Supervisors and managers can inadvertently enter into oral contracts and should receive training to help them avoid such pitfalls.

The following are some examples of oral contracts:

- An in-house recruiter tells a job applicant that this is a great organization and anyone who keeps their record clean "can expect to have a lifelong career here." Within a year, the new employee's division was closed, and all employees were laid off.

- A manager tells a subordinate that "nothing short of stealing from the company" will be cause for termination. Within a year the employee was terminated for inadequate performance.

- A manager tells a new employee, "Sure, you can bet that you'll be here at least five years, so go ahead and sell your house in another state and move your family here." The employee was part of a downsizing 6 months later.

- A supervisor says to an employee, "Don't worry about your performance rating. Nobody pays any attention to them here anyway." Within a few months the employee was terminated because of poor performance.

At-Will Employment   "During the late 19th and early 20th centuries a new set of legal rules emerged in the United States governing the relationship between employer and employee. These rules were called 'employment-at-will' and provided that, absent express agreement to the contrary, employment was for an indefinite time and could be terminated by either party, for any reason, or for no reason at all. This doctrine is a unique product of American common law, created by state and federal judges, and continues, substantially unchanged, until today."[38]

Currently, employment at will exists in most states, and it is state law that usually governs these employee relationships. In other countries, using different legal systems, employment may be terminated only for cause. That means employers must justify their decisions to end the employment relationship with someone. The behavior of the individual is usually the justification.

Employment at will exists only in the absence of a contract that details the employment agreement between employer and employee. Those contracts can be related to a group, as union memorandums of understanding, or to individuals, such as chief executive officers. Since roughly the 1930s, American courts have been instrumental in identifying conditions under which employers may not arbitrarily discharge people, even though they are at-will employees. Some of those restrictions include the following:

- Civil service rules
- Constitutional protections
- Protections against employment discrimination (based on race, color, national origin, religion, sex, age, genetic information, physical disability, mental disability, pregnancy, veteran status, use of Family and Medical Leave)
- Whistle-blowing protections

Employee Relationship Strategy

Employee relations are methods for managing the employer-employee relationship. Strategically managing that relationship calls for consideration of four key elements.

- Union or nonunion status
- Communication
- Company culture
- Compensation and benefits

Union Acceptance/Avoidance Strategies   Employers that have not been unionized have a choice about how they will approach the idea of union organizing. It is possible that an employer would welcome or be neutral toward the idea. Where an employer believes the organization could be well served by having a single voice in representing the employee body, support for unionizing its workforce may be a positive approach. However, if the employer believes that a union would bring lack of flexibility and stringent work rules, then avoidance could be the path of choice.

Accepting the notion of worker organization efforts is rather simple. It could even represent encouragement for the effort. Strategically, the employer would make it known that it supports the union-organizing effort.

Employers that believe unions would not add substantially to their employee management programs will want to use strategies that are intended to show workers that unions are not necessary for their satisfaction on the job. Strategic programs such as honest open-door policies, sincere management attention to employee complaints, promotion from within, employee training programs, employee satisfaction surveys (with appropriate follow-up), competitive benefit programs and wage schedules, and similar policies can help deflect union-organizing efforts.

Global ER Strategies   Each national jurisdiction has its own legal requirements that act as a minimum threshold for employer-employee treatment. Once those minimums have been reached, it is appropriate for employers to ask whether their policies should go beyond to provide enhanced treatment benefits. Perhaps those are insurance programs such as medical, dental, and vision coverage. Sometimes the strategies include higher wage schedules or paid time-off limits than absolutely required. Strategic use of employee benefits can be a strong argument against union-organizing success. Trying to find an appropriate treatment for employee values that can vary by culture in each different country is also a strategic application of union-prevention efforts.

Employee Recognition and Reward

The larger an organization grows, the greater the likelihood that its recognition programs will be structured. In small organizations, recognition can be given in many forms, often as events unfold and accomplishments are achieved.

Forms of Rewards   Employee recognition can include service anniversary awards (watches, clocks, plaques, certificates, pins), employee-of-the-month awards (designated parking space, plaque or bulletin board posting, special benefit like a dinner gift certificate), cost savings suggestions, sales achievement awards, team achievement awards, or individual achievement awards. Obviously, that is not an exhaustive list. You can add others and apply them as your organization finds a fit between the recognition and the accomplishment.

Recognition Systems   Employee recognition systems can be either formal or informal. Formal recognition systems involve programs that are designed to address systemic employee issues such as service awards, retirement awards, and employee-of-the-month recognitions. Informal recognition systems involve supervisor or manager spotlighting of employee accomplishments at an employee meeting or supervisor acknowledgment of an employee accomplishment by giving an extra paid day off.

Recognition and Rewards in Global Organizations   Cultural differences from one country to another mean that the esteem (or value) placed on specific rewards will also vary from one country to another. It may be that employees think a few extra days off are wonderful if they are in the United States. In China, they may place greater value on a free month of health benefits for their extended family. Before offering a recognition to employees in another country, it is a good idea to be sure the recognition will be perceived as positively as it is by the manager offering it.

Feedback as Reward and Recognition   Culture doesn't usually get in the way of a supervisor telling an employee "thank you" for a job well done. Almost everyone, regardless of their location, feels good when receiving positive reinforcement for their work performance. Managers and supervisors who make it a habit to give thanks to employees when it is truly deserved will find that it is quite the motivator. Everyone likes to feel appreciated.

Employee Communication

Here again, there are formal and informal communication systems. Formal systems include an employee bulletin or monthly newsletter and daily intranet blog updates for company work sites. Informal communication systems can involve manager distribution of periodic e-mails updating workers on specific happenings in the realm of employee relations. Employees are always interested in the subjects of benefits, customer feedback, and new customer contract activity. When the company is given an award for safety accomplishments or production goal achievements, the workers want to know about it. Being sure to communicate those things to employees is often the job of the HR manager.

Including Managers and Supervisors

As important as general employee communication, special communication to supervisors and managers cannot be overlooked. When new policies are issued, for example, managers and supervisors are interested because they will have to implement the policies and answer questions from employees about daily implications. It is not uncommon in larger organizations for managers and supervisors to participate in special meetings just for them. They are often venues for these organizational leaders to learn and provide feedback to senior management about what company policies and programs are working and what are not. Communication flows both directions in such a gathering.

Third-Party Influences on Employee Relations

When we think of employee relationships, we normally consider only the two primary parties: employers and employees. There are times, however, when third parties are involved in that process of conducting employee relationships.

Complex Labor Environments

Even in nonunion environments, there can be third parties in the employment relationship. Often those third parties are government agents responsible for enforcing legal compliance requirements having to do with things such as safety, child labor, equal employment opportunity, or workplace security. Things get complicated when labor unions are active representatives of employees in a portion of the organization and there are no unions in other parts of the company.

Labor or Trade Unions

Unions are groups of employees designated to represent interests of those employees through formal negotiation processes. They are responsible for conducting grievances as employee representatives and for protecting against an employer's failure to follow termination procedures.

Labor/Trade Union Strategies   Employers may find it an advantage to have a union represent their workers. Or, they may not want to have to deal with the regimental procedures necessary once a union gains a foothold in the organization. Either way, having a strategy for supporting or avoiding union representation is worthwhile.

Increasing Formal Internationalization of Unions   These days, unions are more often international entities such as the International Brotherhood of _____ (you can fill in the blank with just about any name). So many employer organizations are multi-national that unions are forced into the same mode of operation.

Pressing for National and International Compliance   Legal compliance requirements for unions vary from one country to another. It is incumbent upon employers who work with international unions to understand the requirements of each country in which they have represented employees.

Implementing International Framework Agreements   "An international (or global) framework agreement (IFA) is an instrument negotiated between a multinational enterprise and a Global Union Federation (GUF) in order to establish an ongoing relationship between the parties and ensure that the company respects the same standards in all the countries where it operates… Most framework agreements include follow-up mechanisms involving trade union participation. These mechanisms include specific actions on the part of management and workers' representatives, such as company-wide dissemination (and translation, where necessary) of the agreement or the development of joint training programs. Some agreements provide for joint missions by the relevant national trade union and global union federation in order to carry out on-site monitoring of the implementation of the agreement. Most of them also include mechanisms for the global union federation to raise a case if the company violates the terms of the agreement."[39]

Forming Networks and Alliances   The international labor-organizing effort is relatively new. It is building bridges between union organizations in individual countries to create international organizations with a wider influence. And the organizing effort continues to expand into new countries where there have not yet been union representation of workers. In Ireland, for example, the Irish Congress of Trade Unions is the single umbrella for trade unions in both Northern Ireland and Ireland.

Understanding Individual Labor or Trade Unions   Each trade union is organized to assist the members it attracts. Those members have a unifying interest in their employment relationship with one or more employers. In the case of trade workers (carpenters, electricians, plumbers), journey-level individuals can work for any union-represented employer.

In the case of labor unions not in the trades (electrical workers, telephone workers, state government workers), employees usually work for a single employer doing similar types of work. For example, the Communication Workers of America (CWA) represents technicians in the telephone companies. The Service Employees International Union (SEIU) represents workers in health care (nurses, doctors, lab technicians, home health workers), property services (cleaning, security, building maintenance), and public service workers (bus drivers, state government workers, school workers).

Managing the Union Relationship   Traditionally, unions have been seen as adversaries of management. These days, more focus is being placed on cooperation between the two. That means employee representatives are often invited to participate in the decision-making process along with managers and supervisors. When given an active participative role, unions can become allies of employers.

Work Councils   Originally in Germany beginning in the 1920s, these groups have been common in other European countries since the late 1990s. Either the employer or employees can request formation of a work council. Member states are to provide for the right to establish European Works Councils in companies or groups of companies with at least five employees in the EU. Through work councils, workers are informed and consulted by management on the progress of the business and any significant decision at European level that could affect their employment or working conditions. Members are usually elected from the employee body. Work councils focus their attention on issues dealing with employee status and rights.

Work Council Structures   Work councils are composed of members from the employer's body of workers. In many organizations, those are also union representatives. Typically, a work council can be established once there are five employees in the employer's organization. The following table is an example of how representation of employees can be composed. Notice that there are always an odd number of members to facilitate achievement of a simple majority vote on issues. Senior management are not party to the work council.

Work Council Membership Size	
Number Employed	**Number of Works Council Members**
5–20	1
21–50	3
51–100	5
101–200	7
201–400	9
401–700	11
701–1,000	13
1,000–1,500	15

Codetermination   In organizations having systems of codetermination, employees are given seats on boards of directors and/or supervisory boards. Policy decisions related to employee treatment are addressed by the board of directors with this system in place.

HR and Work Councils   Work councils are sometimes used in multinational corporations outside Europe. Oracle is one example. At Oracle, line managers and HR managers can make recommendations for hiring and firing, but the work council holds the approval stamp. In the United States, establishing work councils in the absence of labor unions is tricky. The National Labor Relations Act prohibits "company unions," which is sometimes a label pinned on work councils.

Governments and Other Groups

Government laws and regulations weigh heavily on employee relations in today's workplace. In every country, laws govern minimum wage, paid time-off allocations or use, safety and health issues, retirement programs, and union relations. It is incumbent upon HR managers to identify the specific legal requirements in each country where they have employees. Compliance, though complicated, can be critical to employee satisfaction.

Collective Bargaining

Collective bargaining is an issue that is generally governed by law. Regulations that implement the law specify how employers are to respond to employee union-organizing activities and ongoing negotiations for contract content. Collective bargaining is negotiation involving how employee relations will be conducted in the employer organization. It results in a formal contract document or resolution of formal workplace practice and procedures.

Contract Negotiation Process   Negotiating a contract requires identifying the subjects to be addressed by the agreement. Then, each party prepares its preferred position on each subject. Then the process of comparing those positions begins. Often, dollars are attached to contract subjects. For example, the length of work shift, the amount of overtime to be paid, and the cost of health care benefits all can be represented by dollar values. If the union wants greater benefits for its members, a dollar value can be assigned to that increase. Employers argue budget restraint and use dollar values to justify their reasoning.

According to the Negotiation Board, there are eight steps in the negotiation process. Here is a list of the process step flow in contract negotiations:

- **Step 1, Prepare**   Do your research ahead of time so that you know your opponent and you know what you want from the negotiation.
- **Step 2, Open**   Let the other side know what you want and let them tell you what they want.
- **Step 3, Argue**   Back up your case with evidence and uncover defects in your opponent's argument.
- **Step 4, Explore**   Search for common ground and agreeable outcomes.

- **Step 5, Signal** Show that you are ready to reach an agreement.
- **Step 6, Package** Put together different acceptable options for both parties.
- **Step 7, Close** Come to an agreement and finalize the negotiation.
- **Step 8, Sustain** Ensure that their side, and yours, follows through with the negotiated agreement.

HR's Role in Contract Negotiations In large organizations, a segment of the HR department will be responsible for labor relations. That responsibility would include duties associated with contract negotiations. In smaller organizations, the HR manager may be the only person in the HR department. Then, that manager is responsible for contract negotiations. Often, there is direct support from the legal department or external legal counsel.

Each component of a contract agreement can be assigned a cost in dollars. Adding all of those component costs can produce the total contract value. For example, health benefits will cost several hundreds of dollars each month to cover an employee and family members. The employer can agree to cover a percentage of that cost, with the balance being paid by the employee. A union will ask for more employer contribution to that formula. And, should the employer agree, the increased contribution can be assigned an incremental cost increase value. Adding that to other cost increases, such as increased pay schedules and overtime rates, will produce a total increase of contract costs. Each time a new proposal is made or received, a cost analysis should be made to determine the budgetary impact. Some costs will be perpetual, such as an increase in pay rates. Other costs can be limited to one time only, such as special bonus payments. There are advantages and disadvantages to costs that will be contained to one period of time (year) versus continuing into future periods of time. Assembling this data is usually the responsibility of the HR manager.

Contract Administration and Enforcement

The thought that only large employers have union contracts is a myth. Many small employers work with union agreements. That is often the case in the construction industry, for example. Operating engineers, teamsters, and laborers, among other unions, will sometimes have agreements with governmental entities that only union-represented workers will be employed on projects funded by that entity. This is common practice for cities and counties, particularly in geographical areas where labor organizations are a strong political influence.

Memoranda of understanding (MOU) and collective bargaining agreements (CBAs) are the written contracts between employer and unions. MOU is a term usually found in the public sector, and CBA is a term normally used in the private sector.

Whether the employer is large or small, someone in the organization must be assigned the responsibility for coordinating work through unions and ensuring the employer abides by all the requirements of the union contract. Sometimes unions require that they process all job requisitions from their employer counterparts. Hiring through union "hiring halls," as it is sometimes called, is the practice of notifying the union of a job opening and receiving a qualified union member as the new hire designee. It is a simple process that can provide staffing quickly, often with only one telephone call or e-mail conveying the employment requisition.

Large employers will have labor relations staff groups that are assigned responsibility for day-to-day interactions with labor unions, as well as carrying responsibility for contract negotiations. Small employers will rely on a part-time job duty assignment for the labor relations function because it doesn't require full-time attention. Small employers sometimes rely on their labor attorneys to fill the role of contract negotiator and grievance handler, while job requisitions are processed part-time by another company employee.

Handling Grievances   Employee grievances can relate to any subject but always indicate a feeling of upset or discontent about something going on in the workplace, such as the way they are being treated, organizational policies, and the big category of "fairness."

In union-represented organizations, the union contract (memorandum of understanding) will usually explain what steps exist in the grievance procedure. They are designed to permit union members the opportunity to formally protest application of any contract provision. Most will deal with working conditions such as hours of work, how shifts are assigned, or seniority practices.

In nonunion organizations, employee handbooks will often detail the steps for submitting and processing an employee complaint.

Note that rarely will such complaints be called *grievances* in nonunion groups. That is usually a term reserved for union contracts.

Here are the typical grievance-handling steps you will find in most organizations:

1. **A written complaint**   The employee describes in writing what is causing the upset or discontent.

2. **Supervisor-level discussion**   The employee's supervisor (or another group's supervisor) will discuss the complaint with the employee, reviewing facts and reasons for the decision that resulted in the complaint. If the explanation is sufficient, the grievance ends here. If the employee presents information that causes the decision to be changed, the grievance can also end here.

3. **Management- or HR-level discussion**   If the supervisor and employee can't agree, the next discussion is with a management person or the human resource department. If an agreement is reached, the matter is settled. If not, it can go to a final step with senior management.

4. **Senior management**   The final management step is usually with a senior management official. Sometimes that is the chief executive officer, but it can be with any other designated official who has authority to make any adjustments or decisions deemed appropriate in settling the grievance.

5. **Mediation or arbitration**   Contracts usually specify whether arbitration will be used to resolve union grievances. Ordinarily, employers and unions will split the cost of hiring an arbitrator. Contracts will also specify the procedures to be used in selecting an arbitrator.

When the Employee Relationship Falters

Things do not always move smoothly in an employment organization. There are times when management and employees do not see things in the same way. Sometimes, feelings get hurt, and people feel like they are being treated unfairly. Whether these conditions constitute a violation of union contract or company policy or are simply examples of miscommunication, they are very real for employees.

Preserving the Relationship at Difficult Times

When disagreements occur and upsets happen, HR managers should focus on preserving their relationships with union officials. The worst thing that can come from disagreements is failure of the communication channel. If parties cease to talk with one another, it is impossible to get back to a normal working relationship. Sometimes simply agreeing to disagree and move to the next step in the resolution process is the best that can be hoped for. But it carries with it agreement to continue working toward cooperation in other areas.

Industrial Actions and Unfair Labor Practices

Either management or union can initiate retaliatory action in the workplace as a response to the other party's failure to agree at the bargaining table. Industrial actions are designed to get the attention of the opposite party. Unfair labor practices are those activities that violate the National Labor Relations Act (NLRA).

Industrial Actions   Industrial actions can be initiated by either employer or employees and almost always result from the breakdown in the negotiation process.

Employee-initiated industrial actions can include work slowdowns (where production rates are decreased from normal), work stoppage (where a portion of the facility stops its production), and "sickouts" (orchestrated absences by calling in "sick" such as the "blue flu" when police officers fail to report for duty).

Employer-initiated industrial action usually involves lockouts, when employees are prevented from reporting to work because the employer has locked the facility or otherwise barred their access to the work area.

Unfair Labor Practices   The National Labor Relations Act (NLRA) explains that unfair labor practices can be blamed on either employers or labor unions. Common among issues evoking such claims are those revolving around the process of union elections. Unions commonly claim the employer is blocking their organizing efforts, and employers claim that the union is harassing employees and electioneering using paid time. Another issue that generates great numbers of complaints is how management and union members behave during a work stoppage (strike).

Complaints of unfair labor practices are formally filed with the National Labor Relations Board (NLRB). The NLRB will investigate the complaints and issue a determination along with any order for corrective action or limitation on activities of the offending party.

In some instances, when an employer believes there has been a violation of civil law requirements, it will go directly to court requesting an injunction against the union to prevent the behavior that is causing the problem. That is common when striking union pickets block access to parking lots, loading docks, or employee building entrances. Municipal laws in many locations govern how public access to property must be maintained and how public sidewalks and roadways can be used appropriately.

In other instances, unions can seek court assistance when employers are being accused of inappropriate controls on picketers. Use of physical force by private security guards could be an example.

In either situation, the remedy sought through the court is an injunction preventing the offending behaviors. With an injunction in hand, it is possible to request help from law enforcement bodies such as the police department or sheriff's department to enforce the injunction.

HR's Role   Human resource professionals are usually the people responsible for monitoring activities in the workplace, documenting the behavior of individuals, and communicating the messages from management and unions to one another.

Managing Conflicts with and Between Employees

Employee conflicts are not always limited to union grievances or discrimination complaints. Sometimes they happen because what happens "just isn't fair," and the American expectation is always that the workplace will operate fairly.

HR's Role in Managing Conflict   Howard M. Guttman, Guttman Development Strategies, Inc., has identified five roles the HR professional should play in managing conflicts within the employer organization.[40]

- *Be a custodian of team alignment.* HR professionals should hold a mirror to team members so they can see how well the team has done in reaching its goals. Part of that reflection should focus on individual accountability for participation and results.

- *Drive/monitor accountability.* Team members become accountable not only for their own performance but for that of their colleagues—even those who do not report to them.

- *Help assess the team's conflict-management behavior.* The HR professional can guide teams through an exploration of effectiveness in handling conflicts. Identifying specific behavior changes that it will take for successful goal accomplishment then follows.

- *Ensure the right capability set on teams.* A major role for HR is ensuring that, after the "should be-as is" analysis, teams receive the skills needed to fill the gaps.

- *Work to make sure that teams are high performers.* The internal HR consultant must wear many hats: consultant, coach, facilitator, trainer, and, perhaps most important, role model to support the team's continued success.

Conflict-Resolution Techniques   Some amount of conflict will always be present in the workplace. The fact that it exists is not necessarily an unhealthy thing. When it is resolved quickly and effectively, it can lead to personal and professional growth. In many cases, effective conflict resolution can make the difference between positive and negative outcomes. The "Leader's 5-Step Guide to Conflict Resolution"[41] recommends five steps in the conflict-resolution process.

1. **Affirm the relationship**   I am here because I value your friendship more than I value the discomfort of confronting my hurt feelings.

2. **Seek to understand**   Covey's thoughts on listening are worth their weight in gold, teaching one to seek the others person's feelings, thoughts, and perspectives first.

3. **Seek to be understood**   After understanding, share one's feelings, thoughts, and perspectives, not in an attacking mode but in an effort for the other party to see one's views.

4. **Own responsibility by apologizing**   Seek to see where any, if not all, of the conflict is one's responsibility, learning to respond differently in the future. A genuine apology not only affirms the relationship but can do wonders in releasing hurt feelings.

5. **Seek agreement**   After both parties have apologized, accepting responsibility for their parts in the conflict, seeking agreement means reuniting on the common vision that drew both sides together in the first place, agreeing that the cause is bigger than the conflict is for both parties.

One-on-One Resolution   Rarely do two parties involved in conflict have the skills to dig themselves out of the pit they find themselves in. That requires help from a coach such as an HR professional. The coach will facilitate one-on-one discussions to help the two people identify what they want and why it is important for the other party to also get what they want. Identifying something that will be satisfactory to each party is what the coaching process is designed to accomplish.

Third-Party Resolution   When something formal is required, mediation or arbitration might be the answer. Outside experts are trained and certified as mediators and arbitrators and are available for hire to bring two parties to a resolution of the conflict. It is important that each party to the process agree to accept the outcome as binding. The American Arbitration Association (www.adr.org) and the American Mediation Association (www.americanmediation.org) are two resources for HR professionals when these services are necessary.

Agency Complaints and Litigation   Internal complaints give an employer the opportunity to resolve issues with employees before they fester further and generate formal external agency complaints. Wise HR professionals will make every effort to encourage employees to file complaints internally so they will have the opportunity to investigate and resolve them. Dealing with issues internally is always preferable to having them registered with third-party law enforcement agencies.

External complaints are those filed with state or federal fair employment practices agencies (for example, Equal Employment Opportunity Commission), wage and hour enforcement agencies (for example, U.S. Department of Labor or Wage and Hour Division), or safety enforcement agencies (for example, Organizational Safety and Health Administration or Mine Safety and Health Administration). When a formal complaint is filed with an external agency, it is often a signal that the employer may no longer speak with their own employee about that issue. All discussions with the employee after a complaint is filed must be handled through the enforcement agency. As a practical matter, that means the employer will face some limitations.

Before a response can be prepared explaining what happened and why, the employer will need to conduct an investigation to determine whether the complaint has merit. Based on that result and with the help from legal counsel, a formal response can be prepared explaining the employer's position.

Remember that these are law enforcement agencies with authority to require employers to take certain actions to remedy complaints if that is warranted. Your legal advisor is always your best ally when working with external agencies. There are usually complaint filing deadlines, designated response deadlines, and deadlines for implementing remedies. Those will vary depending on the agency involved and provisions of the relevant laws.

HR's Role in Complaints and Litigation   HR managers are often the company's designated contact for employee complaints. And the HR professional will usually be the person responsible for conducting the investigation into the complaint's validity. Once the investigation has concluded, it is up to the HR professional to make recommendations to upper management regarding the outcome and any actions that should be taken. It may be necessary for the HR manager to recommend disciplinary action against the offending employee. Or it may be that the HR manager must determine how to help an employee resolve a problem that is not a question of legal compliance, but rather a problem of communication and misunderstanding.

Workplace Retaliation   Every category of federal law that deals with employee relations provides prohibitions against employer retaliation for employees availing themselves of the legal protections against mistreatment. In 2014, the EEOC received nearly 38,000 charges of retaliation from employees who had already filed complaints of discrimination based on a protected class. That was more than 42 percent of all charges filed with the commission in fiscal year 2014. Clearly, people are feeling that filing a complaint with the EEOC has caused follow-on pain.

Conducting Investigations

Investigations are appropriate in several circumstances within an employer's organization. They can be helpful in a grievance-handling effort and are essential in determining the validity of discrimination complaints. Whenever there is a need to determine facts surrounding a complaint, an investigation should be conducted. Some form of this approach should be used when responding to safety or wage and hour complaints. Interviews may or may not be necessary depending upon the availability of records that can explain the facts.

Internal HR professionals are almost always given authority in state and federal law to conduct an investigation on behalf of the employer. If the organization wants to have an external investigator handle the fact finding, there are some limitations imposed by certain state laws. In California, for example, external investigators who are not licensed attorneys must be licensed private investigators. Other states have different requirements.

Legal advisors suggest that internal attorneys are not the best people to conduct investigations because they could be placed in the position of having to testify to their investigative activities while still providing legal advice to their employer.

Whoever is designated as the investigator should normally follow these steps:

1. *Obtain a written complaint.* The employee should write out a complaint that states she was treated differently from others in similar situations based on a legally protected category and that category should be identified. If she can do this, she will have provided a prima facie case, which means it sounds good on its face.

2. *Conduct interviews.* Next it is necessary to interview the complaining employee, the supervisor or management person who is named as the offending decision-maker, and any witnesses the employee says were there at the time. Sometimes it is a peer who has been the offending party. When that is the case, at least one interview of the offending party should be scheduled. The investigation should follow whatever leads are uncovered until the investigator is satisfied that all the facts have been uncovered that can be uncovered. Each step of the process should be documented in writing and maintained in a complaint investigation file.

3. *Make a determination.* Once the facts have been determined as best as possible, a determination should be made about the validity of the complaint. If the complaint is valid, a remedy should be sought based on both legal and reasonable requirements. If the complaint is determined not to have valid grounds, that will be the determination. The decision should be documented in writing and included in the investigation folder.

4. *Give feedback.* The employee who filed the complaint should be given feedback about the investigation results and any decisions made as a result. It may or may not be advisable to provide specific information about disciplinary action taken against an employee. Your legal advisor can give you guidance about that in your specific circumstances.

Disciplining Employees

The progressive discipline model is the one that has been used in American workplaces for more than a century. It is written into many, if not most, union contracts as a requirement to assure management treats its members appropriately when problems arise. Yet some people contend that this model is not as effective as the coaching model. Even the Huffington Post (www.huffingtonpost.com) endorses this approach in its blog article "A Respectful Way to Discipline Employees."

	Progressive Discipline Model	
	Traditional Discipline System	**Counseling Approach**
Goal	Discipline	Problem solve
Problem ownership	Supervisor	Employee
Supervisor's mind-set	Document, build a case for termination	Understand root cause
Communication style	One-way, parent-to-child, ends with a threat	Two-way, adult-to-adult
Outcome	Fear, anger, resentment	Commitment to change behavior and increase performance or, if the employee does not want to make a change, resignation

In small organizations, discipline and termination are handled without many written procedures. The "boss" simply tells one of the employees that they are being disciplined because of a specific infraction. In larger organizations, the procedures for disciplinary action are written down in a step-by-step format and followed by managers.

Usually, discipline and termination are a multistep process. It doesn't have to be a formal process, but it can be. Here are the typical steps in that process:

- **Oral warning**   Observing the employee violating a policy, procedure, or instruction. In a personal discussion with the employee, the boss explains the problem and issues a verbal warning that the problem should not happen again.

- **Written warning**   Observing the employee doing the same behavior for which they received the oral warning. This is an "escalation" of discipline to the next step. A warning in writing should explain the infraction and why it is unacceptable. It should also explain the consequence of the same thing happening again.

- **Suspension**   Although this step is not always included in the process, it is available for use to emphasize to the employee how serious the behavioral problem is. In many cases, a suspension will be unpaid time off. It can last from a day to several weeks. The length of time should be dependent upon the seriousness of the behavioral problem and the employee's length of service.

- **Termination**   The final stage of the disciplinary process is removing the employee from employment. Use of this step acknowledges that the employee cannot be salvaged.

NOTE   Whatever disciplinary procedures you elect to use in your organization, they should be applied consistently in similar situations. It is not a good idea to treat people differently when their situations are similar. That will surely land you in court or present you with a union grievance.

Employers can avoid locking themselves into strict disciplinary procedures if they provide a policy for discretionary disciplinary decisions based on the circumstances of a situation. Policies containing hard rules about steps to be used in the process can prevent flexibility and discretion.

Preventive Measures   The best prevention is great communication. Be sure each employee is clear about the specific expectations you have for their performance. Help them understand how their personal contribution fits into the team and company efforts. Making sure people understand their personal importance to the employer's success is critical in preventing any behavior problems. It is only when expectations are not met that there are problems. So, be sure everyone understands the expectations that relate to them.

Providing Due Process   Due process is making sure employees receive all the protections to which they are entitled and is part of what contributes to the Covenant of Good Faith and Fair Dealing. It means that every employee will be given an opportunity to hear that there is a problem with their behavior, be it conduct or production, and then given be a chance to change the behavior. Progressive discipline is one approach for providing employees with due process.

Constructive Discipline   It's not an oxymoron. Constructive discipline can exist. It is the positive outcome of the disciplinary process. It means that even though employees are being disciplined, they understand why, and the treatment is fair within the circumstances.

HR's Role in Discipline   HR professionals are the coaches for line managers and supervisors. It is HR's responsibility to track disciplinary cases, counsel managers in how to handle disciplinary interviews, encourage employees when they discuss their problems, and nudge all parties toward a positive outcome. HR is the expert in how to do discipline appropriately. As such, teaching supervisors is a key responsibility of the HR department. And, encouraging employees with problems to do better is also part of the role HR plays.

Functional Area 10—Technology Management

Here is SHRM's BoCK definition: Technology Management involves the use of existing, new and emerging technologies to support the HR function, and the development and implementation of policies and procedures governing the use of technologies in the workplace.[42]

Enhancing the effectiveness of HR functions could not be done without the use of technology. HR information systems, applicant tracking systems, self-service portals to company-specific information such as employee handbooks, training programs, benefits—these form the backbone to having HR processes click along seamlessly. HR professionals should fully understand the HR-related technology applications and the potential value of ever-increasing new technologies being developed.

Key Concepts

- Approaches to electronic self-service for basic HR and people management functions (e.g., scheduling, time keeping, benefit enrollment)
- Data and information management (e.g., data integrity, confidentiality, security, disclosure)
- HRIS capabilities and use
- Policies and procedures for procurement
- Policies and practices for technology and social media use (e.g., bring-your-own-device, web sites, computers for personal activity)
- Software for recruiting and applicant tracking

The following are the proficiency indicators that SHRM has identified as key concepts:

For All HR Professionals	Advanced HR Professionals (SCP Exam)
• Implements and uses technology solutions that support or facilitate the delivery of effective HR services and storage or critical employee data	• Evaluates and implements technology solutions that support the achievement of HR's strategic direction, vision, and goals
• Implements an HRIS that integrates with and complements other enterprise information systems	• Evaluates and selects vendors to provide HR technology solutions
• Develops and implements organizational standards and policies for maintaining the confidentiality of employee data	• Designs and implements technology systems that optimize and integrate HR functional areas
• Uses technologies in a manner that protects workforce data	• Develops and implements technology-driven self-service approaches that enable managers and employees to perform basic people-related transactions (e.g., scheduling, time keeping, compensation administration, benefit enrollment, information changes)
• Provides guidance to stakeholders on effective standards and policies for use of technologies in the workplace (e.g., social media, corporate and personal e-mail, Internet messaging)	
• Coordinates and manages vendors implementing HR technology solutions	
• Uses technologies that collect, access, and analyze data and information to understand business challenges and recommend evidence-based solutions	

HR and Technology

Technology is now foundational to any HR function in an organization. It captures more information and makes that information accessible to a variety of needs and people within the organization. It can make analyzing information far quicker and allows for detecting patterns, conditions, and issues. HR's technology provides communication support, which is particularly helpful with a workplace that is geographically broad. And when technology doesn't work as planned or goes on the blink, it can literally cripple the functions of HR.

HR Technology Use

There is no one-size-fits-all technology blueprint for HR. Every organization is going to require HR technology that is specific to the size of organization, geographical and workforce particulars, and industry. The technological platforms and applications will differ, yet the initial blueprint will have the same process flow guidelines for implementation. Think of the computer game *Minecraft;* the rules are the same, yet each player's outcomes in building things are hugely different.

HR uses technology to allow more work to be accomplished with fewer resources and by automating jobs and functions to allow greater accuracy and speed of processing or providing information to stakeholders. This is the true value of HR's technology use. Examples of technology include the following:

- E-signing, the electronic signature to process authorization of documents
- Electronic recordkeeping, a big advantage in the ever-growing field of legal record retention requirements
- Mobile learning, offering instructional content delivered to wireless mobile devices to facilitate information sharing and learning
- Intranet, access to information for the workforce for a broader style of communicating and understanding
- Gamification, a technology offering an approach for enhancing learning
- Blogs, for communicating both internally and externally
- Social media, for customer service and for promoting information/communications for shared purposes
- Self-service systems, portals that allow targeted groups of employees to access their information such as benefits, payroll, and initiating selections and changes

Advances and Leveraging HR Technology

An ever-changing landscape in HR, technology changes the way HR functions and supports the organization in doing its business. HR professionals should be aware of the trends, the capabilities, and the issues associated with technology in order to be strategic partners and help their organizations with their competitive vantage.

HR professionals can leverage technology to increase the efficiency of HR processes and functions by transforming data into sources of immense value to internal stakeholders. We have been experiencing a digital revolution that is a far cry from the industrial revolution and one that is at a rapid pace of constant change. The world has embraced technology, and HR has been on the forefront of the adopting technology within organizations. The many advantages in doing so include streamlining the processes and reducing administrative work; improving efficiencies; reducing costs, especially those related to compliance; providing real-time metrics to facilitate planning and decision-making; improving service to internal and external stakeholders; and enabling the sharing of information.

Information Management

HR's information, largely maintained within technology vehicles, is highly confidential to both the workforce and the organization. As such, there are challenges in how this information is managed and accessed. There is the complexity of too much data—what to use and what not to use. And then there is real-time access where users are interacting with information that is in real time. Transparency of data is another consideration—where the information is sourced and who will have access.

HR in the Era of Big Data

The era of "big data" has been ushered in because of technology. Big data refers to the large amount of dissimilar data such as images and figures, tables, charts, and words. Users can access and do what is known as *data mining*—extracting particular data that serves their needs. In some large organizations, the HR function will have data specialists such as compensation or affirmative action analysts to gather and scrutinize data collected. In his article "The Promise of Big Data for HR," Alex Levenson[43] discusses the likely paths for HR. They are as follows:

- **Collecting data**   New data collection about how employees do their jobs can provide process insights, possibly reducing errors and increasing productivity and efficiencies.

- **Using data effectively**   Data can be used to understand the motivation of employees, their engagement, and why they do what they do.

- **Strategic analysis**   Mapping how information flows in organizations and how it impacts the manner in which people rely on it to do their jobs.

Measures, Metrics, and Analytics

Analytics help HR professionals translate data into action and decisions. HR can use analytics to link HR outcomes to organizational results by starting with a foundation of accurate, consistent, integrate, accessible, and relevant data.

Sample Human Capital Metrics   A sample of human capital metrics would be using an employee database to track the knowledge, skills, and performance of employees; then using the analytics to identify the key performance indicators of high-potential employees to manage critical needs and projections for the workforce, perhaps because of anticipated retirements; and finally using the analytics to assess the marketplace for recruiting replacements and attracting the talent anticipated, along with the budget resources that will be required for workforce planning.

Why Analytics Matter   Analytics have the ability to improve organizational performance because they can improve and drive the planning and forecasting processes, shorten cycles, reduce costs, and direct resources for just-in-time needs.

HR Information Systems

A human resource information system is technology software that supports the functions of HR and is the workhorse of administration for HR data to be gathered, stored, maintained, retrieved, analyzed, and reported. Processing employee data, researching, answering questions—these were the activities that made up the major components of HR's time in the past. Enter HRIS technology and poof, the time-consuming activities of a typical HR professional diminished. An HRIS offers the ability for increased efficiency and accuracy to be disseminated at a lower cost.

HRIS records involve fields of data including those shown in Figure 5-5. This is not an exhaustive list. Many other records are maintained by some employers.

HRIS Selection

Selecting and implementing an HRIS must be done right because errors in selection will have a profound impact. The HRIS software programs range from those serving employee groups up to 100 people to systems that can handle unlimited data fields and unlimited numbers of employees. Obviously, the prices of such software systems vary according to the capabilities they offer. The first thing to do in selecting an HRIS is to identify all the stakeholders and then do a needs analysis to determine what the features are needed for the stakeholders. A complete analysis will involve not only what the HR needs are but also what the user needs are when interacting with an HRIS.

Build, Customize, or Outsource Development   When deciding on an HRIS, you must consider whether the system is going to be developed internally by the organization's IT group or will be an off-the-shelf system such as PeopleSoft. Another choice is to outsource the HRIS to an external vendor because there are many payrolling services available.

Birthdate	Department	Home phone	Original job title
Building code	Educational degree	Home state	Original pay rate
Cell phone	Employee ID number	Home zip	Past job title
Certifications	Exempt/nonexempt	Job group/EEO code	Race/ethnicity
Current job title	Healthcare plan	Last employer	Sex
Current pay rate	Home address	Licenses	Social Security number
Dental plan	Home city	Name	Vision plan

Figure 5-5   Types of data included in employee records

Integrated Solution or "Best-of-Breed" Option A best-of-breed (BoB) option is the "best-fit" solution for each functional area in HR. Although a BoB option performs specialized functions better than an integrated system, this type of system is limited by its specialty area. To fulfill varying requirements, organizations often use best-of-breed systems from separate vendors. An integrated solution features a common interface across applications.

The choice between an integrated or best-of-breed solution comes down to how to deliver the technology. Will it be on-premise where the organization has software supported by internal IT staff, or will it be hosted, where the software is installed at the vendor's site and supported by external IT? There is also software as a service (SaaS), which is where the organization does not purchase any software. Instead, it subscribes to a service that is accessed via the Internet.

Data Access The data in an HRIS is not restricted to just the HR department. This is referred to as *democratization* where HR data is provided with direct access by those who need it. Executives, finance, payroll, managers, hiring managers—there is a stakeholder for just about every source of data. This type of access brings with it both legal and ethical considerations, including the protection of employee private information and the dissemination of it. Creating restrictions on the access to different portions of an HRIS is imperative when considering the design and implementation.

Database Structure An HRIS is a database, and data is a structure that stores information in an organized manner. Access to the information in an HRIS typically happens through the following means:

- **HR portals** A portal is a customized entry point via the intranet or Internet for employees and applicants that allows them to access information such as benefits enrollment.

- **Employee self-service (ESS) web sites that often are accessed via the HR portal** This is normally associated with transactional functions such as updating personal information, filing expense reports, and changing 401(k) selections.

- **Manager self-service (MSS)** These are tools that are like the ESS, via an HR portal, that allows supervisory management to conduct HR-related transactions such as performance appraisals, job descriptions, and attaining reports or viewing information.

Data Protection Personally identifiable information (PII) is a crucial concern with HRIS and other systems in protecting employee data. It has a high-priority status in today's world to protect it from hacking. Risk managers, IT managers, security managers, and audit managers all have a vested interest in HRIS data protection. Unauthorized use or loss of personnel data is a constant threat, and a breach of the HRIS could be catastrophic to an employer.

HRIS Implementation

Most implementations of HRIS systems will use a project management approach. It will take a team of folks from both the internal IT department and the external IT consultants and HR professionals to follow a proven systematic framework over a period of time. Rushing the implementation of an HRIS is a disservice—take the time to be thorough when following the implementation steps. The steps follow this order:

- Assessing whether to flush out and determine the requirements
- Identifying the project parameters such as budget, technology limitations, and time
- Evaluating software packages against the requirements and parameters
- Gathering the project task committee, stakeholders, and implementation group
- Clarifying vendor requirements and putting out an RFP to vendors
- Screening the RFPs
- Selecting the best vendor/software

The Importance of Systems Integration   Implementing an HRIS is complex and expensive, and there are headaches of unforeseen factors that come up. A systems integration approach that is thorough, looking at the entire process well before fingers are put on the keyboard, will be well worth it in the end. You need to look at all the software components involved and how the entire process will integrate into the HRIS. There are two common approaches: a continuous integration, or *waterfall,* approach or a *big bang* approach.

Continuous Integration Approach   With continuous integration, the HRIS components are integrated as they are developed into mini-versions of the HRIS. The developers will build chunks or portions of the system to integrate them into the whole. This causes an incremental building, which eventually creates the larger final HRIS. Throughout the development process, the HR functions can see the workings of what is created and massage the development process. This approach is generally perceived as less risky.

"Big Bang" Approach   Not until everything is ready will the individual components making up the HRIS be integrated—thus the label *big bang*. This approach allows for everything to be finished, and then testing begins. It can be time-consuming using this approach and cause system failures. Smaller organizations will generally adopt this approach, especially when using off-the-shelf or external HRIS implementations.

Policies for Technology Use in the Workplace

Technology use policies can raise some sticky issues for both the organization and the workforce. They can work well when organizations balance security, compliance, and privacy concerns. The key is being collaborative and thorough in the approach to creating policy and ensuring that policies are being updated to keep pace with the continuous growth of new and changing technologies. Just a few years ago smartphones and watches came on the scene, and around the corner will be new technology that will affect policy-making.

Developing Workplace Policies

"A policy is a broad statement that reflects an organization's philosophy, objectives, or standards concerning a particular set of management or employee activities. Policies reflect the employer's employee relationship strategy. They are general in nature and are expressed through more specific procedures and work rules."[44]

There are nine steps involved with developing workplace policies.[45]

1. Identify the need for a policy.

2. Identify who will take the lead responsibility for this policy development.

3. Gather information.

4. Draft the policy.

5. Consult with stakeholders.

6. Finalize and approve policy.

7. Consider whether procedures will be required to implement the policy.

8. Implement the policy.

9. Monitor its success, and review and revise if necessary.

Developing Employee Handbooks   An employee handbook is a document that communicates organizational history, mission, values, policies, procedures, and benefits. It should contain information about all the "way we do things around here" and why we do them that way.

The steps for developing employee handbooks are similar to those involved in developing workplace policies.[46]

1. Review and make required revisions to the current company policies.

2. Create an outline of what to include in the employee handbook.

3. Create summarized versions of each policy and procedure.

4. Add each summary statement in the appropriate sections according to the outline.

5. Review the entire handbook.

6. Provide a finalized version to legal counsel for review.

7. Select a means of publication.

8. Distribute handbooks.

9. Update as necessary.

The majority of organizations are finding it extremely helpful to have their employee handbooks electronic. It allows for the updating (and announcement of updates) to be more frequent and an acknowledgment from employees that they are aware of the policy changes.

Bring-Your-Own-Device Policy   A *bring-your-own-device* (BYOD) policy applies to employee use of personal electronic devices for company purposes. Taking a clear position on employee-owned devices via a policy is critical. A policy should outline the terms for eligibility for BYOD, as well as protocols for using personal devices.

Allowing employees to work on their personal laptops, tablets, and smartphones instead of company-issued equipment has been a trend that has been driven in part by society that now relies on the use of technology for both work and play. While allowing or asking employees to bring their own devices can lower costs and improve efficiency, effectiveness, and morale, it can also raise concerns of security and legal compliance. A well-crafted policy can alleviate those concerns.

From an employee perspective, the largest concern is that BYOD could lead to a loss of employee privacy. Employees may worry that their company will have inappropriate access to their personal data, as well as to their photographs, contacts, and other information—and that they could lose all that information if the company attempts to remove or "wipe" business information from the worker's device, which typically happens after an employee's employment has ended.

On the organization's side, the primary concern is related to security. For example, devices may not have an automatic lock code or timeout function, and some people do not use passwords to protect their devices. Equally troubling are worries that employees may connect to their devices via unsecured Wi-Fi, share them with others, or simply lose them. All of these possibilities raise the risk for the unauthorized disclosure or destruction of business data.

If nonexempt employees are asked to use their own devices for work, the organization opens itself up to exposure under the federal Fair Labor Standards Act and state overtime and wage payment laws. Nonexempt workers can be in a position to respond to e-mails/text messages or to otherwise engage in work activities outside their scheduled work hours.

Collaboration

Because of the globally dispersed and diverse ways of working, technology vendors have created platforms that allow employees to collaborate more efficiently, such as programmers collaborating on coding. Organizations are recognizing this and adopting collaboration policies and tools to facilitate this new form of communication and productivity learning.

Groupware   Groupware is a specialized software application of a collaborative nature that facilitates interaction between people, helping them work together. Webinars, videoconferencing, and online collaboration tools such as Google Docs are just a few examples of groupware.

Effective Collaboration Policies and Approaches   Organizations have established practices that create greater effectiveness for these collaborations. Webinars may be arranged at times that are early in the morning for those on the West Coast and thus later in the day for those located in Europe, allowing participation and recognizing that it's outside the normal 8 A.M. to 5 P.M. routine. Also, the ability to record meetings using webinar technology allows those in Australia to view a meeting presentation instead of participating in the wee hours of the day, for example.

Of course, legal disclaimers and the rights and responsibilities should also be considered in policies that protect trade secrets and confidentiality.

Social Media

Social media policies and practices are land mines in today's world. With the ever-changing technology and new platforms popping up just about every year, social media is an important technology trend that HR professionals need to stay on top of. Policies need to be aligned with the organization's ethical and cultural expectations and its core values. They must reflect the organization's legal and reputational risks too. What will the organization consider as an infraction of ethics with an employee's personal postings? Many situations have popped up challenging this issue within the last few years, causing newsworthy headlines.

Effective Social Media Policies and Approaches for Personal Posting   The types of personal posts that employers should be concerned with by their employees are the ones that disclose proprietary information, harass other employees or customers, reflect poorly on the organization, or are considered inappropriate comments (non-work-related included). There is a balance of restrictive and permissive aspects for personal posting, and a policy that establishes what constitutes both should be evaluated and updated on a frequent basis.

Networking

Social networks are the online clusters of individuals in groups with shared interests. These networking sites connect individuals with shared interests, regardless of their geographical location. An exchange of private and public messages can occur. They may be groups of professionals, such as alumni from a college, or informational, such as people with hobbies or seeking information such as do-it-yourselfers.

Effective Networking Policies and Approaches   Similar to social media policies, networking policies should protect the reputation of the organization and outline expectations of its employees, values, and ethics.

Communications

Policies and practices with regard to communication in technology require a balance between protecting the organization's proprietary information, its security, and its legal interest and getting work done by the workforce. Here again, having expectations well thought out with examples will help the workforce know where the line is drawn for inappropriate communications.

Effective Communications Policies and Approaches   Over the years, employers have discovered that the best approach to technology communication policies is constantly reminding employees of policies such as the monitoring of employee e-mails or browsing histories. Notifying employees, new hires, and even executives about the potential of monitoring can serve as a deterrent for inappropriate communications and resources. Further, when an organization regularly advises employees that their communications are not private, it makes it problematic for employees to contest confidentiality in lawsuits.

Chapter Review

In this chapter, you learned about the structure of the HR function within organizations. You also reviewed organizational effectiveness and development, workforce management, employee relations, and, finally, technology and data. These collectively compose the entity called an employment organization. There are some new approaches now being used in these areas of HR management that the certified professional will need to be cognizant of and consider using in the operation of a contemporary HR management department.

Questions

1. A large technology company has identified a group of key managers in various departments who were hired with employment contracts that included large equity options. The company went public 2 years ago and continues to see a steady increase in stock value. There is a realization that many of these managers may retire when they are eligible to exercise their stock options in three more years. What OD activity should HR be focused on related to this circumstance?

   A. Review the organization's retirement plan and begin counseling discussions.

   B. Expand the vacation policy for this group of managers.

   C. Design a succession plan and identify high-potential employees.

   D. Hire executive coaches to help this group of management with work-life balance.

2. The process of analyzing and identifying the need for availability of human resources so that the organization can meet its objectives is known as:

   A. Strategic planning

   B. PEST analysis

   C. Human resource planning

   D. Organization planning

3. The AB Trucking Co. is expanding its routes and hiring more people. Those changes will mean that employees will have to take on different work assignments. How should the HR manager handle those changes with the workforce?

A. Explain the coming changes to all employees and solicit their help in deciding how to assign the new routes. Prepare a project plan and make sure everyone has a chance to see it before the implementation date.

B. Explain the coming changes and tell the truckers that assignments will be made based on seniority. The new people will be assigned last.

C. Explain the coming changes and let the senior executives handle the questions about how new job assignments will be made.

D. Explain the coming changes and let the employees discuss among themselves how they want to assign routes to the workforce.

4. Mergers and acquisitions (M&A) provide HR managers with special problems of cultural differences. To make sure that the cultures don't clash after the merger, the HR manager should:

A. Assign a subordinate to monitor the complaint levels and report on problems that are being addressed.

B. Conduct meetings with key players from each organization to outline the cultural values of each organization and determine how best to protect them in the blended employer unit.

C. Send memos to department heads that specify the new cultural characteristics and express the expectation that the department heads will "make it happen."

D. Provide written complaint forms to all employees and express a willingness to listen to any comments the employees have to make about the merger.

5. Harriet has just taken over for the HR manager in her group, and her boss is asking for an update on the succession plan. He wants to see the employee skill inventory as soon as possible. Harriet didn't even know there was a succession plan. What should Harriet be looking for in her files?

A. A confidential record that lists each employee's skills and abilities

B. A list of only the top-rated people in the group who have computer skills

C. A list of everyone in the group identifying each person's skills and whether they are currently ready for promotion

D. A list of people showing what individuals are capable of doing now, without regard for any future assignment

6. An employee in Cortez's organization came to him and suggested that she and her co-worker could consolidate their duties into one job and each work part-time, sharing the 40 hours each week so the work got done as always. What would you say if you were Cortez?

   A. Unfortunately, the Fair Labor Standards Act and the Unified Job Consolidation Act say that sharing jobs is not permitted because it would violate union agreements.

   B. There is no reason that it couldn't work if Cortez believes the two people are capable and want to make it work.

   C. Having more than one person and one Social Security number on one job assignment won't work. It makes tax reporting impossible.

   D. It's not a good idea because it doubles the liability for workers' compensation and unemployment insurance.

7. The local county's workforce has been decimated in recent months because the pension plan is changing and folks wanted to get their higher-level calculation before the changes cut that formula. The result, however, has been that a great deal of organizational intelligence walked out the door. The senior staff are suggesting you hire back some of the key personnel as temporary workers until you are able to get replacements trained. Is that a good idea?

   A. Hardly ever. It gives the newly retired people a way to "double dip" and make more money than they would have if they had stayed on the job without retiring.

   B. Sometimes. If the temporary period is truly used to train a replacement, it could get the organization across the institutional knowledge gap, passing along that information to someone new.

   C. Always. There is no downside to bringing back retirees as temporary workers. So what if they make a bit more? The work gets done without interruption.

   D. Maybe, if there is a limit of 6 months on the temporary assignment in compliance with the Fair Labor Standards Act.

8. The Tasty Good Corporation downsized because of intense global competition and modified its strategic business plan for the year. The most important task that the HR department's training and development function needs to do to support the change is to:

   A. Cost-justify training.

   B. Work with employees on accepting the change.

   C. Evaluate the effectiveness of all training programs.

   D. Link training and development to the new strategic plan.

9. One of the most important competencies of an HR professional is:

   A. Skilled project manager

   B. Masterful change agent

   C. Excellent time management skills

   D. Listening

10. Human resource management as a function within employer organizations has developed into a critical business participant because:

    A. Strategic business success can be accomplished only if minor staff functions are given some consideration in planning conferences.

    B. Accomplishment of organizational objectives is dependent upon strategic deployment of all resources, including human resources.

    C. Finding a seat at the table with other senior executives requires HR executives to contribute to strategic efforts and offer accountability for resource management.

    D. HR management is a function closely allied with accounting and finance, so strategic management of finance can't be complete without a contribution from HR.

11. As the HR professional in your organization, you've been asked to submit a recommendation for the best way to convert to the matrix form of organizational structure. What is the most important issue you might encounter?

    A. Matrix organizations don't have strict reporting relationships, so supervisors will be upset at their loss of control.

    B. Because the matrix organizations are "loose" in their management oversight, results may need to be monitored by executives more carefully.

    C. When matrix organizations are formed, it takes some time for people to get used to working in that type of configuration. There is a "break-in" time required.

    D. Unions object to matrix organizations because they impinge on union representation authority.

12. When participating in a merger or acquisition, part of the process includes assembling data from the "due diligence" process. In many jurisdictions much of the information about employer liabilities requires disclosure. These things could include:

    A. The number of parking spaces that have disabled markings and the quantity of fire extinguishers in the building.

    B. The number and type of discrimination complaints, and the number and type of law suits dealing with employee management issues.

    C. The number and type of safety classes held for employees each year.

    D. The amount of budget allocated to overtime versus straight time payroll.

13. HR professionals must be able to explain to employees the status they enjoy with the employer. While some employers operate by specifying that status to every employee in writing, those who opt not to do that will wind up operating with what type of employment relationship?

    A. All employees will have oral contracts based on the promises made during the interview process and conversations about the job offer.

    B. There are never any contracts made in the employment process, oral or otherwise. The default is a relationship based on promises from the employer.

    C. In the absence of contracts, the relationship is "at will" for each party.

    D. "At will" employment is never a default. It must be specified. So, the default employment relationship is "as promised."

14. Employees are sometimes caught up in downsizing efforts that are aimed at budget control. What are employers required to do when designing downsizing programs?

    A. Compare them to programs that were used by other employers with headquarters in their same city.

    B. Analyze their estimated results for age, race, and sex discrimination.

    C. Determine how many people will be affected from each department.

    D. Give the CEO and board of directors a written report on the downsizing impact on the organization's budget.

15. One of your employees has just been discovered stealing large amounts of money from the accounts receivable account. You have the evidence in hand. What should you do about that?

    A. Reason with the employee and try to get them to give the money back.

    B. Suspend the employee for 2 weeks while the employee tries to stop taking drugs.

    C. File a police report of theft/embezzlement and criminal complaint against the employee and then terminate the employer from the payroll.

    D. Call the insurance company to file a claim of loss.

16. One of the unions representing people in your organization has just called for a boycott of your products and services. What can you do about that?

    A. Negotiate with the union whatever will be needed for them to cancel the boycott.

    B. Take the union to court and get a judgment against them.

    C. Begin an advertising campaign that explains how the union is wrong.

    D. Turn the entire problem over to the legal department.

17. A departmental manager has called you to report that a union steward has been behaving badly in grievance meetings. What can you do about that, if anything?

   A. Nothing can be done about that.

   B. Call the steward in for a chat. Explain that they will be disciplined if they don't change their behavior.

   C. Advise the manager to suspend the steward for bad behavior.

   D. Call the union president and discuss the problem. Ask the union president to control the steward's behavior.

18. HR in the twenty-first century embodies:

   A. A tactical administrative role and a strategic operational role

   B. A strategic administrative role and a strategic operational role

   C. A strategic administrative role and a tactical operational role

   D. A support role for corporate strategies only

19. What are three of the six types of strategic differentiation?

   A. Service differentiation, accounting differentiation, employee differentiation

   B. Reputation differentiation, leadership differentiation, employee differentiation

   C. Product differentiation, relationship differentiation, price differentiation

   D. International differentiation, competitor differentiation, banking differentiation

20. BYOD policies must be carefully crafted to make sure these things are addressed:

   A. That dogs brought in the workplace are well behaved and always on a leash

   B. Legal compliance with current technology

   C. Security, legal compliance, and privacy of both employee and organization

   D. That all levels of employees are offered to bring their dogs into the workplace

21. A detailed HR analysis during the HR strategic process serves what purpose?

   A. Creating HR's goals and objectives

   B. Reviewing the code of ethics

   C. Identifying the HR gaps

   D. Identifying key employees

22. What is the main reason HR is considered a valuable player in the strategic planning process?

   A. Ability to provide programs

   B. Total rewards administration

   C. Access to employment laws

   D. Knowledge of the entire organization

23. Besides activities, HR should also measure:

   A. Progress against goals and objectives

   B. Meetings

   C. Results and outcomes

   D. Projects and initiatives

24. What is the goal of an HR audit?

   A. Demonstrating value

   B. Controlling costs

   C. Identifying the existing gaps in HR processes

   D. Comparing human capital to organizational needs

25. Which form of measurement is an overall yet concise picture of the organization's performance?

   A. Balanced scorecard

   B. Internal audit

   C. ROI

   D. External audit

Answers

1. C. A succession plan is a key component for business success and should be part of every organization's human resource development program to be sure that there is no gap in knowledge that cripples an organization because of the departure of key human capital.

2. C. Human resource planning involves all facets of people management issues. Forecasting the need for more or fewer people, budget considerations, and recruiting sources comes into play. How HR can be used to support the organization's strategic plans is critical.

3. A. Whenever possible, involving employees in designing the plan for accommodating organizational changes will be the best for employee morale.

4. B. Involving key managers from each organization can provide a foundation for whatever cultural values the new organization wants to build.

5. C. The list should show what skills each person has now and whether they are ready for promotion now or need further experience or training before being ready for promotion.

6. B. Sometimes, using part-time workers to accomplish one job is a good solution. A great deal depends on the reliability of incumbents.

7. **B**. One reason these arrangements sometimes fail is that they go on and on and on. There is no real replacement training going on. The retired employee is doing the same work as before they retired, and nobody is being transferred, promoted, or hired into that job as a replacement.

8. **D**. Linking training and development activities to the new strategic plan is the first step to ensuring that activities and resources are aligned with the organization's new initiatives.

9. **B**. Although all those skills listed are important to the profession, being a masterful change agent is most important because change agents serve as a catalyst in helping others work through and accept change, along with implementing processes and programs that align with the change.

10. **C**. Only if HR is willing to contribute to strategic planning and implementation and offer accountability for results will HR professionals be allowed to remain at the executive table.

11. **C**. Working on a team with representatives from many departments can take some time to get used to. There is a lag time between implementation and results simply because employees need time to get acquainted with the new working structure.

12. **B**. Liabilities such as lawsuits and discrimination complaints can pose future drains on budget and cash flow. The other party will want to understand what risks might exist as a result of these types of liabilities.

13. **C**. In the absence of contracts, federal (and many state) laws default to "at will" status. It does not require a written notification to employees, but that is always recommended.

14. **B**. The Uniform Guidelines on Employee Selection Procedures and Age Discrimination in Employment Act (ADEA) requires analysis of the impact of selection decisions in downsizing.

15. **C**. Criminal behavior should be reported to the police. In the eyes of most employers, theft/embezzlement is cause for immediate dismissal.

16. **A**. Negotiation is the avenue to lifting the boycott.

17. **D**. Asking the union president to control the steward's behavior is likely to be the most effective approach. Since you can't discipline the employee for union activities, the president is the person who can help the steward understand the advantages of civil behavior.

18. **B**. Transitioning into the new century, HR professionals will find themselves involved more with strategic planning in an administrative role and operational role.

19. **C**. The three types of strategic differentiation are product, relationship, and price.

20. **C**. Security, legal compliance, and privacy need to be addressed in policies about employee's using their personal electronic devices at work in order to protect both the organization and the employee's right to privacy.

audit vs. analysis

21. **C.** HR analysis includes a thorough review of the current systems and processes in place to identify gaps that may exist with current systems/processes and the future system needs. Addressing these gaps aligns with the basis of HR strategy.

22. **D.** The HR function has a pulse on the current workforce and outside influences on the workforce, which is why it adds value to the organization's strategic planning.

23. **C.** The deliverables, or outcomes, for which HR is responsible for producing is what David Ulrich suggests should be measured for HR's true effectiveness.

24. **C.** An HR audit is a comprehensive evaluation of HR's policies and procedures that identify gaps in performance and outcomes.

25. **A.** A balanced scorecard is a performance metric used to identify and improve internal functions effectiveness in an organization.

References

1. The SHRM Body of Competency and Knowledge, page 44.

2. Ulrich, David. *Human Resource Champions: The Next agenda for Adding Value and Delivering Results.* Boston: Harvard Business Press, 1997.

3. Williams, Jodi. "What changes in the workforce mean for the future of workplace design." *Work Design Magazine,* February 9, 2017.

4. https://www.nytimes.com/2010/05/03/business/03merger.html

5. Inside HR. "How HR can fill the accountability vacuum," https://www.insidehr.com.au/how-hr-can-fill-the-accountability-vacuum/, April 7, 2014.

6. 2013 Global Innovation 1000 Study, Booz & Company. https://www.strategyand.pwc.com/media/file/Strategyand_2013-Global-Innovation-1000-Study-Navigating-the-Digital-Future_Media-Report.pdf.

7. Ulrich D., and W. Brockbank. *The HR Value Proposition.* Boston: Harvard Business School Press, 2005.

8. Becker, Brian, Mark Huselid, and Richard Beatty. *The Differentiated Workforce.* Boston: Harvard Business School Press, 2009.

9. The SHRM Body of Competency and Knowledge, page 45.

10. The Office of State Personnel, North Carolina, March 5, 2008.

11. 2015 SHRM Learning System for SHRM-CP/SHRM-SCP, Figure 4: Performance Problems, page 82.

12. www.eXporance.com blog. November 14, 2013.

13. 2015 SHRM Learning System for SHRM-CP/SHRM-SCP, page 84.

14. 2015 SHRM Learning System for SHRM-CP/SHRM-SCP, HR's Role in OED, page 86.

15. https://www.turknett.com/services-and-tools/organization-development/cultural-assessment-and-change/

16. https://www.shrm.org/resourcesandtools/tools-and-samples/toolkits/pages/introorganizationalandemployeedevelopment.aspx

17. Ibid.

18. www.referenceforbusiness.com/management/Gr-Int/Group-Decision-Making.html

19. https://smlr.rutgers.edu/sites/default/files/documents/faculty_staff_docs/UnderstandingTheDynamicsofDiversityInDecisionMakingTeams.pdf

20. https://hbr.org/2016/11/why-diverse-teams-are-smarter

21. https://www.credit-suisse.com/corporate/en/media/news/articles/media-releases/2012/07/en/42035.html

22. http://smallbusiness.chron.com/relationship-between-systems-theory-employee-relations-22465.html

23. http://enterpriseengagement.org/newswire/content/8483139/iso-releases-the-first-standards-on-human-resources-practices/

24. https://www.villanovau.com/resources/six-sigma/six-sigma-methodology-dmaic/#.Wxhc_e4vyUk

25. http://www.ocai-online.com/about-the-Organizational-Culture-Assessment-Instrument-OCAI

26. https://blog.hrcloud.com/is-it-time-for-your-company-to-do-a-cultural-assessment

27. www.ocai-online.com/about-the-Organizational-Culture-Assessment-Instrument-OCAI/Organizational-Culture-Types

28. The SHRM Body of Competency and Knowledge, page 46.

29. Ebert, Ronald J. and Ricky W. Griffin. *Business Essentials*, Chapter 6, 10th Edition, 2014

30. ibid.

31. Kokemuller, Neil. "Definition of Tactical Planning in Business," *Houston Chronicle,* http://smallbusiness.chron.com/definition-tactical-planning-business-14401.html.

32. "Strategic Planning: How can a skills inventory be used for strategic HR planning?" SHRM Templates & Samples, www.shrm.org, September 6, 2012.

33. ADP_NAS Effective Talent Management White Paper, www.adp.com.

34. The SHRM Body of Competency and Knowledge, pages 47–48.

35. www.ilo.org

36. www.britannica.com/

37. https://www.wto.org/

38. Moskowitz, Seymour. *Employment at Will & Code of Ethics: The Professional Dilemma*, 23 Val. U.L. Rev. 33 (1988). Available at http://scholar.valpo.edu/vulr/vol23/iss1/7 as of June 3, 2015.

39. www.ilo.org

40. www.coachyourselftowin.com/

41. www.thesocialleader.com/

42. The SHRM Body of Competency and Knowledge, page 49.

43. The Promise of Big Data for HR, People & Strategy, 2014.

44. SHRM Learning System, 2017.

45. DIY Committee Guide. www.diycommitteeguide.org/resource/how-to-develop-policies-and-procedures, retrieved on August 29, 2017.

46. How to Develop an Employee Handbook. SHRM, May 22, 2015, https://www.shrm.org/resourcesandtools/tools-and-samples/how-to-guides/pages/developemployeehandbook.aspx, retrieved on August 29, 2017.

PART II

Workplace

The HR expertise domain of Workplace Knowledge counts toward 16 percent for both exams. This domain covers the essential HR knowledge needed for relating to the workplace. The following are the functional areas that fall within the Workplace Knowledge domain:

- Functional Area 11—HR in the Global Context
- Functional Area 12—Diversity and Inclusion
- Functional Area 13—Risk Management
- Functional Area 14—Corporate Social Responsibility
- Functional Area 15—U.S. Employment Law and Regulations

HR professionals are expected to know how to perform the following Body of Competency and Knowledge (BoCK) statements for the Workplace Knowledge domain:

- **01**   Fostering a diverse and inclusive workforce
- **02**   Managing organizational risks and threats to the safety and security of employees
- **03**   Contributing to the well-being and betterment of the community
- **04**   Complying with applicable laws and regulations

Functional Area 11—HR in the Global Context

Here is SHRM's BoCK definition: "HR direction required to achieve organizational success and to create value for stakeholders."[1]

Globalization is here. It has been coming for more than half a century. Now, technology has altered our lives and the way we interact so that world markets, world politics, and world education have all come to our personal cell phones. Employers, too, are now tapped into world suppliers, world customers, and world recruiting like never before in history. It is going to be increasingly difficult to locate an employer that doesn't tap into the Internet resources available from these world sources.

Key Concepts

- Best practices for international assignments (e.g., approaches and trends, effective performance, health and safety, compensation adjustments, employee repatriation, socialization)
- Requirements for moving work (e.g., co-sourcing, near-shoring, off-shoring, on-shoring)

The following are the proficiency indicators that SHRM has identified as key concepts:

For All HR Professionals	For Advanced HR Professionals (SCP Exam)
• Addresses global issues that influence day-to-day HR activities and makes recommendations for business solutions	• Recognizes and responds to global issues that influence the organization's human capital strategy
• Maintains up-to-date knowledge of global political, economic, social, technological, legal, and environmental (PESTLE) factors and their influence on the organization's workforce	• Consults with business leaders on global PESTLE factors and their influence on the organization's workforce
• Administers and supports HR activities associated with a global workforce	• Develops a comprehensive organizational strategy that addresses global workforce issues
• Implements and conducts audits of global HR practices	• Consults with business leaders to define global competencies and embed them throughout the organization
• Maintains knowledge of global HR trends and best practices	• Identifies opportunities to achieve efficiencies and cost savings by moving work (e.g., off-shoring, on-shoring, near-shoring)
• Balances with local needs the organization's desire for standardization of HR programs, practices, and policies	• Designs and oversees programs for international (i.e., expatriate) assignments that support the organization's human capital strategy
• Builds relationships with global stakeholders	
• Manages the day-to-day activities with international (i.e., expatriate) assignments	

The Global Context

No longer are we *just* Americans, Mexicans, Canadians, or Swiss. Global interactions mean we must find ways to place our employer issues in a global context while still abiding by the cultural and legal requirements of each country in which we operate. Globalization is a larger version of the U.S. state differences and how they contribute to the American context.

Defining Globalization

Globalization is the trend of increasing interaction between people on a worldwide scale because of advances in transportation and communication technology.[2] Business and governmental requirements are also contributing factors in the new definition of globalization.

Overall, it represents a compression of the world and intensification of the consciousness of the world as a whole.

Forces Shaping Globalization

International economic influences (finance and development), environmental forces, political forces, global insecurity, and a refugee crisis, along with insecure investment trading markets (Dow Jones, Nasdaq, commodities markets), all contribute to shaping the thing we call globalization. Ultimately, these forces boil down to the shift from developed to emerging economies, a global recession and global warming, and hyper-connectivity.

Three Precepts of Global Force Interconnectedness Taking all of the forces into consideration, there are three precepts of global force interconnectedness that become apparent.

- PEST factors can be fully understood only as global impacts.
- Forces may be global, but impacts can be uniquely felt locally.
- We need to distinguish between large-scale forces and trends and more immediate events and "trendy" phenomena.

Globalization in the Twenty-First Century Thomas L. Friedman reminds us, we used to build our towns and factories along rivers because they provided access to neighbors and their ideas, power, mobility, and nourishment. "But the rivers you want to build on now are Amazon Web Services or Microsoft's Azure—giant connectors that enable you, your business, or your nation to get access to all the computing power applications in the [worldwide Internet of Things], where you can tie into every flow in the world in which you want to participate."[3]

HR professionals no longer have the luxury of thinking only about their own local, state, or federal interactive requirements. International requirements are always nearby in terms of off-shore manufacturing, importing rules and procedures, and exporting rules and procedures. Monetary impact comes from all parts of the earth. Workforce recruiting, talent management, and policy influences come from more countries as time goes by.

Some experts have pointed out that the workforce in emerging world economies is primarily young, while the workforce in developed countries is aging. The problems presented by each of those populations are quite different. HR professionals must be able to address both.

Shift from Developed to Emerging Economies

The long-term global economic power shift away from the established advanced economies is set to continue to 2050, as emerging market countries continue to boost their share of world GDP in the long run despite recent mixed performance in some of these economies.[4]

The Diaspora The World Encyclopedia suggests *diaspora* refers to any people or ethnic population forced or induced to leave its traditional homeland, as well as the dispersal of such people and the ensuing developments in their culture. It is especially used with reference to the Jewish population, who have lived most of their historical existence as a *diasporan* people.[5]

Demographic Dichotomy   The workforce in emerging economies is becoming disproportionately young, while the workforce in developed economies is rapidly aging (parallel demographic shift).[6]

Reverse Innovation   Innovations created for or by emerging-economy markets and then imported by developed-economy markets suggests that the "new" economies will have a greater influence over world economic events because they are selling their innovations to markets in developed countries.

Global Recession and Global Warming

Episodes of severe weather in the United States, such as the abundance of rainfall and then drought in California, are brandished as tangible evidence of the future costs of current climate trends. A study by Hsiang et al. (published in the journal *Science*)[7] collected national data documenting the responses in six economic sectors to short-term weather fluctuations. This data was integrated with probabilistic distributions from a set of global climate models and used to estimate future costs during the remainder of this century across a range of scenarios. In terms of overall effects on the gross domestic product, the authors predict negative impacts in the southern United States and positive impacts in some parts of the Pacific Northwest and New England.

Hyper-connectivity

Hyper-connectivity is a state of unified communications (UC) in which the traffic-handling capacity and bandwidth of a network always exceed the demand. The number of communication pathways and nodes is much greater than the number of subscribers.[8] This is evidenced by the increasing digital interconnection of people and things around the clock from anywhere.

Achieving a Public-Private Balance   The government fiscal balance is one of three major financial sectorial balances in the national economy, the others being the foreign financial sector and the private financial sector. The sum of the surpluses or deficits across these three sectors must be zero by definition. Hence, a foreign financial surplus (or capital surplus) exists because capital is imported (net) to fund the trade deficit. Further, there is a private sector financial surplus due to household savings exceeding business investment. By definition, there must therefore exist a government budget deficit so all three net to zero. The government sector includes federal, state, and local.[9]

Measurability   If you can't measure it, why spend time working on it? Each of the issues we are discussing in this functional area can be measured if you take the time to think about them.

Moving Work

Globalization more than anything has resulted in employers finding ways to do their work better, cheaper, and faster by looking outside traditional local recruiting sources. Here are some of the influences we see today:

- **Outsourcing** The transfer of some work to organizations outside the employer's payroll. The vendor may be across the street or across the country.
- **Off-shoring** The transfer of some work to sources outside the United States.
- **On-shoring (home-shoring)** The relocation of business processes or production to a lower-cost location inside the same country as the business.
- **Near-shoring** Contracting part of the business processes or production to an external company located in a country that is relatively close. For the United States, that could mean Mexico or Canada.

HR professionals play a critical role in supporting the decision-making effort involved in moving work from one location to another. In performing due diligence, HR professionals should perform research on each of the following:

- **Talent pool** Languages spoken, cultural differences.
- **Sociopolitical environment** Governmental regulations, the expense involved in meeting them. Quality of life and ethical environment can create certain expenses.
- **Risk levels** IT security, political and labor conflicts, natural disasters, and security for individuals and property.
- **Cost and quality** Wage structure, tax structure, communication facilities, Internet access.

Defining the Global Organization

A global corporation is a business that operates in two or more countries. It also goes by the name *multinational company.*

Defining the Role of Global HR

Global businesses should have a global HR function. At the same time, to compete successfully in diverse markets, companies should recruit, train, and manage people locally—reflecting local culture, local labor markets, and the needs of diverse local business units.[10]

- Business and talent strategies should be global in scale and local in implementation. Effective programs recruit, train, and develop people locally.
- Global HR and talent management is the second most urgent and important trend for large companies around the world (those with 10,000 or more employees), according to Deloitte Insights' global survey.[10]

- Companies face the challenge of developing an integrated global HR and talent operating model that allows for customizable local implementation, enabling them to capitalize on rapid business growth in emerging economies, tap into local skills, and optimize local talent strategies.

Creating a Global Strategy

As firms expand into countries around the world, more and more are deciding that they need to create an overarching, global human resources strategy. This is because HR leaders must adhere to local laws but still meet the needs of regional staff all while maintaining an across-the-board strategy.[11]

The Strategic Attraction of Globalization

Current attitudes toward globalization have resulted in new thinking called *guarded globalization*. Governments of developing nations have become wary of opening more industries to multinational companies and are zealously protecting local interests. They choose the countries or regions with which they want to do business, pick the sectors in which they will allow capital investment, and select the local, often state-owned, companies they want to promote. That's a different flavor of globalization: slow-moving, selective, and with a heavy dash of nationalism and regionalism.[12]

"Push" Factors   These are examples of "push" factors influencing global organizations:[13]

- **Saturation of domestic demand and need for new markets**   The market for a number of products tends to saturate or decline in advanced countries. This often happens when the market potential has been almost fully tapped. For example, the fall in the birth rate implies contraction of a market for several baby products. Businesses undertake international operations to expand sales, acquire resources from foreign countries, or diversify their activities to discover the lucrative opportunities in other countries.

- **Shortfalls in natural resources and talent supply**   When natural resources begin dwindling in developed countries, it seems reasonable for organizations to look to other countries for their raw materials. Creating a physical presence where the resources are located can help reduce the costs of acquisition. Moving to locations where talent can be found is a common solution for dwindling talent supplies in the home country.

- **Trade agreements**   Global expansion is driven by domestic competition from foreign competitors.

- **Technological revolution**   Revolution is a right word that can best describe the pace at which technology has changed in the recent past and is continuing to change. Significant developments are being witnessed in communication, transportation, and information processing, including the emergence of the Internet and the World Wide Web.

- **Globalized supply chain** Moving production facilities closer to supplier locations can help reduce costs involved in moving raw materials before processing.

- **Domestic recession** Domestic recession often provokes companies to explore foreign markets. One of the factors that prompted Hindustan Machine Ltd. (HMT) to take up exports seriously was the recession in the home market in the late 1960s.

- **Increased cost pressures and competition as driving force** Competition may become a driving force behind internationalization. There might be intense competition in the home market but little in certain foreign countries. A protected market does not normally motivate companies to seek business outside the home market.

- **Government policies and regulations** Government policies and regulations may also motivate internationalization. There are both positive and negative factors that could cause internationalization. Many governments offer a number of incentives and other positive support to domestic companies to export and to invest in foreign locations. Tax subsidies or even tax forgiveness can be a strong magnet for international business moves.

- **Improving the image of companies** International business has certain spin-offs too. It may help the company improve its domestic business; international business helps to improve the image of the company. There may be the "white skin" advantage associated with exporting: when domestic consumers get to know that the company is selling a significant portion of the production abroad, they will be more inclined to buy from such a company.

- **Strategic vision** The systematic and growing internationalization of many companies is essentially part of their business policy or strategic management. The stimulus for internationalization comes from the urge to grow, the need to become more competitive, the need to diversify, and the need to gain strategic advantages of internationalization.

"Pull" Factors Here are some factors that make "foreign" markets attractive:[14]

- **Government policies** When policies encourage foreign investment, domestic organizations may find it financially beneficial to locate in foreign markets. There may be tax advantages gained by expanding into foreign locations.

- **Strategic control** Many multinational companies (MNCs) are locating their subsidiaries in low-wage and low-cost countries to take advantage of low-cost production. When it becomes easier to control things such as brand image by having a subsidiary in a foreign country, organizations can be seen taking that leap.

- **Taking advantage of growth opportunities** MNCs are getting increasingly interested in several developing countries as the income and population are rapidly rising in these countries. Foreign markets can flourish in both developed and developing countries.

- **Declining trade and investment barriers**   Declining trade and investment barriers have vastly contributed to globalization. Business across the globe has grown considerably in a free trade regime. Goods, services, capital, and technology all benefit significantly moving across nations.

Regional trading blocs are adding to the pace of globalization. WTO, EU, NAFTA, MERCOSUR, and FTAA are major alliances among countries. Trading blocs seek to promote international business by removing trade and investment barriers. Integration among countries results in efficient allocation of resources throughout the trading area, promoting growth of some business and decline of others, development of new technologies and products, and elimination of old technologies.

Strategic Approaches to Globalization

A firm using a global strategy sacrifices responsiveness to local requirements within each of its markets in favor of emphasizing efficiency. This strategy is a complete opposite of a multidomestic strategy. Some minor modifications to products and services may be made in various markets, but a global strategy stresses the need to gain economies of scale by offering essentially the same products or services in each market.[15]

These are some approaches to strategic globalization:

- Creating a new organization in the foreign country
- Acquiring a subsidiary in the foreign country perhaps through merger or acquisition
- Creating a new partnership
- Outsourcing all or at least some of the production tasks to a supplier in a new work location
- Adding capacity to existing domestic locations by offshoring

Global Integration (GI) vs. Local Responsiveness (LR)   Adjustments for consumer preference is one strategy for the globalization of product marketing. H. J. Heinz adapts its products to match local preferences. Because some Indians will not eat garlic and onion, for example, Heinz offers them a version of its signature ketchup that does not include these two ingredients. On the other hand, such alterations are not needed in products hidden from consumer view. Intel's processing chips are an example. There is no need to modify the chips for various international cultures. The chips will work the same across all cultures. Such is a benefit of global integration.

Achieving Global Integration   Global integration means the decisions are made from a global perspective, and in some cases the meganational firm operates as if the world were one market.

Achieving Local Responsiveness   Local responsiveness is achieved by delegating most of the decision-making responsibility to local units and by appointing a local manager to the top management teams of subsidiaries.

Global integration vs. Local Responsiveness Examples   BASF is a German-based corporation that is one of the largest chemical production companies in the world. It has more than 330 plants producing a host of chemicals for nearly all industries in the world that use chemicals. Its chemicals are standard, regardless of the country where they will be used. That is global integration.

Beverage companies produce various brands and flavors in local markets worldwide. Coca-Cola offers Georgia Coffee in Japan, Café Zu in Thailand, Inca Cola in Peru, and the Burn energy drink in France. Adjustments for local taste are examples of local responsiveness.

Global-Local Models   There is a range of strategic choices available within the global-local concept.

Upstream and Downstream Strategies   A simple metaphor like "upstream and downstream" can help you identify the strategies that you can apply.

- **Upstream**   Decisions are made at headquarters and apply to strategies for focusing on the standardization of processes and integration of resources. That can be a strategy for workforce alignment, organizational development, and sharing knowledge and experience across internal organization boundaries.

- **Downstream**   Decisions are made at the local level and target adapting strategic goals to local realities. That can be a strategy for agreements with local work groups, adjustments to standard policies related to working conditions that reflect local requirements, and adjustments to operations based on local requirements.

Identity Alignment and Process Alignment   As strategies, identify alignment and process alignment offer some possible benefits to multinational organizations.

- **Identify alignment**   This is based on the diversity of people, products/services, and branding; differences among locations; and adjustment of brand identity and products/services based on local culture. Some downside risks are that localized offerings can dilute the brand or product/service image unless the corporate brand is well established, and local approaches can diffuse the core organizational identity. Think of McDonald's hamburgers. In most markets around the world, beef burgers are acceptable. In India, however, religion prevents a large portion of the population from eating beef. In that local market, products with chicken and fish are much more widely accepted.

- **Process alignment**   This is how well common internal functions can work across all locations. Are the same technologies used in all locations for accounting, HR, finance, legal? Are the same performance measurements used in all locations? Is a unified HR system used in all locations? This can be a problem when one organization acquires another. There is great inertia within each organization for continuing to use their own systems. Blending them or replacing them can be and is often problematic.

The FI-LR Matrix: Strategic Options   For many years scholars have been studying the relationships between global integration and local responsiveness.[16] The following table illustrates what they developed.

Global Corporate Strategies	
Global Strategy • Treats world as a single global market • Standardizes global products/advertising strategies • Strong links between HQ and subsidiaries	**Transnational Strategy** • Seeks to balance global efficiencies and local responsiveness • Combines standardization and customization for product/advertising strategies • Strong links between HQ and subsidiaries and among subsidiaries
International Strategy • Domestically focused • Exports a few domestically produced products to selected countries • Weak links between HQ and dependent subsidiaries	**Multidomestic Strategy** • Handles markets independently for each country • Adapts product/advertising to local tastes and needs • Weak links between HQ and autonomous subsidiaries

High / Low — Need for Global Integration

Need for Local Responsiveness — Low ◄────► High

- **International strategy**   All products/services, processes, and strategy at all levels are developed in the home country even though the organization may export products or services to other countries.

- **Multidomestic strategy**   Headquarters has little influence over remote subsidiary units. They develop their own strategies and goals.

- **Global strategy**   Headquarters develops and disseminates strategies, products, and services. All offerings are the same worldwide. Local entities can influence global image or products very little. Customizable elements are kept to a minimum.

- **Transnational strategy**   Remote locations are chosen for their access to supplies, vendors, and local markets. Subsidiaries are permitted to make adaptations to global products for appeal to local markets. Knowledge and practices are shared among all units in the organization. HQ assumes responsibility for certain factors such as advertising and strategies.

Perimutter's Headquarters Orientations   Howard Perlmutter identified a way of classifying alternative management orientations, which is commonly referred as Perlmutter's EPRG model. He states that businesses and their staff tend to operate in one of four ways.[17]

- **Ethnocentric**   These people or companies believe that their home country is superior. When they look to new markets, they rely on what they know and seek similarities with their own country. Overseas subsidiaries or offices in international markets are seen as less able and less important than the head office. Typically, these companies make few adaptations to their products and undertake little research in the international markets.

- **Polycentric**   Polycentric organizations or managers see each country as unique and consider that businesses are best run locally. Polycentric management means that the head office places little control on the activities in each market, and there is little attempt to make use of any good ideas or best practices from other markets.

- **Regiocentric**   Regiocentric sees similarities and differences in a world region and designs strategies around this. Often there are major differences between countries in a region. For example, Norway and Spain are both in Europe but are very different in climate, culture, transport, retail distribution, and so on. Another example of a regiocentric management orientation occurs when a U.S. company focuses on countries included in the North American Free Trade Agreement (NAFTA), the United States, Canada, and Mexico.

- **Geocentric**   Geocentric companies, as truly global players, view the world as a potential market and seek to serve this effectively. Geocentric management recognizes the similarities and differences between the home country and the international markets. It combines ethnocentric and polycentric views; in other words, it displays the "think global, act local" ideology.

Sourcing and Shoring

As a product of globalization, work is moved to the most advantageous location. That can bring off-shoring and outsourcing into play.

Off-shoring   This is the practice of placing production or other elements of the organization in another country. Off-shoring is sometimes chosen because it offers lower costs, it offers production a closer location for raw materials, it offers better tax impact or other financial impact, or there are direct financial incentives, such as government-sponsored loans or cash payments. It can also take advantage of time zone differences, and work can be done on a project without interruption should the appropriate workforce be scattered around the globe.

Disadvantages of off-shoring can include a strong resistance from customers, whom even call the practice "unpatriotic." Other problems that sometimes arise are language difficulties, cultural differences, high turnover rates, quality control issues, and educational degrees that do not offer reliable skills or talents.

On-shoring   When business processes, product manufacturing, or other functions are contracted out to another organization within the home country, it is called *on-shoring*. Having home-country employees can often avoid the problems associated with off-shoring.

Near-Shoring   The practice of contracting part of the organization's business processes to a country that is close to the home country is known as *near-shoring*. A company in the United States selecting manufacturing subcontractors in Mexico for making its auto-mobiles or washing machines is a good example. These arrangements are influenced to a great degree by trade agreements and social or economic stability.

Outsourcing   Almost always outsourcing is evidenced by contracts with vendors in the home country other countries that can provide products or services more cheaply than can be offered at headquarters. A prime example is the use of call centers to support customer service and order processing.

HR's Role in Globalization

Anytime a strategic decision is contemplated that involves placing a workforce in a distant location, HR has some responsibility for contributing portions of due diligence in that process. What is the workforce talent pool? What are the local laws and customs that will influence operations? What will be the approach to product quality in the new location?

HR Global Abilities   Experts say that some of the core competencies international HR careers demand are the same as those for domestic HR professionals—the skills are just on a heightened scale. For example, global HR managers need effective communication skills, including the ability to listen well.[18] It is common for international HR profession-als to be multilingual. It is often a job requirement. Here are some questions you should include in performing due diligence for HR management in a new distant work location:

- What is the wage structure?
- What is the tax structure for payroll in addition to operational taxes?
- What is the real estate situation?
- How will telecommunications, Internet, and transportation be provided?
- How much government regulation will be involved in managing a workforce?
- How ethical are the government, political influences, or business environments?
- What is the quality of life in the new location?
- Is there a history of labor unrest or political upset?
- Have there been any natural disasters? What is that likelihood?
- How can IT security be addressed?
- What are the possibilities for intellectual property rights and personal and property security?
- Is the economy stable? How widely does the currency exchange value fluctuate?

- What cultural differences are there?
- Is there a qualified labor force available?

HR Global Tasks On a global level, HR professionals must work toward helping the organization achieve its maximum value. Strategically, HR must help balance the priorities of headquarters and subsidiaries. How can human resources be distributed and balanced within budget restrictions and still maximize goal achievement? On a tactical level, HR professionals must facilitate management groups so that different disciplines and professions can achieve joint goals within differing cultural and sociopolitical environments.

HR Global Skills HR professionals must be capable of doing a lot of things that require professional HR skills. Here are some of the skills HR professionals must possess in the global workplace:

- **Develop a strategic view of the organization** How does value get created? What can HR contribute to the strategic plan development of the organization?
- **Develop a global organizational culture** Training plays a key role, and HR needs to be the training provider. How can communication issues be overcome?
- **Secure and grow a safe and robust talent supply chain** Work for a ready supply of leaders at each global location. Monitor the availability of qualified workforce candidates at all levels. Support efforts to develop a strong employer brand.
- **Use and adapt HR technology** Assure HR technology can be applied at all locations globally. Work with IT professionals to assure technology supports both domestic and global operations.
- **Develop meaningful metrics** Develop and implement consistent measurement devices and their application at all global locations. Be sure it is obvious that employee investment supports strategic goals.
- **Develop policies and practices to manage risks** Assure health, safety, and security of employees. Protect physical assets and intellectual property of the organization. Assure all legal requirements are being met at all global locations, including safety requirements, nondiscrimination requirements, payroll requirements, benefit requirements, and ethical requirements.

Auditing Global HR Practices It is important to know how your global HR practices are actually serving your organization and its people. To determine that, you will need to assemble a global compliance audit project team. Consider these types of representatives in your team selection process:

- Headquarters HR representative
- Foreign location HR representative
- In-house legal counsel
- Compliance officer

- Outside legal counsel
- Outside international HR expert
- Corporate audit department representative

An audit of global HR practices would be advisable if you have received a lawsuit challenging your HR practices, you are going through a merger or acquisition, you are undergoing corporate restructuring, you want to be sure you are complying with antibribery and insider trading laws, or you simply want to be sure your practices are being followed.

An audit should begin by identifying the countries that are involved. Next, define what focus you want the audit to have. Will it look at legal compliance, union contracts, corporate policies, or simply best practices? It is possible to take in all of these focal areas, but that becomes more complex.

Will your audit look only at local host country employees, or will you include expatriates, consultants, independent contractors, international transfers, temporary workers, or some other group? Will the audit engage in examining international payroll tax laws or data security issues?

Build a master checklist of areas to be examined. Then, expand that into a matrix that includes individual team member assignments, expected completion date for each component, and the ultimate audit report completion. Be sure you include time for a review process by identifying who will be involved in the review and approval sequence and how long each contributor will have to submit approval or additional report requirements. Finally, determine who will receive the final report when it is issued. What role will the report have in legal filings with organizations such as the Securities and Exchange Commission (SEC) or other similar oversight group?

Becoming a Multicultural Organization

 Organizations cannot become multicultural by proclamation. It takes concerted effort.

Developing a Global Mind-Set

Personal development precedes organizational development. First leaders must develop their own global mind-set. Then they will be able to help guide their organization into the same way of thinking. Here are five steps toward that goal:[19]

- **Recognize your own cultural values and biases**   Developing a strong self-awareness has shown to foster a nonjudgmental perspective on differences, which is critical to developing a global mind-set.

- **Get to know your personality traits, especially curiosity**   There are five specific traits that affect your ability to interact effectively with different cultures, listed here:
  - Openness
  - Flexibility
  - Social dexterity
  - Emotional awareness
  - Curiosity

Ask yourself how open you are to different ways of managing a team. Are you flexible enough to attempt a different feedback style? How easy is it for you to strike up a conversation with people from foreign countries?

- **Learn about the workplace and business expectations of relevant countries and markets** Learn about the typical workplace habits, expectations, and best practices in other countries and cultures.

- **Build strong intercultural relationships** Just like when learning to speak a second language, it's helpful to immerse yourself with people from other parts of the world to develop a global mind-set. These relationships facilitate valuable learning about what works and what doesn't. The ability to form relationships across cultures is not a given, but the more positive intercultural relationships you develop, the more comfort you'll have with diverse work styles and the less you'll resort to stereotyping.

- **Develop strategies to adjust and flex your style** What has made you successful in a domestic or local context likely won't help you reach the same level of success on a global scale, which is why learning to adapt your style is often the hardest part of mastering a global mind-set. This step involves expanding your repertoire of business behaviors by learning to behave in ways that may be unusual to you but highly effective when interacting with others.

Defining a Global Mind-Set We would define global mind-set as one that combines an openness to and awareness of diversity across cultures and markets with a propensity and ability to see common patterns across countries and markets.

Benefits of a Global Mind-Set The main benefit of a global mind-set is the organization's ability to combine speed with accurate response. The organizational global mind-set can bring about benefits that can manifest themselves in one or more competitive advantages.

Acquiring a Global Mind-Set Acquiring a global mind-set requires you to recognize situations in which demands from both global and local elements are compelling; you need to be open and aware of diversity across cultures and markets with a willingness and ability to synthesize across this diversity.

Types of Cultures

Some people consider there are seven major cultures in the world today.

- **Western culture** This includes Anglo America, Latin American culture, and the English-speaking world.

- **African American culture** Also known as Black-American culture, this refers to the cultural contributions of African Americans to the culture of the United States, either as part of or as distinct from mainstream American culture.

- **Indosphere**   This is a term coined by the linguist James Matisoff for areas of Indian linguistic and cultural influence in Southeast Asia.

- **Sinosphere**   The Sinosphere, or East Asian cultural sphere, refers to a grouping of countries and regions in East Asia that were historically influenced by the Chinese culture.

- **Islamic culture**   This is a term primarily used in secular academia to describe the cultural practices common to historically Islamic people.

- **Arab culture**   The Arab world stretches across 22 countries and consists of more than 200 million people. Arab is a term used to describe the people whose native tongue is Arabic. Arab is a cultural term, not a racial term, and Arabic people come from various ethnic and religious backgrounds.

- **Tibetan culture**   Buddhism has exerted a particularly strong influence on Tibetan culture since its introduction in the seventh century. Buddhist missionaries who came mainly from India, Nepal, and China introduced arts and customs from India and China.

Definition of Culture   *Culture* is the beliefs, customs, arts, etc., of a particular society, group, place, or time. It's a particular society that has its own beliefs, ways of life, art, and so on, and it's a way of thinking, behaving, or working that exists in a place or organization (such as a business).

How Types of Culture Affect an Organization   Here are five types of corporate culture.[20] Can you find one that describes your organization?

- **Team-first corporate culture**   Team-oriented companies hire for culture fit first, skills and experience second. A company with a team-first corporate culture makes employee happiness its top priority. Frequent team outings, opportunities to provide meaningful feedback, and flexibility to accommodate employee family lives are common markers of a team-first culture. Netflix is a great example; its recent decision to offer unlimited family leave gives employees the autonomy to decide what's right for them.

- **Elite corporate culture**   Companies with elite cultures are often out to change the world by untested means. An elite corporate culture hires only the best because it's always pushing the envelope and needs employees to not merely keep up but lead the way (think Google). Innovative and sometimes daring, companies with an elite culture hire confident, capable, competitive candidates. The result? Fast growth and making big splashes in the market.

- **Horizontal corporate culture**   Titles don't mean much in horizontal cultures. Horizontal corporate culture is common among startups because it makes for a collaborative, everyone-pitch-in mind-set. These typically younger companies have a product or service they're striving to provide yet are more flexible and able to change based on market research or customer feedback. Though a smaller team size might limit their customer service capabilities, they do whatever they can to keep the customer happy—their success depends on it.

- **Conventional corporate culture**   Traditional companies have clearly defined hierarchies and are still grappling with the learning curve for communicating through new mediums. Companies where a tie and/or slacks are expected are, most likely, of the conventional sort. In fact, any dress code at all is indicative of a more traditional culture, as are a numbers-focused approach and risk-averse decision-making. Your local bank or car dealership likely embodies these traits. The customer, while crucial, is not necessarily always right—the bottom line takes precedence.

- **Progressive corporate culture**   Uncertainty is the definitive trait of a transitional culture because employees often don't know what to expect next. Mergers, acquisitions, or sudden changes in the market can all contribute to a progressive culture. Uncertainty is the definitive trait of a progressive culture because employees often don't know what to expect next (see almost every newspaper or magazine). "Customers" are often separate from the company's audience because these companies usually have investors or advertisers to answer to.

Cultural Layers[21]

There are differing interpretations of culture. A metaphor describes it well: culture looks at it like an onion, consisting of layers that can be peeled off.

Schein's Model[22]   In 1980 the American management professor Edgar Schein developed an organizational culture model to make culture more visible within an organization.

- **Artefacts and symbols**   Artefacts mark the surface of the organization. They are the visible elements in the organization such as logos, architecture, structure, processes, and corporate clothing. These are not only visible to employees but also visible and recognizable for external parties.

- **Espoused values**   This concerns standards, values, and rules of conduct. How does the organization express strategies, objectives, and philosophies, and how are these made public? Problems could arise when the ideas of managers are not in line with the basic assumptions of the organization.

- **Basic underlying assumptions**   The basic underlying assumptions are deeply embedded in the organizational culture and are experienced as self-evident and unconscious behavior. Assumptions are hard to recognize from within.

Cultural Dimensions

Social scientist Geert Hofstede suggests that there are six unique cultural dimensions that can be seen anywhere. These dimensions rank cultures on a scale of 1 to 100 for each dimension.[23]

- **Power distance**   This dimension displays how a culture handles inequality, particularly in relation to money and power. In some cultures, inequality and hierarchal statuses are a way of life.

- **Individualism versus collectivism**   This dimension focuses on the unification of culture. In individualistic cultures, the population is less tightly knit, and there is an "every man for himself" mentality.

- **Masculinity versus femininity**   In this dimension, a culture is measured on a scale of masculinity versus femininity, which represents a culture's preferences for achievement, competition, and materialism versus preferences for teamwork, harmony, and empathy.

- **Uncertainty avoidance**   Have you ever been in a situation where a new idea or element is introduced? How did you react to that? For this dimension, cultures are gauged on their response to ambiguity and new ideas and situations. Change in the future can be a terrifying notion for some, while others will see it as an exciting possibility.

- **Long-term orientation versus short-term orientation**   When dealing with the present and future, a culture either will look to innovate when facing new challenges or will look to the past for answers.

- **Indulgence versus restraint**   In the final dimension, all cultures acknowledge that the natural human response in life is the urgent need to gratify desires. However, each culture will answer this need by either enjoying (indulgence) or controlling (restraint) those impulses.

Hall's Theory of High- and Low-Context Cultures   Hall defines intercultural communication as a form of communication that shares information across different cultures and social groups. One framework for approaching intercultural communication is with high-context and low-context cultures, which refer to the value cultures place on indirect and direct communication.[24]

Hofstedes's Dimensions of Culture[25]   Hofstede's cultural dimensions theory is a framework for cross-cultural communication, developed by Geert Hofstede. It describes the effects of a society's culture on the values of its members and how these values relate to behavior, using a structure derived from factor analysis.

Hofstede developed his original model as a result of using factor analysis to examine the results of a worldwide survey of employee values by IBM between 1967 and 1973.

Trompenaars's and Hampde-Turner's Dilemmas   Anglo-Dutch gurus Fons Trompenaars and Charles Hampden-Turner have become the go-to guys on multinational mergers. Their recipe: making opposites attract.[26]

If you followed dilemma theory to its logical conclusion, you would attribute every pernicious culture clash, and most other management problems, to the human habit (especially common in Western cultures) of casting life in terms of all-or-nothing choices: winning versus losing strategies, right versus wrong answers, good versus bad values, and so on. As a manager, when you unconsciously approach a business issue (or any issue) as a contest between good and evil, you lose sight of the potential benefits the "evil" side has to offer. It's far better to interpret, say, the battle between English and French management styles or American dominance and European resistance as a dilemma that can be reconciled when both sides see they have something to learn from the other.

Cross-Cultural Challenges for HR[27]

With the rapid increase in the globalization of business, workforces are becoming increasingly diverse and multicultural. Managing global workforces has increased pressure on human resource managers to recognize and adapt to cultural differences, which when ignored can result in cross-cultural misunderstandings. With the growing significance of developing economies in the global business environment, human resource management is facing increased difficulty in managing cross-border cultural relationships.

Challenges of Culture   As workplaces become more complex and the mingling of cultures becomes more challenging, HR professionals must keep an eye open for these specific challenges:[28]

- Colleagues from some cultures may be less likely to let their voices be heard.
- Integration across multicultural teams can be difficult in the face of prejudice or negative cultural stereotypes.
- Professional communication can be misinterpreted or difficult to understand across languages and cultures.
- Navigating visa requirements, employment laws, and the cost of accommodating workplace requirements can be difficult.
- There may be different understandings of professional etiquette.
- There may be conflicting working styles across teams.

Dilemma Reconciliation   The essence of the reconciliation of a dilemma lies in the recognition that a dilemma is a nonlinear problem and therefore needs a nonlinear problem-solving approach. It replaces "either-or" thinking with "and-and and through-and-through" thinking.[29]

Creating Cultural Synergy   Cultural synergy is a term coined from work by Nancy Adler[30] of McGill University that describes an attempt to bring two or more cultures together to form an organization or environment that is based on combined strengths, concepts, and skills. High-synergy organizations have employees who cooperate for mutual advantage and usually tackle their problems by following a simple structure that focuses on identifying the problem, culturally interpreting it, and, finally, increasing the cultural activity. Contrary to this, there are low-synergy organizations that work with employees who are ruggedly individualistic and insist on solving any problem alone.

Managing Global Assignments

Only 51 percent of companies track the actual total cost of international assignments, yet 69 percent say there is pressure to reduce mobility program costs, according to a recent survey report on global mobility trends and practices. In addition, 76 percent of companies do not compare the actual versus estimated cost at the end of an assignment, and a whopping 94 percent do not measure the program's return on investment.[31]

Strategic Role of Global Assignments

Global assignments can contribute to the organization's strategic plan. They offer cross-training for senior managers and executives. This can enhance cultural exposure and even cultural emersion. Global assignments also provide an opportunity to assess global presence and expansion plans.

Types of Assignments

Specialists in international human resource management identify different types of global assignment. Technical assignments occur when employees with technical skills are sent from one country to another to fill a particular skill shortage. Developmental assignments, in contrast, are typically used within a management development program and are used to equip managers with new skills and competencies. Strategic assignments arise when key executives are sent from one country to another to launch a product, develop a market, or initiate another key change in business strategy. Finally, functional assignments resemble technical assignments but differ in one important respect.[32]

Managing Allegiances

Sometimes people are torn between their parent company and their local company. According to Kate Hutchins and Helen De Cieri, those allegiances can be understood by using the following chart:[33]

Forms of Expatriate Allegiance			
Allegiance to the Parent Firm	High	Expatriates who leave their hearts at home	Expatriates who see themselves as dual citizens
	Low	Expatriates who see themselves as free agents	Expatriates who "go native"
		Low	High
		Allegiance to the Local Firm	

Global Assignment Guidelines

The companies that manage their expats effectively come in many sizes and from a wide range of industries. Yet they all follow three general practices.[34]

- When making international assignments, they focus on knowledge creation and global leadership development. Many companies send people abroad to reward them, to get them out of the way, or to fill an immediate business need. At companies that manage the international assignment process well, however, people are given foreign posts for two related reasons: to generate and transfer knowledge and to develop their global leadership skills (or to do both).

- They assign overseas posts to people whose technical skills are matched or exceeded by their cross-cultural abilities. Companies that manage expats wisely do not assume that people who have succeeded at home will repeat that success abroad.

They assign international posts to individuals who not only have the necessary technical skills but also have indicated that they would be likely to live comfortably in different cultures.

- They end expatriate assignments with a deliberate repatriation process. Most executives who oversee expat employees view their return home as a nonissue. The truth is, repatriation is a time of major upheaval, professionally and personally, for two-thirds of expats. Companies that recognize this fact help their returning people by providing them with career guidance and enabling them to put their international experience to work.

What Managers Should Know   Global human resource managers can use the high failure rates of international job assignments to support investing in up-front and ongoing programs that will make international assignments successful. Selecting the right person, preparing the expat and the family, measuring the employee's performance from afar, and repatriating the individual at the end of an assignment all require a well-planned, well-managed program. Knowing what to expect from start to finish as well as having some tools to work with can help minimize the risk.[35]

The Global Assignment Process

There are five stages involved in the global assignment process.

- **Stage 1: Assessment and selection**   Determining who will be appointed to the international job opening depends on who meets the job requirements in the best way. There may be a formal assessment, or there may be only a single selecting manager who makes the decision.

- **Stage 2: Management and assignee decision**   The selecting manager determines how long the assignee will have to accept or reject the appointment.

- **Stage 3: Predeparture preparation**   Before anyone leaves the home country, there are important considerations to be processed and questions answered. What are the immigrant requirements in the destination country? What visa requirements must be processed? What provisions will be made for the employee's family members (school or spouse work appointment)? What about selling a home before departure? Will a home be purchased in the destination country?

- **Stage 4: On assignment**   When the employee arrives at the new job location, there is a "settling in" process. Are the living arrangements going to be satisfactory? Where is the local grocery store? What about dentists, optometrists, and physicians? What about automobiles?

- **Stage 5: Completing the assignment**   When the expat comes home, there should be a debriefing process that could last several days. Inquiries should be made about the employee's opinion of the job environment, the work itself, the support received from the employer, and what things could be done differently.

Navigating the Global Legal Environment

There are always labor-management laws to be considered regardless of where one works in the world. They vary greatly in their control over the workplace, but both employee and the employer should understand them for the destination country so no one violates one of them even by accident.

World Legal Systems

Around the globe there are several different types of legal systems, and they don't always agree with one another.

Types of Legal Systems

Civil law, common law, and religious law are the three primary kinds of legal systems in the world today.

Civil Law   Civil law systems have drawn their inspiration largely from the Roman law heritage that, by giving precedence to written law, have resolutely opted for a systematic codification of their general law. It is the most widespread system of law in the world.

Common Law   Common law systems are legal systems founded not on laws made by legislatures but on judge-made laws, which in turn are based on custom, culture, habit, and previous judicial decisions throughout the world.

Religious Law   The Muslim law system is an autonomous legal system that is of a religious nature and predominantly based on the Koran.

Key Concepts of Law

While laws bring us some level of consistency in treatment for the same or similar events, there are some key elements that you should recognize in all of them.

Rule of Law   The *rule of law* is the principle that law should govern a nation, as opposed to being governed by decisions of individual government officials.

Due Process   *Due process* acts as a safeguard from arbitrary denial of life, liberty, or property by the government outside the sanction of law.

Jurisdiction   Legal jurisdiction applies to government agencies as well as courts. State courts have jurisdiction only in their state. Federal courts have jurisdiction over federal matters. Federal case law is determined by appellate courts, and those decisions apply only within the jurisdiction of the appellate court. The U.S. Supreme Court has jurisdiction over all matters of the U.S. Constitution.

Levels of Law

Each governmental strata can offer its own laws.

Within a Nation   At the national level, there can be laws created that apply to the entire country and others that apply only to a subset of the nation.

National Laws   Federal laws apply to all governmental subsets such as states in the United States. Nondiscrimination rules apply to all states equally. Of course, there are qualifying thresholds such as the number of employees that can cause certain employers to be exempt from the provisions of the law, but all those who qualify by employee head count will be expected to comply with the national law.

Subnational   Called a nation-state, canton, or province, each smaller entity within the federal umbrella can create its own laws. These laws apply only within its own jurisdiction.

Between and Among Nations   When nations agree that the same laws should apply to each of them, one of the following types of rule would come into existence.

Extraterritorial   Extraterritorial jurisdiction (ETJ) is the legal ability of a government to exercise authority beyond its normal boundaries. Any authority can claim ETJ over any external territory they want. This is the stuff that wars are fought over. The European Union and the World Trade Organization are examples.[36]

Regional/Supranational   A supranational organization is an international group or union in which the power and influence of member states transcend national boundaries or interests to share in decision-making and vote on issues concerning the collective body.

International   This is a body of rules established by custom or treaty and recognized by nations as binding in their relations with one another.

For example, EU law is divided into primary and secondary legislation. The treaties (primary legislation) are the basis or ground rules for all EU action. Secondary legislation—which includes regulations, directives, and decisions—is derived from the principles and objectives set out in the treaties.

Background   The European Union was set up with the aim of ending the frequent and bloody wars between neighbors, which culminated in World War II. As of 1950, the European coal and steel community began to unite European countries economically and politically to secure lasting peace. The six founding countries are Belgium, France, Germany, Italy, Luxembourg, and the Netherlands. The 1950s were dominated by a Cold War between East and West. Protests in Hungary against the Communist regime were put down by Soviet tanks in 1956. In 1957, the Treaty of Rome created the European Economic Community (EEC), or Common Market.[37]

With the collapse of communism across Central and Eastern Europe, Europeans become closer neighbors. In 1993, the single market was completed with the "four freedoms" of movement of goods, services, people, and money. The 1990s was also the decade of two treaties: the Maastricht Treaty on European Union in 1993 and the Treaty of Amsterdam in 1999. People were concerned about how to protect the environment and also how Europeans could act together in security and defense matters. In 1995 the EU gained three more new members: Austria, Finland, and Sweden. A small village in Luxembourg gives its name to the Schengen agreements that gradually allowed people to travel without having their passports checked at the borders. Millions of young people study in other countries with EU support. Communication was made easier as more and more people started using mobile phones and the Internet.

Legal Institutions   Here are the current institutions serving the European Union:

- The **European Parliament (EP)** and its 751 members represent the citizens of the member states and are directly elected every five years. The Parliament makes decisions on most EU laws, together with the Council of the EU, via the ordinary legislative procedure. Parliamentary positions are prepared by 22 committees, which work on different policies, and adopted during plenary sessions held in Strasbourg or Brussels. Seven political groups have been established at the European Parliament for the current term of office.[38]

- The **European Council** comprises the 28 heads of state or government of the member states and sets the EU's overall political agenda. The president of the European Council, whose primary role is to coordinate and drive forward the work of the European Council, is elected by the members of the European Council and can serve for a maximum of 5 years.

- The **European Commission** is the executive branch of the union. It represents the interests of the European Union and is composed of 28 commissioners (one from each member state) and chaired by a president. The latter is nominated by the European Council and appointed by the European Parliament for a term of five years. The commission has 35,000 staff members working in 33 different departments known as *directorate-generals* (which represent specific policies) and 11 other services. The commission is the only EU institution with the right to propose legislation as part of the ordinary legislative procedure. It also ensures that EU legislation and the EU budget are properly implemented, and it represents the European Commission in international negotiations.

- **The Court of Justice of the European Union** reviews the legality of the acts of the institutions of the European Union, ensures that the member states comply with obligations under the treaties, and interprets EU law at the request of the national courts and tribunals.

- **European Central Bank** is the central bank of the 19 European Union countries that have adopted the euro. Its main task is to maintain price stability in the euro area and so preserve the purchasing power of the single currency.

- The **European Court of Auditors** (ECA) mission is to contribute to improving EU financial management, promote accountability and transparency, and act as the independent guardian of the financial interests of the citizens of the union. The ECA's role as the EU's independent external auditor is to check that EU funds are correctly accounted for, are raised and spent in accordance with the relevant rules and regulations, and have achieved value for money.

Legal Instruments   All of those institutions of the European Union rely on various legal instruments as the foundation of their work.

Treaties   The European Union is based on the rule of law. This means every action taken by the European Commission is founded on treaties that have been approved voluntarily and democratically by all EU member countries. For example, if a policy area is not cited in a treaty, the commission cannot propose a law in that area. A treaty is a binding agreement between EU member countries. It sets out EU objectives, rules for EU institutions, how decisions are made, and the relationship between the EU and its member countries. Treaties are amended to make the European Union more efficient and transparent, to prepare for new member countries, and to introduce new areas of cooperation such as the single currency.

Regulations   A regulation is a legal act of the European Union that becomes immediately enforceable as law in all member states simultaneously. Regulations can be distinguished from directives that, at least in principle, need to be transposed into national law.

Directives   A directive is a legal act of the European Union, which requires member states to achieve a particular result without dictating the means of achieving that result. It can be distinguished from regulations that are self-executing and do not require any implementing measures.

Judicial Decisions   EU case law is made up of judgments from the European Union's Court of Justice, which interpret EU legislation.

Recommendations and Opinions   Recommendations are without legal force but are negotiated and voted on according to the appropriate procedure. Recommendations differ from regulations, directives, and decisions, in that they are not binding for member states. Though without legal force, they do have a political weight. An opinion is an instrument that allows the institutions to make a statement in a nonbinding fashion, in other words, without imposing any legal obligation on those to whom it is addressed. An opinion is not binding.

Functional Area 12—Diversity and Inclusion

Here is SHRM's BoCK definition: "Diversity and Inclusion encompasses activities that create opportunities for the organization to leverage the unique backgrounds and characteristics of all employees to contribute to its success." [39]

Diversity and inclusion are linked together both by definition and by practice. Having a diverse workforce will not persist if that diverse group doesn't feel included as individuals.

Key Concepts

- Approaches to developing an inclusive workplace (e.g., best practices for diversity training)
- Approaches to managing a multigenerational/aging workforce
- Demographic barriers to success (e.g., glass ceiling)

- Issues related to acceptance of diversity, including international differences (i.e., its acceptance in foreign nations or by employees from foreign nations)
- Workplace accommodations (e.g., disability, religious, transgender, veteran, active-duty military)

The following are proficiency indicators that SHRM has identified as key concepts:

For All HR Professionals	For Advanced HR Professionals (SCP Exam)
• Provides mentoring, training, guidance, and coaching on cultural differences and practices to employees at all levels of the organization • Consults with managers about distinctions between performance issues and cultural differences • Develops and maintains knowledge of current trends and HR management best practices related to diversity and inclusion • Contributes to development and maintenance of an organizational culture that values a diverse and inclusive workforce (e.g., conducts diversity training) • Identifies opportunities to enhance the fairness of organizational policies and procedures to all employees (e.g., removes demographic barriers to success) • Identifies and implements workplace accommodations • Demonstrates support to internal and external stakeholders for the organization's diversity and inclusion efforts	• Incorporates diversity and inclusion goals into all HR programs, practices, and policies • Advocates for incorporation of diversity goals into the organization's strategic plan • Develops, implements, and oversees, in conjunction with other business leaders, enterprise-wide programs, practices, and policies that lead to a diverse workforce • Designs and oversees HR programs, practices, and policies supporting the development and maintenance of an organizational culture that values and promotes a diverse and inclusive workforce • Designs and oversees HR programs, practices, and policies that encourage employees to take advantage of opportunities for working with those who possess a diverse set of experiences and backgrounds • Ensures that HR staff members have up-to-date knowledge of current trends and HR management best practices related to diversity and inclusion

Overview: Key Terms

The two key terms are *diversity* and *inclusion*. It is helpful to define them to understand how to incorporate them into an organizational culture and management.

Diversity

Diversity is a workforce characteristic. It indicates a mixture of social, cultural, and personal attributes that affect individual attitudes and behaviors. Diversity characteristics impact how others react to individuals "because they are different."

Diversity of Thought Experiences are tightly linked to cultural background. Food, housing, recreation, and life activities are tied to the culture in which one grows up and matures. Thought processes and references are determined by the experiences people have had and the interactions with others that were part of those experiences. If we were rewarded early on for our "fresh ideas," it is easier for us to generate ideas later in life.

If we were encouraged to contain our behavior within strict boundaries of social decorum and not deviate much from those expectations, then it will be more difficult for us to be inventive or creative later in life.

Organizational leaders need to understand each individual's background to understand how to encourage them to fully participate in the organizational workings.

Inclusion

Inclusion is the characteristic of a workplace referring to behaviors within the organization that determine how individuals are valued, engaged, and respected. Inclusion is also linked to "fairness" and equal access to resources and opportunities. You can see the link between inclusion and equal employment opportunity (EEO). While EEO is a legal obligation, inclusion goes further by valuing the importance of being part of the group in every way.

Diversity Without Inclusion   Through a strong outreach program, it is possible that an organization can recruit a diverse group of employees. And it is possible that some of those employees may not be made to feel like a part of the company because they are not invited to contribute their ideas or suggestions. They may not be invited to participate in out-of-hours activities or assigned the really good jobs. Some folks may not be comfortable with co-workers because they look different or come from different cultures.

Any exclusion, whether subtle or overt, can lead to a feeling of being an outsider. So, diversity does not innately result in inclusion. Inclusion comes from conscious efforts. Inclusion depends on more than a lack of bias. It depends on commitment to assuring each person is welcomed as a participant in every facet of work life.

Diversity and Globalization

Not every culture in the world has the same view of diversity and inclusion as found in the United States. Some are theocracies, monocracies, or other monogenic countries. Whatever the circumstance, lack of variety in cultural experience makes it more difficult to accept, let alone encourage, recruiting a diverse group of job candidates. When it comes to selecting new hires, this cultural bias often plays a part in the hiring decision. That bias usually isn't intentional. Yet it exists, and its results are seen in a high percentage of people in the organization that look alike. It may be based on religion or race or even gender. The differences in cultural experience are measured along a broad spectrum. From one country to another, the pointer along that spectrum line can shift dramatically.

Global Legal Distinctions   Legal requirements for equal employment opportunity and diversity vary widely from one country to another. In some cases, imposition of quotas for some groups exists. Here are a few random examples. Equal employment opportunity requires some serious study of local and federal requirements in each political jurisdiction where you will have employees located.

- **Australia**   Australia requires employers with 100 or more workers to report their gender equity plans and submit reports on the participation of women in their workforce and their board of directors.

- **Canada**   Seven provinces and the federal government have pay equity legislation that requires employers to provide equal pay for work of equal or comparable value.

- **Germany**   There are absolute quotas for the employment of severely disabled people based on the size of the employer workforce. Employers with 60 or more employees must have 5 percent of their workforce composed of severely disabled employees. Smaller quotas apply to smaller organizations.

- **Great Britain**   The practice of a fixed retirement requirement at age 65 has been rescinded by law.

- **South Africa**   There is a legal prescription for annual turnover thresholds. Exceed those limits, and affirmative action requirements will apply for recruiting and hiring. Protected groups include black people, women, and people with disabilities.

The Benefits and Costs of Diversity

A few years ago, the European Commission, Directorate-General for Employment, Industrial Relations, and Social Affairs conducted a study using input from 200 companies in four European countries.[40] It identified some specific benefits and costs associated with employment diversity policies and programs.

The benefits of active diversity policies were determined to include the following:

- Strengthened cultural values within the organization
- Enhanced corporate reputation
- Helped attract and retain highly talented people
- Improved motivation and efficiency of existing staff
- Improved innovation and creativity among employees
- Enhanced service levels and customer satisfaction
- Helped overcome labor shortages
- Reduced labor turnover
- Resulted in lower absenteeism rates

The costs of diversity programs were determined to include the following:

- **Costs of legal compliance**   Recordkeeping systems, staff training, policy communication.
- **Cash costs of diversity**   Staff education and training, facilities and diversity support staff, monitoring and reporting processes.
- **Opportunity costs of diversity**   Loss of benefits because a scarce resource cannot be used in other productive activities (diversion of top management time, productivity shortfalls).
- **Business risks of diversity**   Plans taking longer than planned to implement or fail completely. This is known as the *execution risk*. Sustainable diversity policies are an outcome of a successful change in corporate culture.

The Four Layers of Diversity

According to *Color Magazine*,[41] the four layers of diversity can be compiled into the four layers model, which has radiating rings from a center where personality constitutes the core.

- **Personality**   This includes an individual's likes and dislikes, values, and beliefs. Personality is shaped early in life and is both influenced by, and influences, the other three layers throughout one's lifetime and career choices.

- **Internal dimensions**   These include aspects of diversity over which we have no control (though "physical ability" can change over time because of choices we make to be active or in cases of illness or accidents). This dimension is the layer in which many divisions between and among people exist and which forms the core of many diversity efforts. These dimensions include the first things we see in other people, such as race or gender, and on which we make many assumptions and base judgments.

- **External dimensions**   These include aspects of our lives that we have some control over, which might change over time, and which usually form the basis for decisions on careers and work styles. This layer often determines, in part, with whom we develop friendships and what we do for work. This layer also tells us much about whom we like to be with and decisions we make in hiring, promotions, and so on, at work.

- **Organizational dimensions**   This layer concerns the aspects of culture found in a work setting. While much attention of diversity efforts is focused on the internal dimensions, issues of preferential treatment and opportunities for development or promotion are impacted by the aspects of this layer.

The *Color Magazine* article tells us, "The usefulness of this model is that it includes the dimensions that shape and impact both the individual and the organization itself. While the 'Internal Dimensions' receive primary attention in successful diversity initiatives, the elements of the 'External' and 'Organizational' dimensions often determine the way people are treated, who 'fits' or not in a department, who gets the opportunity for development or promotions, and who gets recognized."

Implications of an Inclusive Definition   In its simplest terms, a narrow definition will narrow impact to the organization. A broad definition will increase that organizational impact. There are many things that can be measured to determine whether the definition being used is broad enough for the organization. Some of them are job satisfaction, relations with supervisors and group members, intention to stay with the organization, commitment to the organization, job performance, organizational citizenship behaviors, well-being, creativity, and career opportunities for diverse individuals. For many of these metrics, benchmarks will need to be established so direct application to any given organization can be accurately developed.

Visible and Invisible Diversity Traits

SHRM breaks down diversity into two categories, namely, visible diversity traits and invisible diversity traits. Basically, everyone matters.

Visible diversity traits are the more typical and visible areas associated with diversity such as race, gender, physical abilities, age, body size/type, skin color, behaviors, and physical abilities.

Invisible diversity traits include areas less visible such as sexual orientation, religion, socioeconomic status, education, sexual orientation, military experience, culture, habits, education, native born/non-native, values/believes, and parental status, among other things.

Developing a Diversity and Inclusion Strategy

There is a key question to be answered at the beginning of any organizational policy discussion: What do you want to accomplish and how will you measure it? Strategy involves the plan for implementation. You must look at problems to be anticipated and identify alternatives for dealing with them. You must identify the value to be received from creating an executive steering committee that will monitor the program implementation. Once the alternatives have been assessed, strategy can be cited from the remaining options.

Why a Diversity and Inclusion Strategy?

Three reasons mark the need for a strategy to be used in creating and implementing a diversity and inclusion (D&I) program for any organization.

- **Reason 1: Priority**   Without a strategy, the D&I efforts will always take a backseat to other more immediately urgent matters.

- **Reason 2: Complexity**   D&I programs are not simple. The complexity requires organization-wide strategies if successful implementation is to be achieved.

- **Reason 3: Resistance**   D&I programs require organizational change, regardless of the organization. There will be more change in some organizations than in others. Change is hard. Therefore, making the changes needed for successful D&I programs will take some significant effort.

The D&I Strategic Process

Once the decision has been made to develop and implement a diversity and inclusion program in your organization, you will need to identify the strategic steps you must take to achieve success.

Executive Commitment   Changing organizational behaviors and individual attitudes are results that don't come easily. If they are to be achieved at all, the highest level of executive will be needed to lay out the program, its reasons, and its objectives. Without the constant challenge and reinforcement from the senior leader, there can be no hope for reaching the established goals. "What the boss says is what gets done." If the boss isn't fully behind the program, it will just waste organizational resources and not accomplish what is hoped.

Making the Business Case for D&I The Conference Board published some thoughts in 2008 that still hold true today.[42]

- **Business acumen and external market knowledge** This becomes the foundation of understanding how a D&I program can support business needs. It includes the following characteristics:
  - Executives understand and are current on global and local trends/changes and how they inform and influence D&I.
  - Executives gather and use competitive intelligence.
  - Executives understand diverse customer/client needs.
  - Executives understand and are current with global sociopolitical environments.
  - Executives understand context and lessons learned.

- **Holistic business knowledge** This requires understanding of the impact of the financial, economic, and market drivers on the bottom-line results. Additional requirements include the following:
  - Executives understand core business strategies.
  - Executives possess solid financial acumen.
  - Executives use information from multiple disciplines and sources to offer integrated ideas and solutions on issues important to the organization.

- **Diversity and Inclusion return on investment (ROI)** This is where the financial impact of the D&I program becomes evident. Requirements include the following:
  - Determine and communicate how D&I contributes to core business strategy and results.
  - Create insights on how D&I contributes both to people and HR strategies as well as business results.
  - Design and develop D&I metrics that exhibit the ROI impact.

Preliminary Assessment A quick way to determine how you are doing with your D&I program is to conduct an employee survey. It may take some professional help to identify the specific information you want to gather and the form of the inquiries you craft for each. But, surveying the workforce will help you understand the "state of the enterprise" about diversity and inclusion.

Infrastructure Creation If you are just beginning to address the issues of diversity and inclusion, it is important to recognize that there is going to be a need for some changes in the way you do things within the organization. Sometimes those changes can be uncomfortable for people, and that demands you be ready to give them the support they need to get past their discomfort to participate in the successful implementation of your program.

Diversity Councils Diversity councils are groups of employees who discuss issues of diversity and inclusion. The duties of these councils can vary widely from being an advisory group to having some responsibility for implementing or overseeing program elements such as complaint handling or community involvement.

Employee Resource Groups Employee resource groups can be called many things. Early on in diversity program efforts, they were called *employee affinity groups*. Whatever the name, these are groups of similar employees who can express opinions and requests for consideration that apply to their group. These are some examples: Black Employees Group, Hispanic Employees, Asian Employees, Women Engineers, Employees Using English as a Second Language. There are countless possibilities.

Strategic Alliances D&I programs can make use of linkages to community groups that support efforts to expand or reinforce outreach efforts for particular groups of people. It may be that you need more women in professional jobs. Identifying and then building relationships with these community groups can take some time but will contribute authenticity to your D&I program. They can also be sources for your open job placement opportunities when those occur. Community organizations range from disabled groups to veteran groups and various racial and gender support groups. Some are social, but many are also focused on increasing employment opportunities for their qualified membership.

System Changes D&I programs by their very nature require changes to the way employers operate. Systemic changes will there be needed by definition. That is why there is often discomfort associated with D&I programs. They take us out of our usual and customary routines and demand that we expand our experiences and embrace things that are different.

Recruitment, Sourcing, and Hiring Identifying new sources for qualified job candidates can take some time. There are groups supporting every type of job candidate you can imagine. They are race-based, gender-based, veteran, and disability-support groups. Larger organizations can usually afford to have people on staff who are dedicated to identifying and developing relationship opportunities within the employer's recruiting geography. Smaller organizations can outsource some of this effort to organizations like Local Job Network.com (www.localjobnetwork.com). For an annual fee, the vendor will find and provide the employer with access to D&I community groups that are relevant to the employer. They will also provide reporting on hiring from each of those sources, so through monitoring, the employer can identify the best sources of diverse candidates for its jobs.

Onboarding and Retention Most would argue that hiring a diverse group of employees won't do much good if they can't be made to feel welcome in the organization. So, how they are treated when they first come to work (onboarding) and what is done to make sure they can be retained for longer periods of time will contribute to a larger financial payback and lower turnover rates for the employer. It will also contribute the benefits associated with a vibrant D&I program.

Promotion and Career Development   For those who are interested in and qualified for promotion, nothing will break their spirit faster than seeing others promoted while they "wait in the wings." This used to be blatant discrimination based on religion, race, sex, or other category that is protected under today's laws. On the other hand, using promotion for those who are qualified and interested in advancement can be a solid motivational tool and morale builder when employees see "nontraditional" advancement. It sends the message that "even I have a chance to advance in this company."

Compensation and Benefits   There is a bigger downside to mismanaged compensation and benefits than there is an upside through increased morale. As a function of D&I programs, it is essential that compensation and benefit programs act to constructively balance both the appearance and reality of fairness in employee treatment. These programs can act as a lure in recruiting and an anchor for retention. Their development and ongoing management should embrace participation from all groups within the employee body. It is important that each segment of the workforce feels like part of the process of development for benefits and compensation. To the extent that any employee group is asked to participate, all employee groups should be represented in the participation.

Supply Chain Management and Relations   Vendor and supplier relations are important to D&I programs because spending dollars is an activity that raises sensitivity and a desire to be on the receiving end of the transaction. Outreach programs to encourage participation of minority- and female-owned businesses are part of the D&I process. It should also be possible for businesses owned by veteran or people with disabilities to participate in the contracting or bidding process. There are some governmental jurisdictions that require contractors to meet participation goals for vendors and suppliers to be sure that these various groups have a "piece of the pie." Employers who demonstrate active solicitation from all portions of the vendor community will also have successful relationships with the vendors, assuring that they will be able to meet future requirements as well as current demands for contract participation.

"Beyond that, nurturing a diverse supplier base—including coaching minority-, veteran-, and women-led enterprises on ways to improve their offers—enhances the buying company's image. It can also foster economic strength, as many of these companies tend to hire from within their communities."[43]

Marketing, Branding, and Customer Relations   Broad appeal is the goal of most marketing programs. Establishing a brand that is recognized and valued by multiple cultures is also desirable. Doing that with an eye on healthy customer relations may require addressing each group in special ways. If a portion of the customer base is Hispanic, having customer service representatives who are able to work on the customer hot line while speaking Spanish can help reinforce those customer relationships. The same is true of any other ethnic or cultural group. In some portions of the country, there are fairly large populations of Vietnamese, Chinese, and Korean people. Serving these groups in their own language can build positive relations and increase brand loyalty. Providing literature in languages that are native to customers is another way to address their needs and increase diversity and inclusion of the various nationality groups.

Providing employment posters in languages that are native to employees is a requirement in many instances. That's why in some places such as San Francisco, employment posters can be found in English, Spanish, Chinese, and Tagalog (Philippines).

Training   Training programs for both managers and nonmanagement employees can be a key component of the D&I program. It is more than sensitivity training. It involves the communication of key organizational values. Also, training can help raise the skill levels of supervisor and manager groups so they are able to more effectively deal with issues of D&I.

Initial employee training during the onboarding process can help new workers understand "how we do things around here." Communicating and instilling values of diversity and inclusion early on can help those lessons last for the duration of the employee's tenure.

Measurement and Evaluation   Diversity programs can be measured by looking at demographics of employee composition. How diverse is the incumbent group? How diverse is the recruiting effort? Count the number of recruiting resources that represent various racial or ethnic groups. Are there groups representing women, veterans, and people with disabilities? Recruiting and hiring are just exercises unless they result in employee retention. So, another measurement is turnover rate. What percentage of new hires are still on the payroll after a year?

Inclusion is a bit more difficult. It can be effectively measured, however, through the use of employee surveys. To what extent do employees feel their boss (supervisor) includes them in decisions about their job activities? Do employees feel they are part of the decision-making process when policy changes are being considered?

Why Diversity Initiatives Falter   Most people don't have a clear understanding of diversity. When you ask people what diversity means, you will get as many definitions as the number of people you poll. People plainly don't have a common understanding of it.

If you are going to emphasize diversity and inclusion in your organization, it is not enough to develop a statement to post on the wall next to your company values. How you define diversity and inclusion needs to be in clear enough terms that your workforce can both understand and reiterate the definition and "walk the talk" in all functions of work, demonstrated leadership, policies, systems, and programs.

The intent of annual diversity and inclusion training is helpful, but it isn't enough. Too often, these initiatives fail because they are delivered as a strong-arm tactic. About three-quarters of firms with training still follow the dated advice of the late diversity guru R. Roosevelt Thomas Jr. He said, "If diversity management is strategic to the organization, diversity training must be mandatory, and management has to make it clear that 'if you can't deal with that, then we have to ask you to leave.'" Many firms even see adverse effects because of the use of negative messages in their training, like headlining a legal case for diversity and highlighting stories of huge settlements, which gives an implied threat: "Discriminate, and the company will pay the price." Threats, or "negative incentives," don't win converts. Organizational Development (OD) specialists have told us for years that people often respond to compulsory training with anger and resistance. Do people who undergo training usually shed their biases? Researchers have been examining that question since before World War II. While people are easily taught to respond correctly to a questionnaire about bias, they soon forget the right answers. The positive effects of diversity training rarely last beyond a day or two, and a number of studies suggest that it can activate bias or spark a backlash. Frank Dobbin and Alexandrea Kalev studied 829 midsize and large U.S. firms, and their findings concluded in their report "Why Diversity Programs Fail"[44] that "companies do a better job of increasing diversity when they forgo the control tactics and frame their efforts more positively." In their statistical research, Figure 6-1 highlights three examples of the percent of change over 5 years in representation among managers from their findings.

Evolution and Integration   Deloitte University Press says, "Organizations can start by broadening their understanding of diversity to focus not only on the visible aspects of diversity, such as race, gender, age, and physical ability, but also diversity of thinking. This means deriving value from people's different perspectives on problems and different ways to address solutions. It's a complex world, it's a global world, and maximal participation is required from every workplace participant from the bottom to the top. Thinking of diversity in this way helps organizations to see value and to be conscious of the risk associated with homogeneity, especially in senior decision makers. And this means that diversity is no longer a 'program' to be managed—it is a business imperative."[45]

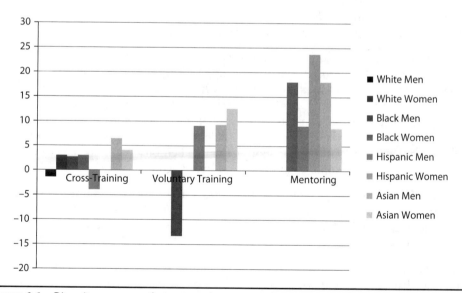

Figure 6-1   Diversity programs that get results: percent change over 5 years

Unless organizations consciously focus on evolution of their inclusion programs, there won't be any integration. After all, integration means that diversity and inclusion become the way things are done. It's no big deal. It's rather the expectation for behavior.

HR's Role in the D&I Process

It was in 2011 that SHRM defined the role of human resources in the diversity and inclusion process. At its annual diversity conference, Doug Harris, CEO of the Kaleidoscope Group, offered these thoughts: "The expectations of human resources in diversity and inclusion is higher than other organization stakeholders. Leaders, managers, and employees often seek out HR for support, coaching, and guidance on how to address challenges and ensure that differences are maximized in the organization. In addition, human resource professionals are often asked to play a key role in the design and implementation of impactful D&I solutions but are rarely given the opportunity to enhance their existing capability and build the D&I expertise necessary to support the overall effort."[46]

Aspects of Organizational Change

Any organizational change effort is dependent upon having clear objectives and implementation assignments. Human resources is often a key player in the change program. There is usually an educational component that HR can take on. And there is the cheerleading role that reinforces over and over the benefits to be achieved by employee support of the change implementation.

Individual Attitudes and Behaviors

There are three major components of personal attitudes and behaviors required of human resource management groups trying to implement a successful D&I program.

Global Mind-Set   The Conference Board is an organization known around the world as a source of insights on the issues facing employer organizations. It publishes *Council Perspectives* to share its research and opinions with its members and the public. In that publication, the Conference Board has concluded the following: "There is no single globally accepted definition of 'diversity.' ... For a diversity and inclusion strategy to be truly global, D&I professionals need to understand the culture, politics, economics, and relevant legislation within the regions in which their businesses operate, all of which underscores the critical importance of being culturally competent."[47]

Emotional Intelligence   Emotional intelligence is the ability to monitor people's emotions, to find distinctions between them, and to use that information to guide behavior. Organizations that have high emotional intelligence are able to achieve greater effectiveness in their work.[48]

Intercultural Wisdom   This is the absence of knowledge. Intercultural wisdom is knowing what we do not know about the values, behavior, and communication styles of people from other cultures.[49] The only way to gain wisdom of this nature is to get input from others.

Managerial Skills and Practices

Management skills are still important in today's workplace. Individual competence in areas of decision-making, leadership, communication (both oral and written), inner work standards, personal ethics, behavior flexibility, creativity, self-objectivity, tolerance for uncertainty, and resistance to stress are some of the key skills still required of today's managers.

The 4 Ts: Travel, Teams, Training, Transfers   In the late 1990s, a team of people studied leadership and concluded that it can be said to consist of the four Ts. Gregson, Morrison, and Black identified each of the categories as critical for international management success today.[50] These four leadership components were elaborated on by Gamaliel Perruci in a paper presented to the International Leadership Association conference held in Atlanta, Georgia, in 1999.[51]

- **Travel**   Travel allows future leaders to see where their followers come from culturally, economically, and politically.

- **Teams**   Teams reflect the need to allow inclusive participation and consensus building.

- **Training**   Training involves four things: language, development, internships, and development of facilitation skills.

- **Transfers**   Transfers provide the opportunity to spend a significant amount of time overseas to immerse oneself in a foreign culture.

Organizational Values and Policies   Organizational values are those things that are important to the organization at its core. They represent the "why we do what we do." Policies should be designed to support the things the organization values. Policies are the guidance for handling issues that arise on a regular or routine basis. For example, most organizations have a policy on safety that includes a statement about why safety is important and also addresses how employees should handle the reporting of safety hazards when they are recognized in the workplace.

Critical Policy Challenge   It is not uncommon to make policy changes. In fact, it is a best practice to review all organizational policies at least once per year. When a policy needs to be changed, it should be rewritten and then distributed to all employees with enough advance notice that the effective date will be far enough in the future to allow proper employee preparation if necessary. An example is changing the policy on expense reimbursement. Employees need enough advance notice so they are able to adapt to the new policy and not be caught off guard with a sudden change of expectations.

Challenge of Details   Details matter, perhaps more in the realm of values and policies than in other aspects of organizational management. The way we do things is important. People have a right to expect that the way we do things will continue from today into the future. When those policies must change or we have a central shift in values, employees need to be given enough detail about the changes so they can adapt and implement the changes appropriately. Details matter, too, in the explanation we offer to workers about the rationale for making the changes they are facing.

Challenge of Dimension-Specific Issues   One way to deal with an issue is to break it into individual components. Diversity can be thought of in terms of individual dimensions or components as well as any other workplace issue. SHRM has created a single list of dimensions it offers as components of diversity. We suggest that you might be better off considering two categories of dimensions: primary and secondary.

Primary diversity dimensions are those we commonly think of when the term *diversity* comes up. They are characteristics found in legal protections at federal, state, and local levels. They include sex/gender (including sexual orientation, sexual preference, LGBT issues), race/ethnicity, culture/nationality, religion, age, disability status, and veteran status.

Secondary diversity dimensions are those that have impact in workplace interactions and achievements but are not as predominant as the primary dimensions. They include marital status, socioeconomic status, personality, educational achievements, and work experience.

These categories are not an exhaustive list. You can add others as you want or find a need in your workplace.

The next question you must ask is, "How can I effectively deal with each of these dimensions?" There are really two avenues of approach to diversity in the workplace. One is the individual approach including personal learning and empathy for others. The second is the organizational approach, which includes assessing the diversity status, training to fill gaps in knowledge and skill discovered in the assessment, and providing mentoring/coaching for individuals and teams that will encourage the necessary changes.

		Diversity Action Plans
Dimension Type	Dimension Category	Action Steps
Primary dimensions	Race/ethnicity	• Training for individuals and work groups • Team building • Recruitment of multilingual workers
	Culture/nationality	• Team building • Individual mentoring efforts • Support of employee resource groups
	Religion	• Training for interfaith awareness • Flextime provisions for religious observance and prayer requirements • Multireligion offerings in company cafeteria

Dimension Type	Dimension Category	Diversity Action Plans
		Action Steps
Primary dimensions	Sex/gender/sexual orientation/sexual preference/LGBT issues	• Inclusion of both women and men in training and development programs • Inclusion of both women and men in promotional opportunities • Benefit programs offered to life partners
	Age	• Intergenerational team membership • Intergenerational mentorship • Phased retirement, medical benefit continuation • Social media privacy and support • Feedback technique adjustment for age groups
	Disability status	• Adjustments to physical work location (work station, restrooms, furniture) • Adjustments to work time to allow medical treatment • Adjustments to instruction delivery (providing written lists of things to be done) • Team training in support techniques to help disabled workers
	Veteran status	• Educational and training opportunities to allow transition into civilian work • Mentorship programs • Health programs that support returning war veterans • Team training in support techniques to help disabled workers
Secondary dimensions	Marital status	• Provisions for on-site daycare • Flextime programs • Parenting leave programs
	Socioeconomic status	• Educational support programs • Mentoring programs
	Personality	• Training for communication skills with various individual styles • Team-building programs
Secondary dimensions	Educational achievements	• Support for individual educational efforts • Benefit programs supporting education
	Work experience	• Mentorship for volunteers • Skill developmental transfer opportunities • International assignment programs

PART II

Functional Area 13—Risk Management

This is SHRM's BoCK definition: "Risk Management is the identification, assessment and prioritization of risks, and the application of resources to minimize, monitor and control the probability and impact of those risks accordingly."[52]

Risk management is a broad functional category. There are so many types of risk management that it is hard to list all of them. Some areas of risk management are liquidity, banking, crisis, supply chain, insurance, software, and strategic reputation risk management. In human resource terms, risk management involves health insurance, discrimination and employee behavior, workplace safety, asset security, and more.

Key Concepts

- Approaches to a drug-free workplace (e.g., testing, treatment of substance abuse)
- Approaches to qualitative and quantitative risk assessment (e.g., single loss expectancy, annualized loss expectancy)
- Business recovery and continuity-of-operations planning
- Emergency and disaster (e.g., communicable disease, natural disaster, severe weather, terrorism) preparation and response planning
- Enterprise risk management processes and best practices (e.g., understand context, identify risks, analyze risks, prioritize risks) and risk treatments (e.g., avoidance, reduction, sharing, retention)
- Legal and regulatory compliance auditing and investigation techniques
- Legal and regulatory compliance auditing and investigation techniques
- Quality assurance techniques and methods
- Risk sources (e.g., project failures) and types (e.g., hazard, financial, operational, strategic)
- Security concerns (e.g., workplace violence, theft, fraud, corporate espionage, sabotage, kidnapping and ransom) and prevention
- Workplace/occupational injury and illness prevention (e.g., identification of hazards), investigation, and accommodations

The following are the proficiency indicators that SHRM has identified as key concepts:

For All HR Professionals	For Advanced HR Professionals (SCP Exam)
• Monitors political, economic, social, technological, legal, and environmental (PESTLE) factors and their influence on the organization	• Develops, implements, and oversees formal and routinized processes for monitoring the organization's internal and external environments to identify potential risks
• Administers and supports HR programs, practices, and policies that identify and/or mitigate workplace risk	• Monitors and evaluated macro-level labor market, industry, and global trends for their impact on the organization
• Implements crisis management, contingency, and business continuity plans for the HR function and the organization	• Examines potential threats to the organization and guides senior leadership accordingly
• Communicates critical information about risks (e.g., safety and security) and risk mitigation to employees at all levels	• Develops, implements, and oversees a comprehensive enterprise risk management strategy
• Conducts workplace safety- and health-related investigations (e.g., investigates workplace injuries)	• Develops crisis management, contingency, and business continuity plans for the HR function and the organization
• Audits risk management activities and plans	• Communicates critical information about risks (e.g., safety and security) and risk mitigation to senior-level employees and external stakeholders
• Maintains and ensures accurate reporting of internationally accepted workplace health and safety standards	• Ensures that risk management activities and plans are audited and that the results inform risk mitigation strategies
• Incorporates into business cases the anticipated level of risk	• Oversees workplace safety- and health-related investigations and reporting
	• Establishes strategies to address workplace retaliation and violence
	• Leads after-action debriefs following significant workplace incidents (e.g., those involving employee safety and security)
	• Evaluates the anticipated level of risk associated with strategic opportunities

Establishing the Context of Risk

Nearly every aspect of HR management impacts the function of risk management in one way or another. Employee satisfaction can be captured through monitoring of complaints. Safety can be expressed in terms of workers' compensation experience. The cost of employee health benefits is impacted by employer programs that support smoking cessation, exercise, and good diet. Computer security programs can block unauthorized access to confidential employee and business records. Privacy of records can be expressed in financial terms. All of these issues are potential impacts on the profit or loss of an employer's organization. Even nonprofits and governmental agencies have budgets they are expected to live within. Huge, unexpected expenses related to risks can cause instant budget failure. HR professionals can have a great impact on the organizational finances by preventing large losses through proper risk management programs.

Focusing Risk Management

Risk management covers many functional areas in the employment world. Some of them are as follows: complying with federal employment laws, identifying workplace hazards, developing safety plans to protect employees and the public, and preparing job descriptions to be used both as a communication tool and as a means to address the physical and mental requirements of each job. Risk management explores how technology can help manage the liability that comes with operating an employment organization. Finally, risk management addresses the rapidly evolving field of social media, Internet, technology, and e-mail use.

There are business risks, and there are employment risks. Risk management addresses issues related to employees, customers, clients, the public, and vendors/suppliers. Risk management is the process of managing liabilities related to these populations in ways that will protect the employer organization and not be so heavy-handed that the organization can't function well in performing its mission. HR professionals are the key to striking a balance in that delicate effort—developing, implementing/administering, and evaluating programs, procedures, and policies to provide a safe, secure working environment and to protect the organization from potential liability. There are lots of exciting things to think about.

Defining Risk

Risk is the potential for losing something of value. As individuals we value our health, our financial well-being, the people we care for, and our happiness. As organizations, we value investment in our workers' training, worker skills, physical plant, assets such as supplies and product material inventories, customer/employee data, financial records, and community goodwill.

Categories of Risk   Risk comes in many forms and can be related to many different issues. There are risks of decision-making, but there are also risks of standing outside as a target for lightning strikes.

What Is Unknown and What Is Not Known About the Unknowns   Planning for risk management is based on the ability to identify anticipated risks. If you are unable to identify the risks in the future, you are not reasonably able to determine how to mitigate them. Consider these examples:

Risk Determinations	
Things You Know The union agreement ends on September 30	**Things You Don't Know** Whether or not the union will agree to our proposals
Things You Know You Don't Know The extent of the union demands for benefits	**Things You Don't Know You Don't Know** The surprises that will happen at the bargaining table

Kaplan and Mike's Categories   Robert S. Kaplan and Annette Mikes are two Harvard Business School professors who wrote an article for the *Harvard Business Review*[53] in June 2012. In it they suggest that risks can be managed using a model containing three categories of risks.

- **Preventable risks**   Internal risks that are controllable and should be eliminated or avoided. They include illegal, unethical, or inappropriate actions and breakdowns in operational processes. These are manageable through rule-based compliance approaches. The best controls involve active prevention such as monitoring operational processes and guiding people's behaviors and decisions toward desirable norms.

- **Strategic risks**   Such risks are identified and accepted in the process of strategic planning. These cannot be managed through a rule-based control model. Instead, it is necessary to reduce the probability that the assumed risks actually materialize and to improve the employer's ability to manage or contain the risk events should they occur.

- **External risks**   These risks generally cannot be prevented from happening. So organizations should forecast what those risks might be and develop ways in which their impact can be minimized. Using key-player discussions to identify how best to handle such risks will take the form of war gaming (simulations) for the near-term issues or scenario analyses for long-term issues. Both offer value from stepping out of individual and group comfort zones, looking around at the bigger picture, and taking the time to plan for the unexpected.

Enterprise Perspective   Risk management can best be performed with an enterprise perspective. Looking at risks solely within a department or division won't reveal the importance of those risks to the entire organization without taking the wider view. When risks are identified, the potential impact on each department can be assessed as well as the impact on the enterprise as a whole. If the risk involves illegal activity, even though only one department is involved, the entire enterprise will be tainted by the bad publicity generated by the bad behavior.

HR and Risk   Human resource management (the HR department) plays a key role in risk management and mitigation. From benefit program management to employee complaint investigations, HR professionals help protect the employer from serious harm and the employees from abuse.

ISO Principles, Framework, and Process

The International Organization for Standardization (ISO) is based in Geneva, Switzerland, and is the world's largest developer and publisher of international standards. In the United States, the oversight organization is called the American National Standards Institute. It publishes standards applying to everything from the size of nuts and bolts (ISO 225:2010) to how to measure the cost per hire (ANSI/SHRM 06001.2012).

Establishing the Context of Risk Management

In 2011, the U.S. Department of Homeland Security (DHS) published a paper on its risk management process.[54] It says, "It is critical to define the context for the decision that the risk management effort will support. When establishing the context, analysts must understand and document the associated requirements and constraints that will influence the decision making process, as well as key assumptions." Here are the key variables DHS says should be considered:

- **Goals and objectives**   Clearly defined goals and objectives are essential to identifying, assessing, and managing those areas that may threaten success.

- **Policies and standards**   Ensure that risk management efforts complement and take into account any risk management policies, standards, or requirements the organization has in place.

- **Scope and criticality of the decision**   The risk analysis and management effort should be commensurate with the criticality of the decision.

- **Decision-makers and stakeholders**   Stakeholders should be engaged and represented throughout the risk management process.

- **Decision time frame**   The time frame in which a decision must be made and executed will dictate a number of the attributes of the risk management effort, including how much time is available for conducting formal analysis and decision review.

- **Risk management capabilities and resources**   At the beginning of the process it is useful to identify the staff, money, skill sets, knowledge levels, and other resources available for risk analysis and management efforts.

- **Risk tolerance**   Risk management efforts often involve trade-offs between positive and negative outcomes.

- **Availability and quality of information**   Consider the anticipated data limitations, including expected levels of uncertainty, so decision-makers can adjust their expectations accordingly.

Risk Criteria   According to ISO 31000, risk criteria are terms of reference and are used to evaluate the significance or importance of an organization's risks. They are used to determine whether a specified level of risk is acceptable or tolerable. Risk criteria should reflect your organization's values, policies, and objectives; should be based on its external and internal context; should consider the views of stakeholders; and should be derived from standards, laws, policies, and other requirements.

Moral Hazard   Moral hazard is a situation in which one party gets involved in a risky event knowing that it is protected against the risk and the other party will incur the cost. For example, shareholders may want to have managers distribute all profits to them. Managers may be more interested in using profits to increase manager compensation.

Principal-Agent Problem   The problem of motivating one party (the agent) to act on behalf of another (the principal) is known as the *principal-agent problem*. For example, shareholders expect managers to oversee profit generation so distributions can be made to the shareholders. Managers may want to hold back some profits to hedge against future problems involving dropping revenues.

Conflict of Interest   A conflict of interest is a conflict between the private interests and the official responsibilities of a person in a position of trust. For example, a manager is responsible for the impartial selection of vendors to maximize value to the employer but has a close relative bidding on the contract. Selecting the relative may represent a conflict of interest for the manager.

Identifying and Analyzing Risk

Risk identification is the process of recognizing and defining risks. Risk analysis is the systematic process to comprehend the nature of the risk and to determine the level of risk.

Risk Assessment Phase

Risk assessment involves evaluating and comparing the level of risk against predetermined standards, target risk levels, or other criteria. For example, the risk identified is associated with managers and supervisors sexually harassing someone in the workforce. Compared to a standard of zero tolerance for such behavior, the risk may be deemed to be strong if there is only one occurrence.

Identifying Risks

Risk identification is the process of determining risks that could potentially prevent the program, enterprise, or investment from achieving its objectives. For example, an employee complains of sexual harassment coming from one manager. The risk has been identified.

Risk Identification Approaches   There are many tools and techniques for risk identification. Here are some of them:

- **Brainstorming**   This is a freewheeling generation of ideas without criticism of any one until later.

- **Delphi technique**   Here a facilitator distributes a questionnaire to experts, and responses are summarized (anonymously) and circulated among the experts for comments. This technique is used to achieve a consensus of experts and helps to receive unbiased data, ensuring that no one person will have undue influence on the outcome.

- **Interviewing**   This is a discussion with individuals using questions to stimulate responses.

- **Root-cause analysis**   This is for identifying a problem, discovering the causes that led to it, and developing preventive action.
- **Checklist analysis**   This involves comparing each item on the checklist with a set of pre-established criteria.
- **Assumption analysis**   This technique may reveal an inconsistency of assumptions or may uncover problematic assumptions.
- **Diagramming techniques**   This includes cause-and-effect diagrams, system or process flow charts, or influence diagrams (graphical representations of situations, showing the casual influences or relationships among variables and outcomes).
- **SWOT analysis**   This is a structured planning method used to evaluate the strengths, weaknesses, opportunities, and threats (SWOT) involved in a project or in a business venture.
- **Expert judgment**   Individuals who have experience with similar projects may use their judgment through interviews or risk facilitation workshops.

Analyzing Risks

Risk analysis involves evaluating vulnerable assets, describing potential impacts, and estimating losses for each hazard. When you buy common stocks, the potential exists for them to lose some or all of their value.

Risk Analysis Tools   It is helpful to have some tools with which to assess risks to your organization. The following are some of the more popular tools available.

Risk Scorecard   The U.S. Army Materiel Systems Analysis Activity developed a "reliability scorecard" that uses eight critical areas to evaluate a given program's reliability progress. Each element within a category can be given a risk rating of high, medium, or low (red, yellow, or green) or not evaluated (gray). The scorecard weights the elements, normalizes the scores to a 100-point scale, and calculates an overall program risk score and eight category risk scores.

- Risk assessment
- Reliability requirements and planning
- Training and development
- Reliability analysis
- Reliability testing
- Supply chain management
- Failure tracking and reporting
- Verification and validation
- Reliability improvements

Risk Matrix   A simplified example, using a single element from the previous list, is shown here:

Overall Risk Assessment			
Reliability Risk	0%–25%	25%–75%	75%–100%
	Low Risk	Medium Risk	High Risk

In general terms, risks can be classified as low, moderate, high, or extreme, as shown here:

		Impact			
		Negligible	**Marginal**	**Critical**	**Catastrophic**
	Certain	High	High	Extreme	Extreme
	Likely	Moderate	High	High	Extreme
	Possible	Low	Moderate	High	Extreme
Liklelihood	**Unlikely**	Low	Low	Moderate	Extreme
	Rare	Low	Low	Moderate	High

Evaluating Risks

A risk evaluation system is a combination of practices, tools, and methodologies within a risk management system used to measure the potential impacts of risk events on the performance metrics of an organization. So, evaluating risks is the act of measuring potential impacts that various risks will have on the organization's ability to accomplish its objectives. For example, you can identify a risk as the possibility of a work stoppage when the union contract expires. Evaluation of that risk can tell you how well you may expect to keep your business operating using only management personnel during the strike.

Key Risk Indicators

A key risk indicator (KRI) is a measure that indicates how risky an activity is. It is different from a key performance indicator (KPI). The KRI indicates the possibility of a future adverse impact. A KPI measures how well something is being done. Indicators are metrics used to monitor identified risk exposures over time. Therefore, any piece of data that can perform this function may be considered a risk indicator. The indicator becomes "key" when it tracks an especially important risk exposure (a key risk) or it does so especially well (a key indicator), or ideally both. An example is the forecasting of the financial impact of expanding the workforce into international offices in multiple countries. Will that be repaid with profits over time, or will it interfere with profitability? Then, how can HR management impact those potential results?

Risk Register

A risk register acts as a central repository for all risks identified by the organization and, for each risk, includes information such as source, nature, treatment option, existing countermeasures, recommended countermeasures, and so on. ISO 73:2009, "Risk management – Vocabulary," defines a risk register to be "a record of information about identified risks. It can sometimes be referred to as a risk log."

Managing Risks

Once risks have been identified and logged, the next logical step is planning for handling those risks believed to bring negative impacts on the enterprise that cannot be accepted.

Responses to Upside and Downside Risks

Upside and downside risks are two sides of the same coin. Possible adverse outcomes represent downside risk. When there is uncertainty about a desirable outcome, there is upside risk.

Eliminate Uncertainty   Risk can be managed if the uncertainty is eliminated. If you know for certain that there will be an undesirable outcome, there is no risk. You simply avoid entering into the activity that will produce that outcome because you know for certain that it will take place. If someone sets fire to a building, that person knows for certain that the fire will happen. There is no risk, simply a certain undesirable outcome. If you can eliminate the uncertainty of an event, you can control the risk.

Redefine Ownership   Only the person or organization that owns the circumstances will own the risk. If you can redefine ownership of the problem, you can reduce your risk exposure.

- **Share**   Sharing the risk of being an employer can be done, for example, by entering into a joint-employer relationship with an employment leasing agency, sometimes called *professional employer organizations* (PEOs). That won't eliminate risk for either party, but it will double the resources available to combat whatever risk may exist because of having an employee workforce.

- **Transfer**   Transferring risk is done by purchasing insurance policies. Employers are able to reduce their exposure to employee liability through the purchase of employment liability insurance. It can lower the potential for financial loss when employees are found to have engaged in harassment, for example. It is much the same as purchasing fire insurance to protect against financial loss if there is a fire in the workplace.

Increase or Decrease Effect   A way to decrease the effect of fire in the workplace is to install a water sprinkler system. So, if a fire does happen, the sprinkler system can limit the damage or effect of the fire. Employee training programs can act in the same way. Teaching employees about the dangers of harassing behavior can help them reduce their personal exposure to liability while at the same time lowering the employer's liability exposure.

Take No Action   In most circumstances, when faced with various possible courses of action, one of those options is to take no action. When a risk is identified and defined, it may be judged to be in the best interest of the organization to do nothing. Usually this is considered if the impact expected would be minimal or the level of certainty for the outcome is low.

- **Accept**   "We will take the risk" is sometimes heard, meaning the decision is to take no action to eliminate the hazard and just wait to see how things develop. If a safety hazard is identified that would not cause serious harm and can be repaired within the near future, it may be best to simply identify the risk by putting out orange cones, for example, than prohibiting all access to the area. Remediation of the hazard will take place in due time. The risk of injury is minimal, and the level of certainty can be lowered by putting out the cones.

- **Ignore**   When a safety hazard is identified, considered, and ignored, there is no credence given to the level of risk or the certainty of loss. Think about the air bag failures that Takata Industries ignored for several years. That was a decision that didn't work out so well for the company.

Implementing the Risk Management Plan

A risk management plan results from analysis of the circumstances that foresees risks, estimates impacts, and defines responses to issues.

Defining Risk Management Performance Objectives   All business enterprise exists in the world of balancing risks and rewards to produce value. Risk management performance objectives should be part of the overall list of performance objectives generated at each level of the organization. Just like EEO compliance or time reporting, risk management for each component of the organization should be identified by those responsible for the component/department/division.

Integration   Is our risk management process aligned with our strategic decision-making process and existing performance measures? Is our risk management process coordinated and consistent across the entire enterprise?

Communication   Does everyone use the same definition of risk? Are all employees involved in some way with the risk management process, sensing a degree of ownership that will result in organizational success? Proper risk management plans will involve employees in training programs and daily discussions, if only brief, about the "risks facing us today." These are sometimes called *tailgate meetings* where safety topics are common. And, they last only five or ten minutes, and then everyone is off to do their work for the day. At higher levels of the enterprise, the topic of risk management should be present on each staff meeting agenda. That way, it becomes a common topic of conversation, and everyone begins to take some level of ownership in the results.

Emergency Preparedness and Business Continuity

A primary safety axiom is that proper planning can save lives and property. It is a good idea to have a written plan specifying what actions will be taken in any of many various scenarios. There are some basic alternatives for dealing with a disaster, large or small.

We are talking about the entire universe of emergency planning.

Crisis Management Planning and Readiness Process   The first step toward having an emergency response plan is to conduct a risk assessment for your work location. Look at the physical facilities, emergency exits, fire suppression systems, electrical and gas shut-off access, hazardous materials used in the workplace, protective equipment needed for operations, employee training for special equipment, use of proper lock-out/tag-out procedures when working on electrical equipment, and proper handling of carcinogenic substances such as copy machine toner. Answer hypothetical questions such as, "What would we do if someone with a gun walked through our front door?"

Engage key personnel in the development process. Ask people on the production line and in the office what they would do in some circumstances. Get input from experts and nonexperts alike. Then list the responses that should happen for each emergency you listed.

Finally, once the plan is developed, be sure everyone in the workplace knows about it and what to do if an emergency happens.

Manage Risk   Initially, it is important to identify the risks. Then you can move on to identifying how to deal with them effectively. So, what types of risks are we concerned with in the world of human resource management? And, what type of involvement does HR have with those risks?

Types of Organizational Risks	
Type of Risk	**HR Involvement**
Safety Risks • Injury hazards • Illness hazards • Workplace violence hazards • Transportation disaster (loss of multiple employee/executive personnel)	Development of safety plans, routine workplace inspections, corrective action oversight, employee training, insurance company interface.
Equipment Risks • Production failures • Protection failures	Inclusion in safety plans, production line procedures when failure occurs, inclusion of protection failure issues in safety plans.
Facility Risks • Systems failure (heating/cooling/sprinklers) • Security access failure	Provision for action plans in the event of system failures, anticipation of security issues, and preventative measures.

Types of Organizational Risks	
Type of Risk	**HR Involvement**
Employment Risks • Background check/wrongful hiring • Wrongful retention • Employee behavior problems (harassment/discrimination/embezzlement/ethics failure) • Loss of key personnel	Establish criteria for screening new hires' background/behavior issues, preparation of procedures for handling behavior problems and termination procedures, discussion with executives about scenario involving loss of key personnel.
Employee-as-Agent Risks • Management interaction with public • Community involvement	Discussion/training of all managers in the legal agent-relationship definition and how they can represent the organization in community groups.
Business Risks • Business continuation • Data security (employee records/customer records/financial records) • Government intervention	Need for essential records backup, including employee, payroll, medical, investigation, and complaint records. Work with finance and sales/marketing to cover preservation of financial and customer records (orders). Create a plan to preserve HR records when government agencies audit the organization.
Natural Disaster Risks • Fire • Flood (rising or falling water) • Earthquake • Temperature (heat or cold) • Drought	Develop procedures for reacting to natural disasters with differences based on the type of disaster.
International Risks • Differences in laws • Differences in customs	Identify the differences in legal response requirements by country. Identify the expectations of each country's customs during disaster responses.

Develop Contingency Plans   If there is a flood or fire and your workplace is destroyed, the computers, hard drives, on-site backup systems, and filing cabinets may no longer be available. How will you open your business tomorrow morning?

Employers must have a plan for how they will continue operating their organization. What about customer records, accounting records, client data, and payroll information?

This is an area of responsibility where HR professionals should work with others in the organization such as professionals in information technology (IT) and accounting. It should be common practice for backups to be made of all technology systems, especially a human resource information system (HRIS). And, those backups, or at least duplicates of them, should be stored off-site at some secure location. It is necessary for the survival of your organization that it be able to continue operations as quickly as possible with all the records it requires for that to happen.

How will you communicate to employees where they should report to work after such a disaster? Do you plan to use e-mail, text messages, or a telephone tree to contact everyone and pass along instructions? How will you keep supervisors and managers informed? Who will handle media inquiries about the disaster and your plans for the future?

Test and Implement Plans   A key element of disaster recovery is practicing the contingent plan to see whether it will actually work. That's what fire drills are all about. People in the military constantly gripe about having to drill all the time. Those drills are nothing more than rehearsals for the time that the actual event will come to pass and the practiced behavior responses will become essential. The same holds true for civilian organizations. Employees need to practice evacuating their work location so they know for sure which exit they should use and what their assigned rallying point is once outside the building. If there is a disaster involving the loss of key personnel, an emergency response plan should be activated. Ideally, it will have been rehearsed so everyone involved understands their roles and how to play them. Who will be the spokesperson for the company when media representatives come asking for answers to their questions? Who will be responsible for interacting with government officials if that becomes necessary? Who will be guiding the instruction of managers and distributing information to the general employee group?

Debrief and Learn   Make plans and then test them by rehearsing. Evaluate the results of the rehearsal and adjust the plans based on those experiences. Identify where improvements can be made and then make them. Debriefing is the process of meeting to discuss what happened during the practice exercise. Debriefing should gather input from individuals as well as the collective input of managers and employees.

Debriefing is the opportunity to be sure all of the communication channels are open and working accurately. Are all telephone number lists up-to-date? Are other contact points noted and verified? What are the emergency contact points for government resources (fire/ambulance/police/sheriff)? If the plan involves coordination with other organizations, they should be represented in the debriefing session so their input can be gathered and evaluated.

Evaluating Risk Management

 At least once per year, all formal risk management plans should be reviewed and adjusted if it is thought necessary. Those reviews are usually chaired by either the chief HR officer or the chief legal officer in the organization.

Providing Oversight

The role of risk management oversight is commonly assumed by the board of directors. It applies to all forms of risk for the entire enterprise. Since the board is the organizational element responsible for the overall success of the company, identifying how risk management is being handled becomes a key element of the board's responsibilities.

Evaluating Effectiveness of Risk Management Policies and Processes

Obviously, the most effective feedback or evaluation comes from having actually experienced the danger (risk) that plans had been developed to address. When disaster strikes, debriefing sessions or critique meetings should be held to establish what worked well and what needs improvement.

Healthy organizations will conduct periodic tests of their risk management plans through exercises designed to probe every element of reaction to the problem anticipated. There should be critique sessions held following each test to determine what updates should be made to the plans. Then, after a reasonable interval, the plans should be tested again. Some plans (evacuation/earthquake/shelter-in-place) should be tested quarterly. Other plans can be tested once a year, or even less frequently. Some tests can be as simple as the CEO walking into an executive staff meeting and announcing that a test scenario will be run in which the top five executives of the enterprise have all been killed in a plane crash. What will the remaining employees do as a result of hearing "The exercise begins now"? Tests of risk management plans must be customized to the plan.

After-Action Debriefs and Incidents Investigations   How to determine the effectiveness of risk management plan test exercises depends on what the plan involves. Fire reactions and building evacuation can be evaluated by using a stop watch and exercise referees who keep track of when each group of employees has assembled at their emergency contact point outside the building. When testing plans for handling embezzlement or product failure/recalls, the exercise will not be as dramatic. But, it should be evaluated after it has completed to determine whether people followed the plan and what issues they discovered need improvement.

If an employee comes to work one morning to find an alligator sitting on the building's front porch blocking the normal route employees use to enter the building, there needs to be a risk management plan/safety plan implementation that can address that issue. The reaction may be as simple as directing workers to a different entrance. But the incident demands there be a reaction to prevent serious harm to humans. After-incident investigations can shed light on how well the plan worked and people reacted. If the plan was good but people didn't implement it properly, there may be a training need. More frequent practice could be called for. The investigation should provide direction for resolving any remaining issues.

Whistle-Blowing   When an employee (or outside person) blows the whistle on bad behavior going on within the organization, it can result in a public relations nightmare. One of the conditions for which emergency plans are prepared should be disclosure of bad behavior such as a cover-up of illegal activity or simply behavior that is ethically wrong and embarrassing to the employer. What can be made of the story by media representatives will be potentially damaging to the company. Someone will need to be positioned to speak for the company on such issues. There needs to be a predesignated group of key employees who will decide quickly how to address the problem and explain the company's reaction to it when addressing the media.

Evaluating Compliance

Compliance with government regulatory requirements is a complex realm. There are compliance requirements for many different topics.

Examples of Government Compliance Issues	
Government contracts for providing service	Government contracts for construction (buildings/roads/dams)
Government contracts for selling goods (pencils/jet engines/Brussels sprouts)	Government requirements for safety reporting
Requirements for logging driving hours for over-the-road truckers	Requirements for logging batch identifications for drug manufacturers
Requirements for handling of meat in slaughterhouses	Labeling requirements for food processors
"Organic" produce category requirements	Bus driver licensing
Health ordinance requirements for restaurants	Banking requirements for cash-handling limits
IRS requirements for tax records and reporting	Affirmative action requirements for government contractors
Employee demographic reporting requirements on EEO-1/EEO-4	Wage and hour requirements/prohibitions for child labor
Minimum wage requirements	Health insurance requirements

Promoting Continuous Improvement

In 1985, Tom Peters wrote a book entitled *Thriving on Chaos.*[55] In it, he highlighted the Japanese management concept of *Kaizen*, the never-ending quest for perfection. American managers have retitled the concept to *continuous improvement*. Whatever it is called, the idea is to strive each day for a little better quality, quantity, and effort. Peters became famous for, among other things, his suggestion that management by walking around (MBWA) was the most effective approach and produced the greatest positive organizational results. Searching for continuous improvements means employees must be involved by very definition. Managers can't be expected to think of everything, and those who work directly with the process are best able to identify how improvements can be made. Employees are truly the best resource for identifying better ways of doing things.

Functional Area 14— Corporate Social Responsibility

Here is SHRM's BoCK definition: "Corporate Social Responsibility (CSR) represents the organization's commitment to operate in an ethical and sustainable manner by engaging in activities that promote and support philanthropy, transparency, sustainability and ethically sound governance practices."[56]

As an HR professional, your role is to help the organization and its employees to integrate corporate social responsibility (CSR) into the everyday business activities of the organization. CSR reflects how the organization integrates and aligns with its communities as a helping hand for sustaining economic prosperity, social equity, and environmental protection.

Key Concepts

- Approaches to community inclusion and engagement (e.g., representation on community boards, joint community projects, employee volunteerism)
- Creating shared value (e.g., definition, best practices)
- Developing CSR-related volunteer programs (e.g., recruiting and organizing participants)
- Organizational philosophies and policies (e.g., development, integration into the organization)
- Principles of corporate citizenship and governance
- Steps for corporate philanthropy and charitable giving (e.g., selecting recipients, types, donation amounts)

The following are the proficiency indicators that SHRM has identified as key concepts:

For All HR Professionals	For Advanced HR Professionals (SCP Exam)
• Acts as a professional role model and representative of the organization when interacting with the community	• Serves as a leader in community-based volunteer and philanthropic organizations
• Engages in community-based volunteer and philanthropic activities	• Develops CSR strategies that reflect the organization's mission and values
• Identifies and promotes opportunities for HR and the organization to engage in CSR activities	• Ensures that the organization's CSR programs enhance the employee value proposition and have a beneficial impact on HR programs (e.g., recruitment and retention) and/or contribute to the organization's competitive advantage
• Helps staff at all levels understand the societal impact of business decisions and the role of the organization's CSR activities in improving the community	• Creates CSR program activities that engage the organization's workforce and the community at large
• Maintains transparency of HR programs, practices, and policies, where appropriate	• Coordinates with other business leaders to integrate CSR objectives throughout the organization.
• Coaches managers to achieve an appropriate level of transparency in organizational practices and decisions	• Coordinates with other business leaders to develop and implement appropriate levels of corporate self-governance and transparency
• Identifies opportunities for incorporating environmentally responsible business practices and shares them with leadership	• Develops, with other business leaders, strategies that encourage and support environmentally responsible business decisions

PART II

The Ever-Changing and Growing CSR

HR can no longer see CSR as an isolated defensive or tactical action. CSR is now seen as a comprehensive strategic initiative for the organization, aligned with business strategy. CSR now has a global reach and impact, enriching and broadening its communities and beyond. As cultural and political landscapes and opinion shift, so does the need for CSR in an organization.

Is Sustainability the New CSR?

Sustainability practice is in every aspect of doing business today and needs to be ingrained in an organization's culture, becoming an ongoing process and way of doing business. Sustainability is a key focus for many organizations as government and regulatory pressures, societal demands, and even climate change have increased its demands on companies. For organizations, this means a conscious way of doing business and how it impacts their communities, employees, and environments. In addition, businesses must assess social and environmental risks and opportunities with their business decisions. This approach is referred to as the *triple bottom line,* which is the simultaneous delivery of positive results for people, the planet, and profit. Sustainability, such as environmental stewardship, workplace responsibility, human rights protection, and good corporate citizenship, are increasingly part of an organization's social legitimacy. The HR function is critical to achieving success in a sustainability-driven organization.

Redefining Sustainability

Sustainability and the associated accountability efforts within sustainability (behavior that is cognizant of depleting resources that the organization is intertwined with) have also become front and center for CSR. Time, labor, and finances are where HR is involved with the design or implementation of programs. An example of a program would be re-entry into the workforce by former stay-at-home parents. "Green initiatives" along with "environmental footprints" are now prime attention grabbers within CSR. HR departments reducing their paper printing needs by converting to online paperless activities such as employment and benefit forms, employee handbooks, and newsletters are green initiatives. Creation of a paid-time-off volunteerism policy for employees is another popular initiative in CSR.

Today's CSR

Corporate social responsibility involves keeping a watchful eye within the organization's communities, including local, national, and even international. CSR strives to enhance the organization's reputation. Strategic relationship and behaviors are elements involved in CSR activities such as being a member of the Chamber of Commerce or sponsoring a local nonprofit fundraiser creating a *corporate citizenship.* Multiple departments may have responsibility, yet HR is typically the department primarily at the core, absent an organization's official CSR or public relations department.

Forces Shaping Today's CSR

The external forces that typically drive goals and objectives in CSR can be better understood by looking at Figure 6-2.

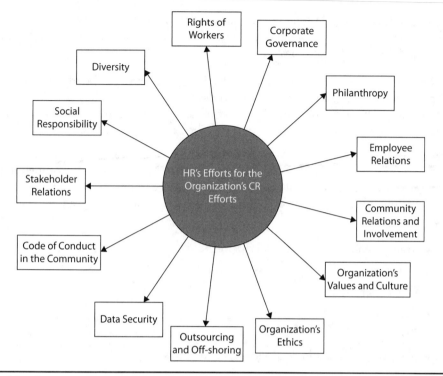

Figure 6-2 Corporate responsibility

According to McKinsey & Company, when identifying the goals and objectives for CSR, it is ideal to use the same analysis tools as used with strategic planning to identify the long-term investment and involvement for the organization.

Creating a CSR Strategy

As mentioned, the CSR of an organization needs to be carefully aligned with the organization's business goals and strategies. As with all strategy initiatives, careful planning must be undertaken. Research into frameworks and existing benchmarks should be involved, and so should the reports of CSR initiatives.

Frameworks, Guidelines, and Examples

Gaining a clear perspective of the work is the best starting point for developing a CSR strategy. There are several international organizations that have provided frameworks and templates, along with guidance for organizations.

- Global Reporting Initiatives' G4 guidelines
- The United Nations Global Compact that developed a broad statement of principles on which a CSR strategy can be based

- The International Organization for Standardization and the Social Accountability International (SA) that created standards addressing specific sustainability issues and social responsibilities

The most widely accepted frameworks and guidelines are briefly described next. Although this are a good starting point to develop your organization's CSR strategy, be sure to tailor them to your organization's industry and unique environments. Review your CSR annually and benchmark against other like organizations.

OECD Guidelines for Multinational Enterprises   The Guidelines for Multinational Enterprises established in 1976 by the Organisation for Economic Co-operation and Development (OECD) is one of the first to address corporate governance. Since 1976 the guidelines have had many revisions; 2008 saw the most recent version, which covered the following:

- Transparency governance and disclosure
- Environment
- Consumer interests
- Workforce relations
- Bribery
- Science and technology application and access

United Nations Global Compact   Introduced in 2000, the United Nations Global Compact has ten principles addressing human rights, labor, environmental, and anticorruption issues. When an organization commits to uphold these principles, it also agrees to annually report on the progress, including specific actions taken.[57]

The UN Global Compact's Ten Principles

Human Rights

Principle 1: Businesses should support and respect the protection of internationally proclaimed human rights.
Principle 2: Make sure they are not complicit in human rights abuses.

Labor

Principle 3: Businesses should uphold the freedom of association and the effective recognition of the right to collective bargaining.
Principle 4: Eliminate all forms of forced and compulsory labor.
Principle 5: Abolish child labor.
Principle 6: Eliminate discrimination in respect to employment and occupation.

Environment

Principle 7: Businesses are asked to support a precautionary approach to environmental challenges.

> Principle 8: Undertake initiatives to promote greater environmental responsibility.
>
> Principle 9: Encourage the development and diffusion of environmentally friendly technologies.

Anti-Corruption

> Principle 10: Businesses should work against corruption in all its forms, including extortion and bribery.

Caux Principles   The Caux Round Table (CRT) principles believe that the world business community should play an important role in improving economic and social conditions. In 1986, a network of business leaders from Japan, Europe, and the United States (aka the Caux Round Table) began meeting because of mounting trade tensions. In 1994 they developed and formalized a set of international business standards based on the values of human dignity and working together for the common good. These became known as the *Caux principles,* which was one of the earliest employer-led efforts for an international code of ethics. The key Caux principles[58] are as follows:

- **Principle 1: Respect stakeholders beyond shareholders.**   Contribute value to society and act with honesty and fairness toward customers, suppliers, competitors, employees, and the community.

- **Principle 2: Contribute to economic, social, and environmental development.**   Maintain investments in the community and its economy that support the environment and social well-being as well as organizational income.

- **Principle 3: Build trust by going beyond the letter of the law.**   Know the spirit and intent of the law and abide by them rather than just the letter of the law.

- **Principle 4: Respect rules and conventions.**   Respect local cultures and traditions everywhere the organization operates.

- **Principle 5: Support responsible globalization.**   Perhaps the most controversial of the Caux principles, this calls for reforming domestic rules and regulations where they impinge global commerce. It supports open and fair multilateral trade.

- **Principle 6: Respect the environment.**   Protect environmental needs while conducting business so the next generations will have the advantage of a secure planet.

- **Principle 7: Avoid illicit activities.**   Corruption of all kinds, bribery, money laundering, drug trafficking, human trafficking, and other illegal and illicit activities are not condoned.

ISO 26000   The ISO is the world's largest developer of voluntary international standards. ISO 26000 is the international standard developed to help organizations effectively assess and address those social responsibilities that are relevant and significant to their mission and vision; operations and processes; customers, employees, communities, and other stakeholders; and the environment. ISO 26000 provides guidance on key themes of social responsibility across a wide spectrum of topics; it's a quality standard, though not a certification. The principles have social and environmental responsibility and guidance for action/implementation. ISO 26000 addresses seven core subjects of social responsibility as shown in Figure 6-3.[59]

SA8000   Social Accountability International (SAI) is the international nongovernmental organization that created SA8000. SA8000 is an auditable certification standard that encourages organizations to develop, maintain, and apply socially acceptable practices in the workplace. It is one of the first certification standards (1997), focusing on human rights and labor relationship, that provides process and performance criteria. It is based on both United Nations and International Labor Organization (ILO) standards.

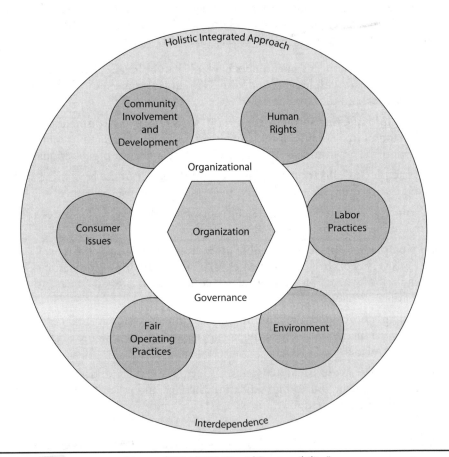

Figure 6-3   The seven core subjects of ISO 26000, "Social Responsibility"

Close to 2,500 facilities with approximately 1.5 million employees around the globe have adopted SA8000. It is frequently used as a tool for ensuring human rights in extended supply chains (aka slave labor). It not only focuses on standards of performance but also on systems that need to be in place for management. In the latest version as of June 2014, nine key areas are the focus of SA8000.

- Human rights and labor relations
- Child labor
- Forced or compulsory labor
- Health and safety
- Freedom of association and right to collective bargaining
- Discrimination
- Disciplinary practices
- Working hours
- Remuneration
- Management systems

GRI G4 Sustainability Reporting Guidelines The Global Reporting Initiative (GRI) G4 Sustainability Guidelines are the universally accepted standard for global reporting or a company's sustainability effort and progress. The main goal is for organizations to identify and report on what GRI terms *mertial aspects* that are significant to a business's economic, environmental, and social impacts that influence the decisions of its stakeholders. The guidelines are divided into two parts.

- Reporting Principles and Standard Disclosures (criteria for preparing the sustainability reporting)
- Implementation Manual (explanations for applying the principles for the reporting)

GRI has other supplementary guidelines, listed here:

- Assistance with G4 efforts
- Guidelines for specific business sectors such as oil and gas, financial services, food processing, media, and so on
- Interactive guides that are online for assisting with specific concerns and issues such as risk management and supply chain
- A sustainability disclosure database providing URL links to corporate CSR reports and scorecards

The G4 list is organized into categories,[60] as shown here:

The G4 Sustainability Reporting Guidelines: Categories	
Category: Economic	**Category: Environmental**
1. Economic Performance 2. Indirect Economic Impacts 3. Market Presence 4. Procurement Practices	1. Compliance 2. Effluents and Waste 3. Emissions 4. Energy 5. Environmental Grievance Mechanisms 6. Materials 7. Products and Services 8. Overall 9. Supplier Environmental Assessment 10. Transport 11. Water Biodiversity

Subcategory: Human Rights	Subcategory: Labor Practices and Decent Work	Subcategory: Product Responsibility	Subcategory: Society
1. Assessment 2. Child Labor 3. Forced or Compulsory Labor 4. Freedom of Association & Collective Bargaining 5. Human Rights Grievance Mechanisms 6. Indigenous Rights 7. Investment 8. Non-discrimination 9. Security Practices 10. Supplier Human Rights Assessment	1. Diversity and Equal Opportunity 2. Employment 3. Equal Remuneration for Women & Men 4. Labor Grievance Mechanisms 5. Labor/ Management Relations 6. Occupational Health & Safety 7. Supplier Assessment for Labor Practices 8. Training & Education	1. Compliance 2. Customer Health & Safety 3. Customer Privacy 4. Marketing Communications 5. Product & Service Labeling	1. Anticompetitive Behavior 2. Anti-corruption 3. Compliance 4. Grievance Mechanisms for Impacts on Society 5. Local Communities 6. Public Policy 7. Supplier Assessment for Impacts on Society

KPMG Survey of Corporate Responsibility Reporting   KPMG has been tracking the trends in corporate responsibility reporting since 1993. KPMG provides a detailed examination of what is being reported and the quality of the reporting. KPMG reporting is helpful with the following:

- Identifying areas that organizations need to address and how to report and measure on the results and outcomes.

- Providing support in making the business case for a sustainability strategy for an organization. This section of the reporting has interviews with industry leaders who discuss how to best maximize the value of sustainability.

You can find more information on KPMG reporting surveys at www.kpmg.com.

Philanthropy and Volunteerism

Corporate philanthropy has been around for decades and was typically the influence of senior management within a corporation. Although corporate philanthropic activities such as monetary donations, percentage of sale, and cooperative programs are still widely in existence, the tide has shifted to a more strategic focus on donations, one that affiliates with the organization's relevant business or branding. A good example of this is the cosmetic company Avon, which is widely known as a corporate sponsor for breast cancer research. The company's customer base is relevant to the majority of affected individuals with breast cancer, women.

Employee Volunteerism

An aspect of CSR is employee volunteerism. It has been growing in popularity in organizations and for good reason. Volunteerism can positively impact employee engagement. Surveys have indicated that when employees frequently participate in company-sponsored volunteer programs, then they are more likely to feel a strong connection and sense of belong at work, which is good for retention. While volunteering sounds like a win-win for everyone, in practice there can be some pitfalls that HR professionals need to be aware of. Chief among them is ensuring that the activities are truly voluntary, especially if the employer is not paying employees to participate.

A great risk for employers centers around the Fair Labor Standards Act (FLSA). An employer can't require an employee to "volunteer." As an example, let's say a company organizes a disaster relief effort for a community recently hit by a hurricane and asks for employees to volunteer to help hand out water and blankets or provide meals. If getting involved is truly voluntary, then that is perfectly fine. But once it's required of any employee, the employee is no longer a volunteer, and it's considered time on the payroll clock. Companies sometimes get so caught up in pushing employees to get involved that they cross this line even though their intentions were for the good of all.

Another related risk for for-profit companies is that there is no such thing as "volunteering" for a for-profit company. If the company "suffers or permits" an employee to work, the employee has to be paid at least minimum wage under FLSA. This issue has shown up recently related to the use of unpaid interns.

Organizations need a program and policy around volunteerism so employees and management completely tow the FLSA line and understand what can and should not be expected of the workforce. Without a policy, there can be misunderstandings and ill-will on the part of employees. Having a policy or process helps to clarify expectations.

Functional Area 15—U.S. Employment Law and Regulations

Here is SHRM's BoCK definition: "U.S. Employment Law and Regulations refers to the knowledge and application of all relevant laws and regulations in the United States related to employment—provisions that set the parameters and limitations for each JR functional area and for organizations overall."[61]

As an HR professional, you are responsible for the compliance of HR programs and policies to be in alignment with employment laws and regulations. You may be educating the workforce and leadership, coaching executives on various matters and options, and tracking compliance with required reporting. It's one of the most important focuses of the HR professional in an organization.

Key Concepts

The key concepts within this functional area are in six broad categories of U.S. laws, regulations, and Supreme Court cases relating to employment. The examples listed here from the SHRM BoCK[62] are not an exhaustive list, nor are the categories. Please refer to Appendix B in this book. Also know that state, municipal, and other local-level laws, regulations, and cases are not included.

- Compensation
  - Employee Retirement Income Security Act of 1974 (ERISA)
  - Fair Labor Standards Act of 1938 (FLSA; Wage-Hour bill; Wagner-Connery Wages and Hours Act) and amendments
  - Equal Pay Act of 1963 (amending FLSA)
  - Lilly Ledbetter Fair Pay Act of 2009
- Employee relations
  - Labor Management Relations Act of 1947 (LMRA; Taft-Hartley Act)
  - National Labor Relations Act of 1935 (NLRA; Wagner Act; Wagner-Connery Labor Relations Act)
  - NLRB vs. Weingarten (1974)
  - Lechmere, Inc. vs. NLRB (1992)
- Job safety and health
  - Drug-Free Workplace Act of 1988
  - Guidelines on Sexual Harassment
  - Occupational Safety and Health Act of 1970
- Equal employment opportunity
  - Age Discrimination in Employment Act of 1967 (ADEA) and amendments
  - Americans with Disability Act of 1990 (ADA) and amendments

- Civil Rights Acts
- Equal Employment Opportunity Act of 1972
- Uniform Guidelines on Employee Selection Procedures (1978)
- Griggs vs. Duke Power Co. (1971)
- Phillips vs. Martin Marietta Corp. (1971)
- Leave and benefits
  - Family and Medical Leave Act of 1993 (FMLA; expanded 2008, 2010)
  - Patient Protection and Affordable Care Act (ACA "Obamacare")
  - National Federation of Independent Business vs. Sebelius (2012)
- Miscellaneous protection laws
  - Employee Polygraph Protection Act of 1988
  - Genetic Information Nondiscrimination Act of 2008 (GINA)

The following are the proficiency indicators that SHRM has identified as key concepts:

For All HR Professionals	For Advanced HR Professionals (SCP Exam)
• Maintains a current working knowledge of relevant domestic and global employment laws • Ensures that HR programs, practices, and policies align and comply with laws and regulations • Coaches employees at all levels in understanding and avoiding illegal and noncompliant HR-related behaviors (e.g., illegal terminations or discipline, unfair labor practices) • Brokers internal or external legal services for interpretation of employment laws	• Maintains current, expert knowledge of relevant domestic and global employment laws • Establishes and monitors criteria for organizational compliance with laws and regulations • Educates and advises senior leadership on HR-related legal and regulatory compliance issues • Oversees fulfillment of compliance requirements of HR programs, practices, and policies • Ensures that HR technologies facilitate compliance and reporting requirements (e.g., tracking employee accidents, safety reports)

HR and the Legislative and Regulatory Environment

Legislatures in state houses around the country, and in Congress at the nation's capital, have been busy in recent years placing more worker protections into law. Where the legislatures would not act, President Obama took the reins and placed requirements on employers through the federal contracting regulations. With approximately 60,000 federal contractors, from small companies with only 50 employees to mega-corporations like Boeing and General Motors, a great many changes can be accomplished through the federal contracting employer community.

Organizational Compliance

Compliance has become expensive for employers, in and out of the federal contracting world. In the first few years of this century, the federal government has enacted the following rules regarding employee management. You will find all of these explained in Chapter 3.

- 2000: The Needlestick Safety and Prevention Act
- 2001: The Economic Growth and Tax Relief Reconciliation Act
- 2001: The USA Patriot Act
- 2002: The IRS Intermediate Sanctions
- 2002: The Sarbanes-Oxley Act
- 2002: The Homeland Security Act
- 2003: The Fair and Accurate Credit Transactions Act
- 2006: The Pension Protection Act
- 2008: Jobs for Veterans Act
- 2008: Americans with Disabilities Act Amendments Act
- 2008: The Genetic Information Nondiscrimination Act
- 2008: The Mental Health Parity and Addiction Equity Act
- 2008: The National Defense Authorization Act
- 2009: The Lilly Ledbetter Fair Pay Act
- 2009: The American Recovery and Reinvestment Act
- 2009: The Health Information Technology for Economic and Clinical Health Act
- 2010: The Dodd-Frank Wall Street Reform and Consumer Protection Act
- 2010: The Patient Protection and Affordable Care Act
- 2012: The FAA Modernization and Reform Act

In addition to these federal laws, states have been busy working on their own versions of employee protections. Those protections vary widely, and HR professionals find themselves faced with having to track and adapt to changing requirements from one state to another. International enterprises have even more challenges with compliance requirements. Other countries have quite different views of employee management requirements. HR professionals must constantly be monitoring the legal updates to be sure they are allocating proper budget amounts for compliance work and covering all of the requirements placed on them by these different jurisdictions.

U.S. Laws and Regulations

Chapter 3 details the federal laws most commonly impacting HR professionals who are responsible for compliance in interstate commerce organizations. You should be familiar with all of these requirements, regardless of your specific corporate obligations.

Employee Records Management

There are increasing obligations for records management in today's climate. It used to be that "good management practices" were the guiding element in determining how an employer established records creation and retention. That's not so any longer.

There are three reasons why proper recordkeeping is a requirement for employers. First, it simply makes good business sense to have accurate information handy and organized when you want to use it. Second, most business owners and managers will eventually encounter the need to produce documentation about employee performance and work history. Having the proper records to retrieve is vital when the need presents itself. Third, some employee records are required by federal or state governments and must be kept somewhere. Organizing them by employee name makes access easy.

There are some important cautions to be given about the subject of identifiable employee information. Generally, state laws permit employees the right to examine their personal employment records. This simply allows individuals the opportunity to confirm information in the file and identify any specific information that is believed to be incorrect. Employees are not universally guaranteed the right to copies of all file contents, however. As the employer, you usually have the right to control the time and location of these examinations as long as you are reasonable in doing so. The objective, of course, is to ensure accuracy of information about each person. In most states, ownership of the personnel file and its contents rests with the employer who maintains it.

Access to information about employees should be strictly limited to those people in your business with a need to use the information in their jobs. Many states are aggressive protectors of employee privacy, and random or unauthorized access to personnel files can bring on severe penalties. Make sure that you store personnel files in a secure location and that they are not left unattended even during the business day. When asked by people outside the company to provide "verification" of certain employment information about your employees, make it a practice to confirm only the information your employees have authorized you to release. Employment verifications are usually required to support such things as mortgage applications, credit applications, and the like. Employee authorization should be in writing and specify the information they want you to reveal. Tell your employee the policy is designed for their protection.

Job applicants may not have decisions about their applications made based on protected categories such as race, color, sex, religion, national origin, and so on. Therefore, having any information on the application that identifies these categories is inappropriate and may be considered illegal. It is permissible, and for some employers required, to request demographic data from job applicants. This information is directed to a location separate from the hiring manager, however, to avoid even the suspicion of discrimination.

For employees (someone you have put on your payroll), it is necessary to have information in the personnel file that would be considered illegal to gather prior to the job offer being made. For example, you need a birth date to enroll your employee in health insurance and life insurance programs. As long as such information is used for legitimate purposes, employers will have no problem (see Chapter 3).

Personnel File

A *personnel file* is often a collection of record files maintained by various people in various locations. The central file is usually maintained by the HR department. However, additional employee records could be located in the training department, in the labor relations department, and in the desk of the immediate supervisor. Each of these files contains different information, yet they all comprise personnel records. Taken together, they represent the personnel file.

The following should be in a personnel file when circumstances require them:

Employment Request for Application

- Employee's original employment application
- Prescreening application notes
- College recruiting interview report form
- Employment interview report form
- Education verification
- Employment verification
- Other background verification
- Rejection letter
- Employment offer letter
- Employment agency agreement if hired through an agency
- Employee handbook acknowledgment form showing receipt of handbook
- Checklist from new employee orientation showing subjects covered
- Veterans/disabled self-identification form
- Transfer requests
- Relocation offer records
- Relocation report
- Security clearance status
- Payroll
- W-4 form
- Weekly time sheets
- Individual attendance record
- Pay advance request record
- Garnishment orders and records
- Authorization for release of private information
- Authorization for all other payroll actions

Performance Appraisals

- New employee progress reports
- Performance appraisal forms
- Performance improvement program records

Training and Development

- Training history records
- Training program applications/requests
- Skills inventory questionnaire
- Training evaluation forms
- In-house training notification letters
- Training expense reimbursement records

Employee Separations

- Exit interview form
- Final employee performance appraisal
- Exit interviewer's comment form
- Record of documents given with final paycheck

Benefits

- Emergency contact form
- Medical/dental/vision coverage waiver/drop form
- Vacation accrual/taken form
- Request for nonmedical leave of absence
- Retirement application
- Payroll deduction authorizations
- COBRA notification/election
- Hazardous substance notification and or reports
- Tuition reimbursement application and or payment records
- Employer concession and or discount authorization
- Annual benefits statement acknowledgment
- Safety training/meeting attendance/summary forms

Wage/Salary Administration

- Job description form
- Job analysis questionnaire
- Payroll authorization form
- Fair Labor Standards Act exemption test
- Compensation history record
- Compensation recommendations
- Notification of wage and or salary increase/decrease

Employee Relations

- Report of coaching/counseling session
- Employee Assistance Program consent form
- Commendations
- Employee written warning notice
- Completed employee suggestion forms
- Suggestion status reports

The following should *not* be in a personnel file:

Medical Records

- Physician records of examination
- Diagnostic records
- Laboratory test records
- Drug screening records
- Any of the records listed previously in the discussion on HIPAA
- Any other medical records with personally identifiable information about individual employees

Investigation Records

- Discrimination complaint investigation information
- Legal case data
- Accusations of policy/legal violations

Security Clearance Investigation Records

- Background investigation information
- Personal credit history

- Personal criminal conviction history
- Arrest record

Insupportable Opinions

- Marginal notes on any document indicating management bias or discrimination (for example, comments about an applicant's race, sex, age, disability, national origin, or other protected class membership)

Medical File

The federal Health Insurance Portability and Accountability Act of 1996 (HIPAA) requires employers and health care providers to protect medical records as confidential, separate, and apart from other business records. That means you may no longer retain medical information in a personnel file. Here are some examples of information you should extract from your personnel files and place in separately protected files as medical information:

- Health insurance application form
- Life insurance application form
- Request for medical leave of absence, regardless of reason
- Personal accident reports
- Workers' compensation report of injury or illness
- OSHA injury and illness reports
- Any other form or document that contains private medical information for a specific employee

Questions about employee access to review their personnel file come up frequently. Each employer should have a policy addressing such questions that complies with state requirements. Federal law does not address the question. Government employees and private sector employers are usually controlled by state laws. So, multistate employers must comply with requirements in all of the states in which they operate.

Investigation File

Any time a complaint is lodged or law enforcement agencies get involved with individual employees, it may be necessary to conduct an investigation of facts. Each time that happens, a written record should be created that documents what investigative steps were taken and what actions resulted from them. Complaints of illegal employment discrimination are a good example.

These files will have specific employee-identifiable information that may be of a sensitive personal nature. Facts may involve criminal activity or behavior that could result in civil action. For the sake of privacy, each investigation file should be held under the same security provisions as medical records. Only those people having a need to access the content of the files should be allowed access. Records should be secured at all times so passersby cannot pull open a file drawer and remove documents.

Recordkeeping Legal Compliance

As with many HR issues, retention requirements do change from time to time. Be sure you confirm the requirements for your situation before destroying any records. Because these requirements are fluid in nature, we suggest you confirm your specific needs through discussion with your management attorney or by checking the Internet for guidance. Be careful about relying on the Internet without knowing your source, however. You still have the responsibility and the liability for proper records retention even if you get bad advice from an Internet source.

Some possible sources include the following:

- www.management-advantage.com/products/retainrecords.htm
- http://nctc.fws.gov/courses/references/job-aids/supervisors/suprefdocs/ documents/FederalRecordRetentionGuidelines.pdf
- www.nationalscanning.com/document-retention-guidelines.html

The following table lists some of the most common federal requirements for record retention:

Federal Records Retention Requirements		
Record Required	**Retention Period**	**Requirement Citation**
Wages, Hours, Working Conditions		
Payroll records • Name • Address • Social Security number • Occupation • Hours worked each day (nonexempt employees) • Wages paid • Payday records • Straight time and overtime • Payroll deductions • Union collective bargaining agreements • Qualified benefit plans • Trust records • Employee notices • Sales and purchasing records	Four years from date of last entry (according to the IRS)	Fair Labor Standards Act of 1938 (29 U.S.C. Sec 201-219)

Federal Records Retention Requirements		
Record Required	**Retention Period**	**Requirement Citation**
Payroll records • Basic time and earnings cards • Wage rate tables • Work time schedules • Order, shipping, billing records • Records of additions to or deductions from wages • Unemployment compensation contributions	Two years from the date of last entry	Fair Labor Standards Act of 1938 (29 U.S.C. Sec 201-219)
Payroll records • Any report required by the Secretary of Labor • All backup data required to prepare required reports (including vouchers, worksheets, receipts, dispute resolutions)	Five years after filing report based on records	Labor Management Reporting & Disclosure Act of 1959 (29 U.S.C. Sec 433-436
Occupational Safety and Health Records		
• Log of occupational injuries or illnesses resulting in medical treatment (other than first aid), loss of consciousness or restriction of work or motion, transfer or termination of employment	Five years minimum following injury or illness	Occupational Safety and Health Act of 1970 (29 U.S.C. Sec 51, *et.sec.*, 29 C.F.R. Sec 1904-2, 1904.4, 12904.6)
• OSHA 300 report posted each year from February 1 through April 30 • Hazardous condition exposures • Medical tests and screening • Employee medical records • Allegations of employee exposure • Heavy equipment operation records	Five years after the year reported; up to 30 years after employment ends	29 C.F.R. 1904.2, 1904.4, 1904.6 Occupational Safety and Health Act of 1970 (29 U.S.C. Sec 51 *et.sec.*, 29 C.F.R. Sec 1904.32(a)(1), 1904.32(b)(6))

Federal Records Retention Requirements		
Record Required	**Retention Period**	**Requirement Citation**
Nondiscrimination, EEO, and Affirmative Action Records		
• Employment records (hiring, promotion, demotion, transfer, layoff, termination, compensation changes, training selection) • Payroll records (name, address, birth date, occupation, rate of pay, days worked each week, compensation earned each week) • Job descriptions • Union agreements and contracts • Retirement, pension, and insurance plans • Seniority and merit system descriptions and records	One year from the date of personnel action, or until any discrimination charge is resolved Three years for affirmative action employers unless employer has fewer than 150 employees or does not have a government contract at least $150,000; then, the retention requirement is 2 years from the date of making the record or the personnel action taken	Civil Rights Act of 1964, Title VII (42 U.S.C. Sec 2000e-5, 2000e-17) Age Discrimination in Employment Act of 1967 (29 U.S.C. Sec 621-634)
• Employment requisitions • Job advertisements • Job applications and testing documents • Affirmative action plans and all supporting evidence of good faith efforts to implement the plans • Standard Form 100 (EEO-1, EEO-4, EEO-3, EEO-5)	One year (same as Title VII) Three years for affirmative action employers with the same exceptions shown for Title VII	Civil Rights Act of 1964, Executive Order 11246 (41 C.F.R. 60-1.12; 60-2.32; 60-250.80; 60-741.80)
• Interviewer records and notes • Selection decisions • Physical exam reports	Three years for affirmative action employers with the same exceptions shown for Title VII	Vietnam Era Veterans Readjustment Assistance Act (41 C.F.R. 60-250; 60-1.12)

Federal Records Retention Requirements

Record Required	Retention Period	Requirement Citation

Family and Medical Leaves

Record Required	Retention Period	Requirement Citation
• Basic payroll data showing additions/deductions from wages and total compensation paid • Dates for FMLA leave • Hours for FMLA leave • Notices given to employees regarding FMLA • Employee requests for FMLA leave • All benefit documents and information about paid/unpaid leave status • Benefit premium information • Any dispute or complaint from employee about FMLA leave	Three years from the making of the record	Family and Medical Leave Act of 1993

Income Tax Records

Record Required	Retention Period	Requirement Citation
• All payroll-related records (including general ledgers, cash, books, journals, voucher registers, etc.); may be retained in magnetic tapes, discs, and other machine-readable data media used in accounting processing; microfilm systems must be complete, used consistently in the business and properly indexed; retrieved data must be legible, and taxpayer must provide IRS with written procedures governing the system and its operation • Name, address, account number, total amount, and date of each payment • Period of services covered by each payment • Amount of wages subject to withholding • Amount of tax collected • Explanation for any discrepancy between total income and taxable income • Fair market value and date of each noncash payment • Form W-4 for each employee • All other supporting documents relating to each employee's individual tax status	15 years (assessment period of 3 years plus collection period of 10 years plus 2 years for payment of refund) W-4 kept for as long as in effect plus 4 years	Treasury Regulations Sec 1.446-1(a)(4); 1.6001-1(a); 1.6001-1(b); 1.6001-1(e); 301.6501(a)-1; 3016501(e)-1; 301.6511(d)-1; 301.6501(c)-1; 31.6001-5 IRS Sec 6502(a); 3402

Federal Records Retention Requirements		
Record Required	**Retention Period**	**Requirement Citation**
Unemployment Tax		
• Total pay, including amounts withheld for any reason • Wages subject to tax • Contributions to state unemployment funds	Four years after tax is due or paid	Federal Unemployment Tax Act (Internal Revenue Code Sec 3301-3311)
Social Security and Medicare Tax		
• Name, address, and Social Security number of all employees • Total amount and date of each payment and period covered by payment • Amount of total wages subject to tax • Amount of employee tax collected for each pay period • Explanation of any difference between total pay and taxable pay • Details of adjustment or settlement of taxes • Records of tips received by employees including statements of tips provided by employees • All employer filing records	Four years after tax is due or paid, whichever is later	Treasury Regulations Sec 6001-2
Work Authorization Records		
• Form I-9 for each employee hired after November 6, 1986 • Forms I-9 kept in a file separate from other personnel records • Student work permits	Three years from date of hire, or 1 year after termination of employment whichever is later	Immigration Reform and Control Act of 1986 (8 U.S.C. Sec 1324a, *et seq.*)
Polygraph Exams		
• Statement of reasons for conducting the examination • Copy of statement given to examinee about time and place of examination • Copies of opinions, reports, etc., to employer from examiner	Three years after exam	Employee Polygraph Protection Act (29 U.S.C. Sec 2001-2009; 29 C.F.R. Sec 801.1-801.75)

Federal Records Retention Requirements

Record Required	Retention Period	Requirement Citation
Public Works Contracts: Prevailing Wages		
• Contract number and period each employee was engaged on the contract • Detailed pay records for each employee for each day worked • Record showing all employees paid prevailing benefits or their equivalent value	Two years	Davis-Bacon Act (40 U.S.C. Sec 276a-276a-5)
• Wage and hour records for all "laborers and mechanics" employed in construction and repair of public works facilities • Records showing all employees paid at least the prevailing minimum wage • Age certificate for each employee younger than 19	Three years	Walsh-Healey Act (41 U.S.C. Sec 34-45) Service Contract Act
Pension Plans		
• Records sufficient to determine benefits due to employees • Welfare and pension records • Supporting documents for ERISA filings	Permanent Five years Six years after filing	Employee Retirement Income Security Act of 1974 (29 U.S.C. Chapter 18, Sec 1001-1381) Welfare and Pension Plans Disclosure Act (29 C.F.R. 308)
Union-Related Records		
• Collective bargaining agreements • Organizing records • Correspondence with union	Seven years from conclusion of contract	National Labor Relations Act
Other Personnel Records		
Some personnel records should be retained for even longer than required by individual laws; here are our recommendations: • Attendance records • Employee training • All verification of job applicant references • Verification of previous employment requests • HIPAA employee advisory record	Three years after termination	Best practices

Federal Records Retention Requirements		
Record Required	**Retention Period**	**Requirement Citation**
• Employee awards • Employee commendations • Disciplinary action records • Requests for transfer	Five years after termination	Best practices
• Job descriptions • Performance evaluations • Wage attachments or garnishment notices	Six years after termination or update	Best practices
• Employer property records showing employee issue of property	Duration of employment	Best practices
• Employment applications • Job offer letters • Records of pay changes since date of hire • Benefits beneficiary designation or changes • Benefits request form • Performance evaluations • Policy receipts with employee signatures • All employee training logs • Leaves of absence taken • Notices of union membership/dues deduction • Education records • Termination records • Exit interviews	Permanent	Best practices

Records Destruction　Once a record has reached its expiration date (been retained for the period required by law), it should be destroyed. Destruction is something that should be done by shredding so that records cannot be reconstructed by someone rifling through the trash bin.

There are commercial records storage and destruction companies almost everywhere in the United States. For a fee, they will come to your work site, collect the records you want to have destroyed, and either shred them in their truck while at your location or take them back to a central location where the documents will be shredded. Some specialize in certain industries such as medical records.

SHRM-SCP

As with other subject areas, the difference between SHRM-CP and SHRM-SCP requirements lies with the level of policy involvement. Strategic policy development is in the realm of the senior HR responsibilities.

For example, developing a records retention policy requires involvement of all operations, departments, and support organizations such as accounting and payroll, benefits administration, legal, and safety administration. Coordinating input from all of those sources requires a level of skill defined as "senior" for the human resource professional.

Senior Certified Professionals (SCPs) must be masters of all the knowledge required of federal laws and regulations. They must also be capable of understanding how those compliance requirements impact their daily interactions with employees and managers. The formulation of strategic policies is the result of a process built on knowledge, skill, and experience.

Chapter Review

In this chapter, you studied workplace issues such as the global context, diversity and inclusion, risk management, and corporate social responsibility. All of these are based on the foundation of employment law and regulations that are thoroughly reviewed in Chapter 3. You saw how contemporary HR organizations are influenced by global issues even if they are not themselves multinational. HR professionals will be expected to increasingly know and manage according to these influences as years pass and societies change.

Questions

1. What is diaspora?
   A. Any medical condition that presents as an upset stomach
   B. Any people or ethnic population forced or induced to leave the traditional homeland
   C. Any common grouping of workers who commute across international borders
   D. Any group of people who are collectively working to upgrade their personal skills

2. What does guarded globalization mean?
   A. Developing nations are wary of opening more industries to multinational companies and are zealously protecting local interests.
   B. Countries are slow to invest in globalization.
   C. Developing nations believe it is unwise to export too much of their national resources.
   D. Developed countries choose not to participate with certain developing countries in trade exchanges.

3. What did Perlmutter identify?
   A. Certain countries don't behave fairly in international trade agreements.
   B. Developing countries are the best type of trade partners.
   C. Unknowns must be revealed before international trade can begin.
   D. Classifying alternative management orientations can be classified into four categories.

4. HR's role in setting up global business presence involves which of the following?

   A. Updating the employee handbook for the new location languages

   B. Providing accounting with the payroll tax withholding rates for the new location(s)

   C. Providing due diligence in issues related to the workforce

   D. Issuing newsletter updates about the progress being made in opening distant locations.

5. When placing an employee on an international assignment, it is important to do what?

   A. Provide ongoing support for the individual and their family in the new location

   B. Provide anything needed before the family lands in the new location

   C. Provide assistance with language issues before the move takes place

   D. Provide publicity in the corporate newsletter showcasing the newly appointed employee and the assignment.

6. Diversity and Inclusion touch:

   A. All organizations in the modern workplace

   B. Only employers with 50 or more workers on the payroll

   C. Only people of color

   D. Only employers settling government complaints

7. Diversity and Inclusion programs:

   A. Explain that minorities and women must be hired at a certain rate

   B. Provide managers with mandates for recruiting only minorities

   C. Make it possible for all employees to contribute to the workforce

   D. Supersede EEO and affirmative action programs

8. Diversity and Inclusion programs should reach out to:

   A. Employees of competitor organizations

   B. Veterans and disabled people for their viewpoints and experiences

   C. Government auditors for validation of the employer's program

   D. News organizations that can provide justification for a diversity program

9. Employee affinity groups can provide:

   A. Mandates for hiring more people like those in the affinity group

   B. Enticement for other employees to form their own groups as a defense

   C. Input on diversity programs and suggestions for changes

   D. Secrets to why language options should be permitted

10. Diversity and Inclusion programs can include:

   A. Special benefits based on cultural background

   B. Special hiring bonus based on minority or female status

   C. Executive endorsement of hiring preferences

   D. Celebrations based on specific cultural groupings

11. Employment risks are the potential for losing things of value. They can include which of the following?

   A. Confidential employee data and complaint investigation records

   B. Job requisition information and published news articles on the organization

   C. Executive biographical summaries and SEC required reports

   D. Visitor comment cards and building maintenance records

12. What are key risk indicators (KRIs)?

   A. Indicators of how well something is being done

   B. Indicators of how much insurance covers the employer

   C. Indicators of future adverse impact

   D. Indicators of company risks compared to competitor risks

13. What is a risk register?

   A. A financial account of insurance costs

   B. A record of information about identified risks

   C. A computer device to monitor IT performance

   D. A record of automotive repairs due to accidents

14. The first step toward having an emergency response plan is to:

   A. Be sure all emergency exits are properly marked

   B. Write a policy for evacuation in an emergency

   C. Conduct a risk assessment for your work location

   D. Assign development for the emergency plan to an HR person

15. Contingency plans explain:

   A. How to handle whistle-blower exposure

   B. How to bring the organization into governmental compliance

   C. How to respond to discrimination complaints

   D. How the organization will continue running in the event of a catastrophe

PART II

16. Which CSR guideline framework was one of the first initiatives relating to corporate governance?

    A. United Nations Global Compact

    B. OECD

    C. The Caux principles

    D. SIO 26000

17. Which social responsibility subject *does not* belong to the ISO 26000?

    A. Animal rights

    B. Labor practices

    C. Consumer issues

    D. The environment

18. What set of sustainability guidelines was created by a network of business leaders from Japan, Europe, and the United States?

    A. ISO 26000

    B. OECD Guidelines for Multinational Enterprises

    C. SA8000

    D. Caux principles

19. Elsie is the plant HR specialist for the Natural Springs Water bottling plant, which is the closest plant to Naples, Florida. Naples just experienced a direct hit from Hurricane Albert. The plant manager has instructed Elsie to round up employees to go with the truck drivers to deliver water to the people of Naples. What should Elsie do in seeking volunteers?

    A. She should ask only management employees to go with the drivers so that there is no overtime pay involved.

    B. She should ask employee volunteers to sign a document stating they are volunteering for this relief work knowingly, without pay, and representing the company.

    C. She should pay only the truck drivers and not the employees helping them.

    D. She should ask the plant manager for budget allocation for overtime pay for the volunteers.

20. What should *not* be in an employee's personnel file?

    A. Job description

    B. EAP consent form

    C. Performance improvement program records

    D. Insupportable opinions

Answers

1. **B**. Relocating any specific population by inducement or force is diaspora.

2. **A**. Protecting local interests is part of guarded globalization.

3. **D**. Perimutter classified management orientations into four categories.

4. **C**. Global business expansion involves more than translating the employee handbook. Due diligence embraces everything from legal requirements to policy differences.

5. **A**. Expatriate employees need support as do their family members.

6. **A**. All units in an employer entity are involved in diversity and inclusion these days.

7. **C**. Diversity and inclusion programs attempt to gain value from the contributions of all employees.

8. **B**. Veterans and disabled workers have been overlooked populations for many years. Including them in recruiting and employment programs is a way to strengthen diversity and inclusion programs.

9. **C**. Employee affinity groups can contribute to diversity with suggestions for program content.

10. **D**. Cultural celebrations are helpful in understanding how others live and celebrate their heritage.

11. **A**. Confidential employee data and complaint investigation records are both considered confidential and private. Losing them would be losing something of value.

12. **C**. KRIs are forecasts of future bad things happening.

13. **B**. A risk register is like a log of identified risks.

14. **C**. Emergency response plans depend on a risk assessment that the response plan is built on.

15. **D**. Contingency plans outline how the organization will continue operating in the event of a catastrophe.

16. **B**. Corporate social responsibility (CSR) was an overall umbrella guideline. The Guidelines for Multinational Enterprises established in 1976 by the Organisation for Economic Co-operation and Development (OECD) is one of the first to address corporate governance.

17. **A**. Animal rights are not part of the ISO 26000 standard on corporate social responsibility.

18. **D**. The Caux principles were created by a joint effort of several countries.

19. **B**. Getting signed documents from employee volunteers in the relief effort is important because the work will be unpaid.

20. **D**. Insupportable opinions, regardless of the source, should never be part of an employee's personnel file.

References

1. The SHRM Body of Competency and Knowledge, page 52.

2. https://en.wikipedia.org/wiki/Globalization, retrieved on March 10, 2018.

3. Friedman, Thomas L. *Thank You for Being Late: An Optimist's Guide to Thriving in the Age of Accelerations,* pp 120–121. New York: Farrar, Straus and Giroux, 2016.

4. https://www.pwc.com/jp/en/press-room/world-in-2050-170213.html, retrieved on March 10, 2018.

5. http://www.newworldencyclopedia.org/entry/Diaspora, retrieved on March 10, 2018.

6. https://quizlet.com/114411913/shrm-cp-hr-in-the-global-context-flash-cards/, retrieved on March 10, 2018.

7. http://science.sciencemag.org/content/356/6345/1362, retrieved on March 10, 2018.

8. Google search, retrieved on March 10, 2018.

9. https://en.wikipedia.org/wiki/Sectoral_balances, retrieved on March 10, 2018.

10. Stephan, Michael, et al. The Global and Local HR Function, Deloitte Insights, https://www2.deloitte.com/insights/us/en/focus/human-capital-trends/2014/hc-trends-2014-global-and-local-hr.html, retrieved on March 12, 2018.

11. https://www.adp.com/spark/articles/2016/12/create-a-global-human-resources-strategy.aspx, retrieved on March 12, 2018.

12. Bremmer, Ian. "The New Rules of Globalization," *Harvard Business Review,* Jan–Feb 2014, https://hbr.org/2014/01/the-new-rules-of-globalization, retrieved on March 12, 2018.

13. Push and pull factors in business, www.ukessays.com/essays/business-strategy/push-and-pull-factors-in-business.php, retrieved on March 12, 2018.

14. Ibid.

15. Mastering Strategic Management, https://opentextbc.ca/strategicmanagement/chapter/types-of-international-strategies/, retrieved on March 12, 2018.

16. Bartlett, C. A., and S. Ghoshal. *Managing Across Borders: The Transnational Solution.* Harvard Business School Press, 1989.

17. https://www.managementstudyhq.com/eprg-framework.html, retrieved on March 13, 2018.

18. Koch, Jennifer. Must-have Global HR Competencies, Workforce, 10/1/1996, retrieved on March 13, 2018.

19. https://trainingindustry.com/articles/strategy-alignment-and-planning/5-ways-to-develop-a-global-mindset/, retrieved on March 13, 2018.

20. https://blog.enplug.com/corporate-culture, retrieved on March 14, 2018.

21. Lee, Kiefer, and Steve Carter. *Global Marketing Management, 3rd Edition.* OUP Oxford, 2012.

22. https://www.toolshero.com/leadership/organizational-culture-model-schein/, retrieved on March 14, 2018.

23. http://daily.unitedlanguagegroup.com/stories/editorials/six-cultural-dimensions, retrieved on March 14, 2018.

24. https://online.seu.edu/high-and-low-context-cultures/, retrieved on March 14, 2018.

25. https://en.wikipedia.org/wiki/Hofstede%27s_cultural_dimensions_theory, retrieved on March 14, 2018.

26. https://www.strategy-business.com/article/17251?gko=444c1, retrieved on March 14, 2018.

27. http://summit.sfu.ca/item/774, retrieved on March 14, 2018.

28. http://www.hult.edu/blog/benefits-challenges-cultural-diversity-workplace/, retrieved on March 14, 2018.

29. http://cognitive-edge.com/blog/a-non-linear-approach-to-reconciling-business-dilemmas/, retrieved on March 14, 2018.

30. https://www.mcgill.ca/desautels/category/tags/nancy-adler

31. https://www.shrm.org/resourcesandtools/hr-topics/talent-acquisition/pages/half-of-employers-report-not-tracking-global-mobility-costs.aspx, retrieved on March 14, 2018.

32. http://www.oxfordreference.com/view/10.1093/oi/authority.20110803095855152, retrieved on March 14, 2018.

33. Hutchings, Kate, and Helen De Cieri. *International Human Resource Management: From Cross-Cultural Management to Managing a Diverse Workforce*, New York: Routledge, 2007.

34. https://hbr.org/1999/03/the-right-way-to-manage-expats?referral=03758&cm_vc=rr_item_page.top_right, retrieved on March 14, 2018.

35. https://www.shrm.org/resourcesandtools/tools-and-samples/toolkits/pages/cms_010358.aspx, retrieved on March 14, 2018.

36. https://www.investopedia.com/terms/s/supranational.asp, retrieved on March 15, 2018.

37. https://europa.eu/european-union/about-eu/history_en, retrieved on March 15, 2018.

38. http://cor.europa.eu/en/welcome/Pages/module-1-part-1.aspx, retrieved on March 15, 2018.

39. The SHRM Body of Competency and Knowledge, page 53.

40. The Costs and Benefits of Diversity: Fundamental Rights and Anti-Discrimination, A Study on Methods and Indicators to Measure the Cost-Effectiveness of Diversity Policies in Enterprises; European Commission Directorate-General for Employment, Industrial Relations and Social Affairs Unit D/3 Manuscript completed in October 2003.

PART II

41. www.colormagazineusa.com

42. https://www.conference-board.org/pdf_free/councils/TCBCP005.pdf

43. "Global Diversity and Inclusion: Perceptions, Practices and Attitudes," Society for Human Resource Management, 2009, http://graphics.eiu.com/upload/eb/ DiversityandInclusion.pdf

44. Dobbin, Frank, and Alexandrea Kalev. "Why Diversity Programs Fail," HRBO.org July/August 2016.

45. www.dupress.com/articles/hc-trends-2014-diversity-to-inclusion

46. http://www.shrm.org/Conferences/Diversity/Documents/11Confsessions/11Div_ Harris.pdf

47. Council Perspectives CP-014, The Conference Board, Inc., 2009.

48. "Emotional Intelligence and Organizational Effectiveness," *Industrial Psychiatry Journal,* Jul–Dec 2013.

49. Fleming, Sherwood. "Exercise Intercultural Wisdom," www.sherwoodfleming.com.

50. Gregersen, Hal B., Allen J. Morrison, and J. Stewart Black. "Developing Leaders for the Global Frontier," *Sloan Management Review,* fall 1998.

51. Gramaliel Perruci, "Leadership Studies Programs in the Context of Globalization," presented at the International Leadership Association conference October 22–24, 1999, in Atlanta, GA, USA. The paper was available online at www.ila-net.org/ Publications/Proceedings/1999/gperruci.pdf.

52. The SHRM Body of Competency and Knowledge, page 54–55.

53. Kaplan, Robert S., and Anette Mikes. "Managing Risks: A New Framework," *Harvard Business Review* 90, No. 6, June 2012.

54. Risk Management Fundamentals, Homeland Security Risk Management Doctrine, U.S. Department of Homeland Security, April 2011. https://www.dhs.gov/xlibrary/ assets/rma-risk-management-fundamentals.pdf.

55. Peters, Thomas J. *Thriving on Chaos,* New York: Harper & Row Publishers, 1987.

56. The SHRM Body of Competency and Knowledge, page 56.

57. Ten Principles of UN Global Compact, www.unglobalcompact.bg.

58. CRT Principles for Responsible Business, www.cauxroundtable.org.

59. ISO 26000 Social Responsibility: 7 Core Subjects, https://www.iso.org/iso-26000-social-responsibility.html.

60. Global Reporting Initiative, G4. Categories and Aspects in the Guidelines https://www.globalreporting.org.

61. The SHRM Body of Competency and Knowledge, page 57.

62. The SHRM Body of Competency and Knowledge, page 57.

Behavioral Competencies

SHRM Certified Professional (SHRM-CP) and SHRM Senior Certified Professional (SHRM-SCP) identify and detail eight behavioral competencies that will be tested for both the SHRM-CP and SHRM-SCP. They make up a whopping 50 percent of both exams. The eight behavior competencies are segregated by SHRM into three clusters: Leadership, Business, and Interpersonal.

A *competency* is a cluster of interrelated attributes that includes knowledge, skills, and abilities (KSAs) that lead to behaviors that have been identified as needed to perform a specific job effectively. Competencies can be either technical (the knowledge required to perform a specific job) or just behavioral in nature. A behavioral competency is the application of knowledge to job-related behavior. Thus, technical competencies for HR professionals reflect *what* knowledge they are expected to apply to their jobs, and a behavioral competency is about *how* they apply the knowledge. Please note that there may be more in-depth information about some of the behaviors within the knowledge topics in Chapters 4 through 6.

In each of the eight behavioral competencies, we have included the outline of SHRM's Body of Competency and Knowledge (BoCK) key concepts[1] (foundational knowledge), which are a description of what HR professionals are expected to know to perform their job. It's important to learn and know the distinction between what SHRM has identified and detailed versus what your organization may have culturally expressed with expectations of behavior because they may be different.

Leadership Cluster

The Leadership cluster represents 13 percent of both exams' weighted scores. There are two competencies that fall within the Leadership cluster:

- Behavioral competency 1—Leadership and Navigation
- Behavioral competency 2—Ethical Practice

Regardless of experience level or job title, all HR professionals need to demonstrate and display strong leadership skills and ability, keeping in mind the focus of a strategic mind-set.

Behavioral Competency 1—Leadership and Navigation

The first competency in the SHRM-identified behavioral competency model is Leadership and Navigation. This competency focuses on understanding leadership and the knowledge/skills needed to be an effective HR leader, along with being an HR business partner in your organization and contributing to initiatives and processes for the organization. Additionally, an effective HR professional builds trust, influences, motivates and has the required level of emotional intelligence to demonstrate those behaviors.

Four subcompetencies comprise the Leadership and Navigation competency. They are defined by SHRM[2] as follows:

- **Navigating the organization** Working within the parameters of the organization's hierarchy, processes, systems, and policies
- **Vision** Defining and supporting a coherent vision and long-term goals for HR that support the strategic direction of the organization
- **Managing HR initiatives** Executing the implementation and management of HR projects or initiatives that support HR and organizational objectives
- **Influence** Inspiring colleagues to understand and pursue the strategic vision and goals of HR and the organization

Key Concepts

- Leadership theories (e.g., situational leadership, transformational leadership, participative leadership, inclusive leadership)
- People management techniques (e.g., directing, coaching, supporting, delegating)
- Motivation theories (e.g., goal-setting theory, expectancy theory, attribution, theory, self-determination theory)
- Influence and persuasion techniques (e.g., personal appeal, forming coalitions, leading by examples, rational persuasion)
- Trust- and relationship-building techniques (e.g., emotional and social intelligence)

Definition

According to SHRM, "*Leadership and Navigation* is defined as the knowledge, skills, abilities, and other characteristics (KSAOs) needed to navigate the organization and accomplish HR goals, to create a compelling vision and mission for HR that aligns with the strategic direction and culture of the organization, to lead and promote organizational change, to manage the implementation and execution of HR initiatives, and to promote the role of HR as a key business partner."[3]

Proficiency Indicators for All HR Professionals

The Leadership and Navigation competency for all HR professionals focuses on understanding leadership and the skills and knowledge needed to be a leader: influencing, building trust, emotional intelligence, and motivation. Yet first there needs to be an understanding as to the difference between managing and leading. Both are needed to get work done through people. Knowing when and how to lead and when to manage is the key to effective leadership and navigation. All HR professionals are expected to conduct themselves according to these expectations.

Conforming to Organizational Culture

Organizations create their own models of leadership, creating a set of expected behaviors, attitudes, and beliefs that become the leadership norm for the organization to fit in with the organization's mission and strategies. The result is a leadership culture. Managers/ leaders are then expected to conform to that identified model, a *norm,* to guide their interactions in managing people.

Organizations desire to identify the type of leadership that is most effective in their workplaces. This self-awareness can then be used to identify individuals with the potential for leadership and to create leadership development programs and use these identified norms when sourcing new hires via branding the leadership culture.

Collaborating Among Stakeholders

There are basically five steps to apply to gain collaboration with stakeholders:

1. *Know the stakeholders.* The first step toward any collaboration process is identifying stakeholders and their roles. Understanding who you are working with is critical to collaborating effectively.

2. *Identify what is at stake.* Every stakeholder has involvement for a specific reason. Use their role and motivation to your advantage. For example, if you are working on an office reconfiguration for HR, consider including the IT manager in every conversation that relates to the new room design, not just those explicitly regarding the movement of PCs. Why? Because they may be affected by the decisions made in those conversations pertaining to the location of cables, connectivity, and other associated matters such as overtime for IT personnel.

3. *Understand each stakeholder's issues and language.* Communicating effectively with stakeholders is linked to their motivation. For example, for decision-makers, every project is an investment because they are normally responsible for their share of the resources. To collaborate effectively, you should discuss plans in relation to the planned outcomes or ROI.

4. *Set the specific expectations.* Once you know who stakeholders are, what their challenges and issues are, and how to talk to them, you can better express your expectations for their involvement, such as when they are expected to provide input for the project and how to provide feedback.

5. *Value their input.* One reason stakeholders can become frustrated is they don't feel "heard." Helping stakeholders to see how their input was incorporated or even why it was not used is essential. It makes them an active part of decision-making without letting them make the decision.

Accomplishing Tasks

Leaders get things done through people, which means managing people and their tasks for producing desired outcomes. Chapter 4 discusses in great detail the techniques, skills, and theories to manage and motivate people with tasks.

Managers do the following with groups:

- Plan activities
- Organize and identify resources required, including people
- Direct work in a way that ensures the best use of resources
- Coordinate to achieve efficiency
- Control resources and activities through monitoring, measuring, and correcting as needed

Leaders perform the following roles with groups:

- They model desired values in all their actions.
- They challenge the status quo and harness the talent in the organization to solve problems, accept change, and move in a new direction.
- They inspire and influence people toward achieving a common vision and goals.
- They maintain employees' motivation and focus.
- They foster growth and develop people to their full potential.

If an organization has ineffective management, it will fail to meet goals. On the other hand, if organizations lack leadership, they often lack innovation and the ability to adapt to change.

Demonstrating Agility and Expertise

Although the concept of learning agility is not new, it is gaining a lot of momentum in today's organizations. There is a clear message from the mounting research around demonstrating agility: you should be either hiring for it, developing it, or, perhaps, doing both. The traits to look for are simple: self-driven motivation to learn, seeking out and using feedback, and an openness to try something new and different (to welcome discomfort). It's not easy, yet having developmental experiences is what leads to a new level of expertise and innovation. Success as a leader depends largely on a willingness and ability to learn because it enables leaders to acquire new behaviors quickly and effectively, which ultimately enables adaptability and resilience. While this overarching concept of learning agility may have always been important, it seems even more so now given the constant turmoil of today's business environment. This can explain why some of the world-renowned management experts are saying now is the time to put your bets on learners.

Setting the Vision

Leaders create energy. They inspire, empower, and support others. And they set vision. Setting a vision of what can be serves as a powerful inspiration, a North Star of sorts for a leader, to move everyone in an organization in the same direction toward that vision's achievement. That vision needs to be clear and achievable—something that inspires others to want to be a part of it. Leaders must continually point to this North Star and remind everyone that this is where we are all headed. The behavior that is most essential with this leadership ability is going to involve inspiring and motivating others.

Leading the Organization Through Adversity

"The best developer of a leader is failure," said Richard Branson, chairman of Virgin Airlines. Business history is full of examples of leaders whose organizations ran into adversity and bounced back to become more successful than before. It was through the leadership that created the survivors. A great example is Steve Jobs who was fired from Apple Computer and then rehired when it was on the brink of despair. When he came back to Apple, he had a new view of the market that caused him to lead Apple with products like the iPod, which ended up redefining the industry. It was through his vision and ability as a leader to paint the picture of what could be, design the strategy, and send in the resources. The rest is history.

Promoting Consensus

Getting people to move together as a unified team toward a common goal has always been challenging. However, with consensus building, management can ensure they have the support of the entire team as they steer the organization in the chosen direction.

This concept is known as *consensus management*. It is not a new concept (Native Americans have been utilizing it for hundreds of years), and now organizations like Starbucks have successfully incorporated it into their management processes. Consensus management is the process where team members work as a group to develop a solution and agree to support whatever decision is made in the best interests of the whole. It requires asking for input from each person on the team, carefully considering that feedback, and making an earnest effort to address any concerns that are raised. This is most commonly accomplished by holding a consensus meeting where staff is empowered to voice their support and concerns. The key to success here is that everyone agrees to support the consensus decision once it is made, regardless of how they feel about it.

Serving as a Transformational Leader

Leadership today is associated with a group role, placing value on behaviors characterized as authentic leadership or transformational leadership.

The following are key elements of this type of approach to leadership:

- **Power** Leaders can be recognized as formal or informal. They often exercise the power to empower other team members, act as their champion, and support their efforts.

- **Orientation** Transformational leaders think in terms of vision, strategy, and values rather than short-term objectives. They believe in challenging and developing for the long term.

- **Emotional intelligence** They have the knowledge and skills that allow transformational leaders to be self-aware of their actions and emotions and to understand others' perspectives and the drivers of other people's behavior.

- **Ethical grounding** They walk the talk of the organization's values, encouraging others, and will sacrifice for those values.

Proficiency Indicators for Senior HR Professionals

Senior HR professionals are expected to be able to do and say the following behaviors over and above the basic behaviors already reviewed.

Leading HR Staff

Leading the HR staff to become a true business partner is one of the most important leadership roles for HR professionals. Demonstrating the behaviors to be a strong HR leader is one of the best training tools for the HR leader. In their book *The Extraordinary Leader: Turning Good Managers into Great Leaders*,[4] Jack Zenger and Joseph Folkman studied the strengths and weaknesses of HR leaders and concluded the following:

Strong HR leaders demonstrate the following behaviors:

- Develop and coach others
- Build positive relationships
- Model their values and fulfill their promises and commitments
- Have functional expertise

Weak HR leaders display these behaviors:

- Focus internally rather than externally, failing to look outside the HR function to the organization's internal and external stakeholders
- Lack strategic perspective, focusing on short-term objectives and daily tasks
- Do not anticipate or react well to change
- Resist "stretch" goals and act as a drag on the organization's attempts to innovate

As an HR professional, consider what your own leadership style is and where you may need to shore up a leadership skill to lead the HR department more effectively so that you and HR can have a more significant role in your organization.

Facilitating Strategic Change

Facilitating strategic change as an HR leader involves employing the three Cs of change leadership.

- **Communicate**   Unsuccessful leaders tended to focus on the "what" behind the change. Successful leaders communicated the "what" and the "why." Leaders who explained the purpose of the change and connected it to the organization's values or explained the benefits created stronger buy-in and urgency for the change.

- **Collaborate**   Bringing people together to plan and execute change is critical. Successful leaders worked across boundaries, encouraged employees to break out of their silos, and refused to tolerate unhealthy competition. They also included employees in decision-making early on, strengthening their commitment to change. Unsuccessful change leaders failed to engage employees early and often in the change process.

- **Commit**   Successful leaders made sure their own beliefs and behaviors supported change, too. Change is difficult, but leaders who negotiated it successfully were resilient and persistent and willing to step outside their comfort zone. They also devoted more of their own time to the change effort and focused on the big picture. Unsuccessful leaders failed to adapt to challenges, expressed negativity, and were impatient with a lack of results.

Serving as the Voice for HR

There is a new agenda for HR in today's business environment, and it is a radical departure from the status quo. It used to be that HR was charged with mainly playing policy police and regulatory watchdog, handling the volumes of paperwork involved in hiring and firing, managing the bureaucratic aspects of benefits, and administering compensation decisions made by others. HR's activities were often disconnected from the real work of the organization. Today HR is defined not by what it does but by what it delivers—results that enrich the organization's value to customers, stakeholders, and employees.

Serving as the voice for HR, more organizations have dispersed their staff as HR business partners in the business units to be closely aligned with the needs of that particular business unit so that HR can help deliver organizational excellence in the following four ways:

- Become a true business partner within the unit with line management in strategy execution

- Become an expert in the way work is organized and executed, delivering administrative efficiency

- Become a champion for employees, representing their concerns to line management and at the same time working to increase employee contribution and engagement

- Become an agent of continuous transformation, shaping processes and a culture that together improve the organization

Ensuring Accountability

As an HR leader, modeling desired behavior and outcomes with the HR staff is vitally important to other employees and management in the organization. When leaders are visibly holding their own direct reports accountable, this sends a powerful leading-by-example message. People struggle to be accountable when roles and processes are ambiguous; thus, having clear roles, responsibilities, and expectations is a vital step in holding others accountable. As an HR professional, how well are you measuring up to doing what you say you are going to do and by when? Holding yourself accountable to delivering the outcomes and the outlined leadership behavior norms is just as important.

Changing Organizational Culture

When embarking on changing organizational culture, the first step is in defining the values and behaviors you're seeking to change. *Culture* is defined as the beliefs and behaviors that govern how people act in an organization, and it is now believed to be a major determinant of a company's success or failure. Culture is considered a potential competitive advantage, if it is perceived as a positive strong culture.

According to the Deloitte Global Human Capital Trends 2016[5] report, here are ten tips for driving a culture change:

- Define desired values and behaviors.
- Align culture with strategy and processes.
- Connect culture and accountability.
- Have visible proponents.
- Define the non-negotiables.
- Align your culture with your brand.
- Measure your efforts.
- Don't rush it.
- Invest now.
- Be bold and lead.

Championing the HR Function

To champion the HR function, HR professionals must build relationships that are known as a reliable expert partner that champions high performance from the workforce.

To champion high performance from the workforce, HR's functions must be deliberately designed to support and be directly linked to the organization's mission, vision, strategy, and goals. When HR is seen as the lever that drives performance upward, then HR lives up to its potential as the most important function in every organization.

Creating Buy-In for Organizational Change

When you're enacting an organizational change, organizational executives most likely already gave a green light for the change you're heading up. You need to create more buy-in for other levels in the organization to help proceed with the change. The following are steps to take to create buy-in.

Working from the Top Down   In addition to obtaining buy-in from the C-suite, consider bringing in mid-level management into the change plans early on. Gaining support from leaders at different levels in the organization will make your pitch stronger and ensure managers have time to prepare for questions from employees from the get go.

Being Transparent   Communication is key to prevent unfounded concerns and gossip about how the change is going to affect people. Be open and transparent early and often. This includes being clear about what's going well and what's not working. Be up-front and specific about what failed throughout the process and was learned.

Asking for Input   It's vital for employees to know their opinions and ideas are being acknowledged when voiced. It can prove to be a challenge to collect and address feedback and questions from everyone. Think of having a task force within each unit to help you communicate details and gather feedback at certain phases of the change process.

Change is key to helping organizations innovate and grow, and your organization's workforce is the needed component for helping changes take place. Ensuring they're informed and can provide input throughout the change transition is essential in earning their support.

Summary

In this portion of Chapter 7, we explored the expertise in leadership and navigation that enables HR professionals to keep their organizations focused on its strategies and goals to lead the workforce talent by creating collaboration and fostering a vision with influence, EQ, and motivation.

Behavioral Competency 2—Ethical Practice

It is important for HR professionals to understand the demand for ethical practice. Everyone expects a level playing field, and that requires employers to be doing what is expected for employees, customers, and shareholders.

Three subcompetencies comprise the Ethical Practice competency. They are defined by SHRM[6] as follows:

- **Personal integrity**   Demonstrating high levels of integrity in personal relationships and behaviors

- **Professional integrity**   Demonstrating high levels of integrity in professional relationships and behaviors

- **Ethical agent**   Cultivating the organization's ethical environment and ensuring that policies and practices reflect ethical values

Key Concepts

- Ethical business principles and practices (e.g., transparency, confidentiality, conflicts of interest)

- Anonymity, confidentiality, and privacy principles and policies

- Codes of conduct

Definition

According to SHRM, "*Ethical Practice* is defined as the ability to integrate core values, integrity, and accountability throughout all organizational and business practices."[7]

Personal integrity is a personal choice to uphold certain moral and ethical standards. *Professional integrity* defines the professional who consistently and willingly practices within the guidelines of a chosen profession under the obligation of a code of ethics. *Ethical agent* means someone who, with strong internal guidance, practices ethical behavior.

What Are Ethics?

Ethics are the rules or standards that govern conduct of individuals within a profession. They are based on a moral philosophy. That philosophy holds that there are differences between right and wrong or good and bad. Ethics are the standards people use to guide their decision-making with the intent that outcomes are fair to those involved.

Unethical behavior is that which is inconsistent with the stated values, norms, and beliefs of the organization's stakeholders.

Proficiency Indicators for All HR Professionals

Ethical practice for all HR professionals relies on these key behaviors. All HR professionals are expected to conduct themselves according to these requirements. SHRM has published a professional *Code of Ethics* for HR professionals. You will find it at https://www.shrm.org/about-shrm/Pages/code-of-ethics.aspx. It is something you should read, understand, and follow in your daily job.

Maintaining Confidentiality

Confidentiality refers to data. Privacy refers to people. So, recognizing that HR professionals work frequently with confidential information, maintaining that confidential status is critical. Handling such information requires respect for the intimate and classified nature of the information. Keeping those secrets is an expectation of all HR professionals.

Acting with Personal, Professional, and Behavioral Integrity

Personal conduct of HR professionals must meet a standard as high or higher than others are expected to meet. Integrity is the inner expectation people have for themselves that causes them to act in accordance with a code. That code expects honesty and forthrightness in all activities. Frequently, organizations publish written ethics codes, specifying exactly the expectations that exist for personal behavior.

Responding Immediately to All Reports of Unethical Behavior or Conflicts of Interest

When other people are suspected of acting unethically, it is up to the HR professional to react with appropriate challenges. That may involve a formal investigation or a simple coaching of the individual involved. Doing nothing is not an appropriate option.

Empowering All Employees to Report Unethical Behavior or Conflicts of Interest Without Fear of Reprisal

Employees at all levels must feel welcome to report observations of unethical behavior exhibited by others, even their bosses. If employees don't feel safe in doing so, it becomes a cancer that can grow and consume the organization over a short period of time.

Showing Consistency Between Espoused and Enacted Values

Everyone in the organization must be able to witness the leaders doing what they demand of others. Organizational values are valid only if they are supported by daily decisions from the executive suite. People notice those things and will be slow to support values that are not supported by executives. "Do as I say, not as I do," doesn't work.

Acknowledging Mistakes

Denial is a reaction that may work in court, but it rarely proves helpful in the employment context. If an HR professional has made an error, it is always preferable to admit the mistake and extend an offer to correct it. Most of us appreciate people who admit that they have goofed. We don't so much appreciate someone stonewalling us. Building confidence and trust in the HR department depends on people admitting and correcting mistakes when they happen.

Driving the Corporate Ethical Environment

Charles D. Kerns writes in Pepperdine University's *Graziadio Business Review*,[8] "Values drive behavior and therefore need to be consciously stated, but they also need to be affirmed by actions. Driving ethical behavior with values and attitudes requires that there be alignment among values, attitudes, and behavior." Table 7-1 shows examples of this alignment between each of the virtuous values, associated attitudes, and behavior.

Applying Power or Authority Appropriately

Abusing power is the shortest route to violate a trust. If employees are to trust and support an employer organization, the leaders must wield power and authority appropriately and with discretion. Decisions must be made in ways that support the employment relationship rather than undermining it. Power can be corrupting; successful HR professionals are people who understand the concepts of fairness and equality.

Mitigating the Influence of Bias

Perhaps the most difficult image to see is the self-image. We tend to see ourselves as we think we are rather than as others see us. That is simply human nature. It is important for HR professionals to make special efforts to seek feedback from those they interact with so they can make adjustments to their behavior that may be appropriate. Identifying personal bias is not always easy. Once identified, assuring that personal bias doesn't influence business decisions is even more difficult. It is not uncommon for individuals to create justifications for their decisions that deny impact of personal bias when in actuality bias is driving the decision. Bias is ingrained and can come from personal experiences reaching back into childhood. Once treated unfairly by someone in a particular group (e.g., race, gender, age, disability), the sense of ill treatment carries over into future relationships and decision-making.

Value	Attitude	Ethical Behavior
Wisdom and knowledge	Experience promotes wisdom that helps convert information to knowledge.	Using knowledge to solve problems ethically and to do what is right.
Self-control	Self-control means effectively managing reactions to challenging situations and temptations.	Putting personal motivations aside and acting with objectivity by doing what is right.
Justice	Acting justly and fairly is a long-term driver of ethical behavior; remember the "Golden Rule."	Establishing just and mutually agreed upon criteria and administering them fairly to all people.
Transcendence	The belief in a power and source outside oneself reduces self-serving actions and increases humility.	Putting institutional and/or stakeholder interests above self-interests. Identifying a personal purpose that is aligned with organizational mission.
Love and kindness	Treating people with kindness helps increase the reservoir of positive affection and love.	Recognizing and encouraging others for their contributions.
Courage and integrity	Ethics requires the courage to do the right things consistently without regard to personal consequences.	Making unpopular decisions based on fair consideration of the facts.

Table 7-1   Values, Attitude, and Ethics and How They Relate

Maintaining Appropriate Levels of Transparency in Organizational Practices

As it has been used in recent times, applied to organizations, transparency means the opposite of secrecy. Related to HR professionals, transparency means making information available to employees, stakeholders, and even sometimes the public, to explain policy changes and even benefit issues. The latest legislative push has been directed at compensation transparency. That means employers are required to permit employees to discuss their compensation openly and that of others in the group. In the private sector, such discussions have been generally prohibited historically. Expectations have changed. Openness is now the order of the day. In truth, such openness makes it more difficult to cover up differences in pay between men and women in the same job or how job schedules are assigned to a racially mixed group of workers.

Ensuring That All Stakeholder Voices Are Heard

An obvious prerequisite is the identification of all stakeholders for the organization. Then, as issues arise, reach out to each for input to the discussion. The downside of not doing this is that people will feel left out and ignored. None of us wants to be ignored. Invite participation and input.

Managing Political and Social Pressures when Making Decisions

HR professionals are in the unique position of brokering compromise between opposite views on issues such as benefits versus budget restrictions, cultural celebration versus production requirements, and confidentiality of records versus transparency of investigation outcomes. There are always going to be pressures from those of higher rank in the organization and sometimes from outside social standings. Many employers are being pressured to permit employee use of recreational marijuana while federal law continues to hold the substance illegal. Reconciling these differences is often the job of the HR professional. Sometimes, it takes the wisdom of Solomon.

There comes a time in most people's lives when there is pressure from a supervisor, manager, executive, or other influential player who would have you do something unethical. While the action may not be illegal, you recognize it as crossing the line on ethics. The question is, "What will you choose to do?" Going against the wishes of the power-holder may cause you a negative career impact. Agreeing to the unethical action may cause harm to someone else. How you choose to handle that conundrum will determine your personal and professional ethics. Professional HR managers must put their jobs on the line from time to time to stand up for ethics. Remember the military comparison. Just because your boss tells you to shoot someone else, you remain responsible for your own actions. "Because my boss gave me an order" is no excuse for doing something you know is wrong.

Proficiency Indicators for Senior HR Professionals

At the senior level in the profession, ethical practice takes on greater importance because of the impact of the decisions being made. These added elements are additions to the basic ethics requirements for all HR professionals.

Empowering Senior Leaders to Maintain Internal Controls and Create an Ethical Environment to Prevent Conflicts of Interest

Executives must be leaders, but they must also follow policies and values established by the CEO and board of directors. From time to time pressures arise to do something expedient that would actually violate a policy or a corporate value. An example is making an exception to the corporate commitment for equal pay when an executive chooses to hire a highly qualified female candidate at a rate below market value simply because she appears willing to accept a low offer. Such exceptions can undermine the organization's declaration that it values equal pay treatment for all of its workforce. Senior leaders need to understand they have a responsibility to oppose such violations of values.

Maintaining Contemporary Knowledge

With changes in local, state, and federal laws added to the changes in research about employee management issues, professionals in human resource delivery positions are challenged every day to maintain current knowledge. It is a never-ending process. If you happen to fall behind, your organization's reputation can suffer, it can lose its ability to recruit top talent, and it can miss important compliance requirements. Maintaining current knowledge is an imperative.

Establishing Credibility

Acceptance at the executive table requires HR professionals to be accepted as credible contributors among organization executives. Credible reputation is based on the ability to inspire belief. Belief is created when experience shows there is more honesty and accuracy than missed expectations. Credibility goes beyond talk and promise. It is based on demonstrated accomplishments.

Challenging Conflicts of Interest

Conflicts of interest occur with more frequency than one might imagine. When the purchasing manager has stock in the vendor organization, there is a potential conflict of interest. When the HR professional has a personal interest in the recasting of a compensation policy because it can result in a substantial pay increase, there is a potential conflict of interest. When the CEO wants to hire her neighbor's daughter on a summer internship even though the company is laying off workers, there is a potential conflict of interest. These situations should be identified and challenged by the HR professional. Conflicts of interest undermine the organization's values and can occur at every level of the organization.

Withstanding Pressure when Developing Strategy

One conflict of interest that arises frequently for management people is the interest to protect or grow their slice of the organization. Getting more budget dollars, more headcount, or more time on the executive committee agenda can be strong motivating forces leading to bias in decision-making about organizational policy. HR professionals have the need to constantly be aware of motivations that cause managers and executives to take policy positions. Counteracting such bias takes skill and commitment to the organization's well-being.

Set the Standard

HR professionals contribute to performance standards by demonstrating behavior that is both legal and ethical. It is hard for employees, let alone managers and supervisors, to follow behavior standards when they see people in HR doing things that violate those standards. If people in HR have poor attendance or tardiness records and suffer no penalty, other departments begin to wonder why they should not also ease up on disciplinary action for the same type of problems in their organization.

Balancing Organizational Success with Employee Advocacy

HR professionals are unique in that they have two masters. The organization relies on HR to help establish and enforce standards and rules. The organization's employees also rely on HR to be an advocate when there has been inappropriate treatment. Complaints of sexual harassment often put HR into that dual role. The employer depends on HR to help control legal liability by conducting an appropriate investigation, gathering all the evidence available. When the management is actually at fault, employees depend on HR to be honest and bring in an investigation finding that supports their complaint as valid.

Developing HR Policies

One of the most exciting parts of the HR management function is the development of employment policies. In organizations such as government agencies, there are extensive rule books that describe procedures and policies for almost any conceivable requirement. In entrepreneurial organizations, initially there are no policies. They have to be written without the benefit of historical references within the organization. HR professionals get to work with executives to identify policy needs and then draft new policies. They have responsibility for gathering data that compares with alternative policies. Ultimately, data supporting whatever policy is recommended should stand out above other alternatives. Data includes input from executives and managers, analysis of industry standards and expectations, and even competitor policies. Cost analysis or forecasting for each option is often helpful.

Creating HR Strategy

Louise Allen offers this, "Deeper knowledge and understanding of your business goals and business model can identify potential threats and opportunities in the quantity and quality of human resource required by your organization. This in turn identifies the key components of your HR strategy and the virtuous circle of providing whatever your organization needs for success."[9] So, once you have your business goals and business model well in hand, the question becomes, "How can we get HR functions to support those business requirements?"

Like any other creative effort, there will likely be multiple drafts and reviews before a final strategy is approved. Remember always that HR has a value-added mission to support the organizational reasons for being if it is to survive as an internal portion of the company. If that isn't done, executives may decide to outsource the HR functions to someone who will provide the necessary support.

Making Decisions Aligned with Organizational Strategies and Values

Consistency of policy interpretation is critical to employees feeling they are being treated fairly. Americans have an innate belief that employers should treat their workers fairly. "Fair" is not a legal requirement, except for the common law requirement that employers offer "good faith and fair dealing." Every individual will be carrying around their own measuring tool to assess decisions based on how fair they are. When a decision doesn't pass the fairness test, discomfort, disgruntlement, and discord soon follow. When one department terminates someone for poor attendance and another department only gives a warning to an employee with a similar attendance record, there will be cries of unfairness. It is up to HR professionals to assure that these opposing conditions don't happen.

You should be able to write down your organization's strategies and values. Based on those lists, you may assess the quality of decisions made in any department on any issue.

Communicating the Vision

Once executives have developed and described the organization's vision, it is up to HR to support and communicate that vision to the workforce. That communication often happens through training sessions. They can be classroom events, online seminars, webinars, or some other form of training. Ultimately, every employee needs to understand and support the vision their leaders put forth. If the vision includes treating employees with dignity, then an open door policy with access to managers and executives on a timely basis may be appropriate. Treating customers with respect may also be part of the vision. Training employees to be courteous in their approach to customers is part of the vision implementation requirement.

Maintaining a Culture of Ethics

"Do as I say and not as I do" doesn't work very well as an ethical model. People will comply with almost any requirement if they see their superiors also complying with that requirement. If the company doesn't allow employees to telecommute and it becomes known that managers are telecommuting, a schism develops in the workforce. How serious it is will depend on how many employees find the behavior contrast distasteful and if discipline has resulted in some employee cases. Remember, a perception of fair treatment is a strong requirement in the employment relationship. Lose that, and you may see turnover rates increase.

Aligning All HR Practices

Ethical behavior requires that all interests under the control or influence of HR professionals be joined in the effort to support those ethical decisions. Think about what HR professionals must cover.

- Legal and regulatory compliance
- Labor union relationships
- Employee motivation
- Employee discipline oversight
- Global and cultural effectiveness
- Organizational leadership
- Support for creation and implementation of organizational vision, mission, policies, and other behavioral expectations
- Recruiting and hiring
- Employee training
- Diversity programs
- Workforce leadership and coaching managers on leadership issues
- Oversight of ethical expectations
- Employee communication
- Consultation on business decisions representing the employee viewpoint
- Periodical review of employee programs to assure effectiveness

Usually, on the job, several of these areas of HR influence will be in play at the same time. Balancing them with one another is an expectation of a certified HR professional.

Summary

In this portion of Chapter 7, we explored ethical requirements for HR professionals. Ethics permeates each segment of HR duties and responsibilities. If HR managers don't demonstrate personal and organizational integrity, employees are likely to also demonstrate absence of integrity. Transparency, honesty, and confidentiality are key components of an effective ethics program. For some people, ethics is simply doing the right thing in each circumstance. For others, ethics represents compliance with professional standards of conduct. Every day, an HR professional is likely to encounter one or more ethics dilemmas. How you react to those problems will determine what your organizational culture really is, not what you claim it is. Decision-making is integral to ethics requirements. It starts with the most senior executive and then applies to each subordinate manager, supervisor, and employee.

HR professional behavioral standards are expected to conform to the HR Professional Code of Ethics, published by SHRM.[10] Key components of the code include the following:

- Professional responsibility
- Professional development
- Ethical leadership
- Fairness and justice
- Conflicts of interest
- Use of information

Interpersonal Cluster

The Interpersonal cluster represents 18.5 percent of both exams' weighted scores. There are three competencies that fall within the Interpersonal cluster.

- Behavioral Competency 3—Relationship Management
- Behavioral Competency 4—Communication
- Behavioral Competency 5–Global and Cultural Effectiveness

This cluster covers the behaviors, attributes, and knowledge required for HR professionals to perform collaboratively and with interpersonal aspects of their roles.

Behavioral Competency 3—Relationship Management

HR's most notable role has been, and continues to be, the "people" job; therefore, managing relationships is a core function for an HR professional. Those who are good at using their relationship skills will foster greater collaboration, understanding, and communication with stakeholders.

Five subcompetencies comprise the Relationship Management competency. They are defined by SHRM[11] as follows:

- **Networking** Effectively building a network of professional contacts both within and outside of the organization
- **Relationship building** Effectively building and maintaining relationships both within and outside of the organization
- **Teamwork** Participating as an effective team member that builds, promotes, and leads effective teams
- **Conflict management** Managing and resolving conflicts by identifying areas of common interest among the parties in conflict
- **Negotiation** Reaching mutually acceptable agreements with negotiating parties within and outside of the organization

Key Concepts

- Types of conflict (e.g., relationship, task, inter- and intra-organizational)
- Conflict-resolution styles (e.g., avoidance, competition, cooperation, conciliation)
- Conflict-resolution techniques (e.g., accommodate, avoid, collaborate)
- Negotiation, tactics, strategies, and styles (e.g., perspective taking, principled bargainer, auction, interest-based bargaining)

Definition

According to SHRM, "*Relationship Management* is defined as the knowledge, skills, abilities, and other characteristics (KSAOs) needed to create and maintain a network of professional contacts within and outside of the organization, to build and maintain relationships, to work as an effective member of a team, and to manage conflict while supporting the organization."[12]

Basic Proficiency Indicators

All HR professionals must be able to establish and maintain positive relationships with people both inside and outside the organization. HR touches all parts of the employer organization and reaches into a myriad of external groups. Each of those contacts requires positive relationships with the people there.

Establishing Credibility

Without credibility, the HR professional has little to offer. Seen as someone who can't be relied on to offer accurate information and advice, the HR professional will find internal managers avoiding them. You must be the "go-to" expert on all matters involving human resources. That means when you don't know an answer, say so and promise to do the necessary research and get back to your contact with accurate information. Do it in a timely way because help that is delayed often is not any help at all. Managers need information quickly so they can deal with the issues they have facing them. Remember, it takes only one incident where you give bad advice and your reputation is damaged. It will take a long time to get it back on the positive side.

Treating Stakeholders with Respect and Dignity

As an HR professional, you have many stakeholders. We reviewed them in Chapter 5. However, remember all organizational employees fall into that category. And all managers within the organization fall into that category. Don't forget your boss. Your boss is a stakeholder, too. Some of these folks will be delightful to work with. Some of them will be difficult to work with. Each of them deserves your respect for the role they play and the person they are. Your job as an HR professional is to treat each individual with dignity. Even if there is someone who has committed a firing offense and you are helping the supervisor terminate them, being kind can go a long way toward decent treatment. Ask yourself each time, "How would I like to be treated?" Then do that. No one deserves to be belittled or shamed for any reason. Even if you have to call the police to deal with a serious behavior issue, you can still be an adult in your approach to that person who is causing the problem.

Building Engaging Relationships

Building relationships is a skill HR people must develop. Some people do it naturally, and others have to work at it. Here are some suggestions from an expert in communication.

Building Engaging Relationships

Proactive communication with your team can serve your business significantly. Done consistently, you'll have access to one of the best, most authentic focus groups for your brand. You'll be given qualified, firsthand perspective into your services and processes. You'll also gain better knowledge of your staff and their strengths. Another bonus, your team will become more inspired and loyal knowing you care about their feedback.

The key is listening. Meet with your HR professionals one at a time. Go into this kind of communication without preconceived thoughts. Listen mindfully and don't dominate the conversation. This is your time to collect insights and information. Remember that you are the final decision-maker, but now is your opportunity to gather data to help in creating strategies to improve your business. Don't be defensive. Remember this person is on your team. When your meeting concludes, let your employee know how appreciative you are and *then* correct or add anything you think will benefit their knowledge of the business.

(continued)

Here are some tips to get started:

- Meetings with each employee should be held on a regular basis such as quarterly or monthly.

- Dedicate a specific time for these discussions and *ink* them in on your schedule. It could be 3 hours one afternoon each week or just one meeting per week. The goal is to schedule meetings that you can attend week after week and not have to reschedule.

- Be prepared. Most likely your employee has thought a lot about this meeting. They'll be more engaged in this and future conversations if you're taking this meeting seriously.

- Ask purposeful questions so at the end of your meeting you've learned something. (In other words, what is the one thing that we do that customers appreciate? What new technology do you think our clients would respond to?)

- Keep to your allotted time so you establish structure and consistency. If meetings tend to always go long, it could lead to burnout.

- If possible, schedule the next meeting right away so your team knows these conversations are now part of the business culture.

- Ask staff to save any follow-up comments or notes for the next meeting, unless urgent. This will keep you both organized and avoid pop-in meetings that could lead to burnout.

- Realize you're building a new process, and it will take time. Don't push yourself to meet with everyone or act on suggestions right away. It's better to be consistent with meetings and actions to effect change that truly improves your business.

This same process can work with your customers/clients and even vendors.

Sheri Nelson
Founder, The Marketing Shop
Welcometotheshop.com
Facebook: TheMarketingShopBayArea
Instagram: the_marketing_shop

Demonstrating Approachability

How do you feel when you walk up to someone and they don't recognize you? Perhaps they continue their current conversation or, worse, actually turn away from you. It hurts when people don't acknowledge you. Others feel the same when we treat them in those ways. While it isn't always easy, particularly with people who are known to be difficult to work with, it is important for HR people to treat others with professionalism. Being discourteous is a sure way to become known as someone who cannot be approached easily.

Ensuring Alignment with HR Strategy

Without doubt, HR strategy will embrace employees, managers, suppliers, customers, and perhaps even stockholders. Each of these groups is important to the successful achievement of the company goals. Strategy is the way those goals will be accomplished. And people are always going to be the force that implements the strategy. There is a direct link to strategic completion of goals with the relationships that can cause that to happen. HR professionals touch each of the stakeholder groups along the way. It is therefore critical that HR professionals be conscious of how they impact their relationships and thus the impact they have on strategic implementation of action plans.

Providing Customer Service

Customers in the corporate sense are those people external to the organization who buy our products or services. They are the clients of governments and nonprofits who receive services. Customers and how we provide for them are the reasons that our organizations exist. Without customers we wouldn't have need for an HR organization.

For HR, our customers are our organizational employees and managers. We provide the products (e.g., insurance programs, career pathing) and services (e.g., complaint investigations, onboarding) that our customers rely on. How we service these people will determine their view of the HR group, not to mention the individuals within that group. If HR is always telling people, "You can't do that," it won't be long before the phones in the HR department stop ringing. People don't like hearing, "You can't do that." They much prefer hearing, "Let's see what we can do." Then explore with the employee and/or supervisor what is possible and what isn't. Your employee will leave with a more positive feeling having received an explanation of the reasons behind each option or prohibition. You will have provided good customer service, even if the employee didn't get exactly what was requested.

Promoting Successful Relationships

These are some basic methods for promoting successful relationships:

- Help employees understand organizational goals and strategies for achieving them.
- Give each employee an understanding about how they personally can contribute to achieving those goals.
- Acknowledge positive accomplishments when they are extraordinary.
- Showcase employee achievements in organizational publications, including the employer web site.
- Say "thank you" when people do the right thing.
- Compliment the boss for achievements of people in the group.

Managing Internal and External Relationships

Internal relationships take the form of employee and management encounters. Often HR is serving these people in some way. Managing those relationships can be best accomplished by offering a positive experience, even if the message HR is required to deliver is not one people want to hear. How it is delivered, its tone, and its level of kindness will go a long way to preserving the relationships.

External relationships exist with shareholders, regulators, enforcement agencies, media contacts, and even membership in community service clubs like Rotary, Kiwanis, and Lyons. Knowing what information can be shared and responding when appropriate will establish positive relationships with each of these groups. There is an expectation that HR professionals are "the face of the corporation" whenever someone is dealing with you in an official capacity. Even if you are on a community baseball team, you carry the flag of your employer organization. People see you as the official representative of that employer. You are an agent in that regard. You carry a large burden when that happens. You must be ready to carry it with pride and professionalism.

Championing Organizational Effectiveness

Being a cheerleader for effectiveness in your organization is another role you must play as an HR professional. When you see things that aren't working because of organizational structure or "red tape," it is incumbent upon you to intervene and suggest change. That can be a bit tricky when people have a sense of "owning" the portion of the organization that isn't working well. Working with your HR boss to identify means for influencing improvements is often a good way to approach the situation. This is another area where spotlighting success is a great way to get other people to agree to do something similar in the future when similar problems exist.

Serving as an Advocate

Employees need an advocate sometimes. When there are policy issues that need attention and large groups of employees are providing feedback that the current policy is inadequate or no longer applicable to the times, HR is responsible for consolidating those employee views and presenting them to senior management. When a discrimination complaint is filed and investigation suggests the manager is at fault, HR is the entity that will usually be responsible for providing the feedback and advocating for a remedy on behalf of the employee. Sure, there is always a need to act as an advocate for what is right. But there are also circumstances that call for an advocate when people just need to be heard. Potentially unsafe working conditions that have yet to be recognized by management can be a reason for HR's involvement. One employee working alone may not be as effective as when HR becomes an advocate for employees in general to deal with the problem.

Fostering Team Building

HR sometimes provides team building training and facilitation programs. And sometimes HR researches and recommends outside vendors for such programs. Every day, HR can support team building by recognizing team accomplishments. Offering rewards for team accomplishments can be effective, and providing acknowledgment and thanks for those accomplishments can be equally effective. An important HR role in fostering team building is in guiding supervisors on effective behaviors for high-performing teams, helping them create internal team cultures that include high trust, common vision, team unity, and accountability.

Building a Network of Contacts

Effective HR professionals will have a notebook full (or cell phone contact list full) of contacts who can help with the wide range of HR problems that can come up from day to day. Who do you call when you need a contact for employee assistance programs, workers' compensation reimbursement problems, or addiction rehabilitation programs? Who can help you set up an employee relocation program or provide in-home medical care following a difficult surgery? Each day another issue will come up, and you will be faced with having to do some research to determine what contact will help you solve your problem with or for the employee. Over time, all those vetted contacts will combine to represent a large database of references when you need to use them again.

Proficiency Indicators for Senior HR Professionals

Beyond the basic proficiency indicators are found behaviors that senior HR professionals are challenged to master.

Designing Metrics

Senior HR managers are usually involved in establishing the measurements that will indicate how they and their department are doing in their job of serving employees. Whether it's computing turnover rates or revenue to expense ratios, there are some critical aspects of HR management that should be measured. Those measurements provide feedback to the HR department but also offer reassurance to the senior executive team that HR is accomplishing its key goals as it has said it would. Designing those measurements (metrics) is a way for HR to demonstrate it is willing to be accountable for its own accomplishments. All other portions of the employer organization are measured in some ways, so, too, should the HR department.

Networking

Developing a professional network outside the organization is as important as maintaining healthy relationships with managers and employees inside the company. Other senior HR professionals at other industry organizations can help suggest solutions to problems you are having that they have already solved. As cultural norms evolve, other HR professionals can provide sounding boards for policy questions and benefit program adjustments. Maintaining a professional network of HR friends is more and more important as time goes on. Not everyone can solve all of the problems. Relying on help from other professionals is an effective way to leverage your time and resources.

Championing Customer Service

While it is a basic HR behavior to champion organizational effectiveness, it is an advanced behavior to champion customer service. Sometimes it is necessary to fight for employee treatment when budget dollars must be allocated. Adding a new paid day off to the offering will expand budget expense by a certain amount. What will be the offsetting benefit to the corporation for making that extra offering? Identifying the business needs is first. Then comes the presentation and response to executive questions about your recommendations. Serving your customers is an important role for you as an HR professional.

Negotiating with Stakeholders

It is not only employees we deal with. You will interact frequently with vendors of insurance programs, with union representatives, with state and federal enforcement agencies, and at executive HR levels with the board of directors. All are stakeholders in how an organization is run. From time to time, you will have a need to negotiate with each one. For example, changing working condition provisions in a union contract can be calculated to have a dollar impact on the budget. Settling discrimination complaints and workers' compensation cases with outside agencies will also have budget impact. Establishing a new policy sometimes requires approval of the board of directors. Persuading them to adopt the new policy is often also an exercise in convincing them to accept the budget impact it will cause.

If you are in an organization that bills its HR costs back to internal client departments, there will be negotiations to support and justify those billings. You will be called upon to discuss your department's performance on a regular basis.

Designing a Customer Service Culture

When HR workers arrive at work each day knowing that they will be expected to provide great customer service, that will be what happens most of the time. It is necessary to create a sense that providing outstanding customer service is "just the way we do things around here." When your HR department believes that, and behaves collectively to deliver that, your internal clients will be happy, and your boss will be happy.

Forbes published a list of key customer service action plan items for those who have yet to develop your own program.[13]

- *Articulate your central philosophy in a few meaningful words.* "The needs of our patients come first."
- *Distill a list of your core values.* Identify how customers, employees, and vendors should be treated at all times.
- *Reinforce your commitment to these values constantly.* Do this daily or weekly, not annually.
- *Make it visual.* Put your values on all e-mails, stationary, vehicles, and in-customer packages.
- *Make your philosophy the focus of orientation.* Make sure your employee orientation messages are reinforced by actual work experiences.
- *Train, hire, support, and if necessary discipline to enforce what's important.* Be sure the messages are consistent.

Creating Conflict-Resolution Strategies

Put two people together in a working environment, and eventually there will be some level of conflict. Put many people together, and those conflicts will happen frequently. According to SHRM,[14] "The human resource team has a leadership responsibility to develop and implement workplace conflict policies and procedures and to create and manage conflict-resolution programs. HR also initiates employee communication on conflict and tracks the metrics and costs of conflict-resolution efforts. Many HR professionals receive conflict-resolution training, often as part of their professional development, and many are accustomed to conducting such training or enlisting outside training resources for supervisors and managers.

"HR professionals often become involved in settling workplace conflicts, particularly if the employees and their supervisors cannot achieve a resolution. If HR cannot resolve a conflict, an outside specialist may be needed to work out a settlement."

Overseeing HR Decision-Making Processes

The entire HR department must be capable of making decisions that are consistent with legal requirements and also company policy. Documentation of those decisions is essential if the employer will be able to defend its actions at some later time. Then, it is necessary to train managers and supervisors to make good decisions and properly document them. Managers and supervisors hate documentation. It takes time that they don't believe they have. And some just hate writing anything. HR is accountable for overcoming those impediments and assuring that the proper standards are met.

Developing Strategic Relationships

Remember, relationships both inside and outside the organization can be strategic. That means they can help you meet your corporate goals. The senior HR professional is responsible for developing relationships that can contribute to those strategies. Think in terms of the insurance program representatives for health care and long-term disability care. How about life insurance, employee assistance contractors, relocation moving companies, and HRIS software vendors? Each of these is an important relationship that senior HR managers must develop and maintain.

Fostering Intra-organizational Culture

Encouraging understanding other of cultures is something HR can facilitate for others in the organization. International interests are obviously going to require such action and support. But within the employee group, there are more and more cultural backgrounds added to our populations. Embracing and supporting the integration of those cultures into your employee body is an important role for senior HR managers. Working with employee affinity groups can help achieve that goal. Those might include women engineers, Hispanic managers, or Black technical professionals just as examples. Hosting meetings of employees who come from outside the United States can help make people feel more comfortable in their new surroundings. Helping them understand how to contribute their cultural features to problem-solving at the company will go a long way to expanding the warm welcome you want them to feel.

Designing Strategic Opportunities

HR should have a prominent attachment to each of the corporate strategic action items. Even if HR is not specifically mentioned, the link to HR must be identified by the senior HR executive. HR must then develop its own strategic plan for supporting those links. Just how that will happen is the process of designing strategic opportunities. You must be creative and invent ways that you can support your customers in other departments.

You must identify ways to actively support their strategic goals by connecting them back to the HR functions. Those actions on your part will prove to your colleagues in other departments that you stand ready to support them as a business partner and that you will help them succeed in their goals.

Proactively Developing Relationships

It does no good to sit on the sidelines and wait for someone to come to your office with a request for help. You have to actively extend yourself to your customers. Offer to attend their departmental staff meetings so you can help people understand the new policies or benefit programs. Help them understand how the new health care laws or income taxes will impact them. Providing information to employees will help your client managers maintain a calm work environment for their employees. Upset only grows through lack of factual input. You can help alleviate such upset by extending your offer to participate personally.

Proactively developing external relationships is also important. Getting to know your vendors and learning about the way they do business can help you analyze how you use them now and in the future. The objective in all relationships is to be well enough acquainted so that when necessary you can pick up the phone and discuss whatever business problem you face.

Summary

You now know about the behavioral competency of Relationship Management. You learned that establishing and maintaining relationships is critical to the HR mission and purpose in an organization. Supporting stakeholders in reaching the strategic goals of the organization can make those achievements less painful and more rewarding.

Behavioral Competency 4—Communication

Being an effective communicator is one of the most important building blocks to a successful career in HR. First, career-level HR professionals will need to hone their oral and written communication skills to handle employee and candidate communications, grievances, and training and presentations, along with investigations. More senior-level HR professionals will require a higher level of communication skills that will be used in developing presentations, programs, policies, and various analysis or other outcomes, along with interactions with a variety of internal and external stakeholders.

Three subcompetencies comprise the Communication competency. They are defined by SHRM[15] as follows:

- **Delivering messages**   Developing and delivering to a variety of audiences communications that are clear, persuasive, and appropriate to the topic and situation
- **Exchanging organizational information**   Effectively translating and communicating messages among organizational levels of units
- **Listening**   Understanding information provided by others

Key Concepts

- Elements of communication (e.g., source, sender, receiver, message feedback)
- General communication techniques (e.g., planning communications, active listening)
- Communication techniques for specialized situations (e.g., giving feedback, facilitating focus groups, facilitating staff meetings)
- Communications media (e.g., phone, e-mail, face-to-face, report, presentation, social media)

Definition

According to SHRM, "*Communication* is defined as the knowledge, skills, abilities, and other characteristics (KSAOs) needed to effectively craft and deliver concise and informative communications, to listen to and address the concerns of others, and to transfer and translate information from one level or unit of the organization to another."[16]

Proficiency Indicators for All HR Professionals

All HR professionals are expected to conduct themselves according to the following behaviors associated with the competency of Communication:

Communicating Clarity

Communication is a vital and critical change management element. To be effective with change management in any leadership position within an organization, and especially in the HR function, will require over-communication to ensure that everyone hears and embraces a message, that they will understand the message and act accordingly. The basics of a communication model is simply:

> *Who* is the **Communicator** → *Says what* **Message** → *in what way* **Medium used** → *to whom* **Intended Receiver** → *with what effect* **Feedback**

Whether the communication is spontaneous (someone dropping into your office) or carefully planned out (all-hands meeting), the same model is applied in order to ensure impactfulness. At each step of the model, something can go south, derailing the intent or purpose of the communication. Clarity of what is intended to be communicated is absolutely of high importance in HR communications—whether they be planned communications or the informal, spontaneous type. A communicator's ability to be clear builds their credibility and helps avoid rumor mills or "noise" within an organization.

Kouzes and Posner, in their book *The Leadership Challenge*,[56] described the following behaviors that contribute to the "credibility factor" with communicators:

- Accuracy, derived from their expertise and preparation
- Consistency

- Reliability, doing what a person says they will do
- Courage to disagree when appropriate and necessary
- Integrity
- Creativity
- Maintaining confidentiality
- Creating an atmosphere that is comfortable

Listening

Effective communicators are excellent listeners. They can interpret and confirm what is being said and use this content to drive the conversation further—for example, through follow-up questions such as, "If I understood what you told me, you feel that the records are incorrect. What makes you think they are incorrect?"

Communicators must also be good observers of nonverbal messages. They can promote a more open and better discussion by using a nonthreatening manner to draw in a person who may be indicating resistance to speak (e.g., sitting with legs crossed and arms are crossed high, perhaps with a scowl on the face). Use an open-ended question that may sound to the receiver as agreement, to help elicit their openness, for example, "Chris, you would be probably one of the best people to ask this question due to your length of time in your job. What do you believe I should review?" Listening has another big benefit in communications too. Focused, authentic attention builds trust and goodwill with others, allowing you to get to the heart of what really matters.

Delivering Critical Information

The delivery of a message, especially critical messages, involves choosing the communication channel that best fits the message and the intended receiver's needs, along with a delivery style that supports the receiver's understanding of the message. Timing plus anticipation of the intended receiver's reactions are important considerations. Circling the wagon and not getting to the core point of the message within the first couple of sentences is highly ineffective. When delivering critical information, get to the factual point quickly. An example would be: "Lee, the ABC project deadline for Friday is not going to be met by my analysis and observation. I believe that if we switch Jan from the implementation group over to the analytics, we have a better chance of making a Monday deadline if we have everyone work overtime 2 hours each night next week."

Providing Constructive Feedback

In constructive feedback, you need to consider ways to be precise but also help the person to hear and apply the feedback. This can be done by framing the message in terms of the ultimate goal of the activity, what is lacking, and what specifically needs improving and what improvement would look like.

The following might be made in a coaching session aimed at helping a manager improve their ability to conduct discipline meetings:

> "You want Jim to know the reason for the meeting and the outcomes. I've observed that when Jim rambles at length and repetitively about various excuses, you lose focus on the point that he's not meeting quota and what Jim has to do to correct his quota deficiency. Yes, allow Jim to respond and explain, but keep it short and draw him back to what he can do, what he is accountable for."

The employee's understanding of the feedback can be confirmed by asking the employee to demonstrate the performance and/or by observing the employee at work. For example, in the situation described earlier, the HR professional might role-play a meeting with the manager.

Ensuring Effective Communication

Impactful communicators are prepared to shorten their message to key points if the audience is rushed or bored, tailor it if the audience has more trouble understanding or accepting a certain point, or expand the message if the audience shows great interest. They engage their audience with not just their words and supporting documentation but also with their voices and nonverbal body presence. Their gestures are appropriate to the message, such as shaking their heads up and down for positive agreement/understanding or side-to-side to signal a disapproval. They establish eye contact and have vocal qualities that amount to speaking clearly, at a pace and volume that can be heard.

Knowing Your Audience

Understanding an audience's needs and perspective relies on building awareness of common interest. This requires seeing situations through the eyes of the audience or intended receiver, an essential skill set within Emotional Intelligence. As discussed earlier, knowing how your message will be framed and delivered for understanding and acceptance will help with a communications impactfulness. Consider the audience, their needs, and perspectives when shaping your communication. This is easier with a cognitive and emotional connection.

Leading Meetings

Communication in meetings often focuses on conveying information, receiving updates, soliciting opinions, improving engagements and morale, and coordinating activities. While these are essential communication activities, meetings can become time wasters that are resented by the employees if they are a one-way street and/or are felt to be a waste of their time. All meeting facilitators would well advised to open up their meeting with the purpose and goal of the meeting and why the people present are attending. Here are additional tips for leading effective meetings:

- Set a clear agenda with defined items. Circulate the agenda before the meeting and specify what individuals may need to do to prepare for the meeting.

- Allot time according to the agenda and stay within the time limit as a show of respect for others' time.

- Start on time. Come early to allow social exchanges that strengthen relationships, but start covering the agenda at the published time.

- Take time to resolve conflicts, but postpone discussion of conflicts that may be difficult to resolve until after the meeting.

- Review any decisions and assignments at the meeting's end.

- Send an e-mail summary if needed for more complex agendas.

Proficiency Indicators for Senior HR Professionals

Beyond the basic proficiency indicators are the following additional behaviors that senior HR professionals are challenged to master.

Negotiating with Stakeholders

When negotiating with stakeholders, it's imperative that you begin dialogue with the stakeholder by asking open-ended questions about the issue at hand, their position and perspective, and the desired outcomes they have. The more information you can gather, the better you will understand what is motivating their position, and the more targeted and effective your negotiations will be. By also building an authentic dialogue with the open-ended question, you will be creating a level of trust that will help you work out a deal when a genuine connection is felt. Stakeholders need to feel that you hear and understand their point of view.

Soliciting Feedback

Significant communication events need to be evaluated as soon as possible to determine if the communication has met its objective or failed. Within the change management process, feedback is the phase of communicating that makes sure the desired outcome or action targeted is going to happen. Allowing the audience a question-and-answer period is most helpful after a presentation. Even within a one-in-one communication when delivering critical information, asking for feedback is a wise thing to do (e.g., "Leslie, so I am confident that I communicated everything that I had planned to discuss with you, will you please give me a recap of our discussion and your next actions?")

A review of what occurred for all major communication initiatives and meetings would include these evaluating questions:

- Did the intended audience react as anticipated?
- Was there confusion and, if so, about what?
- Where did the audience seem most engaged and why?
- Where did the audience seem least interested?
- Were the medium and materials used supportive and understood by the audience?
- What questions were asked? Were there interruptions and when?

Developing Communication Strategies

While not all communications require extensive planning, the costs of not planning are high. Impactful communicators create strategies for critical and/or complex communications. These strategies can include the following considerations:

- *How will the communication take place?* Face-to-face? By phone? In writing, using e-mail, text, or other methods? It is going to be difficult to assess the intended receiver's (or receivers') reactions when they are not personally in front of you. In these cases, communications should be reviewed by multiple people who can point out areas where there may be ambiguity or potential confusion. Complex topics addressed in presentations usually provide visual support materials that allow the audience to see and digest information, especially those involving numerical data. Discussions about sensitive issues may be conducted best in person or at least by phone or video conference call, rather than by e-mail.

- *When will the communication take place?* Some messages require the planning and releasing phases or portions of the message to different groups in a specific sequence. As an HR professional, you need to also consider organizational timing. What other communications might be occurring at this time that can distract from your message?

- *Where will the communication take place?* For sensitive discussions, the setting should safeguard confidentiality. For group communication events, the setting should be comfortably accommodating for the group size. Be sure to minimize the risk of distractions and interruptions with sensitive discussions.

- *Who will communicate?* Some communications will be better delivered by a presenter with authority in the organization, such as the CHRO. Others require expertise and the ability to respond to technical questions, such as the HRIS manager. Still others require communicators who are adept at listening, understanding an audience's changing needs, and responding in a positive, unthreatened way, such as the workers' compensation specialist.

- *What form of media will be used?* HR communications should consider the appropriateness of the media used to deliver the messages and intended receiver's ease with different media types, such as reading level, ability to use and access to technology, and the effects of time zones.

Communicating in various media presents certain challenges and different types of planning. The following table provides the advantages and challenges of various means of communication.

Media	Advantages	Challenges
Face-to-face (or small group)	• Provides immediate verbal and nonverbal feedback • Useful for complex, sensitive issues (e.g., conflicts, negotiations, problem-solving)	• Takes time • Requires good listening skills • Requires care to avoid conveying wrong message
Phone call	• Provides more opportunity for feedback, questions	• Requires good listening skills since there are no visual cues • Faces more competition for attention • Takes more time
Voicemail	• Saves time (when used to relay content, not make direct contact)	• Does not provide feedback or confirmation of understanding
E-mail	• Saves sender time • Allows detail • Includes multiple parties easily • Documents communication	• Requires more care to create accurate message and convey correct tone • Does not necessarily provide desired feedback • Can be missed or perceived as nuisance
Short messaging (e.g., texting, chat)	• Saves time for both parties • Can be broadcast to announce information (e.g., promotional, emergency)	• Limits content that can be communicated • Can be missed or perceived as intrusive
Social media	• Can be broadcast to large audiences • Reaches certain audiences efficiently and can elicit immediate feedback (e.g., quick surveys)	• May not reach all audiences • Requires review since the message will be widely viewed
Written report	• Allows full presentation of topic • Can reach a large audience and encourage thoughtful responses • Provides documentation of communication	• Takes time and care to create • May need to conform to organizational expectations (templates) • Takes time to get a response
Oral presentation	• Can allow immediate questions and feedback and adjustment of message • Can incorporate visuals, video, handouts	• Requires skill and time to practice • Requires time and expense to create support materials

Mastery of Delivery

Framing is often used in discussions of communication. The term reflects the process of getting an audience to see communicated topics and facts in a particular way. *Reframing* is changing the way an audience sees or feels the intended message. When an HR professional manages an employee's discouragement over a change in the workplace by pointing out benefits and opportunities for them created by the change, the HR professional is reframing the facts. Effectively framing the message requires clarity and explanation. This in turn requires:

- Articulating the objective and desired outcome of the communication
- Identifying the benefit to the intended audience
- Identifying the key points of the message and placing them in a logical order
- Providing an explanation for each point that helps the intended audience see these facts in the desired frame

Summary

In this portion of Chapter 7, we discussed the importance of and ability to effectively exchange and communicate information, both oral and written, with stakeholders. When HR information is communicated with clarity and effectiveness, the intended receivers better understand the value and purpose of what is being communicated, be it policies, practices, decisions, or changes. This in turn can have a positive effect with the audiences HR serves, both internal such as employee satisfaction and external such as candidate attraction.

Behavioral Competency 5—Global and Cultural Effectiveness

Even organizations that do not actively participate in direct international exchanges have a stake in how those relationships influence their own organization. What suppliers do does influence the pricing of products used in both manufacturing and as consumers. Follow along as we explore the nuances of a global mind-set in this section. According to SHRM, "In the context of today's increasingly global workforce, HR professionals must be able to effectively and respectfully interact with colleagues, customers, and clients of varying backgrounds and cultures."[17]

Three subcompetencies comprise the Global and Cultural Effectiveness competency. They are defined by SHRM[18] as follows:

- **Operating in a diverse workplace** Demonstrating openness and tolerance when working with people from different cultural traditions
- **Operating in a global environment** Effectively managing globally influenced workplace requirements to achieve organizational goals
- **Advocating for a diverse and inclusive workplace** Designing, implementing, and promoting organizational policies and practices to ensure diversity and inclusion in the workplace

Key Concepts

- Cultural intelligence
- Cultural norms, values, and dimensions (e.g., Hall, Hofstede, Schein, Trompenaars models)
- Techniques for bridging individual differences and perceptions (e.g., barrier removal, assimilation)
- Best practices of managing globally diverse workforces
- Interactions and conflicts of professional and cultural values

Definition

According to SHRM, *Global and Cultural Effectiveness* is defined "as the knowledge, skills, abilities, and other characteristics (KSAOs) needed to value and consider the perspectives and backgrounds of all parties, to interact with others in a global context, and to promote a diverse and inclusive workplace."[19]

Proficiency Indicators for All HR Professionals

Behaviors all HR professionals should be able to demonstrate include each of the following.

Having a Strong Set of Core Values
While Adapting to Conditions, Situations, and People

Appreciating and accepting input from other cultures can be a beneficial management technique. But having a solid foundation in the cultural expectations where we conduct business is paramount. U.S. culture is different from culture in Israel or Chile. Each has its strong points; each can contribute to the success of our enterprise. Yet if you are based in the United States, it is critical for that success to be based on compliance with U.S. requirements and culture.

Maintaining Openness to the Ideas of Others

It only makes sense to take advantage of all the knowledge and abilities other people can offer. So, does it really matter if they are U.S. citizens or from other countries? If they have positive input to the discussions you have about employee issues, shouldn't you be listening? The answer, of course, is "yes." There is no expectation that you will accept 100 percent of their input 100 percent of the time. That is no more realistic than taking 100 percent of the input of U.S. employees. But overlooking valuable resources can cause you to fall short of your effectiveness goals.

Demonstrating Nonjudgmental Respect for the Perspectives of Others

By listening more and talking less, you can learn more from other people about their mind-sets. Listening shows respect for what people have to say. It doesn't obligate anyone to agree with what is being said. It does require strong resistance to preparing rebuttal arguments while pretending to listen. When we listen to others, we can gain the nuggets of value that they have to offer.

Working Effectively with Diverse Cultures and Populations

One of the drivers of our need to communicate across cultures is the ability we now have to work remotely. It is therefore easier to have people participate from distant locations than it used to be. How we communicate effectively with them is now the problem.

Although it is not a cultural issue, time zone differences are a large issue when working with people in other parts of the world. Why? Because of this, there are often delays in responses to phone calls and messaging.

Even within the same language there are sometimes issues because of spelling differences. *Labor* in U.S. English is spelled *labour* in Great Britain and Australia. Sometimes that can confuse things. Part of the communication challenge is to be aware of these differences and encourage people to work with them, not change them for their own convenience. Thinking that someone in a different culture is stupid because they can't spell correctly will block acceptance of any value they have to offer. And believing that someone in a different country is not very smart because they have trouble with vocabulary when speaking English can ignore the fact that they are multilingual. Only about 15 to 20 percent of Americans consider themselves bilingual, compared to 56 percent of Europeans surveyed in 2006 by the European Commission.

Conducting Business with Understanding and Respect for Differences

Our global interactions bring us into contact with customs we may find strange, even unacceptable in our own culture. For example, "Many foreigners new to Saudi Arabia have to adapt to significant limits to public interaction and contact between men and women, even in business environments. Saudi Arabia is one of the most gender-segregated countries in the world. Public places such as shopping malls, restaurants, and the workplace have entire areas that are female-only. Female businesswomen meeting male counterparts in public locations are expected to be accompanied by another male."[20]

Appreciating the Commonalities, Values, and Individual Uniqueness of All Humans

We each market ourselves based on our uniqueness. Our language skills, our business background, and our specific skill demonstration all become our self-expression about who we are. If we do that, wouldn't other people as well? Of course, they do. The trick for HR professionals is to train themselves to recognize, and even encourage, self-expression from others. Getting to know who you deal with is the first stage of developing a healthy relationship. Any sales expert will tell you that it is critical to determine what the customer wants and then speak to that. In HR terms, determining a person's background, experiences, and cultural influences is important to creating a healthy relationship with them. Find out what is important to people and then speak to that topic, and you will build a long-term relationship.

Possessing the Self-Awareness and Humility to Learn from Others

"JetBlue airlines founder and former CEO, David Neeleman, spent one day each week flying on JetBlue planes, working alongside his crew serving passengers drinks and snacks and cleaning planes between flights. By doing this, Neeleman showed his humility and that work he was expecting others to do well was not beneath him. Result: The word spread about Neeleman's leadership and helped JetBlue become an employer of choice.

Two years after JetBlue was founded, it was growing so fast it needed to hire 2,000 new employees. The company received an astounding 130,000 employment applications!"[21] Humility is letting your experiences speak for themselves and not believing that you are more important than you are.

Embracing Inclusion

We would all behave with an attitude of inclusiveness if it weren't for our personal biases. Embracing inclusion begins with recognizing our biases and working to prevent them from blocking other people's contributions. Racial and religious biases are two of the biggest biases in our population today. To embrace inclusion, we must be able to reach out to people of different races and religions. Even though our laws say that we may not use these group memberships in our employment decisions, the biases we carry can often result in unseen discrimination. As HR professionals, we are responsible for leading the way with our organization's staff members and getting them to focus on recognizing their own biases. Employment decision-makers must particularly keep these thoughts in the front of their thinking when selecting people for job openings, assigning training opportunities, and making other employment decisions.

Adapting One's Perspectives and Behaviors to Meet the Cultural Context

In recent times a new term has crept into our lexicon regarding cultural acceptance and inclusion. That term is *cultural quotient* (CQ). It joins intelligence quotient (IQ) and emotional quotient (EQ) in how we think of people. "CQ is a system consisting of three interactive components: cultural knowledge, cross-cultural skills, and cultural metacognition."[22] Sometimes cultural metacognition is described as cultural mindfulness. This is the ability to recognize cultural context, analyze the cultural issues, and develop strategies to work within them.

Navigating the Differences Between Commonly Accepted Practices and Laws

When meeting someone for the first time in Japan, it is customary to present a small gift. Giving gifts in Germany is usually not done and may even be considered offensive. Gifts are seldom presented in the United Kingdom or Belgium. When conducting business meetings in the Middle East, it is expected that small talk will be exchanged before beginning a business discussion.

There are scores of legal differences between countries of the world. Here are just three areas of labor law that have different expectations.

- **Laws on paid time off**   Germany and Spain mandate 34 days of paid vacation and holidays for every worker each year, Italy and France require 31 days of paid time off, Belgium and New Zealand require 30 days, Australia mandates 28 days, and Canada's federal law requires 19 paid days off. Even Japan, which has a reputation for working employees to their limits, requires 10 paid holidays for every worker.[23] In the United States, by contrast, paid time off is mandated only under certain circumstances. For example, states such as California require paid time off for parental leave when the employee has a new child.

- **Laws on paid vacations**   The United States is the only country with an advanced economy that does not guarantee paid vacation to its workers. In the United States, no company is required to provide paid vacations to employees or pay its employees for federal or state holidays. This is considered an optional employee benefit that employers can choose to provide. The law doesn't mandate additional pay for employees who work on holidays unless such work is overtime as defined in state and federal law.[24] Paid holiday entitlement in the European Union is set at a minimum of 4 weeks (20 days) per year, exclusive of bank holidays; however, many countries are more generous. Sweden, France, and Denmark offer the most, at 5 weeks (25 days) for a standard Monday to Friday job.

- **Laws limiting hours worked**   In the United States, the Fair Labor Standards Act defines when overtime must be paid and how much that amount will be. There are few upper limits to employees working overtime. In Mexico, the constitution establishes a maximum of 8 work hours for shift workers, a maximum of 7 work hours for the night shift, and a maximum of 9 hours of overtime per week. For every 6 days of work, Mexico's workers must have 1 day off.

In the European Union, the maximum average working week (including overtime) is capped at 48 hours. The minimum daily rest period is 11 consecutive hours in every 24, and breaks are required when the working day exceeds 6 hours. The European Union requires a minimum weekly rest period of 24 hours plus an 11 hours daily rest period every 7 days.[25]

If you have employees working in other countries, it is critical that you understand the labor laws in those countries. Payroll requirements are also an obligatory focus for HR professionals.

Operating with a Global Mind-Set

Glen Fisher describes mind-sets as "differing ways that the subject at hand is perceived, understood, and reasoned about."[26] Stephen Rhinesmith says, "A mind-set is a filter through which we look at the world."[27] Being open to all cultural contributions doesn't mean accepting everything that comes along. Like any problem-solving effort, it is important to establish criteria that represents the filter you will use in identifying the way forward or solution to your problem.

National norms are one thing; local needs may be slightly different. A classic example can be found in holiday observance. The United States generally observes the following federal holidays: New Year's Day, Martin Luther King, Jr. Day, Presidents Day, Memorial Day, Independence Day, Labor Day, Thanksgiving Day, and Christmas Day. On the local level, Columbus Day in the Eastern portion of the country is an important holiday. Some locations have holidays like Founder's Day and Armistice (or Veterans) Day. In other countries, the same types of examples can be identified. Walpurgis Night, the Friday After Ascension Day, Mother's Day, and Father's Day are celebrated. In Brazil, holiday celebrations include Our Lady of Apparition, All Souls Day, and Public Proclamation Day. Locally, in Rio de Janeiro people celebrate holidays such as Umbanda, the Festival of the Goddess of the Sea, and June Bonfire Festivals (Festas Juninas).

Operating with a Fundamental Trust in Other Humans

Ralph Waldo Emerson said, "Our distrust is very expensive."[28] Without trust, influence wanes, intimacy erodes, relationships crumble, careers derail, organizations fail to prosper (and ultimately, also crumble), and, in short, nothing much works. Wherever trust is missing, opportunity is lost. Opportunity to collaborate, exert influence, deepen intimacy, build understanding, resolve conflict, expand peace, and succeed at the very things that matter most, individually and collectively. It's why building trust is the foundation of every peace negotiation, every business collaboration, and every truly meaningful endeavor.[29]

According to Roderick M. Kramer, human beings are predisposed to trust others. And touch is one way we indicate acceptance of trusting another person. The American handshake is one example. It not only says "hello" and "goodbye," it also says many other things including "I trust we will have a good relationship."[30] Sometimes we are too eager to trust. It is important, Kramer says, to temper our trust with some conscious examination of the circumstances. HR professionals are key players in building trust with stakeholders by demonstrating that HR will do what it says it will do. Making and keeping commitments is part and parcel of a trusting relationship.

Taking the Responsibility to Ensure Inclusion

Respecting individual differences will benefit the workplace by creating a competitive edge and increasing work productivity. Diversity management benefits associates by creating a fair and safe environment where everyone has access to opportunities and challenges. Management tools in a diverse workforce should be used to educate everyone about diversity and its issues, including laws and regulations. Most workplaces are made up of diverse cultures, so organizations need to learn how to adapt to be successful.[31]

Incorporating Global Business and Economic Trends into Business Decisions

Incorporating sustainable development principles into a business's mission can improve its reputation and regain public trust, increase profit margins, open new business opportunities, and reduce risks associated with less sustainable processes. Businesses are influenced to incorporate sustainable development into supply chains by consumer demand and, in some cases, by investor pressure.[32]

HR professionals must be sensitive to economics when analyzing strategies for employee benefits, payroll issues, policy development, and business impact. It is no longer acceptable for HR professionals to work in a vacuum and just make recommendations without support from a business case analysis.

Proficiency Indicators for Senior HR Professionals

 In addition to the "basic" behaviors all HR professionals are expected to master, these behaviors are essential for the success of senior HR people.

Setting a Strategy to Leverage Global Competencies for Competitive HR Advantages

More and more today, business leaders are concluding that competency in human resources is a core requirement for success. Are your human resources ready and able to answer key questions like the following?

- Do you need radical change, or will you move forward with incremental adjustments?
- Will you "rock the boat" today and add more uncertainty to your strategy, or should you wait until things are more settled?
- Is it less risky to mitigate the uncertainty of large and complex organizational changes or the potential downside of the status quo?
- Does your future business need new skills and competences, or are you comfortable with the talent you have today?

Businesses need to answer these questions, and increasingly, HR plays a key role in doing this. Suddenly, HR performance is positioned to influence the overall business performance of a company. HR leaders find themselves under heavy pressure, which calls for new skills, competencies, and profiles across the HR profession. There is also a special focus on HR senior management in charge of driving organizational medium and long-term changes.[33]

Using a Global Economic Outlook to Determine Impacts on the Organization's Human Capital Strategy

Many converging issues are driving the need to rewrite "the rules." Technology is advancing at an unprecedented rate. Individuals are relatively quick to adapt to ongoing innovations, but organizations move at a slower pace. Many still retain an industrial age structure and practices that are long outdated. Even slower moving are public policy issues such as income inequality, unemployment, immigration, and trade.

It's these gaps among technology, individuals, businesses, and public policy that are creating a unique opportunity for HR to help leaders and organizations adapt to technology, help people adapt to new models of work and careers, and help the company, as a whole, adapt to and encourage positive changes in society, regulation, and public policy.[34]

Maintaining Expert Global and Cultural Knowledge/Experience

Learning is a continuous process. It isn't enough to go to a weeklong course about the culture in the country where your company wants to conduct business. It is necessary to keep up with changes in that culture and in the expectations for legal compliance and customer service. HR staffs should maintain that intercultural knowledge and experience. When someone with those talents moves on to another job, it is necessary to identify a qualified replacement so that the needed components of HR strategic contributions can be maintained.

Maintaining Expert Knowledge of Global Economic Trends

How will the global economy impact the countries in which you do business? What are the economic trends in those countries? Who has the knowledge necessary to deal with these issues? What backups do we have for that key contact person? What role does HR play in educating employees about these trends? Answer these questions, and you will be on your way to being in control of your strategic contributions.

Understanding Global Labor Markets and Associated Legal Environments

International trade and workers' rights are two of the most complex issues in which HR can get involved. Laws vary widely around the world when focused on employee rights and treatment. Due diligence is necessary if you plan to expand into a new country. Your international labor attorney can become your best friend when that happens. You need to understand the nuances of labor laws in a new country so you can properly adjust the focus of your company's policies. This is an example of how important HR's contribution can be to the strategic decision-making process. Identifying workforce-related costs in the new country can contribute to a business decision-making exercise that will determine whether the move will be profitable.

Fostering the Organization's Cultural Norms

According to SHRM, "(It) is important to have a culture based on a strongly held and widely shared set of beliefs that are appropriately supported by strategy and structure." That's a mouthful. It means that culture evolves from shared beliefs. And if those beliefs are not supported by strategy and organizational structure (e.g., reporting relationships), the beliefs will ring hollow with employees and others outside the organization.

If a company says, "We believe in customer service at the highest level" and then doesn't behave as though customer service is important, the culture will wind up being based on poor customer service. Managers who say "People are our most important asset" and then cut into policies affecting working schedules and job assignments will have a decided impact on the organization's culture. It isn't what we say that impacts culture as much as what we do.

Proving the ROI of a Diverse Workforce

The consulting firm McKinsey & Company conducted some studies related to the question of return on investment from corporate diversity efforts.[35]

- Companies in the top quartile for racial and ethnic diversity are 35 percent more likely to have financial returns above their respective national industry medians.

- Companies in the top quartile for gender diversity are 15 percent more likely to have financial returns above their respective national industry medians.

Managing Contradictory Practices to Ensure Cross-Cultural Harmony and Organizational Success

If you accept the definition of culture as the patterns of behavior and beliefs shared by a group, then you can examine the impacts of those behaviors within the group. When cultures clash (e.g., religious dress codes, beards, or holiday observance), HR professionals are usually called upon to intercede and find some common-ground resolution that will fit for the entire organization. Doing so respects individual cultural expectations while preserving the employer's need to get work done.

How these conflicts are resolved usually involves gathering data from individuals and examining what common ground exists between conflicting viewpoints. Involving those same individuals in discussions about the issues, with HR playing the facilitation role, can often result in acceptance of the common ground as a way forward.

Integrating Perspectives on Cultural Differences and Their Impact on the Success of the Organization

Some of the elements found to have the strongest impact on cross-cultural or multicultural business include the following:[36]

- **Communicating**   Explicit versus implicit
- **Evaluating**   Direct negative feedback versus indirect negative feedback
- **Leading**   Egalitarian versus hierarchical
- **Deciding**   Consensual versus top-down
- **Disagreeing**   Confrontation versus avoidance
- **Persuading**   Holistic versus specific
- **Scheduling**   Organized time versus flexible time
- **Trusting**   Task versus relationship

Setting the Vision That Defines the Strategic Connection Between Diversity and Organizational Success

Organizational leaders are the ones on whose shoulders rest the need to set and communicate the vision for the company. They must set forth the clear desire to embrace diversity and acknowledge that diversity brings its own set of problems. With an eye on the need to resolve those conflicts, leaders can create a culture of diversity acceptance, knowing they will get a *fair chance* to express their needs and have those needs respected. Leaders, including HR professionals, must communicate that people should not expect to have all of their needs met as they are expressed but, through discussion and negotiation, can meet them in ways acceptable to others in the workforce as well.

Building Cross-Cultural Relationships and Partnerships

Regardless of their background, when cultural representatives interact, they can build strong cross-cultural partnerships if they observe seven tips recommended by Juliette C. Mayers.[37]

- *Seek to understand.* Don't make assumptions. Ideally you want to learn about different cultures through a variety of credible sources such as your own personal relationships, books, travel, research, and ongoing education.
- *Keep an open mind.* Avoid stereotypes. Expand your base by building a broad cross-section of relationships such as gender, race, sexual orientation, country of origin, and people who think differently from you.

- *Start with "who you know."* The best place to start is with others who you know inside and outside of your organization, business, and social organizations.
- *Attend multicultural networking events.* Professional organizations, cultural events, conferences, diversity forums, minority business expos, and community events are all great places to network.
- *Get involved.* Volunteer and partner with groups and organizations where you can add value, while interacting and getting to know others from different backgrounds. It will take time to build trust and to establish authentic relationships, so think long-term.
- *Keep your word.* Establishing trust is the key to sustained successful relationships. If you say you're going to do something, do it!
- *Assume positive intent.* Be positive. At some point miscommunication is likely to occur. When this happens, don't give up. Assume positive intent and continue your journey. Persistence is the key. Stay the course and establish yourself as someone with genuine interest in maintaining relationships across cultures.

Summary

In this segment, we examined global and cultural needs and their impacts when organizations begin the process of operating in other countries. Differences in the speed of work and the way in which respect is shown and expected all play a part in how we help our groups develop the common culture we want to have moving into the future. Each culture has positive contributions to make, and through discussions, those contributions can be discovered and highlighted.

Business Cluster

The Business cluster represents 18.5 percent of both exams' weighted scores. There are three competencies that fall within the Business cluster.

- Behavioral Competency 6—Business Acumen
- Behavioral Competency 7—Consultation
- Behavioral Competency 8—Critical Evaluation

This cluster covers the behaviors, attributes, and knowledge for HR professionals to identify, design, implement, and evaluate HR solutions that meet its organization's goals and objectives. These competencies address HR's ability to understand the business and environment in which the organization does business, create and implement solutions to meet the human capital needs, suggest and lead change initiatives, and gather/analyze data for informed business decisions.

Behavioral Competency 6—Business Acumen

Understanding how the business (organization) runs, what makes it financially viable, and how it can be guided to greater effectiveness is a role for HR managers that gains importance each day.

Three subcompetencies comprise the Business Acumen competency. They are defined by SHRM[38] as follows:

- **Business and competitive awareness**   Understanding the organization's operations, functions, products and services, and the competitive, economic, social, and political environments in which the organization operates
- **Business analysis**   Applying business metrics, principles, and technologies to inform and address business needs
- **Strategic alignment**   Aligning HR strategy, communications, initiatives, and operations with the organization's strategic direction

Key Concepts

- Business terms and concepts (e.g., return on investment [ROI])
- Analyzing and interpreting business documents (e.g., balance sheets, budgets, cash flow statements, profit and loss statements)
- Elements of a business case
- Business intelligence techniques and tools (e.g., online analytical processing, advanced analytics, business intelligence portals)
- Financial analysis and methods for assessing business health

Definition

According to SHRM, *Business Acumen* is defined "as the knowledge, skills, abilities, and other characteristics (KSAOs) needed to understand the organization's operations, functions, and external environment, and to apply business tools and analyses that inform HR initiatives and operations consistent with the overall strategic direction of the organization."[39]

Proficiency Indicators for All HR Professionals

These are the basic behaviors required of all HR professionals in the area of Business Acumen.

Building Strategic Relationships

Strategic relationships are symbiotic. They provide each person or entity with something that they need. Strategic relations can exist with vendors, customers, regulators, and other oversight groups. HR can contribute to those relationships through its policies, planning, and management of the HR functions. Everything HR does should support the organization's strategic planning objectives.

Understanding the Business Operations

Business operations are ongoing activities involved in the production of value for the organization's stakeholders. HR contributes to an organization's business operations by supporting its people assets in ways that enhance the organization's strategic goals and objectives.

Learning the Business and Operational Functions

"Operations management (OM) is the business function responsible for managing the process of creation of goods and services. It involves planning, organizing, coordinating, and controlling all the resources needed to produce a company's goods and services. Because operations management is a management function, it involves managing people, equipment, technology, information, and all the other resources needed in the production of goods and services. Operations management is the central core function for every company. This is true regardless of the size of the company, the industry it is in, whether it is manufacturing or service, or is for-profit or not-for-profit."[40] HR professionals should create "people" policies and practices that contribute to the organization's operational success.

Understanding the Industry

Industries are collections of enterprises doing similar things or serving similar segments of the economy. Examples include energy, retail, restaurant, communications, consumer products, and business services. Organizations within an industry either compete with one another for a portion of the market or serve those who are competing. HR policies and procedures should be constructed to enable rapid response to industry demands and competitive adjustments.

Making the Business Case for HR Management

HR should contribute key elements to organizational success. This requires the development of a business case. There are specific content requirements for a business case.

The ten elements of an HR business case include the following:[41]

- **Problem statement** In one paragraph or less, clearly state the specific business problem.

- **Background** Be sure to include significant information regarding skills, budgeting, and performance that contribute to the business problem. Indicate, in general terms, what's required to resolve or reduce the problem.

- **Project objectives** Use a maximum of seven bullet points to state what the proposed solution is trying to accomplish. Some examples may include purchasing hardware and software or selecting a new vendor.

- **Current process** Identify the organizational processes and units impacted by the proposed solution such as the training department when training is required, as well as other impacted units and relationships with clients, external partners, and the competition.

- **Requirements**   List resources needed to complete the project, such as staff, hardware, software, print materials, time, and budget.

- **Alternatives**   Outline at least four options to implementing the proposed solution. Be sure to include basic requirements for each and estimate project risks, ramp-up time, training costs, and project delays.

- **Compare alternatives**   Compare and contrast each of the alternatives with the proposed solution and the other alternatives. State similarities and differences, benefits, detriments, and costs associated with each option.

- **Additional considerations**   List critical success factors other than return on investment (ROI) metrics; for example, list the effects on partnership agreements with specific vendors or the potential need for help desk or customer support.

- **Action plan**   Propose specific action steps. State your short-term (first 3 months) and long-term (3 months to conclusion) action plans, including major milestones. This section should also include proposed metrics to measure success.

- **Executive summary**   Write a clear, one-page summary of the proposed solution. Tailor it to your audience and offer a high-level overview of research that leads you to make the proposal.

Marketing HR
HR challenges have increased in recent times. Identifying, attracting, and holding onto qualified talent are the number-one priorities in many industries. The trades (carpentry, plumbing, electrical) are in crisis because they don't have a supply of qualified talent from which to draw. That leads to the need to be innovative in how to "grow your own" or support training programs that will graduate qualified people who can be hired. HR plays a key role in those strategies. Letting people inside the organization know that HR is working on their behalf to accomplish these types of critical functions is important to creating HR credibility within the organization.

Applying Organizational Metrics
Metrics are measurements. Organizational metrics are measurements of individual functions or specific business processes within the organization. Applying metrics involves identifying the things to be measured that are critical indicators of success for the organization. Then, once the measurements have been identified, it is necessary to prepare a plan for implementing or applying them.

Business metrics can include things such as creating policies that attract top talent to fill job openings and identifying applications for social media in raising revenues. HR metrics within those business metrics might include annual benchmarking within the industry for employment policies to be sure your organization remains competitive and HR actions that can support social media programs.

Using Organizational Metrics

HR can employ organizational metrics easily enough. Here are two very basic measurements that impact HR:

- **Revenue per employee** Divide the revenue by employee head count.
- **Expense per employee** Divide the expense element (or total expense) by employee head count.

These can be applied to the total organization or to individual elements (divisions, departments) within the organization.

Metrics can be tactical or strategic. Tactical metrics are such things as reasons why people accept job offers, levels of satisfaction with the boss (supervisor, manager), and number of new hires made within the target date on each requisition. Strategic metrics are things like goals or targets met within a period of time (month, quarter, year), value received for HR programs compared to forecast value, and achievement rates for revenue or expense targets and goals.

Leveraging Technology

Technology plays an indispensable role in today's employment world. Yet technology without proper consideration of its impact on the workforce is not helpful. Technology can have a positive effect on human resources. It can play a key role in communicating, interacting, collaborating, and training workers. Making sure technology is working for you and not against you is the process of leveraging technology to its greatest advantage.

Training used to be done in a classroom environment. People would have to travel to the training location, stay in hotels or long-term housing, eat meals out, do laundry, and do other activities that allowed them to remain in the training for the time required. Technology today allows training to be done electronically, so traveling to a central training site is no longer necessary. People can stay at home and participate in training while on the job or away from the workplace. That saves time and money. Measuring the savings is one way to support HR's contribution to organizational economic performance.

Proficiency Indicators for Senior HR Professionals

 Senior HR professionals are expected to be able to do and say these following 19 behaviors over and above the basic behaviors we have already reviewed. If you are studying for the SHRM-SCP exam, pay close attention to these requirements.

Developing ROIs for All HR Initiatives

Return on investment (ROI) is a way of expressing the financial benefit gained from any given business activity. You can talk about ROI of a new paid time off policy when looking at the impact on absence rates and expenses. You can examine ROI for offering employee access to their employment record on the organization's computer network.

It can allow employees to enter their own data changes (marriage name change, birth of a new child for health care enrollment, or updating educational achievements when receiving a new degree). Such programs can reduce the payroll expense in the HR department and thereby offer an opportunity to compare the payroll savings with the expense associated with the technology program permitting employee record access.

Assessing Risks/SWOT

There are two sources of risk for any organization: internal and external. Internal risks come from strengths and weaknesses. External risks come from opportunities and threats. Together, they form the acronym SWOT.

- **Strengths**   Advantages you and your team have that will help you reach project goals. It's important to know your special skills that give you an advantage. Lack of strengths in a specific area can define a risk.

- **Weaknesses**   Anything internal to your organization or team that could prevent you from meeting objectives. Something that gives you a disadvantage relative to others.

- **Opportunities**   External facts that could lead to a positive outcome in meeting objectives. Overlooking opportunities can be described as representing specific risks.

- **Threats**   External elements that could jeopardize your project.

Aligning HR Strategy, Goals, and Objectives

According to SHRM, "Identifying and implementing workforce strategies in a challenging global economy is a high-priority issue for top executives. To be successful, HR professionals and business leaders together must grapple with the many variables that affect the organization's ability to attain its strategic objectives. They must develop quantitative and qualitative approaches to efficiently and effectively attract, engage, and retain human capital."[42] Once HR strategy, goals, and objectives are all in alignment, the outcomes are more likely to be positive. Creating action plans to implement strategies and then achieving specific goals and objectives become easier once they are identified and written. Even more important for other managers in the organization is the ability this will provide for showing how HR can support them in their efforts toward their goals and objectives.

Demonstrating Business Language Fluency

It has become clear that for HR professionals to be accepted as strategic business partners with other executives in the organization, they need to be able to talk about what they do using business terminology. So, expressing the budget impact for a new employee benefit program and then showing the offset that can be accomplished by reducing turnover costs will speed acceptance and credibility for HR. Business language includes profits, loss, cost impact ratios, industry position impact for given programs, and revenue impact ratios for HR programs that can be sold outside the organization.

Examining Organizational Problems

Problem identification is a critical step in the process of finding solutions. Too often, people rush to express their thoughts about solutions without first identifying the problem they face. Problem identification is a process of questioning what is getting in the way of achieving specific goals and objectives. For example, what is preventing us from getting more employee enrollment in the company retirement savings program? Why is the turnover rate in the accounting department above normal? How can we reduce the cost of training managers in the new safety requirements? Once the problem is identified, you can begin working on solutions but not before.

Sometimes, people rush to recommend solutions without a problem having surfaced. That situation presents a solution in search of a problem. If you are to be part of the executive team in your organization, you should get into the habit of clearly laying out the problem before rushing to identify solutions.

Developing Solutions

Problem-solving techniques are many and varied. They all basically have these steps in common:

1. *Define the problem.* What is it that gets in the way of our reaching our goals?

2. *Identify options.* What might we do to eliminate the problem? These are the solutions we think might work.

3. *Evaluate the options.* Develop a list of criteria any solution must meet to be acceptable and then compare each of the options identified against that list of criteria. Any option that doesn't pass this test must be discarded. What remains is a list of those options that can work.

4. *Choose an option and implement it.* Make a judgment about what might be best of all the options that pass the criteria screening. Identify what is necessary for the successful implementation in the form of an action plan.

5. *Evaluate the solution.* Ask if the chosen solution actually solved the problem. Did it create other problems? What other follow-up action might be required?

Evaluating Proposed Business Cases

Business case analysis (BCA) looks at programs, solutions to problems, or other action plans with the eye on how they will impact the business. In every analysis, consideration must be given to the impact the activity or plan will have on the overall business operation. What is the impact on profit or loss? What is the impact on corporate image in the marketplace? What is the impact on product liability? What is the impact on employee retention? Not all of these will be the focus of any one evaluation. But all are eventually going to be part of some business case analysis at some time.

Ultimately, business case analysis is a means of projecting accountability for taking any action. Business case analysis demands accountability. Any senior HR professional these days must be willing to be accountable for the success or failure of their programs.

Putting their job on the line is something HR professionals are expected to do every day. It is no longer acceptable to duck accountability by excusing results as unmeasurable people issues. If it can't be measured, it shouldn't be done.

Benchmarking the Competition

According to Ross Beard, "Competitive benchmarking can be defined as the continuous process of comparing a firm's practices and performance measures with that of its most successful competitors."[43] For HR professionals, that may mean identifying compensation levels through periodic compensation surveys. It could involve comparative analysis of insurance benefits being offered in other organizations within the industry compared to those offered in our organization. What "leading-edge" programs are being offered by competing companies? Might they work here? What would be the business impact of adapting such programs?

Communicating Global Labor Market Direction

Communicating global labor market direction first requires identifying what that direction might be. Is there a trend for exporting manufacturing jobs to Asian countries? Is there a trend to return manufacturing jobs to the United States? What trends are politically motivated, and what are economically motivated?

Once identified, the trends can be articulated and communicated to executives within the organization. Perhaps there is an impact on technology workers because it is suddenly no longer economically viable to produce computer components off-shore. Maintaining a competitive edge in the marketplace requires following those economic benefits and moving production units to locations where the work can be done for less money. The executive team needs input from HR professionals that will allow them to make these types of decisions.

Maintaining Expert Knowledge

HR is responsible for identifying sources of expert knowledge that can be used when job openings occur in any department of the organization. It is also critical that HR protect its own expert knowledge. That is often done through specifying a certification requirement when searching for HR professionals. When expert knowledge leaves through normal turnover, the organization's goals and objectives can be negatively impacted if there is no backup available. Fast replacement is often needed. That means HR must have done its homework and already identified sources for candidates with that knowledge.

Developing HR Business Strategies

In the beginning, there are corporate strategies. These are normally developed by executives representing each of the major organizational work units such as legal, production, research, engineering, accounting, and, of course, HR management. Once organizational strategies are clearly defined and documented, each individual work unit can begin developing their specific strategic plans to support the larger organization.

Administrative support entities are unique in that they serve all operational units in the organization. What they do impacts the internal client groups. So, strategic planning for support groups must be focused on the services they offer to internal clients. That means fancy HR initiatives and the latest fashionable HR programs should take a back seat to delivering the HR support needed by the client groups. Once clients are satisfied, HR professionals can spend time thinking about upgrading to the latest versions of HR management programs.

For each strategy there should be at least one action item in the action plan. Implementing a strategy is necessary to reflect its reason for existing. If you don't plan to take action on the strategy, scratch that strategy off your list because it is going to use energy for monitoring and maintenance without delivering any practical value to your group.

Maintaining Knowledge of Economic Factors

Human resource management is a function that embraces pieces of each organizational unit, carrying some influence over the success or failure of those portions of the internal client functions. If staffing is not done in a timely way by HR management, the production and accounting organizations cannot perform their tasks successfully.

HR's influence is dependent upon knowledge of economic factors. The annual company budget is dependent upon knowing the cost of compensation in all departments. HR holds the key to those numbers and any adjustments that will be required and appropriate in the coming year. The cost of employee benefit plans is also something that HR oversees but shares with client organizations inside the company. If HR professionals don't understand the economic impact of these expenses, the support they provide to other groups cannot be sound or effective. It would be like the legal staff providing bad legal advice to other departments.

HR is often responsible for a large portion of the employer's compliance efforts, from safety to equal employment opportunity. Done improperly, the economic impact to the business can be quite severe, including fines and legal judgments.

Evaluating Critical Activities

Each effort we make in our jobs should be subject to review and evaluation. Review involves checking to be sure we have included the topic in our action planning. Evaluation is the effort to determine the value achieved by the action taken.

Balanced Scorecard

Developed by Robert Kaplan and David P. Norton, a *Balanced Scorecard*[44] helps evaluate HRM effectiveness. The Balanced Scorecard contains four dimensions: financial performance of an organization, its customer service, its internal business processes, and its capacity to learn and achieve growth. Within these four areas, managers need to identify key performance indicators the organization should track. The financial dimension reflects a concern that the organization's activities contribute to improving short-term and long-term financial performance.

Customer service perspective measures such things as how customers view the organization, as well as customer retention and satisfaction. Business process indicators focus on production and operating statistics, such as order fulfillment or cost per order. The final component relates to the human resource and its potential to learn and grow. This perspective seeks to focus on how well resources and human capital are being managed for the company's benefits.

The Balanced Scorecard provides a balanced picture of current performance as well as the triggers for future performance. The scorecard helps managers align their business units, as well as their financial, physical, and human resources, to the firm's overall strategy.

What needs emphasis is that the HR evaluation should not be confined only to the people dimension of the scorecard. The HR professional should be judged on all the dimensions of the scorecard. HR executives tend to believe that their success should be judged only by the extent to which they meet employee needs. As the scorecard indicates, employee commitment is only one criterion for effective HR performance, and HR professionals will be held accountable for all the dimensions like other managers.

Knowing the Business

It is up to HR to understand the business it supports. Are there seasonal workflow fluctuations? Are there peaks and valleys for employment activity? How important are specific educational backgrounds for future employees? What colleges will provide the skills that new hires will require? How much do employee benefit programs contribute to employee retention programs?

How do labor relations efforts work in this employer organization? What type of employee benefits are needed to attract and retain the type of qualified people you need?

Brainstorm the specific questions you must ask so that you understand the business you are supporting. Revisit these questions and others at least annually. Invite critical updates from internal client executives at any time during the year.

Setting Technology Strategy

The information technology (IT) department is responsible for corporate technology initiatives. But HR professionals are responsible for IT developments within their own realm of influence. What programs will permit employees to access and update their own employee records in the human resource information system (HRIS)? What types of programs will give employees the opportunity to do online comparisons of various benefit programs they may want to consider? How can new policies be introduced online so training costs can be controlled?

Overall, HR professionals are given the responsibility of identifying the strategy they will apply for IT within the HR department. Knowing how that will impact and contribute to company strategies is something the HR professional must undertake.

Serving as a Strategic Contributor

For years HR professionals have been clamoring for "a seat at the table," meaning they want to "play with the big boys and girls" in the corporate suite. That is not something that is given to HR. It is something HR must earn. Proving that HR belongs at the executive table can be done only through demonstration of strategic contributions to the corporation. HR professionals have been welcomed into the "C-suite" (corporate executive suite) discussions when they have been able to show they add value to the discussions and programs.

Influencing Government Policy

Compliance with government regulations is often delegated to the HR department. Occupational Safety and Health Administration (OSHA) rules about safety require compliance efforts for all employers, regardless of size. Department of Labor (DOL) regulations about wages and hours of work, federal contracting, and the Equal Employment Opportunity Commission (EEOC) all require compliance efforts.

Employers can influence government policy by monitoring the *Federal Register* postings of proposals for regulatory changes. Identifying how those proposals will impact their employer is a service HR professionals can provide. Submitting those studies with editorial comments to the agency proposing the changes will help by giving "real-world impact" input to the government. Testifying at government hearings at local, state, and federal levels is another way to offer input to government changes governing employee management issues.

Developing Business Strategy with Top Leaders

HR professionals have a great deal to offer their organization's strategic planning process. Participating with the top leaders of the organization in that effort will cement HR's relationship with the executive team. Offering to take on responsibility for key strategic plans will assure the executive team invites HR back to participate in the future.

Defining Strategy for Managing Talent

We know now that any HR strategy must compliment overall employer strategy. Managing talent is a strategic contribution to the organization's interest in maintaining a workforce needed to produce products and services for financial success.

Talent management requires recruiting, onboarding, training, probationary observation periods, and assessment of match for talent to needs. HR can likely develop a strategy for each of these components of workforce oversight.

Summary

In this section, we identified the need for HR professionals to gain and exercise the knowledge and skills associated with business acumen. Assessing financial impacts of business proposals related to employee management is an important HR contribution to executive discussions and proposal considerations. All HR programs should be assessed periodically using business management tools, including profit and loss sheets and balance sheets. HR professionals cannot have credibility with other executives unless they have this ability to analyze programs using business considerations, business and competitive awareness, and an alignment of strategies in HR with corporate strategies.

Behavioral Competency 7—Consultation

Providing advice and counsel to your clients is one of the biggest roles and most important for HR professionals. There are some important components of that effort you should be developing or polishing.

Five subcompetencies comprise the Consultation competency. They are defined by SHRM[45] as follows:

- **Evaluating business challenges**   Working with business partners and leaders to identify business challenges and opportunities for HR solutions
- **Designing HR solutions**   Working with business partners and leaders to design HR solutions and initiatives that meet the business needs
- **Implementing and supporting HR solutions**   Working with business partners and leaders to implement and support HR solutions and initiatives
- **Managing change**   Leading and supporting maintenance of or changes in strategy, organization, and/or operations
- **Interacting with customers**   Providing high-quality customer service and contributing to a strong customer service culture

Key Concepts

- Organizational change management theories, models (e.g., Lewin's change management model, McKinsey 7-6 model, Kotter's eight-step change model), and processes (e.g., leadership buy-in, building a case for change, engaging employees, communicating change, removing barriers)
- Consulting processes and models (e.g., discovery, analysis and solution, recommendation, implementation), including the contributions of consulting to organizational systems and processes
- Effective consulting techniques (e.g., understanding organizational culture, understanding areas and limits of one's own expertise, setting reasonable expectations, avoiding overpromising)
- Key components of successful client interactions (e.g., listening, empathy, communication, follow-up)
- Methods for design and delivery of HR service functions and processes (e.g., issue tracking, client service)

PART II

Definition

According to SHRM, *Consultation* is defined "as the knowledge, skills, abilities, and other characteristics (KSAOs) needed to work with organizational stakeholders in evaluating business challenges and identifying opportunities for the design, implementation, and evaluation of change initiatives and to build ongoing support for HR solutions that meet the changing needs of customers and the business."[46]

Proficiency Indicators for All HR Professionals

Every HR professional should have the ability to behave in ways that will offer their organization these competencies.

Applying Creative Problem-Solving

Of course, there are "old" problems that keep cycling back demanding attention. Those include open insurance benefit enrollment each year. Yet there are even more "new" problems that arise requiring more than compliance. Those problems demand unique approaches that can keep our organizations running smoothly with attention to new requirements. Perhaps the conversion of HR's role to include oversight of electronic employee records is the best example. Each organization has its own needs and cultural expectations demand that the HRIS respond to those needs.

Creative problem-solving for such a company-wide effort should involve representatives from all aspects of company life. Together, identifying the problem ("How do we convert paper record systems into an HRIS?") and exploring possible solutions can result in a superior approach that wouldn't have been possible absent a bit of creativity.

Remember the basics of creative problem-solving and assume the role of facilitator so you can guide your colleagues to a proper conclusion.

Steps to Creative Problem-Solving

These are the steps to creative problem-solving:

1. *Identify the problem.* Rushing into generating a list of solutions without everyone being clear about what problem you are trying to solve will result in a lot of wasted time. It is likely that your committee will generate solutions for many different problems, without any idea how they all fit together.

2. *Generate a list of possible solutions.* This can be done by brainstorming or some other technique you personally prefer. Teach people in your group how to apply the technique you choose and then go to town. Get as many solutions on your list as you can. You can evaluate them in the next step. For now, just make the list as long as possible.

3. *Create a list of criteria for acceptable solutions.* It is necessary to have an idea about how to evaluate the solutions you generate so you can compare each against the criteria and determine which will meet all the requirements and which must be scratched from the list.

4. *Re-evaluate your list of remaining solutions.* Select the one you want to use as your problem solution. Assign responsibilities for communication of the new solution to managers and employees.

5. *Coordinate implementation of the solution across the company.* Perhaps a pilot program could determine whether the solution will really work as expected. If so, you can expand the pilot into a full-blown introduction company-wide.

6. *Evaluate the results.* It is important to measure the results to determine whether they meet your expectations.

Serving as an In-House Expert

No one in the organization knows as much about employee programs as the professionals in the HR department. Being an in-house expert is just part of what HR people do. Remember that being accurate is one of the job demands. Loss of credibility can happen in a heartbeat. So, be sure you are correct before answering questions. Do your homework. Study each of the subject areas you are assigned. They can include wage and hour rules, union contract provisions, discrimination prevention requirements, management skills training, employee relocation services, HRIS administration, and so many more. Become the expert people will look to for answers when they have questions. Again, you should know all applicable U.S. employment laws (found in Chapter 3) and your local laws that apply to where you have employment.

Analyzing Specific Business Challenges

Have you ever had one of your external customers tell the sales and marketing organization that you must attest that your organization is compliant with equal employment opportunity and affirmative action requirements? It is not unusual for customer organizations, particularly local governmental entities, to say they require adherence to stricter requirements than those imposed by the federal government. There are many reasons for such a difference, many of which are not founded in law. They may require release of sensitive employee data to "prove" your organization is doing what the customer's requirements demand. In these situations, along with your sales and marketing people, you have the opportunity to determine whether you are willing to release the data required or push back with objections and negotiate. When the customer is adamant about its submission demands, you are faced with the question about whether you will comply or forego business with that customer. All along the way, you must identify issues, provide assessment of those issues to others in the decision-making group, and offer recommendations with your rationale. The final decision is not going to be made by HR for many of these types of issues. Yet the final decision depends on high-quality staff work by HR professionals.

Generating Organizational Interventions

What happens when the production department and the maintenance department have a conflict over access to machinery? Production wants to use the machinery for production. Maintenance wants to use the machinery for updates and repair. Both cannot prevail without some compromise. HR can help identify how union and wage and hour rules can be used to support a solution to the problem. Scheduling maintenance work during a shift that is not used for production is one approach. HR can facilitate the resolution by knowing legal requirements and offering support to both departments and their own missions. In the end, the only thing that matters is having the company reach its objectives.

Developing Consultative and Coaching Skills

Everyone needs personal help from time to time, even managers and executives. One of the most satisfying and productive HR roles is that of counselor and coach.

Ten Tips for Building Relationships with Your Clients During Meetings[47]

- *Do your homework.* Be sure you know the mission and goals of the organizational unit you will be working with.

- *Listen before you talk.* Ask questions to be sure you understand the client's needs. Tell them you will be taking notes as the meeting progresses. That is so you don't forget a follow-up item and also so you capture key points along the way.

- *Learn about your client's vision of the future.* Where will their portion of the organization be in another few years? Will their role be changing within the company?

- *Provide anecdotes and examples.* Help your clients understand the nuances of HR requirements and options. Always try to relate your message specifically to your clients through conversation and with a storytelling approach. Describe similar situations and offer examples of how others handled situations successfully.

- *Offer to work with other advisors.* Perhaps the legal staff or accounting should be involved in the discussion. Be willing to work with others so your advice can satisfy the client's needs.

- *Save your clients time and effort.* Your client is busy like you are. If you can help them save their time and budget dollars, you will be doing them a favor.

- *Use technology.* Suggest web portals or apps that can help the client with their problem(s).

- *Build a team approach.* Whenever possible, make use of your HR colleagues as backup to your personal participation in the discussions. If you are a sole HR practitioner, this will be more difficult, but it may be possible for your boss to help out.

- *Find out how clients prefer to be contacted.* Not everyone prefers e-mail contact. Some would rather have text messages or even a voice phone call. If the client doesn't have a preference and you do, ask if you can contact them the way you find best for you.

- *Follow up.* After the meeting, follow up with your client to thank them for their time and suggest you are available for additional discussions if they would like to have more sessions.

There are some steps you can take to practice your coaching skills in addition to those you use for consultation.

Coaching Skills[48]

- *Listen with curiosity.* Convey a genuine interest in what others have to say.

- *Take in what you hear.* Concentrate on what the other person is saying. Don't be thinking about what your next comment will be.

- *Reflect with accuracy.* Active listening is a skill that HR professionals must develop. Comments like "So, what you're saying is…" and "What I'm hearing is…" are good ways to recap what you think you heard. If it is incorrect, the other person can make the necessary correction by saying, "No. What I really meant was…."

- *Ask open-ended questions to explore more fully.* Who, what, when, where, and how are the way to begin questions that can't be answered with a simple "yes" or "no." They require an explanation and allow the coach to get additional information that will be helpful in providing the advice necessary.

- *Provide feedback for development.* Understand the individual's strengths and weaknesses and know that feedback is what we all need to be sure we are on track with the journey to our goals. Feedback is not an accusation or complaint. Feedback consists of suggestion and rationale, reinforcement, and praise.

Guiding Employees

Every day, employees will walk into the HR department with questions. Today it will be about life insurance. Tomorrow it will be about a discrimination complaint. Later in the week it will be someone asking how to correct some of the information in their employee records. Guiding employees to a solution that they can implement themselves is going to free you to help others more quickly than if you took on the problem resolution yourself.

Employees are sometimes confused. They don't often know the law and its application. And sometimes they don't even know company policy. Guiding them through understanding where to find the answers they need is a good approach. You may have an employee who wants to file a discrimination complaint because their boss has just told them their work performance must be improved or there will be further steps toward a performance improvement program. Everything is called discrimination when it actually may not be discrimination. Employees don't know that. You can help them understand the legal requirements for something to actually be called illegal discrimination.

Sexual harassment problems are usually just the opposite. People say, "I need to tell you something, but I don't want you to do anything." You have to guide them to understand that once you are aware of the problem, you are obligated to do something about it. You can't keep things to yourself.

Proficiency Indicators for Senior HR Professionals

 Senior HR professionals have much more impact on the business because they are involved in developing strategies that will contribute to the company achieving its goals.

Creating Talent Management Strategies

Managing talent depends on knowing two things. What talent exists in the incumbent workforce, and what talent needs exist in the organization now and into the future?

A strategy is a plan for how you will reach your goal. If the goal is to determine what talent needs exist that can't be met by your incumbent workforce, then the strategy can reflect how you will obtain that talent from external sources. Finding new recruiting sources for minorities, women, disabled, and veterans can be helpful. Utilizing the resources of specific groups such as the Institute for Electrical and Electronic Engineers (IEEE), technical school graduates, or the United States Chef Association can tap into specific talent and skills that you may require. Identify the needs you have and then explore how those needs might be met with a campaign aimed at specific groups.

Listening

Listening is an often-underrated skill. Most people don't do it very well. Senior HR professionals must develop this skill so it can be used to help internal clients and even vendors and recruiting sources from outside.

You will recall our discussion earlier about the communication cycle. It requires a message to be sent from the speaker to the listener. Then, it requires feedback from the listener to the speaker to be sure the message was received and understood in its entirety. The communication cycle embodies the concept of active listening. It requires listening for the meaning of the message, not just the words being used. Feedback to the speaker will allow the speaker to confirm the listener's understanding or give the speaker an opportunity to correct the misunderstanding.

Feedback amounts to comments like "What I hear you saying is…" or "You're telling me…." It is often helpful as the speaker to request feedback from the listener. This is helpful for supervisors and managers who are giving instructions to workers. After the instruction, say something like, "Now, tell me what you are going to do," Or "so I know I have clearly conveyed what I intended, please tell me what you understood and what action you will be taking."

Developing Human Capital Visions

A vision is a statement of what you want for the future. Steve Jobs had a vision that Apple's desktop computer would be the best on the market. He also had a vision that Pixar could become a leader in animated entertainment. He articulated those visions and developed strategic plans to support them. And, guess what? They came to pass.

It is always amazing to hear people talk about "overnight successes." The fact is, not very many successes actually develop overnight. They take years and suddenly appear to have just happened because they broke through the background clutter and are now visible as a force in the world.

Human capital changes, faster in some industries than in others. Yet it changes. When USS-POSCO, the joint venture of U.S. Steel and POSCO steel in Korea, decided to work together, there were some basic requirements they had to meet for the success they wanted. They completely refurbished the factory that U.S. Steel had in Pittsburg, California. It was changed from a steel smelting operation to a plant that would "cold-roll" steel for customer use. Cold-rolled steel is used to make refrigerators, computer housings, automobile parts, and "tin" cans for the food industry. The smelting and hot rolling was to be done in Korea; then the rolls of steel would be shipped to Pittsburg, California, where they would be rolled again but without heating. Some of the stock would be zinc coated to produce galvanized steel. The thing is, none of this can be done by people manually operating the machinery that squeezes the steel smaller and smaller in thickness by thousands of an inch at a time. It is all controlled by computer. That meant employees had to undergo 6 months of training in statistical process control, machinery, and hydraulic operations. The talent requirements for the new factory shifted from laborer and craftspeople to technicians. They had to find their new employees somewhere other than they had been looking historically.

Your vision of human capital in the future of your organization will demand a new strategic plan for attaining the goals associated with that vision.

Maximizing ROI for the Organization

HR Professionals magazine identifies several elements of the effort to maximize return on investment for an organization.[49]

- **Perceptual elements** How we learn and retain new knowledge (auditory, visual, tactile and/or kinesthetic, and verbal)

- **Psychological elements** How we process new information and for making decisions/solving problems (analytic/global, reflective/impulsive)

- **Environmental elements** How the work environment contributes to or detracts from productivity (sound or quiet, bright or low light, warm or cool temperature, informal or formal seating)

- **Physiological elements** How we remain energized and stay alert at work (time of day, intake, and mobility)

- **Emotional elements** How quickly we complete challenging and complex tasks (internal or external motivation, single- or multiple-task persistence, more or less conformity, and more or less structure)

- **Sociological elements** How we prefer to work and interact effectively with others (alone/pair/ small or large group, more or less authority, more or less variety)

Making sure the organization receives the greatest financial return on its investment in HR is the duty of every senior HR professional.

Using Appropriate Analytical Tools

Data analysis is a growing responsibility of the HR professional. Particularly at the senior HR levels, determining and interpreting the data are critical functions. The question is, how do we perform those analyses?

Some of the software available for use in data analyses include Orange Data Mining, R Software Environment, Weka Data Mining, Tableau Public, Arcadia Data, Microsoft R, ITALASSI, Shogun, Trifacta, ELKI, Scikit-learn, Data Applied, Lavastorm Analytics Engine, Gephi, DataMelt, TANAGRA, Julia, RapidMiner Starter Edition, SciPy, KNIME Analytics Platform Community, and Dataiku DSS Community. Most of these are languages that will require programming assistance.

"As enterprises have more and more data at their fingertips, the expectation is now that your average business user can have access to key metrics in real-time—without having to know what SQL means."[50]

This has led to a boom in companies dedicated to building data visualization and analysis tools that can be used by almost anyone within the business. Gone are the days of waiting for an analyst to generate a report that is out of date the minute you get it or spending weeks mired in Excel." The explosion of databases and uncounted web sites gathering information about visitors has led to a boom in the software being offered to do the analysis job. "This boom is reflected in the figures ... that the global business intelligence (BI) and analytics software market could grow further to $22.8 billion by 2020."

Identifying Creative Solutions

Senior HR professionals are the key players in their organizations who can explore alternative solutions for difficult, often new problems. Sure, the old problems about helping employees understand the benefit plan choices will still be around. But now there are issues such as protecting the HRIS data from external hackers. Dealing with industrial espionage, key employees walking away for jobs at competitor companies, and key vendors closing up shop are just three of the types of problems you can face in today's world.

How you deal with these problems will determine whether you are going to survive as an HR department without turnover in key HR personnel. Creative approaches are the ones that explore options. Executives want to know what is possible, not what is impossible. It is up to senior HR executives to help them find those alternatives.

Supervising HR Investigations

One element of HR management that should be consistent is the investigation of employee complaints. There are some legal experts who believe that the employer's legal staff should conduct all the investigations. Other people within the legal community counsel that HR should be the investigating group so there is a separation of investigator and legal counsel.

However you approach the issue in your organization, you will want to be sure that every complaint investigation is handled in the same rigorous and systematic way. Methodology is important. Touchstones during the investigation are important. Discrimination complaints must meet certain requirements. If an employee says she has been discriminated against because of her sex, it is necessary to determine what happened that has resulted in her paying a penalty of some kind. And what was that penalty? If those basic elements are present, the *prima facie* case has been established. Then the investigation must gather evidence to show that the complaint can be substantiated.

Should our organization treat each complaint on its emotional value rather than its evidentiary value, our liability will likely be increased. Ultimately, the complaint will migrate to state or federal enforcement agencies and sometimes to the courts. Senior HR managers must supervise those conducting the investigations to remedy problems when that is appropriate and to explain that the employee does not have the evidence to support her claim if that is the appropriate outcome.

Recognizing HR Liabilities

According to SHRM,[51] these are the top ten employment liabilities in the modern workplace. Some of these may be covered by insurance, and others will not be subject to insurance protections. Some coverage will depend on specific policies designed to cover risks of discriminatory treatment among other issues.

- **Wage and hour claims**   Violations of FLSA and state counterparts can cause employer exposure to financial remedies.
- **Class action lawsuits**   More frequently these days employees are banding together to consolidate their complaints into a class action lawsuit. It means the exposure for employers is higher as a result.
- **FMLA violations**   Not following the Family and Medical Leave Act can bring financial remedies that could be quite costly.
- **Whistleblowers**   These are employees who file complaints that something illegal is happening at the employer's organization.
- **Data breaches**   This is loss of employee data that could lead to identity theft.
- **Social media**   Beware of negative reviews of company policies or employment practices.
- **Alternative work arrangements**   Telecommuting, job sharing, and other alternative work schedules can lead to FMLA complaints and more.
- **Discrimination complaints**   Violations of civil rights laws brings exposure for financial remedies.
- **Sexual harassment**   Also a violation of civil rights law, workplace behavior that is sexual in nature can bring employer liability.
- **Gender and sexual orientation claims**   Most recently defined of the civil rights protections, this type of complaint and financial remedy is just gaining traction.

Coaching Executives

More than any other, this skill will allow HR managers to leverage influence in the employer organization. Teaching line executives how to evaluate problems that have HR implications is a way to help them deal with issues within their own organizational unit.

And there is the personal element of coaching. Executives sometimes need help to adjust their personal approach to managing employees. Sometimes they don't see what their behavior is doing adversely to the workforce. Helping them understand that impact and exploring alternative approaches can give the executive a path to greater effectiveness.

Designing Strategic HR and Business Solutions

Strategy is the plan that you will implement to achieve your goals. HR strategy should always support business solutions. HR must help the organization meet its goals. Proving that link is the duty of a senior HR professional. When problems arise that were not anticipated, HR professionals should be key players in developing the appropriate solutions so company goals will be supported.

Summary

Behavior competency 7, Consultation, has explored the things that HR professionals say and do that will provide quality support to other departments. Collaborative interactions can be rewarding and satisfying when the impact is measured and found to contribute to company goals.

Behavioral Competency 8—Critical Evaluation

The days of "winging it" are in the past. HR professionals are now able to access vast amounts of data to help them in their decision-making. This area of behavioral competency looks at the extent to which that information is gathered, assessed, and used in the decision-making process.

Four subcompetencies comprise the Critical Evaluation competency. They are defined by SHRM[52] as the following:

- **Data advocate**   Understanding and promoting the important and utility of data
- **Data gathering**   Understanding how to determine data utility and identifying and gathering data to assist and inform with organizational decisions
- **Data analysis**   Analyzing data to evaluate HR initiatives and business challenges
- **Evidence-based decision-making**   Using the results of data analysis to inform and decide the best course of action

Key Concepts

- Survey and assessment tools (e.g., development, administration, validation of surveys and assessments)
- Sources of data (e.g., surveys, interviews, focus groups)
- Basic concepts in statistics (e.g., descriptive statistics, correlation) and measurement (e.g., reliability, validity)

- Interpretation of data and charts
- Using data to support a business case (e.g., interpretation, visualization, graphical representation)

Definition

According to SHRM, *Global and Cultural Effectiveness* is defined "as the knowledge, skills, abilities, and other characteristics (KSAOs) needed to collect and analyze qualitative and quantitative data and to interpret and promote findings that evaluate HR initiatives and inform business decisions and recommendations."[53]

Proficiency Indicators for All HR Professionals

Anyone working at the professional level in human resource management is expected to be able to access and interpret information the organization's leaders need to make accurate decisions about the workforce. What follows are the basics in this area of competency.

Making Sound Decisions

It is a rare circumstance for all information needed to be provided in decision-making. In most situations there is only partial data available. Yet, in spite of that, HR professionals are expected to be able to make good, workable decisions in a timely way. For example, from a long list of possible health insurance vendor programs, HR must select only a handful to present as options for employee enrollment. That requires using whatever might be known about the vendor programs, costs of each program, availability in the geography required, and employee likelihood that each program would be deemed attractive. Only some of that information is available, but the selection of a "short list" must happen anyway. If the decisions are not good, employees will reject some or all of the options. There can be impact on morale and even production levels. Turnover may be impacted whether the decisions made by HR are good or bad. And that is just one example of the importance of sound decisions in the presence of uncertainty.

Assessing the Impact of Laws

Federal and state laws change every year to some degree. When those laws impact HR issues, it is important to determine what specific impact they will have on our organization. When minimum wages increase, there is direct financial impact that can be computed and presented for consideration in the budget planning process. When new benefits are mandated, such as paid sick leave, the costs can be estimated and provided for budget consideration. If there are new requirements placed on nondiscrimination, it may be necessary to train all managers and supervisors in those new legal provisions. If the company decides to move into federal contracting or subcontracting, the financial and recruiting impacts must be estimated.

Chapter 3 lists the federal laws involved based on the payroll head count of any employer organization that is involved in interstate commerce. When a company hires its first employee, it becomes subject to 53 federal laws governing employment. Hire more than 14 people, and the exposure to legal requirements continues to grow.

HR professionals are expected to monitor these legal developments and forecast how the organization will comply with those requirements.

Transferring Knowledge

What do benefit enrollment, payroll, and discrimination complaints have in common? The answer is they all can involve historical data for proper handling. Using knowledge gained in handling one issue within the HR arena to apply to another (or even several other) issue is both efficient and smart. Equally important is the need to pass along to others the information gained in handling problems in one issue so that it might help in other areas.

Applying Critical Thinking to Information Received from Organizational Stakeholders

Determining what information can be used to support organizational success is dependent on being able to identify what is important from what is not. There are many pieces of information that flow into our realm every day. Most of those data don't have value in the HR decision-making process. So, you have to sort the valuable from the less valuable.

Of the several phone calls received on a given day,

- One is an alert that the union will be challenging an employee suspension.
- One is an invitation to speak at the local service club luncheon.
- One is a subordinate in the HR department complaining about the lack of hand towels in the restroom.
- One is the boss explaining that the budget estimates are due a week earlier than planned.
- One is describing the progress to date in planning the office holiday party.
- One is from the union president wanting to discuss disciplinary policy.

As each call comes in, your priorities may have to shift. And the information you get from one issue may be helpful in some way when addressing other issues. You have to store, sort, and retrieve each of these pieces of data, applying critical thinking to each in determining what will be helpful and what will not be helpful.

Gathering Critical Information

When a problem has been identified such as "The board of directors has just approved a policy that will give paid sick leave to all employees," it falls to human resources to figure out how to implement that policy. Implementation begins with gathering data. How many employees are going to be impacted? What has been the average absence rate in the past year? What portion of that absence has been due to illness of the employee? What portion has been due to illness of an employee's family member? Will the new policy apply to family members as well as the employee?

Identify the information you want to have and then go get it. If it is not available for some reason, you may need to make some educated guesses about what it might have been if it were available.

Analyzing Data

Once you have the data you think you need, begin the sorting process to determine what will be helpful and what will not be helpful. Then test the data for accuracy. Do the best you can to determine whether there have been any data collection errors introduced to the process. Were there typos or transpositions? When the data is clean, then begin analyzing what it tells you.

Analyzing Best Practices

Having in hand an analysis of the data for your organization, the next step is to define what the best practices are for the issue being considered. What are other similar employers doing about the same issue? Who can you call (e-mail or text) that will be able to give you information about other employers handling of this issue? Once you have determined what other employers are doing, you will know what they consider best practice in the situation.

Delineating Best Practices

Compare the best practices identified by contacting other employers and researching industry data or through some other source. Determine what similarities exist in how other employers handle a situation. Then compare the way other employers handle a situation and what you would like to do in your organization. Information sources can include the following:

- Your organizational history
- Industry data
- Specific data from one other company
- Peer-reviewed research
- Internet information available to the general public
- Response to survey requests sent to other employers

Combine all the input you can gather and construct a description of the best practices being followed by employers similar to you own.

Identifying Leading Indicators

Leading indicators provide evidence that HR is achieving its goal expectations. Human resource management has common measurement areas. Productivity, employee engagement, recruiting, retention, and budget are some of the key areas.

- **Productivity** Translated into dollars, employee productivity offers opportunity for significant savings in company expense. When one employee can produce more this year than last year, the budget will benefit.
- **Engagement** Results from employee surveys can indicate the state of morale and positive feelings about the employer. In turn, these factors can reduce turnover, improve attendance, and improve employee loyalty.

- **Recruiting** Perception of an employer's reputation can impact people's willingness to respond to recruiting efforts.

- **Retention** Employee turnover can represent a sizable amount of expense. Reducing that turnover, or increasing retention, can directly reduce costs.

- **Budget** Some executives see HR as an overhead expense. Achieving success in expense management is represented by the closeness HR can come to hitting budget targets.

Analyzing Large Quantities of Information

There are vast amounts of data that flow to the HR department each year. There are financial data, recruiting data, internal employee data, and training needs data, just to name a few. It is necessary for HR professionals to sort the important information from the less important. Data can drag the HR organization to a halt. Without prioritization and sorting, data as a total can be so overwhelming that it isn't possible to deal with all of it. HR professionals must be able to determine which information should be acknowledged and which ignored.

One technique for dealing with large quantities of information is to only dip into that data in search of specific answers to specific questions. Systems can be developed to house data, permit retrieval by authorized individuals, and allow access to answers as questions arise. Protecting the data with security procedures can meet legal and philosophical obligations for privacy. But first, systems can permit data management that will prevent submerging the HR organization.

Once sorted and stored, HR has responsibility to analyze what the data says. What portions of the organization are experiencing the highest turnover rates? What departments have the lowest absence rates? What is the cost of each benefit program? What should be offered in the next round of union negotiations and why? Who has yet to be trained in sexual harassment prevention? Identifying the problem, defining it properly, and then seeking data to help analyze the potential solutions are the key roles in HR departments.

Proficiency Indicators for Senior HR Professionals

 Evaluation done at the senior level of HR tends to focus more on the impact of policy and strategy. That evaluation can contribute to discussions held by executives about the positioning of the organization in its market, employee issues, and financial performance.

Maintaining Expert Knowledge

HR knowledge is constantly changing. There are new scientific studies being conducted each year and new laws enacted by federal, state, and local entities. It falls to the senior HR professional to know all of these things, keeping that knowledge current. It is often helpful to seek regular input from the legal staff and the accounting staff, for example. Knowing requirements and how they relate to organizational goals can help by identifying areas in which adjustments should be made.

Senior HR professionals must not only keep current in their knowledge but also be able to understand what that knowledge will mean to organizational objectives and how it will impact performance.

Interpreting Data and Make Recommendations

It is rather easy to identify the cost of benefit plans and suggest changes if costs warrant them. It may be a bit more difficult to interpret data about employee satisfaction and formulate recommendations for changes in policies or practices that might be appropriate.

The key question to ask is, "What impact will this data have on our organization?" Answering that question will then suggest what should be done to influence different outcomes. For example, monitoring recruiting efforts for veterans might tell you the goal for identifying sources of qualified people is not producing the results you hoped it would. The impact on your organization is that you will fall short of the target you set for hiring veterans. If you are a federal contractor, that can mean you would need to make adjustments in the use of recruiting sources. It could be necessary to find new sources of qualified veterans.

Making Decisions with Confidence

Decision-making has two components. One is the willingness to make decisions. The other is the quality of the decisions (or, do the decisions actually work)? Senior HR professionals are expected to be able to make decisions, often in the face of uncertainty. Not all the data will be available to guide you when you would like to have it. Sometimes, the quality of data you do have will be questionable. In the face of all the uncertainty, you are still expected to draw conclusions and make choices that will guide senior executives in your organization.

When policy changes are not an absolute requirement but an option, how will you formulate recommendations? Consider, for example, adding protections in your EEO and affirmative action policy that apply to LGBT. Aside from federal contractors, most other employers have the choice about including LGBT in their policy statement. The question is, should you? What will be the outcome if you do include that group among protected categories of people? What recommendation will you make to the senior executives? Likely you will not have all the data you would like to have about the impact of such a policy change. Yet you are still expected to make a professional determination about the question.

Setting the Direction of HR

Where is your HR organization going? What are its objectives? How should those objectives be redefined from year to year? To determine the answers, it is necessary to evaluate risks and economic and environmental factors.

Keeping a list of issues that will have an impact on your employer organization can help determine any adjustments in goals needed during the year. Economic impacts can come from change in benefit plan costs, increases in payroll expense, and increases or decreases in turnover rates. Environmental factors can include legislation, competition, compensation, and employee relations. Legislation impacts HR by imposing requirements such as records retention and compliance requirements, such as the Americans with Disabilities Act. Competition impacts can come from the effort to recruit the same type of talent found in competing organizations. Employee relations brings policy issues, early retirement programs, and different international expectations among the employee workforce. Compensation factors include the effort to maintain competitive positioning in the job market compared to other similar employer organizations.

How HR responds to each of these factors will determine how well it can meet its stated objectives. Altering the direction HR will take can result in the need to change its objectives.

Seeking Information

Obtaining information can be done strategically and systematically. Senior HR professionals are interested in gathering data that can help them run their HR organization, as well as data that can be shared with other executives.

Strategic data might include the results of employee attitude surveys. One strategy is to incorporate employee views into decisions about specific employment-related policies and programs. Knowing how employees feel about specific issues can provide guidance needed for decision-making about those policies and programs. Vacation policies, leave of absence practices, educational support programs, and telecommuting policies are all examples of issues that can benefit from employee input during the decision-making process.

Systematic data gathering can be done using routine systems such as direct employee accessing and updating of the HRIS records. Regular sampling of employee attitudes can be done automatically once the system has been set in place to generate questionnaires to a sampling of the workforce. Questionnaires can be modified as needed to test opinions about evolving issues.

Data is essential to decision-making. When there are routine visitations made to topics such as employee benefits, compensation, and performance appraisal systems, having data gathering processes in place to accumulate information needed makes those discussions easier. Informed decisions are better than those made in the dark.

Analyzing Information for Evaluation

Raw data might be interesting, but it is usually easier to use if it is summarized and transformed into statistics and charts. The number of hours employees are absent because of illness may be interesting, but it is more useful to look at it when it has been summarized into statistics such as absence rates. Displaying the relationship between two or more different data items means more when viewed over time.

Other examples of data that can be useful when evaluated over time can include anything that would permit trend plotting. Median compensation paid to a given job category, average employee training hours per year, and percentage of employees still on the job 1 year after hiring are all examples of data relationships that can be plotted on a graph to represent trends over time, as shown in Figure 7-1.

Figure 7-1
Sample data
summary display
with trend line

EEO Complaints per Year

Sponsoring Process Improvement Initiatives

There is usually more than one way to accomplish a goal. The same can be said of most processes used in the workplace. You tend to use processes because they exist, not because they are the best. What exists and works pretty well takes no effort to change. If you want to make changes, you must invest effort.

Improving processes is not always encouraged precisely because it takes time and effort. It may also take other resources like budget dollars. For example, the recruiting links we have on our company web site are used by people interested in our job openings. If we wish to modify the process to include an invitation to self-identify disabled and veteran status during the application process (which is now required of all federal contractors), we must involve the people who actually write the code for these additional steps in the process.

HR can offer support or withhold support for such changes in processes having to do with employee data. Designing a new employee survey can take considerable time. Hiring an outside consulting firm to do that can cost considerable money. HR can decide to either support or oppose the creation of a new employee survey based on all the factors known at the time.

Sponsoring initiatives to improves processes is an HR opportunity to influence/improve the overall workings of company systems. These initiatives can be spontaneous from employee suggestions ("The handling of new employee orientation would be better if…") or structured (from a study group assigned to assess and improve the performance evaluation process).

Communicating Impact for Data Analysis

Data has no value until it is communicated to those who can use it. Human resource professionals play a critical role in employer organizations because they have ownership of many data elements regarding employment activities. How HR people decide to pass along that data will determine the effectiveness of HR and the impact of the data.

For example, when it is determined that certain recruiting sources are more productive than others, helping the hiring managers understand where candidate riches are is a role

HR can play. When HR explains to senior managers the cost of discrimination complaints, even though they are investigated internally and do not result in external agency complaints, it falls to the executive team to take any policy actions that HR recommends.

Building Effective and Creative Policies

When local, state, or federal legislation specifies how employees are to be treated, HR should craft policies that will ensure the organization is in compliance. When there is no legislation but regulatory rules specify the handling of employee issues, again HR professionals should guide their organizations to implement policies that will ensure compliance.

When managers are making decisions that treat similarly situated employees quite differently, it is time for HR to step in and create policies that can be recommended for standardizing that treatment when those conditions arise.

When no one seems to know how things should be done and the circumstances will likely recur, it should be no wonder that HR is expected to step in and create policies that will address those situations.

Using Environmental Factors in Decision-Making

Political, sociological, economic, technological, legal, and environmental are all factors that influence decision-making within employment organizations. Responsible business leaders look for ways to minimize the impact of their decisions on the environment. That means, for example, that energy consumption and energy sources come into play. Should the company invest in solar or wind power generation to offset carbon-based generation sources? Should systems be developed that will permit the recycling of water in the production of company products? If so, perhaps the overall use of "new" water can be reduced.

Customers are voting with their wallets these days. Organizations that consider the impact on environmental factors will win the race for consumer dollars when compared with sources or products and services that ignore such things.

Challenging Assumptions

Critical evaluation isn't complete until you review your work and identify assumptions that have been made. What happens if you don't check for assumptions? Well, here are some examples:[54]

- IBM focused on mainframe sales in the 1980s while servers and PCs got more sales.
- Blockbuster held onto retail stores when streaming and DVD sales exploded.
- Nokia did not recognize smartphones as important but held onto standard cell phones.

The impacts of these oversights were serious financial penalties. In HR terms, it behooves you to keep track of the leading-edge trends or our competitors will be able to attract the talent that you would like to have. What are you doing for paid parental leave, employee lounge areas for rest breaks, or paid health care benefits that include dental and vision coverage? You can bet your competitors are considering all of these things as tools for recruiting and retaining tomorrow's workforce.

Providing a Strategic View

"Critical analysis of the strategic management process focuses on the way managers develop strategies to achieve company goals. Since carrying out the strategy requires the support of the whole company, you have to evaluate how well you achieve such an acceptance of your strategy. You can build consensus by demonstrating to employees that the strategy looks after their interests, while motivating employees to look beyond their own interests to the well-being of the group as a whole. An example is profit-sharing, which rewards each team member but only to the extent that the team as a whole performs well."[55]

HR professionals provide critical input to strategic development and implementation of the strategic plan. Your problem analysis and decision-making are not complete until you evaluate how the decision will fit into the strategic plan.

Summary

In this section of Chapter 7, we examined the behaviors associated with critical evaluation. All HR professionals will find it necessary to use these behaviors when performing their jobs. Looking past the obvious to what is actually driving people to do what they do is essential. Gathering data, assessing that data, and using the information to make quality decisions is something all HR professionals should be able to do. There is no more "shooting from the hip." Conscious exploration of alternatives and impact now drive the modern HR function.

Chapter Review

Chapter 7 has been about behavioral competencies that apply to HR professionals. These are things that HR people are expected to be able to say and do given any set of circumstances they may face. Proper responses depend on experience, careful thought, and knowledge. It isn't enough to memorize facts. What is important is how those facts can be blended with the situation to produce a proper response or employee treatment. That is called situational awareness. HR professionals must be capable of working with problems within their context. It isn't enough to say, "You can't use that written employment test." There needs to be an analysis of why the test was wanted by the hiring manager in the first place. Situationally, there may be some valid alternative approaches to the real problem of identifying the talent needed. Behavioral competencies are a critical part of an HR professional's life.

NOTE The exam will have 10 percent knowledge-related questions pertaining to the eight behavioral competencies, and 40 percent will be situational judgment type questions stemming from scenarios. The following questions are intended to help you review your understanding of Chapter 7's content and to simulate actual situational judgment practice exam questions. You will find more scenario situational judgment based exam-like questions in the two practice exams available with this book.

Questions

1. Allison is the HR manager in her organization. She has just been told she must find a supplier for employee service awards. As it turns out, she is well acquainted with all of the local companies offering such products. One of them is owned by her husband. Given that circumstance, what should Allison do about placing an order?

   A. Since she knows she can get a good deal from her husband's company, she should select it as the vendor.

   B. The professional HR code that deals with conflicts of interest would prevent her from selecting her husband's company because it could appear as favoritism for personal gain whether this is the case or not.

   C. As long as Allison treats her husband's company as an equal in consideration of vendors, there should be no problem.

   D. Allison should seek vendors outside the local area just to avoid any contamination of her ultimate selection.

2. Shimone has been recently promoted to senior HR representative. On nearly the first day of her work in the new position, one of her internal clients comes to her with a request to approve an expense voucher. When she reads the voucher, she sees it will be a payment to a foreign government agency to help facilitate her company's sale of product to their country. What ethical issues, if any, should Shimone be cognizant of?

   A. There are no ethical issues. It is a legitimate government payment like any permit application process in this country.

   B. There is an ethical issue. HR should support every sales effort regardless where it is taking place around the globe. Yet, Shimone is right to be concerned. She has approval authority only up to a certain amount. In this case, she will "fudge" the limit and sign off anyway.

   C. There are no ethical issues. There is nothing in this transaction that would raise any questions about ethics.

   D. There is an ethical issue. The story sounds like she will be giving a bribe to someone in the foreign government. That is both illegal and unethical.

3. It is Thursday, and just as you reach your desk, the phone rings. On the other end of the line is an employee saying one of the company's executives sexually assaulted her. After a 3-month-long investigation, you have gathered volumes of testimony from the employee's co-workers. But there were no witnesses to the assault. And the executive has denied all charges. He didn't even contend a consensual encounter was behind the current complaint. He just says, "Nothing happened."

   During the complaint investigation you discover this accused executive is the key contact for your company with a major international customer. What will you do at the conclusion of the investigation, assuming the employee has more credibility than the executive in this complaint? There are no witnesses to the assault, but co-worker statements support the employee's credibility as well. The company sees itself as an ethical organization, and it rewards managers for ethical behavior on occasion.

A. The key contact status is a major mitigation of the sexual harassment charges. The company can't afford to lose the customer's business. It would be appropriate to support retention of the executive in the current job until some other person is able to take over as key contact with that customer.

B. Immediate suspension is appropriate in this circumstance. There is no ethical barrier to taking that action.

C. Ethics are not an issue in this type of situation. The best business decision is to keep the executive in his job and reassign the complaining employee to some other work group.

D. Postponing any discipline or corrective action with the executive because of his key contact status with a key customer is wrong. It amounts to treating the executive differently from the way other management people have been treated in similar circumstances if you ignore the key contact component. Inconsistency in treatment is unethical. You decide to recommend appropriate discipline based on the evidence you have and comparable other cases. It doesn't matter how much pressure you are getting to do otherwise.

4. Jose has always been a good employee. He has been at work promptly and worked hard throughout his shift. His manager gives him top marks for his attitude and performance. The manager says, "If I had more like Jose, we would never have to worry about production."

Then one day, Jose gets a call and has to rush home for a family emergency. Later, just about quitting time, he remembered he didn't clock out. He called his buddy Guillermo and asked him to punch out for him. Guillermo says, "Sure, no problem."

A few days later, Jose's manager is reviewing the time cards and finds the time card was altered from actual work hours. Jose didn't work the afternoon, but his time card says he did. Is this a termination offense? Are there any ethical issues for you as the HR director?

A. There are ethical issues if what has happened involves a cover-up at any level. Jose's lack of intention to deceive by having a friend clock him out at the end of the day may be a mitigating factor based on company policy. Endorsing the cover-up by giving Jose a "pass" on his behavior would be unethical. Falsifying time cards is still a serious issue.

B. Falsifying time cards is a disciplinary issue, not an ethical issue.

C. HR should not be involved in this situation. It is up to Jose's manager to dole out whatever discipline is appropriate.

D. What's the big deal? Jose is a good performer. Cut him some slack. Keep him happy.

5. When Achmed became an HR professional, there were only four people in the HR department. The other three staff members were women. Achmed has trouble working with women and giving them the respect they deserve. Nonetheless, he attempts to be careful to make sure that doesn't interfere with his personal job interactions.

Achmed should do the following to be sure his bias doesn't impact his job-related decision-making.

A. Often bias won't surface except in rare circumstances. Achmed should not be worried. He knows his colleagues will tell him when he has become too obnoxious.

B. What does it matter if he is a bit heavy-handed with the women he interacts with on the job? In the end, it is really his decision that counts. As long as it doesn't reflect a bias, there should be no issue.

C. Ask for feedback from women with whom he interacts. Request that they tell him how he can improve his interpersonal skills. Ask for input about his fairness in approaching the problem being discussed. He can work on identifying when his bias is trying to break through and influence his decision-making.

D. The best approach is for him to wait for women to get upset with him so he can get good input about his bias.

6. Juanita is the HR representative for her assigned department. She handles all of the HR issues that come up. Recently, Juanita saw an article in the news about a new requirement that will likely impact her company's workers. She decides that the company lawyers will probably take responsibility for digesting that information and distributing it to the HR professionals. What would you tell Juanita about her decision?

A. Her decision is a good one. She obviously doesn't have time to spend scouring through the news for new HR requirements. And it is the lawyer's responsibility to follow legal changes, right?

B. Her decision is a good one. She doesn't have responsibility for tracking new legal requirements that apply to HR management issues.

C. Her decision is not a good one. She should accept responsibility for detecting and studying new legal requirements as they apply to the HR profession. Certification requirements point out that it is the HR professional, as well as the legal staff, who should be monitoring these changes.

D. Her decision is not a good one. It isn't the inside attorney who should be monitoring these new requirements; it is the outside attorney. What else does that consulting attorney do if not tracking legal requirement changes related to the HR staff?

7. It is commonly known that one of the senior vice presidents in your company has a business on the side that involves maintenance of electronic copy machines, including Xerox and Cannon. When your company begins its search for a new vendor to handle copier maintenance, the senior vice president raises his hand and says he can give the company a really good deal on the cost of a machine maintenance contract. What should you do when you hear this?

A. Confirm that he wants to participate. Identify whatever policies or code of ethics elements may have bearing on the circumstance. If there is a conflict of interest, you can discuss it with the senior vice president and tell him he may not compete for the copier maintenance contract. If there is no conflict-of-interest policy, you can escalate the issue to the president/CEO and recommend against allowing the senior vice president's participation.

B. Making exceptions to any policy when appropriate is something the HR department can recommend. It is OK to permit the senior vice president to compete for the new maintenance contract. As long as the contract is awarded based on random access data about vendor proposals, there won't be a conflict of interest.

C. Identify any policy the company may have on conflict of interest. Once identified, review the conditions under which an officer of the company can submit a vendor proposal to gain revenues from your company. If there isn't such a policy, a discussion with the president/CEO would be appropriate to determine what policy elements could be desirable for future implementation.

D. Why can't the senior vice president own an independent company and participate in the vendor selection process? The person who will make the vendor selection is two levels below the senior vice president, although in the senior VP's management group.

8. As a new venture, your company is doing quite well. When you arrived to head the HR department, however, there were no company policies. You believe they are necessary so everyone on the payroll can know what is expected of them. Almost immediately you set off to create policies for conduct expectations, honesty expectations, time-off rules, and payroll expectations. Then a complaint is filed against your boss claiming he has been having a sexual relationship with one of the HR department clerks. Is this a problem? Why?

A. Yes. It's a problem because complaints mean a lot of people will start nosing around, poking themselves into private affairs.

B. No. It's not a problem. As long as the clerk doesn't report directly to your boss, there can be no negative impact from their consensual relationship.

C. Yes. It's a problem because HR professionals are expected to set the standard for ethical behavior. Having a sexual relationship with someone in his own department says to other employees that it is OK to ignore training about sexual harassment and do whatever you want.

D. No. It's not a problem as long as the relationship is consensual and the clerk is over 21 years old. Where is this complaint coming from anyway?

9. You have been serving as an HR professional for more than 20 years now. In your current assignment you have been working to identify the organization's values and strategies. And you have been working to assess HR policies to be sure they support those organizational values and strategies. Why is that appropriate?

   A. If HR policies don't support values and strategies, it will be difficult to get the employee body to work toward the organizational values. If strategies for the organization are different from HR policies, employees are likely to be left out of the journey to the organization's vision.

   B. If HR policies don't support values and strategies, it will mean that almost all employees will find it hard to link their jobs to the organizational values.

   C. If HR policies don't support values and strategies, the executive team will begin asking questions about the importance of the HR department to the organization. Somewhere along the line the HR department may become irrelevant.

   D. If HR policies don't support values and strategies, there is no problem. HR policies are in place so they can be interpreted in each case as events develop. Nothing is written in stone. It's all good.

10. It's May and the start of your "season of the interns." Your company is a federal contractor and always hires student interns to expose them to actual workday requirements of the job and ideally have them consider working here after they graduate. Yesterday, your CEO came to you and said his next-door neighbor's daughter needs a job, and he said she could work here. He wants you to put her on the payroll. What should you do?

    A. There is no ethical conflict. The executives of the company get to decide how the company will be staffed. Hiring by directive is an acceptable and ethical strategy.

    B. You should explain the ethics of not getting a job requisition number to start with. Once that is done, you can hire the neighbor's daughter and close the job requisition without a problem.

    C. You should explain the ethics of following the company's hiring process. Federal contractors would find it particularly problematic when complying with recruiting and hiring regulations come into play. You need to assess how ethical it would be to open a job requisition and then close it with only one candidate without any announcement of opportunity to others.

    D. You can ignore the normal process and just do what the CEO has asked you to do. The boss is in charge. Anything they want can be done.

11. Sadie is a new HR analyst, and this is her first professional HR job. Her first assignment is to determine how other companies in the area are handling the problem cost of housing is creating for employee recruiting. What should Sadie keep in mind above all else?

   A. Never disclose any information to other companies.

   B. Don't discuss the issue with any of our own employees.

   C. Her credibility will be based on the quality of the work she produces.

   D. She should call her boss each time a question comes up about the project.

12. Renaldo has just been appointed director of HR. At the same time, the company has announced a merger that will result in a new line of business. How can Renaldo make the transition easier for the merging company employees?

   A. Negotiate with the new company executives how the employment policies of the two companies can be merged and on what timeline.

   B. Negotiate with the new company executives what service awards will be presented to people in the new organization.

   C. Negotiate with the current company executives what office space they will be giving up to the new people.

   D. Negotiate with the current company executives how parking spaces will be allocated.

13. HR professionals must be open to the ideas of others based on:

   A. The financial backing that they can offer

   B. The similarities they have to U.S. expectations

   C. Decisions made at headquarters that demand conformity to policies

   D. Experience, data, facts, and reasoned judgment

14. The best way managers and HR professionals can learn from others is to:

   A. Encourage employees to send in anonymous suggestions for improvement

   B. Invite them to correct the manager's decision-making methods

   C. Express self-awareness and humility

   D. Tell them you understand their culture pretty well

15. Industry characteristics should be part of an HR professional's study list because:

   A. Industry requirements can vary considerably based on the type of products and services it demands.

   B. Industry associations demand that HR professionals submit information about employee compensation and benefit programs.

   C. Industry competitors are going to get greater revenues if you don't adjust your programs based on how competitors are doing their work.

   D. Industry representatives dictate the HR programs that must be adopted by each corporate employer.

16. Shirley is new to her job as director of human resources. She has been asked by the CEO to prepare a business case supporting HR's representation in executive strategic planning sessions. What should Shirley do to create that business case?

   A. She should give the job to her lieutenant as a developmental assignment.

   B. She should follow the ten-element process from problem identification to action planning.

   C. She should identify at least five reasons why HR needs to be included in the planning process.

   D. She should call a friend at a competitor's company and ask what they did.

17. Anton has been VP of HR for 3 years now. He has been gradually adding metrics to the HR department since he took over as leader. Are there practical limits to the amount of metrics that can exist in an organization?

   A. Yes. If there are too many metrics, nobody will get anything done other than generating data for the measurements.

   B. No. Any quantity of measurements is acceptable as long as each one can be linked to another department.

   C. Yes. More than ten metrics will choke an HR department and bring its production to a standstill.

   D. No. Any amount of metrics is acceptable as long as they are each measuring a critical component of HR work product.

18. Elliot has just been invited to present an analysis of employee benefit programs that the executive team wants to consider for use beginning next year. How should he do that?

   A. An ROI analysis is the best approach.

   B. Getting anecdotal evidence from competitors who are using the programs is the best approach.

   C. Getting vendor input is critical to the best approach.

   D. Preparing a narrative analysis is the best approach.

19. Latisha is a new HR analyst. She has been tasked with training her contacts in client departments on the changes in medical insurance benefit programs for this year. How should she handle that assignment?

   A. Provide managers the option to sit in on the training or skip the program.

   B. Study the benefit programs so she is an expert in the provisions of each plan and all the changes that will be made this year.

   C. Take the literature from the insurance companies and distribute it to the client managers in the training session.

   D. Ask the registration clerk to come along to the training sessions to answer questions about the plans.

20. Rolly has been director of HR at his company for 2 years. He is now facing the task of making use of all the employee data that is available to him. What should he do?

   A. Delegate the project. Get a clerk to gather all the data and find a way to handle it.

   B. Bring in a consultant to write a computer program that will digest the employee data and spit out comparisons that will help in decision-making.

   C. Review the data personally and determine which analytical tool he should use to "crunch the numbers" and get some comparative results.

   D. Send the data to a consultant off-site for review and analysis.

21. Savanah has just been appointed to the HR staff as an entry-level professional. What should she recognize about the need for critical evaluation in her decision-making?

   A. She must be able to interpret information and make business recommendations to those who will decide on the organization's direction.

   B. She must rely on HR analysts to provide her with evaluation of the issues she faces. Then, she should make any policy decisions needed.

   C. She must recognize that any situation with less than total descriptive information can't be addressed by critical evaluation.

   D. She must depend on her external contacts to provide the evaluation of HR policies in other organizations.

22. Elliott is a senior HR analyst in his organization. What impact do you think new state and federal laws will have on his work?

   A. It depends on whether the new laws have local impact. HR can't make that determination. It is important for HR professionals to get outside legal input.

   B. It is the legal staff that should be paying attention to the new laws. HR really has no significant role to play in that regard.

   C. Each new piece of legislation that impacts HR issues is important and must be a consideration for Elliott's analysis work.

   D. In these days, having an attorney on the HR staff is a good idea. Elliott should always rely on that HR staff lawyer.

23. When inputs to HR on any given workday become so varied and intense, the HR professionals must do what?

   A. Issues should always be handled in the order they were received. "First in, first served" should be the motto.

   B. HR must do triage and determine the priority for each new issue. Then deal with issues in priority order.

   C. Priorities, once set, should not be changed. Commitments must be honored and receive attention as originally determined.

   D. Benefits issues should always be handled first, followed by payroll issues and union issues.

24. Sofia has just been asked to draft a new policy for employee engagement efforts and programs. What key components should her analysis include?

    A. HR, accounting, production, and budget

    B. Office staff, production staff, recruiting staff, and legal staff

    C. Productivity, engagement, recruiting, retention, and budget

    D. Competitors, industrial associations, congressional actions, and budget

25. There is so much data involved in HR problems. How is a new HR professional supposed to handle it all?

    A. Every HR professional must be a certified professional statistician so all the data analysis can be certified as accurate.

    B. There is no need for HR professionals to be certified professional statisticians; they just need to be able to do a defensible regression analysis with 15 or more variables.

    C. When the data elements get to be overwhelming, HR professionals should just pick the most important for their analysis and ignore the rest.

    D. Refining problem statements so they are more specific is one important way to reduce the data overload problem.

Situational Judgment Scenario-Based Questions

Scenario 1 (Questions 26–29): You answer your phone, and it is Nancy, the CEO's executive assistant. She wants to know whether you could come talk with the CEO in 15 minutes. When you reply you will be right up, Nancy hesitates and then adds that she wants you to keep who you are meeting with to yourself. You are intrigued but assure Nancy you will comply with her request.

When you get to the CEO's office, Marian is not there, but Nancy asks you to take a seat in her office, saying Marian will be right back. Sure enough, Marian soon arrives and asks whether she may speak freely and in confidence. You respond, "Absolutely." Marian goes on to say she wants your advice as she thinks she needs to fire one of her C-suite members, so of course she needs to do it right. You are surprised that you've been asked for this help and not your vice president of human resources, Hank, but you keep listening. The CEO has received e-mails from three different employees claiming different degrees of sexual harassment, all naming the same member of the C-suite. These allegations of behavior are different from what Marian has experienced with this executive.

26. What is one of your first questions for the CEO?

    A. Is the C-suite member's performance otherwise okay?

    B. Is this C-suite member a key financial contributor?

    C. What investigatory steps have been taken?

    D. What succession plan do you have in place for this C-suite member?

27. Marian gives you printouts of the three e-mails she referenced and asks you to talk to "who you think you need to talk to, please." Who will that include?

   A. The three employees

   B. The three employees and the accused

   C. The three employees, their supervisors, and the accused

   D. The three employees, their supervisors, the accused, and anyone else who becomes relevant based upon your interviews

28. Marian tells you that if you have any resistance setting up your meetings, you should share that you are doing this at her request. She asks that you meet with her again to give a verbal update as soon as you have news to report. In that second meeting, you share more details from e-mail writers, that every supervisor reported their employee was credible, and that the accused was shocked, outraged, and refused to cooperate once he understood the purpose of the meeting. Based upon this data gathering, what do you report to the CEO?

   A. You will make a recommendation based upon the preponderance of the evidence.

   B. You can't make a recommendation without more information from the accused.

   C. You need your vice president, Hank, to make such an important recommendation.

   D. You want to turn your notes over to the firm's legal counsel to make the recommendation.

29. Marian says you have provided her with enough information and looks forward to quickly receiving your written report. She asks whether you have any additional related comments. How do you respond?

   A. "No, but thank you for the learning assignment."

   B. "Yes, we should do sexual harassment prevention training for all supervisors within the company."

   C. "Yes, why didn't this assignment go to Hank?"

   D. "No," but you wonder the reason this assignment didn't go to Hank.

Scenario 2 (Questions 30–33): You have been tasked to prepare a report the VP of human resources has requested for the senior leadership team. You will need to figure out what data is available, how to display it, and how to interpret what it means.

30. Ideally you will be able to include all the following except which one?

   A. Current organizational turnover rates

   B. Historical organizational turnover rates

   C. Your industry turnover rates

   D. National turnover rates

31. Looking at the data you have gathered on your organizational turnover rates, it would be best to share the data by what feature?

   A. Department

   B. Title

   C. Length of service

   D. Whichever way shares greater insight

32. Looking at the data you have gathered on your organizational turnover rates, it would be best to share the data using which of the following?

   A. A bar chart

   B. A matrix

   C. A Pareto chart

   D. A Six Sigma

33. Looking at the data you have gathered on your organizational turnover rates, when you share the data, you want to be sure to include what?

   A. All the detailed data you collected, so senior management may draw their own conclusions

   B. All the detailed data you collected, so senior management will appreciate all the hard work you have done

   C. Your insights about your turnover rates and whether they are good or bad

   D. Your insights about your turnover rates and whether they are good or bad, plus recommendations on how to make the rates better

Scenario 3 (Questions 34–37): You have been a director of human resources in California for 7 years now. Your firm has just completed an acquisition of a new operations group in Texas that has more employees working at it than your California operations, so you have overnight more than doubled in size. You just got your hands on their current employee handbook and are comparing it to the one you recently updated in California. While the California handbook has a policy that bans firearms from all work locations, the Texas handbook is silent on the issue. Another difference is California's handbook states a zero-tolerance policy for any violence, and again the Texas handbook is silent.

As you FaceTime with the local human resources manager prior to your planned trip to Texas next week, Serena tells you about an operations technician, Martin, who was terminated last week for making threats toward a co-worker as they were both interested in the same woman who is the company's receptionist.

PART II

34. Turning your attention to fired Martin, what follow-up question do you want to ask Serina first?

    A. What is the name of the receptionist?

    B. What security measures are in place at the Texas plant?

    C. What is the name of the co-worker who had threats made against him?

    D. Do you have good operations technician applicants available?

35. What is one of the first steps you are going to take regarding the differences in policies?

    A. Make all the handbooks the same, following the Texas lead, since it has more employees who are familiar with those policies.

    B. Make all the handbooks the same, following the lead of California, since that is the company that did the acquiring.

    C. Make all the handbooks the same, following the lead of California, since California is famous for having more complicated employment laws for compliance.

    D. Engage Serina in conversation about the areas of silence for better understanding.

36. You realize your options for the policies are to keep your policies separate, adopt one of the two for all, integrate the two, or start fresh. What will influence you most in your choice of approach?

    A. The approach you can implement the fastest to get through the change quickly

    B. The values of the combined company going forward

    C. The mission, vision, and values of the combined company going forward

    D. The mission and vision of the combined company going forward

37. What is your best approach to convince the new leadership team of your proposed newly integrated policies related to firearms and workplace violence?

    A. Talk in individual sessions with each leader to explain the risks to the corporation and employees.

    B. Discuss the topic at a meeting of the leadership team, outlining the general risk and what some mitigating measures are.

    C. Share examples and facts from the news and about growing workplace violence and its financial risk with the leadership team and then offer your prepared solutions for your firm.

    D. Share examples and facts from the news and about growing workplace violence and its financial risk with all the stakeholders of the firm.

Scenario 4 (Questions 38–42): Nadine, the director of marketing, is having a serious performance problem with a key marketing analyst, Andrew. Andrew has been with the firm for three years and is a 41-year-old minority. Andrew's initial 6-month review was satisfactory. After that, the appraisals have continued to be satisfactory, but marginally so.

You talked the director of marketing out of firing Andrew for employment at will and got her to agree to put Andrew on a performance improvement plan (PIP). You convinced her that for the PIP to work, she'd need to make expectations for work quantity and quality clear to Andrew and to meet with him weekly to provide regular feedback.

38. It is now 30 days later, and Nadine wants to meet with you concerning Andrew. What will you want to know from Nadine?

   A. How is Andrew's performance in terms of quality?

   B. How often did Nadine meet and give feedback?

   C. How is Andrew's performance in terms of quality?

   D. How often did they meet, and how is Andrew's overall performance?

39. Thirty-two days after Andrew's PIP began, you meet with Nadine. She reports that Andrew's quality is about the same as before and his quantity of analytical reports has gone up slightly. She met with him initially to put him on the PIP and then just met with him a second time 3 days ago. Nadine wants to fire Andrew. What is your counsel to Nadine?

   A. Agree completely and offer to prepare the final check plus remind Nadine it is best practice to have another manager present when she terminates Andrew.

   B. Agree completely and offer to prepare the final check and be in the room with Nadine when she terminates Andrew.

   C. Disagree, saying termination now is premature since there has been some improvement and there has been imperfect feedback.

   D. Disagree, saying termination now is premature as there isn't time to get a special termination check this week.

40. In that meeting 32 days after the start of Andrew's PIP you gently ask Nadine to help you understand the reason she didn't engage in more feedback meetings with Andrew. She tells you work has been overwhelming, especially with marginal performers on her staff, and that she had to go out of state for 2 weeks to arrange for hospice for her father. What is your response?

   A. Condolences for her father's condition and a gentle reminder of her managerial duties

   B. Condolences for her father's condition and your advice on how best to proceed with Andrew

   C. Condolences for her father's condition, your advice on how best to proceed with Andrew, and a reminder of your employee assistance program

   D. Knowing you are to stay professional, you give her a gentle reminder of her managerial duties

41. If Nadine wants to go forward with the termination, what advice do you want to give to her?

    A. Advise Nadine that since all the performance appraisals are satisfactory and improvement was made during the 30-day PIP, you think the paper trail is insufficient to warrant going forward with the termination at this time.

    B. Advise Nadine that since all the performance appraisals are satisfactory and improvement was made during the 30-day PIP, suggest finding an alternate job in another department for Andrew.

    C. Advise Nadine that since all the performance appraisals are satisfactory and improvement was made during the 30-day PIP, direct Nadine to set up a meeting with your legal counsel for suggested possible actions.

    D. Advise Nadine that since all the performance appraisals are satisfactory and improvement was made during the 30-day PIP, since she's going through a lot right now, you will handle the termination for her to provide excellent internal customer service to her.

42. What further advice do you want to give to Nadine, knowing Andrew is in at least two protected groups?

    A. Don't terminate too hastily since Andrew has the right to file a complaint with EEOC, alleging his termination was biased based upon his protected-class status.

    B. Don't get too stressed over Andrew's termination since you have personal issues going on and Andrew is an at-will employee.

    C. Don't terminate too hastily since the director could instead ask Andrew if he'd like to resign.

    D. Don't get too stressed over Andrew's termination since your human resource group has prescreened a number of qualified marketing analyst applicants.

Scenario 5 (Questions 43–46): You are an HR manager in one of the states that have decriminalized marijuana, starting in 3 months. You are getting comments from supervisors concerned that they will have lost productivity and a break room that smells of that "wacky tabacky," and they dread it.

43. What is one of the first steps you are going to take in response to this situation?

    A. Gather data from SHRM chapters in states where marijuana has already been decriminalized.

    B. Research the exact wording of the law in your state.

    C. Confirm the law hasn't changed at the federal level.

    D. Conduct an employee survey to ask how many employees plan to partake.

44. You are revising your internal policies to include your corporate response to marijuana. Part of that process will include what?

    A. Present all the options for a response to your leadership team so they may decide.

    B. Present all the options for a response to your vice president of HR so she may decide.

    C. Run the draft of your new policies past some respected colleagues in other departments.

    D. Post the draft of your new policies in the break room and set up a suggestion box next to it for comments.

45. What is a key message you want everyone to understand in your new policies?

    A. In 3 months, the company parties are going to get a lot more fun.

    B. All employees must be mentally and physically able to execute their responsibilities safely.

    C. All employees should be reminded of your sick time policy.

    D. All employees must be reminded of your attendance policy.

46. The manager with the greatest concerns approaches you with an article in hand stating that marijuana is still a controlled substance under federal law. In response, you do what?

    A. Say thanks for the article, but you already knew that.

    B. Give thanks for the article and realize if illegal at the federal level, there is no need to change your policies.

    C. Assure the manager that the federal law is changing any day now.

    D. Assure the manager your new policies state there will be no ADA nor ADAAA accommodation for medical use of marijuana.

Answers

1. **B**. She should exclude her husband's company from participating in the vendor selection process simply because it may have an appearance of a conflict of interest.

2. **D**. Bribery is possible. And it is one of the specific problems a code of ethics will address and caution against. At the least, before approving the transaction, Shimone should investigate the true nature of the payment demand from the foreign government or its representative.

3. **D**. Withstanding political pressure from above, and fighting for consistent treatment of management employees who have been accused of similar misbehavior, is the ethical approach to the solution. The company will just have to take its lumps until another key contact can be appointed and learns the job. The loss of new revenue in the process may not be considered.

4. A. A review of company policy related to falsifying time cards or generally falsifying any records should be undertaken. Then a review of similar cases of friends clocking out for another employee should be made. Once all the background information has been gathered, you can proceed with any appropriate discipline. Assuring that treatment is the same for Jose as it has been for others in similar circumstances will help avoid ethical conflicts or favoritism claims.

5. C. Requesting feedback from others is a good way to see things through the eyes of other people. Sometimes it is difficult to determine the impact we are having on those we interact with on the job. Asking for feedback is the solution. He can be specific about the type of feedback he wants or can just ask for general observations. He can also increase his personal awareness of his bias trying to break through when he interacts with women.

6. C. Part of a senior HR professional's is to keep current on all new HR requirements that may come to influence the workplace. Juanita should accept the responsibility and do her homework. It is a requirement of certification. A is incorrect. If Juanita abandons her role in maintaining current knowledge about HR requirements, she can have no assurance that her organization will be in compliance should that be necessary. It is not just the legal staff that is responsible for tracking such things but also the professional HR staff.

7. A. Checking for a code-of-conduct policy or a conflict-of-interest policy in your company is always a good idea. If you find one, be guided by its provisions. If you don't find one, identify the most "common-sense" approach to the question of inclusion/exclusion of the senior vice president in the vendor selection process.

8. D. Ethical standards are established as much by behavioral examples as by written policy. HR professionals are charged with setting the standard for ethical behavior. Your boss, in this situation, appears to be setting a low standard.

9. A. If there is a disconnect between policies versus values and strategies, the organization will find it difficult, if not impossible, to demonstrate its values and implement the stated strategies. Having consistent HR policies should be one of the strategies itemized by the organization.

10. C. Federal contractors must meet certain outreach and recruiting requirements. The CEO's request would present an ethical problem for you. Do you abide by the company's policies and meet federal requirements, or do you abandon all that and do what the boss wants? Explaining the situation to the CEO is the best option. Then they can make an informed decision.

11. C. Credibility, both personal and departmental, will rest on the quality of work she produces in this and all future assignments.

12. A. Negotiating the merger of employment policies is critical to successful merger of different workforce groups.

13. **D**. The entire spectrum of possibilities must be considered. Input from experience, data, and facts, combined with reasoned judgment, will best support cultural strength.

14. **C**. "Walk a mile in his shoes" is a motto for executives. Finding out how it feels to actually perform jobs done by subordinates will bring more understanding than a stack of memos.

15. **A**. Retail is different from restaurants. Consumer products are different from business services. Knowing the specifics for your industry is important because it has needs unique to the work being done.

16. **B**. There are ten elements in the process of preparing a business case. She needs to follow those steps to generate the analysis her CEO wants.

17. **D**. As long as each is measuring a critical HR work product, any amount will be acceptable.

18. **A**. A return on investment analysis will provide the financial information necessary to clarify the best benefit program out of the options available.

19. **B**. Latisha must be able to answer all the basic questions that might arise in the training sessions. She also must be willing to take unanswered questions and research them so she can provide answers to the people interested in the answers.

20. **C**. Rolly must prepare a list of data elements that will be important for comparisons and reporting. He then should select the analytical tool that can best perform those comparisons.

21. **A**. As a new HR professional, Savanah must interpret the information she has about the problem situation and design recommendations to higher management people.

22. **C**. Even if there is a legal expert available for advice to the HR staff, Elliott must be able to understand the new laws and how they will impact HR programs and policies.

23. **B**. Priorities must constantly be reassessed and issues handled in the order that new priorities dictate.

24. **C**. While not the only areas to be considered, these are the significant areas every problem analysis should include.

25. **D**. Reducing data overload can be done quickly by narrowing the scope of the problem statement. It is going to be easier to handle data analysis for the cost of a new paid time-off policy rather than trying to deal with the cost of all benefits.

26. **C**. It is never a best practice to terminate an employee based upon allegations. An investigation to get to the truth is required.

27. **D**. You want to be inclusive to gather as many facts as possible. That definitely includes the employees. It also includes their supervisors to get a sense of motivation to make a false allegation, plus the accused. If anyone in their statements mentions a witness, then your investigation should expand to include witnesses as well.

PART II

28. **A**. Once an investigation is undertaken, you are required to make a decision based upon the preponderance of the evidence, which means 51 percent and up.

29. **B**. This is the right response to increase the odds of all supervisors understanding what harassment is and the steps to prevent it going forward.

30. **D**. It is the least useful measurement.

31. **D**. You may need to experiment with all three variables to detect patterns and gain the insight as to what is going on in your organization.

32. **A**. A bar chart showing differences by department, title, or length of service will help tell your story best.

33. **D**. Part of the value you are bringing to senior management from human resources is your interpretation of the data. That is strong and even stronger when coupled with suggestions on what next steps to take.

34. **B**. Your first concern under duty of care is to make sure your new employees at the Texas facility are secure.

35. **D**. While both states are within the United States, there could be some significant cultural differences regarding firearms. It is best to understand a situation before making changes to a situation. There may be local gun use laws that you do not know about to take into consideration as well.

36. **C**. This answer is most complete.

37. **C**. Speaking with facts and then offering solutions for your organization is the best approach.

38. **D**. Yes, you want to know how Andrew is performing across all his defined measurements *and* you want to know that he was getting the regular feedback that was part of the commitment to help him improve.

39. **C**. The PIP commitment was for weekly feedback, and that didn't happen. In spite of a lack of weekly feedback, Andrew's performance is slightly better. We don't know how much better it could have been if management had kept its commitment during the PIP.

40. **C**. The director of marketing has just shared something very personal, so your best response is to acknowledge it with your condolences, remind Nadine of a resource available (EAP), and share your expertise on the matter at hand.

41. **A**. It is completely acceptable to extend the PIP 30 or even 60 days to give Andrew a fair shot at getting better.

42. **A**. Since your documentation is not good right now justifying a termination, Andrew might indeed file a complaint with this outside federal agency.

43. **A**. It is a best practice to have a policy regarding whether you will tolerate someone being under the influence in your work environment. Learning how other human resource professionals have already dealt with this issue is a smart step to take.

44. **C**. You need to take the lead, but getting additional input from a variety of perspectives can only make your final policy better.

45. **B**. Whether it's over-the-counter cough syrup, prescription drugs, alcohol, or marijuana, you as the employer have a fiduciary responsibility to assure that employees on your property are safe to execute their responsibilities.

46. **D**. This is a manager who needs assurance and additional facts. You will put this manager more at ease giving additional information, such as information on the ADA.

References

1. SHRM Body of Competency and Knowledge (BoCK), page 9.

2. SHRM Body of Competency and Knowledge (BoCK), page 13.

3. SHRM Body of Competency and Knowledge (BoCK), page 12.

4. Zenger, Jack, and Joseph Fokman. *The Extraordinary Leader: Turning Good Managers into Great Leaders*, McGraw-Hill Education, May 2009.

5. https://www2.deloitte.com/insights/us/en/focus/human-capital-trends.html

6. SHRM Body of Competency and Knowledge (BoCK), page 15.

7. SHRM HR Competencies Definition, page 14.

8. Kerns, Charles D., Ph.D. *Graziadio Business Review*, Pepperdine University, Volume 6, Issue 3, 2003.

9. Allen, Louise, "Developing HR Strategy," *Personnel Today*, November 19, 2002, retrieved on September 15, 2017.

10. Code of Ethics, Society for Human Resource Management, https://www.shrm.org/about-shrm/Pages/code-of-ethics.aspx, retrieved on September 16, 2017.

11. SHRM Body of Competency and Knowledge (BoCK), page 19.

12. SHRM Body of Competency and Knowledge (BocK), page 18.

13. Solomon, Micah. Forbes, "7 Secrets of Building a Customer-Centric Company Culture," https://www.forbes.com/sites/micahsolomon/2014/07/20/customer-centric-culture/#2ccd76db7582.

14. SHRM Managing Workplace Conflict Toolkit, https://www.shrm.org/resourcesandtools/tools-and-samples/toolkits/pages/managingworkplaceconflict.aspx.

15. SHRM Body of Competency and Knowledge (BoCK), page 21.

16. SHRM Body of Competency and Knowledge (BoCK), page 20.

17. SHRM Learning System, 2017.

18. SHRM Body of Competency and Knowledge (BoCK), page 23.

19. SHRM Body of Competency and Knowledge (BoCK), page 22.

20. Guide to Saudia Arabia: Etiquette, Culture, Customs and Business, www
.kwintessential.co.uk/resources/guides/guide-saudi-arabia-etiquette-customs-
culture-business/.

21. Stallard, Mike. Leading with Character: Humility, http://connectionculture.com/
post/leading-with-character-humility.

22. Why You Need Cultural Intelligence (And How to Develop It), IESE Business
School, https://www.forbes.com/sites/iese/2015/03/24/why-you-need-cultural-
intelligence-and-how-to-develop-it/#44dc66d917d6.

23. McDonnell, Steve. Foreign vs. U.S. Labor Laws, Chron, http://smallbusiness
.chron.com/foreign-vs-us-labor-laws-77421.html.

24. Ibid.

25. Ibid.

26. Fisher, Glen. *Mind-sets: The Role of Culture and Perception in International
Relations*, New York: John Wiley, 1988.

27. Rhinesmith, Stephen H. Global Mind-sets for Global Managers, https://www
.questia.com/magazine/1G1-13528770/global-mind-sets-for-global-managers.

28. Emerson, Ralph Waldo. Essays: Man the Reformer. A Lecture Read before the
Mechanics Apprentices' Library Association, Boston, January 25, 1841.

29. Warrell, Margie. How to Build High Trust Relationships, Forbes Leadership,
https://www.forbes.com/sites/margiewarrell/2015/08/31/how-to-build-high-
trust-relationships/#54ac927415cf.

30. Kramer, Roderick M. "Rethinking Trust," Harvard Business Review, June 2009.

31. Green, Kelli et al., Diversity in the Workplace: Benefits, Challenges, and the
Required Managerial Tools, University of Florida, 2015.

32. Willis, Jennifer. Sustainable Development is Good for Business, American Bar
Association "Trends," May/June 2017.

33. Fogh-Andersen, Karen. 7 Pivotal HR Competencies for Global Business in
2017, Stanton Chase, Copenhagen, Denmark, https://www.stantonchase
.com/wp-content/uploads/2017/03/SC_WP_7_HR_Competencies_A4-1.pdf,
March 2017.

34. 2017 Deloitte Global Human Capital Trends: Rewriting the rules for the digital
age, https://www2.deloitte.com/us/en/pages/human-capital/articles/introduction-
human-capital-trends.html.

35. Hunt, Vivian, Dennis Layton, and Sara Prince. Why Diversity Matters,
McKinsey & Company, January 2015, https://www.mckinsey.com/business-
functions/organization/our-insights/why-diversity-matters.

36. "Understanding Workplace Cultures Globally," SHRM, November 30, 2015,
https://www.shrm.org/resourcesandtools/tools-and-samples/toolkits/pages/
understandingworkplaceculturesglobally.aspx.

37. Mayers, Juliette C. Seven Tips for Building Cross-Cultural Relationships, April 22, 2012.

38. SHRM Body of Competency and Knowledge (BocK), page 27.

39. SHRM Body of Competency and Knowledge (BocK), page 26.

40. Sanders, Nada. The Definitive Guide to Manufacturing and Service Operations, Council of Supply Chain Management Professionals, December 28, 2013.

41. Mayberry, Ed. How to Build an HR Business Case, SHRM, October 28, 2008.

42. Aligning Workforce Strategies with Business Objectives, SHRM, September 14, 2015.

43. Beard, Ross. Competitive Benchmarking 101, Client Heartbeat, http://blog .clientheartbeat.com/competitive-benchmarking-101/, retrieved on October 12, 2017.

44. Management Study HQ, www.managementstudyhq.com/hrm-evaluation-approaches.html, accessed on October 13, 2017.

45. SHRM Body of Competency and Knowledge (BoCK), page 29.

46. SHRM Body of Competency and Knowledge (BoCK), page 28.

47. Alter, Michael. Accounting Web, https://www.accountingweb.com/practice/ clients/top-ten-ways-to-take-a-consultative-approach-to-client-meetings.

48. Bacharach, Yael. Five Essential Skills for Successful Coaching, Inc., https://www .inc.com/yael-bacharach/five-essential-skills-for-successful-coaching.html.

49. Atkins, Richard. How to Maximize Human Capital ROI, HR Magazine, http:// hrprofessionalsmagazine.com/how-to-maximize-human-capital-roi/.

50. Carey, Scott, and Thomas Mccaulay. ComputerWorld UK, "The Best Analytics and Business Intelligence Tools for Enterprises 2018," https://www .computerworlduk.com/galleries/applications/best-self-serve-analytics-software-for-enterprises-3635147/.

51. Andrews, Walter J., and Michael S. Levine. SHRM, Top 10 Employment Liability Concerns, https://www.shrm.org/hr-today/news/hr-magazine/ pages/070815-employment-liability.aspx.

52. SHRM Body of Competency and Knowledge (BoCK), page 31.

53. SHRM Body of Competency and Knowledge (BoCK), page 30.

54. Herbold, Bob. "Challenge Assumptions. Don't Be Afraid of Taking a Different Tack," Entrepreneur, April 6, 2014, https://www.entrepreneur.com/article/232767, downloaded on November 6, 2017.

55. Markgraf, Bert. "Critical Analysis of Strategic Management," http:// smallbusiness.chron.com/critical-analysis-strategic-management-65195.html, accessed on November 6, 2017.

56. Kouzes, James M., and Barry Z. Posner. *The Leadership Challenge: How to Make Extraordinary Things Happen in Organizations*, Jossey-Bass, July 31, 2012.

PART III

Appendixes

- **Appendix A**   List of Common HR Acronyms
- **Appendix B**   Case Laws by Chapter
- **Appendix C**   For Additional Study
- **Appendix D**   About the Digital Content

List of Common HR Acronyms

AA	1) Affirmative Action; 2) Adverse Action
AACU	American Association of Colleges and Universities
AAO	Affirmative Action Officer
AAP	Affirmative Action Plan
AAR	Average Annual Return
ABF	Asset-Based Financing
ABM	Activity-Based Management
ABMS	Activity-Based Management System
ACA	Affordable Care Act
ACH	Automated Clearing House
AD&D	Accidental Death and Dismemberment
ADA	Americans with Disabilities Act
ADAAA	Americans with Disabilities Act Amendments Act
ADEA	Age Discrimination in Employment Act
ADL	Activities of Daily Living
ADP	Automatic Data Processing
ADR	Alternative Dispute Resolution
AFL-CIO	American Federation of Labor and Congress of Industrial Organizations
AFSCME	American Federation of State, County, and Municipal Employers
AI	Appreciative Inquiry
AIDS	Acquired Immunodeficiency Syndrome
AJB	America's Job Bank
ALC	Alien Labor Certification
ALEX	Automated Labor Exchange
ALJ	Administrative Law Judge
ALM	Asset Liability Management
AMPS	Auction Market Preferred Stock

ANSI	American National Standards Institute
AP	Accounts Payable
APA	American Psychological Association
APB	Accounting Principles Board
aPHR	Associate Professional in Human Resources
APR	Annual Percentage Rate
APV	Adjusted Present Value
APY	Annual Percentage Yield
AR	Accounts Receivable
ARRA	American Recovery and Reinvestment Act
ASB	Accounting Standards Board
ASHHRA	American Society for Healthcare Human Resources Administration
ASO	Administrative Services Only Plan
ASTD	American Society for Training and Development
ATB	Across the Board
ATO	1) Administrative Time Off; 2) Asset Turnover
ATOI	After Tax Operating Income
ATU	Annual Tax Unit
AWL	Actual Wage Loss
AWOL	Absent Without Leave
AWW	Average Weekly Wage
BARS	Behaviorally Anchored Rating Scale
BAT	Bureau of Apprenticeship and Training
BB	Base Benefits
BCP	Business Continuity Plan
BCR	Benefit/Cost Ratio
BIA	Business Impact Analysis
BFOQ or BOQ	Bona Fide Occupational Qualification
BLBA	Black Lunch Benefits Act
BLS	Bureau of Labor Statistics
BNA	Bureau of National Affairs
BOD	Board of Directors
BOT	Board of Trustees
BPA	Blanket Purchase Agreement
BRB	Benefit Review Board
BU	Bargaining Unit
C&B	Compensation and Benefits
C&P	Compensation and Pension
CAA	Congressional Accountability Act
CAFTA	Central American Free Trade Agreement

CAI	Computer Assisted Instruction
CAO	Chief Administrative Officer
CAPEX	Capital Expenditures
CASB	Cost Accounting Standards Board
CBA	Controlled Business Arrangement
CBO	Congressional Budget Office
CBP	Cafeteria Benefit Plan
CBT	Computer-Based Testing
CC	Civil Code
CCH	Commerce Clearing House
CCHR	Canadian Council on Human Resources
CCI	Consumer Confidence Index
CCL	Center for Creative Leadership
CCP	Certified Compensation Professional
CCPA	Consumer Credit Protection Act
CDC	Center for Disease Control
CDL	Commercial Driver's License
CEA	1) Commodity Exchange Authority; 2) Certificate of Educational Achievement
CEBS	Certified Employee Benefits Specialist
CEO	Chief Executive Officer
CEPS	Cash Earnings Per Share
CEU	Continuing Education Unit
CFAT	Cash Flow After Taxes
CFO	Chief Financial/Fiscal Officer
CFR	Code of Federal Regulations
CGQ	Corporate Governance Quotient
CGT	Capital Gains Tax
CHRC	1) Canadian Human Rights Commission; 2) Criminal History Records Check
CHRO	Chief Human Resources Officer
CIO	1) Chief Investment Officer; 2) Chief Information Officer
CISO	Chief Information Security Officer
CMO	Chief Marketing Officer
CO	Compliance Officer
COB	Close of Business
COBRA	Consolidated Omnibus Budget Reconciliation Act
COL	Cost of Living
COLA	Cost of Living Adjustment
COO	Chief Operating/Operations Officer

CPA	Certified Public Accountant
CPE	Continuing Professional Education
CPG	Consumer Packaged Goods
CPHR	California Professional in Human Resources Certification
CPI	Consumer Price Index
CPI-U	Consumer Price Index for All Urban Consumers
CPI-W	Consumer Price Index for Urban Wage Earners and Clerical Workers
CPM	Critical Path Method
CR	Corporate Responsibility
CRM	1) Client Relationship Management; 2) Customer Relationship Management; 3) Credit Risk Management
CROGI	Cash Return on Gross Investment
CSHO	Compliance Safety and Health Officer
CSO	Chief Security Officer
CTO	Compensatory Time Off
CTS	Carpal Tunnel Syndrome
CUPA	College and University Personnel Association
CUSFTA	Canada-U.S. Free Trade Agreement
CV	Curriculum Vitae
CWHSSA	Contract Work Hours and Safety Standards Act
CWSP	College Work-Study Program
D&I	Diversity and Inclusion
D&O	Directors and Officers
DB	Defined Benefit
DBA	1) Davis-Bacon Act; 2) Doing Business As
DBPP	Defined Benefit Pension Plan
DC	Defined Contribution
DCA	Dollar Cost Averaging
DCAA	Defense Contract Audit Agency
DCF	Discounted Cash Flow
DCPP	Defined Contribution Pension Plan
DCAP	Dependent Care Assistance Program
DEFRA	Deficit Reduction Act
DFA	Department of Finance and Administration
DFEH	Department of Fair Employment and Housing
DINKS	Dual Income No Kids
DJIA	Dow Jones Industrial Average
DMADV	Define, Measure, Analyze, Design, Verify
DMAIC	Define, Measure, Analyze, Improve, Control
DRIP	Dividend Reinvestment Plan

DRP	Disaster Recovery Plan
DSI	Discretionary Salary Increase
DSPP	Direct Stock Purchase Plan
DOB	Date of Birth
DOC	United States Department of Commerce
DOD	United States Department of Defense
DOH	Date of Hire
DOI	Date of Injury
DOJ	United States Department of Justice
DOL	United States Department of Labor
DOLETA	Department of Labor Employment and Training Administration
DOT	1) Dictionary of Occupational Titles; 2) United States Department of Transportation
DTI	Department of Trade and Industry
DVOP	Disabled Veterans Outreach Program
DW	Dislocated Worker
DWC	Division of Workers' Compensation
E-VERIFY	United States Department of Labor New Hire Screening System
EAC	Employee Advisory Committee/Council
EAP	Employee Assistance Program
EAPA	Employee Assistance Professionals Association
EB	Extended Benefits
EBO	Employee Buyout
EBRI	Employee Benefits Research Institute
EBS	Employee Benefits Security
EBSA	Employee Benefit Security Administration
EBT	Earnings Before Tax
ECI	Employment Cost Index
ECOA	Equal Credit Opportunity Act
ECPA	Electronic Communications Privacy Act
EDA	Economically Depressed Area
EDI	Electronic Data Interchange
EDP	1) Electronic Data Processing; 2) Employee Development Plan
EE	Employee
EEO	Equal Employment Opportunity
EEO-1/EEO-4	EEO-1 or EEO-4 Report/Standard Form 100 Report
EEOC	Equal Employment Opportunity Commission
EEOICPA	Energy Employee Occupational Illness Compensation Program Act
EFT	Electronic Funds Transfer
EFTA	European Free Trade Area

EGTRRA	Economic Growth and Tax Relief Reconciliation Act
EI or EQ	Emotional Intelligence
EIC	Earned Income Tax Credit
EIN	Employer Identification Number
EMT	Executive Management Team
EO	Executive Order
EOB	Explanation of Benefits
EOD	End of Day
EOI	Evidence of Insurability
EOY	End of Year
EPA	1) Equal Pay Act; 2) Environmental Protection Agency
EPLI	Employment Practices Liability Insurance
EPPA	Employee Polygraph Protection Act
EPS	Earnings per Share
ER	Employer
ERISA	Employee Retirement Income Security Act
ERTA	Economic Recovery Tax Act
ESA	Employment Standards Administration
ESL	English as a Second Language
ESO	Employee Stock Option
ESOP	Employee Stock Option Plan
ESOT	Employee Stock Ownership and Trust
ESP	Exchange Stock Portfolio
ESS	Employee Self-Service
ETA	1) Employment and Training Administration; 2) Estimated Time of Arrival
EU	European Union
EV	Enterprise Value
EVA	Economic Value Added
EVM	Earned Value Management
EX	Exempt
FAAS	Financial Assurance and Accountability Standards
FACT	Fair and Accurate Credit Transactions Act
FAQ	Frequently Asked Questions
FAS	Financial Accounting Standards
FASB	Financial Accounting Standards Board
FASAB	Financial Accounting Standards Advisory Board
FASAC	Financial Accounting Standards Advisory Committee
FASB	Financial Accounting Standards Board
FCC	Federal Communications Commission

FCCPA	Federal Consumer Credit Protection Act
FCPA	Foreign Corrupt Practices Act
FCRA	Fair Credit Reporting Act
FDA	Food and Drug Administration
FDCPA	Fair Debt Collection Practices Act
FDIC	Federal Deposit Insurance Corporation
FEA	Fair Employment Act
FECA	Federal Employees' Compensation Act
FEIN	Federal Employment Identification Number
FELA	Federal Employment Liability Act
FEMA	Federal Emergency Management Agency
FEP	Fair Employment Practice
FERS	Federal Employees Retirement System
FES	Factor Evaluation System
FFY	Federal Fiscal Year
FHA	Federal Housing Administration
FICA	Federal Insurance Contributions Act
FICO	Fair Isaac Credit Organization
FIE	Foreign Invested Enterprise
FIFO	First In, First Out
FLC	Foreign Labor Certification
FLRA	Federal Labor Relations Authority
FLSA	Fair Labor Standards Act
FMLA	Family Medical Leave Act
FMSHA	Federal Mine and Safety Health Act
FMV	Fair Market Value
FOIA	Freedom of Information Act
FOM	Field Operations Manual
FOREX	Foreign Exchange
FR	Federal Register
FRA	Federal Reserve Act
FRB	Federal Reserve Board
FROI	First Report of Injury
FRS	Financial Reporting Standards
FSA	Flexible Spending Account
FSB	Fortune Small Business
FSET	Federal State Employment Tax
FSLMRA	Federal Service Labor-Management Relations Act
FT	Full-Time
FTA	Free Trade Agreement

FTC	Federal Trade Commission
FTD	Federal Tax Deposit
FTE	Full-Time Equivalent
FTP	File Transfer Protocol
FUA	Federal Unemployment Account
FUTA	Federal Unemployment Tax ACT
FY	Fiscal Year
GAAC	Government Accounting and Auditing Committee
GAAFR	Governmental Accounting, Auditing, and Financial Reporting
GAAP	Generally Accepted Accounting Principles
GAAS	Generally Accepted Auditing Standards
GAGAS	Generally Accepted Government Accounting Standards
GAO	General Accounting Office
GAS	Governmental Accounting Standards
GASB	Governmental Accounting Standards Board
GATB	General Aptitude Test Battery
GATT	General Agreement on Tariffs and Trade
GDP	Gross Domestic Product
GED	General Equivalency Diploma
GIC	Guaranteed Investment Contract
GICS	Global Industry Classification Standards
GIF	Guaranteed Investment Fund
GINA	Genetic Information Nondiscrimination Act
GIPS	Global Investment Policy Standard
GIS	Geographic Information System
GL	1) General Ledger; 2) General Liability
GLB	Gramm-Leach-Bliley Act
GLSO	Group Legal Services Organization
GM	Gross Margin
GNP	Gross National Product
GPHR	Global Professional in Human Resources Certification
GPROI	Gross Profit Return on Investment
GPS	Global Positioning System
GR	General Revenue
GS	General Schedule
GSI	General Salary Increase
GTL	Group Term Life Insurance
HAS	Highest Average Salary
HAZMAT	Hazardous Material
HB	House Bill

HC	Human Capital
HCE	Highly Compensated Employee
HCFA	Health Care Financing Administration
HCIP	Harmonized Index of Consumer Pricing
HCM	Human Capital Management
HCN	Home-Country Nationals
HCO	Health Care Organization
HCSA	Health Care Spending Account
HCTC	Health Coverage Tax Credit
HHS	Department of Health and Human Services
HIPC	Health Insurance Purchasing Cooperatives
HIPPA	Health Insurance Portability and Accountability Act
HITECH	Health Information Technology for Economic and Clinical Health Act
HIV	Human Immunodeficiency Virus
HMO	Health Maintenance Organizations
HR	Human Resources
HRA	Health Reimbursement Account
HRCI	Human Resource Certification Institute
HRCS	Human Resource Competency Study
HRD	1) Human Resources Development; 2) Human Resources Department
HRIS	Human Resources Information System
HRLY	Hourly
HRM	Human Resources Management
HRMS	Human Resource Management System
HROD	Human Resources and Organizational Development
HSA	Health Savings Account
HTML	Hypertext Markup Language
HUD	United States Department of Housing and Urban Development
I-9	United States Immigration Form I-9
IAG	International Auditing Guidelines
IAS	International Accounting Standards
IASC	International Accounting Standards Committee
ICC	International Chamber of Commerce
ICE	United States Immigration and Customs Enforcement
IFEBP	International Foundation of Employee Benefit Plans
IHRIM	International Association of Human Resource Information Management
IIPP	Injury and Illness Prevention Programs/Plans
ILAB	International Labor Affairs Bureau
ILO	International Labor Organization

IME	Independent Medical Examination
INA	Immigration and Naturalization Act
INS	Immigration and Naturalization Service
IOS	International Organization for Standards
IPA	Inflation Protected Annuity
IPI	Industrial Protection Index
IPMA	International Personnel Management Association
IPO	Initial Public Offering
IPS	1) Inflation Protected Security; 2) Investment Policy Statement
IRA	Individual Retirement Account
IRB	Internal Revenue Bulletin
IRC	Internal Revenue Code
IRCA	Immigration Reform and Control Act
IRR	Internal Rate of Return
IRS	Internal Revenue Service
ISO	1) International Standards Organization; 2) Incentive Stock Option
ISP	Internet Service Provider
ISSA	International Securities Services Association
IT	Information Technology
ITA	United States International Trade Administration
ITIN	Individual Taxpayer Identification Number
IUR	Insured Unemployment Rates
IVR	Interactive Voice Response
J&S	Joint and Survivorship
JAN	Job Accommodation Network
JD	1) Job Description; 2) Juris Doctorate; 3) Job Date
JGTRRA	Jobs and Growth Tax Relief Reconciliation Act
JEEP	Joint Ethics Enforcement Plan
JIT	Just in Time
JOA	Joint Operating Agreement
JPAC	Joint Public Advisory Committee
JPEG	Joint Photographic Experts Group
JSSA	Jury Selection and Service Act
JTPA	Job Training Partnership Act (replaced by WIA)
JV	Joint Venture
JVA	Jobs for Veterans Act
KM	Knowledge Management
KPI	Key Performance Indicator
KSA	Knowledge, Skills, or Abilities
KSOP	401(k) Employee Stock Option Plan

LA	Labor Area
LAN	Local Area Network
LAR	Legislative Appropriations Request
LAUS	Local Area Unemployment Statistics
LBB	Legislative Budget Board
LBO	Leveraged Buyout
LCA	Labor Condition Application
LCD	Labor Cost Distribution
LDI	Liability-Driven Investment
LDP	Last Day Paid
LDW	Last Day Worked
LEI	Leading Economic Indicators
LEO	Long-Term Equity Options
LEPO	Low Exercise Price Option
LF	Labor Force
LFPR	Labor Force Participation Rate
LFY	Last Fiscal Year
LHWCA	Longshore and Harbor Workers' Compensation Act
LIFO	Last In, First Out
LLC	Limited Liability Company
LLP	Limited Liability Partnership
LMA	Labor Market Area
LMI	Labor Market Information
LMRA	Labor Management Relations Act
LMRDA	Labor Management Reporting and Disclosure Act
LMS	Learning Management System
LO	Learning Objectives
LOA	Leave of Absence
LOC	Letter of Commitment
LOI	Letter of Intent
LOR	Letter of Response
LOS	Length of Stay
LOW	Lack of Work
LP	Limited Partnership
LR	Labor Relations
LRO	Labor Relations Officer
LT	Lost Time
LTC	Long-Term Care
LTCM	Long-Term Capital Management
LTD	Long-Term Disability

PART III

LTFP	Long-Term Financial Plan
LTIP	Long-Term Incentive Plan
LTO	Long-Term Option
LTV	Loan-to-Value Ratio
LWDI	Lost Work Day Injury Rate
LWO	Leave Without Pay
LWP	Leave with Pay
M&A	Merger and Acquisition
MBO	Management by Objectives
MBTI	Myers-Briggs Type Indicator
MER	Management Expense Ratio
MEWA	Multiple Employer Welfare Arrangement
MHAEA	Mental Health and Addiction Equity Act
MHPA	Mental Health Parity Act
MHPAEA	Mental Health Parity and Addiction Equity Act
MIRR	Modified Internal Rate of Return
MIS	Management Information System
MLA	Minimum Liquid Assets
MLM	Multilevel Marketing
MLP	Master Limited Partnership
MLR	Monthly Labor Review
MLS	Mass Layoff Statistics
MNC	Multinational Corporation
MOC	Market on Close
MOF	Ministry of Finance
MOU	Memorandum of Understanding
MPPAA	Multiemployer Pension Plan Amendments Act
MRD	Minimum Required Distribution
MSA	1) Medical Savings Account; 2) Metropolitan Statistical Area; 3) Merit Salary Adjustment
MSDS	Material Safety Data Sheet
MSFW	Migrant and Seasonal Farm Worker
MSHA	Mine Safety and Health Act
MSP	Managed Service Provider
MSPA	Migrant and Seasonal Agriculture Worker Protection Act
MSPB	Merit Systems Protection Board
MSPR	Medicare Secondary Payer Rules
MST	Marketable Securities Tax
MTD	Month to Date
MTHLY	Monthly

NAAEC	North American Agreement on Environmental Cooperation
NAALC	North American Agreement on Labor Cooperation
NAB	Nonaccrual Basis
NAFTA	North American Free Trade Agreement
NAFTA-TAA	NAFTA Transitional Adjustment Assistance
NAICS	North American Industry Classification System
NASDAQ	National Association of Securities Dealers Automated Quotations
NASDR	National Association of Securities Dealers Regulation
NATO	North Atlantic Treaty Organization
NAV	Net Asset Value
NAVPS	Net Asset Value Per Share
NAWW	National Average Weekly Wage
NCCI	National Council on Compensation Insurance
NDNH	National Directory of New Hires
NEO	New and Emerging Occupations
NEX	Nonexempt
NFA	Net Financial Assets
NFE	Net Financial Expense
NFI	Net Financial Income
NFO	Net Financial Obligations
NHCE	Non-Highly Compensated Employee
NI	Net Income
NIH	National Institute of Health
NIOSH	National Institute of Occupational Safety and Health
NL	No Load
NLRA	National Labor Relations Act
NLRB	National Labor Relations Board
NMB	National Mediation Board
NMHPA	Newborns' and Mothers' Health Protection Act
NMS	Normal Market Size
NOA	Net Operating Assets
NOI	Net Operating Income
NOL	Net Operating Loss
NOPAT	Net Operating Profit After Taxes
NPV	Net Present Value
NRA	Nonresident Alien
NRET	Nonresident Withholding Tax
NSC	National Security Council
NSTA	National Securities Trade Association
NSX	National Stock Exchange

PART III

NT	Near Term
NVI	Negative Volume Index
NYSE	New York Stock Exchange
O*Net	Occupational Information Network
OA	Operating Assets
OAS	Option-Adjusted Spread
OASDHI	Old Age, Survivors, Disability, and Health Insurance
OASDI	Old Age and Survivors Disability Insurance
OASI	Old Age Survivors Insurance
OBRA	Omnibus Budget Reconciliation Act
OCF	Operating Cash Flow
OD	Organizational Development
ODDS	Online Data Delivery System
OE	Operating Expense
OEBS	Office of Employee Benefits Security (replaced by PWBP)
OER	Operation Expense Ratio
OES	Occupational Employment Statistic
OFCCP	Office of Federal Contract Compliance Programs
OHCA	Organized Health Care Arrangement
OI	Operating Income
OIS	Occupations Information System
OJT	On-the-Job Training
OL	Operating Liabilities
OM	Options Market
OMB	Office of Management and Budget
OOB	Out of Business
OOH	Occupational Outlook Handbook
OPM	Office of Personnel Management
OR	Operating Revenue
OSHA	Occupational Safety and Health Administration
OT	Overtime
OTC	Over the Counter
OTI	OSHA Training Institute
OTS	Office of Thrift Supervision
OWBPA	Older Workers Benefit Protection Act
P&L	Profit and Loss
PAR	Public Accounting Report
PBGC	Pension Benefit Guaranty Corporation
PBO	Projected Benefit Obligation
PBSI	Performance-Based Salary Increase

PBT	Profit Before Tax
PC	1) Personal Computer; 2) Politically Correct
PCAOB	Public Company Accounting Oversight Board
PCE	1) Preexisting Condition Exclusion; 2) Private Commercial Enterprise
PCI	Per Capita Income
PCN	Parent-Country Nationals
PD	Position Description
PDA	1) Pregnancy Discrimination Act; 2) Personal Data Assistant; 3) Public Displays of Affection; 4) Payday Advance Loan
PDF	Portable Document Format
PDQ	Position Description Questionnaire
PE	Price to Earnings Ratio
PEG	Price to Earnings Growth
PEO	Professional Employer Organization
PEPPRA	Public Employee Pension Plan Reporting and Accountability Act
PERT	Project Evaluation and Review Techniques
PEST	Political, Economic, Social, and Technological
PFK	Pay for Knowledge
PHI	Protected Health Information
PHR	Professional in Human Resources Certification
PIK	Payment in Kind
PIP	Performance Improvement Plan
PL	Public Law
PM	1) Profit Margin; 2) Performance Management
PMSA	Primary Metropolitan Statistical Area
PMV	Private Market Value
PNG	Portable Network Graphics
POA	Power of Attorney
POB	Public Oversights Board
POD	1) Payable on Death; 2) Professional and Organizational Development
POP	1) Premium-Only Plan; 2) Public Offering Price
POS	Point of Service Plan
PPA	Pension Protection Act of 1987
PPACA	Patient Protection and Affordable Care Act
PPE	Personal Protective Equipment
PPI	Producer Price Index
PPO	Preferred Provider Organization
PR	Public Relations
PRC	Peer Review Committee
PSI	Performance Salary Increase

PT	Part-Time
PTO	Paid Time Off
PTSD	Post-Traumatic Stress Disorder
PV	Present Value
PW	Present Worth
PWBA	Pension and Welfare Benefits Administration
PWBP	Pension and Welfare Benefit Program
PWC	Public Works Commission
PWD	Prevailing Wage Determination
PY	Program Year
QA	Quality Assurance
QAIP	Quality Assurance and Improvement Plan
QBU	Qualified Business Unit
QC	Quality Control
QCEW	Quarterly Census of Employment and Wages
QCR	Quarterly Contributions Report
QDRO	Qualified Domestic Relations Order
QMAC	Qualified Matching Contributions
QMCSO	Qualified Medical Child Support Order
QME	Qualified Medical Examiner
QNEC	Qualified Nonelective Contributions
QPAM	Qualified Professional Asset Manager
QR	1) Quarterly Report; 2) Quality Review
QREC	Quality Review Executive Committee
QTD	1) Qualified Total Distribution; 2) Quarter to Date
QWI	Quarterly Workforce Indicators
R&C	Reasonable and Customary
R&D	Research and Development
RA	Resident Alien
RAP	Regulatory Accounting Principles
RCR	Recruiting Cost Ratio
RE	Residual Earnings
REA	Retirement Equity Act
RFB	Request for Bid
RFI	Request for Information
RFID	Radio Frequency Identification
RFP	Request for Proposal
RFQ	Request for Quote
RIC	Regulated Investment Company
RICO	Racketeer Influenced and Corrupt Organizations Act

RIF	Reduction in Force
RIPA	Retirement Income Policy Act
RMP	Risk Management Plan
RNFA	Return on Net Financial Assets
ROA	Return on Assets
ROC	Return on Capital
ROI	Return on Investment
ROIC	Return on Invested Capital
ROM	Range of Motion
RONA	Return on Net Assets
ROOA	Return on Operating Assets
ROR	Return on Revenue
ROS	Return on Sales
ROTA	Return on Total Assets
ROTC	Reserve Officer Training Corps
RPI	Retail Price Index
RR	Retention Rate
RRSP	Registered Retirement Savings Plan
RSU	Restricted Stock Unit
RTO	Reverse Takeover
RTW	1) Return to Work; 2) Right to Work
RWA	Risk-Weighted Asset
RYR	Recruitment Yield Ratio
S&P	Standard and Poor's
SAAR	Seasonally Adjusted Annual Rate
SAR	1) Summary Annual Report; 2) Stock Appreciation Right
SARSEP	Salary Reduction Simplified Employee Pension
SAS	Statement of Accounting Standards
SAT	Scholastic Aptitude Test
SB	Senate Bill
SBA	Small Business Administration
SBAP	Small Business Assistance Program
SBBA	Sales and Buy-Back Agreement
SBD	Small Disadvantaged Business
SBJPA	Small Business Job Protection Act
SBLC	Standby Letter of Credit
SBO	Small Business Ombudsman
SC	Securities Commission
SCA	McNamara-O'Hara Service Contract Act
SCM	Supply Chain Management

PART III

SDI	State Disability Insurance
SE	1) Salaried Exempt; 2) Self-Employed
SEA	Securities Exchange Act
SEC	Securities and Exchange Commission
SEP	Simplified Employee Pension
SEPPAA	Single Employer Pension Plan Amendments Act
SERP	Supplemental Executive Retirement Plan
SESA	State Employment Security Agency
SFAS	Statements of Financial Accounting Standards
SHRM	Society for Human Resource Management
SIA	Securities Industry Act
SIB	Securities and Investment Board
SIC	Standard Industrial Classification
SIPA	Securities Investment Protection Act
SITC	Standard International Trade Classification
SLA	Service Level Agreement
SLOB	Separate Lines of Business
SMART	Specific, Measureable, Attainable, Realistic, Timed
SMI	Supplemental Medical Insurance
SMM	Summary of Material Modifications
SMS	Standard Metropolitan Statistical Area
SMT	Senior Management Team
SNAP	Supplemental Nutrition Assistance Program
SNE	Salaried Nonexempt
SOC	Standard Occupational Classification
SOL	Statute of Limitations
SOP	Statement of Position
SOX	Sarbanes-Oxley Act
SPD	Summary Plan Description
SPHR	Senior Professional in Human Resources Certification
SPX	Standard and Poor's Index
SRA	Supplemental Retirement Annuity
SRO	Self-Regulatory Organization
SROI	Subsequent Report of Injury
SS	Social Security
SSA	Social Security Administration
SSB	Securities Supervisory Board
SSD	Social Security Disability
SSDI	Social Security Disability Indemnity
SSI	Supplemental Security Income

SSN	Social Security Number
STD	Short-Term Insurance
STEEPLED	Social, Technological, Environmental, Economic, Political, Legal, Ethics, and Demographics
STF	Summary Tape File
STIP	Short-Term Industry Projections
STW	School-to-Work
SUB	Supplemental Unemployment Benefit
SUTA	State Unemployment Tax Act
SWOT	Strengths, Weaknesses, Opportunities, and Threats
T&D	Training and Development
TAMRA	Technical and Miscellaneous Revenue Act of 1988
TANF	Temporary Assistance to Needy Families
TBD	To Be Determined
TCN	Third Country National
TDA	Tax-Deferred Annuity
TDB	Temporary Disability Benefits
TEA	Transportation Efficiency Act
TEFRA	Tax Equity and Fiscal Responsibility Act
TER	Total Expense Ratio
TESSA	Tax-Exempt Special Savings Account
TEUC	Temporary Extended Unemployment Compensation
TEV	Total Enterprise Value
TIL	Truth in Lending
TIP	Transportation Improvement Program
TL	Time and Labor
TN	Temporary Visitor Visa
TOC	Theory of Constraints
TOM	Traded Options Market
TPA	Third-Party Administrator
TPD	Temporary Partial Disability
TPL	Third-Party Liability
TQM	Total Quality Management
TRA	Tax Reform Act
TRASOP	Tax Reduction Act ESOP
TSA	Tax-Sheltered Annuity
TSB	Targeted Small Business
TSP	Thrift Savings Plan
TTD	Temporary Total Disability
TUR	Total Unemployment Rates

PART III

TVI	Trade Value Index
TWA	Time-Weighted Average
UAW	United Auto Workers
UBTI	Unrelated Business Taxable Income
U&C	Usual and Customary
UCA	Unemployment Compensation Amendments Act
UCC	Uniform Commercial Code
UCI	Unemployment Compensation Insurance
UCR	Usual, Customary, and Reasonable
UFW	United Farm Workers
UGESP	Uniform Guidelines on Employee Selection Procedures
UGMA	Uniform Gifts to Minors Act
UI	Unemployment Insurance
UIC	Unemployment Insurance Commission
ULP	Unfair Labor Practice
UN	United Nations
UNCITRAL	United Nations Commission on International Trade Law
UR	1) Utilization Review; 2) Unemployment Rate
URL	Uniform Resource Locator (Web Site Address)
URO	Utilization Review Organization
USCIS	United States Citizenship and Immigration Services
USDA	United States Department of Agriculture
US DOL	United States Department of Labor
US DOJ	United States Department of Justice
USC	United States Code
USERRA	Uniform Services Employment and Reemployment Rights Act
USITC	United States International Trade Commission
USM	Unlisted Securities Market
USTC	United States Tax Court
UTMA	Uniform Transfers to Minors Act
VA	Veterans Administration/Affairs
VBIA	Veterans Benefits Improvement Act
VEBA	Voluntary Employees' Beneficiary Association
VETS	Veterans Employment and Training Service
VETS-4212	VETS-4212 Report (replaced VETS-100)
VEVRA	Vietnam-Era Veterans Readjustment Act
VOC-ED	Vocational Education
VOC-REHAB	Vocational Rehabilitation
VPN	Virtual Private Network
VPT	Volume Price Trend

VWAP	Value-Weighted Average Price
VWPT	Value-Weighted Price Trading
VWPX	Volume-Weighted Price Uncrossing
WACC	Weighted Average Cost of Capital
WAI	Wealth-Added Index
WARN	Worker Adjustment and Retraining Notification Act
WC	Workers' Compensation
WCB	Workers' Compensation Board
WDC	Workforce Development Center
WHCRA	Women's Health and Cancer Rights Act
WIA	Workforce Investment Act
WIP	Work in Progress
WKLY	Weekly
WOTC	Workforce Opportunity Tax Credit
WPE	Workforce Planning and Employment
WPI	Wholesale Price Index
WPOA	Wagner-Peyser Act
WPPDA	Welfare and Pension Plan Disclosure Act (repealed by ERISA)
WRA	Weighted Risk Assets
WRAEA	Workforce Reinvestment and Adult Education Act
WTO	World Trade Organization
WTW	Welfare to Work
XML	Extended Markup Language
XRA	Expected Retirement Age
YTD	Year to Date
YTM	Yield to Maturity
ZBB	Zero-Based Budgeting

PART III

Case Laws by Chapter

Generally speaking, there are three types of federal laws. First are the acts taken by Congress to legislate mandates. Congressional actions, when completed, become the "law of the land." Second are the implementing regulations promulgated by the federal agencies and departments that specify in detail how the laws, passed by Congress, will be administered. Third are the court interpretations of those congressional actions and regulatory rules. When the U.S. Supreme Court, or an agency such as the National Labor Relations Board (NLRB), issues a ruling about how the laws should be applied and interpreted, the ruling becomes "case law." It establishes precedent that must be followed by everyone within the court's jurisdiction. This appendix lists cases that interpret important issues that have influence on human resource management and summarizes key case law decisions. We recommend that you review each case in its entirety by going to the link listed and searching by the citation title. HR professionals should have a working knowledge of these cases and their impact on the workplace. This information may appear on the certification exam in one way or another.

Chapter 4: People

Year	Citation	Decision
1987	*Leggett v. First National Bank of Oregon* (739 P.2d. 1083) http://law.justia.com	The employer invaded privacy of employee when a company representative contacted the employee's psychologist (to whom the employee had been referred by an employee assistance program [EAP]), inquiring about the employee's condition.
2000	*Erie County Retirees Association v. County of Erie* (2000 U.S. App. LEXIS 18317 3rd Cir. August 1, 2000) http://www.buypeba.org/publications/Eriecase.pdf	If an employee provides retiree health benefits, the health insurance benefits received by Medicare-eligible retirees cost the same as the health insurance benefits received by younger retirees.
2005	*IBP, Inc. v. Alvarez* (546 U.S. 21) http://www.law.cornell.edu	Time spent donning or doffing unique safety gear is compensable, and the FLSA requires payment of affected employees for all the time spent walking between changing and production areas.

Year	Citation	Decision
2008	*LaRue v. DeWolff* (No. 06-856, 450 F. 3d 570) http://www.law.cornell.edu	When retirement plan administrators breach their fiduciary duty to act as a prudent person would act in investment of retirement funds, the employee whose retirement account lost money can sue the plan administrators.
2009	*Kennedy v. Plan Administrators for DuPont Savings* (No. 07-636) https://supreme.justia.com	This decision awarded retirement benefits to an ex-spouse even though she had agreed to disclaim such benefits, because the retiree had never changed the beneficiary designation on the retirement plan. This points out the need for retirement plan administrators to pay attention to divorce decrees and qualified domestic relations orders.

Chapter 5: Organization

Year	Citation	Decision
1971	*Griggs v. Duke Power Co.* (401 U.S. 424) http://www.law.cornell.edu	When an employer uses a neutral test or other selection device and then discovers it has a disproportionate impact on minorities or women, the test must be discarded unless it can be shown that it was required as a business necessity.
1973	*McDonnell Douglas Corp. v. Green* (411 U.S. 792) http://caselaw.findlaw.com	In a hiring case, the charging party has to show only that 1) the charging party is a member of a Title VII protected group, 2) he or she applied and was qualified for the position sought, 3) the job was not offered to him or her, and 4) the employer continued to seek applicants with similar qualifications. Then the employer must show a legitimate business reason why the complaining party was not hired. The employee has a final chance to prove the employer's business reason was really pretext for discrimination.
1974	*Espinoza v. Farah Manufacturing Co.* (414 U.S. 86) https://supreme.justia.com	Noncitizens are entitled to Title VII protection. Employers who require citizenship may violate Title VII if it results in discrimination based on national origin.
1974	*Corning Glass Works v. Brennan* (417 U.S. 188) http://supreme.justia.com	Pay discrimination cases under the Equal Pay Act require the employee to prove that there is unequal pay based on sex for substantially equal work.

Year	Citation	Decision
1975	*Albermarle Paper v. Moody* (422 U.S. 405) http://supreme.justia.com	This decision requires the employer to establish evidence that an employment test is related to the job content. Job analysis could be used to show that relationship, but performance evaluations of incumbents are specifically excluded.
1976	*Washington v. Davis* (426 U.S. 229) http://www.law.cornell.edu	When an employment test is challenged under constitutional law, intent to discriminate must be established. Under Title VII there is no need to show intent, just the impact of test results.
1976	*McDonald v. Santa Fe Transportation Co.* (427 U.S. 273) http://supreme.justia.com	Title VII prohibits racial discrimination against whites as well as blacks.
1987	*Johnson v. Santa Clara County Transportation Agency* (480 U.S. 616) http://supreme.justia.com	The employer was justified in hiring a woman who scored 2 points less than a man because it had an affirmative action plan that was temporary, flexible, and designed to correct an imbalance of white males in the workforce.
1987	*School Board of Nassau v. Arline* (480 U.S. 273) http://supreme.justia.com	A person with a contagious disease is covered by the Rehabilitation Act if the person otherwise meets the definitions of "handicapped individual."
1988	*Watson v. Fort Worth Bank & Trust* (487 U.S. 977) http://supreme.justia.com	In a unanimous opinion, the Supreme Court declared that disparate impact analysis can be applied to subjective or discretionary selection practices.
1989	*City of Richmond v. J. A. Croson Company* (488 U.S. 469) http://supreme.justia.com	Affirmative action programs can be maintained only by a showing that the programs aim to eliminate the effects of past discrimination.
1989	*Price Waterhouse v. Hopkins* (490 U.S. 288) http://caselaw.findlaw.com	This decision established how to analyze an employer's actions when the employer had mixed motives for an employment decision. If an employee shows that discrimination played a motivating part in an employment decision, the employer can attempt to prove as a defense that it would have made the same employment decision even if discrimination were not a factor.
1989	*Wards Cove Packing Co. v. Antonio* (490 U.S. 642) http://www.law.cornell.edu	An employee is required to show the disparate impact violation of Title VII in specific employment practices, not the cumulative effect of the employer's selection practices. When a showing of disparate impact is made, the employer only has to produce evidence of a business justification for the practice, and the burden of proof always remains with the employee.

(continued)

PART III

Year	Citation	Decision
1993	*Harris v. Forklift Systems Inc.* (510 U.S. 17) http://www.law.cornell.edu	In a sexual harassment complaint the employee does not have to prove concrete psychological harm to establish a Title VII violation.
1993	*St. Mary's Honor Center v. Hicks* (509 U.S. 502) http://www.law.cornell.edu	Title VII complaints require the employee to show that discrimination was the reason for a negative employment action.
1993	*Taxman v. Board of Education of Piscataway* (91 F.3d 1547, 3rd Circuit) http://caselaw.findlaw.com	Race in an affirmative action plan cannot be used to trammel the rights of people of other races.
1995	*McKennon v. Nashville Banner Publishing Co.* (513 U.S. 352) http://www.law.cornell.edu	"After-acquired" evidence collected following a negative employment action cannot protect an employer from liability under Title VII or the Age Discrimination in Employment Act (ADEA), even if the conduct would have justified terminating the employee.
1996	*O'Connor v. Consolidated Coin Caterers Corp.* (517 U.S. 308) http://www.law.cornell.edu	To show unlawful discrimination under the Age Discrimination in Employment Act, a discharged employee does not have to show that he or she was replaced by someone outside the protected age group (that is, younger than 40).
1997	*Robinson v. Shell Oil* (519 U.S. 337) http://www.law.cornell.edu	Title VII prohibition against retaliation protects former as well as current employees.
1998	*Faragher v. City of Boca Raton* (524 U.S. 775) http://www.law.cornell.edu	This distinguished between supervisor harassment which results in tangible employment action and that which does not. When harassment results in tangible employment action, the employer is liable. Employers may avoid liability if they have a legitimate written complaint policy, it is clearly communicated to employees, and it offers alternatives to the immediate supervisor as the point of contact for making a complaint.
1998	*Oncale v. Sundowner Offshore Service, Inc.* (523 U.S. 75) http://www.law.cornell.edu	Same-gender harassment is actionable under Title VII.
1998	*Bragdon v. Abbott* (524 U.S. 624) http://www.law.cornell.edu	An individual with asymptomatic HIV is an individual with a disability and therefore is protected by the Americans with Disabilities Act (ADA). Reproduction is a major life activity under the statute.
1998	*Wright v. Universal Maritime Service Corp.* (525 U.S. 70) http://supreme.justia.com	Collective bargaining agreements must contain a clear and unmistakable waiver if they are to bar an individual's right to sue after an arbitration requirement.
1999	*Kolstad v. American Dental Association* (527 U.S. 526) http://www.law.cornell.edu	Title VII punitive damages are limited to cases in which the employer has engaged in intentional discrimination and has done so "with malice or with reckless indifference."

Year	Citation	Decision
1999	*Gibson v. West* (527 U.S. 212) http://caselaw.findlaw.com	This decision endorsed the position of the Equal Employment Opportunity Commission (EEOC) that it has the legal authority to require federal agencies to pay compensatory damages when the EEOC has ruled during the administrative process that the federal agency has unlawfully discriminated in violation of Title VII.
2001	*Circuit City Stores v. Adams* (532 U.S. 105) http://www.law.cornell.edu	The court ruled that a prehire employment application requiring that all employment disputes be settled by arbitration was enforceable under the Federal Arbitration Act.
2001	*Ronald Lesch v. Crown Cork and Seal Company* (334 NLRB 699) http://www.nlrb.gov/cases-decisions/board-decisions?volume=334&sort_by=case_nameSort&sort_order=ASC	This NLRB decision lifted some restrictions on the employer's use of employee participation committees.
2002	*EEOC v. Waffle House* (534 U.S. 279) http://www.law.cornell.edu	The Supreme Court ruled that even if there is a mandatory arbitration agreement in place, a relevant civil rights agency can still sue on behalf of the employee.
2002	*Phoenix Transit System v. NLRB* (337 NLRB 510) http://www.nlrb.gov/cases-decisions/board-decisions?volume=337&sort_by=case_nameSort&sort_order=ASC	This NLRB ruling struck down an employer rule prohibiting employees from discussing among themselves an employment complaint—in this instance, a complaint of sexual harassment—on the grounds that the prohibition was not limited in time and scope and interfered with a protected concerted activity.
2004	*NLRB v. Weingarten, Inc.* (420 U.S. 251, 254 1975) overturned by *IBM Corp. v. NLRB* (341 NLRB No 148, June 9, 2004) http://www.hawaii.edu/ and http://www.nacua.org/documents/IBM_Corp_and_KennethPaulSchult.pdf	NLRB ruled by a 3–2 vote that employees who work in a nonunionized workplace are not entitled to have a co-worker accompany them to an interview with their employer, even if the affected employee reasonably believes that the interview might result in discipline. This decision effectively reversed the July 2000 decision of the Clinton board, which had extended Weingarten rights to nonunion employees.
2007	*Toering Electric Company v. NLRB* (351 NLRB 225) http://www.nlrb.gov/cases-decisions/board-decisions?volume=351&sort_by=case_nameSort&sort_order=ASC	NLRB ruled that an applicant for employment must be genuinely interested in seeking to establish an employment relationship with the employer in order to be protected against hiring discrimination based on union affiliation or activity; this creates greater obstacles for unions attempting salting campaigns.

PART III

(continued)

Year	Citation	Decision
2007	*Oil Capitol Sheet Metal, Inc., v. NLRB* (349 NLRB 1348) http://www.nlrb.gov/ cases-decisions/board- decisions?volume=351&sort_ by=case_nameSort&sort_ order=ASC	This NLRB decision provided employers relief in salting cases by announcing a new evidentiary standard for determining the period of back pay; it required the union to provide evidence that supports the period of time it claims the salt would have been employed.
2007 and 2011	*Dana Corporation / Metaldyne Corporation v. NLRB* (351 NLRB 434) http://www.nlrb.gov/ cases-decisions/board- decisions?volume=351&sort_ by=case_nameSort&sort_ order=ASC	NLRB ruled that a recognition bar, which precludes a decertification election for 12 months after an employer recognizes a union, does not apply when the recognition is voluntary, based on a card check. This was overruled in 2011 in *Lamons Gasket*, which restored the recognition bar for voluntary recognition but revised the prohibited time period from 1 year to a minimum of 6 months up to a year.
2007	*Syracuse University v. NLRB* (350 NLRB 755) http://www.nlrb.gov/ cases-decisions/board- decisions?volume=351&sort_ by=case_nameSort&sort_ order=ASC	NLRB found that an employee grievance panel did not violate the National Labor Relations Act (NLRA) because the purpose of the panel was not to deal with management but to improve group decisions.
2010	*KenMor Electric Co., Inc. v. NLRB* (355 NLRB No. 173) http://www.nlrb.gov/ cases-decisions/board- decisions?volume=351&sort_ by=case_nameSort&sort_ order=ASC	NLRB ruled that a system developed and operated by an association of electrical contractors violated the NLRA because it discriminated against individuals who were salts. The board held that an individual's right to be a salt is protected under the NLRA.
2011	*Staub v. Proctor* (131 U.S. 1186) http://supreme.justia.com	The Supreme Court applied the "cat's paw" principle to a wrongful discharge case, finding that an employer was culpable because the HR manager did not adequately investigate supervisors' charges against the fired employee.
2011	*AT&T Mobility v. Concepcion* (S.Ct. No 09-893) http://www.supremecourt.gov	The Supreme Court ruled that some state statutes restricting the enforceability of arbitration agreements in a commercial context may be preempted by the Federal Arbitration Act.
2011	*Kepas v. eBay* (131 S. Ct. 2160) http://www.ca10.uscourts.gov	The Supreme Court refused to review a lower court decision that held in an employment case that a cost provision was severable from the balance of an arbitration agreement. The cost provision was unenforceable, but the agreement to arbitrate was enforceable.

Year	Citation	Decision
2011	*Specialty Healthcare and Rehabilitation Center of Mobile v. NLRB* (15-RC-008773) http://www.nlrb.gov/ case/15-RC-008773	NLRB indicated that, in nonacute health care facilities, it will certify smaller units for bargaining unless the employer provides overwhelming proof of a community of interest.
2011	*UGL-UNICCO Service Company v. NLRB* (01-RC-022447) http://www.nlrb.gov/case/ 01-RC-022447	NLRB reestablished the successor bar doctrine, allowing unions a window of 6 months to 1 year of presumed majority support after the transfer of ownership of a business.
2012	*D. R. Horton, Inc., v. NLRB* (12-CA-25764) http://www.cozen.com/ cozendocs/outgoing/alerts/2012/ labor_011012_link.pdf	NLRB ruled that requiring employees to agree to a class action waiver as a term and condition of employment violates Section 7 of the National Labor Relations Act.

Chapter 6: Workplace

Year	Citation	Decision
1971	*Phillips v. Martin Marietta Corp.* (400 U.S. 542) https://supreme.justia.com	Sex discrimination means employers may not have different policies for men and women with small children of similar age.
1977	*Hazlewood School District v. U.S.* (433 U.S. 299) http://caselaw.findlaw.com	An employee can establish a *prima facie* case of class hiring discrimination through the presentation of statistical evidence by comparing the racial composition of an employer's workforce with the racial composition of the relevant labor market.
1977	*Trans World Airlines, Inc., v. Hardison* (432 U.S. 63) http://supreme.justia.com	Under Title VII employers must reasonably accommodate an employee's religious needs unless doing so would create an undue hardship for the employer. The court defines hardship as anything more than *de minimis* cost.
1978	*Regents of University of California v. Bakke* (438 U.S. 265) http://caselaw.findlaw.com	Medical school admission set-asides (16 of 100 seats) are illegal if they discriminate against whites and there is no previous discrimination against minorities established.
1979	*United Steelworkers v. Weber* (443 U.S. 193) http://supreme.justia.com	Affirmative action plans are permissible if they are temporary and intended to "eliminate a manifest racial imbalance."

(continued)

PART III

Year	Citation	Decision
1982	*Connecticut v. Teal* (457 U.S. 440) http://caselaw.findlaw.com	An employer is liable for racial discrimination when any part of its selection process, such as an unvalidated examination or test, has a disparate impact even if the final result of the hiring process is racially balanced. In effect, the court rejected the "bottom-line defense" and made clear that the fair employment laws protect the individual. Fair treatment to a group is not a defense to an individual claim of discrimination.
1984	*EEOC v. Shell Oil Co.* (466 U.S. 54) http://supreme.justia.com	The Supreme Court affirmed authority of EEOC commissioners to initiate charges of discrimination through "Commissioner Charges."
1986	*Meritor Savings Bank v. Vinson* (477 U.S. 57) http://www.law.cornell.edu	This defined "Hostile Environment Sexual Harassment" as a form of sex discrimination under Title VII. It also further defined it as "unwelcome" advances of a sexual nature. The victim's failure to use the employer's complaint process does not insulate the employer from liability.
1988	*DeBartolo Corp. v. Gulf Coast Trades Council* (known as DeBartolo II) (485 U.S. 568) https://supreme.justia.com	The Supreme Court ruled that bannering, hand billing, or attention-getting actions outside an employer's property were permissible.
1991	*United Auto Workers v. Johnson Controls* (499 U.S. 187) http://www.law.cornell.edu	The Supreme Court held that decisions about the welfare of future children must be left to the parents who conceive, bear, support, and raise them, rather than to the employers who hire their parents.
1992	*Electromation Inc., v. NLRB* (Nos. 92-4129, 93-1169, 7th Circuit) http://www.leagle.com/decision/ 1994118335F3d1148_11017	NLRB held that action committees at Electromation were illegal "labor organizations" because management created and controlled the groups and used them to deal with employees on working conditions in violation of the NLRA.
1993	*E. I. DuPont & Company v. NLRB* (311 NLRB 893) http://law.justia.com	NLRB concluded that DuPont's six safety committees and fitness committee were employer-dominated labor organizations and that DuPont dominated the formation and administration of one of them in violation of the NLRA.
1995	*PepsiCo, Inc. v. Redmond* (No. 94-3942 7th Cir) http://caselaw.findlaw.com	This was the case in which a district court applied an inevitable disclosure doctrine even though there was no noncompete agreement in place. An employee who had left his position in marketing PepsiCo's All Sport sports drink to work for Quaker Oats Company and market Gatorade and Snapple drinks was enjoined from working for Quaker because he had detailed knowledge of PepsiCo's trade secrets pertaining to pricing, market strategy, and selling/delivery systems.

Year	Citation	Decision
2003	*Grutter v. Bollinger* (539 U.S. 306) http://supreme.justia.com	The diversity of a student body is a compelling state interest that can justify the use of race in university admissions as long as the admissions policy is "narrowly tailored" to achieve this goal. University of Michigan did not do so for its undergraduate program, but the law school admissions program satisfied the standard.
2004	*General Dynamics Land Systems Inc., v. Cline* (540 U.S. 581) http://www.law.cornell.edu	The ADEA does not protect younger workers, even those older than 40, from workplace decisions that favor older workers.
2004	*Pennsylvania State Police v. Suders* (542 U.S. 129) http://www.law.cornell.edu	In the absence of a tangible employment action, employers may use the Ellerth/Faragher defense in a constructive discharge claim when supervisors are charged with harassment.
2005	*Smith v. Jackson, Mississippi* (544 U.S. 228) http://www.law.cornell.edu	The ADEA, like Title VII, offers recovery on a disparate impact theory.
2005	*Leonel v. American Airlines* (400 F.3d 702, 9th Circuit) http://www.ca9.uscourts.gov	To make a legitimate job offer under the ADA, an employer must have completed all nonmedical components of the application process or be able to demonstrate that it could not reasonably have done so before issuing the offer.
2007	*Ledbetter v. Goodyear Tire & Rubber Co.* (550 U.S. 618) http://www.law.cornell.edu	A claim of discrimination must be filed within 180 days of the first discriminatory employment act, and the clock does not restart after each subsequent act (e.g., issuance of a paycheck with lower pay than co-workers if based on sex). Congress overruled this decision with passage of the Lilly Ledbetter Fair Pay Act of 2009, which says the clock will restart each time another incident of discrimination occurs.
2009	*Ricci v. DeStefano* (No. 07-1428) http://www.supremecourt.gov	"Under Title VII, before an employer can engage in intentional discrimination for the asserted purpose of avoiding or remedying an unintentional disparate impact, the employer must have a strong basis in evidence to believe it will be subject to disparate-impact liability if it fails to take the race-conscious, discriminatory action."
2013	*Vance v. Ball State Univ.* (No. 11-556) http://www.supremecourt.gov	This case determined that an employee is a "supervisor" of another employee for the purposes of liability under Title VII of the Civil Rights Act of 1964 only if he or she is empowered by the employer to take tangible employment actions against the other employee.

(continued)

PART III

Year	Citation	Decision
2013	*University of Texas Sw. Med. Ctr. v. Nassar* (No. 12-484) http://www.law.cornell.edu	Retaliation claims brought under Title VII of the Civil Rights Act of 1964 must be proved according to principles of "but-for-causation," not the lesser causation test applicable to bias claims.

Chapter 7: Behavioral Competencies

There are no case laws that directly relate to these competencies.

For Additional Study

This appendix lists additional resources that can be helpful in your study for the SHRM-CP and SHRM-SCP exams and for future reference as an HR professional. The resources listed may apply to several domains.

Ashbaugh, S., and R. Miranda. "Technology for Human Resources Management: Seven Questions and Answers." Public Personnel Management, 31(1), 7–17, 2002.

Badgi, Satish. *Practical Guide to Human Resource Information Systems.* Delhi: Phi Learning Pvt. Ltd., 2012.

Becker, Brian E., Mark A. Huselid, and David Ulrich. *The HR Scorecard: Linking People, Strategy, and Performance.* Boston: Harvard Business School Press, 2001.

Benjamin, Steve. "A Closer Look at Needs Analysis and Needs Assessment: Whatever Happened to the Systems Approach?" *Performance Improvement* 28, no. 9, 12–16, Wiley Periodicals, Inc., 1989.

Bennett-Alexander, Dawn D., and Laura B. Pincus. *Employment Law for Business.* Chicago: Irwin Publishing, 1995.

Bingham, B., and N. Davidson. "Great Candidates Fast: On-Line Job Application and Electronic Processing: Washington State's New Internet Application System." Public Personnel Management, 31(1), 53–62, 2002.

Bliss, Wendy (Series Advisor). *The Essentials of Finance and Budgeting.* Boston: Harvard Business School Press, and Alexandria, Virginia: Society for Human Resource Management, 2005.

Blosser, Fred. *Primer on Occupational Safety and Health.* Washington, D.C.: The Bureau of National Affairs, 1992.

Carrell, Michael R., and Christina Heavrin. *Collective Bargaining and Labor Relations*, 3rd ed. New York: Merrill, 1985.

Cherrington, David J. *The Management of Human Resources*, 4th ed. Englewood Cliffs, New Jersey: Prentice-Hall, 1995.

Cofey, Robert E., Curtis W. Cook, and Phillip L. Hunsaker. *Management and Organizational Behavior*. Boston: Austen Press, 1994.

Dawes, S. *Human Resource Implications of Information Technology in State Government*. Public Personnel Management, 23(1), 31–46, 1994.

DeLuca, Matthew J. *Handbook of Compensation Management*. Englewood Cliffs, New Jersey: Prentice-Hall, 1997.

DeMers, A. *Solutions and Strategies for IT Recruitment and Retention: A Manager's Guide*. Public Personnel Management, 5/(1), 27–37, 2002.

DeNisi, A., and R. Griffin. *HR*. Boston: Cengage Learning, 2011.

Doherty, Neil. *Integrated Risk Management: Techniques and Strategies*. New York: McGraw-Hill Education, 2000.

Feldacker, Bruce. *Labor Guide to Labor Law*, 3rd ed. Englewood Cliffs, New Jersey: Prentice-Hall, 1990.

Fitz-Enz, Jac. *How to Measure Human Resource Management*, 2nd ed. New York: McGraw-Hill Education, 1995.

Glaser, Judith E. *Conversational Intelligence*. Brookline, MA: Bibliomotion, Inc., 2014.

Grant, Phillip. *Multiple Use Job Descriptions: A Guide to Analysis, Preparation, and Applications for Human Resources Managers*. Westport, Connecticut: Praeger, 1989.

Hayes, John. *The Theory and Practice of Change Management*. London: Palgrave Macmillan, 2010.

Herzberg, Frederick. *The Motivation to Work*. Piscataway, NJ: Transaction, 1993.

Kahan, Seth. *Getting Change Right: How Leaders Transform Organizations from the Inside Out*. San Francisco: Jossey-Bass, 2010.

Kavanaugh, Michael, Mohan Thite, and Richard D. Johnson (Eds.). *Human Resource Information Systems: Basics, Applications, and Future Directions*. Thousand Oaks, California: Sage Publications, 2011.

Kirkpatrick, Donald L. *How to Manage Change Effectively*. San Francisco: Jossey-Bass, 1985.

Knowles, Malcolm. *The Adult Learner: The Definitive Classic in Adult Education and Human Resource Development*. Oxford: Butterworth-Heinemann, 2005.

Kushner, Gary. *Health Care Reform: The Patient Protection and Affordable Care Act of 2010*. SHRM/Kushner and Company, 2010.

Kutcher, David. "What Is a RFP, Where to Find RFPs, and Are RFPs Relevant?" *Confluent Forms*, May 13, 2013. Retrieved February 7, 2014, from www.confluentforms .com/2013/05/requests-for-proposals-rfp.html.

Lawler, Edward E., III. *Strategic Pay: Aligning Organizational Strategies and Pay Systems.* San Francisco: Jossey-Bass, 1990.

Lewis, Jackson. *Employer's Guide to Union Organizing Campaigns.* New York: Aspen Publishers, 2007.

Mantel Jr., S., J. Meredith, S. Shafer, and M. Sutton. *Project Management in Practice.* Hoboken, New Jersey: John Wiley & Sons, 2010.

Mathis, R., J. Jackson, and S. Valentine. *Human Resource Management.* Boston: Cengage Learning, 2013.

Maslow, Abraham H. *A Theory of Human Motivation.* Eastford, Connecticut: Martino Fine Books, 2013.

McGregor, Douglas. *The Human Side of Enterprise* (annotated edition). New York: McGraw-Hill Education, 2005.

Michaud, Patrick A. *Accident Prevention and OSHA Compliance.* Boca Raton, Florida: Lewis Publishers, 1995.

Milkovich, George T., Jerry M. Newman, and Carolyn Milkovich. *Compensation*, 7th ed. Boston: McGraw-Hill Education, 2002.

"Models and Techniques of Manpower Demand and Supply Forecasting: A Strategic Human Resource Planning Model." Retrieved February 7, 2014, from http://corehr .wordpress.com/hr-planning/53-2/.

Porter, Michael E. *Competitive Strategy: Techniques for Analyzing Industries and Competitors.* New York: Free Press, 1980.

Richardson, Blake. *Records Management for Dummies.* Hoboken, New Jersey: For Dummies, 2012.

Rogers, Everett. *Diffusion of Innovations.* New York: Free Press, 2003.

Scott, Mark, JD, CFE. "Managing Risks in Vendor Relationships." *The Fraud Examiner.* March 2012. Retrieved February 7, 2014, from www.acfe.com/fraud-examiner .aspx?id=4294972428.

SHRM Code of Ethical and Professional Standards in Human Resource Management. www.shrm.org.

Tolbert, P., and R. Hall. *Organizations: Structures, Processes, and Outcomes.* New York: Pearson, 2008.

Truesdell, William H. *Secrets of Affirmative Action Compliance.* Walnut Creek, California: Management Advantage, Inc., 2017.

Ulrich, David. *Delivering Results: A New Mandate for Human Resource Professionals.* Boston: Harvard Business Review, 1998.

PART III

Waddill, Deborah, and Michael Marquardt. *The e-HR Advantage: The Complete Handbook for Technology enabled Human Resources.* Boston: Nicholas Brealey America, 2011.

The following material is available on www.youtube.com by searching by author and topic:

Goleman, Daniel. *Introduces Emotional Intelligence.*

Goleman, Daniel. *The Secret to High Performance and Fulfilment.*

Welch, Jack. *People Management.*

About the Digital Content

This book comes complete with TotalTester Online customizable practice exam software as well as a secured PDF copy of the book.

System Requirements

The current and previous major versions of the following desktop browsers are recommended and supported: Chrome, Microsoft Edge, Firefox, and Safari. These browsers update frequently, and sometimes an update may cause compatibility issues with the TotalTester Online or other content hosted on the Training Hub. If you run into a problem using one of these browsers, please try using another until the problem is resolved.

Your Total Seminars Training Hub Account

To get access to the online content, you will need to create an account on the Total Seminars Training Hub. Registration is free, and you will be able to track all your online content using your account. You may also opt in if you wish to receive marketing information from McGraw-Hill Education or Total Seminars, but this is not required for you to gain access to the online content.

Privacy Notice

McGraw-Hill Education values your privacy. Please be sure to read the Privacy Notice available during registration to see how the information you have provided will be used. You may view our Corporate Customer Privacy Policy by visiting the McGraw-Hill Education Privacy Center. Visit the **mheducation.com** site and click on **Privacy** at the bottom of the page.

Single User License Terms and Conditions

Online access to the digital content included with this book is governed by the McGraw-Hill Education License Agreement outlined next. By using this digital content you agree to the terms of that license.

Access   To register and activate your Total Seminars Training Hub account, simply follow these easy steps.

1. Go to **hub.totalsem.com/mheclaim**.

2. To register and create a new Training Hub account, enter your email address, name, and password. No further information (such as credit card number) is required to create an account.

3. If you already have a Total Seminars Training Hub account, select **Log in** and enter your email and password.

4. Enter your Product Key: `z07c-t7pq-hwz0`

5. Click to accept the user license terms.

6. Click **Register and Claim** to create your account. You will be taken to the Training Hub and have access to the content for this book.

Duration of License   Access to your online content through the Total Seminars Training Hub will expire one year from the date the publisher declares the book out of print.

Your purchase of this McGraw-Hill Education product, including its access code, through a retail store is subject to the refund policy of that store.

The Content is a copyrighted work of McGraw-Hill Education and McGraw-Hill Education reserves all rights in and to the Content. The Work is © 2019 by McGraw-Hill Education, LLC.

Restrictions on Transfer   The user is receiving only a limited right to use the Content for the user's own internal and personal use, dependent on purchase and continued ownership of this book. The user may not reproduce, forward, modify, create derivative works based upon, transmit, distribute, disseminate, sell, publish, or sublicense the Content or in any way commingle the Content with other third-party content without McGraw-Hill Education's consent.

Limited Warranty   The McGraw-Hill Education Content is provided on an "as is" basis. Neither McGraw-Hill Education nor its licensors make any guarantees or warranties of any kind, either express or implied, including, but not limited to, implied warranties of merchantability or fitness for a particular purpose or use as to any McGraw-Hill Education Content or the information therein or any warranties as to the accuracy, completeness, correctness, or results to be obtained from, accessing or using the McGraw-Hill Education content, or any material referenced in such content or any information entered into licensee's product by users or other persons and/or any material available on or that can be accessed through the licensee's product (including via any hyperlink or otherwise) or as to non-infringement of third-party rights. Any warranties of any kind, whether express or implied, are disclaimed. Any material or data obtained through use of the McGraw-Hill Education content is at your own discretion and risk and user understands that it will be solely responsible for any resulting damage to its computer system or loss of data.

Neither McGraw-Hill Education nor its licensors shall be liable to any subscriber or to any user or anyone else for any inaccuracy, delay, interruption in service, error or omission, regardless of cause, or for any damage resulting therefrom.

In no event will McGraw-Hill Education or its licensors be liable for any indirect, special or consequential damages, including but not limited to, lost time, lost money, lost profits or good will, whether in contract, tort, strict liability or otherwise, and whether or not such damages are foreseen or unforeseen with respect to any use of the McGraw-Hill Education content.

TotalTester Online

TotalTester Online provides you with a simulation of the SHRM-CP and SHRM-SCP exams. Follow the instructions provided in the previous section to register and activate your Total Seminars Training Hub account. When you register, you will be taken to the Total Seminars Training Hub. From the Training Hub Home page, select **SHRM-CP/ SHRM-SCP Certification All-in-One** from the "Study" drop-down menu at the top of the page, or from the list of "Your Topics" on the Home page.

TotalTester Online Practice Exam Software

The TotalTester Online practice exam software includes more than 320 practice exam questions. Select the SHRM-CP Practice Exam or the SHRM-SCP Practice Exam Total-Tester icons to launch a full-length, timed practice exam. These exams are intended to simulate the actual SHRM-CP and SHRM-SCP certification exams. Only one full-length exam is available for each, and these exams cannot be customized.

Separate TotalTesters are also provided for the knowledge domain questions and the situational judgment questions, although all question types will be delivered together in the real certification exams. The Knowledge exams and the Situational Judgment exams can be customized as described next.

Knowledge Exams

The Knowledge exams can be taken in Practice Mode or Exam Mode. Practice Mode provides an assistance window with references to the book, explanations of the correct and incorrect answers, and the option to check your answer as you take the test. Each time you take a test, a different set of questions will be generated from the total pool of questions. The number, distribution, and types of questions are intended to be an accurate representation of the Knowledge questions you will encounter on the real exam. Note that the 4-hour time allotment is the total time you will receive to complete all questions on the full exam, including the Situational Judgment questions. Be sure you are able to complete the Knowledge exams in Exam Mode with enough time left over to complete a Situational Judgment exam.

The option to customize your quiz allows you to create custom exams from selected functional areas or chapters, and you can further customize the number of questions and time allowed.

Situational Judgment Exams

The Situational Judgment exams can also be taken in Practice Mode or Exam Mode. Practice Mode provides an assistance window with references to the book, explanations of the correct and incorrect answers, and the option to check your answer as you take the test.

Whether taken in Practice Mode or Exam Mode, each Situational Judgment exam will always present the same questions in the same order. The number of questions and types of questions in the Situational Judgment exams are intended to be an accurate representation of the Situational Judgment questions you will encounter on the real exam. As with the Knowledge exams, the 4-hour time allotment is the total time you will receive to complete all questions on the full certification exam. Whether you begin with the Situational Judgment exam or the Knowledge exam, be sure you are able to complete both exams within the total time allotment. For example, if you spend 140 minutes on the Knowledge exam, you would only have 100 minutes left to complete the Situational Judgment exam.

The option to customize your quiz allows you to create custom exams from selected behavioral competencies, and you can further customize the number of questions and time allowed.

Secured Book PDF

The entire contents of the book are provided in secured PDF format on the CD-ROM. This file is viewable on your computer and many portable devices. Adobe Acrobat, Adobe Reader, or Adobe Digital Editions is required to view the file on your computer. A link to Adobe's web site, where you can download and install Adobe Reader, has been included on the CD-ROM.

 NOTE For more information on Adobe Reader and to check for the most recent version of the software, visit Adobe's web site at www.adobe.com and search for the free Adobe Reader or look for Adobe Reader on the product page. Adobe Digital Editions can also be downloaded from the Adobe web site.

To view the book PDF on a portable device, copy the PDF file to your computer from the CD-ROM and then copy the file to your portable device using a USB or other connection. Adobe offers a mobile version of Adobe Reader, the Adobe Reader mobile app, which currently supports iOS and Android. For customers using Adobe Digital Editions and an iPad, you may have to download and install a separate reader program on your device. The Adobe web site has a list of recommended applications, and McGraw-Hill Education recommends the Bluefire Reader.

Technical Support

For questions regarding the TotalTester Online or operation of the CD-ROM, visit **www.totalsem.com** or **e-mail support@totalsem.com**.

For questions regarding the secured book PDF, e-mail **techsolutions@mhedu.com** or visit **http://mhp.softwareassist.com**.

For questions regarding book content, e-mail **hep_customer-service@mheducation .com**. For customers outside the United States, e-mail **international_cs@mheducation.com**.

This glossary is composed of terms you will likely encounter as you move through your life in human resource management. Many of the terms you already know. Some of them, like *andragogy, Delphi technique, histogram,* or *pedagogy,* may be new to you. Yet each of the terms here can be important to HR professionals.

Here is a suggestion. As you work through the book and discover a term that is new to you, pause long enough to flip to the glossary and look it up. Knowing how a word or phrase is used can be helpful in understanding its meaning. It won't be long before you are using these terms in your everyday encounters.

80% rule   The measurement known as a "rule of thumb" used to test for disparity in treatment during any type of employment selection decisions; also identified as *adverse impact.*

401(k) plan   A salary reduction retirement plan for employees. Contributions reduce one's taxable income, and investment income accumulates tax-free until the money is withdrawn.

ADDIE   A five-step instructional design process consisting of assess, design, development, implementation, and evaluation.

administrative exemption   Exemption from overtime payment based on several qualifying factors including minimum pay requirement, and exercise of discretion and independent judgment performing work directly related to management of general business operations.

administrative services–only plan   Health insurance programs in which all of the risk is assumed by the employer.

adult learning   The process of learning associated with people who are older than 18 to 25 and generally referred to as nontraditional learners; also identified as andragogy.

adverse impact   A legal category of illegal employment discrimination involving groups of workers and statistical proofs.

adverse selection   When bad-risk employees choose a benefit and good-risk employees do not under a flexible benefits plan.

adverse treatment   A legal category of illegal employment discrimination involving individual treatment or "pattern and practice" treatment of groups of workers.

affirmative action   Use of special outreach and recruiting programs to assure participation of qualified job candidates, vendors, or students in employment, employer purchasing programs, or college admissions.

aggregate stop-loss coverage   The health plan is protected against the risk of large total claims from all participants during the plan year.

aging   A technique used to make outdated data current.

alternative dispute resolution (ADR)   A variety of processes that help parties resolve disputes without a trial. Processes include mediation, arbitration, neutral evaluation, and collaborative law.

analytics   The discovery and communication of meaningful patterns in data.

andragogy   The study of how adults learn.

applicant tracking system   A method for retention of detailed information about job applicants either manual or computer based.

apprenticeship   A system of training a person in a trade or profession with on-the-job training.

arbitration   The process of submitting a labor dispute to a third party for resolution. The third party is called an *arbitrator*. Both parties agree beforehand to accept the arbitrator's decision.

assessment centers   A method for assessing aptitude and performance applied to participants using various aptitude diagnostic processes in order to obtain information on abilities or potential. Participants are measured against a norm group of successful people in the same job category.

assets   The properties an organization owns, tangible and intangible.

at-will employment   A legal employment relationship in which an employee may quit at any time for any reason and may be dismissed at any time for any reason. No "just cause" is required. This relationship is limited by prohibitions on employer actions related to public interest.

auditory learners   A learning style in which a person learns through listening.

automatic step rate   Division of the pay range into several steps that can be advanced by an employee when time-in-job has met the step requirement.

average   Arithmetic average or mean arrived at by giving equal weight to every participant's actual pay; also, a number that is arrived at by adding quantities together and dividing the total by the number of quantities.

back pay   Payment of salary or wages that should have been paid initially, usually as a form of remedy for a complaint of discrimination.

background checks   Investigation of an individual's personal history, including employment, educational, criminal, and financial.

balance sheet   A statement of a business's financial position.

balanced scorecard   A big-picture view of an organization's performance as measured against goals in areas such as finance, customer base, processes, learning, human capital, and growth.

BARS   Behaviorally anchored rating scales.

base-pay systems   Single or flat-rate systems, time-based step rate systems, performance-based merit pay systems, productivity-based systems, and person-based systems.

behavioral interview   A technique that queries job applicants to describe their specific behaviors or actions they've taken in particular past situations as a basis for determining the individual's demonstrated skill sets.

bell curve   Used to describe the mathematical concept called "normal distribution."

benchmarking   Process by which an organization identifies performance gaps and sets goals for improvement via comparing data and processes against others.

benefits-needs assessment or analysis   Collection and analysis of data to determine whether the employer's benefits programs actually meet their objectives.

bereavement leave   Paid or unpaid time off to attend a funeral.

bias   Prejudice in favor of or against one thing, person, or group compared with another, usually in a way considered to be unfair.

"Big Data"   Extremely large data sets that may be analyzed computationally to reveal patterns, trends, and associations, especially relating to human behavior and interactions.

bill   A proposal presented to a legislative body in the U.S. government to enact a law.

blended learning   A formal education program in which a student learns at least in part through delivery of content and instruction via digital and online media with some element of student control over time, place, path, or pace.

blue ocean strategies   The pursuit of creating a new market space where there are no competitors.

bona fide occupational qualification (BFOQ)   A factor that is reasonably necessary to carry out a particular job function.

boycott   A protest action that encourages the public to withhold business from an employer that is targeted by a union.

brain drain   The departure of educated or professional people from one country, economic sector, or field for another, usually for better pay or living conditions.

branding   The process of conveying key organizational values.

broadbanding   Combination of several pay grades or job classifications with narrow range spreads and a single band into a wider spread.

budgeting   Forecasting income and expenses by category and subcategory.

business acumen   Knowledge and understanding of the financial, accounting, marketing, and operational functions of an organization.

business case   An argument, usually documented, that is intended to convince a decision maker to approve some kind of action.

business concepts   An idea for producing goods or services that identifies the benefits that can be achieved for prospective customers or clients.

business continuity   The ability to continue conducting business following an interruption of some sort.

business ethics   Generally accepted norms and expectations for business management behavior.

business intelligence (BI)   An umbrella term that refers to a variety of software applications used to analyze an organization's raw data. BI as a discipline is made up of several related activities, including data mining, online analytical processing, querying, and reporting.

business unit   A segment of a company (such as accounting, production, marketing, sales) representing a specific business function. This can also be called a department, division, or functional area.

cafeteria benefit plans   Employees who choose the benefits they desire subject to certain limitations and total cost constraints.

career development   A concept that individuals expand their knowledge, skills, and abilities as they progress through their careers.

career management   Planning, preparing, and implementing employee career paths.

career mapping   Process by which organizations use visual tools or guides for career possibilities and paths, sequential positions, roles, and phases in a career.

career pathing   Process in which employees are given a clear outline for moving from a current position to a desired position.

career planning   Activities and actions that individuals follow for a specific career path.

case studies   Simulation of real-world problems that calls for an application of skill or knowledge to resolve.

cash awards   Rewards for exceeding performance goals, a formula-based bonus based on a percentage of profits or other preestablished measurement.

cash flow statement   A mandatory part of a company's financial reports since 1987; records the amounts of cash and cash equivalents entering and leaving a company.

cause-and-effect diagram   Also called a *fishbone diagram* and *Ishikawa diagram,* identifies possible causes for an effect or problem.

center of excellence (COE)   Refers to a team, a shared facility, or an entity that provides leadership, evangelization, best practices, research, support, and/or training for a focus area.

central tendency error   When managers and interviewers rate all or most of the employees or interviewees as average.

certification of a union   Formal recognition of a union as the exclusive bargaining representative of a group of employees.

chain of command   The order in which authority and power in an organization is wielded and delegated from top management to every employee at every level of the organization.

change management   Transitioning individuals, groups, teams, and institutions to a desired future state.

change programs   Strategic approach to organizing and implementing specific changes (e.g., policies or procedures) within an organization.

childcare services   Programs designed to help working parents deal with the ongoing needs of preschool or school-aged children.

civil law   One of the two major legal systems of the modern Western world (the other is common law).

clawback   A provision of the Dodd-Frank Act that requires executives to return ill-gotten bonuses.

cloud computing   Application software that is on central servers and accessed or operated using Internet-enabled devices.

code of conduct   An employment policy listing personal behaviors that are acceptable and required in the workplace.

cobots   A robot intended to physically interact with employees in the workplace.

code of ethics   Principles of conduct that guide behavior expectations and decisions.

cognitive learning   The refining of knowledge by adding new information and thereby expanding prior knowledge.

collective bargaining   A formal process of negotiating working conditions with an employer for a work group represented by a union.

collective bargaining agreements Union contracts for a represented group of employees and designated employers. This is a term usually used in the private sector.

combination step-rate and performance Employees receive step-rate increases up to the established job rate. Above this level, increases are granted only for superior job performance.

common law Law developed over time from the rulings of judges as opposed to law embodied in statutes passed by legislatures (statutory law) or law embodied in a written constitution (constitutional law).

communication skills Verbal and written abilities that enable an individual to transmit and receive messages.

commuter assistance Employer assistance programs designed to help defray public transportation costs associated with going to and from work.

comparable worth A pay discrimination theory where workers in a job classification dominated by one sex are paid less than workers in a classification dominated by the opposite sex, where both job classifications are of equal value or worth to the employer or the underpaid classification is of greater value to the employer.

compa-ratio An indicator of how wages match, lead, or lag the midpoint of a given pay range computed by dividing the worker's pay rate by the midpoint of the pay range.

compensatory damages A monetary equivalent awarded for pain, suffering, and emotional distress as a result of a legal proceeding.

competencies Measurable or observable knowledge, skills, abilities, and behaviors critical to successful job performance.

competency-based interview An interview where the style of question forces candidates to give situational examples of times in the past when they have performed particular tasks or achieved particular outcomes using certain skills.

competency-based system Pay is linked to the level at which an employee can perform in a recognized competency.

compliance evaluation Formal audit by the Office of Federal Contract Compliance Programs (OFCCP) of a federal contractor subject to OFCCP oversight.

compliance program Systematic procedures instituted by an organization to ensure that the provisions of the regulations imposed by a government agency are being met.

computer employee exemption Exemption from overtime payment based on several qualifying factors, including minimum pay requirement, job duties involving computer programming, software analysis, or software engineering.

computer-based testing (CBT)   Testing delivery method via computer, in person, at a testing center.

conciliation   A binding written agreement between an employer and the EEOC or the OFCCP that details specific employer commitments to resolve the alleged violations set forth in the agreement.

conflict of interest   A situation that has the potential to undermine the impartiality of a person because of the possibility of a clash between the person's self-interest and professional interest or public interest.

construct validity   The degree to which a test measures what it claims to measure.

constructive discipline   Discipline that imposes increasingly severe consequences and penalties. This is also called *progressive discipline*.

consumer price index   The average of prices paid by consumers for goods and services.

content validity   The extent a test measures all aspects of a given job.

contingency plan   A coordinated set of steps to be taken in an emergency or disaster.

contingent workers   Workers who do not have an ongoing expectation of full-time employment such as part-time workers, independent contractors, temporary workers, consultants, leased employees, and subcontractors.

contract labor   Work performed under the terms of a legally enforceable contract.

contract negotiation   The process of give and take related generally to content details and provisions of an employment contract such as a union agreement or memorandum of understanding (MOU).

contrast effect   An error made in interviewing when strong candidates are interviewed after weak candidates, causing them to appear overly qualified because of the contrast.

contrast error   In interview or performance appraisal process, error caused by the effect of previously interviewed or appraised applicants on the interviewer.

control chart   A chart that illustrates variation from normal in a situation over time.

controlling   A management function involving monitoring the workplace and making adjustments to activities as required.

cooperative learning   A strategy in which a small group of people work on solving a problem or completing a task in a way that each person's success is dependent on the group's success.

copyright   A legal form of protection for authors of original works.

core competency   A unique capability that is essential or fundamental to a particular job.

corporate citizenship   A self-regulatory mechanism where an organization monitors and ensures its active compliance with the spirit of the law, ethical standards, and international norms.

corporate governance   The mechanisms, processes, and relations by which corporations are controlled and directed.

corporate social responsibility (CSR)   Strategic goals achieved through local community relationships around social needs and issues.

cost-benefit analysis (CBA)   A business practice in which the costs and benefits of a particular situation are analyzed as part of the decision process.

cost containment   Efforts or activities designed to reduce or slow down the cost of expenses and increases.

cost-of-living adjustment (COLA)   Pay increase given to all employees on the basis of market pressure, usually measured against the consumer price index (CPI).

cost per hire   The measurement of dollar expense required to hire each new employee.

credit reports   Reports obtained from one of the major credit reporting agencies that explains the individual's personal rating based on financial history.

criterion-related validity   Empirical studies producing data that show the selection procedure(s) are predictive or significantly related with important elements of job performance.

critical path math (CPM)   A sequence of activities in a project plan that must be completed on time for the project to be completed by the due date.

cross-functional work team   A group of people from different functions working together to generate production or problem resolution.

cultural blending   The blending of different cultural influences in the workforce.

cultural noise   In interview or performance appraisal process, error caused by the effect of previously interviewed or appraised applicants on the interviewer. It results in a conscious or subconscious comparison of one applicant with another and tends to exaggerate the differences between the two.

cultural relativism   The principle that an individual human's beliefs and activities should be understood by others in terms of that individual's own culture.

culture   Societal forces affecting the values, beliefs, and actions of a group of people.

dashboards   A data visualization tool that displays the current status of metrics and key performance indicators (KPIs).

database   Systematically organized or structured repository of indexed information (usually as a group of linked data files) that allows easy retrieval, updating, analysis, and output of data.

database management system (DBMS)   Computer program that catalogs, indexes, locates, retrieves, and stores data; maintains its integrity; and outputs it in the form desired by a user.

deauthorization of a union   Removal of "union security" from the contract. The union remains as the exclusive bargaining representative, and the collective bargaining agreement remains in effect, but employees are not forced to be members or pay dues to the union.

decertification of a union   Removal of a union as the exclusive bargaining representative of the employees.

defamation   Publication of something about an individual that the writer knows is untrue.

defined benefit plan   A pension plan that provides retirement income to retirees based on a formula that usually combines years of service and an average annual income for a set number of years.

defined contribution plan   An individual pension fund created for each employee into which the company invests a specified amount of money each year until the employee retires.

Delphi technique   A systematic forecasting method that involves structured interaction among a group of experts on a subject. The Delphi Technique typically includes at least two rounds of experts answering questions and giving justification for their answer.

demand analysis   Estimation of what customers, clients, or patrons will want in the future.

demonstration   Showing students how something is done.

dental plans   Insurance programs that cover some or all of the cost of dental services for subscribers.

departmentalization   Manner or practice in which related individual tasks and their allocation to work groups is combined to form a specialized functional area that is distinct from other functional areas in an organization.

developmental activities   The part of human resource management that specifically deals with training and development of employees.

differential pay   An addition to base pay that results from special job circumstances such as shift assignment, commute distance required, temporary responsibility assignments, and similar "extras."

differential piece rate system   Employee receives one rate of pay up to the production standard and a higher rate of pay when the standard is exceeded.

dilemma reconciliation   Process of seeking solutions to issues involving cultural differences.

direct compensation   Base pay, commissions, bonuses, merit pay, piece rate, differential pay, cash award, profit sharing, gainsharing.

directing   Managing or controlling people to willingly do what is wanted or needed.

disability   Medically determinable impairment of body or mind that restricts, or causes loss of, a person's functional ability to carry on his or her normal activities.

disaster recovery plans   A set of procedures used to protect and recover a business from a natural or other disaster that has impacted the organization or employer.

discipline   Forms of punishment to assure obedience with policies.

disparate impact   Adverse effect of a practice or standard that is neutral and nondiscriminatory in its intention but nonetheless disproportionately affects individuals with a disability or belonging to a particular group based on their age, ethnicity, race, sex, or other protected class.

disparate treatment   A discrimination theory that holds an individual is treated differently from others, based on protected group membership, who are similarly situated under similar circumstances.

distance learning   Learning that uses television, audio/video tapes, computers, the Internet, etc., instead of physical attendance at classes in a centralized facility.

diversity and inclusion   The practice of embracing differences of race, culture, and background, ensuring that everyone is a participant in workplace processes.

diversity council   Task force of various levels of employees created to work on diversity and inclusion initiatives in an organization.

diversity dimensions   Framework for diversity, including personality, internal dimensions, external dimensions, and organizational dimensions.

diversity of thought   Different types of cognitive processes.

diversity programs   Methods for recognizing and honoring various types of employee backgrounds.

divestiture   The sale of an asset.

domestic partners   Two adults who have chosen to share one another's lives in an intimate and committed relationship of mutual caring.

dual-ladder   A system that enables a person to advance up either the management or technical career development ladder in an organization.

due diligence   The first step in mergers and acquisitions involving a broad scope of research and investigation.

due process   Conduct of legal proceedings strictly according to established principles and procedures, laid down to ensure a fair trial for every accused.

duty of care   The responsibility or the legal obligation of a person or organization to avoid acts or omissions (which can be reasonably foreseen) to be likely to cause harm to others.

elder care   Programs to help employees deal with responsibilities for care of family elders.

e-learning   Internet-based training programs that can be instructor led or self-paced.

emotional intelligence (EQ or EI)   The ability of an individual to have understanding and sensitivity for another's emotions and control over their own.

employee   A person in the service of another under any contract of hire, express or implied, oral or written, where the employer has the power or right to control and direct the employee in the material details of how the work is to be performed.

employee assistance programs   Employer-sponsored benefits that provide a number of services that help promote the physical, mental, and emotional wellness of individual employees who otherwise would be negatively impacted by health-related crises.

employee complaints   Written or verbal statements of dissatisfaction from an employee that can involve charges of discrimination, lack of fairness, or other upset.

employee engagement   Where employees are fully absorbed by and enthusiastic about their work and so take positive action to further the organization's reputation and interests.

employee leasing   Contracting with a vendor that provides qualified workers for a specific period of time at a specific pay rate.

employee life cycle   A human resources model that identifies stages in employees' careers to help guide their management and optimize associated processes.

employee relations programs   Methods for management of the employer-employee relationship.

employee resource group (ERG)   A group of employees who share a diversity dimension, also called an *affinity group*.

employee stock ownership plans   Retirement plans in which the company contributes its stock, or money to buy its stock, to the plan for the benefit of the company's employees.

employee stock purchase plans (ESPP)   Programs allowing employees to purchase company stock at discounted prices.

employee surveys   Tools used to gather opinions of employees about their employment experiences.

employee value proposition (EVP)   An employee's perceived value of the total rewards (tangible and intangible benefits) they receive from an organization as part of their employment.

employee-management committees   Problem-solving groups of management and nonmanagement employees focused on specific issues within the workplace.

employer sick leave   Paid leave for a specified number of hours or days absent from work because of medical conditions.

employment affirmative action   Programs required by federal regulations for some federal contractors to implement outreach and recruiting programs when the incumbent workforce is significantly less than computed availability.

employment at will   A legal doctrine that describes an employment relationship without a contract where either party can end the relationship at any time for any reason.

employment branding   A targeted strategy to manage the awareness and perceptions of employees, potential employees, and related stakeholders with regard to an organization.

employment policies   Rules by which the workplace will be managed.

employment reference checks   Verification of references, both personal and professional, provided by a job candidate on an application form or résumé.

employment testing   Any tool or step used in the employment selection process. Commonly includes written tests, interviews, résumé reviews, or skill demonstration.

encryption   Scrambling sensitive information so that it becomes unreadable to everyone except the intended recipient.

enterprise resource planning (ERP)   Accounting oriented, relational database based, multimodule but integrated software system for identifying and planning the resource needs of an enterprise.

environmental footprints   The effect that a person, company, activity, etc., has on the environment.

environmental scanning   A process of studying the environment to pinpoint potential threats and opportunities.

e-procurement   An electronic web application for transacting and purchasing supplies and services.

Equal Employment Opportunity (EEO)   Equal access to employment opportunities based on qualifications regardless of federal or state protected class membership.

equal pay Providing equal compensation to jobs that have the same requirements, responsibilities, and working conditions regardless of the incumbent's gender.

equity The difference between income and liabilities in a for-profit organization.

essential functions The fundamental, crucial job duties performed in a position.

ethical universalism A concept that implies there are fundamental ethical principles applying across cultures.

ethics Principles and values that set expectations for behaviors in an organization.

ethnocentric A policy calling for key management positions to be filled by expatriates.

evacuation plan A written procedure for moving employees out of the work location to a safer location in case of fire or natural disaster.

evaluation The ability to judge.

E-Verify A government database that employers access to confirm a match between a new employee's name and Social Security number.

executive coaching Coaching senior- and executive-level management by a third party.

executive exemption Exemption from overtime payment based on several qualifying factors, including supervision and minimum pay requirements.

executive incentives Variable compensation additives for executive employees that may include company stock and use of company facilities such as vacation timeshares. These are usually variable based on the profitability of the company.

exempt employees Employees exempt from overtime compensation by federal wage and hours guidelines.

exempt job A job with content that is exempt from the FLSA requirement to pay overtime for work exceeding 40 hours per week. Exemption can be based on several designated factors.

exit interviews Discussions with departing employees to explore how they feel about their experience as an employee and what recommendations they might have for the employer.

expatriates Employees working in a country other than that of their origin.

external coaching Coaching that is provided by a certified third-party coach.

external equity Employees' perception of the conditions and rewards of their employment, compared with those of the employees of other firms.

extraterritoriality Being outside the territory of the country where you are living and so not subject to its laws.

extrinsic rewards   Rewards such as pay, benefits, incentive bonuses, promotions, time off, etc.

factor-comparison job evaluation   A process that involves ranking each job by each compensable factor and then identifying dollar values for each level of each factor to develop an actual pay rate for the evaluated job.

fast-track program   A career development program that identifies high-potential leaders for rapid career growth and organizational knowledge.

fee-for-service plans   Allows health plan members to go to any qualified physician or other health care provider, hospital, or medical clinic and submit claims to the insurance company.

fiduciary responsibilities   A legal and ethical relationship between two or more parties.

final warning   Last step in the disciplinary process progression prior to removing the employee from the payroll.

first impression error   Occurs when a manager or interviewer bases his or her entire assessment of an employee or applicant on the first impression that the employee or applicant made.

flat-rate or single system   Each worker in the same job has the same rate of pay regardless of seniority or job performance.

flexible spending account   Allows employees to set aside a preestablished amount of money on a pre-tax basis per plan year for use in paying authorized medical expenses.

floating holidays   Designated paid time off that can be used at any time during the year with the employer's approval.

flow analysis   How processes operate and how flows of products, data, or other items go through these processes.

focus group   A group of people brought together with a moderator where they share their point of view on a specific topic or problem. Focus groups aim at a discussion instead of individual responses to formal questions and produce qualitative data (preferences and beliefs) that may or may not be representative of the general population.

force-field analysis   Technique for identifying and analyzing the positive factors of a situation that help ("driving forces") and negative factors that hinder ("restraining forces") an entity in attaining its objectives.

forced choice   An evaluation method in which the evaluator selects two of four statements that represent "most like" and "least like."

formalization   The extent to which work roles are structured in an organization and the activities of the employees are governed by rules and procedures.

frequency distribution   Listing of grouped pay data from lowest to highest.

frequency tables   Number of workers in a particular job classification and their pay data.

front pay   Payment of salary or wages that could have been earned had the individual continued to work on the job in question or had the person been employed for a future period of time.

full-time   Employees who work a designated number of hours per week, usually 30 to 40 hours.

fully funded plans   Health insurance programs paid for entirely by the employer.

functional HR   A structure where HR generalists are located within business units such as HR business partners and implement the policies and interact with management and employees in the unit and where headquarters HR staff create policies and strategy.

functional structure   A common type of organizational structure in which the organization is divided into smaller groups based on specialized functional areas, such as IT, finance, HR, and marketing.

functional work team   A group of people from the same function working together to generate production or resolve problems.

gainsharing plans   Extra pay provided to individual or groups of employees based on the gain in performance results in one measurement period over another period.

gamification   Elements of game playing (e.g., point scoring, competition with others, rules of play) to other areas of activity that encourage employee engagement.

Gantt chart   A project planning tool that scopes and monitors the activities of a project, the timeline, and accountability.

gap analysis   Measurement of the difference between where you are and where you want to be.

gender   Culturally and socially constructed difference between men and women.

general duty clause   A provision in OSHA regulations that imposes a duty on all subject employers to assure a safe and healthy working environment for their employees.

general pay increases   A pay increase given to all employees regardless of their job performance and not linked to market pressures.

geocentric   A staffing policy wanting to place the best person in the job regardless of their country of origin.

geographic structure   Used as an organizational structure by organizations that have locations in different geographic locations which define their regions.

geographic-based differential pay   Adjustment to base pay programs based on cost-of-living requirements in various geographic locations where employees work.

geography   Adjustments to survey numbers based on geographic differences with original survey content.

Giganomics   The creation of employment through the piecing together of several projects, or "gigs."

gig worker   Employees or independent contractors who move from job to job (gig to gig) and are employed for a particular need or a defined time.

glass ceiling   A discriminatory practice that has prevented women and other protected class members from advancing to executive-level jobs.

global integration strategy (GI)   A term used to denote an organization that fashions its strategy, its management, and its operations in pursuit of a new goal: the integration of production and value delivery worldwide.

global mind-set   An openness to and awareness of diversity across cultures and markets.

Global Professional in Human Resources (GPHR)   Credential that is global competency based, validating the skills and knowledge of an HR professional who operates in a global marketplace.

global remittances   A transfer of money from migrant workers to his or her home country.

globalization   The worldwide movement toward economic, financial, trade, and communications integration.

golden parachutes   Provisions in executive employment contracts that provide special payments or benefits to the executives under certain adverse conditions such as the loss of their position or otherwise adversely impacted actions by organizational changes.

governance   Establishment of policies, and continuous monitoring of their proper implementation by the members of the governing body of an organization.

graphic organizers   Diagrams, maps, and drawings/webs as illustrations of learning materials.

green circle rates   Pay at a rate lower than the minimum rate for the assigned pay range.

green initiatives   Relationships around community and social issues.

grievance procedure   Step-by-step process an employee must follow to get his or her complaint addressed satisfactorily. This is typically included in union (collective bargaining) agreements.

grievances   Formal employee complaints handled by a structured resolution process usually found in a union-represented work group.

gross domestic product (GDP)   The total value of goods and services produced in a country.

group incentive program   Pay to all individuals in a workgroup for achievement by the entire workgroup.

group term life insurance   Provides lump-sum benefit to beneficiaries on the death of an insured.

halo effect   This occurs when an evaluator scores an employee high on all job categories because of performance in one area.

harassment   Persecution, intimidation, pressure, or force applied to employees by supervisors, co-workers, or external individuals that interferes with the employee's ability to perform the job assignment.

Hay method   A widely used job evaluation method that addresses three compensable factors (knowledge, problem solving, and accountability) to determine how many points should be assigned to different jobs in determining compensation categories.

hazard   Situation that may lead to a danger, emergency, or disaster.

hazard pay   Additional pay for working under adverse conditions caused by environment or because of specific circumstances.

head count   Number of individuals carried on a firm's payroll.

health insurance purchasing cooperatives   Purchasing agents for large groups of employers.

health maintenance organization   Health care program where the insurer is paid on a per-person (capitated) basis and offers health care services and staff at its facilities.

health reimbursement accounts   Employer-funded medical reimbursement plans.

health savings account   A tax-advantaged medical savings account available to taxpayers in the United States who are enrolled in a high-deductible health plan.

high-context culture   A culture of people that emphasizes interpersonal relationships and close connections over a long period of time.

high-deductible health plans   Programs that help employers lower their costs and allow employees with set-aside money to pay for out-of-pocket medical and medical-related expenses.

histogram   A graphic representation of the distribution of a single type of measurement using rectangles.

horn effect   This occurs when an employee receives a low rating in all areas because of one weakness influencing the evaluator.

host-country nationals (HCNs)   Employees originating in the country where a remote work location is being established.

hostile environment harassment   Occurs when an employee is subject to unwelcome advances, sexual innuendos, or offensive gender-related language that is sufficiently severe or pervasive from the perspective of a reasonable person of the same gender as the offended employee.

HR audit   An objective look at the company's HR policies, practices, procedures, and strategies to protect the company, establish best practices, and identify opportunities for improvement.

HR business partner   HR staff that acts as an internal consultant to senior management.

HR Certification Institute (HRCI)   A nonprofit professional certifying organization for the human resources profession.

HR service model   An approach for delivering HR services to support an organization.

HR professional certification   Status awarded to HR professionals by a recognized certifying agency after satisfying qualifying requirements.

HRCI Body of Knowledge (BOK)   The description of a set of concepts, tasks, responsibilities, and knowledge associated with HRCI credentialing.

HRIS   Human resources information system. This is usually a computer-based collection of personal data for each employee.

human capital   The value of the capabilities, knowledge, skills, experiences, and motivation of a workforce in an organization.

Human Resource Business Professional (HRBP)   A global, competency-based credential designed to validate generally accepted professional-level core HR knowledge and skills.

Human Resource Management Professional (HRMP)   A global, competency-based credential designed to validate generally accepted HR principles in strategy, policy development, and service delivery.

human resources development   Systematically planned activities that help the organization's workforce meet the current and future job and skills needs.

human resource management (HRM)   The direction of organizational systems to ensure that human talent is used effectively and efficiently to accomplish organizational goals.

hybrid structure   An approach to designing the internal operating structure of a company or other entity in a manner that makes use of several different organizational patterns, rather than relying on one particular model.

identity alignment   The extent to which diversity is accepted and embraced in an organization.

IIPP   Injury and illness prevention programs.

incentive pay   Pay designed to promote a higher level of job performance than otherwise included in the basic design of the job.

incentive stock options   Awards of rights to purchase company stock in the future at a price determined at the time of the grant.

incentives   Inducement or supplemental reward that serves as a motivational device for a desired action or behavior.

inclusion   The state of including or of being included within a group or structure.

income statement   A summary of management's performance as reflected in the profitability (or lack of it) of an organization over a certain period.

independent contractor   One who, in the independent exercise of his/her business affairs, contracts to do a piece of work according to his/her own methods and is subject to his/her principal's control only as to the end product or final result of his/her work.

indirect compensation   Social Security, unemployment insurance, disability insurance, pensions, 401(k), and other similar programs; health care; vacations; sick leave; and paid time off such as holidays.

individual development plan (IDP)   A written document that outlines goals and professional growth for an employee.

individual incentive program   An offer to individual employees in a workgroup to receive extra pay based on achievement of clearly defined objectives.

information management (IM)   Application of management techniques to collect information, communicate it within and outside the organization, and process it to enable managers to make quicker and better decisions.

inpatriates   Employees working at corporate headquarters who originated in a different country.

insourcing   Delegating a job to someone within a company, as opposed to someone outside of the company (outsourcing).

instructional methods   Approaches to training that are either teacher-centered or learner-centered.

intellectual property (IP)   Knowledge, creative ideas, or expressions of human mind that have commercial value and are protectable under copyright, patent, service mark, trademark, or trade secret laws from imitation, infringement, and dilution.

intercultural wisdom   The knowing what you do not know about the values, behavior, and communication styles of people from other cultures.

internal coaching   A training or developmental process whereby organizational leaders support the achievement of a personal or professional goal.

internal equity   Employees' perception of their responsibilities, rewards, and work conditions as compared with those of other employees in similar positions in the same organization.

internal investigation   Gathering verbal and written information dealing with an issue that needs to be clarified.

intrinsic motivation   Stimulation that drives an individual to adopt or change a behavior for his or her own internal satisfaction or fulfillment.

intrinsic rewards   Rewards such as meaningful and fulfilling work, autonomy, and positive feedback that lead to high levels of job satisfaction.

investigation   A detailed search for facts involving records, witnesses, and other inputs.

investigation file   A collection of documents related to complaints or charges of discrimination, policy violation, or criminal behavior assembled by an employer about an employee or event.

involuntary separations   Individuals leaving the payroll for involuntary reasons, including such things as performance deficiencies, policy violations, or unauthorized absence.

ISO 9000 standards   Standards and guidelines on quality management and quality assurance developed by the International Organization for Standardization (ISO).

item response theory (IRT)   Method used to preequate the difficulty level of questions on an exam.

job analysis   A process to identify and determine the particular job duties and requirements for a given job.

job application   A form used to gather information significant to the employer about an individual candidate for employment.

job classification   A system for objectively and accurately defining the duties, responsibilities, tasks, and authority level of a job.

job-content-based job evaluation   A job evaluation method in which the relative worth and pay of different jobs are based on their content and relationship to other jobs within the same organization.

job description   A document that contains a summary of duties and responsibilities of a given job assignment and a description of the physical and mental requirements of the job.

job enlargement   Broadening the scope of a job by expanding the number of tasks.

job enrichment   Increasing the depth of a job by adding responsibilities.

job evaluation   A systematic determination of the relative worth of jobs in an organization.

job evaluation method   Quantitative or nonquantitative programs allowing sorting or categorizing jobs based on their relative worth to the organization.

job ranking   Comparison of jobs based on each job's measurable factors.

job rotation   The process of shifting a person from job to job.

job sharing   Two or more employees who work part-time in the same job to create one full-time equivalent person.

job specifications   A statement of employee characteristics and qualifications required for satisfactory performance of defined duties and tasks comprising a specific job or function.

judgmental forecasts   Projections based on subjective inputs.

judgment-based forecasting   Simple estimates, the Delphi technique, focus group or panel estimates, or historically based estimates used in human resource management.

jurisdiction   Power or right of a legal or political agency to exercise its authority over a person, subject matter, or territory.

key performance indicators (KPIs)   Key business statistics such as number of new orders, cash collection efficiency, and return on investment (ROI), which measure a firm's performance in critical areas.

key risk indicators (KRIs)   A measure used in management to indicate how risky an activity is.

kinesthetic learners   These are the "hands-on learners" or the "doers" who actually concentrate better and learn more easily when movement is involved.

knowledge   Facts and information gathered by an individual.

knowledge management   The way an organization identifies knowledge in order to be competitive and for the design of succession plans.

knowledge-based system   Pay is based on the level of knowledge an employee has in a particular field.

KSAs   Knowledge, skills, and abilities needed to perform a job.

KSAQs   Knowledge, skills, abilities, and other characteristics.

K-W-L table   Display of what students know (K), what they want to know (W), and what they actually learned (L).

labor cost differentials   Adjustment to pay structures based on local competitive comparisons.

labor unions   A group of people who represent workers in different occupations and work to protect the rights of the workers, such as working conditions, and wages.

lagging indicator   Measures the results of a process of a change, such as sales, profits, and customer service levels, a metric commonly used in the Balanced Scorecard.

layoffs   Suspension or termination of employment (with or without notice) by the employer.

leadership

   1. The individuals who are the leaders in an organization, regarded collectively.
   2. The activity of leading a group of people or an organization, or the ability to do this.

leadership concepts   The study of leadership styles and techniques.

leadership development   Teaching of leadership qualities, including communication, ability to motivate others, and management, to an individual.

leading indicator   A measure that precedes, anticipates, or predicts future performance, a measure commonly used in the Balanced Scorecard.

learning management system (LMS)   A comprehensive system that tracks training content, employee skill sets, training histories, and career development planning.

learning objects (LOs)   Defined learning elements that may be used in other contexts in the organization, i.e., animated graphics and training aids.

learning organization   Organizations that quickly respond and adapt to changes.

lecture   An oral presentation intended to teach or present information.

leniency errors   This occurs when ratings of all employees fall at the high end of the range.

leveling   Adjustments to survey numbers by an appropriate percentage needed to achieve a match with specific jobs.

liabilities   An organization's debts and other financial obligations.

local responsiveness (LR) strategy   A strategy that adapts to the needs of local markets, allowing an organization's units to meet the needs of their unique market.

location-based differentials   Adjustment to base pay programs based on work location remoteness, lack of amenities, climatic conditions, and other adverse conditions.

lockout   Employer action that prevents workers from entering the workplace to do their normal jobs.

long-term care insurance   Covers cost of long-term care at home, in an assisted living facility, in a nursing home, or as an inpatient in a hospice.

long-term disability   Begins where short-term disability ends. Covers some or all of an employee's income for up to a specified period, usually from 6 months to age 65 or an alternative number of years.

long-term incentives   Rewards for attaining results over a long measurement period.

low-context culture   A communication style that relies heavily on explicit and direct language.

lump-sum increases   Either a standalone performance bonus or part of an annual pay increase.

managed care plans   Insurance that provides plan subscribers with managed health care, with the purpose of reducing costs and improving the quality of care.

management by objectives (MBO)   A method of performance appraisal that specifies the performance goals that the employee and manager identify.

management skills   The abilities required to succeed at a management job. They include such skills as leadership, communication, decision making, behavior flexibility, organization, and planning.

managerial estimates   Projections based on managerial experience alone.

mandatory bargaining issues   Issues that must be discussed by the employer and union when negotiating a contract of representation.

market-based job evaluation   Key jobs are measured and valued against the market, and the remaining jobs are inserted into a hierarchy based on their whole-job comparison to the benchmark jobs.

marketing   The process of encouraging people to purchase the organization's products or services.

mathematically based forecasting   Staffing ratios, sales ratios, or regression analysis used in human resource management analysis of data elements.

matrix structure   Multiple command-and-control structure in which some employees have dual responsibilities and dual bosses.

maturity curves   Measures salaries based on years of directly related experience in the profession such as research or teaching.

mean (average)   Arithmetic average or mean arrived at by giving equal weight to every participant's actual pay.

measuring   Collecting and tabulating data.

median   The middle number in a range.

mediation   Use of an independent, impartial, and respected third party in settlement of a dispute, instead of opting for arbitration or litigation.

medical file   A collection of documents related to medical evaluations or status of an employee.

memorandum of understanding   Union contracts for a represented group of employees and designated employers. A term usually used in the public sector.

mentoring   A career relationship with an experienced individual with another who has less experience.

mergers and acquisitions (M&A)   The joining together of two separate organizations (merger) or by acquiring another organization (acquisition).

merit pay   Basing an employee's salary on his or her performance, over a predetermined period and according to an agreed-upon criteria.

metrics   Standards of measurement by which efficiency, performance, progress, or quality of a plan, process, or product can be assessed.

minimum premium plans   Health insurance programs paid for in part by the employer and in part by the employee.

mission statement   A statement describing what an organization does, who its customer/client base is, and how it will do its work.

mobile learning   Learning across multiple contexts, through social and content interactions, using personal electronic devices.

mode   The most frequently appearing number in a range.

modified duty   Temporary alteration of job duties that can be performed by an employee who is medically restricted for a designated period of time.

moral hazard   Lack of incentive to guard against risk where one is protected from its consequences.

motivation concepts   Notions about what motivates individuals, which have come about as a result of scientific studies. Examples of researchers involved with such studies include Herzberg, Maslow, and McGregor.

multicriteria decision analysis (MCDA)   A subdiscipline of operations research that explicitly considers multiple criteria in decision-making environments.

multinational enterprise (MNE) An enterprise operating in several countries but managed from one (home) country.

multiple linear regression A statistical technique based on an assumed linear relationship between a dependent variable and a variety of explanatory or independent variables.

national origin Nation of origin. This usually means national heritage and is a protected category within Title VII of the Civil Rights Act of 1964.

needs analysis See "needs assessment."

needs assessment Determining through analysis what gaps exist between a standard or an objective and existing capabilities.

negative emphasis The rejection of a candidate based on a small amount of negative information.

negligent hiring A legal tort claim against an employer for injury to someone inside or outside the organization in a way that should have been predicted by the employer if a proper background check had been completed.

negligent retention A legal tort claim against an employer for keeping someone on the payroll who is known to be a danger to others inside or outside the organization.

net assets The difference between income and liabilities in a nonprofit organization.

new employee orientation The process of welcoming new workers into the organization that may include completing payroll or benefits documents and a tour of the workplace.

nominal group technique Development of forecasts based on input from several groups of people.

noncash awards Prizes, gifts, and awards presented in recognition of service or production or other designated achievement.

nonexempt job A job with content that requires payment of overtime for work in excess of 40 hours per week under the FLSA.

objective measurement Impartial assessment of a result.

objectives End-result intentions.

occupational categories Groupings of job titles with similar levels of responsibility or skill requirements.

occupational illness A physical or mental malady caused by job-related conditions.

occupational injury A physical or mental injury caused by job-related conditions.

offboarding Moving employees out of the organization, off the payroll.

offshoring The relocation of functions or work to another country.

on-the-job training (OJT) Training that takes place while the employee is performing the job. This usually involves a co-worker or supervisor providing the coaching or training while job content is being learned.

onboarding Moving employees onto the payroll, into the organization.

oral employment contract Verbal agreement involving promises of duration or conditions in the employment relationship.

oral warning Verbal notice that a rule or policy has been violated and further discipline will result if the behavior is repeated.

organization exit Final formal meeting between the management and an employee leaving the firm; usually called an exit interview.

organizational culture The way an organization treats its employees, customers, and others.

organizational development The process of structured analysis and planning for strategic organizational accomplishment.

organizational effectiveness The degree to which an organization is successful in executing its strategic objectives and mission.

organizational learning Organization-wide continuous process that enhances its collective ability to accept, make sense of, and respond to internal and external change.

organizational restructuring Radical change to an organization's internal and external relationships.

organizational values The operating philosophies or principles that guide an organization's internal conduct as well as its relationship with its customers, partners, and shareholders. These are core values.

organizing

1. The process of bringing order out of chaos.
2. Union efforts to convince employees to support a union as the designated bargaining agent for a workgroup.

orientation An introductory process or program of new employees to their jobs, organization, and facility.

OSHA Occupational Safety and Health Administration (OSHA); also, the Occupational Safety and Health Act (OSHA).

outplacement A program that assists employees in finding jobs when their job is eliminated.

outside sales exemption   Exemption from overtime payment based on several qualifying factors, including the primary duty being making sales or obtaining orders for products or services. Work must be customarily and regularly engaged away from the employer's place of business.

outsourcing   Contracting for services with a third party rather than having them performed in the organization.

overtime pay   An additional amount of money paid in accordance with federal law to hourly employees who work more than 40 hours in a workweek.

paid holidays   Designated days each year that are awarded to employees as paid time off.

paid leaves   Paid time off for a specific designated reason.

paid sick leave   Accrued paid time off for medical reasons and usually based on length of service.

paid time off (PTO)   A bank of hours in which an employer pools sick days, vacation days, and personal days that employees can use as the need arises.

paid vacation   Accrued paid time off, usually based on length of service.

paired comparison   Method of evaluation in which each employee and job is compared with each other employee and job.

parent-country nationals (PCNs)   Employees sent from the home country to a remote country for a work assignment.

Pareto chart   One of the seven tools of quality control, it is a bar graph that displays variances by the number of their occurrences.

partially self-funded plans   Health insurance programs where the employer purchases one or two types of stop-loss insurance coverage.

part-time   Employees who work fewer than the number of hours required to be considered full-time.

pass rates   The number of people, shown as a percentage, who were successful in passing an exam.

pay compression   Pay inequities that arise when new employees demand and get wages higher than those being paid to the current employees.

pay differentials   Additional compensation paid to an employee as an incentive to accept what would normally be considered adverse working conditions, usually based on time, location, or working conditions.

pay equity   Degree to which the actual pay of an employee matches what he or she thinks to deserve. High pay equity means high employee satisfaction with his or her job; low pay equity increases the potential for absenteeism, grievances, strikes, and turnover. This is often called pay satisfaction.

pay for performance (P4P, PfP)   The notion that employees are compensated based on the results they achieve on their job.

pay grades   The way an organization organizes jobs of a similar value into job groups or pay grades as a result of the job evaluation process.

pay ranges   Pay amounts constrained by the upper and lower boundaries of each pay grade.

pay survey   Collections of data on prevailing market pay rates and information on starting wage rates, base pay, pay ranges, overtime pay, shift differentials, and incentive pay plans.

payroll   The function of recordkeeping and computation of compensation for each employee that results in issuance of a check or electronic deposit and collection and deposit of payroll taxes and other withholdings.

payroll administration   The act of managing the payroll function.

payroll systems   Usually computerized software programs designed to accept work time data and generate paychecks or electronic deposits.

pedagogy   The method and practice of teaching, especially as an academic subject or theoretical concept.

Pension Benefit Guaranty Corporation   A federal corporation established under ERISA that insures the vested benefits of pension plan participants.

percentiles   Distribution of data into percentage ranges such as top 10 percent and so on.

performance appraisal   A process of evaluating how employees perform their jobs.

performance bonus   Compensation in excess of base pay that is paid in recognition for exceeding performance/results objectives.

performance grants   Stock-based compensation that is linked to organizational performance.

performance improvement program (PIP)   A written plan that a supervisor provides an underperforming employee that specifies performance results required by a date.

performance management   The process used to identify, measure, communicate, develop, and reward employee performance.

performance measures   Methods for identifying quantities and qualities for job performance.

performance standards   Indicators of what a job is to accomplish and how it is to be performed.

performance-based merit pay system A system with pay determined based on individual job performance.

permissible bargaining issues Issues that may be discussed by the employer and union during contract negotiations. They are neither required nor prohibited.

perquisites (better known as perks) Special privileges for executives, including club memberships, company cars, reserved parking, use of the company airplane, and other such benefits.

personal protective equipment (PPE) Equipment worn by employees as protection against injury or illness hazards on the job.

person-based system Employee capabilities rather than how the job is performed determine the employee's pay.

personnel file One or more sets of documents held by an employer that contain information about the employee's employment status, performance evaluations, disability accommodations, and so forth, collectively considered one personnel file.

PESTEL Analysis Used in SWOT analysis, a framework or tool used to analyze and monitor the external environment factors that have an impact on an organization.

phantom stock plan Employee benefit program giving selected senior management employees pretend stock rather than actual stock, with the same financial benefits over time.

phased retirement Partial retirement while continuing to work a reduced schedule.

PHR HRCI's credential for experts in employment regulations and legal mandates.

PHRca Specific HRCI credential to the state of California.

picketing Technique used by unions to announce to the public a problem with an employer over issues involving working conditions or benefits.

pilot programs A small-scale, short-term experiment that helps an organization learn how a large-scale project might work in practice. This is also called a feasibility study or experimental trial.

plateau curve A type of learning curve in which learning is fast at first but then flattens out.

pluralism A work environment in which differing groups each have an agenda and conflict is overcome via negotiations as in a labor environment.

point-of-service plan A type of managed care plan that is a hybrid of HMO and PPO plans.

point-factor job evaluation   An approach using specific compensable factors as reference points to measure relative job worth.

policies   Statements describing how an organization is to be managed.

polycentric   A condition that occurs when jobs at headquarters are filled with people from other countries and positions in remote countries are filled with people from the headquarters country.

portal to portal   From door to door. This is usually applied to employees traveling from home to work or home to remote job site.

preferred provider organization   Health care program including an in-network and an out-of-network option for services.

premium-only plans   Authorized under the IRS Code, Section 125, allows employer-sponsored premium payments to be paid by the employee on a pre-tax basis instead of after-tax. These are sometimes called *POP plans*.

premium pay   Payment at rates greater than straight pay for working overtime or other agreed-upon condition.

premiums   Excess over apparent worth.

prepaid legal insurance   Employer financial support for cost of routine legal services such as developing a will, real estate matters, divorces, and other services.

prescription drug plans   Medical insurance programs that cover some or all of the cost of prescription drugs for subscribers.

primacy error   Tendency of an employee performance evaluator or an interviewer to rely on early cues for the first impressions.

principal agent problem   A conflict arising when people entrusted to look after the interests of others use the authority or power for their own benefit instead.

procedures   Methods to be used in fulfilling organizational responsibilities and policies.

process alignment   The linking an organization's structure and resources with its strategy and business environment.

process-flow analysis   A diagram of the steps involved in a process.

product structure   A representation of the way in which the parts of a product fit together and interact, organized in levels of detail based on structure.

productivity-based system   Pay is determined by the employee's production output.

professional employer organization   Vendor who, as a co-employer, provides qualified workers to a client organization.

professional exemption   Exemption from overtime payment based on several qualifying factors, including minimum pay requirement, advanced knowledge or education, and use of professional discretion and judgment.

Professional in Human Resources PHR   Credential that demonstrates mastery of the technical and operational aspects of HR practices and U.S. laws and regulations.

profit-and-loss statement (P&L)   A financial statement that summarizes the revenues, costs, and expenses incurred during a specific period of time.

profit-sharing plans   Direct or indirect payments to employees that depend on the employer's profitability.

program evaluation and review technique (PERT)   A project management tool used to organize, coordinate, and schedule tasks and people.

progressive discipline   A system of penalties involving increasing sanctions that can be taken if unwanted behaviors recur.

prohibited bargaining issues   Issues that may not be discussed by the employer and union during contract negotiations. These are illegal issues under the NLRA.

project hire   An employee who is hired for the duration of a project. Once the project is completed, the employee is dismissed or laid off. See "term employee."

project management   Guiding the implementation of a program from beginning to end.

project management concepts   The study of project management styles and techniques.

project team   A group of people with specific talent or experience brought together to resolve a problem or accomplish some other organizational goal.

promotion   Usually considered to be an increase in responsibility or compensation or both.

proof of identity   Document such as a passport or driver's license that contains a photo of the individual that proves that person is who they claim to be.

proof of work authorization   Document such as a Social Security card or alien work registration authorization that proves the individual is authorized to work in the United States.

protected class   Any group of people designated as such by the Department of Housing and Urban Development (HUD) in consideration of federal and state civil rights legislation.

prudent person rule   Basic principle for investment decisions by institutional investors and professional money managers.

punitive damages   Damages intended to deter a defendant from engaging in conduct similar to that which was the basis of a lawsuit.

qualified domestic relations order (QDRO)   A court-issued order that instructs a plan administrator to pay all or a portion of a pension plan benefit to a divorced spouse or child.

qualitative analysis   Research that explores the reasoning behind human behavior; often uses open-ended interviewing.

quantitative analysis   Research based on quantifiable data.

quartiles   Distribution of data into four quadrants: bottom quarter, lower-middle quarter, upper-middle quarter, and top quarter.

quid pro quo harassment   Insisting on sexual favors in exchange for some job benefit, be it promotion, compensation, or just retaining employment. This normally occurs between supervisor and subordinate. Literally, it means "this for that."

radicalism   A management-labor concept that conflict is an inherent characteristic of capitalism and can be resolved only with a change in the economic system.

range spreads   Dispersion of pay from the lowest boundary to the highest boundary of a pay range.

ratio analysis   Comparison of current results or historic results at a specific point in time.

realistic job preview (RJP)   A recruiting approach used by an organization to communicate the important aspects of the job prior to the offer of a position.

reasonable accommodation   Adjustment to a job condition or workplace that will allow an employee to perform the essential job duties.

reasonable cause   One possible determination from a state or federal enforcement agency concerning an investigation of a charge of illegal discrimination.

recency error   This occurs when an evaluator gives greater weight to recent events of performance.

recognition   Acknowledgment of accomplishments by individual employees.

recordkeeping   Documentation involving any aspect of employee management from discussions to personal employee information.

recruitment   Process of seeking out qualified job candidates for open positions.

red circle rates   Pay at a rate higher than the maximum for the assigned pay range.

redeployment   Assignment to a new job, often at a remote work location.

regiocentric   Orientation to culture in a specific region or collection of countries such as Asian, South American, or European.

regression analysis   A statistical process of estimating the relationships among variables.

regulation   Rule of order issued by an administrative agency of government, which usually has the force of law behind it.

rehire   A former employee who is hired back onto the payroll.

reliability   Consistency and validity of test results determined through statistical methods after repeated trials.

remediation   A process by which an unacceptable action or behavior is corrected.

remuneration surveys   Surveys that collect information on compensation and benefit practices in the prevailing market.

repatriates   Employees who return to their home country following a work assignment in a different country.

replacement planning   Succession planning using a snapshot assessment of existing qualified talent for key positions.

request for proposal   A written document asking for vendor input and suggestions along with cost estimates for any given work to be performed in the establishment.

residual risk   Exposure to loss remaining after other known risks have been countered, factored in, or eliminated.

responsibility   A required part of a job or organizational obligation.

restructuring   Redesigning the organization structure and altering reporting relationships and responsibility assignments.

results measurement   Methods for monitoring the amount of progress that has been accomplished toward a stated goal or objective.

retention   Measurement of the quantity of new employees remaining with the employer over a given period of time.

retiree   An ex-employee who met the qualification requirements for retirement under the organization's definition or plan.

return on investment (ROI)   The calculation showing the value of expenditures versus the investment.

return to work   Clearance to return to active employment activities following an illness, injury, or other absence.

reverse innovation   Also known as trickle-up innovation; a term referring to an innovation seen first, or likely to be used first, in the developing world before spreading to the industrialized world.

risk   A probability or threat of damage, injury, liability, loss, or any other negative occurrence that is caused by external or internal vulnerabilities and that may be avoided through preemptive action.

risk appetite   The level of risk that a person or corporation is willing to take in order to execute a strategy.

risk control   Probability of loss arising from the tendency of internal control systems to lose their effectiveness over time and thus expose (or fail to prevent the exposure of) the assets they were instituted to protect.

risk management   Identifies and manages potential liabilities that come from operating a business.

risk position   Extent of exposure to a particular risk, expressed usually in monetary terms.

risk scorecard   The gathering of individual characteristics of risk and keeping track.

risk tolerance   Capacity to accept or absorb risk.

role-play   Technique for simulating individual participation in real-life roles involving performance or action involved with solving a problem.

Rucker plan   A company-wide incentive plan in which compensation is based on a ratio of income to value added by employees engaged in the production process.

rule of law   Absolute predominance or supremacy of ordinary law of the land over all citizens, no matter how powerful.

safety audit   The process of evaluating the workplace for safety hazards and determining any needed corrective action.

sales personnel incentive programs   Bonuses or commissions based on predetermined formulas involving performance and time.

scaffolding   Teacher modeling skills and thinking for students, allowing students to take over those expressions based on the initial structure provided by the teacher.

Scanlon plan   Cost-saving productivity-incentive plan in which any saving (computed per unit of output) compared with an agreed-upon standard labor cost is shared equally between the workers and the firm.

scatter diagram   A graphical tool that depicts the relationship among variables.

scenario "what if " analysis   The process of determining the effects on outcomes with altering details to determine a likely outcome.

seasonal employee   A worker hired for a specific seasonal surge in work levels, common in the retail industry and also agriculture and other food processing businesses.

Section 125 cafeteria plans   Allows employees to pay certain qualified expenses on a pre-tax basis. (See "premium-only plans.")

selection   The ultimate choice in a field of multiple choices. This is usually applied to job candidate selection.

selection screening   The process of sorting out job candidates based on specified criteria of job requirements. This is accomplished through the use of interviews, tests, and demonstrations.

self-directed team   A group of people with a specific assignment permitted to select its own leadership and direction to take toward the problem or task.

self-directed work teams   Assignment of employee groups with multiple knowledge and skill specialties represented from multiple disciplines.

self-funded plans   Health insurance programs where the employer assumes all of the risk as a self-insured entity.

Senior Professional in Human Resources (SPHR)   Credential for those who have mastered the strategic and policy-making aspects of HR management in the United States.

seniority   Length of service in a job, employer organization, industry, or union.

seniority pay increases   A pay increase given based solely on length of service.

service level agreement (SLA)   Contract between a service provider and a customer; it details the nature, quality, and scope of the service to be provided. This is also called *service level contract*.

severance package   Voluntary payment by some employers to laid off employees. It may include pay for designated number of work days, job retraining, outplacement services, and paid benefits premium assistance.

shared services HR model   An HR organizational structure where specific functions of HR expertise develop HR policies and units of HR can determine what it needs for the menu of services.

short-term disability   Begins where sick leave ends. This covers some or all of an employee's income for up to a specified period, usually 6 months.

simple linear regression   A technique in which a straight line is fitted to a set of data points to measure the effect of a single independent variable. The slope of the line is the measured impact of that variable.

simulations   Imitation of real-world systems or processes. Learning exercises designed to be as realistic as possible without the risk of a real-life circumstance.

single or flat-rate system   Each worker in the same job has the same rate of pay, regardless of seniority or job performance.

situational judgment tests (SJTs)   A type of psychological test that presents the test-taker with realistic, hypothetical scenarios and asks the individual to identify the most appropriate response or to rank the responses in the order they feel is most effective.

Six Sigma   A data-driven approach and method for eliminating defects.

skill-based system   When pay is based on the number and depth of skills that an employee has applicable to their job.

SMART goal model   Model for creating goals that are Specific, Measurable, Attainable/Achievable, Relevant/Realistic, and Timed.

social media   Contemporary methods of communicating with other individuals or groups. A term applied to Internet services such as Facebook, Pinterest, LinkedIn, and Twitter as examples.

social movement unionism   A type of union activity devoted to topics associated with social issues.

socialization   An onboarding initiative where employees learn the knowledge, language, social skills, culture, and values required for assimilating into a new group or organization.

Society of Human Resource Professionals (SHRM)   The world's largest HR membership organization devoted to human resource management, representing more than 275,000 members in over 160 countries.

software as a service (SaaS)   Software rental from a centralized location, described as the "cloud," as opposed to having software installed on a desktop computer.

solution analysis   Statistical comparison of various potential solutions.

sourcing   The process of finding applicants and suppliers of goods or services.

span of control   The number of subordinates reporting to a supervisor or manager.

specific stop-loss coverage   The health plan is protected against the risk of a major illness for one participant, or one family unit, covered by the plan.

SPHR-CA   SPHR credentials for experts in employment regulations and legal mandates specific to the state of California (no longer recognized effective April 1, 2016; see PHRca).

staff units   Specialized services provided to work groups.

staffing   Filling job openings with qualified applicants.

stakeholder concept   A conceptual framework of business ethics and organizational management that addresses moral and ethical values in the management of a business or other organization.

stakeholders   Individuals with an interest in an organization's success or outcomes.

standard deviation   Scores in a set of data that spread out around an average.

standards   The yardstick by which amount and quality of output are measured.

state employment service   The agency responsible for assisting citizens with job placement and unemployment benefits in each state.

statistical forecasts   Use of mathematical formulas to identify patterns and trends.

stay interviews   A structured interview with existing employees for the purpose of determining what aspects of their job causes retention or can be improved to cause future retention.

step rate with performance considerations   A system allowing performance to influence the size or timing of a pay increase along the step system.

stereotyping   Broadly classifying people into groups based on characteristics that may not be accurate. "All blonds are dumb," for example.

storytelling   Use of multimedia technology such as PowerPoint to present interactive opportunities involving any subject.

straight piece rate system   Employee receives a base rate of pay and is awarded additional compensation for the amount of output produced.

strategic business management   That which formulates and produces HR objectives, programs, practices, and policies.

strategic fit   A situation that occurs when a specific project, target company, or product is seen as appropriate with respect to an organization's overall objectives.

strategic planning   Identifying organizational objectives and determining what actions are required to reach those objectives.

strategies   Specific direction that outlines objectives to achieve long-term plans.

strategy   1. A method or plan chosen to bring about a desired future, such as achievement of a goal or solution to a problem. 2. The art and science of planning and marshalling resources for their most efficient and effective use.

stress interview   Emotionally charged interview setting where the interviewee is put under psychological stress to evaluate how he or she performs under pressure.

strictness   An error in which a manager is too strict in evaluating the performance of employees, leading to decreases in motivation and performance.

strike   Work stoppage resulting from a failed negotiation between the employer and union.

structured interview   Fixed-format interview in which all questions are prepared beforehand and are put in the same order to each interviewee.

subject matter expert   A person who is well versed in the content of a specific knowledge area.

subjective measurement   Assessment of a result using opinion or perception.

substance abuse   Personal use of alcohol or drugs in excess of amounts prescribed by a medical professional, or any use of illegal substances. Abuse generally results in an impairment of the individual's physical or mental capacities.

succession planning   A process of identifying a plan for the replacement of key employees.

supplemental unemployment benefits   An unemployment benefit in addition to government benefits offered by some employers.

supply analysis   Strategic evaluation of job candidate sources, plant locations, and other factors.

supply chain   Entire network of entities directly or indirectly interlinked and interdependent in serving the same consumer or customer.

suspension   Temporary hiatus of active employment, usually as a disciplinary step, that can be paid or unpaid.

sustainability   Ability to maintain or support an activity or process over the long term.

SWOT analysis   A process in strategic planning that looks at an organization's strengths, weaknesses, opportunities, and threats.

systems thinking   Understanding how independent units within a larger organization interact with and influence each other.

talent management   The management and integration of all HR activities and processes that aligns with the organization's goals and needs.

talent retention   The retention of key talent, those employees who are the strongest performers, have high potential, or are in critical jobs.

taskforce   A group of people assembled to address major organizational issues.

teacher exemption   Exemption from overtime payment based on several qualifying factors, including the primary duty of teaching in an educational establishment.

teams   A group of people focused on specific organizational issues.

temp-to-lease   Conversion of a temporary agency–provided employee to regular employee status in the client organization.

term employee   An employee who is hired for the duration of a project. Once the project is completed, the employee is dismissed or laid off. See "project hire."

termination   End of the employment relationship.

theory of constraints (TOC)   Concepts and methodology aimed mainly at achieving the most efficient flow of material in a plant through continuous process improvement.

third-country nationals (TCNs)   Employees who are moved from one remote location to another remote location for a work assignment.

third party   Someone other than the two primary parties involved in an interaction.

third-party administrator plan   Health insurance programs in which the employer assumes all of the risk but hires an independent claims department.

time-based differential pay   Shift pay that is generally time-based rewards for employees who work what are considered undesirable shifts like night shifts.

time-based step rate system   Determining pay rate based on the length of time in the job.

total quality management (TQM)   A management system for achieving customer satisfaction using quantitative methods to improve processes.

total rewards   Financial inducements and rewards as well as nonfinancial inducements and rewards, such as the value of good job content and good working environment.

total rewards strategy   An integrated reward system encompassing three key elements that employees value from their employment: compensation, benefits, and work experience that attracts and retains talent.

totalization agreements   Agreements between several nations that avoid double taxation of income for workers who divide their working career between two or more countries.

trade union   An organization whose membership consists of workers and union leaders, united to protect and promote their common interests.

trainability   The readiness and motivation to learn.

training   The process whereby people acquire skills, knowledge, or capabilities to perform jobs.

training effectiveness   Measurement of what students are expected to be able to do at the end of the training course or module.

training techniques   Approaches to training, including virtual, classroom, on-the-job, and one-on-one tutoring.

transactional leadership   A leadership style that focuses on either rewards or threat of discipline in an effort to motivate employees.

transfer   Movement of current employee to a different job in a different part of the organization.

transfer of learning   Ability of a trainee to apply the behavior, knowledge, and skills acquired in one learning situation to another.

transformational leadership   A leadership style that motivates employees by inspiring them.

transparency   When an organization's dealings, information, practices, transactions, and agreements are open to disclosure and review by others.

travel pay   Extra pay provided for travel time, either under legal requirement or by other agreement.

trend analysis   Comparison of historical results with current results to determine a trend.

triple bottom line   Financial, social, and environmental effects of a firm's policies and actions that determine its viability as a sustainable organization.

tuition reimbursement   Employer financial support for employee continuing education efforts.

turnover analysis   Comparison of the reasons for employees leaving the workforce and the organizational problems that may be causing them.

unfair labor practice (ULP)   Legally prohibited action by an employer or trade union such as refusal to bargain in good faith.

uniform guidelines   Federal regulations that specify how job selection tools must be validated.

unitarism   When employers and employees act together for their common good.

unpaid sick leave   Accrued unpaid time off, usually based on length of service.

unweighted average   Raw average of data that gives equal weight to all factors, with no regard to individual factors.

validity   The extent to which a test measures what it says it measures.

value   Resulting benefits created when an organization meets its strategic goals.

value chain   Interlinked value-adding activities that convert inputs into outputs, which, in turn, add to the bottom line and help create competitive advantage.

value drivers   Entities that increase the value of a product or service by improving the perception of the item and essentially providing a competitive advantage.

values   The principles or standards of behavior that are most important to either an individual or entity.

variable pay   Performance-based pay that includes individual performance bonuses, executive bonuses, profit sharing, gainsharing, group incentives, and other incentives tied to productivity as opposed to base pay.

variance analysis   Process aimed at computing variance between actual and budgeted or targeted levels of performance and identification of their causes.

veteran   A former member of the US military service in any branch.

veto   The action of canceling or postponing a decision or bill in the US legislature.

vicarious liability   Obligation that arises from the relationship of one party with another.

vision care plans   Medical insurance programs that cover some or all of the cost of vision care (exams and corrective lenses) for subscribers.

vision statement   A statement that describes the desired future of an organization.

visual learners   A learning style in which ideas, concepts, data, and other information are associated with images and techniques.

voluntary separations   Individuals leaving the payroll for voluntary reasons, including such things as retirement, obtaining a different job, returning to full-time education, or personal reasons.

wage compression   A reduction in the relative wage differentials between high- and low-paying jobs resulting in insufficient incentives required for higher-level job responsibilities and skills.

weighted average   An average result taking into account the number of participants and each participant's pay.

Weingarten rights   A term used that refers to a union employee's right to have a union representative or co-worker present during an investigatory interview.

well-being   A good or satisfactory condition of existence; a state characterized by health, happiness, and prosperity; welfare.

work councils   An organization that represents employees on a local level. A works council often provides a useful collective bargaining tool for employees that require an organization that is more familiar with their particular situation than a national labor union, for example.

work-life balance (WLB)   A comfortable state of equilibrium achieved between an employee's primary priorities of their employment position and their personal lifestyle.

workers' compensation   Program that provides medical care and compensates an employee for part of lost earnings as a result of a work-related disability.

workforce analysis   Assessment of the workforce and things that are influencing it.

workforce management   Managing employees' work activities and responsibilities, work hours, planning, scheduling, and tracking results of the work effort.

workforce planning and employment   The process of recruiting, interviewing, staffing, assuring equal employment opportunity, affirmative action, new employee orientation, retention, termination, and employee records management performed by an employer.

workplace accommodation   The modification of a job or way of doing a job so that a person with a disability can have equal access to opportunity in all aspects of their work and perform the essential functions of a job.

workplace violence   Personal behavior that ranges from shouting to hitting or worse taking place on an employer's premises.

workweek   A period of 7 days that always begins at the same hour of the same day each week.

written employment contract   Written agreement involving promises of duration or conditions in the employment relationship.

written warning   Written notice that a rule or policy has been violated and further discipline will result if the behavior is repeated.

zero-based budgeting   A model of budgeting that is based on expenditures being justified for each budget year.

zero-sum   Whatever is gained by one side is lost by the other.

INDEX

A

ability tests in talent selection process, 153
Accelerating Implementation Methodology (AIM), 104–105
accept action in risk response, 421
accountability
    HR increases for, 280–281
    as proficiency indicator, 466
accounting function, 282
acronyms list, 553–573
action-centered leadership, 126
action learning leadership, 203
action plans in HR business case, 503
active disengaged employees, 162
activities
    staffing plans, 320–321
    training and development, 191
activity-based budgeting, 283
activity logs in strategy implementation, 110
actual damages in Civil Rights Act (Title VII), 54
ADA (Americans with Disabilities Act), 49–53
Adair, John, 126
ADDIE (Analyze, Design, Develop, Implement, and Evaluate) model
    OED initiatives, 306
    phases, 190–192
additional considerations in HR business case, 503
address of residence as interview question, 149
ADEA (Age Discrimination in Employment Act), 58
adhocracy culture, 311
Adler, Nancy, 391
administrative services, 277
adult learning
    obstacles, 188
    overview, 186

retention effects, 187
styles, 186–189
adverse impact in talent selection process, 154
adversity, leadership in, 463
advisor role
    career development, 194
    change management, 112
    HR staff, 275
advocate role, 480
affirmative action
    executive orders, 60–61
    record-keeping requirements, 446
Affordable Care Act, 62–63
African American culture, 387
after-action debriefs in risk management, 425
Age Discrimination in Employment Act (ADEA), 58
age in interview questions, 149
agency complaints, 347–348
agility as proficiency indicator, 462–463
aging technique in compensation analysis, 228
agreements in negotiations, 295
agricultural workers, employment visas for, 68
alignment
    decisions with organizational strategies and values, 473
    globalization, 381
    HR function and strategic plans, 295–297
    HR goals and objectives, 98, 505
    HR practices, 475
    HR strategy with relationship management, 479
    objectives with strategy, 114
    organizational structures, 284–285, 303, 313
    strategic planning for, 87

total rewards and global staffing, 211–212
total rewards and organizational strategy, 217
allegiances in global assignments, 392
alliances
    diversity and inclusion, 404
    employee and labor relations, 340
alternative staffing, 323–326
alternative work arrangement liabilities, 519
alternatives in HR business case, 503
American Management Association (AMA), 127
American Recovery and Reinvestment Act (ARRA), 59
American Society for Training and Development (ASTD), 200
Americans with Disabilities Act (ADA), 49–53
analysis
    appropriate tools, 518
    BCA, 506–507
    compensation structure, 221–224, 228–230
    data analysis methods, 116–118
    gap, 246, 318
    job, 136–137, 221–224
    risks, 418–419
    training and development, 190
ancestry in interview questions, 149
anecdotes and examples in meetings, 514
anti-corruption in United Nations Global Compact, 431
aPHR (Associate Professional in Human Resources), 6
aPHRi (Associate Professional in Human Resources, International), 6

applicant reactions in talent selection process, 154
application deadlines, 16
application forms, 146–147
appraisal methods, 175–179
appraiser role in career development, 194
apprenticeships, 196
approachability in relationship management, 478
approval function in job descriptions, 137
Arab culture, 388
arbitration for grievances, 344
ARRA (American Recovery and Reinvestment Act), 59
arrests or convictions in interview questions, 150
artefacts in cultures, 389
assessment
    employee engagement, 164–168
    organizational gap development, 305–306
    talent selection process, 153–155
    total rewards strategy, 206–207
assessment centers in leadership development, 201–202
assignments, global, 391–393
Associate Professional in Human Resources (aPHR), 6
Associate Professional in Human Resources, International (aPHRi), 6
associate's degree requirements, 14
associations in career development, 199
assumptions
    challenging, 528
    cultures, 389
    risk identification, 418
ASTD (American Society for Training and Development), 200
at-will employment
    global issues, 211
    overview, 337
attainability as SMART goal setting, 98
attitudes and behaviors in diversity and inclusion, 408
attrition metric in recruiting effectiveness, 142
audience in communication, 487
auditory learners, 187
audits
    global HR policies, 385–386
    HR value, 292

Australia
    diversity, 399
    health plans, 249
authentic leadership in employee engagement, 163
authority, appropriate application of, 469
authorization to test (ATT) letters, 17
auto didacticism, 191
automatic step rate systems, 232
availability and quality of information in risk management, 416
avoidance strategies in employment relationship, 337–338

B

bachelor's degree requirements, 14–15
background in HR business case, 502
background investigations in talent selection process, 155
bad habits in leadership, 120–121
balanced scorecards
    dimensions, 508
    HR value, 291–292
    strategy performance, 114
bank holidays, 247
bargaining powers in strategy formulation, 95
barriers in globalization, 380
BARS (behaviorally anchored ratings), 176–177
base pay systems, 232–234
base periods in unemployment insurance, 255
BCA (business case analysis), 506–507
Beard, Ross, 507
Beatty, Richard, 296–297
Becker, Brian, 296–297
behavior in Four-Level Training Evaluation Model, 193
behavioral competencies, 9, 11–12
    Business Acumen, 501–511
    chapter review, 529
    Communication, 484–491
    Consultation, 511–520
    Critical Evaluation, 520–529
    Ethical Practice, 467–475
    Global and Cultural Effectiveness, 491–500
    Leadership and Navigation, 460–467
    overview, 459
    questions, 530–548
    Relationship Management, 475–484

behavioral engagement, 161
behavioral interviews, 148
behavioral problem in OED, 300
behavioral reinforcement theory, 172
behavioral school for leadership, 122
behavioral strategy in OED, 300
behaviorally anchored ratings (BARS), 176–177
bell curves in performance management, 176
Bell System divestiture
    downsizing, 314
    overview, 106
belonging and love in Maslow's hierarchy of needs, 170–171
benchmarking
    competition, 507
    strategy performance, 114
benefits
    determining, 245–246
    diversity and inclusion, 405
    employment contracts, 336
    family-oriented, 248
    health and welfare, 249–252
    legislation, 257–261
    metrics, 257
    needs assessment, 245–246
    overview, 244
    personnel files, 441
    retirement, 254–255
    severance packages, 253–254
    Social Security, 255–256
    structure, 244–245
    total rewards, 206
    types, 246–247
    unemployment insurance, 255
    workers' compensation, 252–253
benefits statements in total rewards strategy, 218
best-of-breed (BoB) option in HR information systems, 356
best practices
    analyzing and delineating, 523
    audits, 292
    employment branding, 136
bias errors in performance appraisal, 177
biases
    in interviews, 152–153
    mitigating, 469
big bang approach, 357
big data era, 354–355
birthplace in interview questions, 149
Black, J. Stewart, 409

Black-American culture, 387
Blake, Robert R., 122
Blake-Mouton behavioral leadership theory, 122
blended learning, 191
BoCK Advisory Panel, 11
Body of Competency and Knowledge (BoCK), 9–10
    description, 13
    Society for Human Resource Management, 6
Body of Knowledge (BoK), 5–6
Boston boxes, 95–96
brain drain, 132
brainstorming
    OED initiatives, 307
    risk identification, 417
branding
    diversity and inclusion, 405
    employment, 135–136, 140
Branson, Richard, 463
bring-your-own-device (BYOD) policies, 359
broadbanding pay ranges, 232
Brockbank, W., 290
budgeting analysis function, 282–283
budgets as leading indicators, 524
burial benefits, 252
Buros Center for Testing, 10
Business Acumen competency, 9
    definitions, 501
    description, 12
    key concepts, 501
    proficiency indicators, 501–510
    summary, 510–511
business case
    diversity and inclusion, 403
    employee engagement, 167–168
    HR management, 502–503
    retention, 181
    strategy implementation, 108–109
business case analysis (BCA), 506–507
business challenges, analyzing, 513
Business Cluster competency
    Business Acumen, 501–511
    Consultation, 511–520
    Critical Evaluation, 520–529
business continuity, 422–424
business intelligence (BI), 115–116
business language fluency, 505
business lifecycles as organizational staffing challenge, 132
business results and employee growth in employee engagement, 180

business strategy, developing, 99–102
business unit level strategy, 88
buy-in for organizational change as proficiency indicator, 466–467
BYOD (bring-your-own-device) policies, 359

C
Cameron, Kim, 311
Canada
    diversity, 400
    health plans, 250
capabilities and resources in risk management, 416
career development
    cultural influences, 195
    diversity and inclusion, 405
    forms, 195–199
    managing, 194
    roles, 194–195
    trends, 199
cars as perquisites, 256
cash awards, 237
cash car allowances, 256
cash flow metrics, 115
cause-and-effect diagrams, 309
Caux Round Table (CRT) principles, 431
CBAs (collective bargaining agreements)
    description, 343
    global issues, 211
Center for Creative Leadership, 200–202
Centers of Excellence, 291
central errors in performance appraisal, 179
central tendency measures in compensation analysis, 229–230
centralized organizational structure, 285–286
Certificate program, 14
Certification Commission, 11
certification program
    BoCK Advisory Panel, 11–13
    Body of Competency and Knowledge, 13
    chapter review, 21
    exam. See exam
    HR Expertise, 11
    overview, 9–10
Certified Professional, 6
chain of command organizational structure, 285

challenging assignments in leadership development, 202
championing
    HR function as proficiency indicator, 466
    organizational effectiveness, 480
change
    corporate social responsibility, 428–429
    diversity and inclusion, 404–406, 408
    HR impact, 278–279
    mergers and acquisitions, 104
    organizational, 466–467
    strategic, 465
    strategy implementation, 110–113
change facilitation as proficiency indicator, 465
change readiness in organizational gap development, 305
changing needs in talent management, 322
check sheets in OED quality initiatives, 309
checklists
    performance management, 176
    risk identification, 418
cherry picking in organizational staffing, 133
chief human resource officer (CHRO) title, 275–276
citizenship in interview questions, 150
civil law systems in global context, 394
Civil Rights Act (1991), 55
Civil Rights Act (Title VII), 54
Civil Service Reform Act, 64–65
clan culture in OED assessment, 311
clarity in communication, 485–486
class action law suits, 519
classification, jobs, 225
Clayton Act, 24
club memberships, 257
coach role in career development, 194, 199
coaching executives, 519–520
coaching skills, developing, 514–515
COBRA (Consolidated Omnibus Budget Reconciliation Act), 59
Code of Ethics, 468
Codes of Fair Competition, 34
codetermination in labor relations, 342
cognitive problem in OED, 300
COLAs (cost-of-living adjustments), 235

collaboration
  with stakeholders, 461–462
  strategic change, 465
  technology management,
    359–360
collective bargaining
  process, 342–343
  total rewards strategy, 213
collective bargaining agreements (CBAs)
  description, 343
  global issues, 211
colleges in career development, 199
commission for direct sales personnel,
    242–243
commitment
  incentive pay systems, 242
  strategic change, 465
committees, career development, 197
common law systems in global
    context, 394
Common Market, 395
communication
  data analysis, 118
  employee, 339
  employee surveys, 167
  global and cultural effectiveness, 499
  global labor market direction, 507
  impact for data analysis,
    527–528
  leadership, 128
  mergers and acquisitions, 105
  OED, 302, 310
  policies, 360–361
  risk management, 421
  staffing plans, 321
  strategic change, 465
  strategy development, 106–107
  total rewards strategy, 216–219
  vision, 473–474
Communication competency, 9
  definitions, 484–485
  description, 12
  framing, 491
  key concepts, 485
  proficiency indicators,
    485–491
  summary, 491
communities in organizational strategy
  role, 294
compa-ratios
  compensation structure, 244
  pay ranges, 231
company cars, 256
comparing alternatives in HR business
  case, 503

compensation
  diversity and inclusion, 405
  employment contracts, 336
  legislation, 257–261
  for termination, 254
  total rewards, 205–206
compensation structure
  data analysis, 228–230
  differential pay, 236–237
  incentive pay, 237–243
  job analysis, 221–224
  job documentation, 224
  job evaluation, 224–228
  metrics, 244
  overview, 220
  pay adjustments, 235–236
  pay structure, 230–232
  pay variations, 234–235
  system design, 220–221
  systems, 232–243
compensatory damages in Civil Rights
  Act (Title VII), 54
competencies
  behavioral. See behavioral
    competencies
  business cluster. See Business
    Cluster competency
  communication. See
    Communication competency
  Ethical Practice, 467–475
  job analysis, 223
competency-based interviews, 148
competency-based pay systems, 234
Competency Model, 9
competition
  benchmarking, 507
  globalization, 379
  strategy development, 99–101
competitive advantages in global and
  cultural effectiveness, 497
competitive labor market in total
  rewards strategy, 213
complaints in employee and labor
  relations, 343–344
complex labor environments, 339
complexities in compensation and
  benefits legalities, 258–261
compliance
  audits, 292
  complexities, 258–261
  diversity, 400
  employee records, 444–450
  risk management, 426
  U.S. employment law and
    regulations, 438

compressed workweeks, 249
concessions in HR role, 295
Conference Board for diversity and
  inclusion, 403, 408
confidentiality, 468
conflict management
  agency complaints and litigation,
    347–348
  HR roles, 346
  leadership, 128–130
  relationship management, 476
  resolution techniques, 347
  strategies, 482–483
conflicts of interest
  challenging, 472
  dealing with, 468–469
  preventing, 471
  risk management, 417
Congressional Accountability Act, 65
consensus management as proficiency
  indicator, 463
consistency in ethical behavior, 469
consistent key messages in total rewards
  strategy, 219
Consolidated Omnibus Budget
  Reconciliation Act (COBRA), 59
construct validity in talent selection
  process, 155
constructive discipline, 351
constructive feedback, communicating,
  486–487
Consultation competency, 9
  definitions, 511–512
  description, 12
  key concepts, 511
  proficiency indicators, 511–520
  summary, 520
Consumer Credit Protection Act, 24
contact building in relationship
  management, 481
contemporary knowledge,
  maintaining, 471
content revisions in training, 192
content validity in talent selection
  process, 155
contingency leadership style, 123–126
contingency plans in risk management,
  423–424
contingent assessment methods in
  talent selection process, 154
continuing education programs, 199
continuous improvement
  OED, 302
  risk management, 426
  staffing plans, 321

continuous integration approach in HR information systems, 357
contract administration and enforcement, 343–344
contract labor, 324
contract negotiation process, 342–343
contracts
    employment, 335–336
    talent selection process, 156
contradictory practices in global and cultural effectiveness, 498–499
contrast effect in interviews, 153
contrast errors in performance appraisal, 179
contribution-oriented culture in total rewards strategy, 208
control charts, 309
control support by HR staff, 275
conventional corporate culture, 389
Copeland "Anti-Kickback" Act, 24
Copyright Act, 25
core business functions in HR function organization, 281–284
core values in global and cultural effectiveness, 492
corporate citizenship, 428
Corporate Social Responsibility (CSR)
    Caux Round Table principles, 431
    changes, 428–429
    definitions, 426–427
    Global Reporting Initiative G4 Sustainability Guidelines, 433–434
    ISO 26000, 431–432
    key concepts, 427
    KPMG survey, 434–435
    OECD guidelines, 430
    philanthropy and volunteerism, 435
    Social Accountability International, 432–433
    strategy, 429–435
    United Nations Global Compact, 430–431
corporate strategy development, 102–106
cost and yield ratios in recruiting effectiveness, 143
cost leadership strategy, 100
cost of hire/cost per hire metric in recruiting effectiveness, 142
cost-of-living adjustments (COLAs), 235

costs
    diversity, 400
    globalization, 377
    talent selection process, 154–155
counseling
    career development, 199
    job analysis, 223
Court of Justice of the European Union, 396
credibility
    establishing, 472
    relationship management, 476–477
Credit Suisse diversity analysis, 308
crisis management planning, 422–424
criteria
    risk management, 416
    talent selection process, 154
critical activities, evaluating, 508
Critical Evaluation competency, 9
    definitions, 520–521
    description, 12
    key concepts, 520–521
    proficiency indicators, 520–529
    summary, 529
critical incidents in performance management, 177
critical information
    delivering, 486
    gathering, 522
critical policy challenges in diversity and inclusion, 409
critical thinking, 522
Cross, K. P., 188
cross-border situations for incentive pay, 242
cross-cultural assessment tools in talent selection process, 154
cross-cultural challenges, 391
CRT (Caux Round Table) principles, 431
CSR. See Corporate Social Responsibility (CSR)
cultural assessment
    OED, 311
    organizational gap development, 305–306
cultural influences in career development, 195
cultural issues
    leadership, 127, 204
    learning and development, 186
    training and development, 190, 192

cultural knowledge, maintaining, 497
cultural noise in interviews, 153
cultural quotient (CQ), 494
culture change as proficiency indicator, 466
culture of ethics, maintaining, 474
cultures
    cross-cultural challenges, 391
    definitions, 388
    dimensions, 389–390
    effects of, 388–389
    intra-organizational, 483
    layers, 389
    OED, 301
    strategic planning for, 88
    total rewards strategy, 208, 213
    types, 387–388
current process in HR business case, 502
curricula vitae (CV) in talent selection process, 146
customer feedback metrics, 115
customer relations in diversity and inclusion, 405–406
customer service in relationship management, 479, 481

D

damages in Civil Rights Act (Title VII), 54
data
    breeches, 519
    HR information systems access, 356
    interpreting, 525
    mining, 354
    privacy and protection, 334, 356
data analysis
    compensation structure, 228–230
    employee engagement, 167
    impact for, 527–528
    OED, 303
    strategy performance, 116
data collection in big data era, 354
database structures in HR information systems, 356
Davis-Bacon Act, 25
days to fill metric in recruiting effectiveness, 142
De Cieri, Helen, 392
death benefits in workers' compensation, 252
debriefs in risk management, 424–425

decentralized organizational structure, 285–286
decision-making
    aligned with organizational strategies and values, 473
    confident, 525
    global and cultural effectiveness, 499
    movement of, 279
    OED, 303, 307
    relationship management, 483
    risk management, 416
    sound decisions, 521
    talent selection process, 156
decision timeframe in risk management, 416
decline phase in industry lifecycle, 94
decreasing returns in adult learning, 189
defined benefit plans, 254
defined contribution plans, 254
degree requirements, 14–15
delegating tasks, 125
delivery, training, 191
Delphi technique
    OED initiatives, 307
    risk identification, 417
demand analysis in workforce planning, 318
democratization in HR information systems, 356
demographic dichotomy in globalization, 376
demographics
    organizational staffing challenge, 131
    recruiting effectiveness, 142
demonstrator role in change management, 112
demotions, 197
Department of Homeland Security (DHS), 416
departmental organizational structure, 285
design in total rewards strategy, 207
destruction of records, 450
detail challenges in diversity and inclusion, 409–410
determinations in investigations, 349
developing relationships, 484
DHS (Department of Homeland Security), 416
diagramming techniques in risk identification, 418
dialectical inquiry in OED initiatives, 307

diaspora, 375–376
differences, respect for, 493
differential pay, 236–237
differential piece rate pay systems, 234
Differentiated Workforce, 296–297
differentiation in competitive strategies, 100
difficult times, employee and labor relations in, 345
dilemma reconciliation as cross-cultural challenges, 391
dimension-specific issues in diversity and inclusion, 410
direct sales personnel incentive pay, 242–243
direction, setting, 525–526
directives in global context, 397
directorate-generals in European Commission, 396
disabilities
    Americans with Disabilities Act, 49–53
    interview questions, 150
disability benefits
    compliance, 260
    overview, 251
disagreements in global and cultural effectiveness, 499
disciplining employees, 349–351
discounted products and services, 256–257
discretionary assessment methods in talent selection process, 154
discretionary incentives, 237
discrimination complaints, 519
disengaged employees, 162
dispersed leadership, 126
dispositional obstacles to adult learning, 188
diverse cultures and populations, working with, 493
diverse markets, sourcing and recruiting in, 139–140
diverse workforce, return on investment, 498
Diversity and Inclusion (D&I)
    attitudes and behaviors, 408
    benefits and costs, 400
    definitions, 397
    diversity layers, 401
    diversity traits, 402
    globalization, 399–400
    HR roles, 408–411

    key concepts, 397–398
    key terms, 398–399
    managerial skills and practices, 409–410
    organizational change, 408
    program failures, 406–407
    strategy, 402–408
diversity councils, 404
diversity of thought, 398–399
diversity programs in OED initiatives, 308
divestiture
    strategy development, 105–106
    workforce management, 314–315
divisional HR structure, 280
Dobbin, Frank, 407
documentation
    job, 137–139, 224
    performance management, 179
Dodd-Frank Wall Street Reform and Consumer Protection Act, 25
domestic recessions in globalization, 379
downside risk responses, 420–421
downsizing, 314, 316
downstream strategies in globalization, 381
drift, strategic planning for, 87
Drive: The Surprising Truth About What Motivates Us, 173
Drucker, Peter, 114, 202
Drug-Free Workplace Act, 55–56
dual-career ladders
    career development, 197–198
    incentive pay, 243
due diligence
    HR role, 295
    mergers and acquisitions, 315
due process
    discipline, 351
    global context, 394

E

e-learning, 191
e-mail communication, 490
E Nonimmigrant Visas, 67
EAPs (employee assistance programs), 251
early career establishment, 196
EB visas, 69–70
ECA (European Court of Auditors), 396
economic cycles as organizational staffing challenge, 132

economic factors
   knowledge of, 508
   strategy formulation, 93
   total rewards strategy, 214–215
Economic Growth and Tax Relief
   Reconciliation Act (EGTRRA), 25
economic trends in global and cultural
   effectiveness, 496–498
ecosystems in OED, 303
ECPA (Electronic Communications
   Privacy Act), 26
education
   interview questions, 150
   as perquisite, 256
   talent selection process, 155
educational requirements in job
   descriptions, 137
educator role in change
   management, 112
EEC (European Economic
   Community), 395
EEO (Equal Employment
   Opportunity)
   employer and employee rights, 332
   record-keeping requirements, 446
EEOA (Equal Employment
   Opportunity Act), 56
EEOC (Equal Employment
   Opportunity Commission)
   discrimination guidelines, 57
   talent selection process, 146
effect risk control, 420
effective communication, 487
effectiveness
   risk management, 425–426
   talent management measures, 326
EGTRRA (Economic Growth and Tax
   Relief Reconciliation Act), 25
Electronic Communications Privacy
   Act (ECPA), 26
elite corporate culture, 388
emergency contact information in
   interview questions, 152
emergency preparedness, 422–424
emergency temporary standards in
   Occupational Safety and Health
   Act, 39
emergent leadership, 126
Emerson, Ralph Waldo, 496
emotional elements in ROI
   maximization, 517
emotional intelligence
   diversity and inclusion, 408
   leadership, 119, 200

   tools, 202
   transformational leadership, 464
emotional quotient (EQ), 494
empathy in leadership, 119
employee advocacy vs. organizational
   success, 472
employee affinity groups, 404
Employee and Labor Relations
   conflicts, 346–348
   definitions, 330
   discipline, 349–351
   employment relationship, 332–339
   faltering, 345–351
   investigations, 348–349
   key concepts, 330–331
   third-party influences, 339–344
employee assistance programs
   (EAPs), 251
employee development
   OED, 302
   overview, 321–326
Employee Engagement and Retention
   assessing, 164–168
   benefits, 162
   business case, 167–168
   business results and employee
    growth, 180
   challenges, 163–164
   data analysis, 167
   employee life cycle, 168–174
   evaluating, 183
   focus groups, 166
   information gathering, 164–167
   interviews, 166
   key concepts, 159–161
   as leading indicator, 523
   motivation theories, 170–174
   organizational culture, 162–163
   overview, 161–162
   performance management,
    174–179
   retention, 180–183
   separation process, 174
   strategy, 164
employee feedback metrics, 115
employee handbooks, 358
employee leasing, 324
employee lifecycle (ELC)
   employee engagement, 168–174
   organizational staffing challenge, 132
   total rewards strategy, 216
Employee Polygraph Protection Act, 26
employee recognition and reward,
   338–339

employee records management
   investigation files, 443–444
   medical files, 443
   overview, 439
   personnel files, 440–443
   retention requirements, 444–450
employee relations in personnel
   files, 442
employee resource groups for diversity
   and inclusion, 404
Employee Retirement Income Security
   Act (ERISA), 26, 258
employee satisfaction in total rewards
   strategy, 210
employee self-service (ESS) software
   career development, 196
   HR information systems, 356
   total rewards strategy, 218
employee separations in personnel
   files, 441
employee stock ownership plans
   (ESOPs), 240
employee stock purchase plans
   (ESPPs), 240
employee surveys, 164–167
employee value propositions (EVPs), 136
employee volunteerism, 435
employees
   guiding, 515–516
   organizational strategy role, 294
employment branding, 135–136, 140
employment checks in talent selection
   process, 155
employment contracts, 335–336
employment equity in total rewards
   strategy, 209
employment law and regulations in
   U.S. See U.S. Employment Law and
   Regulations
employment protections in Civil
   Rights Act (Title VII), 54
employment relationship
   employee communication, 339
   employee recognition and reward,
    338–339
   employer and employee rights,
    332–337
   manager and supervisors, 339
   programs overview, 332
   strategy, 337–338
employment requests for application in
   personnel files, 440
employment visas for foreign nationals,
   67–70

enforcement
    Americans with Disabilities Act, 53
    Drug-Free Workplace Act, 56
    Fair Labor Standards Act, 31
    Mine Safety and Health Act, 34
    Occupational Safety and Health
      Act, 38
    Sarbanes-Oxley Act, 42
engagement, employee. *See* Employee
    Engagement and Retention
engaging relationships, building,
    477–478
enterprise perspective in risk
    management, 415
enterprise social media (ESN), 330
entitlement-oriented culture in total
    rewards strategy, 208
environment considerations
    external, 288
    internal, 287
environment in United Nations
    Global Compact, 430–431
environmental factors
    job descriptions, 137
    ROI maximization, 517
    strategy formulation, 93
environmental scanning in strategy
    formulation, 92–96
EPA (Equal Pay Act), 27, 209
EPRG model, 383
Equal Employment Opportunity Act
    (EEOA), 56
Equal Employment Opportunity
    Commission (EEOC)
    discrimination guidelines, 57
    talent selection process, 146
Equal Employment Opportunity (EEO)
    employer and employee rights, 332
    record-keeping requirements, 446
Equal Pay Act (EPA), 27, 209
equal pay compliance, 259
equity
    talent selection process, 155
    total rewards strategy, 208–209
ERISA (Employee Retirement Income
    Security Act), 26, 258
errors in appraisal methods, 177–179
ESOPs (employee stock ownership
    plans), 240
espoused values in cultures, 389
ESPPs (employee stock purchase
    plans), 240
essay format in performance
    management, 177

essential job functions
    Americans with Disabilities Act, 51
    job descriptions, 137
esteem in Maslow's hierarchy of needs,
    170–171
ethical agents, 468
ethical behavior in leadership, 128
ethical grounding in transformational
    leadership, 464
Ethical Practice competency, 9
    definitions, 467–468
    description, 12
    key concepts, 467
    proficiency indicators, 468–474
    summary, 475
ethics and HR changes, 279
ethnocentric operation in
    globalization, 383
ethnocentric orientation in total
    rewards strategy, 212
ETJ (extraterritorial jurisdiction), 395
European Central Bank, 396
European Commission, 396
European Council, 396
European Court of Auditors
    (ECA), 396
European Economic Community
    (EEC), 395
European Parliament (EP), 396
European Union, 395
"Evaluating Training Programs," 193
evaluation
    critical activities, 508
    diversity and inclusion, 406
    employee engagement, 183
    global and cultural effectiveness, 499
    job, 224–228
    mergers and acquisitions, 105
    retention, 182
    risk management, 424–426
    risks, 419
    strategy performance, 113–118
    talent selection process,
      153–155
    total rewards strategy, 207, 219
    training and development, 193
evolution
    diversity and inclusion, 407
    HR professionals, 275–278
EVPs (employee value propositions), 136
exam
    application deadlines, 16
    content outline, 16–17
    delivery, duration, and format, 16

    identification and conduct
      guidelines, 17–18
    personal experience, 18–20
    scoring, 20–21
executive commitment in diversity and
    inclusion, 403
Executive Order 11246—Affirmative
    Action, 60–61
executive summaries in HR business
    case, 503
executives
    coaching, 519–520
    employment visas for, 68
    incentive pay, 239–242
exempt employees
    compliance, 259
    description, 138
expectations with stakeholders, 461
expense per employee metric, 504
experience in adult learning, 186
expert judgment in risk
    identification, 418
expert knowledge, maintaining, 507,
    524–525
expertise as proficiency indicator,
    462–463
extended organizations
    HR impact, 279
    restructuring, 314
external dimensions in diversity, 401
external environment considerations, 288
external equity in total rewards
    strategy, 209
external job evaluation, 227–228
external market knowledge in diversity
    and inclusion, 403
external recruiting, 140
external relationships, managing,
    479–480
external risks, 415
external staffing factors, 135
external strategies in knowledge
    management systems, 329–330
*Extraordinary Leader: Turning Good
    Managers into Great Leaders*, 464
extraterritorial jurisdiction (ETJ), 395

F

FAA Modernization and Reform
    Act, 27
face-to-face communication, 490
FACT (Fair and Accurate Credit
    Transactions Act), 27

factor comparison job evaluation methods, 224–225, 227
factor evaluation system (FES), 226
Fair and Accurate Credit Transactions Act (FACT), 27
Fair Credit Reporting Act (FCRA), 27
Fair Labor Standards Act (FLSA)
employee volunteerism, 435
enforcement, 31
overtime pay, 30–31
provisions and protections, 28
recordkeeping, 28–30
fairness orientation in total rewards strategy, 208
False Claims Act, 65–66
Family and Medical Leave Act (FMLA)
overview, 61
violations, 519
family and medical leaves records, 447
family-oriented benefits, 248
fashion models, employment visas for, 67
fatalities and catastrophes in Occupational Safety and Health Act, 38
FCPA (Foreign Corrupt Practices Act), 31
FCRA (Fair Credit Reporting Act), 27
Federal Equal Pay Act, 209
federal government employees, laws and regulations for, 64–67
Federal Insurance Contributions Act (FICA), 44
Federal Labor Relations Authority (FLRA), 65
Federal records retention requirements, 444–450
feedback
constructive, 486–487
investigations, 349
metrics, 115
performance management, 175–179
as recognition and reward, 339
soliciting, 488–489
FI-LR matrix for globalization, 382
FICA (Federal Insurance Contributions Act), 44
fiduciary responsibility, 261
Fiedler, Fred, 125
Fiedler contingency theory, 125–126
finance metrics, 115
financial analysis function, 282–283

financial statements, 115
financial status in interview questions, 150
Finkelstein, Sydney, 200
first-impression errors in interviews, 153
fishbone diagrams, 309
fishbowl interviews, 148
Fisher, Glen, 495
flat organizational structure, 285
flat-rate pay systems, 232
flexible staffing, 323
flexible work hours, 248
flow analysis in workforce planning, 317–318
FLRA (Federal Labor Relations Authority), 65
FLSA. See Fair Labor Standards Act (FLSA)
FMLA (Family and Medical Leave Act)
overview, 61
violations, 519
focus
competitive strategies, 100–101
strategic planning for, 87
focus groups for employee engagement, 166
Folkman, Joseph, 464
follow-ups
meetings, 515
Occupational Safety and Health Act, 38
forced choices in performance management, 176
forecasts
workforce management, 312
workforce planning, 318
Foreign Corrupt Practices Act (FCPA), 31
foreign nationals, employment visas for, 67–70
formula budgeting, 283
foundational knowledge items (FKIs) in exam, 16
Four-Level Training Evaluation Model, 193
Fox, Erica, 118–119
frameworks for corporate social responsibility, 429–435
framing in communication, 491
free products and services, 256–257
Freeman, R. Edward, 90–91
frequencies distributions and tables in compensation analysis, 229

Friedman, Thomas L., 375
fringe benefits, 206
full-time employees, 139
function-specific audits, 292
functional structure
new HR structure, 280
organizational design, 286–287
"Future Insights," 304

G

gainsharing plans, 238–239
Gantt charts, 110
gap analysis
benefits needs assessment, 246
workforce planning, 318
gap development, organizational, 305–306
GE-McKinsey nine-box matrix, 96–97
gender and sexual orientation claims, 519
gender in talent selection process, 146
general pay increases, 235–236
generalists, HR, 290
Genetic Information Nondiscrimination Act (GINA), 56–57
geocentric operation in globalization, 382
geocentric orientation in total rewards strategy, 212
geographic differential pay, 237
geographic structure in organizational design, 287
geography in compensation analysis, 229
Germany
diversity, 400
health plans, 250
GINA (Genetic Information Nondiscrimination Act), 56–57
Global and Cultural Effectiveness competency, 9
definitions, 491–492
description, 12
key concepts, 492
proficiency indicators, 492–500
summary, 500
global assignments, 391
guidelines, 392–393
process, 393
strategic role, 392
types, 392
global basis in talent acquisition planning, 134–135

global considerations in leadership development, 203–204
global context
    definitions, 373
    global assignments, 391–393
    global organizations, 377–378
    global strategies, 378–386
    globalization factors, 374–377
    key concepts, 374
    legal environment, 394–397
    multicultural organizations, 386–390
global engagement drivers in employee engagement, 163
global integration (GI) vs. local responsiveness, 380–383
global labor market direction, communicating, 507
Global Leadership and Organizational Behavior Effectiveness (GLOBE) Research Program, 127
global leadership models, 126–127
global-local models, 381
global mind-set
    diversity and inclusion, 408
    multicultural organizations, 386–387
    operating with, 495
global organizations
    defining, 377–378
    employee recognition and reward, 338–339
Global Professional in Human Resources (GPHR), 6
global recession, 376
global remuneration issues and challenges in total rewards strategy, 211–212
Global Reporting Initiative (GRI) G4 Sustainability Guidelines, 433–434
global strategies, 378
    approaches, 380–383
    employment relationship, 338
    EPRG model, 383
    pull factors, 379–380
    push factors, 378–379
    sourcing and shoring, 383–384
Global Union Federations (GUFs), 340
global warming, 376
globalization
    diversity, 399–400
    forces shaping, 375
    global recession and global warming, 376

HR impact, 278–279
HR roles, 384–386
learning & development, 185–186
shift from developed to emerging economies, 375–376
goals and objectives
    risk management, 416
    strategy formulation, 97–98
    strategy performance, 114
    training and development, 190
golden parachutes, 239
Goldsmith, Marshall, 118
Goleman, Daniel, 118–119
government and regulatory barriers in organizational staffing, 132
government policies and regulations
    globalization, 379
    influencing, 510
governments
    employee and labor relations, 342
    organizational strategy role, 294
GPHR (Global Professional in Human Resources), 6
grades, pay, 230–232
graduate degree requirements, 14
graphic presentation in strategy performance, 117–118
graphic scales in performance management, 176
Great Britain, diversity in, 400
green circle pay rates, 235
Gregersen, Hal B., 409
grievances, 343–344
group decision-making in OED initiatives, 307
group interviews in recruitment, 148
groups
    incentive pay, 238
    recruiting effectiveness, 141
groupware, 359
growth opportunities in globalization, 379
growth phase in industry lifecycle, 94
Growth Share Matrix, 95–96
growth strategies
    staffing, 134
    strategy development, 102–105
guarded globalization, 378
GUFs (Global Union Federations), 340
guidelines
    corporate social responsibility, 429–435
    interview questions, 149

Guidelines for Multinational Enterprises, 430
Guidelines on Discrimination Because of Sex, 57

H

H Visas, 67–68
Half, Robert, 181
Hall's theory for cultures, 390
halo errors
    interviews, 153
    performance appraisals, 177
Hampden-Turner, Charles, 390
handbooks, employee, 358
hard negotiation style in conflict management, 130
hardship testing, 202
Harris, Doug, 408
Hay plan for job evaluation, 226
headcounts in recruiting effectiveness, 141
health and welfare plans, 249–252
health care laws and regulations
    compliance, 260
    Consolidated Omnibus Budget Reconciliation Act, 59
    Patient Protection and Affordable Care Act, 62–63
Health Information Technology for Economic and Clinical Health Act (HITECH), 31
Health Insurance Portability and Accountability Act (HIPAA)
    medical files, 443
    overview, 32
health records record-keeping requirements, 445
height and weight in interview questions, 151
Heneman, Herbert G., III, 221
Hersey-Blanchard situational leadership theory, 123–125
Herzberg's motivation-hygiene theory, 171
hierarchy culture in OED assessment, 311
high-context cultures, 390
HIPAA (Health Insurance Portability and Accountability Act)
    medical files, 443
    overview, 32

hiring process. *See also* talent
  selection process
    diversity and inclusion, 404
    employee engagement, 168–169
histograms, 309
history, organizational, 296
HITECH (Health Information
  Technology for Economic and
  Clinical Health Act), 31
Hofstede, Geert, 127, 390
holiday pay compliance, 259
holidays, 246–247
holistic business knowledge in diversity
  and inclusion, 403
home purchase/lease escape fees, 325
home-shoring, 377
Homeland Security Act, 66
horizontal corporate culture, 388
horn effect
  interviews, 153
  performance appraisals, 177
hours of work
  compliance, 259
  country differences, 495
  flexible, 248
  job descriptions, 137
  Portal-to-Portal Act, 40
  record-keeping requirements, 444
  shortened workweeks, 323
housing as perquisite, 256
How to Manage Change Effectively, 111
HR Certification Institute (HRCI),
  4–6
HR Expertise (HR Knowledge)
  competency, 9, 11
HR function organization.
  See Structure of the HR Function
HR information systems (HRIS),
  355–357
HR management business case,
  502–503
HR metrics in recruiting
  effectiveness, 141
HR-related degree requirements,
  14–15
HR roles
  conflict management, 346
  diversity and inclusion, 408–411
  employee engagement, 174
  leadership development, 200
  strategies, 293–297
HR Strategic Planning, 85
  key concepts, 86
  leadership, 118–130

strategy, 87–91
strategy development, 98–107
strategy formulation, 92–98
strategy implementation
  production, 107–113
strategy performance evaluation,
  113–118
HRCI (HR Certification Institute), 4–6
HRIS (HR information systems),
  355–357
human capital
  global and cultural effectiveness, 497
  metrics in big data era, 354
  vision development, 516–517
human resource certification, 3
  benefits, 4
  chapter review, 6–7
  choosing, 15
  description, 3–4
  organizations, 4–6
human rights in United Nations
  Global Compact, 430
Huselid, Mark, 296–297
Hutchins, Kate, 392
hybrid structure in organizational
  design, 287
hyper-connectivity in globalization, 376

I

ICE (Immigration and Customs
  Enforcement), 66
ideas, openness to, 492
identification and conduct guidelines
  for exam, 17–18
identify alignment in globalization, 381
identifying risks, 417–418
IFAs (international framework
  agreements), 340
ignore action as risk response, 421
illness, leave for, 247
ILO (International Labor
  Organization), 333
immigrant investors, employment visas
  for, 70
Immigration and Customs
  Enforcement (ICE), 66
Immigration and Nationality
  Act (INA), 32
Immigration Reform and Control
  Act (IRCA), 32
imminent danger situations in
  Occupational Safety and Health
  Act, 38

impact
  business strategies, 101–102
  change, 278–281
  for data analysis, communicating,
    527–528
  of laws, assessing, 521–522
implementation
  mergers and acquisitions,
    104–105, 316
  risk management plans, 424
  strategy, 107–113
  total rewards strategy, 207
  training and development,
    192–193
improshare plans, 239
in-house experts, serving as, 513
INA (Immigration and Nationality
  Act), 32
incentive pay
  cross-border situations, 242
  direct sales personnel, 242–243
  executives, 239–242
  gainsharing plans, 238–239
  groups, 238
  individual, 237
  outside directors, 243
  professionals, 243
  profit-sharing plans, 238
incentive stock options (ISOs), 240
incentives in total rewards, 206
incidents investigations in risk
  management, 425
inclusion. *See also* Diversity and
  Inclusion (D&I)
  embracing, 494
  ensuring, 496
income benefits in workers'
  compensation, 252
income tax record-keeping
  requirements, 447
increased communication in OED, 302
increased profits in OED, 302
increasing returns in adult learning, 189
incremental budgeting, 283
indirect compensation. *See* benefits
individual incentive pay, 237
individual perspective in leadership
  development, 200
individualism
  vs. collectivism in culture, 389
  leadership, 127
individualized compensation in total
  rewards strategy, 218
Indosphere culture, 388

indulgence vs. restraint in cultures, 390
industrial actions in employee and labor relations, 345
industry analysis in strategy formulation, 94–96
industry lifecycle, 94
industry rivalry in strategy formulation, 95
industry understanding as proficiency indicator, 502
influencing as HR role, 294–295
information
    analyzing, 526–527
    risk management, 416
    seeking, 526
information exchange in HR role, 294
information gathering
    employee engagement, 164–167
    strategy formulation, 92
information systems, HR, 355–357
information technology
    core business functions, 284
    staffing, 135
infrastructure creation in diversity and inclusion, 403
initiatives
    OED, 306–310
    retention, 181–182
    return on investment, 504–505
inner team, 119
input, stakeholders, 462
institutional obstacles to adult learning, 188
instructor-led training, 191
instructor selection in training, 192
insupportable opinions in personnel files, 443
integration
    diversity and inclusion, 407
    mergers and acquisitions, 104, 316
    risk management, 421
integrity
    acting with, 468
    personal and professional, 468
    talent selection tests, 154
intellectual property, 332
inter-rater or inter-observer reliability in talent selection process, 154
intercultural wisdom, 408
internal dimensions in diversity, 401
internal environment considerations, 287
internal equity in total rewards strategy, 209

internal job evaluation, 224–227
internal mobility in career development, 197–198
internal recruiting, 140
internal relationships, managing, 479–480
internal strategies in knowledge management systems, 329
international assignments in career development, 197
international background checks in talent selection process, 155
international framework agreements (IFAs), 340
international human rights and labor standards, 333–334
International Labor Organization (ILO), 333
international laws, 395
International Organization for Standardization (ISO) standards
    OED quality initiatives, 308–309
    risk principles, 415
internationalization of unions, 340
Internet recruiting, 144
interns, 139
Interpersonal Cluster
    communication, 484–491
    Global and Cultural Effectiveness, 491–500
    relationship management, 475–484
interventions
    generating, 514
    organizational, 317
interviews, 147
    biases, 152–153
    employee engagement, 166
    guidelines, 148
    investigations, 349
    job analysis, 222
    questions, 149–152
    risk identification, 417
    types, 147–148
intra-company transferee visas, 68
intra-organizational culture, fostering, 483
intrinsic motivation in employee engagement, 173
introduction phase in industry lifecycle, 94
inventories for leadership skills, 200–201

investigations
    employee and labor relations, 348–349
    in personnel files, 442–444
    supervising, 518–519
investment barriers in globalization, 380
investment decisions in strategy formulation, 95–96
invisible diversity traits, 402
IRCA (Immigration Reform and Control Act), 32
IRS Intermediate Sanctions, 33
Ishikawa diagrams, 309
Islamic culture, 388
ISO 26000 for corporate social responsibility, 431–432
ISO (International Organization for Standardization) standards
    OED quality initiatives, 308–309
    risk principles, 415
ISOs (incentive stock options), 240

J

JAN (Job Accommodation Network), 52
Japanese management style, 172
JetBlue airlines, 493–494
job accommodation in Americans with Disabilities Act, 51–52
Job Accommodation Network (JAN), 52
job analysis
    compensation structure, 221–224
    overview, 136–137
job boards, 140
job descriptions
    elements, 137–139
    employment contracts, 335
    job analysis, 222
job documentation, 224
job evaluation, 224–228
job openings as organizational staffing challenge, 133
job previewing in talent selection process, 157–158
job rotation, enlargement, and enrichment in career development, 197
job sharing, 323
job-to-predetermined-standard comparison, 225–226
judgmental forecasts in workforce planning, 318
judicial decisions in global context, 397
jurisdiction in global context, 394

K

Kaizen
    risk management, 426
    staffing plans, 321
Kalev, Alexandrea, 407
Kaplan, Robert S., 415, 508
Katzenbach, Jon, 126
Kerns, Charles D., 469–470
key risk indicators (KRIs), 419
kinesthetic learners, 187
Kirkpatrick, Donald, 111, 193
knowledge
    maintaining, 471
    transferring, 522
knowledge-based pay systems, 234
knowledge items in exam, 16
knowledge management (KM)
    learning & development, 185
    organizational, 327–328
    strategy, 329–330
    systems, 328–329
    workforce management, 327
Kouzes, James M., 118, 485–486
KPMG survey for corporate social
    responsibility, 434–435
Kramer, Roderick M., 496
Kubler-Ross, Elisabeth, 110

L

L-1 Intra-Company Transferee visas, 68
labor
    global markets, 498
    in United Nations Global
        Compact, 430
labor laws, country differences, 494
Labor-Management Relations Act
    (LMRA), 33
Labor-Management Reporting and
    Disclosure Act, 33–34, 49
labor relations. *See* Employee and
    Labor Relations
labor unions
    employee and labor relations,
        340–345
    organizational strategy role, 294
    record-keeping requirements, 449
lag market pay strategies, 210
lagging indicators in OED, 310
late-career in career development, 196
laws and statutory regulations
    case law summary by chapter,
        575–584
    employment, 334–335

global context, 397
impact assessment, 521–522
total rewards strategy, 214
U.S. *See* U.S. Employment Law
    and Regulations; U.S. laws and
    regulations
Lawson v. FMR LLC., 42
layers
    cultures, 389
    diversity, 401
layoffs
    Worker Adjustment and Retraining
        Notification Act, 63
    workforce management, 314
lead market pay strategies, 210
leader development, 199
    global considerations, 203–204
    needs assessment, 200–202
    programs, 200
    strategies, 202–203
leaders
    HR, 289
    leader-member relations, 125
    OED, 302
Leaders and Followers theory, 126–127
leadership
    change management, 112
    characteristics, 118–121
    employee engagement, 163
    leaders description, 118
    theories, 121–130
Leadership and Navigation
    competency, 9
    definitions, 460
    description, 12
    key concepts, 460
    proficiency indicators, 461–467
Leadership Challenge, 485–486
Leadership cluster
    Ethical Practice, 467–475
    Leadership and Navigation,
        459–467
    overview, 459
leading element in global and cultural
    effectiveness, 499
leading indicators
    identifying, 523–524
    OED, 310
leading meetings, 487–488
Learning and Development
    adult learning, 185–189
    career development, 194–199
    definitions, 183
    factors, 185–186

key concepts, 183–184
leadership development,
    199–204
overview, 184–185
training and development,
    189–193
learning curves for adult learning,
    188–189
learning management systems
    (LMSs), 191
learning portals, 191
leasing employees, 324
leave
    compliance, 259–260
    types, 247–248
legal environment in global context,
    394–397
legal factors in strategy formulation, 93
legal institutions in global context, 396
legal instruments in global context,
    396–397
legislation for compensation and
    benefits, 257–261
length of employment contracts, 335
leniency errors in performance
    appraisals, 179
leveling in compensation analysis, 228
levels
    employee engagement, 162
    global legal environment,
        394–395
    strategy, 88–89
leveraging technology, 353–354, 504
liabilities, recognizing, 519
life insurance, 251–252
Light Duty Assignments provision, 61
Lilly Ledbetter Fair Pay Act, 57
limiting hours worked, country
    differences, 495
listening
    communicating, 486
    listener needs and expectations, 128
    during meetings, 514
    proficiency indicator, 516
    relationship management, 477
litigation in conflicts, 347–348
LMRA (Labor-Management Relations
    Act), 33
local responsiveness (LR)
    vs. global integration, 380–383
    talent acquisition strategy, 134
logistical considerations in training, 193
logs in strategy implementation, 110
long-term incentives, 239

long-term orientation
  leadership, 127
  vs. short-term orientation in
    cultures, 390
low-context cultures, 390
lump-sum pay increases (LSIs), 236

M

Maastricht Treaty on European
  Union, 395
major life activities in Americans with
  Disabilities Act, 51
managed service providers (MSPs),
  324–325
management
  employee engagement, 163
  OED, 302
Management by Objectives, 114
management by objectives (MBO) in
  performance management, 176
management by walking around
  (MBWA), 426
manager self-service (MSS) tools, 356
managerial skills and practices in
  diversity and inclusion, 409–410
managers
  employment relationship, 339
  employment visas for, 68
  HR, 289
marital status in interview questions, 151
market-based job evaluation, 227–228
market-based pay increases, 236
market culture in OED assessment, 311
marketing
  core business functions, 284
  diversity and inclusion, 405
  HR, 503
  metrics, 115
masculinity
  vs. femininity in cultures, 390
  leadership, 127
Maslow's hierarchy of needs, 170–171
mass layoffs, 63
match market pay strategies, 210
material safety data sheets (MSDSs), 34
maternity leave, 247
Matisoff, James, 388
matrices
  GE-McKinsey nine-box matrix,
    96–97
  Growth Share Matrix, 95–96
  risk analysis, 419

matrix HR structure, 280
matrix organizational structure, 286
maturity curves in incentive pay, 243
maturity phase in industry lifecycle, 94
Mayers, Juliette C., 499
MBO (management by objectives) in
  performance management, 176
MBWA (management by walking
  around), 426
McGregor's theory
  employee engagement,
    171–172
  leadership, 122
McKinsey report on diversity
  programs, 308
meal allowances, 257
means in compensation analysis,
  229–230
measurability in globalization, 376
measurement and metrics
  benefits, 257
  big data era, 354
  compensation structure,
    229–230, 244
  diversity and inclusion, 406
  globalization, 385
  HR value, 291–293
  mergers and acquisitions, 316
  OED, 310–311
  organizational, 503–504
  performance management,
    175–179
  recruiting effectiveness, 141–144
  relationship management, 481
  retention, 182
  SMART goal setting, 98
  strategy performance, 113–118
  talent management effectiveness, 326
  total rewards strategy, 219
media in communication, 489–491
medians in compensation analysis, 229
mediation for grievances, 344
medical benefits in workers'
  compensation, 252
Medical Certification Process
  provision, 61
medical conditions in interview
  questions, 150
medical files, 443
medical records in personnel
  files, 442
Medicare tax record-keeping
  requirements, 448

meetings
  appraisal, 179
  leading, 487–488
  relationship building during,
    514–515
memoranda of understanding
  (MOUs), 343
Mental Health Parity Act (MHPA), 62
Mental Health Parity and Addiction
  Equity Act (MHPAEA), 62
mental requirements in job
  descriptions, 137
mentoring, 199
mergers and acquisitions (M&As)
  restructuring, 315–316
  strategy development, 103–105
merit pay, 233
Merit Systems Protection Board
  (MSPB), 64
mertial aspects in GRI, 433
MHPA (Mental Health Parity Act), 62
MHPAEA (Mental Health Parity and
  Addiction Equity Act), 62
midcareer in career development, 196
Mikes, Annette, 415
milestone charts, 110
Military Caregiver Leave provision, 61
military service in interview
  questions, 151
Mine Safety and Health Act, 34
minimum wage compliance, 259
Mintzberg, Henry, 87, 118
mission
  strategy formulation, 96–97
  total rewards strategy, 208
mistakes acknowledging, 469
mobile devices as perquisites, 256
mobile learning, 192
modes in compensation analysis,
  229–230
monitoring mergers and acquisitions,
  105, 316
moral hazard in risk management, 416
Morrison, Allen J., 409
mortgage subsidies, 326
Mossevelde, Chris, 135
motivation
  adult learning, 186
  leadership characteristics, 119
  theories, 170–174
  total rewards strategy, 210
MOUs (memoranda of
  understanding), 343

Mouton, Jane, 122

moving work in globalization, 377

MSDSs (material safety data sheets), 34

MSPB (Merit Systems Protection Board), 64

MSPs (managed service providers), 324–325

multicultural organizations
  cultural issues, 387–391
  global mind-set, 386–387

multidomestic strategy, 382

multinational organizations, recognition in, 173

multiple jobs in career development, 199

N

NAHRMA (North American Human Resource Management Association), 6

name in interview questions, 151

narrative evaluations in performance management, 177

National Defense Authorization Act, 62

National Guard and Military Reserve Family Leave provision, 61

national holidays, 247

National Industrial Recovery Act, 35

National Labor Relations Act (NLRA)
  overview, 35
  unfair labor practices, 345

National Labor Relations Board (NLRB), 345

national laws, 395

national origin in interview questions, 149

near-shoring, 377, 384

Needlestick Safety and Prevention Act, 35–36

Neeleman, David, 493

negative emphasis in interviews, 153

negotiation
  conflict management methods, 130
  HR role, 294–295
  relationship management, 476, 482

Nelson, Sheri, 478

Netherlands, health plans in, 250

networking
  policies, 360
  relationship management, 476, 481

networks in employee and labor relations, 340

new entrants in strategy formulation, 95

new HR organizational structures, 280

nine-box matrix, 96–97

NLRA (National Labor Relations Act)
  overview, 35
  unfair labor practices, 345

NLRB (National Labor Relations Board), 345

no action as risk response, 421

nominal group technique in OED initiatives, 307

non-agricultural workers, employment visas for, 68

noncash awards, 237

nondiscrimination records record-keeping requirements, 446

nonexempt employees, 138

nonfinancial organizational performance metrics, 115

nonjudgmental respect for perspectives of others, 492

nonquantitative job-content job evaluation, 224–225

nonselected candidates in talent selection process, 156–157

nontraditional employment in career development, 199

nonverbal bias in interviews, 153

normal standards in Occupational Safety and Health Act, 39

Norris-LaGuardia Act, 36

North American Human Resource Management Association (NAHRMA), 6

Norton, David P., 508

not engaged employees, 162

notice requirements in Worker Adjustment and Retraining Notification Act, 64

O

O-1 visas, 69

objectives in strategy performance, 113

OBRA (Omnibus Budget Reconciliation Act), 39

observation in job analysis, 222

OCAI (Organizational Culture Assessment Instrument), 311

occupational preparation in career development, 196

Occupational Safety and Health Act (OSHA), 36–39

occupational safety record-keeping requirements, 445

ODEP (Office of Disability Employment Policy), 157

OECD (Organization for Economic Cooperation and Development)
  corporate social responsibility guidelines, 430
  overview, 333

OED. *See* Organizational Effectiveness and Development (OED)

OFCCP (Office of Federal Contract Compliance Programs), 146

off-shoring, 377, 383

offers in talent selection process, 156

Office of Disability Employment Policy (ODEP), 157

Office of Federal Contract Compliance Programs (OFCCP), 146

Office of Personnel Management (OPM), 64

Older Workers Benefit Protection Act (OWBPA), 59–60

Omnibus Budget Reconciliation Act (OBRA), 39

on-call employees, 139

On Death and Dying, 110

on-shoring, 377, 384

on-site visits in Occupational Safety and Health Act, 38

on-the-job training, 191

onboarding
  diversity and inclusion, 404
  employee engagement, 168–169
  employee lifecycle, 216
  Talent Acquisition, 159

one-on-one conflict resolution, 347

one-on-one interviews for employee engagement, 166

online employee surveys, 165

open-ended questionnaires in job analysis, 222

openness to ideas, 492

operational level in strategy, 88

operational services in HR function, 277–278

operations function, 284

operations management as proficiency indicator, 502

OPM (Office of Personnel Management), 64

opportunities in SWOT analysis, 94, 505

opportunity costs in diversity, 400

oral employment contracts, 335–336

oral presentations, 490

oral warnings for discipline, 350

Organization for Economic
 Cooperation and Development
 (OECD)
  corporate social responsibility
   guidelines, 430
  overview, 333
organization incentive pay plans,
 240–242
Organization Knowledge domain, 273
  chapter review, 361
  Employee and Labor Relations. *See*
   Employee and Labor Relations
  Organizational Effectiveness and
   Development, 297–311
  questions, 361–371
  Structure of the HR Function. *See*
   Structure of the HR Function
  Technology Management, 351–361
  Workforce Management. *See*
   Workforce Management
organization learning, 185
organization memberships in interview
 questions, 151
organizational change in diversity and
 inclusion, 408
organizational compliance for U.S.
 employment law and regulations, 438
organizational cultural norms,
 fostering, 498
organizational culture
  conforming to, 461
  employee engagement, 162–163
Organizational Culture Assessment
 Instrument (OCAI), 311
organizational culture change as
 proficiency indicator, 466
organizational design
  core business functions, 284
  OED, 301
organizational dimensions in
 diversity, 401
organizational effectiveness,
 championing, 480
Organizational Effectiveness and
 Development (OED)
  benefits, 301–302
  definitions, 297–298
  HR roles, 304
  initiatives, 306–310
  key concepts, 298
  measurement, 310–311
  opportunities, 303–304

organizational gap development,
 305–306
 overview, 299–304
 process, 299–300
 strategies, 300–304
organizational entry in career
 development, 196
organizational gap development,
 305–306
organizational growth and retraction in
 HR impact, 279–280
organizational interventions,
 generating, 514
organizational level strategy, 88
organizational metrics, 503–504
organizational perspective in leadership
 development, 200
organizational problems, examining, 506
organizational staffing requirements,
 131–133
organizational strategy
  HR role, 293–297
  total rewards, 205–219
organizational structures, 284–287
organizational success vs. employee
 advocacy, 472
organizational values
  diversity and inclusion, 409
  performance management, 175
  strategy formulation, 97
organizations for human resource
 certification, 4–6
orientation
  adult learning, 186
  employee lifecycle, 216
  staffing, 134
  talent acquisition, 158
  transformational leadership, 464
OSHA (Occupational Safety and
 Health Act), 36–39
Ouchi, William, 172
outside directors, incentive pay for, 243
outsourcing
  alternative staffing, 324
  globalization, 377, 384
oversight in risk management, 424
overtime pay
  compliance, 259
  Fair Labor Standards Act, 30–31
OWBPA (Older Workers Benefit
 Protection Act), 59–60
ownership of risk, 420

P

P visas, 69
packing/shipping/unpacking
 payments, 326
paid holidays, 246–247
paid time off (PTO)
  country differences, 494
  holidays and vacations, 246–247
paid vacations, country differences
 in, 495
paired-comparison method for jobs, 225
panel interviews, 148
parental status in interview
 questions, 151
Pareto charts, 309
part-time employees, 139
participating tasks in leadership, 125
partnerships, cross-cultural, 499–500
paternity leave, 247
Patient Protection and Affordable Care
 Act (PPACA), 62–63
PATRIOT Act, 66–67
pay. *See also* compensation
  adjustments, 235–236
  compression, 235
  strategies, 209–210
  structure, 230–232
  surveys, 228
  variations, 234–235
pay equity in total rewards strategy, 209
pay for performance, 233
payments, retirement, 255
payroll record-keeping requirements,
 444–445
payrolling alternative staffing, 324
penalties in Civil Rights Act (Title
 VII), 54
pension compliance, 260
pension plans record-keeping
 requirements, 449
Pension Protection Act (PPA), 39
People Knowledge expertise domain, 85
  chapter review, 261
  Employee Engagement and
   Retention. *See* Employee
   Engagement and Retention
  HR Strategic Planning. *See* HR
   Strategic Planning
  Learning and Development.
   See Learning and Development
  questions, 261–267

Talent Acquisition. *See* Talent Acquisition
Total Rewards. *See* Total Rewards
peoplepower reporting for recruiting effectiveness, 141
PEOs (professional employer organizations)
    alternative staffing, 324
    risk, 420
percentiles for pay ranges, 230
perceptual elements in ROI maximization, 517
performance appraisals
    job analysis, 223
    personnel files, 441
performance-based merit pay systems, 233
performance grants, 241
performance improvement in OED, 300
performance management, 174
    appraisal methods, 175–179
    HR value, 291–292
    measurement and feedback, 175–179
    organizational values and goals, 175
    standards, 175
performance objectives in risk management, 421
performance requirements in employment contracts, 336
performance strategy, 113–118
performance tests in talent selection process, 153
Perlmutter, Howard V., 211, 383
perquisites
    incentive pay, 239
    total rewards, 206
    types, 256–257
Perruci, Gamaliel, 409
person-based pay systems, 234
personal growth and development in total rewards strategy, 210
personal integrity, 468
personal postings policies, 360
Personal Responsibility and Work Opportunity Reconciliation Act, 39–40
personality layer in diversity, 401
personality tests in talent selection process, 153
personally identifiable information (PII), 356
personnel file contents, 440–443

perspectives
    cultural context, 494
    embracing, 494
perspectives of others, nonjudgmental respect for, 492
persuasion
    global and cultural effectiveness, 499
    HR role, 294
PEST factors
    organizational staffing challenge, 132
    total rewards strategy, 215
PESTEL analysis in strategy formulation, 92–93
Peters, Tom, 426
phantom stock plans, 240
phased retirement, 323
philanthropy, 435
phone call communication, 490
photographs in interview questions, 151
physical description in interview questions, 151
physical factors in job descriptions, 137
physiological elements in ROI maximization, 517
pilot testing in training, 192
Pink, Daniel, 173
planned and programmed investigations in Occupational Safety and Health Act, 38
planning and management requirements in strategy, 87–88, 91
plans
    HR strategy. *See* HR Strategic Planning
    risk management, 421–424
    staffing, 319–321
    workforce, 317–319
plant closings, 63
plateau curves in adult learning, 189
point-factor job evaluation methods, 224–227
policies
    building, 528
    developing, 473
    diversity and inclusion, 409
    employee engagement, 169–170
    globalization, 385
    risk management, 416, 425
    technology management, 357–361
policy challenges in diversity and inclusion, 409

political factors
    managing, 471
    strategy formulation, 92
    total rewards strategy, 215
polycentric operation in globalization, 383
polycentric orientation in total rewards strategy, 212
polygraph exams record-keeping requirements, 448
Portal-to-Portal Act, 40
portals in HR information systems, 356
Porter, Michael, 89–90
Porter's competitive strategies, 100–101
Porter's Five Forces, 95
position power in leadership, 125
Posner, Barry Z., 118, 485–486
power
    appropriate application, 469
    transformational leadership, 464
power distance
    cultures, 389
    leadership, 127
PPA (Pension Protection Act), 39
PPACA (Patient Protection and Affordable Care Act), 62–63
practitioners, HR, 290
Pregnancy Discrimination Act, 57
preliminary assessment in diversity and inclusion, 403
prevailing wages record-keeping requirements, 449
preventable risks, 415
preventive measures in discipline, 351
previews in talent selection process, 157–158
primacy errors in performance appraisal, 177
principal-agent problem, 417
principled negotiation style in conflict management, 130
principles and practices in strategy implementation, 109–110
Privacy Act, 66
private health insurance, 250
problem-solving techniques, 506
    creative, 512–513, 518
    leadership development, 203
problem statement in HR business case, 502
problems, organizational, 506
process-related problem in OED, 301

processes
    alignment in globalization, 381
    HR, 288–289
    improvement initiatives, 527
    OED, 299–300
    risk management, 425
product and service enhancement in
    OED, 302
product structure in organizational
    design, 287
production incentives, 237
productivity as leading indicator, 523
productivity-based pay systems, 234
professional employer organizations
    (PEOs)
    alternative staffing, 324
    risk, 420
Professional in Human Resources
    (PHR), 6
Professional in Human Resources,
    California (PHRca), 6
Professional in Human Resources,
    International (PHRi), 6
professional integrity, 468
professionals, incentive pay for, 243
profit-sharing plans, 238
profits in OED, 302
progressive corporate culture, 389
project employees, 323
project management tools, 110
project objectives in HR business
    case, 502
projects in career development, 197
promotions
    career development, 197
    diversity and inclusion, 405
    employee lifecycle, 216
provisions and protections
    Americans with Disabilities Act, 50
    Drug-Free Workplace Act, 55
    Fair Labor Standards Act, 28
    Mine Safety and Health Act, 34
    Occupational Safety and Health
        Act, 36–37
    Sarbanes-Oxley Act, 41–42
psychological elements in ROI
    maximization, 517
public-private balance in
    globalization, 376
public works contracts record-keeping
    requirements, 449
pull factors in global strategies,
    379–380

punitive damages in Civil Rights Act
    (Title VII), 54
push factors in global strategies,
    378–379

Q

quality
    globalization, 377
    OED control tools, 309
    OED initiatives, 308–310
    OED standards, 308–309
quantitative methods in job evaluation,
    226–227
quartiles for pay ranges, 230
questionnaires for job analysis, 222
questions in interviews, 149–152
Quinn, Robert, 311

R

race/ethnicity
    interview questions, 151
    talent selection process, 146
RACI matrix organizational
    structure, 286
Radjasa, Satya, 181
Railway Labor Act, 40
ranges, pay, 230–231
ranking
    decisions, 156
    jobs, 225
reaction in Four-Level Training
    Evaluation Model, 193
readiness
    adult learning, 186
    risk management, 422–424
real estate processing fees, 325
real-life problem-solving, 203
realism in SMART goal setting, 98
reasonable accommodation in talent
    selection process, 157
recency errors in performance
    appraisals, 177
recession, global, 376
recognition
    employee engagement, 173
    forms, 338–339
recommendations
    in global context, 397
    making, 525
recordkeeping
    Americans with Disabilities Act,
        52–53

Drug-Free Workplace Act, 55–56
    employee records, 445–450
    Fair Labor Standards Act, 28–30
    Mine Safety and Health Act, 34
    Occupational Safety and Health
        Act, 37
    Sarbanes-Oxley Act, 42
recruiting cost ratio (RCR), 143
recruitment
    and benefits, 245
    in diverse markets, 139–140
    diversity and inclusion, 404
    effectiveness, 141–144
    employee lifecycle, 216
    job analysis, 223
    leading indicator, 524
    methods, 140–141
red circle pay rates, 234–235
redefining sustainability, 428
redistribution of decision-making
    authority, 314
references
    interview questions, 151
    talent selection process, 155
referral agents in career development, 194
referrals
    Occupational Safety and Health
        Act, 38
    recruiting, 140
reframing communication, 491
regiocentric operation in
    globalization, 383
regiocentric orientation in total rewards
    strategy, 212
regional laws, 395
registered nurses, employment visas
    for, 67–68
regression analysis, 116
regular full-time employees, 139
regular part-time workers, 139
regulations. *See* laws and statutory
    regulations
Rehabilitation Act, 40–41
rehires, 325
reinforcements in mergers and
    acquisitions, 105
Relationship Management
    competency, 9
    definitions, 475–476
    description, 12
    key concepts, 476
    proficiency indicators, 476–484
    summary, 484

relationships
  cross-cultural, 499–500
  HR role, 294
relatives in interview questions, 152
reliability factor in talent selection
  process, 154
reliability scorecard in risk analysis, 418
reliable data availability for staffing, 132
religion in interview questions, 152
religious law systems in global
  context, 394
relocations
  alternative staffing, 325–326
  career development, 197
remuneration surveys for job
  evaluation, 228
reports
  in communication, 490
  strategy performance, 113
required actions in Worker Adjustment
  and Retraining Notification Act, 63
requirements
  HR business case, 503
  total rewards strategy
    communication, 217
  workforce, 312–317
research and development (R&D), 284
resistance in mergers and
  acquisitions, 105
resources
  staffing plans, 320
  strategy implementation, 108–109
respect
  for differences, 493
  relationship management, 477
"Respectful Way to Discipline
  Employees," 349
responses to risk, 420–421
restricted stock units (RSUs), 241
restructuring, corporate, 313–316
results in Four-Level Training
  Evaluation Model, 193
résumés in talent selection process, 146
retaliation, workplace, 348
retention
  adult learning, 187
  business case, 181
  diversity and inclusion, 404
  employee engagement, 180–183
  evaluating, 182
  leading indicator, 524
  practices and strategies, 181–182
  total rewards strategy, 210

retention period requirements for
  employee records, 444–450
retirement
  benefits, 254–255
  phased, 323
Retirement Equity Act (REA), 41
return on investment (ROI)
  diverse workforce, 498
  diversity and inclusion, 403
  initiatives, 504–505
  maximizing, 517
  training and development, 193
Revenue Act, 41
revenue per employee metric, 504
reverse innovation in globalization, 376
rewards
  employee engagement, 173
  forms, 338–339
Rhinesmith, Stephen, 495
rightsizing, 314
Risk Management
  definitions, 412
  emergency preparedness and
    business continuity, 422–424
  evaluating, 424–426
  focusing, 414
  ISO principles, 415
  key concepts, 412–413
  leadership development, 202
  plans, 421–424
  risk assessment, 417–420
  risk context, 413–417
  risk definition, 414–415
  risk responses, 420–421
risk matrices, 419
risk registers, 420
risk scorecards, 418
risks
  in business acumen, 505
  diversity, 400
  globalization, 377, 385
robust sourcing strategies for
  recruiting, 140–141
Rohm, Howard, 114
ROI. See return on investment (ROI)
roles in career development,
  194–195
root-cause analysis in risk
  identification, 418
Rucker Plan, 238
rule of law in global context, 394
rules of conduct for exam,
  17–18

S

S-shaped learning curves in adult
  learning, 189
SA8000 certification, 432–433
safety and security in Maslow's
  hierarchy of needs, 170–171
SAI (Social Accountability
  International), 432–433
salary levels in organizational
  staffing, 133
salary plus commission for direct sales
  personnel, 243
sales
  core business functions, 284
  metrics, 115
Sarbanes-Oxley Act (SOX), 41–42
SBJPA (Small Business Job Protection
  Act), 43–44
Scanlon Plan, 238
scatter diagrams, 309
schedules for global and cultural
  effectiveness, 499
Schein, Edgar, 389
Schein's model for cultures, 389
Schengen agreements, 395
scope and criticality of decisions in risk
  management, 416
scorecards
  dimensions, 508
  HR value, 291–292
  risk analysis, 418
  strategy performance, 114
scoring, exam, 20–21
screening in talent selection process,
  145–146
Securities and Exchange Act, 42–43
security clearance investigation records
  in personnel files, 442–443
select and offer process in talent
  selection, 155–157
selection in job analysis, 223
self-actualization in Maslow's hierarchy
  of needs, 170–171
self-assessment
  career development, 196
  performance management, 177–178
self-awareness
  global and cultural effectiveness, 493
  leadership characteristics, 119
self-concept in adult learning, 186
self-directed study, 191
self-regulation in leadership, 119

self-service technologies in total
rewards strategy, 218
selling tasks in leadership, 125
Senior Certified Professional
certification, 6
senior HR professionals proficiency
indicators
business acumen, 504–510
communicating, 488–491
consultation, 516–520
critical evaluation, 524–529
ethical, 471–475
global and cultural, 496–500
leadership, 464–467
relationship management,
481–484
senior management role in
grievances, 344
Senior Professional in Human
Resources (SPHR), 6
Senior Professional in Human
Resources, International (SPHRi), 6
seniority pay increases, 236
separation process
employee engagement, 174
employee rights, 335
Service Contract Act (SCA), 43
service support by HR staff, 275
"Seven Habits of Spectacularly
Unsuccessful People," 200
severance
compliance, 260
packages, 253–254
sex in interview questions, 152
sexual harassment, 516, 519
shadow stocks, 240
shadowing in talent selection
process, 157
shared services, 290–291
sharing
jobs, 323
risk, 420
Sherman Anti-Trust Act, 43
shift differential pay, 236
SHOP (Small Business Health
Options Program), 62
short messaging communication, 490
shortened workweeks, 323
SHRM Certified Professional
(SHRM-CP), 5
description, 9
exam eligibility, 13–14

SHRM Senior Certified Profession
(SHRM-SCP), 5
description, 9
exam eligibility, 13–14
SHRM (Society for Human Resource
Management), 4–6
similar-to-me error in interviews, 153
simulations
talent selection process, 157
training and development, 192
single-rate pay systems, 232
Sinosphere culture, 388
situational judgment items (SJIs),
16–17
situational judgment tests (SJTs), 201
situational leadership model, 123–126
situational obstacles to adult
learning, 188
Six Sigma methodologies, 310
SJIs (situational judgment items),
16–17
SJTs (situational judgment tests), 201
skill-based pay systems, 234
skill requirements in job
descriptions, 137
skilled labor
employment visas for, 70
organizational staffing challenge, 131
skills assessment centers, 201–202
Skinner, B. F., 172
Small Business Health Options
Program (SHOP), 62
Small Business Job Protection Act
(SBJPA), 43–44
SMART goals
strategy formulation, 98
strategy performance, 114
smart-sizing, 314
Smith, Douglas, 126
Social Accountability International
(SAI), 432–433
social factors
strategy formulation, 93
total rewards strategy, 215
social media
communication, 490
employment branding, 136
metrics, 115
policies, 360
recruiting, 140, 144
training and development, 192
violations, 519

social pressures, managing, 471
social responsibility
corporate, 426–436
staffing, 135
Social Security
compliance, 260
concepts, 255–256
Social Security Act, 44
Social Security tax record-keeping
requirements, 448
social sharing of knowledge, 330
social skills in leadership, 119
Society for Human Resource
Management (SHRM), 4–6
sociological elements in ROI
maximization, 517
sociopolitical environment in
globalization, 377
soft negotiation style in conflict
management, 130
solution analysis in workforce
planning, 319
sourcing and recruiting
in diverse markets, 139–144
diversity and inclusion, 404
leveraging technology, 144
South Africa, diversity in, 400
span of control organizational
structure, 285
special considerations in talent
selection process, 157
special immigrants, employment visas
for, 70
special occupations and fashion
models, employment visas for, 67
specialists, HR, 290
specialized knowledge, employment
visas for, 68
specifications
job analysis, 222
job descriptions, 138
specificity in SMART goal setting, 98
spelling differences, 493
sponsorship in mergers and
acquisitions, 105
stability in talent selection process, 155
stable base pay plans, 241
staffing. *See also* Talent Acquisition
organizational requirements,
131–133
plans, 319–321
strategic, 133

stage engagement, 161
stakeholder information for critical
  thinking, 522
stakeholders
  collaboration with, 461–462
  communication, 488
  listening to, 470
  relationship management, 477
  risk management, 416
  staffing plans, 319
standardization vs. localization in total
  rewards strategy, 213
standards
  establishing, 472
  Occupational Safety and Health
    Act, 38–39
  performance management, 175
statements of authority in employment
  contracts, 335
statements of purpose in staffing
  plans, 319
statistical forecasts in workforce
  planning, 318
step rate variability considerations,
  232–233
stereotyping in interviews, 152
stock options, 240
Stored Communications Act, 26
straight commission for direct sales
  personnel, 242
straight piece rate pay systems, 234
straight salary for direct sales
  personnel, 242
strategic administrative role, 277
strategic alliances in diversity and
  inclusion, 404
strategic audits, 292
strategic change facilitation as
  proficiency indicator, 465
strategic operational role, 278
strategic opportunities in relationship
  management, 483–484
strategic process in HR, 297
strategic risks, 415
strategic role
  global assignments, 392
  HR function, 275–281
strategic solutions, designing, 520
strategic staffing, 133
strategic view, providing, 529
strategies
  benefits, 88
  communication, 489–490

contributing, 510
corporate social responsibility,
  429–435
description, 87
developing, 98–107, 507–508
diversity and inclusion, 402–408
employee engagement, 164
employment relationship, 337–338
formulation in HR Strategic
  Planning, 92–98
global, 378–386
HR roles, 89, 293–297
HR Strategic Planning roles, 87–91
implementation, 107–113
knowledge management systems,
  329–330
leadership development, 202–203
levels, 88–89
mistakes, 88
OED, 300–304
performance evaluation, 113–118
planning and management
  requirements, 87–88
retention, 181–182
stakeholder concept, 90–91
talent management, 322, 516
technology, 509
total rewards, 205–219
unions, 340
value in, 89–90
stratification charts, 309
strengths in SWOT analysis, 94, 505
stress interviews, 148
strictness errors in performance
  appraisals, 179
structural alternatives
  HR function organization,
    290–291
  organizational design, 286–287
structural principles in organizational
  design, 285
structure, strategic planning for, 88
Structure of the HR Function
  change impacts, 278–281
  core business functions, 281–284
  definitions, 273
  evolving role, 275–278
  external environment
    considerations, 288
  HR processes, 288–289
  HR team, 289–290
  internal environment
    considerations, 287

key concepts, 274
organizational design, 284
organizational strategy role, 293–297
organizational structures, 284–285
proficiency indicators, 274–275
strategic role, 275–281
value measurements, 291–293
structured interviews in talent selection
  process, 148, 154
student eligibility, 15
study resources, 585–588
subnational laws, 395
substantially limits in Americans with
  Disabilities Act, 51
successful relationships, promoting, 479
succession planning, 326–327
summarizing information in talent
  selection process, 156
supervisor-level discussions in
  grievances, 344
supervisors in employment
  relationship, 339
suppliers in organizational strategy
  role, 294
supply analysis in workforce
  planning, 317
supply chain
  diversity and inclusion, 405
  globalization, 379
supportive leadership in employee
  engagement, 163
supranational organization, 395
surveys
  compensation structure, 228–230
  employee engagement, 164–167
suspension for discipline, 350
sustainability practice in corporate
  social responsibility, 428
Sweden, health plans in, 249
SWOT analysis
  business acumen indicator, 505
  risk identification, 418
  strategy formulation, 94
symbols in cultures, 389
synergy, cultural, 391
system changes in diversity and
  inclusion, 404–406
systems integration in HR information
  systems, 357
systems theory in OED quality
  initiatives, 308
systems thinking, strategic planning
  for, 88

T

tactical objectives in workforce
  planning, 318
tactile learners, 187
Talent Acquisition
  definitions, 130
  employment branding, 135–136
  global basis planning, 134–135
  job analysis, 136–137
  job documentation, 137–139
  key concepts, 130–131
  onboarding, 159
  organizational staffing
    requirements, 131–133
  orientation, 158
  selection. *See* talent selection
    process
  sourcing and recruiting, 139–144
  strategic staffing, 133
talent development in OED, 300
talent management
  effectiveness measures, 326
  learning and development,
    185–186
  overview, 322–326
  strategies, 510, 516
talent pool in globalization, 377
talent selection process, 144
  application forms, 146–147
  assessing and evaluating, 153–155
  factors chart, 144–145
  interviews, 147–153
  screening, 145–146
  select and offer, 155–157
talented employees, total rewards
  strategy for attracting, 210
targeted investigations in Occupational
  Safety and Health Act, 38
targets in organizational gap
  development, 305–306
task accomplishments as proficiency
  indicator, 462
task structure in leadership, 125
tasks for staffing plans, 320–321
Tax Reform Act, 45
taxes
  alternative staffing, 326
  and benefits, 245
  compliance, 259
  record-keeping requirements,
    447–448
  total rewards strategy, 214

Taxpayer Relief Act, 45
team approach in meetings, 514
team building
  OED initiatives, 307
  relationship management, 480
team-first corporate culture, 388
team interviews, 148
team members in staffing
  plans, 320
team participation in career
  development, 197
teams
  diversity and inclusion, 409
  HR, 289–290
teamwork in relationship
  management, 476
technical competencies, 11
technical strategy in OED, 300
technological factors
  strategy formulation, 93
  total rewards strategy, 215
technological revolution in
  globalization, 378
technology
  leveraging, 504
  meetings, 514
  OED, 301
  sourcing and recruiting, 144
  strategy, 509
Technology Management
  big data era, 354–355
  definitions, 351
  and HR, 352–354
  information management, 354
  information systems, 355–357
  key concepts, 352
  leveraging, 353–354
  policies, 357–361
technology shifts and organizational
  staffing, 133
telling tasks for leadership, 125
temp-to-lease programs, 325
temporary agricultural workers,
  employment visas for, 68
temporary contract and contingent
  work in career development, 199
temporary employees, 139, 324
termination
  compensation for, 254
  discipline, 350
  employee lifecycle, 216
  employment contract provisions, 336

test center administrators (TCAs), 18
test-retest reliability in talent selection
  process, 154
testing risk management plans, 424
theories
  cultures, 390
  employee engagement,
    171–172
  leadership, 121–130
  OED quality initiatives, 308
Theory of Constraints (TOC), 309
third-party conflict resolution, 347
third-party contractors, 291
third-party influences in employee and
  labor relations, 339–344
Thomas, R. Roosevelt, Jr., 406
threats
  strategy formulation, 95
  SWOT analysis, 94, 505
360-degree appraisals, 175
Thriving on Chaos, 426
Tibetan culture, 388
time-based differential pay, 236
time-based step rate systems, 232
time zone differences, 493
timing in SMART goal setting, 98
TOC (Theory of Constraints), 309
tolerance in risk management, 416
total company compensation
  expense, 244
Total Rewards
  benefits, 244–256
  compensation structure,
    220–232
  compensation systems, 232–244
  definitions, 204
  key concepts, 204–205
  organizational strategy, 205–219
  perquisites, 256–257
  special considerations, 212–216
  strategy communication,
    216–219
  strategy development, 206–207
  strategy evaluation, 219
  strategy objectives, 207–212
tracking applicants in talent selection
  process, 146
trade agreements, 378
trade barriers in globalization, 380
trade unions, 340–345
Trademark Act, 45
trainees, employment visas for, 68

training and development, 189
    ADDIE model, 190–192
    diversity and inclusion, 406, 409
    evaluating, 193
    implementation, 192–193
    job analysis, 223
    leadership development, 203
    as perquisite, 256
    personnel file records, 441
traits
    diversity, 402
    employee engagement, 161
    leadership, 121–122
"Traits of Truly Agile Businesses," 302
transactional leadership, 126
transferring
    knowledge, 522
    risk, 420
transfers
    alternative staffing, 325
    career development, 197
    diversity and inclusion, 409
transformational leadership
    employee engagement, 163
    overview, 126
    proficiency indicator, 463–464
transition tactics in restructuring, 316
translation and interpretation in
    training, 192
transnational strategy, 382
transparency
    maintaining, 470
    organizational change, 467
    total rewards strategy, 217–219
travel in diversity and inclusion, 409
treaties and trade agreements
    employer and employee rights, 334
    global context, 397
treaty investors, employment visas
    for, 67
Treaty of Amsterdam, 395
Treaty of Rome, 395
treaty traders, employment visas for, 67
trends
    career development, 199
    strategy performance analysis,
      116–117
    workforce planning analysis, 317
triple bottom line approach, 428
Trompenaars, Fons, 390
trust in global and cultural
    effectiveness, 496, 499
turnover analysis, 317

U

UCA (Unemployment Compensation
    Amendments Act), 45
Ulrich, David, 278, 290
unbundling, 314
uncertainty avoidance, 127, 390
uncertainty in risk, 420
Unemployment Compensation
    Amendments Act (UCA), 45
unemployment insurance, 255
unemployment tax record-keeping
    requirements, 448
unethical behavior, dealing with,
    468–469
unfair labor practices, 345–346
*Uniform Guidelines on Employee
Selection Procedures*, 57–58, 155
Uniformed Services Employment
    and Reemployment Rights Act
    (USERRA), 45–46
unions
    employee and labor relations,
      340–345
    employment relationship, 337–338
    record-keeping requirements, 449
United Kingdom, health plans in, 250
United Nations Global Compact,
    430–431
universities in career development, 199
unknowns in risk, 414–415
unplanned activities in job
    descriptions, 137
unstructured interviews, 148
upside risks, responses for, 420–421
upstream strategies in globalization, 381
U.S. Employment Law and
    Regulations
    definitions, 436
    employee records management,
      439–450
    key concepts, 436–437
    legislative and regulatory
      environment, 437
    organizational compliance, 438
U.S. laws and regulations, 23
    Age Discrimination in Employment
      Act, 58
    American Recovery and
      Reinvestment Act, 59
    Americans with Disabilities Act,
      49–53
    chapter review, 70
    Civil Rights Act (1991), 55

Civil Rights Act (Title VII), 54
Civil Service Reform Act, 64–65
Clayton Act, 24
Congressional Accountability
    Act, 65
Consolidated Omnibus Budget
    Reconciliation Act, 59
Consumer Credit Protection
    Act, 24
Copeland "Anti-Kickback" Act, 24
Copyright Act, 25
Davis-Bacon Act, 25
Dodd-Frank Wall Street Reform
    and Consumer Protection Act, 25
Drug-Free Workplace Act, 55–56
Economic Growth and Tax Relief
    Reconciliation Act, 25
Electronic Communications
    Privacy Act, 26
employee management overview,
    23–24
Employee Polygraph Protection
    Act, 26
Employee Retirement Income
    Security Act, 26
employment visas for foreign
    nationals, 67–70
Equal Employment Opportunity
    Act, 56
Equal Pay Act, 27
Executive Order 11246—Affirmative
    Action, 60–61
FAA Modernization and Reform
    Act, 27
Fair and Accurate Credit
    Transactions Act, 27
Fair Credit Reporting Act, 27
Fair Labor Standards Act, 28–31
False Claims Act, 65–66
Family and Medical Leave Act, 61
federal government employees,
    64–67
Foreign Corrupt Practices Act, 31
Genetic Information
    Nondiscrimination Act, 56–57
Guidelines on Discrimination
    Because of Sex, 57
Health Information Technology for
    Economic and Clinical Health
    Act, 31
Health Insurance Portability and
    Accountability Act, 32
Homeland Security Act, 66

U.S. laws and regulations (*cont.*)
  Immigration and Nationality
    Act, 32
  Immigration Reform and Control
    Act, 32
  IRS Intermediate Sanctions, 33
  Labor-Management Relations
    Act, 33
  Labor-Management Reporting and
    Disclosure Act, 33–34, 49
  Lilly Ledbetter Fair Pay Act, 57
  Mental Health Parity Act, 62
  Mental Health Parity and
    Addiction Equity Act, 62
  Mine Safety and Health Act, 34
  National Defense Authorization
    Act, 62
  National Industrial Recovery
    Act, 35
  National Labor Relations Act, 35
  Needlestick Safety and Prevention
    Act, 35–36
  Norris-LaGuardia Act, 36
  Occupational Safety and Health
    Act, 36–39
  Older Workers Benefit Protection
    Act, 59–60
  Omnibus Budget Reconciliation
    Act, 39
  Patient Protection and Affordable
    Care Act, 62–63
  Pension Protection Act, 39
  Personal Responsibility and Work
    Opportunity Reconciliation Act,
    39–40
  Portal-to-Portal Act, 40
  Pregnancy Discrimination Act, 57
  Privacy Act, 66
  questions, 70–81
  Railway Labor Act, 40
  Rehabilitation Act, 40–41
  Retirement Equity Act, 41
  Revenue Act, 41
  Sarbanes-Oxley Act, 41–42
  Securities and Exchange Act, 42–43
  Service Contract Act, 43
  Sherman Anti-Trust Act, 43
  Small Business Job Protection Act,
    43–44
  Social Security Act, 44
  Tax Reform Act, 45
  Taxpayer Relief Act, 45
  Trademark Act, 45
  Unemployment Compensation
    Amendments Act, 45
  Uniform Guidelines on Employee
    Selection Procedures, 57–58
  Uniformed Services Employment
    and Reemployment Rights Act,
    45–46
  USA PATRIOT Act, 66–67
  Vietnam Era Veterans
    Readjustment Assistance Act,
    46–47
  Wagner-Peyser Act, 47
  Walsh-Healey Act, 47
  whistleblowing, 49
  Work Opportunity Tax Credit,
    47–48
  Worker Adjustment and Retraining
    Notification Act, 63–64
  Workforce Investment Act, 47
USA PATRIOT Act, 66–67
USERRA (Uniformed Services
  Employment and Reemployment
  Rights Act), 45–46
USS-POSCO joint venture, 517

V

vacations
  country differences, 495
  paid leave, 247
validity in talent selection process,
  154–155
value
  measurements, 291–293
  in strategy, 89–90
value chain, 89–90
values
  OED measurement, 310–311
  strategy formulation, 97
variability considerations in step rate
  compensation, 232–233
variance analysis, 116
video previews in talent selection
  process, 157
Vietnam Era Veterans Readjustment
  Assistance Act (VEVRAA), 46–47
virtual-world simulations, 192
visa requirements, 67–70, 135
visible diversity traits, 402
vision
  communicating, 473–474
  strategy formulation, 97
vision setting as proficiency
  indicator, 463
visual learners, 187
voice of HR as proficiency indicator, 465
voicemail communication, 490
voluntary communications in total
  rewards strategy, 218
volunteerism, 435

W

wage and hour claims, 519
wage/salary administration in
  personnel files, 442
wages
  compliance, 259
  record-keeping requirements, 444
Wagner-Peyser Act, 47
Walsh-Healey Act, 47
WARN (Worker Adjustment and
  Retraining Notification Act), 63–64
warnings
  discipline, 350
  talent selection process, 147
waterfall approach in HR information
  systems, 357
weaknesses in SWOT analysis, 94, 505
web sites in recruiting, 140
Webb, Geoff, 139
webinars, 192
weighted averages in compensation
  analysis, 229–230
wellness programs, 251
Western culture, 387–388
WFPMA (World Federation of People
  Management Associations), 6
"What Employers Are Looking for in
  HR Positions," 4
whistleblowing
  legal protections, 49
  risk management, 425
  violations, 519
white knights, 313
whole-job evaluation methods,
  224–225
Why Smart Executives Fail, 200
WIA (Workforce Investment Act), 47
Wiretap Act, 26
work authorization record-keeping
  requirements, 448
work councils, 341–342
work diaries and logs for job analysis, 222
work hours. *See* hours of work
work-life balance (WLB)
  alternative staffing, 326
  employee engagement, 169

Work Opportunity Tax Credit (WOTC), 47–48
work samples in talent selection process, 153
work schedule in interview questions, 152
work specialization organizational structure, 285
Worker Adjustment and Retraining Notification Act (WARN), 63–64
worker complaints in Occupational Safety and Health Act, 38
workers' compensation, 252–253
workforce
    OED initiatives, 306–307
    planning, 317–319
    in total rewards strategy, 208
workforce analytics in recruiting effectiveness, 144
Workforce Investment Act (WIA), 47
Workforce Management
    definitions, 311
    employee development, 321–326

key concepts, 311–312
knowledge management, 327–330
organizational structure, 313
restructuring, 313–316
staffing plans, 319–321
succession planning, 326–327
workforce planning, 317–319
workforce requirements, 312–317
workforce/workplace changes, HR impact from, 278
working conditions record-keeping requirements, 444
Workplace Knowledge domain, 373
    chapter review, 451
    Corporate Social Responsibility, 426–435
    Diversity and Inclusion, 397–411
    global context. *See* global context questions, 451–455

Risk Management, 412–426
U.S. Employment Law and Regulations, 436–451
World Federation of People Management Associations (WFPMA), 6
world legal systems, 394–397
World Trade Organization (WTO), 334
WOTC (Work Opportunity Tax Credit), 47–48
written complaints, 349
written reports communication, 490
written warnings, 350
WTO (World Trade Organization), 334

Y

Yoder, Dale, 221

Z

Zenger, Jack, 464
zero-based budgeting, 283